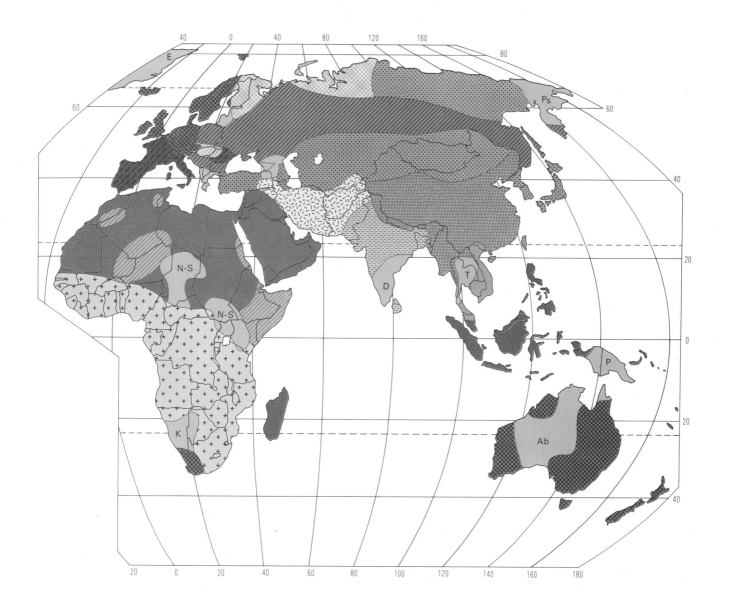

Fifth Edition

The
Human Mosaic

A Thematic Introduction to Cultural Geography

Terry G. Jordan
University of Texas at Austin

Lester Rowntree
San Jose State University

Cartographic Design by Mei-Ling Hsu
University of Minnesota

1817

HARPER & ROW, PUBLISHERS, New York
Grand Rapids, Philadelphia, St. Louis, San Francisco,
London, Singapore, Sydney, Tokyo

Director of Development: Mary Falcon
Project Editor: Donna DeBenedictis
Art and Cover Direction: Teresa J. Delgado
Text Design: Teresa J. Delgado
Cover Design: Circa 86, Inc.
Cover Photograph: © George Holton, Photo Researchers, Inc.
Cartographer: R. R. Donnelley & Sons Cartographic Services
Photo Research: Susan Kaprov
Production Manager: Jeanie Berke
Production Assistant: Paula Roppolo

THE HUMAN MOSAIC
A Thematic Introduction to Cultural Geography, Fifth Edition

Library of Congress Cataloging-in-Publication Data

Jordan, Terry G.
    The human mosaic: a thematic introduction to cultural geography /
Terry G. Jordan, Lester Rowntree; cartographic design by Mei-Ling
Hsu.—5th ed.
      p. cm.
    Bibliography: p.
    Includes index.
    ISBN 0-06-043460-0 (teacher's ed.).—ISBN 0-06-043481-3
(student's ed.)
    1. Anthropo-geography.   2. Ethnology.   I. Rowntree, Lester, 1938–
II. Title.
GF41.J67 1990
900—dc20   89-15358
                                           CIP

90 91 92 9 8 7 6 5 4 3 2

Credits

Contents

Preface   ix

About the Authors   xiii

About the Cartographic Designer   xiv

CHAPTER 1   **THE NATURE OF CULTURAL GEOGRAPHY**   **1**

What Is Cultural Geography?   4

Themes in Cultural Geography   6

The Cultural Geographical Past   30

Conclusion   31

Suggested Readings   32

PHOTO ESSAY   **A PREVIEW OF THE CONCEPTS OF CULTURAL GEOGRAPHY**

CHAPTER 2   **PEOPLE ON THE LAND**   **36**

Demographic Regions   38

Diffusion in Population Geography   53

Population Ecology   59

Cultural Integration and Population Patterns   64

Settlement Patterns in the Landscape   68
Conclusion   76
Suggested Readings   77

CHAPTER 3   **THE AGRICULTURAL WORLD**   **80**
Agricultural Regions   81
Agricultural Diffusion   95
Agricultural Ecology   101
Cultural Integration in Agriculture   104
Agricultural Landscapes   110
Conclusion   117
Suggested Readings   117

CHAPTER 4   **POLITICAL PATTERNS**   **121**
Political Culture Regions   122
Diffusion of Political Innovations   134
Political Ecology   139
Cultural Integration in Political Geography   144
Political Landscapes   149
Conclusion   154
Suggested Readings   154

CHAPTER 5   **THE BABEL OF LANGUAGES**   **157**
Linguistic Culture Regions   158
Linguistic Diffusion   166
Linguistic Ecology   170
Linguistic Cultural Integration   174
Linguistic Landscapes   180
Conclusion   185
Suggested Readings   186

CHAPTER 6   **RELIGIOUS REALMS**   **189**
Religious Culture Regions   190
Religious Diffusion   198
Religious Ecology   203
Cultural Integration in Religion   208
Religious Landscapes   217
Conclusion   223
Suggested Readings   224

CHAPTER 7   **FOLK GEOGRAPHY**   **227**
Folk Culture Regions   229
Folk Cultural Diffusion   234
Folk Ecology   240

Cultural Integration in Folk Geography 245
Folk Architecture in the Cultural Landscape 249
Conclusion 257
Suggested Readings 258

CHAPTER 8 **POPULAR CULTURE** **261**
Popular Culture Regions 263
Cultural Diffusion in Popular Culture 270
The Ecology of Popular Culture 276
Cultural Integration in Popular Culture 279
Landscapes of Popular Culture 282
Conclusion 290
Suggested Readings 290

CHAPTER 9 **ETHNIC GEOGRAPHY** **293**
Ethnic Regions 295
Cultural Diffusion and Ethnic Groups 306
Cultural Ecology and Ethnicity 310
Cultural Integration and Ethnicity 312
America's Ethnic Landscapes 319
Conclusion 324
Suggested Readings 325

CHAPTER 10 **THE CITY IN TIME AND SPACE** **328**
Culture Region 330
Origin and Diffusion of the City 333
Evolution of Urban Landscapes 341
The Ecology of Urban Location 366
Cultural Integration in Urban Geography 370
Conclusion 373
Suggested Readings 373

CHAPTER 11 **THE URBAN MOSAIC** **376**
Urban Culture Regions 377
Cultural Diffusion in the City 380
The Cultural Ecology of the City 390
Cultural Integration and Models of the City 399
Urban Landscapes 405
Conclusion 415
Suggested Readings 415

CHAPTER 12 **INDUSTRIAL GEOGRAPHY** **418**
Industrial Regions 421
Diffusion of the Industrial Revolution 428

Industrial Ecology   434
Industrial Cultural Integration   439
Industrial Landscapes   445
Conclusion   449
Suggested Readings   449

PHOTO ESSAY　　**TAKING CULTURAL GEOGRAPHY BEYOND THE CLASSROOM**

CHAPTER
13

APPLYING CULTURAL GEOGRAPHY: A CASE STUDY APPROACH

APPLYING CULTURAL GEOGRAPHY: A CASE STUDY
APPROACH   452
Common Themes in the Case Studies   453
Problems of Regional Landscape Change: Bolinas Lagoon,
    California   454
Settlement Change and Health in West Malaysia   457
Cultural Diffusion in India: Problems with the Green
    Revolution   459
The Cultural Ecology of Desertification: Drought in the Great
    Plains   462
The Amish Culture Region: A Study in Energy Efficiency   465
The Cultural Geography of Drought, Famine, and Conflict:
    The Case of Ethiopia   469
Conclusion   472
Suggested Readings   473

Glossary   475
Index   485

Preface

The Human Mosaic is intended as the basic text for a college-level, introductory course in cultural or human geography. It is an outgrowth of our quarter-of-a-century experience in teaching cultural geography to college undergraduates. We have found that beginning students learn best when provided with a precise framework. They need to know, at any given time in the course, exactly how the material they are studying relates to the geographic whole. Most introductory textbooks, we feel, lack such a framework. That we have reached the remarkable milestone of a fifth edition can perhaps be regarded as an affirmation of the pedagogical value of our structured-thematic approach.

▇ STRUCTURED-THEMATIC FRAMEWORK

The Human Mosaic is built around five themes: culture region, cultural diffusion, cultural ecology, cultural integration, and cultural landscape. These five themes are introduced and explained in the first chapter and serve as the framework for the topical chapters that follow. The themes are applied to a variety of geographic topics: demography, agriculture, the city, religion, language, ethnicity, politics, industry, folklife, and popular culture. Students are able to relate to one of the five themes at every point in *The Human Mosaic*.

We do not claim to have invented this structure. Its roots run deep in cultural geography, as deep as Carl O. Sauer's "The Morphology of Landscape," August Meitzen's classic work on European settlement forms, Eduard Hahn's publications on agricultural origins and dispersals, and

George Perkins Marsh's nineteenth-century writings on environmental modification. Much inspiration was derived from the innovative *Readings in Cultural Geography,* written in 1962 by Philip L. Wagner and Marvin W. Mikesell.

Nor do we propose that our framework is the only one possible. We *can* say that in our classroom experience we have found this approach to be highly successful. The enthusiastic reception enjoyed by the four previous editions of *The Human Mosaic* have led us to believe that our thematic approach to cultural geography is educationally sound. Our culture region theme appeals to students' natural human curiosity about the differences among places. The dynamic aspect of culture—particularly relevant to an age of incessant and rapid change—is conveyed through the theme of cultural diffusion. Students acquire an appreciation for how cultural traits spread—or don't spread—from place to place. The topics employed to illustrate the concepts of diffusion include many that college students can quickly relate to—for example, country-western music, football, and migration. Cultural ecology, also highly relevant in our age, addresses the complicated relationship between culture and physical environment. Cultural integration permits students to view culture as an interrelated whole, in which one facet acts upon and is acted upon by other facets. Lastly, the theme of cultural landscape heightens students' awareness of the visible expressions of different cultures.

■ CARTOGRAPHIC DESIGN

The cartography displayed in *The Human Mosaic* is of the highest standard. As map designer, we were fortunate to obtain the services of Professor Mei-Ling Hsu, a woman famous for the beauty, intricacy, and clarity of her work. Dr. Hsu is the preeminent cartographer in American academic geography today. Each of her maps in *The Human Mosaic* is worth at least 10,000 words. Dr. Hsu's designs were ably rendered by the highly professional and detail-oriented staff of R. R. Donnelley & Sons Cartographic Services.

■ LEARNING DEVICES

The book offers a variety of special learning devices to motivate and assist students:

- A glossary at the end of the book, giving students concise definitions of terms and concepts.
- Boxes scattered throughout most chapters, elaborating on concepts, presenting illustrative examples or case studies, and introducing famous personalities who contributed to the rise of this discipline.
- Extensive, updated lists of suggested readings at the end of each chapter, of special value to motivated students who wish to probe more deeply into cultural geography on their own.
- Figure captions written to stimulate critical thinking; many captions ask questions intended to elicit a response or to heighten awareness of geographic facts or issues. Illustrations are included for their instructional value rather than as mere decoration.

■ NEW TO THIS EDITION

We have tried to take full advantage of the opportunity offered by a new edition to correct errors of fact, interpretation, or omission, and to update statistical data. Our primary goal in the fifth edition has been to incorporate suggestions for improvement made by users of previous editions. We have revised and expanded our treatment of the theme of cultural ecology, including increased attention to adaptive systems, to crises such as acid rain and the greenhouse effect, and to environmental degradation in a third-world setting; we have devoted more attention to cities in developing countries, especially in Latin America; and we have included findings contained in recently published geographic research.

To enhance the visual impact of our illustration program, we have added color photographs at various places in the text, not merely for decorative purposes, but to convey more effectively themes such as cultural landscape and to make various geographic concepts come alive.

Color-photograph essays have been designed to introduce and summarize, in a vivid and visual manner, some of the major geographic issues raised in *The Human Mosaic* — such as overpopulation, the world military power balance, the ecological value of traditional versus modern farming systems, the links between our environment and our religious faiths, the concepts of place and placelessness, the durability of ethnicity, and destructive environmental alteration.

■ NEW SUPPLEMENTS PACKAGE

The following teaching aids are available free to adopters of *The Human Mosaic*, Fifth Edition:

- **Instructor's Manual.** Written by Lester Rowntree, this new manual for teachers includes essay questions, student projects, and ideas for elaboration of text material.
- **Test Bank.** Completely new, a separate test-item file contains approximately 1,300 multiple-choice, fill-in, and true-false questions, written by Brock J. Brown, University of Colorado at Boulder.
- **Harper Test.** Available on disks, the *Test Bank* utilizes our popular Harper Test program for the Apple or IBM PC.
- **Transparency Acetates.** A package of 26 illustrations selected from the map program in the text.

While there is no doubt in our minds that the fifth is the most polished and attractive edition yet, we think most users will be pleased to know that we have enhanced but not changed the basic features of the text. Combining a thematic approach with a wide variety of topics and learning devices, we believe, produces a disciplined approach to an inherently interesting and important subject. We are confident that beginning students will develop an appreciation and understanding of our academic discipline from *The Human Mosaic*.

■ ACKNOWLEDGMENTS

No textbook is ever written single-handedly (or even "double-handedly"). In particular, an introductory text covering a wide range of topics must draw heavily on the research and help of others. In various chapters, we have not hesitated to mention a great many geographers on whose work we have drawn. We apologize for any misinterpretations or oversimplifications of their findings that may have resulted due to our own error or to the limited space available. Numerous geographers have contributed advice, comments, ideas, and assistance as this book moved from outline to draft, from first through fourth editions, and now to the fifth.

Special thanks go to James P. Allen, California State University, Northridge; John Alwin; George Aspbury, Illinois State University; Nancy R. Bain, Ohio University; Brock J. Brown, University of Colorado; John A. Carthew, Pierce College; Robert Christopherson, American River College; Michael D. Cummins, Normandale Community College; Richard D. Dastyck, Fullerton College; Donald R. Floyd, California Polytechnic State University; Larry Ford, San Diego State University; Thomas O. Graff, University of Arkansas; Charles F. Gritzner, South Dakota State University; Peter D. Herrem, University of Calgary; Sam B. Hilliard, Louisiana State University; Rex Honey, University of Iowa; Richard Hough, San Francisco State University; Fred B. Kniffen, Louisiana State University; James E. Landing, University of Illinois at Chicago Circle; Ann Larimore, University of Michigan, Ann Arbor; George Lewis, Boston University; Michael Libbee, Central Michigan University; Bonnie Loyd, *Landscape* Magazine; Risa Palm, University of Colorado; John Ressler, Central Washington University; John F. Rooney, Jr., Oklahoma State University; Christopher L. Salter, University of Missouri; James Scott, Western Washington University; James B. Sellers, Douglas College; Joseph Velikonja, University of Washington; Howard Vogel, Shoreline Community College; Philip L. Wagner, Simon Fraser University; Gene Wilken, Colorado State University; Nancy Wilkinson, San Francisco State University; and Wilbur Zelinsky, Pennsylvania State University. The authors remain fully responsible for any errors found within the text.

We also thank John Milbauer of Northeastern State University for dropping everything to go out and take some color photographs for us of his local vernacular region, "Green Country."

Our thanks, too, go to various members, past and present, of the College Department staff at Harper & Row whose encouragement, skills, and suggestions have created a special working environment and to whom we express our deepest gratitude. We are particularly grateful to Donna DeBenedictis, who has so ably served as project editor for the last two editions, and to Mary Falcon, Director of Development, who greatly smoothed the way to the fifth edition and allowed the introduction of full color. They are true professionals.

TERRY G. JORDAN
LESTER ROWNTREE

About the Authors

Terry G. Jordan is currently the Walter Prescott Webb Professor of History and Ideas in the Department of Geography at the University of Texas at Austin. He earned his Ph.D. at the University of Wisconsin–Madison. A specialist in the cultural and historical geography of the United States, Dr. Jordan is particularly interested in the various transfers of Old World culture to North America that ultimately produced the vivid geographical mosaic evident today. He has served as president of the Association of American Geographers in 1987–1988 and earlier received an honors award from that organization. He has written on a wide range of American cultural topics, including forest colonization, cattle ranching, folk architecture, and German ethnicity. His scholarly books include *The American Backwoods Frontier: An Ethnic and Ecological Interpretation* (with Matti Kaups, 1989), *American Log Buildings: An Old World Heritage* (1985), *Texas Graveyards: A Cultural Legacy* (1982), *Trails to Texas: Southern Roots of Western Cattle Ranching* (1981), and *German Seed in Texas Soil* (1966). Having been fascinated with maps and landscapes since childhood, Dr. Jordan became a geography major during his freshman year. For him, the most rewarding aspect of geography has been the field research of cultural landscape relics. His only hobby is travel, "the more often the better," and he is often able to combine travel with field research.

Lester Rowntree lives in Berkeley, California, where he is a Professor of Geography and Environmental Studies at nearby San Jose State University and a Research Associate in the Department of Anthropology at the University of California. His Ph.D. (1971) is in cultural geography from the University of Oregon. Rowntree's research and publications have concentrated on symbolism and landscapes, urban problems, social theory, and the cultural ecology of climatic fluctuations. Current work continues on these topics, in addition to a growing interest in the cultural ecology of Third World countries. After trying several different undergraduate majors in the 1960s, he chose geography because it integrated the natural and social sciences in a way that gave him an effective understanding of global environmental problems; he still finds this perspective compelling and rewarding, given his interests and concerns about the global environment.

About the Cartographic Designer

Mei-Ling Hsu is Professor of Geography at the University of Minnesota, Minneapolis, where she teaches and does research on computer-assisted cartography, cartographic/ quantitative analysis, cartographic design and communication, and the history of cartography. She received her B.A. from National Taiwan Normal University, and her M.A. and Ph.D. from the University of Wisconsin–Madison. Her publishing endeavors include *Fidelity of Isopleth Maps;* articles in *Annals of Association of American Geographers,* the *American Cartographer, Cartographica, Imago Mundi,* and *International Yearbook of Cartography;* and cartographic design in textbooks.

The
Human Mosaic

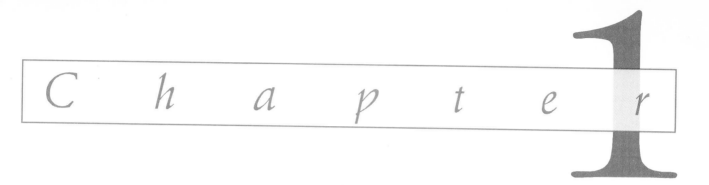

Chapter 1

The Nature of Cultural Geography

WHAT IS CULTURAL GEOGRAPHY?

THEMES IN CULTURAL GEOGRAPHY
   The Theme of Culture Region
   The Theme of Cultural Diffusion
   The Theme of Cultural Ecology

The Theme of Cultural Integration
The Theme of Cultural Landscape

THE CULTURAL GEOGRAPHICAL PAST

CONCLUSION

Geography is the science of place. Its vision is grand, its view panoramic. It sweeps the surface of the Earth, charting the physical, organic and cultural terrains, their areal differentiation, and their ecological dynamics with man. Its foremost tool is the map.

Leonard Krishtalka
Carnegie Museum of Natural History

Humans are, by nature, geographers. That is, we possess an awareness of and curiosity about the character of places and can think territorially or spatially; these attributes encompass the essential geographical qualities and dimensions. As a result, nongeographers such as Leonard Krishtalka often possess a fundamentally accurate idea of what geography involves, though they work in other academic disciplines. Even children are so endowed. They create carefully mapped realms in tiny spaces—rooms, backyards, neighborhoods (see box, "Sizing Up the World"). As we grow, our concepts of spatial relationships change constantly, gaining a partially magical quality. Always beyond what we have explored lies the unknown, the mysterious lands that we move into at our own peril and that we often populate with our fears and dreams. The academic discipline of geography is basically the product of human nature, of our ancient and insatiable curiosity about lands other than our own.

In time this natural curiosity was strengthened by the practical motives of traders and empire builders, who wanted information about the

1

SIZING UP THE WORLD: THE MAPS CHILDREN DRAW

"In the Mission Hill area of Boston, . . . Florence Ladd asked a number of black children to draw a map of their area, and then she tape-recorded her conversation with them. On Dave's map, the Mission Hill project is where the white children live, and he has drawn it as the largest, completely blank area on his map. From his taped conversation it is clear that he is physically afraid of the area and has never ventured near it. On his map the white residential area is literally *terra incognita*, while all the detail on the map is immediately around his home and school on the other side of Parker Street. Ernest also puts in Parker Street dividing his area

from the white Mission [Hill] project, and uses about a quarter of his sheet of paper to emphasize, quite unconsciously, the width of this psychological barrier. Both of these boys going to the local neighborhood schools have never ventured across this barrier to the unknown area beyond."

From Peter Gould and Rodney White, *Mental Maps* (Baltimore: Penguin, 1974), pp. 31–33. Maps from F. Ladd, "A Note on 'The World Across the Street,'" *Harvard School of Education Association Bulletin,* 12 (1967), 47–48.

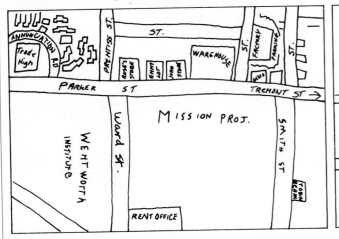

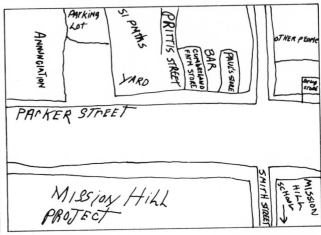

world for the purposes of commerce and conquest. It is not surprising, then, that a concern for certain practical aspects of geography in Western culture first arose among the ancient Greeks, Romans, Mesopotamians, and Phoenicians, the greatest traders and empire builders of their time. They cataloged factual information on locations, places, and products. Indeed, *geography* is a Greek word meaning literally "to describe the earth." Not content, however, merely to chart and describe the known world, these ancient geographers soon began to ask questions about why cultures and environments differ from place to place. By the end of the Roman era, geographers had developed theories of a spherical earth, latitudinal climate zones, environmental influences on humans, and people's role in modifying the Earth.

During Europe's Dark Ages, a newly expanding Arab empire took over academic geography. Muslim Arab scholars, following in the wake of trade and conquest as their Greek and Roman predecessors did, further expanded geographical knowledge. These Arab geographers were great travelers, ranging from China to Spain in search of new knowledge. Although they tended to be even more practical than the Greeks and Romans, they did not entirely ignore the theoretical side of learning. For example, Arab geographers proposed theories about the evolution of mountain ranges.

With the European cultural reawakening known as the Renaissance and the beginning of the Age of Discovery, the center of geographical learning shifted again to Europe. The modern scientific study of geography arose in Germany during the seventeenth, eighteenth, and nineteenth centuries, during the time European power was slowly spreading over much of the globe. In the 1700s, the German philosopher and geographer Immanuel Kant (see biographical sketch) defined **geography** as the study of interrelated *spatial* patterns—that is, describing and explaining the differences and similarities between one region and another. Kant compared geography and history, because he recognized that both disciplines thrive on variations. Just as geographers emphasize the differences between places or areas, so historians emphasize the differences between periods of time. If every year were identical—and the same events occurred over and over again—no academic study of history would be needed. In the same way, if every place on earth were identical, we would not need geography.

Let us extend Kant's comparison. When geographers consider the differences and similarities between places, or when historians study different points in time, they want to understand what they see. Historians compare two periods and try to find reasons for the change or lack of change from one period to the other. Geographers study spatial patterns in the same way. They first find out exactly what the variation between the areas is by describing differences and similarities as precisely as possible. Then they try to interpret the data and to decide what forces made these two areas different or alike. This process merely reflects the basic human curiosity that makes us all geographers. No one needs special training to wonder why things are where they are, and that is the geographer's key question. Historians ask the questions What? When? and Why? Geographers ask What? Where? and Why? In both disciplines, Why? is the all-important question, because it leads to interpretations. This type of analytical geographic research was begun in the nineteenth century by the German geographers Alexander von Humboldt and Carl Ritter (see biographical sketches), who are generally recognized as the fathers of modern geography.

Another similarity between geographers and historians is the way they subdivide their disciplines. Historians divide time into manageable sections called periods: the Napoleonic period, the Civil War period, the Elizabethan period, and so on. The geographic equivalent of the period is the *region*, a subdivision of the earth. Examples of regional divisions are the geography of Europe, of Latin America, or of California. Both periods and regions are characterized by certain unifying traits that justify picking them out of time and space.

Another way of dividing subject matter common to both geography and history is the **topical** or *systematic* method. Using this method, the geographer or the historian singles out a certain topic rather than a region or period. A geographer might choose to study political geography, urban geography, or agricultural geography; a historian might select military history, agricultural history, or economic history. Within geography, the two principal topical divisions are physical and cultural. Each of these is, in turn, separated into smaller topical divisions. In this book, we use mainly a topical approach to cultural geography. However, as the "culture region" theme discussed later in this chapter indicates, the regional approach is not ignored.

It is our aim in this textbook to teach you to see the human world through your geographer's eyes. If we succeed, you will have a new perspective of the world—a useful one, we believe. Analysis and answer-seeking are important, and we will show you how geographers solve problems. Equally important, though, is the geographer's perspective of the world, a unique perspective that we regard as essential for any truly educated person.

IMMANUEL KANT
1724–1804

Kant is best known as a philosopher, but he taught a course in physical geography between 1756 and 1798 at the University of Königsberg in East Prussia. Königsberg, today called Kaliningrad, was on the far edge of the Prussian state, much as Alaska is on the far edge of the United States. Kant brought international attention to this provincial German town and university. He organized geography into such categories as mathematical, "theological," commercial, political, and "moral" (an account of differing customs of peoples). In addition, he developed the distinction between geography and history described in the text. Kant defined geography as the study of spatial variations.

ALEXANDER VON HUMBOLDT
1769–1859

Humboldt, a world-famous German scientist, traveled widely and wrote extensively on geographical topics. In 1797, with the permission of the Spanish crown, he sailed to South America. For the next five years, he explored from Mexico to the Andes. Later, at the age of 60, he accepted an invitation from the czar of Russia to explore mineral resources. He traveled by carriage through Siberia, carefully recording and describing the landscape. His interests were in physical geography — the study of climate, terrain, and vegetation — but Humboldt's writings reveal his belief that humans are part of the ecological system. His main contribution to geography was his attention to cause-and-effect relationships. Most geographies of earlier times merely compiled facts. When Humboldt tried to explain spatial patterns of certain physical phenomena, he found geography useful. Because he brought the prestige and methods of science to geography, he is considered one of the founders of modern geography. Humboldt never held a university position, but he was widely respected as a scholar. His single most important geographical publication was *Cosmos*, a five-volume work. (For more on Humboldt's remarkable life and achievements, see Loren McIntyre, ''Humboldt's Way,'' *National Geographic*, 168 (1985), 318–351.)

■ WHAT IS CULTURAL GEOGRAPHY?

The term **cultural geography** implies an emphasis on human cultures rather than on the physical environment people live in. To understand the scope of cultural geography, we must first agree on what the word *culture* means. Social scientists and humanists have suggested many definitions of culture, some broad and some narrow. Furthermore, even within some disciplines not all scholars agree on a common definition. For our purposes, we will define culture as learned collective behavior, as opposed to instinctive, or inborn, behavior. These learned traits form a total way of life held in common by a group of people. Learned similarities in speech, behavior, ideology, livelihood, technology, value system, and society bind people together in a culture. It involves a communication system of acquired beliefs, perceptions, and attitudes that serves to supplement and channel instinctive behavior.

Cultural geography, then, is the study of spatial variations among cultural groups and the spatial functioning of society. It focuses on describing and analyzing the ways language, religion, economy, government, and other cultural phenomena vary or remain constant from one place to another and on explaining how humans function spatially (Figure 1.1). Cultural geography is, at heart, a celebration of human diversity. Because cultures are formed by groups of people, the cultural geographer

FIGURE 1-1
Geographers seek to learn how and why cultures differ, or are similar, from one place to another. Often those differences and similarities have a visual expression. In what ways are these two structures — one a rural Lutheran church in the treeless tundra of Iceland and the other a Greek Orthodox chapel amidst the olive groves of Crete — alike and different?

is necessarily concerned with humans in the aggregate. However, you should not make the mistake of assuming that the individual person is culturally unimportant or powerless. A culture, after all, is not an organism or an irresistible force compelling its members to behave in a certain way. At the most basic level, culture is simply people interacting with one another. An individual is therefore potentially able to modify the culture he or she shares with others. Partly for this reason, change is an ever-present cultural phenomenon.

Anthropologists, historians, and sociologists share geographers' fascination with culture. Geographers' attention to cultures overlaps that of many of these other social scientists and humanists. Even so, it is still possible to discern a focus of concern that sets geographers apart from other students of culture: our previously mentioned concern with the ways cultures and societies vary and function *spatially*. Geographers are trained to observe spatial patterns of all kinds, both human and environmental. Therefore, they are particularly well qualified to describe and interpret spatial variations in culture. Geographers recognize that any differences and similarities in cultures are the result of complex forces. As a result, they can rarely find easy explanations for the questions raised by spatial patterns in culture, causing them to adopt a rather holistic or integrative view of culture.

The complexity of the forces that affect culture can be illustrated by an example drawn form agricultural geography: the distribution of wheat cultivation in the world. Looking at the map in Figure 1.2, you can see important wheat cultivation in Australia but not Africa, the United States but not Brazil, China but not Southeast Asia. Why does this spatial pattern exist? Partly it is due to environmental factors such as climate, terrain, and soils. Some regions have always been too dry for wheat cultivation, others too steep or infertile. Indeed, there is a strong correlation between wheat cultivation and midlatitude climates, level terrain, and good soil. Still, do not place too much importance on such physical factors. People can now modify the effects of climate through irrigation, the use of hothouses, or the development of new, specialized strains of wheat. They can conquer slopes through terracing, and they can make infertile soils productive through fertilization. For example, farmers in mountainous parts of Greece wrest an annual harvest of wheat from tiny, terraced plots where soil has been trapped behind hand-built stone retaining walls. Even in the United States, environmental factors alone cannot explain the curious fact that major wheat cultivation is concentrated in the semiarid Great Plains, some distance from states such as Ohio and Illinois, where the climate for wheat is better.

The cultural geographer knows that wheat has to survive in a cultural as well as physical environment. Agricultural patterns cannot be explained by the characteristics of the land and climate alone. Many factors complicate the distribution of wheat, including people's tastes, desires, and traditions. Food preferences and taboos, often backed by religious beliefs, strongly influence the choice of crops to plant. Some cultural groups, such as the Poles, prefer dark bread made from rye flour. Other groups, particularly American Indians, would rather eat breads made from corn. Obviously, wheat will not "thrive" in such cultural environments. Where wheat bread *is* preferred, people are willing to put great efforts into overcoming hostile physical surroundings. They have even created new strains of wheat, thereby decreasing the environment's influence on distribution. Economics also enters the picture. Wheat cultivation can be encouraged or discouraged by tariffs like those protecting the

CARL RITTER
1779–1859

Ritter, a longtime and close associate of Alexander von Humboldt, was a professor of geography at the University of Berlin beginning in 1820. He began his career as a tutor for a wealthy family in Frankfurt. In these comfortable surroundings, he was able to meet other intellectuals and study geography. During the long period he taught in Berlin, his work influenced the thinking of many people, including military leaders. In contrast to Humboldt, his chief concern was cultural geography, the geography of humans. He sought to bring the rigor of science to the study of human geography and believed that laws of human spatial behavior could be discovered. His first book discussed Africa, then a little-known continent, but he is best known for the massive work entitled *Die Erdkunde (Geography)*, which appeared in 19 volumes between 1822 and his death. Ritter is widely regarded as a cofounder, with Humboldt, of the academic discipline of geography.

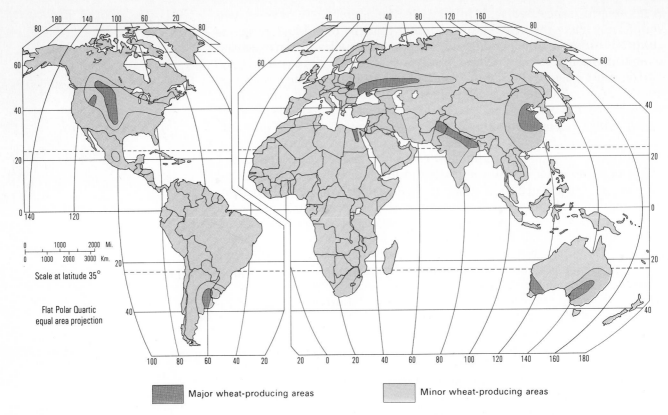

Major wheat-producing areas   Minor wheat-producing areas

FIGURE 1-2
This map shows areas of wheat production in the world. These culture regions are based on a single trait — the importance of wheat in the agricultural system.

wheat farmers of Germany and other Common Market countries from competition with more efficient American and Canadian producers. In addition, wheat farming is a less profitable use of the land than dairying or fattening livestock. For this reason, wheat is sometimes not grown in the most suitable regions, such as the American Midwest.

This is by no means a complete list of the forces that affect wheat distribution. It should be clear, though, that the contemporary map of wheat reflects the pushing and pulling of many factors. The distribution of all cultural elements, not only the distribution of wheat, is a result of the constant interplay of diverse causal factors.

▮ THEMES IN CULTURAL GEOGRAPHY

Our study of cultures will be organized around five geographical concepts or themes. These are **culture region, cultural diffusion, cultural ecology, cultural integration,** and **cultural landscape.** These themes will be stressed throughout the book, giving structure to each chapter. They represent only one of many possible ways to study cultural geography, and not all cultural geographers employ them. However, we find them to be useful devices for teaching the concepts of cultural geography.

The Theme of Culture Region

Places provide the main stuff of geography. How and why are places alike or different? How are they meshed together into functioning spatial networks? How do their inhabitants perceive and identify with them? These are all essential geographical questions. **Region** is the word and concept used by geographers to mean a grouping of like places or the functional union of places to form a spatial unit. Maps are an essential tool used to describe and reveal regions. If, as is often said, one picture is worth a thousand words, then a well-prepared map is worth at least ten thousand words to the geographer. No description in words can rival the descriptive force of maps. Maps are valuable tools particularly because they so concisely portray spatial patterns in culture. Three types of regions are recognized by cultural geographers.

Formal Culture Regions. A **formal culture region** can be defined as a uniform area inhabited by people who have one or more cultural traits in common. If cultural geography, above all, is a celebration of human diversity in the spatial dimension, then the formal culture region is a depiction of that mosaic. You cannot go into the street and find a formal culture region, yet there is nothing mysterious about it. Geographers find the formal culture region useful for grouping people with similar cultural traits. It is a tool geographers can use to describe spatial differences in culture. For example, a German-language culture region can be drawn on a map of languages, and it would include the area where German is spoken. Or a wheat-farming region could describe the parts of the world where wheat is a major crop (look again at Figure 1.2).

The examples of German speech and wheat cultivation represent the concept of formal region at its simplest level. Each is based on a single cultural trait. More commonly, culture regions depend on multiple related traits (see Figure 1.3). Thus an Eskimo culture region might be based on

FIGURE 1-3
In this market in Morocco, various facets of a multitrait formal culture region are apparent. Agricultural products, marketing, architecture, and clothing all contribute to the region's identity.

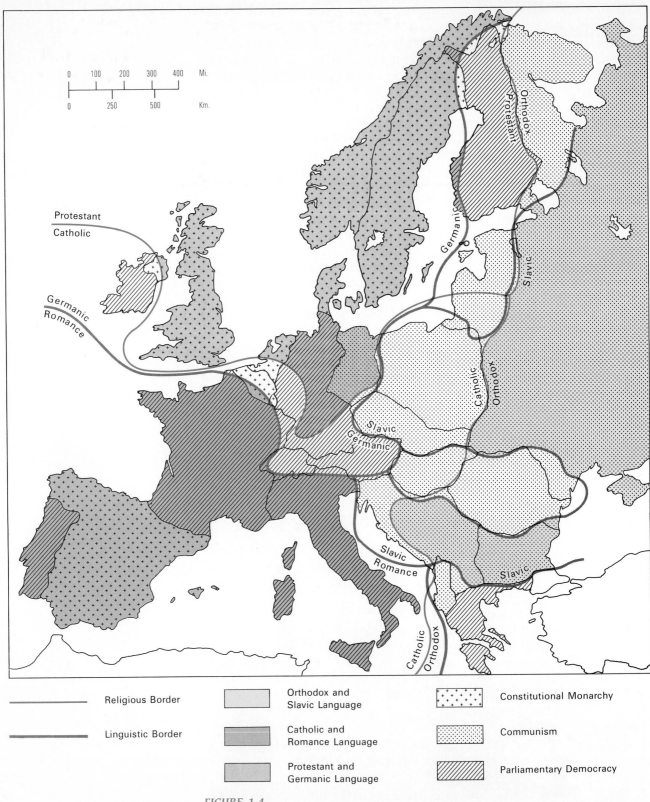

FIGURE 1-4
Multitrait formal culture regions of Europe, based on language and traditional religion. Notice how transitional areas appear between such culture regions even when only two traits are used to define them. How much wider would the transition zone become if a third trait, type of government, were added—Communism for the Slavic-Orthodox region, constitutional monarchy for the Germanic-Protestant region, and parliamentary democracy for the Romance-Catholic region?

language, religion, type of economy, type of social organization, and typical form of dwellings. The culture region would reflect the spatial distribution of these five Eskimo cultural traits. Districts where all five of these traits are present would be part of the culture region. A more complex culture, such as that of Europe, can also be subdivided into multitrait regions (see Figure 1.4).

Formal culture regions are the geographer's somewhat arbitrary creations. No two cultural traits have the same distribution and the territorial extent of a culture region depends on what defining traits are used (Figure 1.5). For example, Greeks and Turks differ in language and religion. Culture regions defined on the basis of speech and religious faith would separate these two groups. However, Greeks and Turks hold many other cultural traits in common, partly because of the long Turkish rule of Greece and the lengthy coexistence of Greeks and Turks in Asia Minor. Both groups are monotheistic, worshiping a single god. In both groups, male supremacy and patriarchal families are the rule. Certain folk foods, such as shish kebab, are enjoyed in common. Whether Greeks and Turks are placed in the same formal culture region or in different ones depends entirely on how the geographer chooses to define the culture region. That choice in turn depends on the specific purpose of research or exposition that the culture region is designed to serve. Thus an infinite number of formal culture regions can be created. It is unlikely that any two geographers would use exactly the same distinguishing criteria.

Often cultural geographers attempt to delimit culture regions based on the totality of traits displayed by a culture. The term **culture area** is sometimes used for such regions. Because of the greater complexity of traits involved, culture areas are typically even more arbitrarily delimited than are formal regions based on fewer characteristics. Often they are based more on the geographer's intuition, derived from intimate knowledge of an area, than on carefully marshaled facts. Figure 1.6 shows a ninefold division of the United States and southern Canada into traditional rural culture areas. The "Yankee" region, sometimes referred to as "New England extended," was originally settled by colonists largely from England in the period before American independence. Their agricultural technology was poorly suited to such cold, infertile lands. Marginal success in farming caused many colonists to turn to fishing, trading, manufacturing, and lumbering as occupations. In its early stage, the Yankee area was a theocracy, controlled by Puritan leaders. In contrast, the Midland culture area embraced a great variety of ethnic groups. English, Scotch-Irish, Germans, Swedes, Finns, Welsh, and other European groups met and mingled here, importing rich and diverse agricultural heritages into a fertile land. The middle-class family farm was instituted here. Quakers, Lutherans, German and Dutch Reformed, Presbyterians, Mennonites, and various other Protestant sects were represented. Here was America's first **melting pot** (see Chapter 9). The result was a farming culture that shaped the face of much of the rural United States from then on. In the Lower South, British, French, and African traits were combined in a plantation system of agriculture. Large estates, specializing in subtropical cash crops and depending on a large body of slave laborers, gave rise to a landed aristocracy that quickly assumed political control of the plantation colonies. The other six culture areas on the map also developed uniquely, formed by interactions among diverse cultural groups in particular environmental and temporal settings.

The geographer who identifies a formal culture region or area must locate cultural borders. Because cultures are fluid, such boundaries are

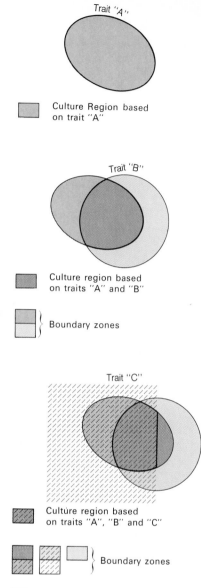

Trait "A"

▨ Culture Region based on trait "A"

Trait "B"

▨ Culture region based on traits "A" and "B"

▨ } Boundary zones

Trait "C"

▨ Culture region based on traits "A", "B" and "C"

▨ ▨ ▨ } Boundary zones

FIGURE 1-5
Hypothetical formal culture regions based on one, two, and three traits. Notice that no two traits have the same spatial distribution. Thus with each additional trait, the core of the region grows smaller and the boundary zone broader.

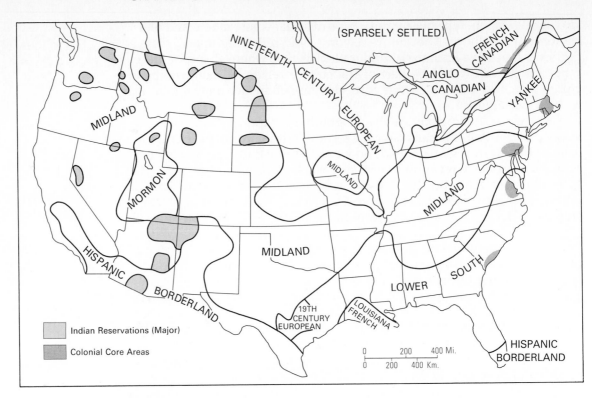

FIGURE 1-6
Traditional rural culture areas of the continental United States and southern Canada. An attempt was made to consider a totality of traits in drawing the borders, making the delimitation by necessity highly subjective.

rarely sharp, even if only a single culture trait is being mapped. For this reason, geographers often speak of cultural border zones rather than lines. Naturally, these zones broaden with each additional cultural trait that is considered, because no two traits have the same spatial distribution.

No matter how closely related two elements of culture seem to be, careful investigation always shows that they do not exactly cover the same area. This is true regardless of what degree of detail is involved. Thus, just as the map of languages does not duplicate the distribution of religions, governments, or economies, so also no two words or pronunciations within a single dialect or language cover precisely the same area.

What does this mean to the cultural geographer in practical terms? First, it means that every feature and detail of culture is unique to an area and that the explanation for each spatial variation is different in some degree from those for all other cultural phenomena. Second, it means that culture changes continually through an area, and that every inhabited place on the Earth has a unique combination of cultural features, differing from every other place in one or more respects.

Does this cultural uniqueness of each place prevent geographers from seeking explanatory theories? Does it doom them to explaining each distribution separately? The answer must be no. The fact that no two hills or rocks, no two planets or stars, no two trees or flowers are identical has not prevented geologists, astronomers, and botanists from formulating theories based on generalizations.

The lack of areal covariation does mean that multitrait formal regions cannot have sharp borders. Instead, they reveal a core, where the defining traits are all present, and away from which the regional characteristics weaken and disappear, as is suggested in Figures 1.4 and 1.5. Thus formal regions display a **core/periphery** pattern.

Cultural boundary zones are often extremely durable, surviving long after the causal forces that created them have vanished. Central Europe provides a good example of this persistence (see Figure 1.7).

Functional Culture Regions.   A **functional culture region** is quite different from a formal culture region. The hallmark of the formal type is cultural homogeneity, and the formal culture region is abstract rather than concrete. By contrast, the functional culture region is generally not culturally homogeneous. Instead, it is an area that has been organized to function politically, socially, or economically. A city, an independent state, a precinct, a church diocese or parish, a trade area, a farm, and a Federal Reserve Bank district are all examples of functional regions. Functional culture regions have **nodes,** or central points where the functions are coordinated and directed. Examples of such nodes are city halls, national capitals, precinct voting places, parish churches, factories, farmsteads, and banks. In this sense, functional regions also possess a core/periphery configuration, in common with formal regions.

Some functional regions have clearly defined borders and are concrete units. A farm is a functional region that includes all land owned or leased by the farmer (see box, "Culture Regions in a Microcosm"). Its operation is directed by the farmer, who has organized the land to function

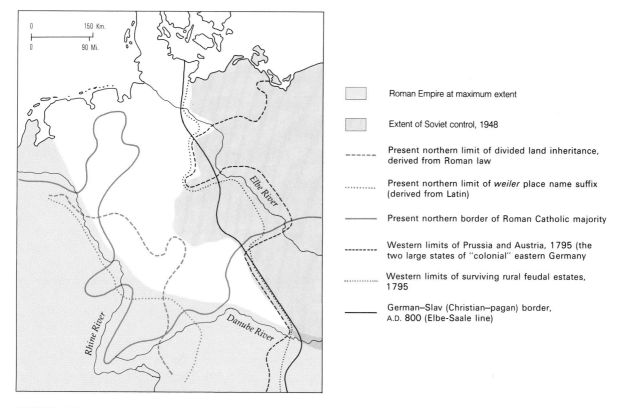

▨	Roman Empire at maximum extent
▨	Extent of Soviet control, 1948
– – – –	Present northern limit of divided land inheritance, derived from Roman law
··········	Present northern limit of *weiler* place name suffix (derived from Latin)
————	Present northern border of Roman Catholic majority
- - - - - -	Western limits of Prussia and Austria, 1795 (the two large states of "colonial" eastern Germany
············	Western limits of surviving rural feudal estates, 1795
————	German–Slav (Christian–pagan) border, A.D. 800 (Elbe-Saale line)

FIGURE 1-7
This map displays the persistence of a cultural border zone in central Europe. Since Roman times, an east-west cultural division has characterized central Europe. This ancient cultural divide has taken many forms—political, legal, religious, social, economic, and place-names. It has persisted in spite of repeated German attempts to unify central Europe. (Derived in part from Werner B. Cahnman, "Frontiers Between East and West in Europe," *Geographical Review,* 39 (1949), 605–624.)

CULTURE REGIONS IN A MICROCOSM

Imagine a valley filled with farms. Each farm consists of a strip of land reaching from the center of the valley up to the adjacent ridge crest (see map). Farmsteads are at the fronts of the farms, along a road that bisects the valley. On each farm, the slope of the land becomes steeper as we go away from the road. On the most level land, at the front of each farm, wheat is raised, and with the steadily increasing slope toward the rear of each farm, we encounter vineyards, then pastures, and finally, on the steepest slopes at the rear of the farm, forest. Thus each farm in the valley consists of wheat fields, vineyards, pastures, and woodland with increasing distance from the road. Each of these types of land use occupies a continuous strip running lengthwise through the valley.

In this situation, both formal and functional culture regions are present. Each farm constitutes a functional region, and the strips of wheat, vineyards, pasture, and woodland are each formal culture regions, defined by the homogeneity of land use.

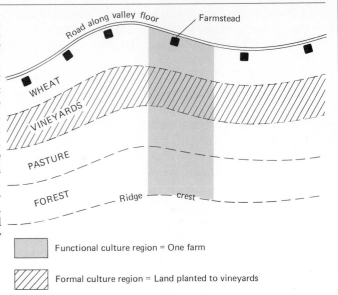

as a distinct spatial unit. The node is the farmstead, which contains the home of the farmer and various structures essential to farming, such as barns, implement sheds, and silos. The borders of this functional region will probably be clearly marked by fences, hedges, or walls. Similarly, each state in the United States is a functional region, coordinated and directed from the state capital and extending government control over a fixed area with clearly defined borders.

It is misleading to think all functional culture regions have fixed, precise borders. It is better to imagine these borders in terms of increasing or diminishing flows of energy out of or into nodes. On a map, this motion might be represented by directional arrows rather than boundary lines—as a network, not a territory. A good example is a daily newspaper's trade area. The node for the paper would be the plant where it is produced. Every morning, trucks move out of the plant to distribute the paper throughout the city. The newspaper may have a sales area extending into the city's suburbs, local bedroom communities, nearby towns, and rural areas. There its sales area overlaps the sales territories of competing newspapers published in other cities. It would be futile to try to define borders for such a process. How would you draw a sales area boundary for *The New York Times*? Its Sunday edition is sold in some quantity even in California, thousands of miles from its node.

The sales areas for manufactured goods present similar problems. Every time you buy a soft drink or a bottle of beer, you are a part of a dynamic functional culture region. Which bottle you choose depends on the regions you are in. Some beer manufacturers have gone nationwide in their marketing, establishing branch breweries in various parts of the country. Schlitz, Budweiser, and Pabst are in this category. Certain others confine sales activity to selected multistate regions, and some, such as Lone Star of Texas, are marketed largely within a single state. Finally, some beers are sold in small, local areas, as Pittsburgh's Iron City beer is. Each beer has a unique market area—a functional region—and these often overlap one another. The node for each beer's functional area is the brewery.

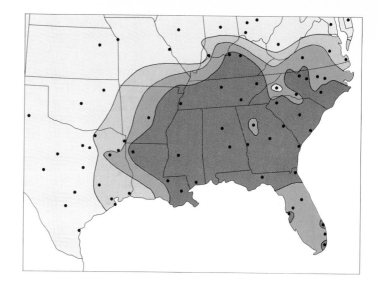

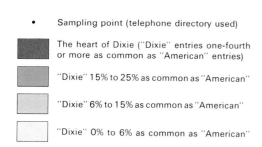

- Sampling point (telephone directory used)

The heart of Dixie ("Dixie" entries one-fourth or more as common as "American" entries)

"Dixie" 15% to 25% as common as "American"

"Dixie" 6% to 15% as common as "American"

"Dixie" 0% to 6% as common as "American"

FIGURE 1-8
Dixie: a vernacular region. "Dixie" is a more restrictive regional term than is "South," and it is loaded with historical and cultural connotations. The territorial extent of "Dixie" was determined by counting the number of times it apeared in telephone directories as part of the name of business establishments. The total for each city was then divided by the entries for "American," to adjust for the different population sizes of the cities, producing the numbers on the map. The higher the number, the more common the use of "Dixie." Make a count of regional terms in your telephone directory. Does the place where you live lie within a vernacular region such as Dixie? How does the perceived "Dixie" compare to the formal region "Lower South" in Figure 1.6? (After John Shelton Reed, "The Heart of Dixie: An Essay in Folk Geography," *Social Forces,* 54 (1976), 932, with modifications for Texas.)

Vernacular Culture Regions.   Geographers recognize a third type of culture region, the **vernacular** or **perceptual.** This is a region perceived to exist by its inhabitants, as evidenced by the widespread acceptance and use of a regional name. The map, Figure 1.8, reveals one such popular region in the United States, "Dixie," and the photograph, Figure 1.9, shows a visible expression of that region. Some vernacular regions are based on physical environmental features, while others find their basis in economic, political, historical, or promotional aspects. Vernacular regions, like most culture regions, generally lack sharp borders, and the inhabitants of any given area may claim residence in more than one such region. These perceived regions are often created by publicity campaigns, and their use in the communications media has a lot to do with acceptance by the local population.

FIGURE 1-9
Notice the "Heart of Dixie" symbol on this Alabama state license plate.

The element of regional self-consciousness, through which people are aware of their regional identity and endow it with symbols and emotions, is inherent in the vernacular type of region. By contrast, many formal or functional regions lack this attribute and are, as a result, far less potent geographical entities. Self-conscious regional identity can have major political and social ramifications.

Vernacular culture regions, as you can see, are rather different from the functional or formal types. They often lack the organization necessary for functional regions, though often they are centered on a single urban node, and they frequently do not display the cultural homogeneity that characterizes formal regions. They are a type unto themselves, a type rooted in the popular or folk culture, as we will see in Chapter 8.

The Theme of Cultural Diffusion

The culture regions of the world, regardless of type, evolved through communication and contact among people. In other words, they are the product of **cultural diffusion,** the spatial spread of learned ideas, innovations, and attitudes, As Figure 1.10 shows, each element of culture originates in one or more places and then spreads. Some innovations occur only once, and therefore geographers can sometimes trace a cultural element back to a single place of origin. In other cases, **independent invention** occurs. The same or very similar innovation is independently developed at different places by different peoples. The study of cultural diffusion—the origin and spread of ideas and innovations throughout an area—is a very important theme in cultural geography. Through the study of diffusion, the cultural geographer can begin to understand how spatial patterns in culture evolved.

Any culture is the product of almost countless innovations that spread from their points of origin to cover a wider area. Some of these innovations occurred thousands of years ago, others very recently. Some spread widely (see box, "Cultural Diffusion: A 100 Percent American"), while others remained confined to their area of origin. Geographers, drawing upon the research of Torsten Hägerstrand (see biographical sketch), recognize several different kinds of diffusion. Two important types are **expansion diffusion** and **relocation diffusion.** In expansion

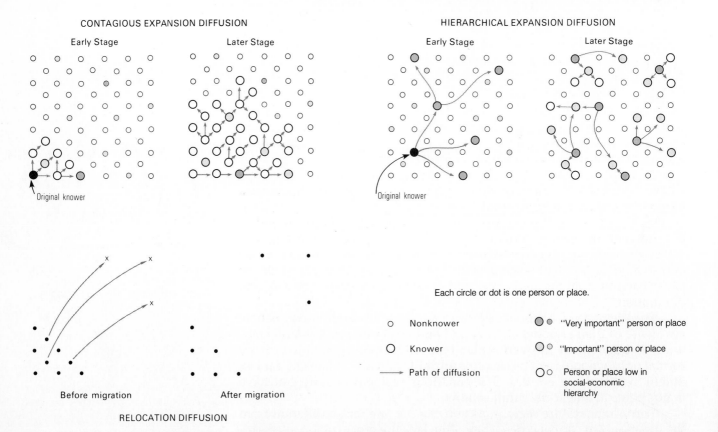

FIGURE 1-10
Types of cultural diffusion are presented here. These diagrams are merely suggestve; in reality, spatial diffusion is far more complex. In hierarchical diffusion, different scales can be used, so that, for example, a "very important person" could be replaced by "large city."

diffusion, ideas spread throughout a population, from area to area, in a snowballing process, so that the total number of knowers and the area of occurrence become ever greater. Relocation diffusion occurs when individuals or groups with a particular idea move bodily from one location to another, thereby spreading the innovation to their new homeland. Religions are frequently spread this way. An example is the migration of Christianity with European settlers who came to America. Indeed, the entire process of European-based colonialism, lasting from about 1500 to 1950, constituted perhaps the most important occurrence of relocation diffusion in all of history.

Expansion diffusion can be further divided into subtypes called **stimulus diffusion, hierarchical diffusion,** and **contagious diffusion.** In hierarchical diffusion, ideas leapfrog from one important person to another or from one urban center to another, temporarily bypassing other persons or rural territory. We can see hierarchical diffusion at work in everyday life by observing the acceptance of new modes of dress or hairstyles. By contrast, contagious diffusion involves the general spread of ideas, without regard to hierarchies, in the manner of a contagious disease. Sometimes a specific trait is rejected, but the underlying idea is accepted. This is **stimulus diffusion.** For example, it is generally believed that early Siberian cultures domesticated reindeer only after exposure to the domesticated cattle and horses raised by cultures to their south. The Siberians had no use for these animals, but the idea of domesticated herds appealed to them and they began domesticating reindeer.

If you throw a rock into a pond and watch the spreading ripples, you can see them become gradually weaker as they move away from the point of impact. While these ripples are not cultural, they are similar to diffusion because the acceptance of a cultural innovation decreases with distance. An innovation will be accepted most thoroughly in the areas closest to where it originates. Time is also a factor, since it takes increasing time for innovations to spread outward. Because acceptance decreases with distance, acceptance also decreases with time. This is what geographers mean by **time-distance decay.** Modern mass media have greatly speeded diffusion, diminishing the impact of time-distance decay.

In addition to the "natural" weakening or decay of an innovation through time and distance, barriers tend to retard its spread. **Absorbing barriers** completely halt the diffusion, allowing no further progress. For example, television was for decades prevented from entering the Republic of South Africa because the government there outlawed it. The border of the Republic thus served as an absorbing barrier to the spread of television. Few absorbing barriers exist in the world. More commonly, barriers are **permeable,** allowing part of the innovation wave to diffuse through but acting to weaken and retard the continued spread. For example, when a school board objects to long hair on boys, the principal of a high school may set a limit on hair length for male students. This length will likely be longer than the haircuts before the long-hair innovation, but it will be shorter than the length of the new hairstyle. In this way, the principal and school board act as a permeable barrier to a cultural innovation. Barriers may be either cultural—in the form of social or governmental taboos and restrictions—or environmental. The old joke about selling refrigerators to Eskimos as the ultimate test of a salesperson's ability reveals the environmental barrier that can be encountered by innovations.

Acceptance of innovations at any given point in space can be depicted with an S-shaped curve that includes three distinct stages. The first stage

TORSTEN HÄGERSTRAND 1916–

A native and resident of Sweden, Hägerstrand is professor emeritus of geography at the University of Lund, where he received a doctorate in 1953. His doctoral research was on innovation diffusion, and his findings were published in 1953. His work on diffusion is significant because it is based on models and statistical techniques. As a result, it has been the basis for many theories and has elevated cultural geographers' research on diffusion to a higher, more scientific level. Sweden, and particularly Lund, has become a major center of innovative work in cultural geography. In 1968 Professor Hägerstrand received an Outstanding Achievement Award from the Association of American Geographers, and in 1985 he was awarded an honorary doctor of science degree from Ohio State University. The commendation accompanying the honorary degree noted that "his work on innovation diffusion, carried out in the 1950s and 1960s, continues to be cited as a standard against which current research is measured" and that "this distinguished individual . . . inspired a generation of scholars around the world."

Mc Donalds? delayed response

CULTURAL DIFFUSION: A 100 PERCENT AMERICAN

"Our solid American citizen awakens in a bed built on a pattern that originated in the Near East but that was modified in Northern Europe before it was transmitted to America. He throws back covers made from cotton, domesticated in India, or linen, domesticated in the Near East, or silk, the use of which was discovered in China. All of these materials have been spun and woven by processes invented in the Near East. He slips into his moccasins, invented by the Indians of the Eastern woodlands, and goes to the bathroom, whose fixtures are a mixture of European and American inventions, both of recent date. He takes off his pajamas, a garment invented in India, and washes with soap, invented by the ancient Gauls. He then shaves—a masochistic rite that seems to have been derived from either Sumer or ancient Egypt.

". . . On his way to breakfast, he stops to buy a paper, paying for it with coins, an ancient Lydian invention. At the restaurant, a whole new series of borrowed elements confronts him. His plate is made of a form of pottery invented in China. His knife is of steel, an alloy first made in southern India; his fork, a medieval Italian invention; and his spoon, a derivative of a Roman original.

". . . When our friend has finished eating, . . . he reads the news of the day, imprinted in characters invented by the ancient Semites upon a material invented in China by a process invented in Germany. As he absorbs the accounts of foreign trouble, he will, if he is a good, conservative citizen, thank a Hebrew deity in an Indo-European language that he is 100 percent American."

From Ralph Linton, *The Study of Man: An Introduction.* Copyright © 1936, renewed 1964, pp. 326–327. Adapted by permission of Prentice-Hall, Inc., Englewood Cliffs, N.J.

---

sees acceptance taking place at a steady, yet slow, rate, perhaps because the innovation has not yet caught on, the benefits have not been adequately demonstrated, or the trait is not physically available. Then during the second stage, there is rapid growth in acceptance, and the trait will spread widely, as with a fashion style or dance fad. Often diffusion on a microscale will exhibit what is called the **neighborhood effect,** which means simply that acceptance is usually most rapid in small clusters around an initial adopter. Think of a fad that first appeared in your neighborhood one day; a few days later it seemed that everyone on the block was doing the same thing. Direct exposure to an innovation is the best advertisement. The third stage of growth shows a slower rate than the second, perhaps because the fad is passing, or because an area is already saturated with the innovation.

While all places and communities hypothetically have equal potential for innovation, it is nevertheless true that invention and diffusion normally produce a core/periphery spatial arrangement, the same pattern observed earlier in our discussion of culture regions (Figures 1.4, 1.5). Recently, Hägerstrand has offered an explanation of how diffusion produces such a regional configuration. While the distribution of innovations can be random, the *overlap* of new ideas and traits as they diffuse through area and time is greatest toward the center and least on the peripheries (Figure 1.11). In this manner, cores develop based on the greater availability of innovations in the central region.

Some other cultural geographers, most notably James M. Blaut, have criticized this Hägerstrandian concept of diffusion. They regard it as too narrow and mechanical, since it does not give enough emphasis to cultural variables. As a result, wrote Professor Blaut, "Serious difficulties arise whenever efforts are made to generalize the . . . Hägerstrand theory or to apply it in realms and epochs which are culturally distant from the modern Western world." Nondiffusion—the failure of innovations to spread—is perhaps more prevalent than diffusion, a condition Hägerstrand's system cannot successfully accommodate. Furthermore, Blaut argued, the Hägerstrand concept lacks explanatory power.

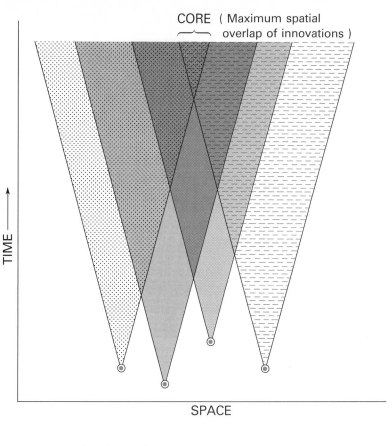

CORE (Maximum spatial overlap of innovations)

TIME →

SPACE

⊚   Innovation

◗   Diffusion of innovation through space and time

FIGURE 1-11
Evolution of regional core and periphery from a random distribution of innovations and an equal rate of cultural diffusion in space and time. This scheme was proposed by Torsten Hägerstrand at a symposium on diffusion held at Texas A&M Universtiy in 1984.

The Theme of Cultural Ecology

Cultural geographers look on people and nature as interacting. Cultures do not exist in a vacuum. Each human group and the way of life it has developed occupy a piece of the physical earth. Cultures, as you might expect, interact with the environment, and it is necessary for the cultural geographer to study this interaction in order to understand spatial variations in culture. This study is called **cultural ecology.** The word **ecology,** as used here, refers to the two-way relationship between an organism and its physical environment. It comes from two ancient Greek words. *Oikos* means "house" or "habitat"; *logia* means "words" or "teachings." Thus the Greek *oikologia* could be rendered "teachings about the habitat." Cultural ecology, then, is the study of the cause-and-effect interplay between cultures and the physical environment. A **physical environment** is understood to include climate, terrain, soil, natural vegetation, wildlife, and other aspects of the physical surroundings. Another frequently used word is **ecosystem.** By this, we seek to describe the functioning ecological system in which biological and cultural *Homo sapiens* live and interact with the physical environment. In sum, we may define cultural ecology as the study of (1) environmental influence on culture and (2) the impact of people, acting through their culture, on the ecosystem. Cultural ecology, then, implies a "two-way street," with people and the environment exerting influence on one another.

The theme of cultural ecology is the meeting ground of cultural and physical geographers and has traditionally provided a focal point for the academic discipline of geography. In fact, some geographers have proposed that geography *is* cultural ecology. They argue that study of the intricate relationships between people and their physical environments constitutes a valid academic discipline. While few accept this narrow definition of geography, most will agree that appreciating the complex people-environment relationship is necessary for concerned citizens of the late twentieth century. Through the years, cultural geographers have developed various perspectives on the spatial interaction between humans and the land. In a broad sense, four schools of thought have developed: environmental determinism, possibilism, environmental perception, and humans as modifiers of the Earth.

Environmental Determinism.   During the first quarter of the twentieth century, many English-speaking geographers adhered to the doctrine of **environmental determinism.** These geographers believed that the physical environment, especially the climate and terrain, was the active force in shaping cultures—that humankind was essentially a passive product of the physical surroundings. According to the logic of the determinist, humans were clay to be molded by nature. Similar physical environments were likely to produce similar cultures. In effect, environmental determinists view cultural ecology as a "one-way street."

There are many examples of determinist beliefs. Determinists believed that peoples of the mountains were predestined by the rugged terrain to be simple, backward, conservative, unimaginative, and freedom loving. Dwellers of the desert were likely to believe in one god, but to live under the rule of tyrants. Temperate climates produced inventiveness, industriousness, and democracy, whereas coastlands pitted with fjords produced great navigators and fishermen. Environmental determinists had a handy explanation for England's preeminent position in the world at that time: The surrounding waters demanded seamanship, and an optimum climate produced genius for government and a work ethic.

From the perspective of the late twentieth century, we can see that the determinists overemphasized the role of environment in human affairs. This does not imply that environmental influence is inconsequential or that the cultural geographer should not study such influence. Rather, it suggests that the physical environment is only one of many forces affecting human culture and is rarely the sole determinant of human behavior and beliefs.

Possibilism.   Since the 1930s, environmental determinism has fallen from favor among cultural geographers. **Possibilism** has taken its place. Possibilists do not ignore the influence of the physical environment, and they realize that the imprint of nature shows in many cultures. However, possibilists stress that cultural heritage is at least as important as the physical environment in affecting human behavior (see box, "The Facts Are Incontestable").

According to possibilists, people, rather than their environment, are the primary architects of culture (see Figure 1.12). Possibilists claim that any physical environment offers a number of possible ways for a culture to develop. How people use and inhabit an area depends on the choices they make among the possibilities offered by the environment. These choices

---

"THE FACTS ARE INCONTESTABLE": AN ENVIRONMENTAL DETERMINIST'S AND A POSSIBILIST'S VIEWS OF CREATIVE GENIUS

An Environmental Determinist's View

"The absence of artistic and poetic development in Switzerland and the Alpine lands [may be ascribed] to the overwhelming aspect of nature there, its majestic sublimity which paralyzes the mind. . . . This position [is reinforced] by the fact that . . . the lower mountains and hill country of Swabia, Franconia and Thuringia, where nature is gentler, stimulating, appealing, and not overpowering, have produced many poets and artists. The facts are incontestable. They reappear in France in the geographical distribution of the awards made by the Paris Salon of 1896. Judged by these awards, the [people of the] rough highlands . . . are singularly lacking in artistic instinct, while art flourishes in all the river lowlands of France. . . . French men of letters, by the distribution of their birthplaces, are essentially products of fluvial valleys and plains, rarely of upland and mountain."

A Possibilist's View

"All [European] patent offices report the Swiss as the foremost inventors. . . . A partial list of books published in different countries showed Switzerland to be far ahead of any other country in this sphere. . . .

"The Swiss themselves attribute much importance in the growth of their industries to the religious persecutions in neighboring countries in the sixteenth and seventeenth centuries—persecutions which drove thousands of intelligent men . . . into Switzerland. The revocation of the Edict of Nantes . . . in 1685 is credited with driving sixty thousand Huguenots from France into Switzerland. They founded the silk industry of Zurich and Bern. It was a Huguenot who founded the watch business at Geneva. . . . Spanish persecution in the Low Countries and Swiss neutrality during the Thirty Years' War added to the human resources of Switzerland."

First selection from Ellen Churchill Semple, *Influences of Geographic Environment.* Copyright 1911 by Holt, Rinehart and Winston. Copyright © 1939 by Carolyn W. Keene. Second selection from Mark Jefferson, "The Geographic Distribution of Inventiveness," *Geographical Review,* 19 (1929), 660–661.

---

are guided by cultural heritage. Possibilists, then, see the physical environment as offering opportunities and limitations; people make choices among these in order to satisfy their needs. In short, local traits of culture and economy are the products of culturally based decisions made within the limits of possibilities offered by the environment.

Most possibilists feel that the higher the technological level of a culture, the greater the number of possibilities and the weaker the influences of the physical environment. Technologically advanced cultures, in this view, have achieved near total mastery of the physical surroundings. Geographer Jim Norwine, however, warns that even in these advanced societies "the quantity and quality of human life are still strongly influenced by the natural environment," especially climate. He argues that humankind's control of nature is anything but supreme and perhaps even illusory. An unusually favorable climatic cycle has characterized the twentieth century and witnessed the rise of possibilist thought. The present world population of over 5 billion and the unprecedentedly high living standard typical of advanced countries may be untenable when a deterioration of the weather regime occurs. Perhaps, in our zeal to discard environmental determinism, we have overstated the possibilist view.

A Narrower Definition. Many cultural ecologists within geography, particularly those who study traditional rural peoples, employ a somewhat narrower definition of the theme. Their type of cultural ecology is based upon the premise that culture is the human method of meeting physical environmental challenges—that culture is an adaptive system. This outlook borrows heavily from the biological sciences, with the assumption that plant and animal adaptations are relevant to the study of humans, that **cultural adaptation** is the essential concept for geographical research. In their view, culture serves to facilitate long-term, successful, nongenetic human adaptation to nature and to environmental change. Adaptive strategy is based in culturally transmitted, or learned, behavior that permits a population to survive in its natural environment.

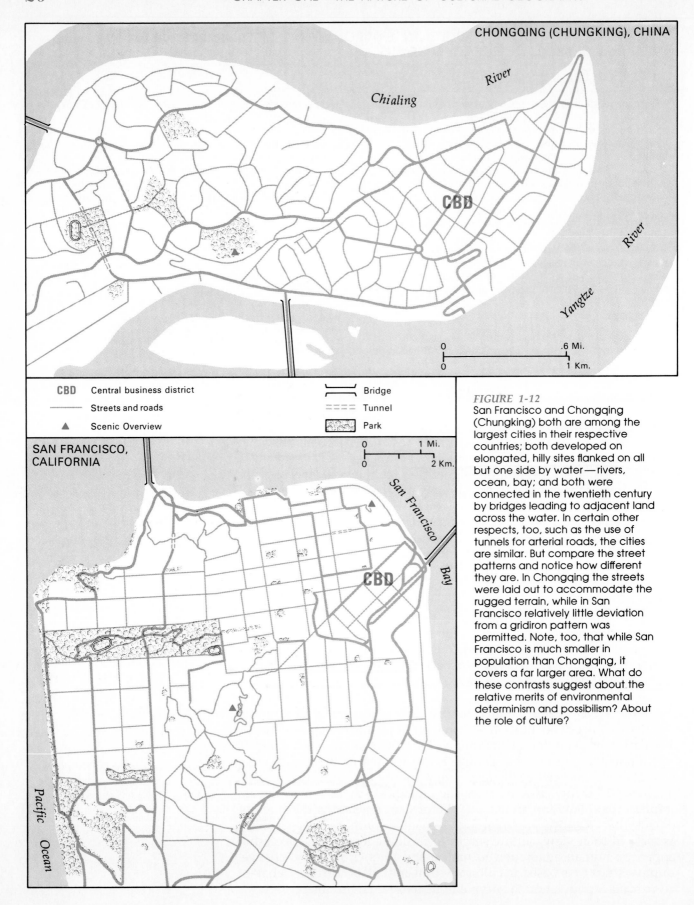

CHONGQING (CHUNGKING), CHINA

CBD   Central business district

⎯⎯⎯   Streets and roads

▲   Scenic Overview

⎯⎯   Bridge

= = = =   Tunnel

▨   Park

SAN FRANCISCO, CALIFORNIA

FIGURE 1-12
San Francisco and Chongqing (Chungking) both are among the largest cities in their respective countries; both developed on elongated, hilly sites flanked on all but one side by water—rivers, ocean, bay; and both were connected in the twentieth century by bridges leading to adjacent land across the water. In certain other respects, too, such as the use of tunnels for arterial roads, the cities are similar. But compare the street patterns and notice how different they are. In Chongqing the streets were laid out to accommodate the rugged terrain, while in San Francisco relatively little deviation from a gridiron pattern was permitted. Note, too, that while San Francisco is much smaller in population than Chongqing, it covers a far larger area. What do these contrasts suggest about the relative merits of environmental determinism and possibilism? About the role of culture?

This more narrowly defined cultural ecology can easily lapse into environmental determinism, but most of its practitioners are possibilists, who recognize that more than one path of successful adaptation exists in any environment and that the choice among them is a function of culture. Individual adaptive pathways result from interplay between the unique character of cultures and their physical environments. Culture channels the adaptive strategy by helping to determine what is meaningful as resources in a particular setting, but the individual person gains considerable decision-making and innovative power.

Adaptive strategies vary greatly in versatility. In general, stable and fruitful environments tend to diminish behavioral or adaptive variability, engendering conservatism and intolerance of deviant behavior, and producing a condition called **stabilizing selection.** By contrast, stressful marginal environments, where considerable areal and temporal contrasts in climate, soils, or terrain exist, tend to encourage a large, nonspecialized adaptive repertoire, or **diversifying selection.** In such stress zones, where nature is volatile, rather considerable behavioral variability and individualism are tolerated and new ideas or strategies always welcome. Two or more adaptive norms may coexist even within a single cultural population.

Environmental Perception. Another very productive approach to the broader theme of cultural ecology came to geography from psychology and focuses on human perception of nature. Each person and cultural group has mental images of the physical environment. To describe such mental images, cultural geographers use the term **environmental perception.** Whereas the possibilist sees humankind as having a choice of different possibilities in a given physical setting, the environmental perceptionist declares that the choices people make will depend more on what they perceive the environment to be than on the actual character of the land (see box, "Buffalo No Bigger than Insects"). Perception, in turn, is colored

---

BUFFALO NO BIGGER THAN INSECTS: THE PYGMY AND THE RAIN FOREST

The sun is a network of flickering lights dotting the ground, not a bright disk moving across the sky. The stars are not visible at night. The seasons hardly vary. The chief landmark of the area is no landmark at all—no distant rise of ground, no special tree standing out against the sky, nothing. Sound is supreme. In hunting, game is merely heard until it appears yards away from the hunter. The clearest idea of the supernatural that the inhabitants of this land have is not God, not a visual land to which the dead depart, but a sound: the "Beautiful Song of a Bird."

Although this may seem like science fiction, it is in fact the world of the Ba Mbuti pygmies, who live in the Congo rain forest. As an environment, the rain forest is all-enveloping and naturally affects every aspect of pygmy life, even the way they see. Living underneath a thick, almost impenetrable canopy of branches and leaves, hemmed in on all sides by lush, green foliage, the pygmies never have the experience of seeing anything from a distance. As a result, their sense of perspective is severely curtailed.

Can you imagine what it would be like to step out of that all-sustaining world for the first time? Kenge, a pygmy of the Ba Mbuti tribe, actually had the experience. Field researcher Colin Turnbull took him to an area of open grasslands. A flock of buffalo grazed several miles away, far below where they were standing. Familiar with the size of buffalo in the forest, Kenge could make no sense of these tiny dots in front of him. He asked Turnbull, "What insects are those?" "When I told Kenge that the insects were buffalo," Turnbull wrote, "he roared with laughter and told me not to tell such stupid lies." When Turnbull tried to explain how far away they actually were, Kenge "began scraping mud off his arms and legs, no longer interested in such fantasies."

Later, as the men approached the herd in a car, Kenge became frightened. He could see the animals growing bigger and bigger and feared that a magic trick was being played on him. In fact, his eye/brain had never learned something we take for granted: the ability to correct for changes in the size of the retinal image when looking at an object, so that the image remains relatively the same size as the object moves closer or farther away. Bewildered by distance, the lack of trees, and the sharpness of relief, Kenge's brain was making wrong guesses based on inadequate experience. Used to the environment of the rain forest, Kenge, for a moment at least, found the world a less stable and predictable place.

Adapted from Colin M. Turnbull, *The Forest People.* Copyright © 1961 by Colin M. Turnbull. Reprinted by permission of Simon & Schuster, Inc.

GEORGE PERKINS MARSH
1801–1882

Some few among us are gifted with the ability to perceive trends and their future consequences long before others do. George Perkins Marsh was such a person. Born to demanding Calvinist parents when America was still very young, when wilderness and open frontier were abundant and parts of his native Vermont still bore the mark of pioneering, Marsh nevertheless came to realize that the physical environment was being drastically altered by people, to the extent that the future of humankind was gravely endangered. At a time when the United States possessed seemingly limitless natural resources and huge expanses of fertile open land for settlement, in an era of almost unbounded optimism and belief in the steady progress of humankind toward a higher and better condition, Marsh intruded with a stern warning of future ecological disaster. His message was most effectively presented in a book, *Man and Nature; or, Physical Geography as Modified by Human Action,* published in 1864. Subsequently, after Marsh's death, it made a major impact on the academic discipline of cultural geography in America. It was a geographer who wrote Marsh's biography.

Based on David Lowenthal, *George Perkins Marsh, Versatile Vermonter* (New York: Columbia University Press, 1958).

by the teachings of culture. The perceptionist maintains that people cannot perceive their environment with exact accuracy and that decisions are therefore based on distortions of reality. To understand why a cultural group developed as it did in its physical environment, geographers must know not only what the environment is like, but also what the members of the culture think it is like.

An excellent example is **geomancy,** an East Asian world view and art. Geomancy, called *feng-shui* in Chinese, is a traditional system of land-use planning dictating that certain environmental settings deemed by the sages to be particularly auspicious should be chosen as the sites for houses, villages, temples, and graves. Particular configurations of terrain, compass directions, textures of soil, and patterns of watercourses are perceived to be more auspicious than others. Belief in geomancy has significantly affected the location and morphology of villages and cities in countries such as China and Korea. For more on this particular mode of environmental perception, see Chapter 6.

Some of the most productive research done by environmental perceptionists has been on the topic of natural hazards, such as floods and droughts. Different cultural groups react to the same hazards in varied ways. Some reason that natural disasters are unavoidable acts of the gods; others seek to cope with environmental hazards by placating the gods; and still others place responsibility for preventing calamities on the government. In Western cultures, people tend to regard hazards and disasters as natural phenomena that they can manipulate and control through technology.

The perceptionists' ideas are particularly striking when applied to migrations. They have found that people migrating from one environment to another usually imagine their old and new homelands to be environmentally more similar than is actually the case. For example, American farmers migrating from the humid eastern regions of the United States onto the semiarid Great Plains consistently overestimated the rainfall of their new homeland. Accustomed by the experience of many generations to living and farming in moist climates, they were initially unable to perceive the realities of their new climatic setting. They made decisions based on their experience and had to learn by trial and error that the realities of the Great Plains climate were not what they imagined (see Chapters 3 and 9).

Different cultures, surveying their environment, treat the natural resources around them quite differently. What to one cultural group is a major resource may be completely worthless or even a nuisance to another. To hunters and gatherers, the principal resources of an area may be wild berries, game animals, and flint deposits from which weapons can be fashioned. An agricultural group in the same environment may regard level land, fertile soils, and reliable sources of water as their most valuable resources. An industrial society may cherish the oil, coal, and other minerals buried beneath the land. In this way, people of three cultures perceive the resources of the same environment in different ways.

Humans as Modifiers of the Earth.   Some cultural geographers, observing the changes people have wrought in this physical environment, have chosen to study humans as modifiers of the Earth. This exposes yet another facet of cultural ecology. In a sense, this human-as-modifier theme is the opposite of environmental determinism. Whereas the determinists proclaim that nature molds humankind, those cultural geographers who study the human impact on the land emphasize that humans mold nature (see biographical sketch of George Perkins Marsh).

Even in ancient times, perceptive observers realized that people influenced their environment, and this theme often appears in the great literature of the Western world. Plato, commenting on the soil erosion around Athens around 400 B.C., lamented that the once fertile district had been stripped of its soil so that ''what now remains compared to what formerly existed is like the skeleton of a sick man, all the fat and soft earth having wasted away, and only the bare framework of the land being left'' (see Figure 1.13).

Cultural geographers began to concentrate on the human role in changing the face of the Earth long before North Americans gained their present level of ecological consciousness. They found, not surprisingly, that different groups have widely different outlooks on humankind's role in changing the Earth. Some, such as those rooted in the Judeo-Christian tradition, tend to regard environmental modification as divinely approved, viewing humans as God's helpers in completing the task of creation. Humans are seen as creatures apart from, and often at war with, nature. Some other groups are much more cautious, taking care not to offend the forces of nature. To many of these latter groups, humans are part of nature, meant to be in harmony with their environment. For more on this intriguing subject, see Chapter 6.

The Theme of Cultural Integration

The relationship between people and the land, the theme of cultural ecology, lies at the heart of traditional geography. However, the explanation of human spatial variations requires consideration of a whole range of cultural factors. The cultural geographer recognizes that all facets of culture are systemically and spatially intertwined, or **integrated.** In short, cultures are complex wholes rather than series of unrelated traits. They are integrated units in which the parts fit together causally. All aspects of

FIGURE 1-13
Human modification of the earth includes such severe soil erosion as on this farm in Kentucky. The erosion could have been caused by poor farming methods, overgrazing the cattle, or other careless abuses of the land.

culture are functionally interdependent on one another. The theme of cultural integration reflects the geographer's awareness that the immediate causes of some cultural phenomena are other cultural phenomena. Nor is the concept static, for a change in one element of culture almost requires an accommodating change in others. It is impossible to understand the distribution of one facet of culture without studying the variations in other facets of that culture, in order to see how they are interrelated and integrated causally and spatially with one another.

For example, religious belief has the potential to influence a group's voting behavior, diet, shopping patterns, type of employment, and social standing. Traditional Hinduism, the religion of India, segregates people into social classes called *castes* and specifies what forms of livelihood are appropriate for each. The Church of Jesus Christ of Latter-day Saints forbids the consumption of alcoholic beverages, tobacco, and certain other products, thereby influencing both the diet and shopping patterns of its members. There are countless other ways in which one facet of a culture influences other facets. The cultural integration theme allows the geographer to see how these intracultural causal forces help determine variations.

Indeed, it is through the theme of cultural integration that geographers, often using mathematical techniques, have developed theories to explain spatial variations and systems. **Space** is the word often used to describe this scientific theme in geography, much as **place** connotes the theme of culture region. Most spatial analysis has been economic in focus, though it need not be.

To get at the ways culture is integrated, at how space is organized by humans, geographers generally seek to strip down reality, separating different causal factors. They are aware that in the real world, so many causal factors are involved in any problem that confusion may result, and so they have employed a simpler way of testing how a culture works. It is called **model building.** Unlike physical scientists, scholars studying cultures are unable to achieve laboratory conditions, where certain causal forces can be isolated from forces surrounding them. To simulate a laboratory, social scientists set up model situations in which they can observe certain isolated forces. For example, the nineteenth-century scholar Johann Heinrich von Thünen created a model consisting of a single country isolated from all others and consisting of a flat plain surrounding a central city. He declared the soils and climate uniform throughout the country and assumed that all persons living a given distance from the city could transport goods to it in equal time and at equal rates. Von Thünen's purpose in creating this model was to study the effect of transportation costs and increased distance from the market on agricultural land use. The result was a theory that could then be applied to more complex real situations. His model is still recognized as valid and helpful by today's geographers (see Chapter 3).

Similarly, several geographers recently proposed a model for Latin American cities, in an effort to stress similarities among them and to understand certain underlying causal forces (Figure 1.14). Obviously, no actual city in Latin America conforms precisely to their uncomplicated geometric plan. Instead, they deliberately generalized and simplified, in order that an urban type could be recognized and studied. The task of building models and formulating theories goes on with increased vigor in modern cultural geography. In the following chapters, you will be introduced to some other models that geographers have built. Hägerstrand's concept of diffusion, discussed earlier, provides another example.

Theorists and model builders tend to regard geography as a **nomothetic,** or law-giving, science, believing that the chief purpose of geographical scholarship should be the discovery of universal principles. They feel that cultural geography belongs among the social sciences, alongside economics. Indeed, they are often accused of **economic determinism,** the belief that human behavior is largely dictated by economic motivation. In their emphasis on economically based quantitative data, some critics feel, they are led to an essentially acultural analysis. The previously mentioned von Thünen model and the body of land-use theory that has sprung from it could well be criticized on these grounds. In modern cultural geography, we look beyond what seem to be imperatives of the economic system, just as we earlier learned to be wary of reputed controls of the physical environment, and seek to learn more about the cultural qualities, aims, and perceptions of people.

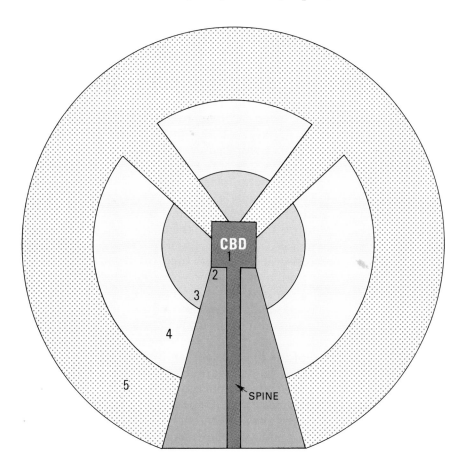

Commercial/Industrial Areas
CBD = Central Business District, the original colonial city
SPINE = High quality expansion of the CBD, catering to the wealthy

Elite Residential Sector

Zone of Maturity
Gradually improved, upgraded, self-built housing

Zone of Accretion
Transitional between zones 3 and 5, modest housing, improvements in progress

Zone of Peripheral Squatter Settlements
Slum housing

FIGURE 1-14
A generalized model of the Latin American city. Urban structure differs from one culture to another, and in many ways the cities of Latin America are distinctive, sharing much in common with each other. Geographers Ernst Griffin and Larry Ford developed the model diagramed here to help describe and explain the processes at work shaping the cities of Latin America. In what ways would this model not be applicable to cities in the United States and Canada? (After Griffin and Ford, "A Model of Latin American City Structure," *Geographical Review,* 70 (1980), 406.)

At the heart of much of nomothetic, social science-oriented geography is **logical positivism,** the attempt to apply the methods of science to the study of humankind. Knowledge, in this view, is derived from an analysis of the properties and relationships of phenomena, as verified by scientific methods. This knowledge can provide the basis for the law-giving stage. Other advocates of logical positivism, perhaps the majority, regard geography as an **idiographic** rather than a nomothetic science. They argue that the phenomena studied by cultural geographers are never identical and therefore are not susceptible to the type of generalization required for formulating theories and laws. Many idiographic geographers often also regard themselves as social scientists, but they go about the job of explaining cultural-spatial variations without attempting to apply their findings to situations other than the one they are studying.

Some geographers have rejected positivism to embrace **structuralism.** They believe that all cultural phenomena rest upon a few basic structures that are universal to the human mind and provide the motivating forces in society. The basis of these structures lies in the material conditions of existence, and the search for explanations must be directed accordingly. However, the structures are not generally accessible to scientific, positivistic analysis, which treats outward spatial appearances and manifestations that do not necessarily reveal causal mechanisms and mainsprings. Instead, structures can be discovered by looking beneath superficial spatial patterns to seek basic economic, social, ideological, and institutional processes. In other words, an explanation of spatial patterns is impossible to achieve from a study of the patterns themselves. Marxists, for example, are structuralists who focus upon the search for socioeconomic structures that they feel guide human behavior. In geography, Marxists emphasize the organization of production as the shaping structurer of society. They too are susceptible to the danger of economic determinism.

Still other cultural geographers stress the **humanistic** aspect of the discipline, rejecting the notion of human geography as a social science. Daniel W. Gade beautifully expressed this viewpoint recently, declaring that "two decades of economic determinism and logical positivism have failed to dispel the sense that humanistic understanding of places lies near the heart of the geographical enterprise." To these geographers, an understanding of culture and of the individuality and subjectivity of people is essential to an analysis of spatial variations. Humanists feel that all knowledge is subjective and perceived, and that no universal truth is attainable. Instead, they advocate the search for *meaning* on the individual level, placing research on a very personal plane, where intuition and imaginative interpretation prevail. Some humanistic geographers promote **phenomenology,** the objective of which is the direct investigation and description of phenomena as consciously experienced, without regard to theories about their causal explanation and as free as possible from unexamined preconceptions and presuppositions. In contrast to logical positivism, phenomenology does not restrict the subject of study to the range of sense-experience, but instead admits on equal terms such nonsensuous data as cultural values. Many human values cannot be measured.

The theme of cultural integration can also lead the geographer to **cultural determinism.** Advocates of this extreme viewpoint, developed in reaction to the earlier environmental determinism, maintain that the physical environment is inconsequential as an influence on culture. Any facet of a culture, they would argue, is shaped entirely by other facets of culture. Cultural integration, for them, offers all the answers for spatial variations.

People and culture are the active forces; nature is passive and easily conquered. You should be as wary of cultural determinism as of environmental determinism.

The Theme of Cultural Landscape

The **cultural landscape** is the artificial landscape that cultural groups create in inhabiting the Earth. Cultures have shaped their own landscapes out of the raw materials provided by the Earth. Every inhabited area has a cultural landscape, fashioned from the natural landscape, and each uniquely reflects the culture that created it (see Figure 1.15). Landscape mirrors culture, and the cultural geographer can learn much about a group of people by carefully observing the landscape. Indeed, so important is this visual record of cultures that some cultural geographers regard landscape study as the core of geographical concern, geography's central interest.

Why is such importance attached to the cultural landscape? Perhaps part of the answer is that it visually reflects the most basic strivings of humankind: for shelter, food, clothing, and entertainment. Too, geography by definition deals with the Earth's surface, and landscape constitutes that surface. The cultural landscape also reflects different attitudes concerning modification of the Earth by people. In addition, the landscape contains valuable evidence about the origin, spread, and development of cultures, since it usually preserves relic forms of various types (Figure 1.16). It is partly this potential for interpretive analysis that most attracts

FIGURE 1-15
Rice cultivation on the lower slopes of the Sierra Madre, island of Luzon, Philippines, is the basis of a highly distinctive cultural landscape.

FIGURE 1-16
A relic form embedded in the modern urban landscape of Brooklyn, New York, this Dutch colonial farmhouse is a valuable visual index of a now-vanished culture and way of life. The cultural landscape abounds in such relics, though they are often more subtle, and many possess diagnostic power in understanding past cultures and diffusions. (Photo by Terry G. Jordan, 1988.)

the geographer to study the landscape. Properly studied, this visible evidence can teach the observer much about the aspects of culture that are invisible, about a past long forgotten by the present inhabitants, and about the choices made and changes wrought by a people. The idea that cultural landscapes possess diagnostic interpretive potential was introduced into geography by the great German scholar August Meitzen (see biographical box in Chapter 3). Although we may not notice it in our daily lives, the cultural landscape constantly changes across both space and time. The unraveling of its mysteries has occupied the attention of many of the foremost cultural geographers. In the words of a famous French cultural geographer, Paul Vidal de la Blache, "All humanized landscapes have cultural meaning, [and] it follows that one can read the landscape as we do a book. The cultural landscape is our collective and revealing autobiography, reflecting our tastes, values, aspirations, and fears in tangible forms." Modern geographers agree. O. F. G. Sitwell and O. S. E. Bilash recently proposed that "the spatial organization of settlements and the architectural form of buildings and other structures can be interpreted as the expression of the values and beliefs of the people responsible for them." That is, the landscape can serve as a means to study nonmaterial aspects of culture. Certain other geographers, particularly some of the humanists, are content to study the cultural landscape for its intrinsic artistic value, to obtain highly subjective and personal messages from the textures, colors, and forms of the built environment that help describe the essence of place.

The content of the cultural landscape is both varied and complex. Most geographical studies have focused on three principal aspects of this landscape: settlement patterns, land-division patterns, and architecture. In the study of settlement patterns, cultural geographers describe and explain the spatial arrangement of buildings, roads, and other features that people construct while inhabiting an area. Land-division patterns reveal the way people have divided the land for economic and social uses. Such patterns vary a great deal from place to place. They range from huge corporate-owned farming complexes to small family-operated farms composed of tens or even hundreds of separate tiny parcels of land; from the fenced, privately owned home lots of American suburbs to the city's public squares. Perhaps the best way to glimpse settlement and land-division patterns is through an airplane window. Looking down, you can see the multicolored abstract patterns of planted fields, as vivid as any modern painting, and the regular checkerboard or chaotic tangle of urban streets.

Perhaps no other aspect of the human landscape is as readily visible from ground level as the architectural style of a culture. In North American culture, contrasting building styles cannot help catching the eye: modest white New England churches and giant urban cathedrals; hand-hewn barns and geodesic domes; New York City's Empire State Building, a monument to the doctrine of progress; the last of the little red schoolhouses and the new windowless school buildings of the urban areas. This architecture provides a vivid record of the resident culture. For this reason, cultural geographers have traditionally devoted considerable attention to such structures.

We can distinguish two basic types of architecture in the cultural landscape, as Figure 1.17 shows; folk architecture (see Chapter 7) and professional architecture. Folk architecture includes all buildings erected without professional architectural help. The styles and methods used to build them are derived from the folk culture rather than from drawing boards and schools of architecture. The resultant structures are monuments to traditional practices and skills. Folk houses are often faithful copies of dwellings built in the same style for perhaps thousands of years. The works of professional architects and draftsmen also reflect their culture, although on a different level of technology. The professionally designed skyscraper or the mass-produced mobile home is as revealing of the North American material culture and way of life as the Brazilian Indian farmer's thatched hut is of that culture.

Professor Sitwell has also speculated concerning the processes by which transpositions are made from culture to landscape, the processes creating humanized landscapes. He proposed that three figurative expressions of human worth, three cardinal virtues, are height, durability, and central location. Idioms such as "the high point of my visit," "she's at the peak of her career," "diamonds are forever," and "I love to be in the middle of things" reveal the virtues of height, durability, and centrality. If we apply these expressions of worth to architecture, to buildings, then it follows that structures centrally located, tall, and built of steel, brick, or stone are the worthiest and most important to the particular culture in question. In medieval Europe, cathedrals and churches best exemplified the three virtues, built of stone on the central square and towering above other structures. A visitor from another land, using Sitwell's method, would correctly conclude that the church dominated and defined medie-

FIGURE 1-17
The Swiss log structure is an example of folk architecture. It stands in sharp contrast to the professional architecture of the New York skyline. (Swiss photo by Terry G. Jordan, 1978.)

val culture. What conclusion might the perceptive stranger reach in interpreting the urban landscape shown in Figure 1.17? Vidal de la Blache was correct; like books, cultural landscapes convey messages.

◼ THE CULTURAL GEOGRAPHICAL PAST

We must now discard Kant's neat division of geography and history. The spatial distribution of cultural features is the result of changes through time, and cultural geographers have traditionally been concerned with areal patterns as they evolved through time. Cultural landscapes are usually the products of centuries of human action. Ecological decisions made by humans are rooted in their past interactions with the environment, and cultural diffusion by its very nature depends on the passage of time. In short, if cultural geographers hope to understand and explain spatial similarities and variations in culture, they must adopt a historical perspective and delve into the past for answers. Truly, culture is time-conditioned and cannot profitably be studied devoid of its temporal dimension.

The cultural landscape illustrates this point. Much of what meets the eye in that landscape comes from vanished causal forces and circumstances. To see this, all you have to do is stroll through any large American city. Like the ancient cities that archaeologists sometimes discover, built one on top of the other over thousands of years, American cities are really layered by time, cities inside cities inside cities. The modern office buildings of two decades ago are already being covered over by new steel and glass giants. The buildings they had once replaced are often still standing, although perhaps less noticed today. Even the use of buildings changes over time. New York City's Academy of Music, in the 1890s an elegant meeting place for high society, still exists. Today, however, it shows Spanish-language films to Puerto Rican immigrants who inhabit the now run-down neighborhood. In some other areas of the world, geographers must often delve thousands of years into the past to explain elements in the cultural landscape. Cultural geographers are interested in determining when and especially where cultural artifacts, practices, and beliefs originated.

The cultural landscape theme is a valuable tool for examining the sequence of settlement by different groups in an area, for usually each group of inhabitants and phase of land use leaves some sorts of visible reminders of its presence that show up in the landscape. This concept of **sequent occupance**—or the sequence of settlement—is an important part of the cultural-historical method. For example, in California it is still possible today to pick out traces of past cultures and land-use episodes in the landscape. Grassland and forest vegetation show the effects of prehistoric Indian burning; Spanish roads and missions still appear in the countryside, as do the land-division lines from the Mexican rancho period. Reminders of the early American period are everywhere, from eucalyptus trees covering parts of the state to the mine tailings and dredging deposits of the gold rush days. All of these parts of the cultural landscape tell us something about how past cultures interacted with their environment.

If cultural geographers study spatial patterns and ecological interactions through time, why are they geographers rather than historians? The answer is that their first concern is always ecological and spatial; they study changes through time mainly because that study helps them understand patterns and adaptive processes.

■ CONCLUSION

The interests of cultural geographers are, as we have seen, quite diverse. It might seem to you, confronted by the various themes, viewpoints, and methodologies described in this chapter, that cultural geographers are running off in all directions, that they lack unity of purpose. What does a geographer studying folk architecture have in common with a colleague studying the human role in shaping the Earth? What interests do an environmental perceptionist and a student of cultural diffusion share? Why do scholars with such apparently different interests belong in the same academic discipline? Why are they all geographers?

The answer is that regardless of the particular topic the cultural geographer studies, he or she necessarily touches several or all of the five themes we have mentioned. The themes are all closely related segments of a whole. Spatial patterns in culture, as revealed by maps of culture regions, are reflected in the cultural landscape, require an ecological interpretation, imply cultural diffusion, and suggest cultural integration.

As an example of how the various themes of cultural geography overlap and intertwine, let us look at one element of folk architecture—the American log house. Once found widely on the American frontier, many log cabins can still be found in the mountains of the South and West. They are obviously part of the cultural landscape, and their spatial distribution constitutes a formal culture region that can be mapped. In addition, geographers studying such houses need to employ the other themes of cultural geography to gain a complete understanding. They can use the concept of cultural diffusion to learn when and by what routes these techniques diffused and what barriers retarded their diffusion. In this particular case, the geographer would be led back to the history of the Neolithic period in central and northern Europe and, later, to the early Swedish and German colonies in the Delaware Valley. Further, the cultural geographer would need an ecological interpretation of the log house. How does the environment influence the log cabin? Is the form of the house related to types of trees? How do houses built of pine differ from those built of oak? Does the use of logs for houses decline as the forests become thinned out? Do log houses differ from one climatic zone to another? Finally, the cultural geographer wants to know how the use of log houses is integrated with other facets of the culture. Did changes in the economy and standard of living lead people to reject log houses? Did changes in technology lead to more elaborate houses? Are American political images linked to log cabins? Thus the geographer interested in folk housing is firmly bound by the total fabric of cultural geography, unable to segregate a particular topic such as log houses from the geographic whole. In this way, culture region, cultural landscape, cultural integration, cultural ecology, and cultural diffusion are interwoven.

The five themes are complementary in another way, too. Some are descriptive, others analytical. The themes of region, diffusion, and landscape are inherently nonexplanatory. They help geographers describe where different aspects of culture are located and how they spread to occupy that location. Even the diagnostic potential of landscape remains, in the final analysis, descriptive of what happened rather than explanatory of why it occurred. Geographers therefore turn to the themes of cultural ecology and integration in seeking explanations, to concepts such as adaptation and spatial models. Thus, in seeking to progress from description to explanation, the cultural geographer passes from one set of themes to another, again demonstrating the holistic nature of the discipline. In no small measure, it is this holism, this broad, multithematic approach, that distinguishes the cultural geographer from other students of culture.

We will be applying the five complementary themes to a variety of topics, concepts, and issues that possess geographical content. You will be reading about such matters as overpopulation, food production, the world power balance, religious and linguistic strife, the concept of place, environmental destruction, ethnicity, and urban congestion. The color photo essay following this chapter will acquaint you with these and other timely topics, with suggestions of how geographers perceive them.

Suggested Readings

Nigel J. R. Allen, Gregory W. Knapp, and Christoph Stadel (eds.). *Human Impact on Mountains.* Totowa, N.J.: Rowman & Littlefield, 1988.

James M. Blaut. "Diffusionism: A Uniformitarian Critique," *Annals of the Association of American Geographers,* 77 (1987), 30–47.

James M. Blaut. "Two Views of Diffusion," *Annals of the Association of American Geographers,* 67 (1977), 343–349.

Lawrence A. Brown. *Innovation Diffusion: A New Perspective.* New York: Methuen, 1981.

Anne Buttimer (ed.). *The Practice of Geography.* London: Longman, 1983.

Anne Buttimer and David Seamon (eds.). *The Human Experience of Space and Place.* New York: St. Martin's Press, 1980.

A Preview of Concepts in Cultural Geography

The five themes described in Chapter 1 will be applied to a number of important geographical concepts and problems throughout the book, and this first color photograph section is designed to introduce some of these.

Crowding due to **overpopulation** is one of the great crises facing the world today, and by its very nature this problem is spatial and geographical (Chapter 2). How much **personal space** do we need, and how might increased crowding affect life-styles, cultures, and environment? Are we all destined to endure overpopulation, or is **zero population growth** possible? Is family planning, long promoted by governments in countries such as India, a viable solution to the problem? Perhaps, but you will learn of cultural barriers to the diffusion of birth control and become aware that Western technological solutions rarely work in non-Western settings.

Food constitutes the very basis of our existence. In an inherently geographical process, farmers and herders must provide from the land enough for the growing world population to eat (Chapter 3). A cultural ecology is at the root of such production. How can we best produce our food? Even the same crops, such as rice, can be raised in fundamentally different ways. That is,

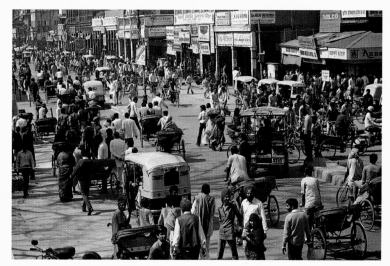

A crowded world: India

Coping with the population explosion: India

Hand threshing of rice: Bali, Indonesia

Machine rice harvest: Arkansas

Intertillage in an Amerindian field: Brazil

contrasting **adaptive strategies** can be employed by farmers belonging to different cultures. In Indonesia, for example, rice is planted, tilled, harvested, and threshed in a labor-intensive adaptive strategy that does not depend on machines or pesticides, while American rice farmers, as in Arkansas, take exactly the opposite approach. "Our way is better," you may say. But is it really? Our system compacts the soil, consumes precious fossil fuels, poisons the Earth with pesticides, causes farmers to run substantial debt risks, forces small family farmers out of agriculture, promotes large-scale **agribusiness**, and provides very few jobs, while yielding less rice per acre than does the Indonesian way. Similarly, Brazilian Indians for millennia have grown a complicated mixture of plants in small, burned clearings, producing all of the crops they need in a sustainable system that does not destroy the Amazonian rain forest where they live—yet you will be tempted to call their farming primitive. Perhaps our North American methods yield more crops, but is the more massive application of chemicals ecologically better in the long run? At this point, no one

Guerrillas know their mountains: Afghanistan

really knows the answer. We hope you will learn
never to assume that the ways of our own
culture are necessarily best, and always to
question the wisdom of imposing our methods
on others.

　　Political disputes, revolutions, and wars are
usually geographical by nature (Chapter 4).
Territory, the most basic geographical commodity,
lies at the root of many such crises. An intimate
knowledge of terrain is often essential to guerrilla
fighters, allowing them to challenge far more
powerful opposing forces, as in Vietnam and
Afghanistan. The countryside can also be affected
by those in power, for instance when they
produce vivid political/ideological images that
add to the world's diversity. Political slogans,
colors, and symbols influence our lives through
the cultural landscape, both subtly and overtly.

An ideological landscape: Soviet Union

A scarcity of English words: Arizona

We become illiterate in an alien linguistic landscape: India

The very languages we speak are geographical in various ways (Chapter 5). Our own English tongue developed originally in a wet, flat land of marshes and floods, and as a result we have relatively few words in our vocabulary to describe mountains and deserts. As an English speaker, then, you are at a disadvantage in trying to describe an Arizona scene. You will verbally ignore the subtleties of the scene altogether: "Mountain," yes, but what type of mountain? "Cactus," yes, but what kinds? If you spoke Spanish, your task would be far easier: The vocabulary describing such places is much larger because the Spanish language evolved in a semiarid, mountainous country. Should everyone speak English, or some other international language, so that there would be no linguistic barriers? The cultural geographer would say no, partly because each language is adapted to its particular place or region, where it functions better than any other tongue.

One might make a far better case for using only one alphabet in the world. As it is, whenever we venture beyond the geographical region of our own familiar alphabet, we lapse into illiteracy, and linguistic landscapes become vaguely discomfiting, as in India. But do we truly want every place and culture to be alike? Variety is the spice of life, and geography thrives on areal variation. Cultural geography instructs us that human diversity is good.

Different religions occupy their own geographical regions, possessing distinctive adaptive strategies and cultural landscapes (Chapter 6). The diversity of faiths helps make the world more interesting than it would be if we

Not everyone worships the same god:
Muslims at prayer in Pakistan

Still a sacred place: Teotihuacán, Mexico

were all alike. True, Christianity is a **universalizing faith** that seeks to convert all of humankind, but you should be aware that certain other faiths, such as Islam, have the same goal and that in the last thousand years no notable number of converts has been won away from the Muslim faith. Too, some scholars believe that the distinctive Judeo-Christian world view, in which people and God are not part of nature, leads to more massive environmental destruction and may be ecologically maladaptive. We hope that religious toleration will be one result of a cultural geographical study of religion.

Also in Chapter 6, we will learn of the mystical power of **sacred places**, a power that often persists even when the faiths that created these special entities perish. Teotihuacán, which means "the place of the gods," is a defunct Aztec sacred site retaining even today an ability to inspire awe and hush the visitor. Sacred places that still hold

Some rivers are holy: The Bagmati in Nepal

Folk houses belong to the land: Papua, New Guinea

Placelessness exemplified: Anywhere, United States

Retaining a sense of place: Portuguese hill town

their full vitality, such as a holy river in Nepal, can draw throngs of pilgrims.

People also differ greatly in their closeness to nature, as we will learn in Chapters 7 and 8, and cultural geographers are, predictably, interested in such differential ecological connections. **Folk cultures** (Chapter 7) involve living intimately with the physical environment. Long ago cultural geographers learned that the dwelling, the house, is one of the most revealing facets of culture, because shelter is a basic human need. **Folk architecture** reflects ancient ancestral memories, forgotten diffusions, and carefully developed adaptive strategies; we can learn much from it. Folk houses, as in New Guinea, spring from locally available natural materials, fit their surroundings, and function well in the local climate. They seem to "belong" to the locales where they are built, helping create a distinctive **sense of place**, the most basic cultural geographical expression. By contrast, we live in the **popular culture** (Chapter 8), a way of life that fosters **placelessness**. Where is the colorful commercial strip shown in the picture—Florida? Idaho? Maine? A Portuguese hill town, on the other hand, retains a vivid sense of place. In the study of cultural geography, place and placelessness are central concepts. Chapters 7 and 8 should cause you to ponder the comparative advantages and disadvantages of folk versus popular cultures. As before, you should emerge less likely to proclaim, automatically, the superiority of your own way of life. Cultural geography teaches humility.

Ethnicity (Chapter 9) helps many among us avoid the placelessness fostered by the popular culture. Not long ago, many social scientists predicted the demise of ethnic groups in countries such as the United States and Canada and the advent of a homogenized mass popular culture. Instead, ethnic identity and attachment to ethnic regions have experienced a resurgence throughout the developed world, from North America to the Soviet Union. Geographers, naturally, are interested in this phenomenon.

Enduring ethnicity: New Brunswick, Canada

The city (Chapters 10 and 11), an increasingly dominant human institution, should also be studied geographically. Different cultures create different kinds of cities. Munich, for example, is far more compact in area than American cities of the same population. The citizens of Munich obviously put a high value on the preservation of historic buildings, and they maintain a lively, attractive center city largely devoid of urban decay and street crime, with abundant pedestrian districts. Americans, by contrast, tend to flee the central city, choosing to live largely in dispersed suburbs facilitated by and designed for the automobile. Greater Baltimore, a typical American urban area, struggles valiantly against blight and crime in its center while its peripheries thrive. In part, these contrasts may be linked to different needs for personal space. Americans require a lot of such space, as reflected in suburban yards; Germans seem to need less.

Industry (Chapter 12) also demands geographical analysis, especially from the standpoint of cultural ecology, because, as our dominant Western adaptive strategy, it seems unsustainable. The evidence of industrial destruction of habitat is increasing at every hand, from the blackened beaches of Alaska to

Cherishing the urban past: Munich

Automobile worship and personal space: Baltimore suburbs

Oil and water *do* mix: Exxon's Alaska

Acid rain kills trees: North Carolina

Appalachian forests devastated by acid rain, from the **greenhouse effect** to overflowing trash landfills. Can we find a way to make our industrial activities compatible with habitat retention? Geographers can help provide an answer.

In this manner, cultural geography, through its five themes, causes us to address such major issues as human diversity, overpopulation, food supply, adaptive strategies, political conflict, ethnicity, religious differences, place and placelessness, the city, and environmental destruction. The discipline of cultural geography implicitly promotes tolerance, humility, and stewardship of the land. Studying it should make for a valuable and interesting semester.

Karl W. Butzer (ed.). *Dimensions of Human Geography: Essays on Some Familiar and Neglected Themes.* University of Chicago, Dept. of Geography, Research Paper No. 186, 1978.

A. D. Cliff and J. K. Ord. *Spatial Processes: Models and Applications.* London: Pion Ltd., 1981.

William M. Denevan. "Adaptation, Variation, and Cultural Geography," *Professional Geographer,* 35 (1983), 399–407.

James S. Duncan. "The Superorganic in American Cultural Geography," *Annals of the Association of American Geographers,* 70 (1980), 181–198.

James S. Duncan and David Ley. "Structural Marxism and Human Geography." *Annals of the Association of American Geographers,* 72 (1982), 30–59.

J. Nicholas Entrikin. "Contemporary Humanism in Geography," *Annals of the Association of American Geographers,* 66 (1976), 615–632.

Daniel W. Gade. "The French Riviera as Elitist Space," *Journal of Cultural Geography,* 3 (1982–1983), 19–28.

Andrew Goudie. *The Human Impact on the Natural Environment.* Cambridge, Mass.: M.I.T. Press, 1986.

Peter Gould and Rodney White. *Mental Maps,* 2nd ed. Winchester, Mass.: Allen & Unwin, 1986.

Derek Gregory. *Ideology, Science and Human Geography.* New York: St. Martin's Press, 1978.

Charles F. Gritzner, Jr. "The Scope of Cultural Geography," *Journal of Geography,* 65 (January 1966), 4–11.

Larry Grossman. "Man-Environment Relationships in Anthropology and Geography," *Annals of the Association of American Geographers,* 67 (1977), 126–144.

Donald L. Hardesty. "Rethinking Cultural Adaptation." *Professional Geographer,* 38 (1986), 11–18.

David Harvey. *Explanation in Geography.* New York: St. Martin's Press, 1970.

J. B. Jackson. *Landscapes: Selected Writings of J. B. Jackson.* Ervin H. Zube (ed.). Amherst: University of Massachusetts Press, 1970.

R. J. Johnston, Derek Gregory, and David M. Smith (eds.). *The Dictionary of Human Geography,* 2nd ed. Oxford: Basil Blackwell, 1986.

Terry G. Jordan. *The European Culture Area,* 2nd ed. New York: Harper & Row, 1988.

The Journal of Cultural Geography. The only English-language journal devoted exclusively to cultural geography. Published semiannually by the Department of Geography, Bowling Green State University, Ohio. Volume 1 was published in 1980.

Journal of Regional Cultures. Published by the Popular Culture Association, Bowling Green State University, Ohio. Volume I was published in 1983.

Robert W. Kates and Ian Burton (eds.). *Geography, Resources, and Environment,* 2 vols. Chicago: University of Chicago Press, 1986.

Landscape. Published at Berkeley, California, edited by Bonnie Loyd, and published by Blair Boyd. An interdisciplinary journal devoted to the cultural landscape. Cultural geographers regularly contribute articles. Volume I was published in 1951.

Peirce Lewis. "Learning from Looking: Geographic and Other Writing About the American Cultural Landscape," *American Quarterly,* 35 (1983), 242–261.

David Ley. "Cultural/Humanistic Geography," *Progress in Human Geography,* 5 (1981), 249–257; 7 (1983), 267–275; 9 (1985), 415–423.

David Ley and Marwyn S. Samuels. *Humanistic Geography: Prospects and Problems.* Chicago: Maaroufa Press, 1978.

David Lowenthal and Martyn J. Bowden. *Geographies of the Mind.* New York: Oxford University Press, 1976.

William E. Mallory and Paul Simpson-Housley (eds.). *Geography and Literature: A Meeting of the Disciplines.* Syracuse, N.Y.: Syracuse University Press, 1987.

James R. McDonald. "The Region: Its Conception, Design and Limitations," *Annals of the Association of American Geographers,* 56 (1966), 516–528.

D. W. Meinig. "Geography as an Art," *Transactions of the Institute of British Geographers,* 8 (1983), 314–328.

D. W. Meinig (ed.). *The Interpretation of Ordinary Landscapes: Geographical Essays.* New York: Oxford University Press, 1979.

Marvin W. Mikesell. "Tradition and Innovation in Cultural Geography," *Annals of the Association of American Geographers,* 68 (1978), 1–16.

W. B. Morgan and R. P. Moss. "Geography and Ecology: The Concept of the Community and Its Relation to Environment," *Annals of the Association of American Geographers,* 55 (1965), 339–350.

Richard Morrill, Gary L. Gaile, and Grant I. Thrall. *Spatial Diffusion* (Volume 10 in the Scientific Geography Series). Newbury Park, Calif.: Sage Publications, 1988.

North American Culture, Publication of the Society for the North American Cultural Survey, Dept. of Geography, Oklahoma State University. Cultural geographers are major contributors to this journal, which focuses upon cultural patterns in North America. Editorship is currently at the Dept. of Geography, University of Florida. Volume 1 was published in 1985.

Jim Norwine. "Geography as Human Ecology? The Man/Environment Equation Reappraised," *International Journal of Environmental Studies,* 17 (1981), 179–190.

Anssi Paasi. "The Institutionalization of Regions: A Theoretical Framework for Understanding the Emergence of Regions and the Constitution of Regional Identity," *Fennia,* 164 (1986), 105–146.

Edmund C. Penning-Rowsell and David Lowenthal (eds.). *Landscape Meanings and Values.* London: Allen & Unwin, 1986.

Progress in Human Geography. A quarterly journal providing authoritative and critical appraisal of developments and trends in the discipline. It aims to report on and stimulate research and progress in both traditional and new aspects of human geography. Volume 1 was published in 1977.

Massimo Quaini. *Geography and Marxism,* Alan Braley (trans.), Russell King (ed.). New York: Barnes & Noble, 1982.

Edward Relph. *Rational Landscapes and Humanistic Geography.* New York: Barnes & Noble, 1981.

G. W. S. Robinson. "The Geographic Region: Form and Function," *Scottish Geographical Magazine,* 69 (1953), 49–58.

Everett M. Rogers. *Diffusion of Innovations,* 3rd ed. New York: Free Press, 1983.

John F. Rooney, Jr., Wilbur Zelinsky, Dean R. Louder, et al. (eds.). *This Remarkable Continent: An Atlas of North American Society and Culture.* College Station: Texas A&M University Press, 1982. The first work of its kind, this atlas contains over 400 maps illustrating the cultural geography of the United States and Canada, and is an indispensable reference for students of North American human geography.

Lester B. Rowntree. "Orthodoxy and New Directions: Cultural/Humanistic Geography," *Progress in Human Geography,* 12 (1988), 575–586.

Lester B. Rowntree. "Cultural/Humanistic Geography," *Progress in Human Geography,* 10 (1986), 580–586; 11 (1987), 558–564.

Lester B. Rowntree and Margaret W. Conkey. "Symbolism and the Cultural Landscape," *Annals of the Association of American Geographers,* 70 (1980), 459–474.

Thomas F. Saarinen. *Perception of Environment.* Resource Paper No. 5. Washington, D.C.: Association of American Geographers, Commission on College Geography, 1969.

Christopher L. Salter. *The Cultural Landscape.* Belmont, Calif.: Duxbury Press, 1971.

Carl O. Sauer, "Morphology of Landscape," *University of California Publications in Geography,* 2 (1925), 19–54.

O. F. G. Sitwell. "Elements of the Cultural Landscape as Figures of Speech," *Canadian Geographer,* 25 (1981), 167–180.

O. F. G. Sitwell and Olenka S. E. Bilash. "Analyzing the Cultural Landscape as a Means of Probing the Non-Material Dimensions of Reality," *Canadian Geographer,* 30 (1986), 132–145.

David M. Smith. *Patterns in Human Geography: An Introduction to Numerical Methods.* New York: Crane, Russak & Co., 1975.

Joseph E. Spencer. "The Growth of Cultural Geography," *American Behavioral Scientist,* 22 (1978), 79–92.

D. R. Stoddart. *On Geography and Its History.* Oxford: Basil Blackwell, 1986.

William L. Thomas, Jr. (ed.). *Man's Role in Changing the Face of the Earth.* Chicago: University of Chicago Press, 1956.

Joy Tivy and Greg O'Hare. *Human Impact on the Ecosystem.* Edinburgh and New York: Oliver & Boyd, 1981.

Yi-Fu Tuan. "Humanistic Geography," *Annals of the Association of American Geographers,* 66 (1976), 266–276.

Yi-Fu Tuan. *Man and Nature.* Resource Paper No. 10. Washington, D.C.: Association of American Geographers, Commission on College Geography, 1971.

Philip L. Wagner, "Cultural Landscapes and Regions: Aspects of Communication," in H. J. Walker and W. G. Haag (eds.), *Man and Cultural Heritage,* vol. 5 of *Geoscience and Man.* Baton Rouge: School of Geoscience, Louisiana State University, 1974, pp. 133–142.

Philip L. Wagner. "The Themes of Cultural Geography Rethought," *Yearbook of the Association of Pacific Coast Geographers,* 37 (1975), 7–14.

Philip L. Wagner and Marvin W. Mikesell. *Readings in Cultural Geography.* Chicago: University of Chicago Press, 1962, pp. 1–24.

Whole Earth Review. No. 58 (Spring 1988). Special section on cultural geography, "A Wedding of People and Place," 2–47.

Larry S. Yapa and Robert C. Mayfield. "Non Adoption of Innovations: Evidence from Discriminant Analysis," *Economic Geography,* 54 (1978), 145–156.

Hong-Key Yoon. "The Image of Nature in Geomancy," *GeoJournal,* 4 (1980), 341–348.

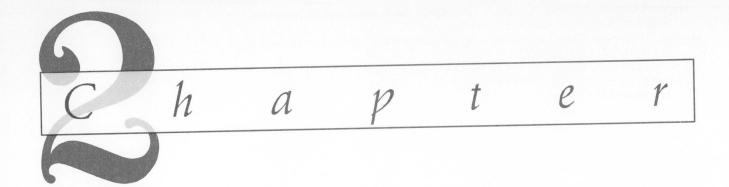

Chapter 2

People on the Land

DEMOGRAPHIC REGIONS

Population Density
Patterns of Natality
Patterns of Mortality
The Population Explosion
Age and Sex Distributions
Standard of Living
Migration Regions

DIFFUSION IN POPULATION GEOGRAPHY

Migration
Diffusion of Population Control
Disease Diffusion

POPULATION ECOLOGY

Environmental Influence
Environmental Perception and
    Population Distribution

Population Density and Environmental
    Alteration

CULTURAL INTEGRATION AND
POPULATION PATTERNS

Cultural Factors
Political and Economic Factors

SETTLEMENT PATTERNS IN THE LANDSCAPE

Clustered Rural Settlement: The Farm
    Village
Dispersed Rural Settlement:
    The Isolated Farmstead
Semiclustered Rural Settlement
Reading the Cultural Landscape

CONCLUSION

Population geographers study the spatial aspects of **demography,** a name given to the statistical analysis of human population. At present, well over 5 billion humans are alive on the earth, producing an average *population density* of about 92 per square mile of land area (36 per square kilometer). The central geographical fact, however, is that people are quite unevenly distributed. Population densities range from zero in the uninhabited expanses of Antarctica to the high levels found in compactly settled places such as Macao, a Chinese territory belonging to Portugal, where 52,000 persons live on each square mile (20,000 per square kilometer).

Geographers study these variations in density of people. So basic and important is population distribution that some cultural geographers even regard it as "the essential geographical expression," a worthy focus for the entire academic discipline. Most geographers would at least agree that the uneven spatial distribution of people is a vitally important phenomenon. It provides us an appropriate point of departure for our study of cultural geography. Population geographers also devote attention to the spatial variation of certain other demographic qualities or characteristics. They, together with the closely related **social geographers,** are interested in the differences from one place to another in demographic features such as birth rates, death rates, growth rates, health, sex ratios, age groups, marriage, divorce, crime, quality of life, and human mobility (see Figures 2.1 and 2.2). In sum, the geographer seeks to describe and explain the significance of spatial differences in the number of people, their living standards, and social conditions.

All these topics will receive our attention in this chapter, and our study of population geography will make use of the five themes outlined in Chapter 1. Accordingly, this chapter will delimit demographic regions, consider cultural diffusion as it relates to population, probe the ecology of population, investigate the ways population characteristics are integrated with other cultural patterns, and view the settlement landscapes produced by differing densities and distributions of people.

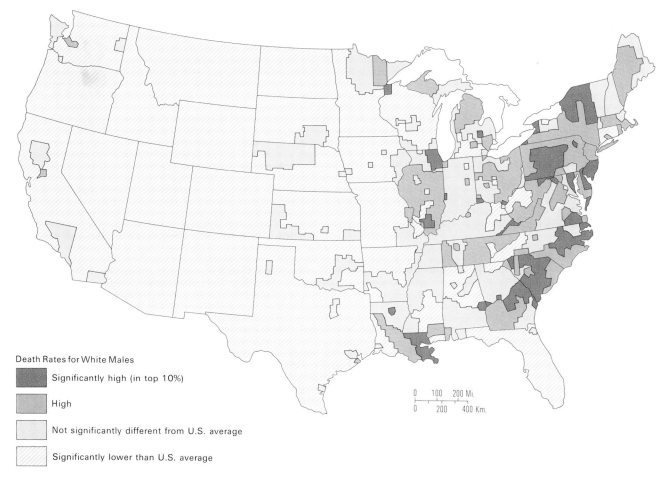

Death Rates for White Males

█ Significantly high (in top 10%)

▓ High

░ Not significantly different from U.S. average

▨ Significantly lower than U.S. average

FIGURE 2.1
Coronary heart disease, death rates for white males. The highest male death rates from coronary heart disease occur in the East. Why? (Source: Thomas J. Mason et al., *An Atlas of Mortality from Selected Diseases,* Washington, D.C.: U.S. Dept. of Health & Human Services, May 1981.)

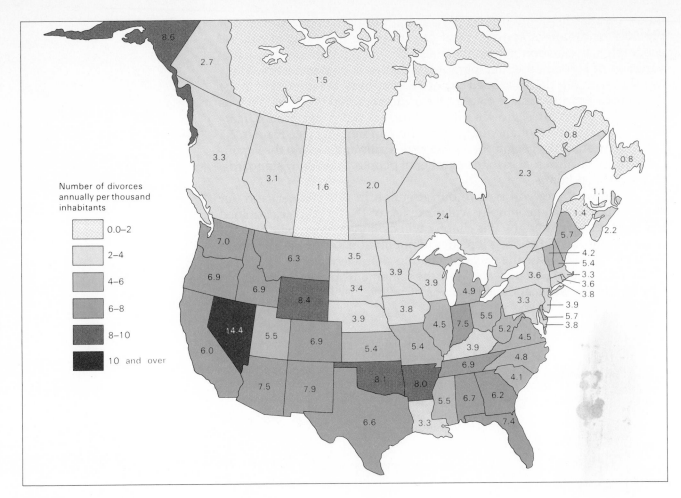

FIGURE 2.2
Divorces per thousand inhabitants, by state, province, and territory in the United States and Canada. The U.S. data are for 1978 and 1981; the Canadian data for 1977. What might account for the higher divorce rate in the South and West? Why did no state in the United States have a rate lower than the *highest* rate for a Canadian province? (Sources: National Center for Health Statistics, August 1980 and August 1982; *Canada Year Book 1980–81*, pp. 141–143.)

■ DEMOGRAPHIC REGIONS

The regions devised by population geographers can be called **demographic regions.** They are very helpful in describing spatial variations in population density, growth, and characteristics. In this way, geographers learn how humankind is distributed over the earth's surface and how other demographic and social traits differ from place to place.

Population Density

There are many ways to view the regionality of population density. If we study the distribution of people by continents, we find that 75 percent of the human race live in Eurasia. The continent of North America is home to only 8 percent of all people; Africa, to 11 percent; South America, to 5 percent; and Australia and the Pacific islands, to less than one-half of 1 percent. If we consider population distribution by political units, we find that approximately 22 percent of all humans reside in the People's Republic of China; 16 percent in India; 5½ percent in the Soviet Union; and only 5 percent in the United States (Table 2.1). Should present trends continue, by the year 2035 India will have surpassed China as the world leader and Nigeria will become the third most populous country.

We can also divide population density into categories such as (1) densely settled areas, which have 250 or more persons per square mile

TABLE 2.1
The Ten Most Populous Countries, 1986

Country	Population
People's Republic of China	1,100,000,000
India	818,000,000
USSR	280,000,000
United States	242,000,000
Indonesia	167,000,000
Brazil	139,000,000
Japan	122,000,000
Bangladesh	101,000,000
Pakistan	99,000,000
Nigeria	99,000,000

Source: United Nations, *Demographic Yearbook, 1987–1988.*

(100 or more per square kilometer); (2) moderately settled areas, with 60 to 250 persons per square mile (25 to 100 per square kilometer); (3) thinly settled areas, inhabited by 2 to 60 persons per square mile (1 to 25 per square kilometer); and (4) largely unpopulated areas, with fewer than 2 persons per square mile (fewer than 1 per square kilometer). These categories represent demographic regions based on the single trait of population density. As Figure 2.3 shows, a fragmented crescent of dense settlement

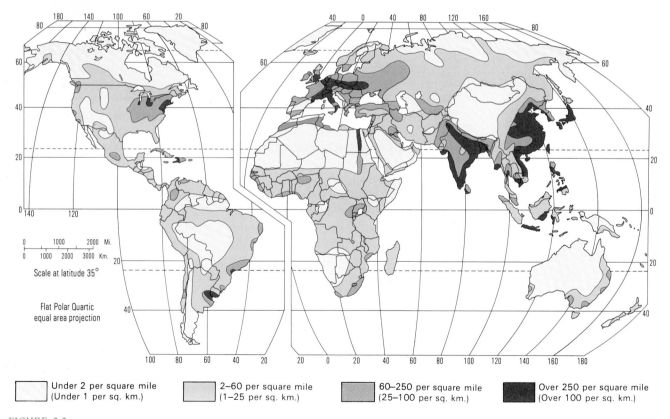

Under 2 per square mile (Under 1 per sq. km.)   2–60 per square mile (1–25 per sq. km.)   60–250 per square mile (25–100 per sq. km.)   Over 250 per square mile (Over 100 per sq. km.)

FIGURE 2.3
This map shows population density in the world. Despite our concern with overpopulation, large areas of the world are thinly settled. Within the densely settled zones, some areas, such as the United States, consume large amounts of the world's resources and maintain a high standard of living. Meanwhile, other areas with similar densities are unable to provide enough food for the population.

IS THE WORLD REALLY OVERCROWDED?

Those who fear overpopulation often conjure up the specter of a world in which people are elbow-to-elbow, with no open space left. How crowded is the present world, really? If all of humanity stood in such a crowd, how much area would be covered?

Allowing 4 square feet for each human, the present world population of 5.3 billion would require 21.2 billion square feet (1.95 billion m²). The square root of 21.2 billion is ap-

proximately 145,600, meaning that a square area 145,600 feet on a side could contain our world crowd. Converted into miles, the square is seen to have about 27.5 miles (44km) on a side, roughly the size of only one typical Midwestern American county.

Adapted from William W. Bunge, "The Geography of Human Survival," *Annals of the Association of American Geographers*, 63 (1973), 288.

stretches along the western, southern, and eastern edges of the huge Eurasian continent. Two-thirds of the human race is concentrated in this crescent, which stretches through the southern half of Japan, the plains and hills of eastern China, the monsoon coasts and great Ganges River plain of India, to the industrial districts of Europe. Outside of Eurasia, only scattered districts are densely settled. These include the most highly industrialized parts of the United States and the irrigated farmlands along the lower Nile River in Africa. Despite our image of global overpopulation, sparsely settled regions are much more extensive than heavily settled ones and appear on every continent (see box, "Is the World Really Overcrowded?"). Thin settlements dot the northern sections of Eurasia and North America, the interior of South America, and most of Australia, and another major zone of sparse population reaches through North Africa and Arabia into the heart of Eurasia.

Although population density allows us to view the distribution of people, it does not tell us anything about standard of living, overpopulation, or underpopulation. Some of the most densely populated areas in the world have the highest standards of living—and even suffer from labor shortages. For example, this has been true of the major industrial areas of West Germany and the Netherlands. In certain other cases, regions designated as thinly settled may actually be severely overpopulated, marginal agricultural lands. Although 1000 persons per square mile (400 per square kilometer) is a "dense" population for a farming area, it is "sparse" for an industrial district.

Density is also a static concept. It does not allow us to see the changes that constantly occur or indicate the pronounced regional differences in birth rate, death rate, and population growth. Nor does density indicate migration. In order to underscore the dynamic aspects of population, we will next explore culture regions based on birth and death rates.

Patterns of Natality

No less than population density, **birth rates,** the number of births in a year per thousand people, vary greatly from one area to another, as Figure 2.4 shows. In many ways, the map of birth rates does not correspond to the map of population density. In fact, the inverse situation occurs in certain areas of the world. Some densely populated areas, such as western Europe and Japan, have very low birth rates, while some sparsely settled regions, such as Arabia and interior Africa, have very high birth rates. In general, high birth rates are concentrated in a belt through the lower latitudes, especially the tropics and subtropics. As a rule, midlatitude and high-latitude countries currently have low birth rates.

Viewed economically, birth rates tend to be highest in countries that are less industrialized and urbanized, belonging to the so-called underde-

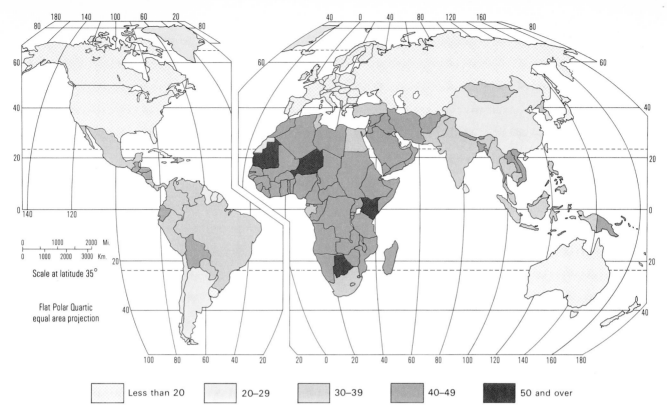

| | Less than 20 | | 20–29 | | 30–39 | | 40–49 | | 50 and over |

FIGURE 2.4
The annual crude birth rate per thousand inhabitants, by country. In general, the highest birth rates occur in the most impoverished, rural nations, while the lowest are found in urbanized, industrialized countries. (Source: United Nations, *Demographic Yearbook,* 1985.)

veloped world. By contrast, the main manufacturing countries, where most people live in cities, generally have low or very low birth rates. Indeed, population geographers recognize birth rates as one of the best single socioeconomic variables for distinguishing between developed and underdeveloped countries. Birth rates are also linked to women's roles and options, which vary from one culture to another. It seems that the lowest birth rates are usually found in European countries and lands peopled by European emigrants, such as the United States, Canada, Argentina, and Australia. However, the low birth rates now typical of Europeans and their overseas kin are relatively recent, coinciding with urbanization and industrialization. Population maps of the nineteenth rather than the twentieth century would show quite a different picture. Giant waves of emigration drew millions of "excess" Europeans out of their own countries to settle distant areas of the earth. Yet this massive surge of colonial migration did little to hold down population growth. Europe's population rose from 194 million in 1840 to 463 million in 1930, approximately double the rate for the world as a whole. It has been estimated that between 1750 and 1930, the number of Caucasians increased 5.4 times; Asians, only 2.3 times; and blacks, less than 2 times. Early in the twentieth century, at the close of its period of rapid population growth, Europe contained 25 percent of all human beings on earth, and its importance was felt almost everywhere. Today, Europe's proportion of the world population has fallen to only 14 percent and the children of the European birth-rate "explosion" now watch the non-European world far surpass them in numbers. In the process, the European culture becomes less influential, demonstrating a link between demography and other aspects of society.

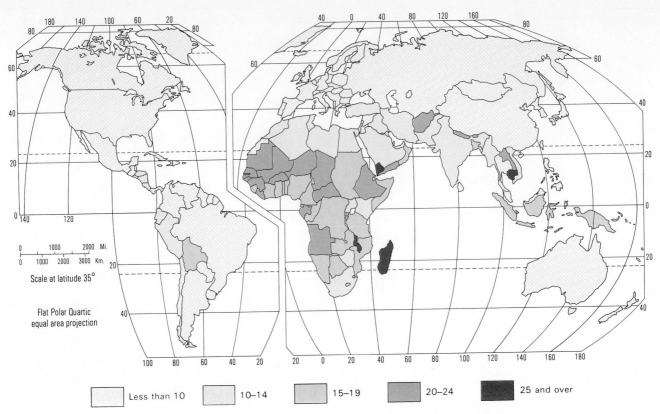

| | Less than 10 | | 10–14 | | 15–19 | | 20–24 | | 25 and over |

FIGURE 2.5
The annual death rate per thousand inhabitants, by country. Compare to Figure 2.4, and note that sub-Saharan Africa ranks very high in both birth and death rates. (Source: United Nations, *Demographic Yearbook,* 1985.)

Patterns of Mortality

The global pattern of **death rates,** the number of deaths in a year per thousand people, reveals both similarities and differences to the map of birth rates. As Figure 2.5 shows, the most striking feature of the mortality map is the concentration of high figures in tropical Africa, the worst area in the world for serious diseases. On the other hand, urban and industrial nations have low death rates, just as they have low birth rates. However, low death rates are also found in such countries as Thailand, Turkey, and Ecuador, where urbanization and industrialization are not well developed and where birth rates are moderate to high.

Many factors contribute to the death rate — from suicide to disease, from starvation to traffic accidents. The greatest reshaper of the global death-rate map, though, has been Western medical technology. In the twentieth century, this technology in one form or another reached almost every part of the world, carried by colonial governments, missionaries, and other agencies. The net result has been greatly lowered death rates, even in areas such as tropical Africa, where the rate is still comparatively high.

The Population Explosion

The spatial contrasts in population density, birth rates, and death rates, when considered together, underscore the dynamic aspect of population. They provide the background for a discussion of the **population explo-**

sion. The crucial element triggering this explosion has been a dramatic decrease in the death rate, particularly for infants and children, in most of the world, without an accompanying decline in the birth rate. Traditionally, only two or three offspring in a family of six to eight children might live to adulthood, and when improved health conditions allowed more of the children to survive, the cultural norm encouraging large families persisted.

On a global scale, we can easily describe the population crisis. The number of people in the world has been increasing geometrically, doubling in shorter and shorter periods of time. Table 2.2 shows the progression. The overall effect of even a few population doublings is startling. An example of a geometric progression is provided by the legend of the king who was willing to grant any wish to the person who could supply a grain of wheat for the first square of his chessboard, two grains for the second square, four for the third, and so on. To cover all 64 squares and win, the candidate would have had to present a cache of wheat many times larger than today's worldwide wheat crop.

The same phenomenon seems to apply to population growth. Humans have actually reproduced at an extraordinarily modest rate throughout history—about 0.02 additional persons per thousand per year. Since A.D. 1, the population has doubled about once every 500 years. At present, about 75 million more people come into the world each year than go out of it. The time span between doublings of the world population has grown progressively shorter and now stands at about 35 years.

For the most part, this population explosion did not come to light until the twentieth century. Nevertheless, some scholars foresaw long ago that an ever-increasing population would eventually present difficulties. As early as the 1600s, Sir William Petty, an Englishman who pioneered the science of statistics, predicted that an overpopulation crisis would develop one thousand years in the future. According to Petty, in the year 2600 there would be one person for each three acres of land. Then, in the 1700s, the Prussian army chaplain Johann Süssmilch estimated the world population at 1 billion, a reasonably accurate figure. He believed that God was steadily reducing the average human life span to accommodate the increasing number of people. Süssmilch reached this conclusion by comparing the life expectancy for people of his own day with the 969-year life span attributed to Methuselah in the Old Testament.

The most famous early-day observer of population growth was an English clergyman. In 1798, Thomas Malthus published *An Essay on the Principles of Population* (see biographical sketch). Malthus believed that the human ability to multiply far exceeds our ability to increase food production (see box, "Excerpts from the Writings of Thomas Malthus").

TABLE 2.2
The World Population Growth

Year	World Population
40,000 B.C.	1,500,000
8,000 B.C.	10,000,000
Birth of Christ	200,000,000
1000	275,000,000
1300	380,000,000
1500	450,000,000
1650	500,000,000
1750	700,000,000
1800	910,000,000
1850	1,200,000,000
1900	1,600,000,000
1950	2,600,000,000
1960	3,000,000,000
1965	3,200,000,000
1970	3,610,000,000
1975	4,000,000,000
1980	4,400,000,000
1985	4,850,000,000
1990	5,300,000,000
2000 (est.)	6,200,000,000

EXCERPTS FROM THE WRITINGS OF THOMAS MALTHUS

"I think I may fairly make two postulata.

"First, that food is necessary to the existence of man.

"Secondly, that the passion between the sexes is necessary, and will remain nearly in its present state.

". . . Assuming, then, my postulata as granted, I say, that the power of population is indefinitely greater than the power in the earth to produce subsistence for man.

"Population, when unchecked, increases in a geometrical ratio. Subsistence only increases in an arithmetical ratio. A slight acquaintance with numbers will show the immensity of the first power in comparison of the second.

"By that law of our nature which makes food necessary to the life of Man, the effects of these two unequal powers must be kept equal.

"This implies a strong and constantly operating check on population . . ."

From Thomas Malthus, *An Essay on the Principles of Population* (London, 1798), chap. 1.

THOMAS R. MALTHUS
1766–1834

Born in the shire of Surrey, England, Malthus studied theology at Cambridge and became an ordained minister. While still a minister, he began writing his essay on population. Gradually, writing and lecturing became his major interest. In 1805, he was appointed a professor of modern history and political economy at Haileybury College, a position he held until his death. Long before most scholars were concerned with overpopulation, Malthus warned of it. His famous *Essay on the Principles of Population* was published in 1798. Marx, Darwin, and many others read and commented on his work. Malthus rejected most artificial birth-control techniques as theologically unacceptable, approving only delayed marriage and moral restraint. He believed warfare, famine, and disease would solve the problem if people failed to seek a more humane solution. In recent decades, his ideas have received renewed attention as the world approaches a population crisis. (For more on Malthus, see the book by Dupâquier and Fauve-Chamoux in the suggested readings section.)

Consequently, Malthus maintained, "a strong and constantly operating check on population" will necessarily act as a natural control on numbers. Malthus felt that famine and war are inevitable because they curb population growth (see Figure 2.6). Today, almost two centuries after Malthus penned his warnings, his basic argument is still accepted in many quarters. Geographers, accordingly, have devoted considerable attention to the spatial aspects of food availability and famine, as suggested by the works of Currey, Dando, Watts, and Grigg listed in the readings at the end of this chapter.

At the present rate of increase, the world population would, within a relatively few centuries, reach a level where each person had only 1 square foot (less than one-tenth of a square meter) of land area. Obviously, conditions could never become this crowded (see box, "Is the World Really Overcrowded?"). It would be impossible to feed and house such a dense clustering of people. Indeed, some population scholars tend to see the extraordinary rise in human fertility rates at the present time as something of a historic oddity. They expect the world population to level out, perhaps early in the twenty-first century, at somewhere between 8 and 15 billion people. Indeed, evidence now suggests that the world birth rate will begin declining by about the year 2000, for the first time in recorded history, though actual population stabilization would lag far behind the onset of this decline. Some feel that stabilization will occur before any catastrophic depletion of resources, but others, convinced that the earth cannot support many more people without an ecological disaster, argue for **zero population growth.** Each couple, they feel, should merely "replace" themselves

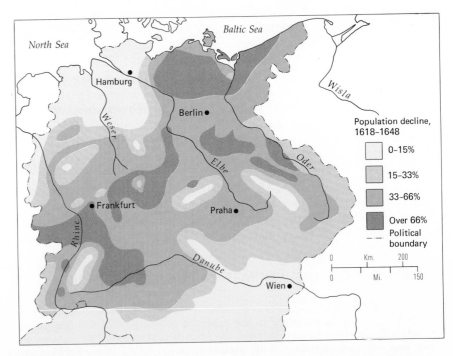

FIGURE 2.6
War as a device for population control in central Europe, 1618–1648. Thomas Malthus regarded war as inevitable, since it was necessary to help control population growth. He would understand this map, which reveals how effective war can be in destroying people. The Thirty Years' War, with its attendant killing, starvation, and disease, drastically reduced the population in some central European provinces, leaving few districts untouched. Population density was greatly altered. (After *Westermanns Grosser Atlas Zur Weltgeschichte*, Braunschweig: Georg Westermann, 1956, p. 107.)

by having only two children. Even if adopted, this idealistic policy would require many years actually to halt population growth.

A global perspective on the population explosion is useful, but it does not provide a complete picture by itself. We also need a geographical perspective. The term *population explosion* is generally applied to underdeveloped countries with a large difference between birth and death rates, yet many countries in this category, such as Brazil, are not overpopulated. Others may be reaching the point where additional population will spell disaster. However, we must also take into account regional variations in forms of livelihood. Would an additional 500 million people overpopulate India? Very likely it would if India remains an agrarian land; perhaps not if India were to become industrialized. Certainly Tokyo and New York City now contain more people per square mile than most areas of India.

Facing the Population Crisis. How will the population explosion be controlled? We know that the continued growth of human numbers must end sometime. Are war, famine, and disease the only answers? Are there viable alternatives to the fearsome "natural" controls envisioned by Malthus? The answer to these questions may well differ from one culture to another.

Starting in the eighteenth century, a number of European countries began to undergo what population geographers now call the **demographic transformation.** In other words, they underwent certain changes in birth and death rates that seem to accompany the movement from a rural, agrarian society to a primarily urban and industrial one. In preindustrial societies, birth and death rates are both normally high, leading to almost no population growth. With the coming of the industrial era, such medical discoveries as inoculations with cowpox serum to prevent smallpox, improvements in diet, and other factors set the stage for the drastic drop in death rates. Human life expectancy in the industrialized countries soared from an average of 35 years in the eighteenth century to 75 years or more at present. The result in Europe was a population explosion as fertility outran mortality. Eventually, after a lag, a decline in the birth rate followed the decline in the death rate, as is shown in Figure 2.7.

Today, from Japan to the United States, industrialized, technologically advanced nations have achieved an almost universally low fertility

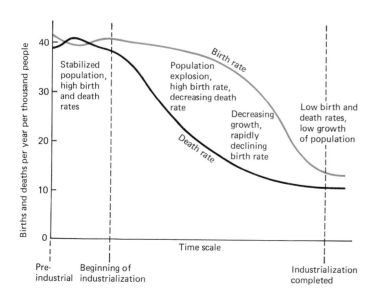

FIGURE 2.7
The demographic transformation as a graph. The "transformation" occurs in several steps, as the industrialization of a country progresses. Initially, the death rate declines rapidly, causing a population explosion as the gap between the number of births and deaths widens. Then the birth rate begins a sharp decline. The transformation ends when both birth and death rates have reached low levels, by which time the total population is many times greater than at the beginning of the transformation.

rate. This universal change is even more remarkable because it has been accomplished in countries with quite different cultures and with quite different birth-control strategies. At present, low growth rates and low birth rates exist throughout the industrialized world.

It is tempting, but not necessarily accurate, to credit this universal lowering of the birth rate to the introduction of modern birth-control methods — the pill, intrauterine devices, vasectomies — and to the legalization of abortion. However, methods of achieving a lowered rate — intercourse without ejaculation, celibacy, **infanticide,** the use of abortifacients, and late marriages — were known for centuries. This implies that lowering the birth rate is a cultural, not a technical, problem. The birth rate declines when people decide that it is personally beneficial to have a smaller family, not when they are convinced of the dangers of overpopulation. The fact is that in an urban, industrial society, children lose much of their economic significance to the family. Thus, having fewer of them can be a benefit. Even so, Western population scientists, politicians, and others are today approaching the global population problem as a matter of technology. They are offering the rest of the world technological solutions rather than cultural ones and ignoring the cultural geography of population and demography.

The Western Technological "Solutions."   Western technological and scientific innovations, in no small measure, caused the population explosion. Their principal effect was to lower death rates without lowering birth rates. This same technological civilization, centered in Europe and America, has now produced techniques and devices for birth control. Western experts in a variety of academic fields have offered many proposals for controlling population growth. These proposals fall into several categories.

A first category involves voluntary fertility control. Experts propose to provide free contraceptive devices, remove all remaining legal restrictions on abortion, encourage vasectomies, and develop improved contraceptive devices. Many of these proposals are familiar to us because they are already being used. In addition, much research is in progress to improve voluntary birth-control methods and to discover new ones.

A second category of possible ways to control population includes various proposals for incentive programs. For example, taxes could be raised as each child is born to a family, with the lowest tax rate reserved for childless couples. Monetary rewards for voluntary sterilization could be offered, and the government could guarantee old-age care to people with no children. Parents might be required to pay a set amount of tax for the birth of each child, beginning with the third-born. In a third category we find laws aimed at changing basic traditions. The law could be changed to encourage more women to go to work. Special legal recognition could be given to the childless marriage. For instance, laws could be changed to make it easier for childless couples to obtain divorces.

Most of these proposals are feasible only in industrially advanced, urbanized nations with well-developed technologies and relatively efficient central governments. Even there, many are unworkable. Most could succeed only among literate, educated, relatively prosperous peoples. As we have already seen, such peoples have, in the main, already significantly lowered their birth rates. In effect, most Western proposals for population control are applicable only in industrial cultures, those that have already "spontaneously" adopted birth control.

Solutions in the Underdeveloped World.   Looking at Figure 2.8, you can
see that exploding populations are found mainly in economically underdeveloped countries. Many of these agrarian lands can hardly afford the
rapid increase in population, and yet their populations are not responsive
to Western birth-control solutions, even though Western methods of
death control were gratefully accepted.

An American, Canadian, or European of the 1990s might find it hard
to understand how the scientific solutions of Western scholars can be
rejected. The problem of overpopulation seems so clear and rational.
However, what is rational and scientific to an urban Westerner may appear to be little short of lunacy to an Asian peasant. For a farmer in India,
children may appear the only way out of a life of poverty and an old age of
solitary begging. An urban society puts large sums of money into the
formal education of its children and forbids child labor, making children a
financial burden (as any parent who has financed a college education for a
son or daughter knows all too well). In a rural society, the costs of raising
and educating a child are minimal and grow smaller the more children
there are in a family. The advantages are enormous. The children can work
from an early age, replace otherwise expensive hired laborers in the fields,
and provide a form of support for the parents in old age. To suggest to an
Indian villager that he or she practice birth control without also suggesting

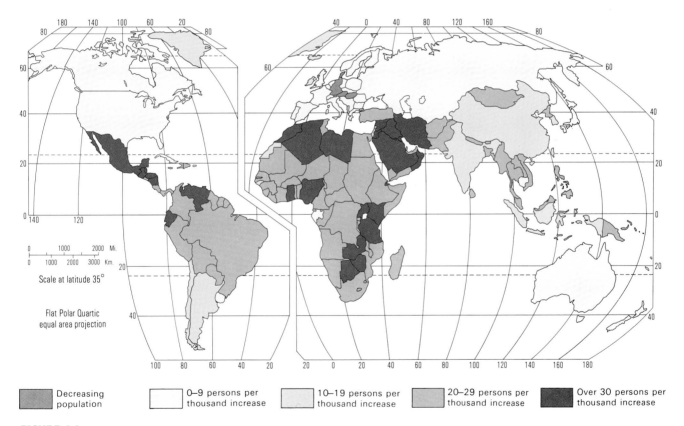

| Decreasing population | 0–9 persons per thousand increase | 10–19 persons per thousand increase | 20–29 persons per thousand increase | Over 30 persons per thousand increase |

FIGURE 2.8

The annual natural increase of population, by country, measured by comparing the
number of births and deaths, but excluding emigration and immigration. Note the
contrast between tropical areas and the middle and upper latitudes. In several places,
countries with very slow increase border areas with extremely high growth. (Source:
United Nations, *Demographic Yearbook,* 1985.)

WHY BIRTH CONTROL FAILED IN MANUPUR

" '[They] were trying to convince me in 1960 that I shouldn't have any more sons,' commented Thaman Singh, water carrier in Manupur village, part of India's Punjab state. 'Now, you see, I have six sons and two daughters and I sit at home in leisure. They are grown up and they bring me money. One even works outside the village as a laborer. [They] told me I was a poor man and couldn't support a large family. Now, you see, because of my large family, I am a rich man. . . . Time has proven me right.'

"Thaman Singh, along with the rest of Manupur's villagers, was the subject of a multiyear birth control project sponsored by Harvard University, the Rockefeller Foundation, and the Indian government. The project attempted to get Manupur's villagers to adopt modern birth control methods, and voluntarily limit family size. Often, the villagers politely accepted the birth control tablets offered by the study's field workers. 'But they were so nice, you know,' commented one villager. 'And they came from distant lands to be with us. Couldn't we even do this much for them? Just take a few tablets?' However, many never actually used the foam tablets. In fact, the villagers considered the whole project bizarre, and were constantly looking for 'the clue' to what the project workers were really doing. In the end, the project failed to dent the area's birth rate. Project workers attributed this to peasant illiteracy, ignorance, or prejudice. The villagers, particularly the poor farmers and tenant farmers of Manupur who resisted the project most strongly, looked on the matter quite differently.

" 'A rich man invests in his machines. We must invest in our children. It's that simple,' said Manupur blacksmith Hakika Singh. The arithmetic of land and labor makes this easy to understand. With a tractor, three people can work about fifty acres. Without a tractor, the same land would take fourteen people year around and twenty at sowing, weeding, and harvesting time. Hakika Singh, like other Manupur villagers, is aware that people are not stuck in poverty because they have large families. Rather they have large families because they are poor, and desperate to change that situation. Sons and daughters in Manupur cost little to raise, replace far more expensive hired laborers in a farmer's fields, can emigrate to other areas or even the city to get jobs augmenting the family's overall income, and support the parents in old age. As one villager put it: 'Without sons, there is no living off the land. The more sons you have, the less labor you need to hire and the more savings you can have.' "

From Mahmood Mamdani, *The Myth of Population Control, Family, Caste, and Class in an Indian Village* (New York: Monthly Review Press, 1972). Copyright © 1972 by Mahmood Mamdani. Reprinted by permission of Monthly Review Press.

a method for attacking the root of the high birth rate—the structure of peasant poverty, tenancy, and insecurity—is to offer less than nothing (see box, "Why Birth Control Failed in Manupur"). Many people in such cultures fear that their offspring might die. Large numbers of children mitigate that fear.

In the People's Republic of China, the powerful central government adopted a very strict policy in an attempt not merely to halt population growth but, ultimately, to decrease the number of people. All over China today one sees billboards and posters admonishing the citizens that "one

FIGURE 2.9
The government of the People's Republic of China is aggressively promoting a policy of "one couple, one child," in an attempt to relieve the pressures of overpopulation. This billboard in Lanzhou (Lanchow), a provincial city in the interior of China, conveys the government's message. Violators, who have more than one child, are subject to fines, loss of job and old-age benefits, loss of access to better housing, and other penalties. Recently, governmental enforcement of the policy has weakened. (Photo by Terry G. Jordan, 1983.)

couple, one child" is the ideal family (see Figure 2.9). Violators face huge monetary fines, cannot request new housing, lose the rather generous old-age benefits provided by the government, forfeit their children's access to higher education, and may even lose their jobs. Late marriages are encouraged. In response, between 1970 and 1980, the total fertility rate in China plummeted from 5.9 births per woman to only 2.7. Even so, the Chinese birth rate turned upward in 1986, rising, for the first time in over a decade, from 18 to 21 in only one year. A significant relaxation in some aspects of the one-child policy, coupled with the entry into the childbearing population of persons born in the middle 1960s, when China experienced a "baby boom," have caused the recent trend.

Age and Sex Distributions

Some countries have overwhelmingly young populations, with close to half of their people under 15 years of age. Mexico is such a country, as are many other nations in Latin America, Africa, and tropical Asia. Others, generally the countries that industrialized early, have a great preponderance of people in the over-20/under-60 age bracket.

A very useful graphic device for depicting such national age characteristics is the **population pyramid.** (Figure 2.10 compares four pyramids.) Careful study of such pyramids not only reveals the past progress of birth control, but also allows geographers to predict future population

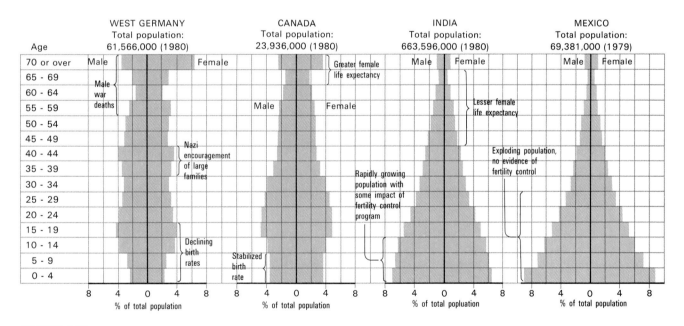

FIGURE 2.10

Population pyramids for West Germany, Canada, India, and Mexico are shown for about 1980. West Germany's "pyramid" looks more like a precariously balanced pillar, an indication that its population is approaching stability. Mexico, by contrast, displays the classic stepped pyramid of an exploding population. Note, too, how population explosion in recent past decades in Mexico would continue to fuel rapid growth in the future, even if birth rates dropped rapidly, since the number of women in the child-producing age span is so much larger than it was previously. The Canadian pyramid reveals recent sharp declines in the birth rate. The modest progress of birth control in India can also be seen. More recent figures, from 1985, indicate that Mexico's latest birth group, aged 0–4, is smaller than expected, causing the base of its pyramid to narrow, while India's group is considerably larger, reversing an apparent trend. West Germany is now experiencing actual population decline. (Sources: United Nations, *Demographic Yearbook*, 1981, 1985.)

trends. Youth-weighted pyramids, broad at the base, suggest the extremely rapid growth typical of the population explosion. Those excessively narrow at the base represent countries approaching population stability.

Population pyramids also allow a graphic portrayal of **sex ratios.** These differ from one country to another and within individual countries. "Frontier" areas typically have far more males than females, as is evident in parts of Alaska and northern Canada. In Alaska, 56 percent of the population 16 years of age or older were male, according to the 1970 census. By contrast, 47 percent were male in Mississippi, where many young men had left for other places. The same is true of many economically depressed rural areas and agrarian nations. For instance, many prime-age males have emigrated from Spain and Portugal. They reside for most of the year in industrialized countries such as France and West Germany, often leaving their families behind. Similarly, in the African nation of Malawi, according to the United Nations *Demographic Yearbook,* the attraction of jobs in the cities has made the urban population 53 percent male. Only 46.5 percent of rural people are men. Figure 2.11 shows sex ratio by country. In part, the ratio is influenced by warfare, by differential migration or health conditions for males and females, and in some extreme cases by female infanticide. Certain fatal diseases strike men or women more frequently, and these illnesses also reveal a striking regionality (Figure 2.1). For more detail on the geographical study of sex

FIGURE 2.11
Number of women per hundred males, by country. What cultural practices might explain this curious pattern? (Source: Seager and Olson, *Women in the World,* p. 13.)

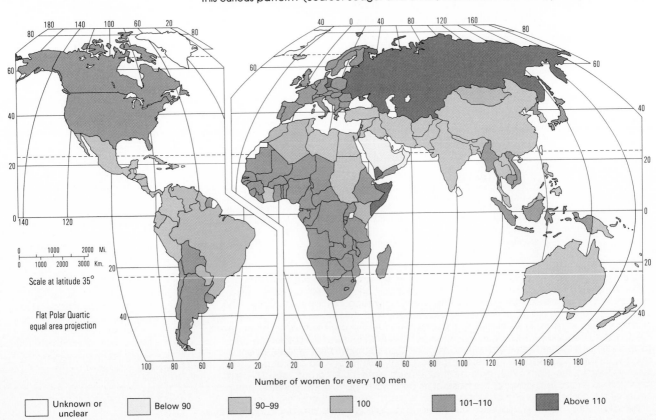

ratios and the spatial aspects of the status of women, see the atlases by Shortridge and by Seager and Olson, as well as the article by Andrews, all of which are listed in the readings at the end of this chapter.

Age structure, too, differs spatially. For example, rural populations in the United States are usually older than those in urban areas. Indeed, the flight of young people to the cities has left some rural counties in the United States with populations 45 years or older in median age. Some warm areas of the United States have become retirement havens for the elderly, so that parts of Arizona and Florida have populations far above average in age. Communities such as Sun City near Phoenix, Arizona, legally restrict residence to the elderly. In Great Britain, coastal districts have a much higher proportion of elderly than does the interior, causing the map to resemble a hollow shell and suggesting that the aged often migrate upon retirement to seaside locations (see Figure 2.12).

Standard of Living

The demographic traits discussed above begin to sketch a picture revealing the standard of living, or quality of life. If other traits such as health, income, housing, food, crime rates, and education are taken into consideration, a more meaningful demographic pattern emerges, one describing the overall quality of life. Population geographers have long been interested in regional health patterns, as is suggested by the books by Professors Cliff, Haggett, and Ord; Eyles; Howe; Pyle; Meade; and others listed in the readings at the end of this chapter. Disease invariably takes on a geographical character that can very strikingly be revealed through maps (Figure 2.13).

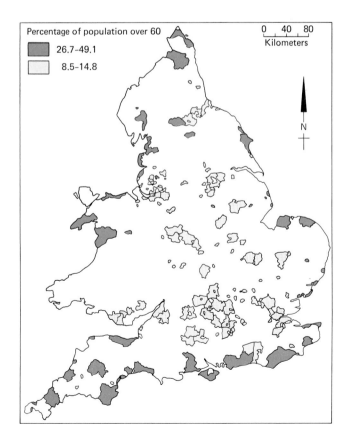

FIGURE 2.12
Proportion of elderly in the population of England and Wales, 1971, by census district. Why do elderly people form a larger part of the population in the coastal regions than in the interior? Does the seaside environment encourage longevity; have the elderly migrated to the shore; or have younger people moved away from the sea? (After C. M. Law and A. M. Warnes, ''The Changing Geography of the Elderly in England and Wales,'' *Transactions of the Institute of British Geographers,* New Series 1 (1976), 461.)

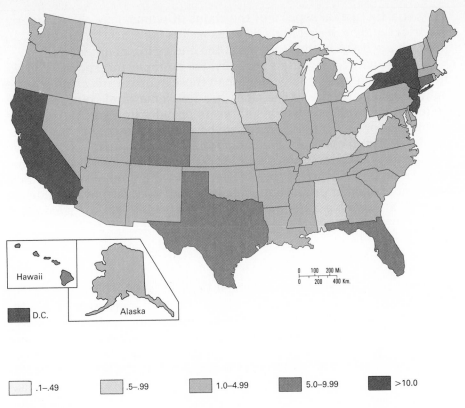

| | .1–.49 | | .5–.99 | | 1.0–4.99 | | 5.0–9.99 | | >10.0 |

FIGURE 2.13
Reported AIDS cases annually per 100,000 persons in the United States, by state, 1987. Why might this pattern of AIDS regions have developed? Is hierarchical diffusion at work? (Sources: Dutt et al., "Geographical Patterns of AIDS in the United States," *Geographical Review*, 77 (1987), 459; U.S. Centers for Disease Control.)

In an attempt to measure and map the standard of living, many criteria could be included. The accompanying map, Figure 2.14, employs infant mortality, life expectancy at age 1, and the literacy rate. Upon that pattern has been superimposed the border between rich and poor nations, as determined by a variety of economic measures. The great spatial variation in living standards is one of the most fundamental geographical facts of our time and one of the most troubling. It could be the basis of future mass migrations or conflicts, particularly in those areas where the rich border the poor.

Migration Regions

Migration is a major subject within population geography and will be dealt with at greater length in the section immediately following, under the theme of diffusion. At the outset, however, it is important to recognize the relevance to migration of the theme of culture region. A **migration region,** in the jargon of demography, is a contiguous geographical area within which movers tend to stay; that is, when people in such areas migrate, they tend not to leave the region. Many larger islands and peninsulas are known to function as migration regions. Newfoundland in Canada and the Delmarva peninsula of Delaware, Maryland, and Virginia provide examples. Sometimes ethnic ties cause the migration region to function, because people are reluctant to leave their group. Acadiana (the Cajun triangle of Louisiana) and the San Luis Valley of Colorado, an Hispanic stronghold, function as ethnic migration regions. The Connecticut Valley is also a migration region, for reasons less clearly understood. In contrast,

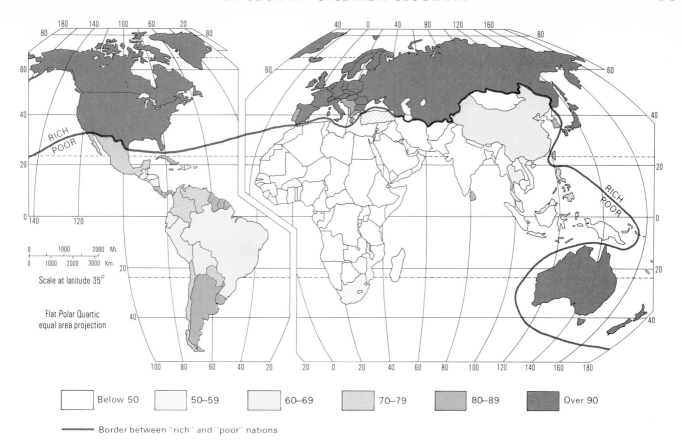

FIGURE 2.14
Rich and poor nations, with the physical standard of living index by country, 1980, on a scale of 0 to 100. The Washington-based, nonprofit Overseas Development Council prepared the index, basing it on three criteria: infant mortality, life expectancy at age 1, and the literacy rate. The highest-ranking country was Sweden with 97; the lowest was Guinea-Bissau with 12. Income, housing, type of government, and other characteristics were not considered. How might the pattern differ if these and other traits had been considered? The classification of rich and poor nations is based on the Seventh Economic Summit meeting of developed nations, held at Ottawa in 1981.

many other areas do not function as migration regions. Southern California, Florida, and Montréal draw and send migrants widely, functioning as cosmopolitan locations in migration. The cultural geographical implications of this contrast for regionalism are profound.

DIFFUSION IN POPULATION GEOGRAPHY

In population geography, cultural diffusion operates on many levels. Migration of people, or relocation diffusion, is perhaps the most basic type. With their concern for spatial processes, geographers have a natural interest in the movement of population, and the territorial redistribution of people is therefore a major concern of population geographers.

Migration

Humankind is not tied to one locale. Although our species probably evolved in tropical Africa, we have proven remarkably adaptable to new and different physical environments. We have made ourselves at home in all but the most inhospitable climates, shunning only such places as ice-sheathed Antarctica and the shifting sands of Arabia's "Empty Quarter." Even there, temporary migrants frequently come to stay for a while. Our permanent habitat extends from the edge of the ice sheets to the seashores, from desert valleys a thousand feet (300 meters) below sea level to mountain slopes 16,000 feet (5,000 meters) or more up. This far-flung distribution is the product of migration.

For those human beings who migrate, the process generally ranks as one of the greatest events of their lives. Even prehistoric migrations often remain embedded in folklore for centuries or millennia (Figure 2.15). Geographers, recognizing the fundamental importance of migration, have long devoted much attention to it, and you will find several books on this aspect of population geography listed in the readings at the end of the chapter.

Migration takes place when people decide that it is preferable to move rather than to stay, when the difficulties of moving seem more than offset by the expected rewards. Although migration is relocation diffusion, the decision to migrate can spread by means of expansion diffusion. For more detail on these processes, see Chapter 9. Every migration, from the ancient dispersal out of Africa to the present-day movement toward urban areas, is governed by a host of **push-and-pull factors.** These act to make the old home unattractive or unlivable and the new land attractive or at least an alternative. When voluntary migration occurs, the combination of push-and-pull factors has obviously become stronger than the desire to stay at home among one's own kind. Generally, the push factors are the key ones, since a basic dissatisfaction with the homeland is prerequisite to voluntary migration. Perhaps the most important factor prompting migration throughout the thousands of years of human existence is economic. More often than not, migrating people are seeking greater prosperity.

In the nineteenth century, more than 50 million European emigrants, seeking better lives outside their native lands, changed the racial and ethnic character of much of the earth. By 1970, about one-half of all Caucasians did not live in the European homelands of the ancestors. Between about 1950 and 1970, about 20 million people migrated into 11

FIGURE 2.15
Redrawn segments of an Aztec codex, or pictograph map, depicting the prehistoric migration of the Aztecs from an island (possibly in northwestern Mexico) to another island in a lake located at the site of present Mexico City, where they founded their great capital, Tenochtitlán. Clearly, the epic migration was a central event in their collective memory. (Source: Modified from María Teresa de Gutiérrez de Macgregor, "Population Geography in Mexico," in Clarke, *Geography and Population,* p. 217.)

AZTLÁN
The original home

ATZCAPOTZALCO
("Place of the ant hill"),
stopped four years here

New World and European industrial nations from the more agrarian areas of the world. They, like their emigrating European predecessors, were looking for jobs, better wages, and a new and more secure economic life.

International migration often occurs because a country has a negative image in the minds of some of its people. Foreign lands seem more attractive to them. Great Britain, for many years a goal of emigrants, especially from Ireland, now loses about 60,000 of its people per year. Many British emigrants are attracted to Australia and New Zealand, in part because these countries are British in culture, yet lack many of the economic and social problems that plague Great Britain. Whether deserved or not, Australia and New Zealand are perceived as something of an earthly paradise by much of the British middle class, an image promoted by publicity offices throughout Britain.

From a geographical standpoint, the central fact concerning international migration is that the sources and destinations both reveal marked spatial variation. Even in so small an island as Ireland, long a major source of emigrants, the proportion of the population leaving has varied greatly from one small district to another (Figure 2.16). The same is true of migration within individual countries, and the United States provides a good example. From the country's beginnings, Americans have been migrating people. The nation has "tilted west," with most migration occurring from east to west. The spectacular growth of California, especially in this century, is the culmination of the westward movement. By contrast, black migration in the United States long flowed mainly from south to north as rural blacks were attracted to large northern cities. In fact, throughout the past century or more, there has been a general movement of Americans from rural to urban areas, although recent censuses suggest that this migration to cities may be ending. Also, both the south-to-north movement of American black people and the east-to-west shift of whites seem to have ended, being replaced by a north-to-south migration of both races to the "Sunbelt" states.

While human migration may be the most fundamental type of diffusion, other demographic phenomena may profitably be studied through the concept of cultural diffusion. For example, we can apply the principles

ACALHUACAN
("Place of canoes"),
stopped four years here

TENOCHTITLÁN
(Founded about 1325 A.D.)

FIGURE 2.16
Emigration from Ireland, 1846–1851, as a percentage of total population, by country. The essential geographical question raised by this map is: Why was the emigration proportionately greater in the interior counties? Because emigration generally does vary greatly spatially, this form of diffusion reshapes the density patterns. (After S. H. Cousens, ``The Regional Pattern of Emigration During the Great Irish Famine, 1846–1851,'' *Transactions of the Institute of British Geographers*, 28 (1960), 121.)

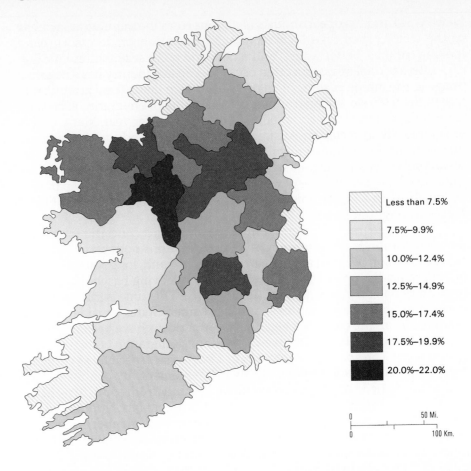

Less than 7.5%

7.5%–9.9%

10.0%–12.4%

12.5%–14.9%

15.0%–17.4%

17.5%–19.9%

20.0%–22.0%

of diffusion to some of the proposed methods of population control that were discussed earlier.

Diffusion of Population Control

How can we determine which, if any, of the proposals for population control are likely to succeed? Cultural geographers can best approach this question by using the theme of cultural diffusion and, in particular, the concept of absorbing and permeable barriers. After all, most methods of population control are simply cultural innovations. Different barriers to those innovations are present in different cultures.

For example, it is impossible to raise the taxes of people living in abject poverty, because they simply do not have the money. In fact, many of the population-control proposals outlined earlier in this chapter require huge bureaucracies, and these could be inefficient and ineffective, making many measures hard to oversee. Moreover, any government other than dictatorship would not be able to carry out unpopular birth-control schemes.

Birth-control programs can also run into social barriers. In India, the cultural preference for large numbers of children is so deeply entrenched that a woman has traditionally been considered immoral if she dies without having mothered at least one son and inadequate if she mothers only a small family. Children provide old-age security, and a son must perform certain rituals at the death of his father. In some other cultures, particularly in Latin America, large numbers of children prove the husband's virility.

Organized religions often block the control of population growth. For instance, the Roman Catholic Church opposes modern methods of artificial birth control, including abortion. This opposition is based on the belief that such controls constitute a human disruption of the divine order. Partly as a result, many, though by no means all, areas of strong Catholicism have high birth rates. In studying Northern Ireland, for example, geographer P. A. Compton found that "significant disparities exist between Roman Catholics and Protestants," to the extent that continuation of current birth-rate patterns would produce a Catholic majority there at some time in the first half of the twenty-first century. Some sects encourage large families as a means of expanding their membership.

International rivalries and nationalist feelings sometimes affect population growth. The leaders of a country may not encourage birth control for fear that their population will become smaller than that of a hostile neighbor country. They look at each newborn child as a future soldier, a defender of the homeland. Similarly, in some diplomatic quarters power and influence in international affairs are seen as linked to the size of population. China's diplomatic victories, in particular its displacement of Nationalist China (Taiwan) in the United Nations, are related to its huge population. Diplomats were repeatedly reminded that "you can't ignore a quarter of the human race," a reference to China's 1.1 billion people. The same problem often arises within countries where two or more ethnic groups compete for influence.

Even within areas as small as western Europe, geographers have found major regional contrasts in attitudes toward population growth. In France, the revolution of 1789 reduced Roman Catholic influence and gave individuals more of a chance to advance economically and socially on the basis of their native ability. Partly as a result of these developments, the birth rate in nineteenth-century France declined rapidly. However, neighboring countries, such as Germany, Italy, and the United Kingdom, did not experience the same decline. Consequently, the French population did not keep pace numerically with that in nearby lands (see Figure 2.17). Table 2.3 compares the populations of five countries from 1720 to 1985. France, the most populous of these countries in 1800, was the least populous of the four European countries included in the table in 1985. During this same period, millions of Germans, Britishers, and Italians emigrated overseas, whereas relatively few French left their homeland. At the same time, the French Canadians of Québec, whose ancestors had left France long before, still favored large families. Consequently, the 10,000 people who settled in Québec between 1608 and 1750 multiplied into today's population of 7 million. This number does not include many French Canadians who migrated from Canada to New England and the other areas. In order to promote population growth in the colony, the Québec government at times supported this enthusiasm for parenthood by offering tax deductions for large families.

Disease Diffusion

In the section on the culture region theme, the uneven distribution of diseases was described (Figures 2.1, 2.13). The theme of cultural diffusion permits us to add a dynamic quality to such maps, demonstrating the movement of diseases across geographical space. For contagious diseases, we might expect only contagious expansion diffusion to be at work, but that is far from the case. Figure 2.18, constructed by geographer Gerald F. Pyle, clearly reveals that in the great influenza epidemic of 1918–1919,

Birthrate 25.0 per 1000 and under

Birthrate 25.0 per 1000 and over

Germanic/Romance language border

International borders

FIGURE 2.17
Birth-rate pattern in western Europe, 1910. Notice how the birth-rate border paralleled the linguistic rather than the political boundary. French-speaking people in France, southern Belgium, western Switzerland, and northwestern Italy, together with their Romance-language kinsmen, the Romanish-speaking people of eastern Switzerland, were reproducing at a lower rate than their German-speaking neighbors. What cultural factors might have helped produce this contrast? (Adapted from Terry G. Jordan, *The European Culture Area: A Systematic Geography,* 2nd ed., New York: Harper & Row, 1988, p. 159.)

TABLE 2.3
Population Growth in France, French Canada, Germany, Italy, and the United Kingdom (Population in Millions)

Country	1720	1800	1850	1900	1930	1985	Increase from 1720 to 1985
France	19	27	36	38	42	55	2.9 Times
Québec	0.02	0.2	0.9	1.7	2.8	6.6	330 Times
Germany	14	25	35	56	64	78[a]	5.6 Times
Italy	13	18	23	32	41	57	4.4 Times
United Kingdom	7	11	27	37	46	56	8.0 Times

[a]East and West Germany together.

hierarchical diffusion allowed the disease to spread from one large city to another. Such a movement, in turn, implies relocation diffusion, as infected persons carried the influenza traveling between urban areas. Most typically, the different types of spatial diffusion are merged in this manner, regardless of whether the item being transmitted is a disease, an idea, an innovation, or a material object.

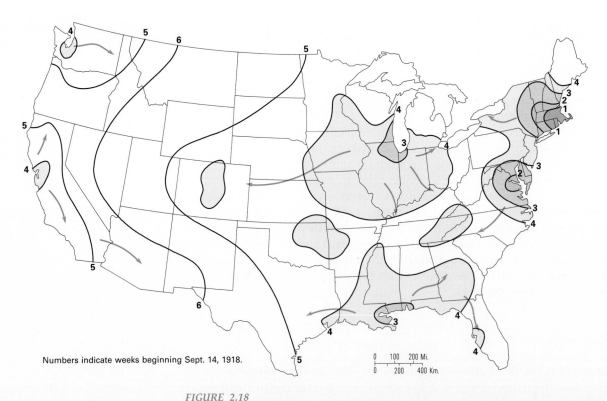

Numbers indicate weeks beginning Sept. 14, 1918.

0   100   200 Mi.
0   200   400 Km.

FIGURE 2.18
Diffusion of the first autumnal wave of influenza in the United States during the pandemic of 1918–1919. Worldwide, this unusually severe pandemic killed perhaps 20 million persons and in the United States it was fatal to over half a million. Contagious diffusion was, of course, at work, but there is also evidence of relocation and hierarchical diffusion, as the disease skipped from one large metropolitan center to another. Why might that have occurred? (Source: Pyle, *Diffusion of Influenza*, p. 48.)

▉ POPULATION ECOLOGY

The theme of cultural ecology is quite relevant to the study of population geography. At the most basic level, a successful adaptive strategy permits a people to reproduce in a given environment. Population size and growth offer an index to successful adaptation, cultural ecologists believe. Maladaptive strategies can lead to a dwindling of numbers, or even extinction for a people. Similarly, when groups migrate to new places as settlers, their success or failure will depend in no small part upon **preadaptation.** To what extent did the groups' way of life, their adaptive strategy, in the old home precondition them for success in the new land? Successful cultural preadaptation is often a matter of chance, particularly when prior knowledge of the new land is sketchy or when migrants have little control over their destinations.

Even a successful adaptive strategy may lead to demographic catastrophe, however. The key is sustainability. If practiced over many decades or generations, does the strategy cause such significant environmental alteration and destruction as to undermine livelihood? This consideration introduces the "humans as modifiers" issue into population ecology. In other ways, too, the theme of cultural ecology bears upon demography, as we will see.

Environmental Influence

Population, regardless of its adaptive strategy, is influenced in a possibilistic manner by the local abundance of resources. Densities, in the middle latitudes, tend to be greatest where terrain is level, the climate mild and humid, the soil fertile, mineral resources abundant, and the sea accessible. Conversely, population tends to thin out with increasing elevation, dryness, coldness, ruggedness of terrain, and distance from the coast (see Figure 2.19).

Climatic factors affect where people settle. Most of the sparsely populated zones in the world have, in some respect, "defective" climates, from the human viewpoint. The thinly populated northern edges of Eurasia and North America are excessively cold, and the belt from North Africa into the heart of Eurasia matches the major desert zones of the Old World. Humans remain creatures of the humid and subhumid tropics, subtropics, or midlatitudes and have not fared well in excessively cold or dry areas. Small populations of Eskimos, Lapps, and other peoples live in some of the undesirable areas of the Earth, but these regions do not support large populations. Humans are remarkably adaptable in the biological sense, and our cultures offer enhanced adaptive strategies, allowing us to live in many different physical environments, but perhaps, as a species, we have not fully forgotten the climatic features of sub-Saharan Africa, where we began. In avoiding cold places, we may reveal even today the tropical origin of our species.

Humankind's preference for lower elevations holds especially true for the middle and higher latitudes. Indeed, most mountain ranges in those latitudes stand out as regions of sparse population (see Figure 2.20). By contrast, inhabitants of the tropics often prefer to live at higher elevations, concentrating in dense clusters in mountain valleys and basins. By doing so, they escape the humid, hot climate of the tropical lowlands. For example, in tropical portions of South America, more people live in the Andes Mountains than in the nearby Amazon lowlands. The capital cities of many tropical and subtropical nations lie in mountain areas above about 3000 feet (900 meters) in elevation.

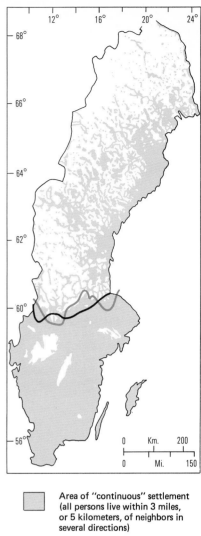

Area of "continuous" settlement (all persons live within 3 miles, or 5 kilometers, of neighbors in several directions)

Area of "discontinuous" settlement (nearest neighbors are more than 3 miles, or 5 kilometers, away)

Southern border of subarctic climate and infertile soils

Northern border of main zone of "continuous" settlement

Discontinuous	Settlement
Continuous	boundary

FIGURE 2.19
Environment and population distribution in Sweden. The northern boundary of the thickly settled area corresponds closely to the southern limit of the bitterly cold subarctic climate and the infertile, acidic soils of the coniferous forests. (Adapted from Kirk H. Stone, "Swedish Fringes of Settlement," *Annals of the Association of American Geographers,* 52 (1962), 379.)

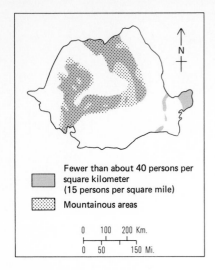

FIGURE 2.20
This map presents population distribution in Romania, based on population data for the early 1960s. Environmental features, such as mountain ranges, may discourage settlement. In Romania, the mountainous areas are also the areas of sparse settlement. In what ways might mountains in midlatitude areas repel population?

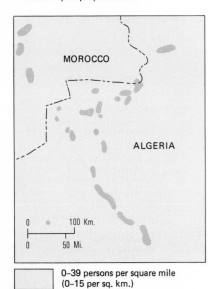

FIGURE 2.21
Environmental factors—in this case, water in the midst of the desert— mold population distribution. These scattered clusters of people are in the Sahara of North Africa, but the pattern is typical of many arid regions. Dot clusters indicate the presence of oases. (After Paul F. Mattingly and Elsa Schmidt, "The Maghreb: Population Density." Map Supplement No. 15, *Annals of the Association of American Geographers*, 61 (1971).)

Our tendency to settle on or near the seacoast is also quite striking. If you look again at Figure 2.3, you can see that the continents of Eurasia, Australia, and South America resemble hollow shells, with the majority of the population clustered around the rim of each continent. In Australia, half the total population lives in just five port cities, and most of the remainder is spread out over nearby coastal areas. This preference for living by the sea can be partly explained by the trade and fishing opportunities the sea offers. At the same time, continental interiors tend to be regions of climatic extremes. For example, Australians speak of the "dead heart" of their continent, an interior land of excessive dryness and heat. People are also attracted to those places where fresh water is available. In desert regions, population clusters reflect the locations of scattered oases and occasional rivers, such as the Nile, that rise from sources outside the desert. Figure 2.21 shows this settlement pattern.

Still another environmental factor that affects population distribution is disease. In the Mediterranean region, especially in Italy, thickly settled, agriculturally productive coastal lands were virtually depopulated by the spread of malaria after Roman times. Only in recent times, as malaria was eradicated by modern scientific methods, were these districts reclaimed and repopulated. Other diseases attack valuable domestic animals, depriving people of food and clothing resources. Such diseases have an indirect but profound effect on population density. For example, in parts of East Africa, livestock are attacked by a form of sleeping sickness. This particular disease is almost invariably fatal to cattle but not to humans. The people in this part of East Africa depend heavily on cattle, which provide food, are symbols of wealth, and serve a semireligious function in some tribes. Thus, the spread of a disease fatal to cattle has caused entire tribes to migrate away from infested areas, leaving them unpopulated (see Figure 2.22).

Environmental Perception and Population Distribution

The most telling geographical commentary on a place is made when people perceive it as a suitable home and choose to live there. Perception of the physical environment plays a role in this choice. Different cultural groups often "see" the same physical environment in different ways. These varied responses to a single environment may influence the distribution of people. A good example appears in a part of the European Alps shared by German- and Italian-speaking people. The mountain ridges in that area—near the point where Switzerland, Italy, and Austria join— run in an east-west direction, so that each ridge has a sunny, south-facing slope and a shady, north-facing side. German-speaking people, who rely on dairy farming, long ago established permanent settlements some 650 feet (200 meters) higher on the *shady* slopes than the settlements of Italians, who are culturally tied to warmth-loving crops, on the *sunny* slopes. This example demonstrates contrasting cultural attitudes toward land use and different perceptions of the best use for one type of physical environment.

Sometimes, the same cultural group changes its perception of an environment through time, with a resulting redistribution of its population. The coal fields of western Europe provide a good case in point. Before the industrial age, many coal-rich areas—such as southern Wales, the lands between the headwaters of the Oder and Vistula rivers in Poland, and the Midlands of England—were only sparsely or moderately settled. However, the development of steam-powered engines and the increased use of coke in the iron-smelting process created a tremendous demand for coal. Industries grew up near the European coal fields, and people flocked to these areas to take advantage of the new jobs. In other words, once a technological development had given a new cultural value to coal, many sparsely populated areas containing that resource acquired heavy concentrations of people.

How people view their environment often plays a key role in determining their voluntary migration and, consequently, the population density of an area. For a variety of reasons, migrants develop positive or negative perceptions of possible new homelands. Any person will view some regions as highly desirable and others as less livable. When people have a negative view of their home areas and a positive view of one or more other regions, then they are prime candidates for migration. That is, people have in their minds what can be called **mental maps** that lay out various places to live in terms of their perceived attractiveness. The mental map in Figure 2.23 is a composite of the individual perceptions of Pennsylvania university students, and it might be used to help predict emigration flows from that state.

Recent studies indicate that much of the interregional migration in the United States today is prompted by a desire for pleasant climate and other desirable physical environmental traits, such as beautiful scenery. Surveys of immigrants to Arizona revealed that its sunny, warm climate is a major reason for migration. Attractive environment was seen as the dominant factor in the growth of the population and economy of Florida in a study covering the 1939–1954 period. Another study ranked desirable environmental traits in the following order as stimulants for American migration: (1) mild winter climate and mountainous terrain, (2) a diverse natural vegetation that includes forests and a mild summer climate with low humidity, (3) the presence of lakes and rivers, and (4) nearness to the seacoast. Similarly, migrating New Zealanders are drawn to mild coastal districts, and many Britishers prefer the south and southwest coast, where

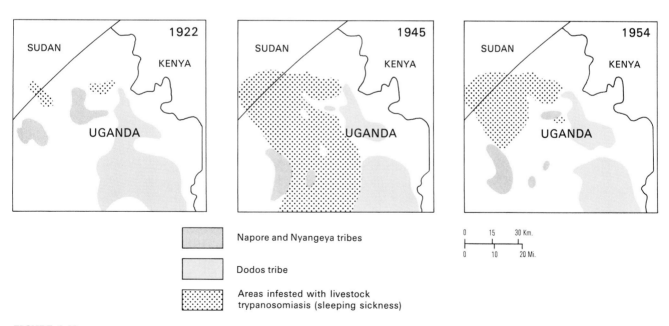

Napore and Nyangeya tribes

Dodos tribe

Areas infested with livestock trypanosomiasis (sleeping sickness)

FIGURE 2.22
Disease is an environmental factor that influences settlement. The effect is apparent in this example in northeastern Uganda, East Africa. Note in particular the changing distribution of the Napore and Nyangeya groups based on the spread and eradication of sleeping sickness. (Adapted from Walter Deshler, "Livestock Trypanosomiasis and Human Settlement in Northeastern Uganda," *Geographical Review*, 50 (1960), 549.)

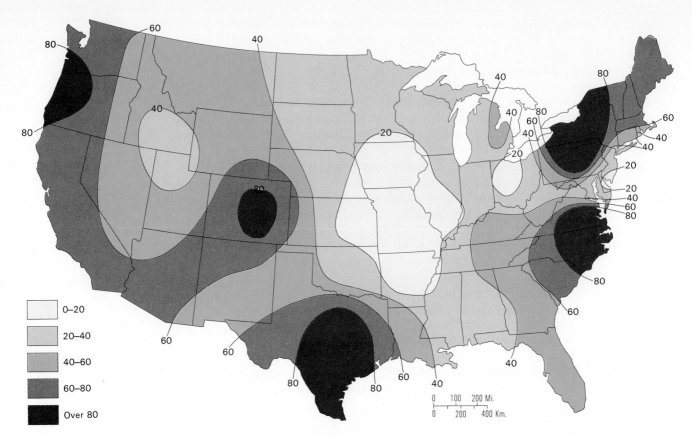

FIGURE 2.23
The residential preference mental map of students at the Pennsylvania State University main campus, 1982. A simple scaling was employed that gave the most preferred state, Colorado, a score of 100 and the least preferred, Iowa, 0. Each student ranked every state on a scale from 1 (most like to live there) to 50. Such mental maps can help predict future migration patterns, but they also are in continual flux. Would the profound economic difficulties of Texas and Oregon since 1982 have changed the map? Both environmental and cultural factors affect the students' perceptions of the states. Compare this pattern with your own mental map of the United States. (After Peter R. Gould, "Getting Involved in Information and Ignorance," *Journal of Geography*, 82 (1983), 161.)

the climate is not so rainy and cloudy as elsewhere in Britain. Different age and cultural groups often display different preferences, but all are influenced by their perceptions of the physical environment in making decisions about migration.

Many elements go into shaping a mental map. Misinformation is at least as important as accurate impressions, because a person will often form strong images of an area without ever visiting it. Many Europeans, particularly in the nineteenth century, were urged to leave their homelands by land speculators who depicted the United States as a second paradise, a new land whose golden streets flowed with milk and honey. Present-day land developers often create distorted, overly favorable environmental images in order to sell their lots.

Population Density and Environmental Alteration

Through their adaptive strategies, people modify their habitats, often in order to enhance habitability. Particularly in areas where population is dense, radical alterations are not uncommon. This can happen in fragile environments even at relatively low densities, since the carrying capacity of the Earth varies greatly from one place to another. We can best say,

THE VALLEY OF THE ASHES

The environmental impact of huge urban agglomerations is considerable. "Out of sight, out of mind" may reduce this impact for many of us, but even as early as the 1920s a leading American novelist was repelled by what he saw on Long Island, near New York City.

About half-way between West Egg and New York [City] the motor road hastily joins the railroad and runs beside it for a quarter of a mile, so as to shrink away from a certain desolate area of land. This is a valley of ashes — a fantastic farm where ashes grow like wheat into ridges and hills and grotesque gardens. . . . Occasionally a line of grey cars crawls along an invisible track, gives out a ghastly creak, and comes to rest, and immediately ash-grey men swarm up with leaden spades and stir up an impenetrable cloud, which screens their obscure operations from your sight. . . . The valley of ashes is bounded on one side by a small foul river, and, when the drawbridge is up to let barges through, the passengers on waiting trains can stare at the dismal scene for as long as half an hour.

If you think this problem has been solved in the intervening years, visit the western end of Staten Island in New York City.

From F. Scott Fitzgerald, "The Valley of Ashes" from *The Great Gatsby.* Copyright © 1925 Charles Scribner's Sons; copyright renewed 1953 Frances Scott Fitzgerald Lanahan. Reprinted by permission of Charles Scribner's Sons.

then, that the density of population relative to the carrying capacity of the land can be of crucial importance in environmental alteration and the issue of sustainability. (See box, "The Valley of the Ashes.")

We now face a worldwide ecological crisis for the simple reason that, at present densities, many of our adaptive strategies are not sustainable. The continued existence of humankind and many other species is now in question. Some experts concerned with the spreading destruction of the human habitat feel that the population explosion and the ecological crisis are closely related. They believe that attempts to restore the balance of nature will not succeed until we halt population growth, although they recognize that other causes are at work in ecological crises. Others feel that adaptive strategy is far more crucial than mere density.

The changes in the vegetation of western and central Europe since medieval times demonstrate how a region's population density and adaptive strategy can have a long-term effect on the environment. During the Middle Ages, farmers cleared vast forests from the plains and valleys of western and central Europe. In time, these fertile agricultural districts became densely populated. Interspersed among these lowlands were small areas of forested hills and low mountains, which the medieval farmers found unsuitable for agriculture and spared from the ax. As a result, surviving woodlands were so often limited to the hilly areas in Europe that the term *forest* is frequently used simply to describe areas of rough terrain, as in Germany's famous Black Forest. Whenever population was on the decline, particularly in times of warfare and plague, these surviving forests expanded, spilling onto the lowland plains. The spread of the forests that accompanied the Hundred Years' War, a conflict between England and France lasting from 1337 to 1453, can be linked to the numerous deaths caused by the war. In fact, surviving peasants coined the saying that "the forests came back to France with the English." Recently, the fate of the European woodlands took another, far more sinister turn, when industrial-derived air pollutants began rapidly destroying the remnant forests (see Chapter 12).

Although population density can affect an area's environment, these environmental modifications can, in turn, affect the area's population density. For instance, in a place where human activity has severely damaged the land in some way, some or all of the inhabitants may abandon the area. Some evidence suggests that the Sahara has steadily expanded since Roman times because domestic sheep and goats have overgrazed the short-grass steppes that border the desert. In the same way, a crust of mineralized "hardpan" has developed on the land's surface as a result of badly planned irrigation projects in some desert regions. This, in turn, has caused a decline in the population.

It would be misleading to say that the worldwide ecological crisis is strictly a function of overpopulation. It might be more accurate to call it a crisis of consumption. A relatively small percentage of the world's population controls much of the world's industrial technology and absorbs a gargantuan percentage of the world's productive capacity each year. For example, Americans, who make up less than 6 percent of humankind, account for about 40 percent of the world's resources consumed each year. Thus a child born in the United States has more of an impact on the global environment than one born in India or China.

◼ CULTURAL INTEGRATION AND POPULATION PATTERNS

Population patterns are closely tied to both the physical environment and numerous facets of culture. The theme of cultural integration allows us to look at some of these relationships among culture, population density, migration, and population growth. Inheritance laws, food preferences, politics, differing attitudes toward migration, and many other cultural features all can influence the pattern of population distribution (see Figure 2.24).

Cultural Factors

Many of the forces that influence the distribution of people are basic characteristics of a group's culture (see box, "Culture and Population"). For example, we must understand the rice preference of people living in Southeast Asia before we can try to interpret the dense concentrations of

---

CULTURE AND POPULATION

A study of the Tenetehara and the Tapirapé, two Tupi-speaking Indian tribes of central Brazil, shows the range of population choices available to different cultures within the same physical and material environment. Before European contact, both tribes inhabited similar tropical forest areas, had the same level of technology, and were horticulturists who depended on hunting, fishing, and wild fruits to supplement their diets. Yet the Tapirapé population was, by choice, relatively small and stable, whereas the Tenetehara population of perhaps 2000 was at least twice as large and probably expanding.

Among the Tenetehara, there was little effort to limit family size. Men took pride in the number of children they fathered. Women, eager to bear children, would leave a husband whom they considered sterile. There seem to have been few cultural values in the tribe that would discourage large families.

The Tapirapé, however, had an explicit idea of maximum family size. When asked why their families were no larger, they would say, "The children would be hungry." In Tapirapé society, this meant "hungry for meat," which was sometimes scarce — but no scarcer than for the more numerous Teneteharas. In other words, Tapirapé population controls were based not on possible starvation levels, but on a specific desire for a larger quantity of meat in their diets.

Other cultural factors also played a role in the Tapirapé decision. As a result, the tribe set limits on how many children a woman should have (no more than three living and no more than two of the same sex). To keep their society within its desired limits, they practiced infanticide, the killing of newborn infants.

The arrival of the Europeans in Brazil highlighted each tribe's population choice. The Teneteharas' first contacts with Europeans in the seventeenth century were violent. Slavery, massacres, war, and epidemics decimated tribal ranks. Yet by 1945, after 300 years of contact with Europeans, their population still numbered 2000. In 1947 the Tapirapés, after less than 40 years of contact — mainly with European diseases — numbered no more than 100. Their society was in shambles; their social organization ruined. Unlike the Tenetehara, their age-old population policies worked against them in this new situation. Culturally unable to replenish themselves fast enough, they were on the road to extinction.

Adapted from Charles Wagley, "Cultural Influences on Population: A Comparison of Two Tupi Tribes," in Daniel R. Gross (ed.), *Peoples and Cultures of Native South America* (Garden City, N.Y.: Doubleday, 1973), pp. 145–156. Reprinted by permission.

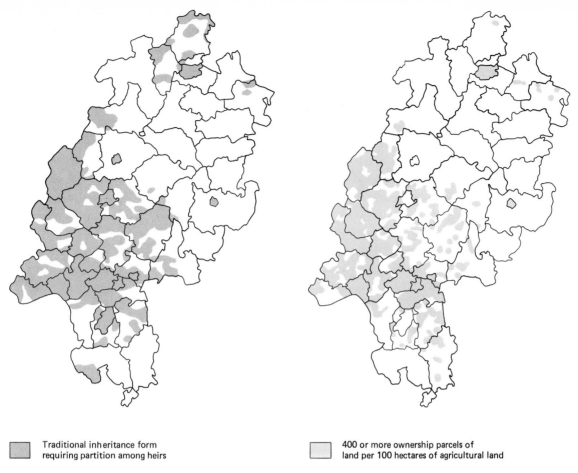

Traditional inheritance form
requiring partition among heirs

400 or more ownership parcels of
land per 100 hectares of agricultural land

FIGURE 2.24
Inheritance systems and land fragmentation in the West German province of Hessen, 1955. In the southern and western parts of Hessen, the tradition, dating to Roman times, was to divide the farms among the various heirs. As a result, the farms there became ever smaller over the centuries, with excessive fragmentation of the holdings. What impact would this have on population density and agricultural prosperity? Northern and eastern Hessen, by contrast, clung to the ancient Germanic custom of primogeniture, by which the farm passes intact to the eldest son. (Adapted from E. Ehlers, "Land Consolidation and Farm Resettlement in the Federal Republic of Germany," in Robert C. Eidt et al. (eds.), *Man, Culture and Settlement: Festschrift to Prof. R. L. Singh,* New Delhi and Ludhiana, India: Kalyani Publishers, 1977, p. 124.)

people in Southeast Asia rural areas. The population in the humid lands of tropical and subtropical Asia expanded as this highly prolific grain was domesticated and widely adopted. Environmentally similar rural zones elsewhere in the world, where rice is not the staple of the inhabitants' diet, never developed such great population densities. Similarly, the introduction of the potato into Ireland in the 1700s allowed a great increase in rural population, because it yielded much more food per acre than did traditional Irish crops. Failure of the potato harvests in the 1840s greatly reduced the Irish population, both through starvation and emigration.

Cultural groups also differ in their tendency to migrate. Religious ties bind some groups to their traditional homelands. Sometimes travel outside the sanctified bounds of the motherland is considered immoral, and religious duties, in particular the responsibilities to tend ancestral graves and perform rites at parental death, kept many Chinese in their native land. The Navaho Indians of the American Southwest practice the custom of burying the umbilical cord in the floor of the *hogan* (house) at birth.

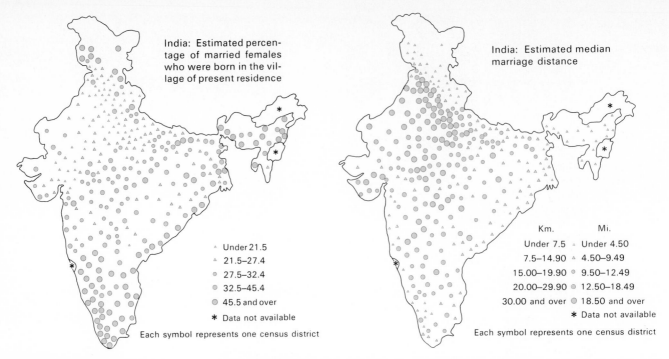

India: Estimated percentage of married females who were born in the village of present residence

- ▵ Under 21.5
- ▴ 21.5–27.4
- ○ 27.5–32.4
- ◍ 32.5–45.4
- ● 45.5 and over
- ✳ Data not available

Each symbol represents one census district

India: Estimated median marriage distance

Km.	Mi.
Under 7.5 ▵	Under 4.50
7.5–14.90 ▴	4.50–9.49
15.00–19.90 ○	9.50–12.49
20.00–29.90 ◍	12.50–18.49
30.00 and over ●	18.50 and over
✳ Data not available	

Each symbol represents one census district

FIGURE 2.25
Female marriage migration in rural India. Major differences in the tendency of women to migrate for the purpose of marriage and in the distance of migration can be seen from one part of India to another. What might some of the cultural causes of this spatial pattern be? (Maps by M. J. Libbee, in Libbee and D. E. Sopher, "Marriage Migration in Rural India," in Kosinski and Prothero (eds.), *People on the Move*, pp. 352, 354.)

Psychologically, this seems to strengthen the Navaho attachment to the home and retard migration. Other religious cultures place no stigma on emigration. In fact, some groups consider migration a way of life. The Irish, unwilling to accept the rural poverty of their native land, have proved so prone to migration that the population of Ireland today is only about half the total of 1840.

Migration tendencies can also differ between the sexes, for cultural reasons. In some parts of rural India, particularly the north and west, marriage is typically between persons from different villages. Since it is traditional in those parts of India for the woman to move into the household of her husband, females are much more likely to migrate than are males. As Figure 2.25 shows, a fifth or fewer of all married women in northern and western India live in the village of their birth; and in many districts their marriage migration has taken them 18 miles (29 kilometers) or more from their original home, a considerable distance in a society with few automobiles. In south and east India and in Kashmir in the far north, by contrast, females are much less likely to marry outside their village. Cultural differences lie at the root of these contrasts. In some parts of south India, for example, matrilineal societies, those that trace lineage primarily through the mother, encourage females to remain close to their place of birth. Even in patrilineal south Indian communities, a preference for marriage within the village prevails, so marriage migration is uncommon. The net result is to reduce cultural diffusion between villages in southern India.

Culture can also condition a people to accept or reject crowding. Studies have been made to determine the dimensions of **personal space,** the amount individuals feel "belongs" to them as they move about their everyday business. Personal space seems to vary from one cultural group to another. For example, when Americans talk with each other, they typically stand farther apart than, say, Italians do. The large personal space demanded by the American may well come from a heritage of sparse settlement. Early pioneers reportedly felt uncomfortable when they first saw smoke from the chimneys of neighboring cabins. Perhaps this is why American cities sprawl across large areas, with huge suburbs dominated by separate houses surrounded by private yards. Most European cities are compact, and their residential areas consist largely of row houses or apartments. Perhaps as more and more Americans are obliged to accept apartment living, our personal space will diminish.

Political and Economic Factors

The pattern of population distribution often arises from actions of governments or world economic conditions. For instance, nations have displaced or expelled cultural groups for thousands of years. The Romans dispersed the Jews from Palestine. However, twentieth-century governments certainly take the laurels in this category. One estimate of worldwide population displacements between 1913 and 1968 comes to an extraordinary 71 million people, many millions higher than the voluntary European emigration to the New World the century before.

During World War II, Nazi Germany directed the forced migration of millions of people. After the war, partly in retribution, nearly all the German-speaking people of western Czechoslovakia and eastern pre-1939 Germany, perhaps 12 million in all, were forcibly expelled from their ancestral homelands. Many districts were left largely unpopulated. Expulsions were carried out by the governments of Poland, Czechoslovakia, and the Soviet Union when German territory was annexed by these countries after the war. Czechs, Slovaks, Poles, and Russians resettled these regions, but even today many districts involved have lower population densities than in 1945.

For centuries, forced mass migration, motivated by either economic or political forces, has been a potent factor in the growth and decline of populations. It has been estimated that 9.6 million slaves, almost all from Africa, were imported into slave-using areas of the Old and New Worlds between 1451 and 1870. Up to one-fourth of the Africans died on the way, so between 11 and 13 million Africans were actually enslaved during that period. For the population geographer, the most startling result of this mass forced migration was probably that by 1930 more than a fifth of all blacks did not live in Africa.

Governments can also restrict voluntary migration. The two independent nations of Haiti and the Dominican Republic share the tropical Caribbean island of Hispaniola in the West Indies. Haiti, which supports about 500 persons per square mile (190 per square kilometer), is far more densely settled than the Dominican Republic, which has only 332 persons per square mile (128 per square kilometer) (see Figure 2.26). Government restrictions make migration from Haiti to the Dominican Republic difficult and thus help produce the different population densities. If Hispaniola were one nation, its population would probably be much more evenly distributed over the island.

Every culture has a set of laws to maintain order within the society, and these laws can affect population density. In most cases, these bodies of law include regulations about inheritance. In Europe, the legal code derived from Roman law requires that all heirs of a deceased person divide land and other property equally among themselves. Germanic law, on the other hand, favors the custom of primogeniture, or inheritance of all land and property by the firstborn son. In areas where divided inheritance is the tradition, farms fragment as the generations pass, causing rural population density to increase. Where primogeniture is the rule, on the other hand, emigration by landless sons retards the growth of population. It is not surprising, then, that the most severe rural overpopulation in Germany during the mid-nineteenth century was in the southern lands along the Rhine River and its tributaries. In that area, the custom of primogeni-

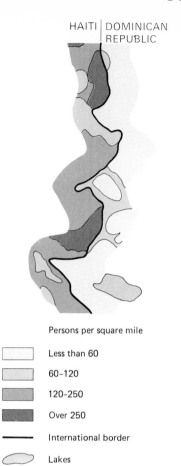

HAITI | DOMINICAN REPUBLIC

Persons per square mile

Less than 60

60–120

120–250

Over 250

International border

Lakes

FIGURE 2.26
Population density contrast along the Haiti-Dominican Republic boundary on the island of Hispaniola in the middle 1970s. Migration across this frontier has been restricted, causing the political boundary to become also a demographic border. (Adapted from John P. Augelli, "Nationalization of Dominican Borderlands," *Geographical Review*, 70 (1980), 32.)

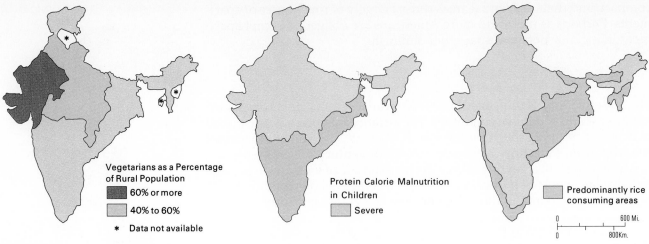

FIGURE 2.27
Protein malnutrition, vegetarianism, and rice consumption in India. In studying cultural integration, the geographer sometimes finds that the "obvious" answers are wrong. The disease and death that can result from protein deficiency are apparently unrelated to vegetarianism; instead, a link to rice consumption is suggested. (After Aninda K. Chakravarti, "Diet and Disease: Some Cultural Aspects of Food Use in India," in Allen G. Noble and Ashok K. Dutt (eds.), *India: Cultural Patterns and Processes*, Boulder, Col.: Westview Press, 1982, pp. 301–323.)

ture had not deviated from the tradition of divided inheritance that the Romans had implanted over 1500 years earlier (Figure 2.24).

Economic conditions often influence population density in profound ways. Indeed, the process of industrialization over the past 200 years has caused the greatest voluntary relocation of people in world history. Within industrial nations, people have fled from rural areas to cluster in manufacturing regions. Commercialized agriculture has attracted people in a similar way. For example, the Indonesian island of Java is one of the most densely settled rural areas in the world, with a population density greater than that of other large islands nearby. This concentration of people on Java results partly from the efforts of the Dutch, who ruled Indonesia until 1949, to concentrate tropical plantations there. Employment opportunities offered by these plantations drew people from the surrounding islands to Java. Consequently, Java's population expanded.

Application of the theme of cultural integration by geographers in their demographic research often produces negative results that are as enlightening as positive correlations. For example, many experts had long assumed that vegetarianism in India, based in the religious belief of numerous Hindus, was largely to blame for protein deficiency, malnutrition, and resultant health problems in many rural areas of that country. Recently, a study by A. K. Chakravarti, a cultural geographer at the University of Saskatchewan in Canada, revealed no spatial correlation between the vegetarian population and the consumption of animal protein (Figure 2.27). That is, nonvegetarians also eat little or no meat. Instead, the greatest protein deficiency occurs in areas where rice, rather than wheaten bread, accounts for the greater part of the cereal consumption.

■ SETTLEMENT PATTERNS IN THE LANDSCAPE

The distribution of people is clearly reflected in the cultural landscape. Differing densities and arrangements of population are revealed, at the largest scale, by maps showing the distribution of dwellings. We can illustrate these cultural landscape contrasts by using the example of rural settlement types. Farm people differ greatly from one culture to another, one place to another, in how they situate their dwellings. The range from tightly clustered villages on the one extreme to fully dispersed farmsteads on the other is shown in Figure 2.28.

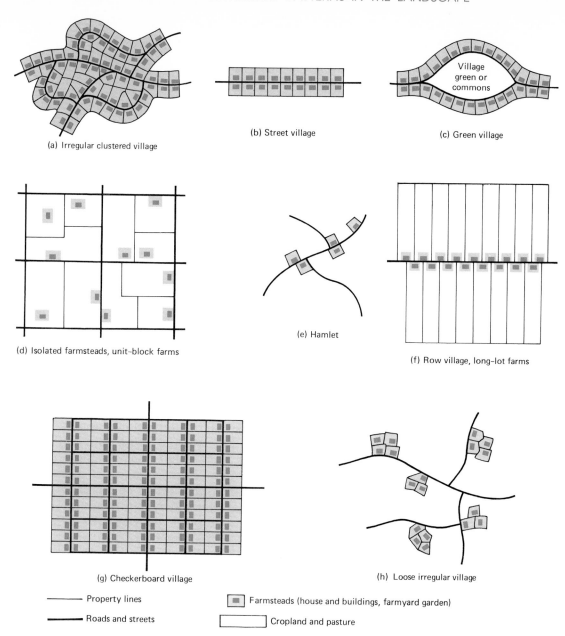

(a) Irregular clustered village

(b) Street village

(c) Green village

Village green or commons

(d) Isolated farmsteads, unit-block farms

(e) Hamlet

(f) Row village, long-lot farms

(g) Checkerboard village

(h) Loose irregular village

———— Property lines

▬▬▬▬ Roads and streets

■ Farmsteads (house and buildings, farmyard garden)

☐ Cropland and pasture

FIGURE 2.28
The way individual farmers choose to locate their farmsteads leads to a general settlement pattern on the land. In some areas, farmsteads are scattered and isolated. In areas where farmsteads are grouped, there are several possible patterns of clustering.

Clustered Rural Settlement: The Farm Village

In many parts of the world, farming people group themselves together in clustered settlements called **farm villages.** These settlements vary in size from a few dozen inhabitants to as many as 25,000 in large agrarian settlements called **agro-towns.** Contained in the village **farmstead** are the house, barn, sheds, pens, and sometimes the garden. The fields, pastures, and meadows lie out in the country beyond the limits of the village, and there are no dwellings in the surrounding farmland. The farmers must journey out from the village each day to work the land.

Farm villages are the most common form of settlement in much of Europe; in many parts of Latin America; in the densely settled farming regions of Asia, including much of India, China, and Japan; and among the

OVERLOOKING A VILLAGE IN INDIA

"On the steep ascent of the first range of hills bordering the southern edge of the great Ganges Valley in the Indian state of Madhya Pradesh, we ask our hired driver to stop the car, overlooking a tightly clustered farm village in the plain below. The village, tucked up against the foot of the hill, is open to our view from above. We look down upon a disorderly jumble of tile-roofed, mud-walled farmsteads, each consisting of single-story buildings grouped protectively around a central courtyard. So compact is the settlement that it is difficult to tell where one farmstead leaves off and the neighboring ones begin. Rounded mounds of threshed rice straw rise from many courtyards, and an occasional shade tree conceals parts of the village from our view. From the narrow dusty lanes and tiny courtyards, a rich variety of village noises drifts up to us on our god-like perch—the noises of animals and people going about their daily routines, noises unchanged for thousands of years. Off into the hazy distance stretch tan fields, another reminder that it is December, a month of gathering. Near the village are bright green rectangles of vegetables, irrigated and lush in the subtropical winter sun. Here is simplicity, continuity, attachment to place.

"The twentieth century returns abruptly and disagreeably with the noise of a loaded truck rumbling along the narrow asphalt highway skirting one side of the village, gearing down for the steep slope ahead. Like proper citizens of the new age, we return to the hired automobile and continue our journey."

From the travel journal of Terry G. Jordan, 1975.

---

sedentary farming peoples of Africa and the Middle East (see box, "Overlooking a Village in India"). These compact villages come in many forms, as Figure 2.28 shows. Most are irregular clusterings—a maze of winding, narrow streets and a jumble of farmsteads (Figure 2.29). Such *irregular clustered* farm villages developed spontaneously over the centuries, without any orderly plan to direct their growth. They are found in lands as diverse as China, India, and western Europe. Other types of farm village are very regular in their layout and reveal the imprint of planned design. The *street village* is the simplest of these planned types and consists of tightly clustered farmsteads lined up along either side of a single, central street, producing an elongated settlement. Street villages are particularly common in Slavic eastern Europe, including much of Russia. Another type, known as the *green village*, is characterized by farmsteads grouped in an orderly fashion around a central open place, or green, which forms a village commons. Green villages occur through most of the plains areas of northern and northwestern Europe, including England, and English immigrants laid out some such villages in colonial New England. Also very regular in layout is the *checkerboard village*, based on a gridiron pattern of streets meeting at right angles. Mormon farm villages in Utah are often of this type, and checkerboard villages are also the dominant type in most of rural Latin America and northeastern China.

Why do people who live in farm villages tend to huddle together in this way? In the past, a nucleus-type community filled many of the needs of rural people (see box, "Notes from a French Village"). Traditionally, the countryside was unsafe, threatened by roving bands of outlaws and raiders. Farmers could better defend themselves against such dangers by grouping together in villages. In many parts of the world, the populations of villages have grown larger during periods of insecurity and have shrunk again when peace was restored. Many farm villages occupy the most easily defended sites in their vicinity. These are referred to as strong-point settlements.

In addition to defense, the quality of the environment helps determine whether people settle in villages. In deserts and in limestone areas where the ground absorbs moisture quickly, farmsteads huddle together at the few sources of water. Such "wet-point" settlements tend to cluster around oases or deep wells. Conversely, a superabundance of water—in

FIGURE 2.29
Different rural settlement types are revealed in the accompanying photo montage. An unplanned irregularly clustered farm village in western Europe, a type found widely in the Old World, contrasts sharply with the regular layout of an East German street village. Both differ from the green village of African cattle herders in Uganda, with its circular houses clustered around a communal cattle pen. Typically American is this isolated farmstead on the Great Plains of North Dakota.

NOTES FROM A FRENCH VILLAGE

"Where do the people live who care for all this splendid farming country? We see them working in the fields, these superb wheat-fields, or harvesting the oats, but you can drive your car for mile after mile and never see a human habitation. . . . The people who till the fields all live in the villages. If you inhabit such a settlement you hear every morning, very, very early, the slow heavy tread of the big farmhorses and the rumble of the huge two-wheeled carts going out to work. . . .

"Of course this arrangement whereby country folk all live in villages turns inside out and upside down most of those conditions which seem to us inevitable accompaniments of country life; for instance, the isolation and loneliness of the women and children.

"There is no isolation possible here, when, to shake hands with the woman of the next farm, you have only to lean out of your front window and have her lean out of hers, when your children go to get water from the fountain along with all the other children of the region, when you are less than five minutes walk from church and the grocery store, when your children can wait till the schoolbell is ringing before snatching up their books to go to school. . . . And if one of the children breaks his arm, or if a horse has the colic, or your chimney gets on fire, you do not suffer the anguished isolation of American country life. The whole town swarms in to help you in a twinkling of an eye. . . ."

From Dorothy Canfield, *Home Fires in France* (New York, 1918). Copyright © 1918 by Holt, Rinehart and Winston. Copyright © 1945 by Dorothy Canfield Fisher. New York: Holt, Rinehart and Winston, Publishers.

marshes, swamps, and areas subject to floods—prompts people to settle together on available dry points of higher elevation.

Various communal ties bind villagers strongly together. Groups of farmers linked to one another by blood relationships, religious customs, communal landownership, or other similar bonds are likely to form clustered villages. Mormon farm villages in the United States provide an excellent example of the clustering force of religion. In addition, nearly all the numerous utopian experiments in rural America, including the "hippie" communes of the 1960s, formed around a nucleus. Communal or state ownership of the land—as in China, the Soviet Union, and parts of Israel—has encouraged the formation of some larger farm villages and agro-towns.

In Marxist Ethiopia, a government-directed plan of "villagization" had relocated more than 3 million peasants from their scattered hilltop farms in Harar and adjacent provinces to centralized villages by 1986, reputedly to permit provision of running water and medical services. Written into the new Ethiopian constitution, villagization would ultimately involve 30 million farmers, if plans were realized.

The people who settle in these tightly knit villages generally depend on crops for their livelihood. Farming requires less land than raising livestock does. Thus a farming economy permits villagers to live close together without having to travel an undue distance from farmstead to field. For this reason, villages are very common in areas of paddy rice farming and plantation agriculture but normally absent in dairy and ranch zones, where dwellings are generally scattered over the land. Exceptions are the irregular clustered villages of African cattle herders, one of which is shown in Figure 2.29.

Dispersed Rural Settlement: The Isolated Farmstead

In many other parts of the world, the rural population lives in dispersed, isolated farmsteads, often a mile or more from their nearest neighbors. These dispersed rural settlements grew up mainly in Anglo-America, Australia, New Zealand, and South Africa, that is, in the lands colonized by emigrating Europeans, but even in areas dominated by village settlements—such as Japan, Europe, and parts of India—some isolated farmsteads appear.

The conditions encouraging dispersed settlement are precisely the opposite of those favoring village development. These include (1) peace and security in the countryside, removing the need for defense; (2) colonization by individual pioneer families rather than by socially cohesive groups; (3) agricultural private enterprise, as opposed to some form of communalism; (4) unit-block farms, in which all land belonging to a farmer is in one block rather than fragmented into many parcels, as is typical in most farm villages (see Chapter 3); (5) rural economies dominated by livestock raising; and (6) well-drained land where water is readily available.

We have seen that clustered rural settlements developed over centuries and were molded by cultural necessities, some of which have since disappeared. On the other hand, most dispersed farmsteads originated rather recently. They date primarily from the colonization of new farmland in the last two or three centuries. During the same period, dispersed farmsteads replaced villages in some older settled areas. In Scandinavia, for example, governments abolished fragmented holdings and thereby promoted the dispersal of the rural population in the late 1700s and early 1800s. Sweden and Denmark deliberately encouraged the movement of farmers from villages to isolated farmsteads because such a migration reduced the amount of travel between home and field, increasing efficiency. Farm families abruptly torn away from the social life of villages in this way often have difficulty adjusting to their isolated dwellings. A study in Italy, where some dispersal has occurred in recent times, revealed that mental depression was more common among such relocated rural persons.

Semiclustered Rural Settlement

Some forms of rural settlement are neither clustered nor dispersed. Instead, they share characteristics of both, and may best be referred to as semiclustered settlements.

The most common type of semiclustered settlement is the *hamlet,* which consists of a small number of farmsteads grouped loosely together. As in farm villages, the hamlet farmsteads lie in a settlement nucleus separate from the cropland, but the hamlet differs from the farm village because it is smaller and less compact. Farmsteads are not so tightly clustered as are the dwellings within villages. In such semiclustered settlements, there are from 3 or 4 up to as many as 15 to 20 houses.

In many countries, hamlets have developed most frequently in poorer hill districts. This is true in parts of western Europe, China, India, the Philippines, and Vietnam.

Occasionally, several clusters of farmsteads lie close to one another, sharing a common name and administration. These constitute what amounts to a *loose irregular village.* The individual clusters in such a group are often linked to various clans or religious groups. These loose villages are especially typical of the Balkan region of southeastern Europe, and they also appear in parts of Malaya, Bangladesh, southern Japan, and India. Loose irregular villages involve a deliberate segregation of rural people, either voluntary or involuntary. In India, farmers of the "untouchable" caste are occasionally segregated from other people by means of loose irregular villages.

The *row village* is a third common type of semiclustered settlement. In this settlement pattern, a line of farmsteads is spaced at intervals along a road, a river, or a canal. A group of farmsteads along a transportation artery suggests the clustering typical of a true village, but the houses of a row village fall in a loose chain that often extends for many miles. The individual farmsteads that make up a row village are spaced farther apart than those in a street village and do not abut one another. Row villages are common in the hills and marshlands of central and northwestern Europe; along the waterways in French-settled portions of North America, especially Québec and Louisiana; and in southern Brazil and adjacent parts of Argentina. In the extensive French "Cajun" row villages along Bayou Lafourche in Louisiana, dwellings are sufficiently close to one another that "a baseball could be thrown from house to house for more than a hundred miles."

Reading the Cultural Landscape

The rural settlement forms described above provide a chance to "read" the cultural landscape. In so doing, we must always be cautious, looking for the subtle as well as the overt and not jumping to conclusions too quickly.

For example, the Maya Indians of the Yucatan peninsula in Mexico live in checkerboard villages, a rural settlement landscape that is both revealing and potentially misleading (Figure 2.30). Before the Spanish conquest, Mayas had lived in templed villages of the irregular clustered type, often situated alongside *cenotes,* natural karst sinkholes that provided water in a land with no surface streams and that possessed religious significance. The Spaniards destroyed these settlements, replacing them with checkerboard villages. Wide, straight streets were intended to accommodate the wheeled vehicles of the European conquerors.

The checkerboard landscape, superficially, suggests a cultural victory by the Spaniards. But if you look more closely, you will see that, in fact, Mayan culture prevailed. For example, many Mayas make little use of wheeled vehicles even today in village life, and many of the Spaniards' "streets" serve merely as rights-of-way for Indian footpaths that wind among boulders and outcroppings of bedrock. Irregularities in the checkerboard, coupled with a casual distribution of dwellings, suggests Mayan resistance to the new geometry. Spanish-influenced architecture—flat-roofed houses of stone, the town hall, a church, and a hacienda mansion—remain confined to the area near the central plaza, with newer examples along highway entrances to the village. A block away, the traditional Maya pole huts with thatched, hipped roofs prevail, echoed by cook houses of the same design. Indian influence increases markedly with distance from the plaza.

In the dooryard gardens surrounding each hut, traditional Indian plants thrive, such as papayas, bananas, peppers, ramon nuts, yucca, and corn, with only a few citrus trees to reveal Spanish influence. In the same yards, each carefully ringed with dry rock walls, as in pre-Columbian times, pigs descended from those introduced by the conquerors must

FIGURE 2.30
A hypothetical Mayan checkerboard farm village of about 1000 inhabitants in Yucatan province, Mexico, at the present. Spanish influence, seen in the grid pattern, plaza, church, hacienda, and flat-roofed buildings, weakens with distance from the center, and the rigid checkerboard masks a certain irregularity of farmstead layout. (Source: Composite of 1987 field observations by Terry G. Jordan in some 15 villages east and southeast of Mérida.)

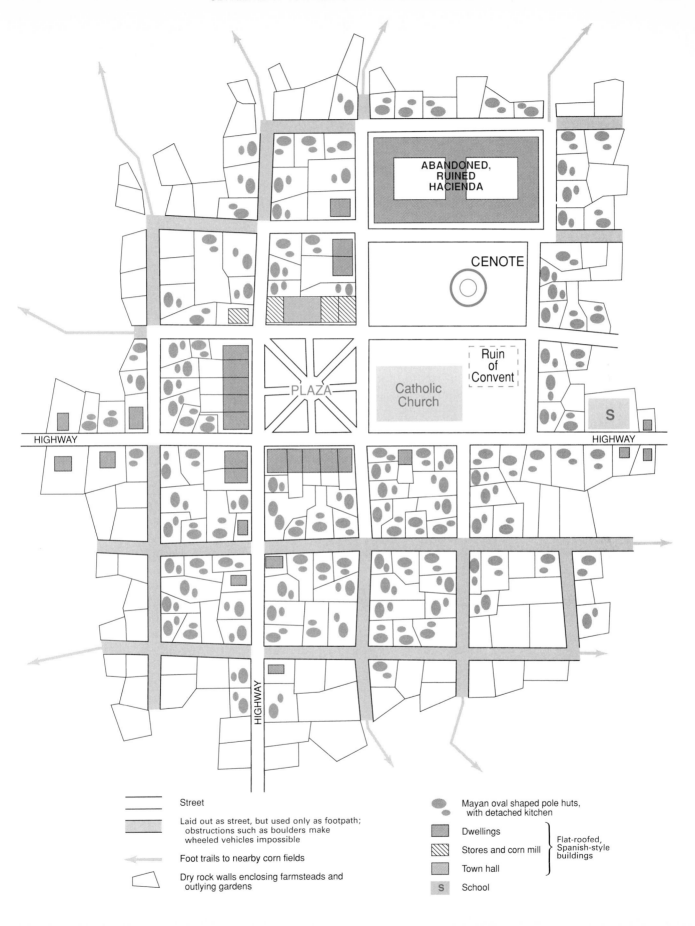

ABANDONED, RUINED HACIENDA

CENOTE

Ruin of Convent

PLAZA

Catholic Church

S

HIGHWAY

HIGHWAY

HIGHWAY

Street

Laid out as street, but used only as footpath; obstructions such as boulders make wheeled vehicles impossible

Foot trails to nearby corn fields

Dry rock walls enclosing farmsteads and outlying gardens

Mayan oval shaped pole huts, with detached kitchen

Dwellings

Stores and corn mill

Flat-roofed, Spanish-style buildings

Town hall

S School

share the ground with the traditional turkeys of the Maya, and space is still devoted to apiaries for the indigenous stingless bees. Occasionally, the Mayan language is heard drifting from hammocks in the pole huts, though Spanish prevails. So does Catholicism, but the absence of huts around the *cenote* suggests a lingering pagan sanctity.

Sometimes, then, the overt aspects of cultural landscape are a façade. We should always look deeper and become sensitive to what is subtle.

■ CONCLUSION

In our brief study of population geography, we have seen that humankind is unevenly distributed across the Earth. Despite the pressures of the population explosion, vast areas of the Earth remain sparsely settled. Spatial variations also exist for birth rates, death rates, rates of population growth, age groups, sex ratios, and standards of living.

Human beings have traditionally been mobile. This human diffusion, or migration, has been part of the human experience from the time of our earliest emergence as a biological species, and mobility remains part of our way of life today. Although our ancestors migrated to find more abundant game animals, better soil to till, or freedom on a new frontier, we migrate to go to school, to find jobs, and to enjoy the amenities of life. Particularly in the United States, mobility has become part of the fabric of life, and the average American family moves every few years. The principles of cultural diffusion are useful in analyzing human migration. They also help explain the spread of birth-control innovations.

By adopting the viewpoint of cultural ecology, we have seen how the environment influences the distribution of people and sometimes helps guide migrations. Whatever the real environment, each person has a perception of it—a mental map on which some areas are viewed as desirable and others as undesirable. Migration is guided, in part, by such mental images of the environment, however distorted they might be. Humans are clearly part of a dynamic ecological system. They migrate to new areas, alter the environment, and readjust their adaptations and perceptions to the changed environment.

Cultural integration is the device used to suggest ways that demography and mobility are linked to such elements of culture as legal systems, food preferences, migration taboos, international political disputes, and economic opportunity. Cultural attitudes can encourage people to be mobile or to stay in one place, and can encourage people to accept crowding or to feel uncomfortable without plenty of room for their personal space. Governments can also encourage or restrict movements of people, force migration or prohibit it. Cultural attitudes, governments, and religion can all help to promote birth control or encourage large families. In many ways, then, spatial variations in demographic traits are enmeshed in the fabric of culture. The understanding of any aspect of demography demands an investigation of many aspects of human culture.

How people distribute themselves across the Earth's surface is expressed visibly in the cultural landscape, most strikingly in rural areas. Using the example of the farm settlement landscape, we have seen how different cultures have developed distinctive forms, each of which reflects a unique distribution of population on the local level.

In these ways, our five themes have been applied to the study of population geography. In the remaining chapters, you will see how we can apply them to a variety of other geographical topics.

Suggested Readings

Alice C. Andrews. "The State of Women in the Americas," *Journal of Cultural Geography,* 2 (1981), 27–44.

Jacqueline Beaujeu-Garnier. *Geography of Population,* 2nd ed. S. H. Beaver (trans.). London: Longman, 1978.

William H. Berentsen. "German Infant Mortality, 1960–1980," *Geographical Review,* 77 (1987), 157–170.

Ian Burton and Robert W. Kates. "The Floodplain and the Seashore: A Comparative Analysis of Hazard-Zone Occupance," *Geographical Review,* 54 (1964), 366–385.

Aninda K. Chakravarti. "Diet and Disease: Some Cultural Aspects of Food Use in India," in Allen G. Noble and Ashok K. Dutt (eds.), *India: Cultural Patterns and Processes.* Boulder, Colo.: Westview Press, 1982, pp. 301–323.

A. G. Champion. *Population Deconcentration in Britain, 1971–84.* Newcastle upon Tyne: University of Newcastle, Dept. of Geography, Publication No. 49, 1987.

W. A. V. Clark. *Human Migration.* Newbury Park, Calif.: Sage Publications (Volume 7 in the Scientific Geography Series), 1986.

John I. Clarke (ed.). *Geography and Population: Approaches and Applications.* Oxford: Pergamon Press, 1984.

John I. Clarke. *Population Geography,* 2nd ed. Elmsford, N.Y.: Pergamon Press, 1972.

John I. Clarke. *Population Geography and the Developing Countries.* Elmsford, N.Y.: Pergamon Press, 1971.

A. D. Cliff, Peter Haggett, and J. K. Ord. *Spatial Aspects of Influenza Epidemics.* London: Pion, 1986.

Hugh Clout. "Rural Settlements," *Progress in Human Geography,* 5 (1981), 408–413.

J. P. Cole. *The Development Gap: A Spatial Analysis of World Poverty and Inequality.* Chichester, England: Wiley, 1981.

P. A. Compton. "Religious Affiliation and Demographic Variability in Northern Ireland," *Transactions, Institute of British Geographers,* N.S. 1 (1976), 433–452.

Stuart Corbridge. "The Economic Value of Children: A Case Study from Rural India," *Applied Geography: An International Journal,* 5 (1985), 273–295.

Bruce Currey and Graeme Hugo (eds.). *Famine as a Geographical Phenomenon.* Dordrecht, Netherlands: D. Reidel, 1984.

William A. Dando. *The Geography of Famine.* New York: Wiley, 1980.

George J. Demko, Harold M. Rose, and George A. Schnell (eds.). *Population Geography: A Reader.* New York: McGraw-Hill, 1970.

J. Dupâquier and A. Fauve-Chamoux (eds.). *Malthus Past and Present.* New York: Academic Press, 1983.

Ashok K. Dutt, Charles B. Monroe, Hiran M. Dutta, and Barbara Prince. "Geographical Patterns of AIDS in the United States," *Geographical Review,* 77 (1987), 456–471.

John Eyles and Kevin J. Woods. *The Social Geography of Medicine and Health.* New York: St. Martin's Press, 1983.

Ronald Freedman and Bernard Berelson. "The Human Population," *Scientific American,* 231, No. 3 (September 1974), 30–39.

Alice Garnett. "Insolation, Topography, and Settlement in the Alps," *Geographical Review,* 25 (1935), 601–617.

Daniel E. Georges-Abeyie. *Crime, a Spatial Perspective.* New York: Columbia University Press, 1980.

David Grigg. "Counting the Hungry: World Patterns of Undernutrition," *Tijdschrift voor Economische en Sociale Geografie,* 73 (1982), 66–79.

Brian Heenan. "Population Studies," *Progress in Human Geography,* 11 (1987), 275–285; 12 (1988), 282–292.

David Herbert. *The Geography of Urban Crime.* New York: Longman, 1982.

David J. M. Hooson. "The Distribution of Population as the Essential Geographical Expression," *Canadian Geographer*, 4:17 (November 1960), 10–20.

William F. Hornby. *An Introduction to Population Geography.* New York: Cambridge University Press, 1980.

G. Melvyn Howe (ed.). *Global Geocancerology: A World Geography of Human Cancers.* Edinburgh: Churchill Livingstone, 1986.

G. Melvyn Howe (ed.). *A World Geography of Human Diseases.* London, New York, and San Francisco: Academic Press, 1977.

Mei-Ling Hsu. "Growth and Control of Population in China: The Urban-Rural Contrast," *Annals of the Association of American Geographers*, 75 (1985), 241–257.

Graeme Hugo. *Third World Populations.* New York: Basil Blackwell, 1989.

R. J. Johnston. "Population Distributions and the Essentials of Human Geography," *South African Geographical Journal*, 58 (1976), 93–106.

R. J. Johnston. "Resistance to Migration and the Mover/Stayer Dichotomy: Aspects of Kinship and Population Stability in an English Rural Area," *Geografiska Annaler*, 54B (1971), 16–27.

Huw R. Jones. *A Population Geography.* New York: Harper & Row, 1981.

Kelvyn Jones and Graham Moon. *Medical Geography: An Introduction.* London: Routledge & Kegan Paul, 1987.

Leszek A. Kosiński. *The Population of Europe: A Geographical Perspective.* Harlow, England: Longman, 1970.

Leszek A. Kosiński and R. Mansell Prothero (eds.). *People on the Move: Studies on Internal Migration.* London: Methuen & Co., 1975.

Andrew Learmonth. *Disease Ecology.* New York: Basil Blackwell, 1988.

Melinda Meade, John Florin, and Wilbert Gesler. *Medical Geography.* New York: Guilford, 1988.

P. E. Ogden. *Migration and Geographical Change.* New York: Cambridge University Press, 1984.

Gary L. Peters and Robert P. Larkin. *Population Geography: Problems, Concepts, and Prospects.* Dubuque, Iowa: Kendall-Hunt, 1979.

Gerald F. Pyle. *The Diffusion of Influenza: Patterns and Paradigms.* Totowa, N.J.: Rowman and Littlefield, 1986.

Andrei Rogers. *Regional Population Projection Models.* Newbury Park, Calif.: Sage Publications (Volume 4 in the Scientific Geography Series), 1985.

Joni Seager and Ann Olson. *Women in the World: An International Atlas.* New York: Simon & Schuster, 1986.

Barbara G. Shortridge. *Atlas of American Women.* New York: Macmillan, 1987.

Mohamed I. Siddiqi. "Population Growth and Food Supply Margin in Pakistan," *GeoJournal*, 10 (1985), 83–90.

Paul B. Slater. *Migration Regions of the United States: Two County-Level 1965–70 Analyses.* Santa Barbara: Community and Organization Research Institute, University of California at Santa Barbara, 1983.

L. Dudley Stamp. *The Geography of Life and Death.* Ithaca, N.Y.: Cornell University Press, 1964.

Kirk H. Stone. "Geographical Aspects of the Limits to Growth Concepts," *Professional Geographer*, 28 (1976), 336–340.

Larry M. Svart. "Environmental Preference Migration: A Review," *Geographical Review*, 66 (1976), 314–330.

Robert J. Tata and Ronald R. Schultz. "World Variation in Human Welfare: A New Index of Development Status," *Annals of the Association of American Geographers*, 78 (1988), 580–593.

Harry Thorpe. "The Green Village as a Distinctive Form of Settlement on the North European Plain," *Bulletin de la Société Belge d'Études Géographiques*, 30 (1961), 93–134.

My T. Vu. *World Population Projections 1985: Short- and Long-Term Estimates by Age and Sex with Related Demographic Statistics.* Baltimore, Md.: Johns Hopkins University Press, 1986.

Anthony M. Warnes (ed.). *Geographical Perspectives on the Elderly.* New York: Wiley, 1982.

Michael J. Watts. "Conjunctures and Crisis: Food, Ecology and Population, and the Internationalization of Capital," *Journal of Geography,* 86 (1987), 292–299.

Paul E. White and Robert Woods (eds.). *Geographical Impact of Migration.* London, New York: Longman, 1980.

William B. Wood. "AIDS North and South: Diffusion Patterns of a Global Epidemic and a Research Agenda for Geographers," *Professional Geographer,* 40 (1988), 266–279.

Robert Woods. *Population Analysis in Geography.* New York: Longman, 1979.

Robert Woods. "Population Studies," *Progress in Human Geography,* 7 (1983), 261–266; 9 (1985), 278–286; 10 (1986), 258–266.

Robert Woods and Philip Rees (eds.). *Population Structures and Models: Developments in Spatial Demography.* London: Allen & Unwin, 1986.

Wilbur Zelinsky, Leszek A. Kosinski, and R. Mansell Prothero (eds.). *Geography and a Crowding World.* New York: Oxford University Press, 1970.

Chapter 3

The Agricultural World

AGRICULTURAL REGIONS

Shifting Cultivation
Paddy Rice Farming
Peasant Grain and Livestock Farming
Mediterranean Agriculture
Nomadic Herding
Plantation Agriculture
Market Gardening
Commercial Livestock Fattening
Commercial Grain Farming
Commercial Dairying
Livestock Ranching
Nonagricultural Areas

AGRICULTURAL DIFFUSION

**The Origin and Diffusion of Plant
  Domestication**
**The Origin and Diffusion of Animal
  Domestication**
Modern Innovation in Agriculture

AGRICULTURAL ECOLOGY

Environmental Influence
**Agriculturalists as Modifiers of the
  Environment**
**The Agricultural Element in Environ-
  mental Perception**

CULTURAL INTEGRATION IN
AGRICULTURE

Selected Cultural Influences
The von Thünen Model

AGRICULTURAL LANDSCAPES

**Traditional Survey, Cadastral, and
  Field Patterns**
Land Reform and Consolidation
Fencing and Hedging

CONCLUSION

The huge population of the world seeks its livelihood in various ways, and it seems appropriate, following upon the discussion of farm villages at the end of Chapter 2, to look next at agricultural activity. **Agriculture,** the tilling of crops and rearing of animals to produce food, drink, fibers, and other necessities of life, has been the principal enterprise of humankind through most of recorded history and even today remains by far the most important economic activity in the world, occupying most of the land area and employing 45 percent of the working population. In some parts of Asia and Africa, over 80 percent of the labor force is devoted to agriculture. It is we North Americans who are unusual, living in an urban society in which less than 3 percent are agriculturists. We easily forget that our entire urban, industrial society rests, none too securely, upon the base of the food

FIGURE 3.1
Agricultural landscapes now dominate most rural areas, though not generally as spectacularly as this aqueduct near Tepotzotlán in central Mexico. Similar structures in Iberia mark this as a Spanish influence in the Mexican rural landscape. (Photo by Terry G. Jordan, 1986.)

surplus generated by farmers, and that without agriculture there would be no cities or universities.

Over thousands of years, agricultural pursuits have become highly diverse regionally, and cultivators and herders have altered the environment on a massive scale. The cultural landscape over much of the Earth's surface became largely agricultural (Figure 3.1). The geographical themes of culture region, diffusion, ecology, integration, and landscape are thus highly relevant to the study of agriculture.

■ AGRICULTURAL REGIONS

The practice of raising plants and animals has spread to most parts of the world. Cultures living in differing environments adopted and developed new farming methods, creating numerous spatial variations in agriculture. Agricultural geographers attempt to capture these regional contrasts by using the culture region concept, in particular, formal **agricultural regions.** Figure 3.2, which shows one particular classification of agricultural regions, should be referred to as we discuss each type. It is useful to divide the various types into two categories: subsistence and commercial. In **subsistence agriculture,** the major purpose is to provide food for the family and local community, whereas commercial agriculture produces for distant markets. The first five types discussed fall in the subsistence category, while the last six are commercial.

Shifting Cultivation

The native peoples of remote tropical lowlands and hills in the Americas, Africa, Southeast Asia, and Indonesia practice an agricultural system known as **shifting cultivation.** Essentially, this is a land rotation system. Farmers, using machetes or other bladed instruments, chop away the undergrowth from small patches of land and kill the trees by cutting off a strip of bark completely around the trunk. After the dead vegetation has dried out, the farmers set it on fire to clear the land (see Figure 3.3). These clearing techniques have given shifting cultivation the name of "slash-

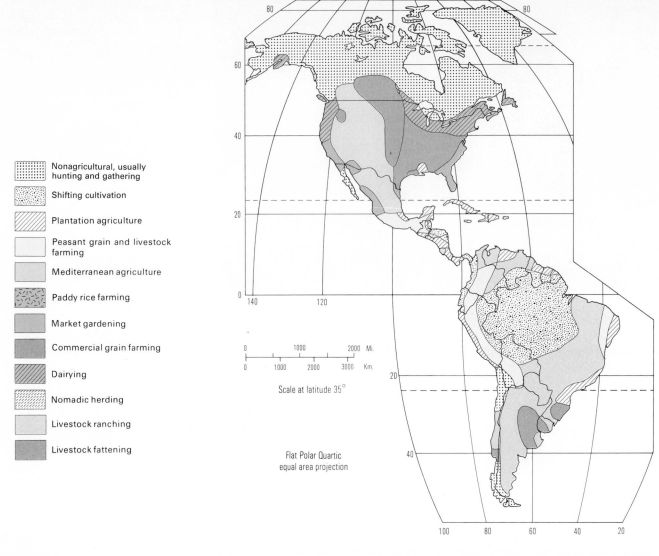

Nonagricultural, usually hunting and gathering

Shifting cultivation

Plantation agriculture

Peasant grain and livestock farming

Mediterranean agriculture

Paddy rice farming

Market gardening

Commercial grain farming

Dairying

Nomadic herding

Livestock ranching

Livestock fattening

Scale at latitude 35°

Flat Polar Quartic
equal area projection

FIGURE 3.2
Major agricultural regions of the world. (Based on Whittlesey, with modifications.)

and-burn'' agriculture. Working with digging sticks or hoes, the farmers then plant a variety of crops in the clearings, varying from the corn, beans, bananas, and manioc of American Indians to the yams and nonirrigated rice grown by hill tribes in Southeast Asia. Different crops are typically planted together in the same clearing, a practice called **intertillage.** This allows taller, stronger crops to shelter lower, more fragile ones from the tropical downpours and reveals the rich lore and learning acquired by shifting cultivators over many centuries. Relatively little tending of the plants is necessary until harvest time, and no fertilizer is applied to the fields. Farmers repeat the planting and harvesting cycle in the same clearings for perhaps four or five years, until the soil has lost much of its fertility. Then these areas are abandoned, and the farmers prepare new clearings to replace them. The abandoned fields lie unused for 10 to 20 years before farmers clear and cultivate them again. Shifting cultivation is one form of subsistence agriculture.

Farm animals play a very small role in shifting cultivation. Farmers keep few if any livestock, often relying on hunting and fishing for much of their food supply. The technology of shifting cultivation may seem crude and poorly developed, but it has proved an efficient adaptive strategy for

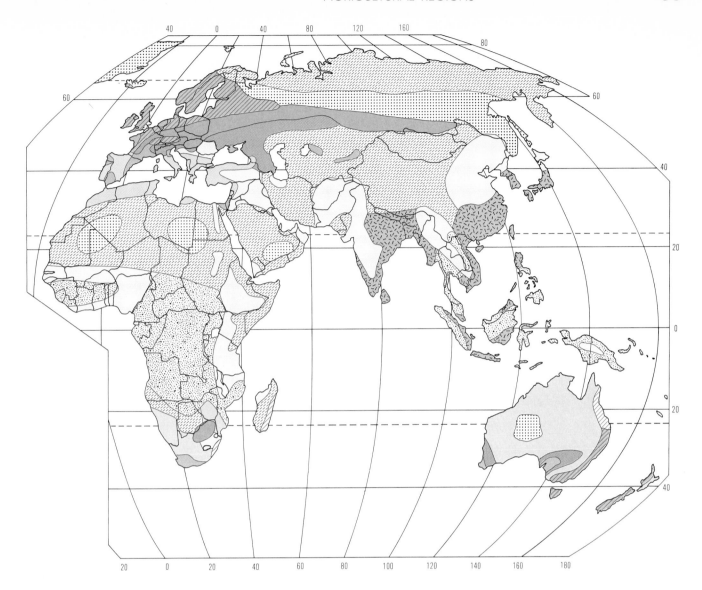

the people who practice this system. Slash-and-burn farming may well return more calories of food for the calories spent on cultivation than does modern mechanized agriculture. We should never assume that modern Western agricultural methods are superior to those of traditional non-Western farming systems. The methods of shifting cultivators and other Third World farmers merit serious consideration, for they, unlike our modern systems, have endured for millennia.

Paddy Rice Farming

Peasant farmers in the humid tropical and subtropical parts of Asia developed a highly distinctive and intensive type of agriculture called paddy rice farming. From the monsoon coasts of India through the hills of southeastern China and on to the warmer parts of Japan stretches a broad region of tiny, mud-diked, flooded rice fields, or **paddies,** many of which are perched on terraced hillsides. These fields form a strikingly uniform cultural landscape that is the hallmark of this type of agriculture.

Irrigated rice accounts for over half of the cultivated acreage in the paddies. Often farmers also cultivate a second, normally unirrigated crop

FIGURE 3.3
An Indian in the Amazon Basin of Brazil is preparing a field for new cultivation by cutting and burning the forest cover. Although slash-and-burn agriculture appears to be disorganized and primitive, it is actually a carefully planned system of crop combinations and field rotation.

for cash, such as tea, sugar cane, mulberry bushes for silkworm production, or the fiber crop jute. Asian farmers also raise pigs, cattle, and poultry and maintain fish in the irrigation reservoirs. Pork is a favorite food among the Chinese. As we will see in Chapter 6, religious dietary taboos prevent Asian Indians from eating most livestock products, but they use draft animals such as the water buffalo to a greater extent than do other paddy farmers. Only the Japanese have mechanized paddy rice farming to any major degree.

Most paddy rice farms outside the Communist areas of Asia are tiny. A 3-acre (about 1 hectare) landholding is considered adequate to support a farm family. Asian farmers can survive on such a small scale of operation partly because irrigated rice provides a very large output of food per unit of land. Still, the paddy farmers must till their small patches most intensively in order to harvest enough food. This means they must carefully transplant by hand the small rice sprouts from seed beds to the paddy (see Figure 3.4). They must also plant and harvest the same parcel of land two or three times each year—a practice known as **double-cropping**—while applying large amounts of organic fertilizer to the land. So intensive and productive is this system that per-acre yields exceed those of American agriculture and the name *garden cultivation* is sometimes applied to paddy farming.

Traditionally, the high intensity of land use in paddy rice farming was achieved through the massive application of human labor. Those from Western cultures can scarcely imagine the magnitude of tedious hand labor involved. More recently, through the so-called **green revolution,** intensity was further heightened through the introduction of improved, higher-yielding varieties of **hybrid** rice, which in turn required various chemical fertilizers and pesticides. That is, additional intensity was achieved through capital, as opposed to labor investment. The green revolution, though not without its own serious problems, has allowed nations such as India to approach self-sufficiency in food production, in spite of their huge populations.

FIGURE 3.4
Laborers plant wet rice shoots by hand in an irrigated paddy in the Orient. In Japan, machines have been introduced to take over the labor in rice farming; but in most Asian paddies, rice still requires hours of stoop labor.

Peasant Grain and Livestock Farming

In colder, drier Asiatic farming regions, climatically unsuited to paddy rice farming, as well as in the river valleys of the Middle East, parts of Europe, Africa, and Latin America, farmers practice a system of semisubsistence plow agriculture based on bread grains and herd livestock (see Figure 3.5). The dominant grain crops in these regions are, variously, wheat, barley, millet, oats, and corn. Other subsistence crops include grain sorghums, soybeans, and potatoes. Many farmers in these areas also raise a cash crop, such as cotton, flax, hemp, or tobacco.

Along with tilling crops, these farmers also raise herds of cattle, pigs, sheep, and, in South America, llamas and alpacas. The livestock pull the plow; provide milk, meat, and wool; serve as beasts of burden; and produce manure for the fields. They also consume a portion of the grain harvest. In some areas, such as the Middle Eastern river valleys, the use of irrigation helps support this peasant-grain-livestock system. Although these peasant farmers work their land intensively, they are generally not as productive as the paddy rice growers.

Mediterranean Agriculture

In the lands bordering the Mediterranean Sea, a truly distinctive type of peasant subsistence agriculture took shape in ancient times, and much of this system survives intact today. Traditional Mediterranean agriculture is based on wheat and barley cultivation in the rainy winter season; raising drought-resistant vine and tree crops like the grape, olive, and fig; and small-scale livestock herding, particularly of sheep, goats, and pigs (Figure 3.6). In recent times, farmers have begun using irrigation in a major way, which has led to the expansion of crops such as the citrus fruits.

Mediterranean farmers do not integrate stock raising with crop cultivation. They rarely raise feed, collect animal manure, or keep draft ani-

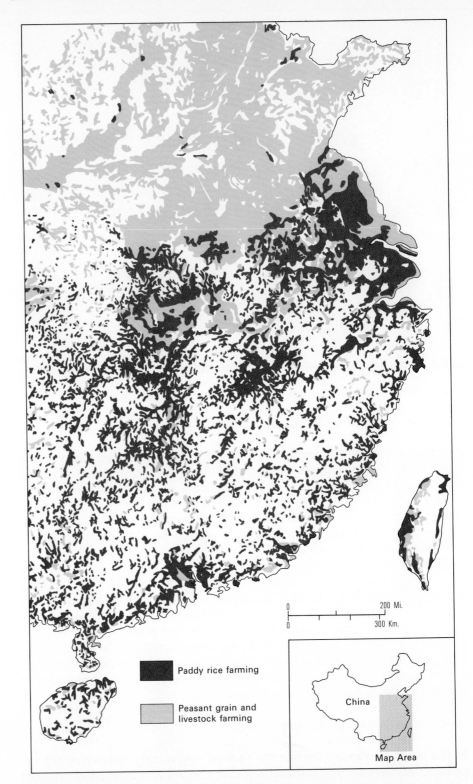

FIGURE 3.5
The intricacies of culture regional boundaries are suggested by the distribution of two types of agriculture in Taiwan and the eastern part of the People's Republic of China. What might account for the more fragmented distribution of paddy rice farming, as contrasted to peasant grain and livestock farming? (Source: "China Land Utilization," a map in Chinese edited by Wu Chuan-jun and published in 1979 by the Institute of Geography, Academica Sinica, Beijing.)

FIGURE 3.6
Mediterranean agriculture combines grain cultivation with vine and tree crops, in addition to herding. Often the grain is raised in the orchards, as in this scene of intertillage from the island of Crete, where newly harvested wheat lies in sheaves amid the olive trees. The mountains in the distance provide range for the farmers' sheep and goats. (Photo by Terry G. Jordan, 1971.)

mals. Instead, they pasture their livestock in communal herds on rocky mountain slopes, while they cover the valleys and gentler slopes below with vineyards, orchards, and grain fields. Because the Mediterranean farmers do not fertilize their land with collected manure, the grain fields must lie fallow every other year to regain their fertility.

All three of these basic enterprises—wheat and barley cultivation, vine and tree cultivation, and livestock herding—are generally combined on each small farm. From this diverse, unspecialized trinity, the Mediterranean farmer can reap nearly all of life's necessities, including wool and leather for clothing, and bread, beverages, fruit, milk, cheese, and meat. Since about 1850, however, many Mediterranean agricultural areas have changed as commercialization and specialization of farming have replaced the traditional diversified system. In such areas, the present-day agriculture is better described as market gardening.

Nomadic Herding

In the dry or cold lands of the Eastern Hemisphere, particularly in the deserts, steppes, and savannas of Africa, Arabia, and the interior of Eurasia, nomadic livestock herders graze cattle, sheep, goats, and camels (see box, "The Wandering Life of the Tartars"). The bitterly cold tundra north of the tree line in the Soviet Union is another zone of nomadic herders. The main characteristic of nomadic herding is the continued movement of people with their livestock in search of forage for the animals. Some nomadic herders migrate from lowlands in winter to mountains in summer, while others shift from desert areas in winter to adjacent semiarid plains in summer, or from tundra in summer to nearby forests in winter. Many nomads place a high value on the horse, which has traditionally been kept for use in warfare, or the camel. Nomads in sub-Saharan Africa are the only ones who depend mainly on cattle, while those in the tundras of northern Eurasia are distinctive because they raise domestic reindeer (Figure 3.7).

Necessity dictates that the few material possessions the nomads have be portable, including the tents they use for housing. Normally, the

"THE WANDERING LIFE OF THE TARTARS"

"The Tartars never remain fixed, but as the winter approaches remove to the plains of a warmer region, in order to find sufficient pasture for their cattle; and in summer they frequent cold situations in the mountains, where there is water and verdure, and their cattle are free from the annoyance of horseflies and other biting insects. During two or three months they progressively ascend higher ground, and seek fresh pasture, the grass not being adequate in any one place to feed the multitudes of which their herds and flocks consist. Their huts or tents, formed of rods covered with felt, exactly round, and nicely put together, can be gathered into one bundle, and made up as packages. . . . They eat flesh of every description, horses, camels, and even dogs, provided they are fat. They drink mare's milk, which they prepare in such a manner that it has the qualities and flavor of white wine."

From *The Adventures of Marco Polo, as Dictated in Prison to a Scribe in the Year 1298; What he experienced and heard during his twenty-four years spent in travel through Asia and at the Court of Kublai-Khan.*

nomads obtain nearly all of life's necessities from livestock products, or by bartering with the sedentary farmers of adjacent river valleys and oases. Traditionally, powerful male chieftains led tribes of nomads in frequent mounted raids against farming peoples, especially in times of drought. Until almost the modern age, nomads presented a periodic military threat to even the greatest sedentary civilizations. With their swift horse-mounted warriors, central Asian nomads established one empire after another. In the thirteenth century, the Mongols, led by Genghis Khan, conquered much of Eurasia. Their gigantic imperial domain extended from the Korean peninsula to the edges of eastern Europe, and from present-day Siberia to the Indian plains.

Today, nomadic herding is almost everywhere in decline. A number of national governments have established policies encouraging nomads to become sedentary. A practice begun in the nineteenth century by British and French colonial administrators in North Africa, the settling of nomadic tribes allows greater control by the central governments. The Soviet Union has adopted such a policy and pursued it with considerable success. Moreover, many nomads are voluntarily abandoning their traditional life

FIGURE 3.7
Kenya is a country of nomadic herding. The Masai people maintain large herds of cattle in part as a symbol of wealth and power.

in order to seek jobs in urban areas or in the Middle Eastern oil fields. Further impetus to abandon nomadic life has recently come from the severe drought in sub-Saharan Africa, which has decimated nomadic livestock herds. Nomadism survives mainly in remote areas today, and this traditional way of life may soon vanish altogether.

Plantation Agriculture

In certain tropical areas, Europeans and Americans desiring to supply themselves with tropical crops imposed a commercial agricultural system on the native types of subsistence agriculture. This system is called **plantation** agriculture. A plantation is a huge landholding devoted to the efficient, large-scale, specialized production of one tropical or subtropical crop for market. Such a system relies on large amounts of hand labor. Most workers live right on the plantation, where a rigid social and economic segregation of labor and management produces a two-class society of the wealthy and the poor. Traditionally, as in the antebellum southern United States, many plantation owners relied on slaves to provide the needed labor. Today, because of the capital investment necessary, corporations or governments are usually the owners of plantations.

Most plantations are located on or near the seacoast, in order to be close to the shipping lanes that carry their produce to nontropical lands such as Europe, the United States, and Japan. Scholars believe that the plantation system originated in the 1400s on Portuguese-owned islands off the coast of tropical west Africa. The greatest concentration of plantations is now in the American tropics.

The plantation provided the base for European and American economic expansion into Asia, Africa, and Latin America. As such, it played havoc with the traditional agricultural economies of those areas by promoting the production of nonessential crops for the luxury diet of Europeans and Americans: sugar cane, bananas, coffee, coconuts, spices, tea, cacao, and tobacco. Similarly, Western textile factories required cotton, sisal, jute, hemp, and other fiber crops from the plantation areas. Profits from these plantations were usually exported along with the crops themselves to Europe and North America, impoverishing the colonial lands where plantations were located.

Owners in each plantation district in the tropical zone tend to specialize in one particular crop. Coffee and tea, for instance, grow in the tropical highlands, with coffee dominating the upland plantations of tropical America and tea confined mainly to the hill slopes of India and Sri Lanka. Today, coffee is the economic lifeblood of about 40 underdeveloped countries, while sugar cane and bananas are the major lowland plantation crops of tropical America. In most cases, plantation workers at least partially process the crop before sending it to the distant market. For example, sugar is generally milled and cotton ginned on the plantation. This combination of raising and partially processing the crop is a major distinguishing trait of the plantation system.

One of the greatest negative impacts of the plantation system is its emphasis on exported crops, at the expense of subsistence agricultural systems that feed local populations. As the national debts of underdeveloped countries rise, enormous pressure is brought to bear by the World Bank and other lending institutions to increase export-oriented plantation agriculture. The best land is thereby removed from local food production. Since many plantations are now mechanized—a type referred to as the *neo-plantation*—less labor is required, causing underemployment and displacement of the local people, who then leave the land and flock to urban centers, contributing to the massive growth of Third-World cities.

Market Gardening

The growth of urban markets in the last few centuries has also given rise to other commercial forms of agriculture, including **market gardening,** also known as truck farming. Unlike plantations, these farms are located in developed countries and specialize in intensively cultivated fruits, vegetables, and vines. They do not raise livestock. Typically, each farm and district concentrates on a single product such as wine grapes, table grapes, raisins, oranges, apples, lettuce, or potatoes, and the entire farm output is raised for sale rather than for consumption on the farm. Many truck farmers participate in cooperative marketing arrangements and depend on migratory seasonal farm laborers to harvest their crops.

Market garden districts are common in most industrialized countries and often lie near major urban centers. In the United States, a broken belt of market gardens extends from California eastward through the Gulf and Atlantic coast states, with scattered districts in other parts of the country. These farms produce everything from wine and raisins to citrus, apples, tomatoes, and spinach.

Commercial Livestock Fattening

In commercial livestock fattening, farmers raise and fatten cattle and hogs for slaughter. One of the most highly developed fattening areas is the famous Corn Belt of the midwestern United States, where farmers raise immense amounts of corn and soybeans to feed cattle and hogs. A similar system prevails over much of western and central Europe, though the feed crops there are more commonly oats and potatoes. Smaller zones of commercial livestock fattening are found in overseas European settlement zones such as southern Brazil and South Africa.

One of the main characteristics of commercial livestock fattening has traditionally been the combination of crop and animal raising on the same farm. This has led some geographers to refer to this type of agriculture as mixed crop and livestock farming. Farmers typically bred many of the animals they fattened, especially the hogs. In recent years, commercial livestock farmers have begun to specialize their activities, some concentrating on breeding animals, others on fattening them for market. The most recent development has been the factorylike **feedlot,** where farmers raise imported cattle and hogs on purchased feed (see Figure 3.8). Such feedlots are most common in the western and southern United States, in part because winters are less severe there.

Although commercial livestock fattening is often organized with assembly-line precision and has proved extremely profitable, the specter of famine in recent years has brought its nutritional efficiency into question. Actual world grain production has risen significantly faster than world population growth, and cereals provide 85 percent of the protein intake of most of the world's people. Yet in the last 50 years, meat eating has soared in the Western world, particularly in the United States, wiping out most of these gains. At least one-half of America's harvested agricultural land is planted with feed crops for livestock, and over 70 percent of the grain raised in the United States is used for livestock fattening. However, livestock are not an efficient method of protein production. A cow, for instance, must eat 21 pounds (9.5 kilograms) of protein to produce 1 pound

[Handwritten marginal notes:]

What is Market Gardening? cult. fruit, veg, vines / truck farming. Where? Industrialized countries

What is Comm. Livestock Fatt. "Raise cattle for slaughter.
1. What is Corn Belt in US.
2. Where? Corn Belt does it produce.
3. What problems does it produce.
— As Amer. fastfoods increase, Beef is raised, which takes over land formerly used for raising crops — grains. Grains being a much better source of protein. 70% of grain in US raised for cattle.

FIGURE 3.8
Six thousand cattle can be fed at this feedlot in Omaha, Nebraska. The operation is run by a company that specializes in fattening cattle for market.

(0.5 kilogram) of edible protein. Plants are far more efficient protein converters. It has been estimated that the protein lost through conversion from plant to meat could make up almost all of the world's present protein deficiencies. The food that today feeds 230 million Americans would feed 1.5 billion at the consumption level of China. This basic inefficiency is now being imposed upon some poorer nations, such as Costa Rica and Brazil, where rain forest is being destroyed and shifting cultivators displaced to make way for cattle pasture to fatten beef for America's fast-food restaurants.

Commercial Grain Farming

Commercial grain farming is another market-oriented type of agriculture in which farmers specialize in growing wheat or, less frequently, rice or corn. Great wheat belts stretch through Australia, the plains of interior North America, the steppes of Russia, and the pampas of Argentina. Together, the United States, Canada, and the Soviet Union produce 45 percent of the world's wheat. Farms in these areas are generally very large. They range from family-run wheat farms of 1000 acres (400 hectares) or more in the American Great Plains to giant state farms in the Soviet Union, some of which exceed 100,000 acres (40,000 hectares) (see Figure 3.9). Extensive rice farms, maintained under the same commercial system, cover large areas of the Texas-Louisiana coastal plain and lowlands in Arkansas and California.

Widespread use of machinery enables commercial grain farmers to operate on this large scale. Indeed, planting and harvesting grain is more completely mechanized than any other form of agriculture. Commercial rice farmers employ such techniques as sowing grain from airplanes. Perhaps the ultimate development is the **suitcase farm,** a post-World War II innovation in the wheat belt of the northern Great Plains of the United States. The people who own and operate these farms do not live on the land. Most of them own several suitcase farms, lined up in a south-to-

FIGURE 3.9
Mechanized grain farming looks much the same throughout the world. This is a view of harvest time on a state farm in the Soviet Union. There the use of machinery can be centrally planned. In North America, teams of workers and equipment move south and contract with individual farmers to harvest the crop.

north row through the plains states. They keep fleets of farm machinery, which they send north with crews of laborers along the string of suitcase farms to plant, fertilize, and harvest the wheat. The progressively later ripening of the grain toward the north allows these farmers to maintain crops on all their farms with the same crew and the same machinery. Except for these visits by migratory crews, the suitcase farms are uninhabited.

Such a highly mechanized, large-scale, commercialized operation is often called an **agribusiness** (see box, "Agribusiness and the Family Farm"). With agribusiness, farming has entered the industrial age. Land, organized in larger and larger units, is monopolized by fewer and fewer owners. Typically, these owners are no longer farm families or even farmers, but corporations located at some place distant from the land. In this way, the traditional human-land linkage has been severed, and a distant corporate relationship set up in its place.

The heavy reliance on large machines and pesticides implicit in commercial grain farming may be inflicting serious damage on the rich soils of these areas, through soil compaction and poisoning. Moreover, the system is heavily dependent on fossil fuels and contributes to the decline of the American small town through depopulation.

Commercial Dairying

In many ways, the specialized production of dairy goods closely resembles commercial livestock fattening (see box, "Thomas Hardy on the Geography of Dairying"). In the large diary belts of the northeastern United States, western and northern Europe, southeastern Australia, and northern New Zealand, the keeping of dairy cows depends on the large-scale use of pastures. In colder areas, some acreage must be devoted to winter feed crops, especially hay. Dairy products vary from region to region, depending in part on how close the farmers are to their markets. Dairy

AGRIBUSINESS AND THE FAMILY FARM

Agribusiness, though most closely linked to commercial grain farming, is rapidly spreading, at the expense of family farms, into other types of agriculture. Ingolf Vogeler, a geographer at the University of Wisconsin-Eau Claire, in a recent book, argues that this spread is neither necessary nor desirable. Some excerpts:

The family farm is an important part of American folklore extending back to the eighteenth century. Nominally, farm families own the land they work, . . . manage their farms, . . . provide the working capital, and take the risks of harvests and markets. In contrast, large-scale, capital-intensive farms — often owned by absentee landlords and operated by managers and farm workers — have traditionally been considered undesirable in American culture. Consequently, writers and politicians have exalted the virtues of the family farm. . . .

Family farming is a myth . . . [that] . . . obscures the dominance of agribusiness and the root causes of rural problems. [For example:]

1.   The concentration of land into large-scale and industrial farms has been facilitated by government policies that were purported to support family farmers.

2.   Large-scale farms are more profitable than family farms, even though they are no more efficient.

3.   Family farmers are heavily in debt for real estate and other productive resources.

4.   Family farmers must rely on off-farm employment to survive.

5.   Contract farming has eroded the independence of family farmers, who are now effectively employees of agribusiness.

6.   Federal tax laws result in higher land prices, over-production of certain crops, expansion of larger-than-efficient farm sizes, absentee ownership, and the demise of family farms.

7.   Federal farm programs disproportionately benefit large-scale farmers. . . .

From Ingolf Vogeler, pp. 4–5, 9, 229.

belts near large urban centers usually produce fluid milk, which is more perishable, while those further away specialize in butter, cheese, or processed milk. New Zealanders, remote from world markets, produce mainly butter.

As with livestock fattening, in recent decades a rapidly increasing number of dairy farmers have adopted the feedlot system and now raise their cattle on feed purchased from other sources. Feedlots are especially common in the southern United States. Often situated on the suburban fringes of large cities in order to have quick access to market, the dairy feedlots are essentially factory farms. Farmers buy feed and livestock replacements, instead of breeding and raising them on the farm. In these large-scale automated operations, the number of cows is far greater than on family-operated dairy farms. Like industrial factory owners, feedlot dairy owners rely on hired laborers to help maintain their herds. While less pleasing to the eye and nose than traditional dairy farms, the feedlots are highly profitable establishments, representing still another stage in the rise of agribusiness and the decline of the American family farm. Rural North America has departed radically from a traditional image of farm life, thus becoming much more factory-like

Livestock Ranching

Ranching, superficially, might seem similar to nomadic herding, but in reality it is a fundamentally different livestock raising system. Although both the nomadic herders and the livestock ranchers specialize in animal husbandry to the exclusion of crop raising, and even though both live in arid or semiarid regions, livestock ranchers have fixed places of residence and operate as individuals rather than within a tribal organization. In addition, ranchers raise livestock for market, not for their own subsistence, and they are typically of European ancestry rather than being an indigenous people.

THOMAS HARDY ON THE GEOGRAPHY OF DAIRYING

Farming culture regions are readily observable, and you need not be a professional geographer to observe them. Some of the finest "geography" has been written by novelists. Among these writers, none surpasses Thomas Hardy, who penned beautiful descriptions of the countryside of southern England. Here is his word picture of a late nineteenth-century commercial dairy region, the Vale of Frome:

> She found herself on a summit commanding the . . . Valley of the Great Dairies, the valley in which milk and butter grew to rankness. . . . It was intrinsically different from the Vale of Little Dairies, Blackmoor Vale, which . . . she had exclusively known till now. The world was drawn to a larger pattern here. The enclosures numbered fifty acres instead of ten, the farmsteads were more extended, the groups of cattle formed tribes hereabout; there only families. These myriads of cows stretching under her eyes from the far east to the far west outnumbered any she had ever seen at one glance before. The green lea was speckled as thickly with them as a canvas by Van Alsloot or Sallaert with burghers. . . .
>
> Suddenly there arose from all parts of the lowland a prolonged and repeated call—Waow waow waow. It

was . . . the ordinary announcement of milking-time— half-past four o-clock, when the dairymen set about getting in the cows. The red and white herd nearest at hand, which had been phlegmatically waiting for the call, now trooped towards the steading in the background, their great bags of milk swinging under them as they walked. . . .

> Long thatched sheds stretched round the enclosure, . . . their eaves supported by wooden posts rubbed to a glossy smoothness by the flanks of infinite cows and calves of bygone years. . . . Between the posts were ranged the milchers. . . . The dairymaids and men had flocked down from their cottages and out of the dairyhouse with the arrival of the cows from the meads. . . . Each girl sat down on her three-legged stool, her face sideways, her right cheek resting against the cow. . . .

From Thomas Hardy, *Tess of the d'Urbervilles* (New York: Harper & Brothers, 1891).

Livestock ranchers, faced with the advance of farmers, have usually fallen back into areas climatically too harsh for crop production. There they raise only two kinds of animals in large numbers: cattle and sheep. Ranchers in the United States and Canada, tropical and subtropical Latin America, and the warmer parts of Australia specialize in cattle raising. Midlatitude ranchers in the Southern Hemisphere specialize in sheep, to the extent that Australia, New Zealand, South Africa, and Argentina produce 73 percent of the world's export wool. In Australia, sheep outnumber people 8 to 1.

Nonagricultural Areas

Some lands do not support any form of agriculture. These are typically areas of extreme climate, in particular deserts and subarctic forests, as in much of Canada and Siberia. Often such areas are inhabited by **hunting and gathering** groups of native peoples, such as the Eskimo and Australian aborigine, who gain a livelihood by hunting game, fishing where possible, and gathering edible and medicinal wild plants. Once, before agriculture began, all humans were hunters and gatherers; it is the ancestral occupation of our species. Today, far fewer than 1 percent of all humans are so employed, preserving the ancient ways. Even fewer depend entirely on such a food-producing system, given the various inroads of the modern world. In most hunting and gathering societies, a division of labor by gender is almost universal. Males perform most of the hunting and fishing, while females carry out the equally important task of gathering harvests from wild plants. Hunters and gatherers can either be specialized, depending upon only a few sources for their food, or, much more commonly, unspecialized and reliant upon a great variety of animals and plants.

AGRICULTURAL DIFFUSION

The various agricultural regions that we have just discussed, reflecting the spatial variations in agriculture, are the result of cultural diffusion. Agriculture and its many components are inventions; they arose as innovations in certain source areas and diffused to other parts of the world.

The Origin and Diffusion of Plant Domestication

The beginnings of agriculture apparently occurred with plant rather than animal domestication. A **domesticated plant** is one deliberately planted, protected, and cared for by humans. In addition, it is genetically distinct from its wild ancestors due to deliberate improvement through selective breeding by the people who raise it. As a result, domesticated plants tend to be bigger than wild species, bearing larger, more abundant fruit or grain. For example, the original wild Indian corn grew on a cob only 0.75 inch (2 centimeters) long — that is, one-tenth to one-twentieth the size of the cobs of domesticated corn.

Plant domestication was a process, not an event. It came as the gradual culmination of hundreds, or even thousands, of years of close association between humans and the natural vegetation that surrounded them. The first step in domestication was the perception that a certain plant had usefulness for people, a usefulness leading initially to protection of the wild plant and eventually to deliberate planting. Cultural geographer Carl L. Johannessen suggests that the domestication process can still be observed today. He believes that by studying current techniques used by native subsistence farmers in places such as Central America, we can gain insight into the methods of the first farmers of prehistoric antiquity. Professor Johannessen points out that two steps are normally required to develop and improve plant varieties: (1) selection of seeds or shoots only from superior plants; and (2) genetic isolation from other, inferior plants to prevent cross-pollination. He believes we can see these processes still under way among American subsistence farmers. Johannessen's study of the present-day cultivation of the pejibaye palm tree in Costa Rica revealed that native cultivators are actively engaged in seed selection. All choose the seed of fresh fruit from superior trees, those which bear particularly desirable fruit, as determined by size, flavor, texture, and color. Such trees are often given personal names, an indication of the value placed on them. Superior seed stocks are built up gradually over the years, with the result that elderly farmers generally have the best selections. Seeds are shared freely within family and clan groups, allowing speedy diffusion of desirable traits.

Dr. Johannessen also reported that some American Indian groups were clearly aware of the need for genetic isolation to reduce contamination from cross-pollination in corn plants. In Panama, for example, one Indian tribe of shifting cultivators raised 14 varieties of corn, each in a field separated from all the others by intervening forest.

When, where, how, and by whom were these processes of plant domestication developed? The answers are not known with certainty, but cultural geographers have been among those who have done research on this problem. Early leaders were the German geographer Eduard Hahn and the famous American cultural geographer Carl O. Sauer (see biographical sketch). Their theories, as well as the contributions of numerous other scholars, are suggested in Figure 3.10.

CARL O. SAUER
1889–1975

Sauer, a native of the Missouri Ozarks and a graduate of the University of Chicago, was widely regarded as the most prominent American cultural geographer. For over half a century, he was associated with the University of California at Berkeley. His works were so diverse as to defy simple classification, but important themes in much of his research were (1) humans as modifiers of the earth, (2) the cultural landscape, and (3) cultural origins and diffusion. As a geographer his work took him on many field trips. He studied by looking at the land, examining archaeological finds, and talking to the residents. In his classic book *Agricultural Origins and Dispersals* he presented some new and stimulating ideas concerning the domestication of plants and animals, some of which are presented in this chapter. His concern for the environment began when he was a student, and throughout his career he argued for "humane" use of the Earth. Professor Sauer twice served the Association of American Geographers as president and in 1974 received an award from that organization for meritorious contributions to the discipline of geography. (For more information on Sauer, see Martin S. Kenzer, ed., *Carl O. Sauer: A Tribute*. Corvallis: Oregon State University Press and the Association of Pacific Coast Geographers, 1987.)

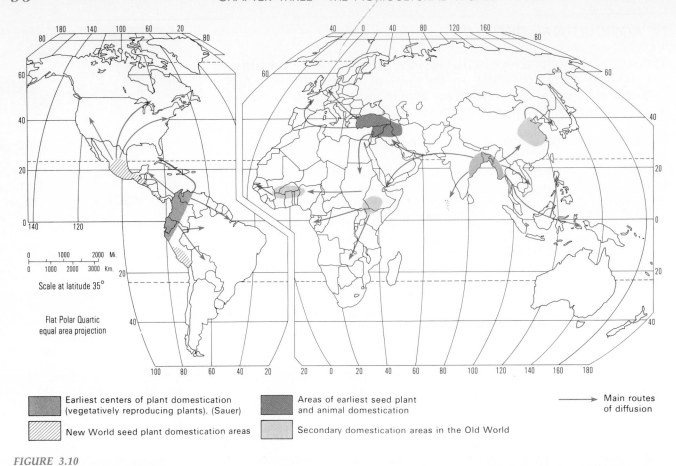

Earliest centers of plant domestication (vegetatively reproducing plants). (Sauer)

New World seed plant domestication areas

Areas of earliest seed plant and animal domestication

Secondary domestication areas in the Old World

Main routes of diffusion

FIGURE 3.10
Centers of early agriculture and routes of diffusion are shown on several continents. Much of the information shown on this map is speculative or controversial because we have no definitive record of when or where farming began. Using archaeological finds, climatic patterns, and biological information, Carl Sauer pieced together this tentative map of early centers of domestication.

Sauer suggested that domestication probably did not develop in response to hunger. He maintained that necessity was not the mother of agricultural invention, because starving people must spend every waking hour searching for food and have no time to devote to the centuries of leisurely experimentation required to domesticate plants. Instead, it was accomplished by a people who had enough food to remain settled in one place and devote considerable time to plant care. Thus, the first farmers were probably sedentary folk, rather than migratory hunters and gatherers.

Sauer reasoned that domestication probably did not initially occur in grasslands or large river floodplains. In such areas, primitive cultures would have had difficulty coping with the thick sod and periodic floodwaters. Sauer also felt that the hearth area of domestication must have been in a region where many different kinds of plants were growing, providing abundant vegetative raw material for experimentation and crossbreeding. Such areas typically appear in hilly districts, where climates change with differing sun exposure and altitude.

Sauer found it useful to distinguish between two different means of reproducing plants. One method, perhaps the more familiar to you, is to plant seeds derived from the fruit of the plant. The other, called vegetative reproduction, involves propagation by breaking off a piece of the fruit and planting it or by transplanting shoots. The white potato and banana are examples of vegetatively reproduced plants. Some domesticated plants can be reproduced either way. Professor Sauer believed that the first plants to be domesticated were those that could be vegetatively reproduced. Such reproduction, particularly the transplanting of shoots, was perhaps easier for primitive folk to understand. Moreover, vegetative reproduction is asexual, eliminating the need for genetic isolation and the danger of cross-pollination.

This initial domestication of plants, Sauer concluded, may have occurred from 14,000 to 35,000 years ago, most likely in the wet-dry monsoon climate of southeastern Asia, among sedentary fishing and gathering people who lived in forests bordering freshwater streams. Recent archaeological discoveries in Thailand and neighboring countries lend some support to his proposal.

Some other scholars have suggested that the constantly wet tropical rain forests were best suited to initial plant domestication because no seasonal adjustments to temperature or rainfall are necessary in these areas. Planting can be done at any time of year. In climates that have pronounced seasonal differences, farmers must plant at a specific time of year. This implies the use of some sort of calendar.

Domestication of plants reproduced by seed, Sauer believed, first occurred in areas of Eurasia peripheral to the older vegetative domestication zone. Virtually all scholars, including Sauer, agree that southwestern Asia was of monumental importance in this respect, in particular the hilly fringe along the northern perimeter of the Tigris-Euphrates plain, part of the so-called Fertile Crescent. They have devoted special attention to sites in northern Iraq. If, as Sauer proposed, the domestication of seed reproductive plants began later and was peripheral to the zone of vegetatively reproducing plants, then the process of stimulus diffusion was apparently at work (see Chapter 1). That is, the idea of domestication was applied to a quite different kind of plant without the seed domesticators even accepting the vegetatively reproduced crops.

Perhaps most notable among the seed domesticates of this region were the small grain crops, wheat and barley. In the moister climatic conditions of 14,000 or more years ago, when scholars estimate that plant domestication began here, this hilly belt seemingly had many of the environmental qualities favored by Sauer. In fact, the entire area from Asia Minor to the borders of India is an agricultural hearth of great antiquity, and domestication of grains such as wheat and barley may have occurred repeatedly throughout this southwestern Asian region.

To the east in China and Indochina, on the northeastern periphery of the old vegetative crop zone, a secondary seed-plant domestication zone developed, with rice as the principal grain domesticate. Indeed, China is now viewed by some experts as a very important secondary center of early domestication. There, too, stimulus diffusion apparently took place.

In the Americas, said Sauer, parallel developments occurred. A vegetative domestication zone lay in northwestern South America, involving such crops as the white potato and manioc. Middle America was the great peripheral seed-plant domestication area, in which the Amerindian staple crop, corn (maize), first entered agriculture. Some regard Peru as a second, less important American seed-plant hearth.

Controversy has long raged over the question of whether plant domestication was independently invented in Eurasia and America or whether the idea spread by cultural diffusion in ancient times from the Old World to the New. The fact that most American domesticates, such as corn, squash, tomatoes, pumpkins, and potatoes, were seemingly unknown in the Eastern Hemisphere even as late as the time of Columbus strongly suggests independent invention, though stimulus diffusion could be responsible. Independent domestication may have occurred even *within* the Old World. In any case, the Amerindians domesticated a com-

CULTURAL DIFFUSION: THE POTATO IN GERMANY

How does a domestic plant spread into new areas and gain wider acceptance? The progress is often slow and not without resistance, as the following eyewitness account from the province of Pomerania, Kingdom of Prussia, shows:

In 1743, through the goodness of King Frederick the Great, the people of Kolberg district received a present completely unknown to us. A large freight wagon full of potatoes arrived at the market square, and, by a beating of drums, the announcement was made that all farmers and gardeners were to assemble before the town hall. The town councillors then showed the new fruit to the assembled crowd. Detailed instructions were read aloud concerning the planting, cultivation, and cooking of the potato. However, few of the people paid attention to the oral instructions, choosing instead to take the highly-praised tubers in their hands, smelling, licking, and tasting them. Shaking their heads, they passed them around, eventually throwing them to the dogs, who also sniffed and rejected them. "These things," they said, "have no smell or taste. What good are they to us?" Hardly anyone understood the instructions for planting. Quite general was the belief that potatoes would grow into trees from which you could gather like fruit in due time. Those who did not throw the potatoes on the rubbish heap, but instead planted them, did so incorrectly.

The town councillors learned that some sceptics had not entrusted their tuberous treasures to the earth. For that reason they instituted a strict potato inspection during the summer months and levied a small monetary fine on those found to be obstinate.

The next year the king renewed his benevolent gift, but this time the authorities sent along a man familiar with raising potatoes, and he helped the people plant and cultivate. In this manner, the new product first came to my district, and ever since has spread rapidly. Now a general famine can never again devastate the province.

Translated and condensed from *Ein Mann: Des Seefahrers und aufrechten Bürgers Joachim Nettelbeck wundersame Lebensgeschichte von ihm selbst erzählt* (Ebenhausen near München: Wilhelm Langewiesche-Brandt, 1910), pp. 8–10.

---

plex of crops superior in overall nutritional value to those developed by all Eastern Hemisphere peoples combined.

The widespread association of female deities with agriculture in the Old World suggests that women were the first people to work the land. We may assume this because of the previously described, almost universal division of labor in hunting-gathering-fishing societies. Since women had day-to-day contact with wild plants and stayed closer to home, it is reasonable to assume that they initiated plant domestication. Only when farming began to supply the community with more food than hunting and fishing did men join women as tillers of crops.

From the original hearths of plant domestication, agriculture spread gradually over much of the Old and New Worlds. Along the routeways of diffusion, secondary domestication centers developed and new crops were added to the agricultural inventory.

The diffusion of domesticated plants did not end in antiquity (see box, "Cultural Diffusion: The Potato in Germany"). Only within the past century did crop farming reach its present territorial extent, completing the diffusion begun many millennia ago. The introduction of the lemon, orange, grape, and the date palm by Spanish mission fathers in eighteenth-century California is a recent example of relocation diffusion. This was part of a larger diffusion—the introduction of European crops that accompanied the mass emigrations of farmers from Europe to the Americas, Australia, New Zealand, and South Africa.

The Origin and Diffusion of Animal Domestication

A **domesticated animal** is one dependent on people for food and shelter, differing also from wild species in physical appearance and behavior, a result of controlled breeding and daily contact with humans. Animal domestication apparently occurred later in prehistory than did the first planting of crops, with the probable exception of the dog, whose companionship with people is seemingly much more ancient. Typically, people value domesticated animals and take care of them for some utilitarian purpose. Yet the original motive for domestication may not have been economic. People perhaps first domesticated cattle, as well as some kinds of birds, for religious reasons. Certain other domesticated animals, such as the pig and dog, perhaps attached themselves voluntarily to human settlements to feast on garbage. At first, perhaps humans merely tolerated these animals, later adopting them as pets. It may have been much later that economic functions were found for such pets.

Farmers of the vegetatively reproductive crop hearth in southern Asia apparently did not excel as domesticators of animals. The taming of certain kinds of poultry may be attributed to them, but probably little else. Seed cultivators of southwestern Asia seemingly deserve credit for the first great animal domestications, most notably the herd animals.

The wild ancestors of major herd animals, such as cattle, pigs, sheep, and goats, lived primarily in a belt running from Syria and southeastern Turkey eastward across Iraq and Iran to central Asia. Most animal domestication seems to have taken place in that general region or in adjacent areas. There in southwestern Asia, farmers first combined domesticated plants and animals into an integrated system, the antecedent of the peasant grain and livestock farming we described earlier. These people began using cattle to pull the plow, a revolutionary invention that greatly increased the acreage under cultivation. In turn, the farmers out of necessity began setting aside a portion of the harvest as livestock feed.

As the grain-herd livestock farming system continued to expand, particularly in the Fertile Crescent area, marginal lands were settled where crop cultivation was difficult or impossible. Population pressures forced people into these districts. The herd animals became more important to the occupants of these inferior lands, and they abandoned crop farming. They began wandering with their herds so as not to exhaust local forage. In this manner, nomadic herding was probably born long ago on the margins of the Fertile Crescent. Similarly, but in very recent times, livestock ranching may have arisen when herder-farmers retreated into inferior environments under pressure from crop-oriented agriculturists, in the process abandoning all crop raising because of the difficulty of raising plants in these inferior lands.

The Amerindian, who made superior contributions to plant domestication, was largely unsuccessful in taming animals, in part because suitable wild animals were less numerous. The llama, alpaca, and turkey were among the few American domesticates.

Modern Innovations in Agriculture

Innovation diffusion in agriculture did not end with the original spread of farming and herding. New ideas arose often during the succeeding millennia and spread through agricultural space as innovation waves. The nineteenth and twentieth centuries, in particular, have witnessed many such farming innovations and diffusions.

The spread of hybrid corn (maize) through the United States in the present century provides a good example of expansion diffusion (see Figure 3.11). Such desirable agricultural innovations are often first accepted by wealthier, large-scale farmers, a clear case of hierarchical diffusion. In the pre-Civil War South, for example, the wealthier plantation owners maintained closest contact with the innovations of the "agricultural revolution" then under way in northwestern Europe.

One of the major innovation diffusions in twentieth-century American agriculture involved the spread of pump irrigation through many parts of the western Great Plains. A detailed study of this irrigation innovation was made in the Colorado Northern High Plains by the geographer

FIGURE 3.11
The spread of hybrid corn in the United States from 1936 to 1948 began from a core area of initial acceptance in Iowa and Illinois. The innovation spread by expansion (or contagious diffusion) throughout most of the eastern United States in little over a decade. Can you explain the barriers to this innovation encountered in New England, the South, and the Great Plains? (After Zvi Grillches, "Hybrid Corn and the Economics of Innovation," *Science*, 132 (July 26, 1960).)

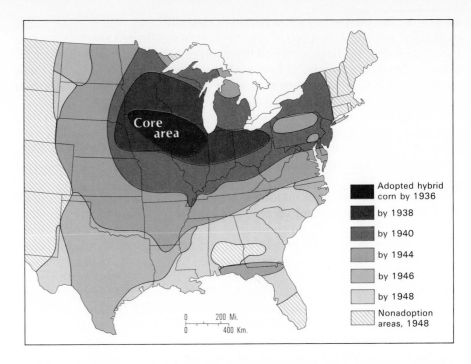

Adopted hybrid corn by 1936

by 1938

by 1940

by 1944

by 1946

by 1948

Nonadoption areas, 1948

Leonard Bowden. Farmers there were deciding much more than whether to irrigate, because irrigation brought with it different crops, different markets, and different farming techniques. The Colorado High Plains farmers were, in effect, deciding whether they wanted an entirely different system of agriculture from the one they had traditionally practiced.

The first irrigation well was in operation by 1935, but initial diffusion was retarded in part by the barrier imposed by a shortage of investment capital in the Great Depression years. Beginning in 1948, irrigation spread quite rapidly. In studying this spread, Bowden observed contagious diffusion from the core area of initial acceptance and distance decay. The closer a potential irrigation site was to an existing irrigated farm, the more likely its owner was to accept the innovation. Some barriers to the diffusion of irrigation weakened through time. Banks and other moneylending institutions were initially reluctant to lend money to farmers for investment in irrigation. However, once the technique proved to be economically successful, loans were easier to obtain and interest rates were lowered.

Not all innovations spread wavelike across the land, in the manner of pump irrigation and hybrid corn. More typical is a much less orderly pattern. The previously mentioned green revolution in Asia provides an example. In some countries, most notably India, acceptance of the hybrid seed, chemical fertilizers, and pesticides associated with the green revolution spread widely in a relatively short time span, becoming almost the normal type of farming. By contrast, countries such as Burma resisted the revolution, favoring traditional methods. A splotchy pattern of acceptance still characterizes the paddy rice areas today. In the lamentable jargon of diffusion studies, nonaccepters are called "laggards" and the inevitability of innovations is assumed, but in reality the green revolution is plagued by ecological and economic problems associated with the use of expensive and damaging pesticides and chemicals. In the long run, the laggards may be proven correct.

Clearly, barriers frequently operate to retard or block agricultural innovations. Some barriers are cultural, others physical or environmental. Religious belief has served as a barrier, preventing old-order Amish farmers in Pennsylvania from accepting tractors, pickup trucks, and other agricultural machinery. Members of this sect will not adopt items of material culture or technological advances they interpret as being anti-scriptural, such as personal photographs; threatening to their traditional lifestyle, as in the case of automobiles; or lacking in merit, particularly luxury items. This is not to say that they totally reject the modern age, for the Amish use windmills, hybrid seed, antibiotic medicines, and other innovations that do not, in their view, conflict with Biblical principles. Similarly, the Communist type of state-owned farm has not diffused to western Europe, the United States or other free-enterprise areas because its structure is based on a different political-economic philosophy from the capitalist system. Physical barriers, such as climate, blocked the continued northward expansion of hybrid corn and the westward movement of the boll weevil.

AGRICULTURAL ECOLOGY

Agricultural types or systems are adaptive strategies, and as a result the theme of cultural ecology is very important to a geographer's study of farming and herding. Some types, such as plantation agriculture, are highly specialized, reflecting stabilizing selection, while others, such as shifting cultivation, retain the varied base typical of diversifying selection. In either case, because farmers and herders work and live on the land, there is a very close relationship between agriculture and the physical environment. In many ways, the map of agricultural regions reflects environmental influences. At the same time, thousands of years of agricultural use of the land have led to massive alterations in our natural environment. This interplay between humankind and the land provides the substance of agricultural ecology.

Environmental Influence

Weather and climate have had perhaps the greatest influence on the location and development of different forms of agriculture. For example, the cultivation of many crops sensitive to frost becomes prohibitively expensive outside tropical and subtropical areas. This is one reason why plantation agriculture has thrived. Plantation farmers in warm climates can produce cash crops desired by peoples in the middle latitudes, where such crops cannot be grown. Much market gardening in the southern and southwestern United States depends on a similar climatic advantage to produce citrus fruits, winter vegetables, sugar cane, and other crops that will not grow in areas closer to the large urban markets of the Northeast. In turn, the need for abundant irrigation water to flood the fields confines paddy rice farming to its present limits within Asia.

Soils can play an influential role in agricultural decisions. Shifting cultivation reflects in part an adaptation to poor tropical soils, which rapidly lose their fertility when farmed. Groups practicing rudimentary sedentary agriculture often owe their superior farming status to the fertility of local volcanic soils, which are not so quickly exhausted.

Terrain can also affect agricultural development. As a general rule, farmers tend to practice crop farming in areas of level terrain, leaving the adjacent hills and mountains forested. In the United States, commercial wheat, rice, and corn farming is concentrated in the flattest areas, partly because such farmers are dependent on heavy machines, and, in the case of rice, on large-scale irrigation (Figure 3.12).

Often environmental influence is more subtle. For example, in paddy areas near the margins of the Asian wet rice region, where unreliability of

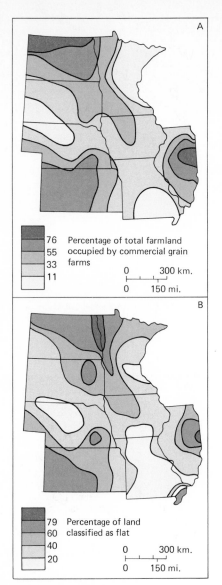

76
55   Percentage of total farmland
33   occupied by commercial grain
11   farms

0   300 km.

0   150 mi.

79   Percentage of land
60   classified as flat
40
20

0   300 km.

0   150 mi.

FIGURE 3.12
The spatial relationship of commercial grain farming and flat terrain in the American Midwest. "Flat" land is defined as any with a 3° slope or less. Commercial grain farming is completely mechanized, and flat land permits more efficient machine operation. The result is this striking correlation between a type of agriculture and a type of terrain. What other factors might attract mechanized grain farming to level land? (After John J. Hidore, "Relationship Between Cash Grain Farming and Landforms," *Economic Geography*, 39 (1963), 86, 87.)

rainfall causes harvests to vary greatly from one year to the next, farmers developed quite complex cultivation strategies to avert periodic famine, including the use of many varieties of rice. That is, their adaptive system is one of diversified selection. Such farmers have, almost universally, rejected the green revolution, as in parts of Thailand. The simplistic advice given to them by agricultural experts working for the Thai government, speaking for the green revolution, is not appropriate for their marginal lands. In their folk wisdom, the local farmers know that the traditional diversified way is superior. A similarly subtle environmental influence can be observed in West Africa, where peasant grain and livestock farmers raise a multiplicity of crops in the more humid lands near the coast. These fall away one by one toward the drier interior of the continent, where the careful observer finds instead numerous drought-resistant varieties of only a few basic crops.

Agriculturists as Modifiers of the Environment

After the domestication of plants and animals, humankind began to alter the environment in a major way (see Figure 3.13). This is particularly evident in the treatment of natural vegetation. To the preagricultural hunter and gatherer, the forest was a friend that harbored valuable wild plants and animals. To the agriculturist, however, the woodland became less valuable as a source of food and had to be cleared to make fields. Over the millennia, as dependence on agriculture grew and as population increased, humans made ever larger demands on the forests. Farmers expanded small patches of cleared land until these areas merged with other clearings. They used ax and fire in their assault on the woodlands, with devastating effect. In many parts of China, India, and the Mediterranean lands, forests virtually vanished. In trans-Alpine Europe, the United States, and some other areas, they were greatly reduced. Figure 3.14 illustrates the clearing of the forests in central Europe over a thousand-year period.

FIGURE 3.13
Millennia of grazing by sheep and goats have helped turn parts of the Greek Aegean Island of Patmos into a rocky wasteland. Four thousand years ago this slope was probably forested with a scattering of live oaks and covered with a mantle of soil. Cacti and low shrubs now grow in the few remaining patches of thin soil. In this manner, traditional farmers practicing Mediterranean agriculture have largely destroyed the land. (Photo by Terry G. Jordan, 1971.)

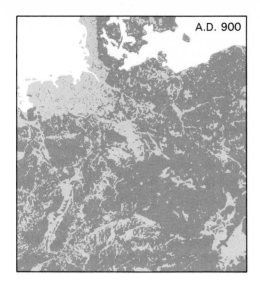

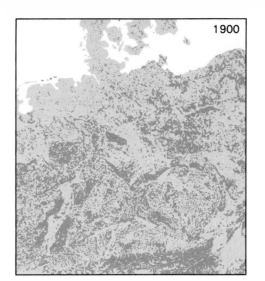

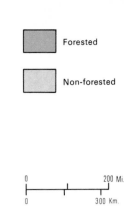

Forested

Non-forested

Grasslands suffered similar modifications (see box, "The Dust Bowl"). Herders often allowed their livestock to overgraze prairie and steppe lands, causing deserts like the Sahara to expand. In the Sahel region, south of the Sahara, severe drought in recent years, coupled with overgrazing, have led to an alarming rate of *desertification* and coincident famine.

In some regions, farmers eventually displaced herders and plowed the grasses under to make way for crops. In the United States, one of the greatest transformations of a grassland area took place in California. Prior to the arrival of the first Spanish settlers, the California prairie lands were perhaps the most productive grasslands in North America. Covering 22 million acres (9 million hectares) and filled with native American grasses, they had a very high grazing capacity. However, Spanish settlers brought with them sheep, cattle, and, unintentionally, Mediterranean grasses. The grass seeds were inadvertently carried in hay on the ships or in sheep's wool. These hardy, lower-quality Old World grasses established themselves initially around the Spanish missions and settlements and then slowly spread across the state as overgrazing and drought years threw the less hardy California grasses into retreat. After about 1850, American farmers and ranchers continued the destruction begun by the Spaniards and Mexicans. The grazing lands were flooded with sheep and cattle, far

FIGURE 3.14

In these maps we see the agricultural impact on the forest cover of central Europe from A.D. 900 to 1900. Extensive clearing of the forests, mostly in the period before 1350, was tied largely to expansion of farmland. The forests survived best in hilly and mountainous areas, because these areas were less attractive to farmers. The map of forests for 1900 closely resembles maps of hills and mountain ranges in the same area. Where have forests survived best in North America? (Redrawn from H. C. Darby, "The Clearing of the Woodland in Europe," in William L. Thomas (ed.), *Man's Role in Changing the Face of the Earth,* Chicago: University of Chicago Press, 1956, pp. 202–203.)

THE DUST BOWL

The "Dust Bowl" of the 1930s devastated the American Great Plains, in large part because farmers had plowed up the grasses that originally protected the soil from wind erosion. A nonsustainable adaptive strategy had come to grief. Woody Guthrie, the great folk balladeer, captured the disaster in his song "The Great Dust Storm":

The storm took place at sundown
It lasted through the night.
When we looked out next morning
We saw a terrible sight.
We saw outside our window
Where wheatfields they had grown,
Was now a rippling ocean

Of dust the wind had blown.
It covered up our fences,
It covered up our barns,
It covered up our tractors
In this wild and dusty storm.
We loaded our jalopies
And piled our families in,
We rattled down the high-way
To never come back again.

"The Great Dust Storm" (Dust Storm Disaster), words and music by Woody Guthrie. TRO—Copyright © 1960 and 1963 by Ludlow Music, Inc., New York, N.Y. Used by permission.

more than they could reasonably support. By the time the California livestock industry had peaked in the late nineteenth century, the grazing capacity of California's ranges had been cut in half due to soil erosion, overgrazing, and the invasion of European weeds and grasses. The native June grass, bluegrass, and oat grass were gone. In some areas, only tarweed, star thistle, or cheat grass was left. The transformation of the California grasslands by humans and their animals has been so total that today it is almost impossible to imagine what the original prairies were like.

Irrigation is another very common environmental modification wrought by farmers (Figure 3.1). Artificial watering can have both intentional and unintentional impacts on the land. Obviously, the intended effect is to circumvent deficiencies in precipitation by importing water from another area, using dams and canals, or from another era, using deep wells and pumps to exploit groundwater accumulated over decades and centuries. Unfortunately, the beneficial effect of irrigation is often offset by unintentional environmental destruction. Ditch and canal irrigation can cause the local subsurface water table to rise, waterlogging the soil, and the mineral content of the water frequently salinizes the ground. In Pakistan, for example, the water table rose 10 to 30 feet (3 to 10 meters), and 800 to 2000 pounds of salt were added per acre of land (900 to 2200 kilograms per hectare), as a result of dam-and-ditch irrigation. Conversely, the water table has been drastically lowered by well and pump irrigation in parts of the American Great Plains, particularly Texas, causing ancient springs to go dry and promising an early end to intensive agriculture there.

The Agricultural Element in Environmental Perception

People perceive the physical environment through the lenses their culture fashions for them. Each person's agricultural heritage can be very influential in shaping these perceptions. This is not surprising, because human survival depends upon how successfully people can adjust their ways of making a living to environmental conditions.

As we saw in Chapter 1, the American Great Plains provide a good example of how an agricultural experience in one environment influenced farmers' environmental perceptions and subsequent behavior in another environment. A study made by geographer Thomas Saarinen in the 1960s revealed that although the oldest and most experienced Great Plains farmers had the most accurate perception of drought, almost every farmer still underestimated the actual frequency of such dry periods. In addition, the study found that livestock ranchers on the Great Plains tend to be less aware of drought hazard than are commercial grain farmers. This suggests that the kind of farming practiced in an area can often mold the inhabitants' environmental perceptions according to the needs of their own livelihood.

■ CULTURAL INTEGRATION IN AGRICULTURE

In the preceding section, we concentrated on how human agricultural pursuits shape and are shaped by the physical environment. Now we turn to the ways cultural and economic forces can influence the distribution of agricultural activities. Religious taboos, politically based tariff restrictions, rural land-use zoning policies, population density, and many other

what are the Cultural Influences Impacting Agriculture?

human factors influence the distribution of agricultural activities (see Figure 3.15). Among some peoples, the system of crop and livestock raising is so firmly enmeshed in the culture that both society and religion are greatly

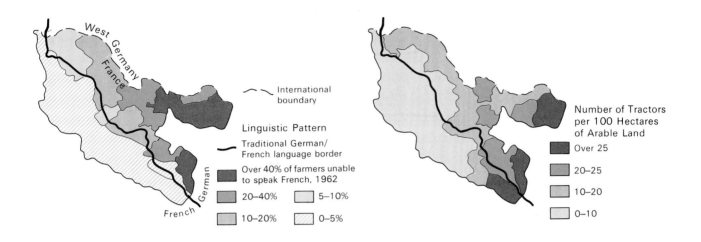

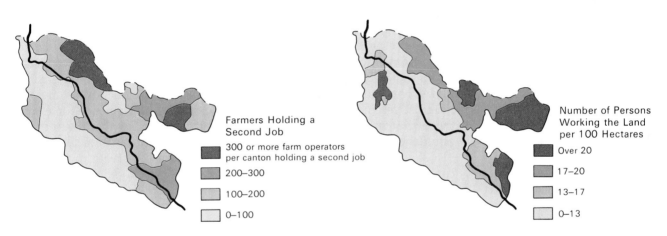

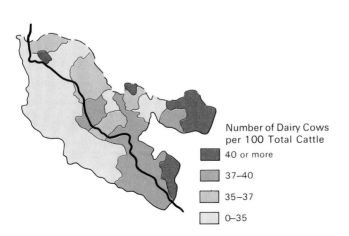

FIGURE 3.15
Agriculture and culture in France. In the northeastern border region of France, part of the old district known as the Lorraine, lies one segment of the German/French language border. Many agricultural features virtually duplicate the language pattern. On the German-speaking side of the line, farms are smaller and more fragmented, causing the farmers to seek second jobs to support their families. Dairy cattle and swine are more important among the German-speaking farmers. The causes of these differences lie in the respective cultures. Try to guess what they might be. (After Michel Cabouret, "Aperçus Nouveaux sur l'Agriculture de la Lorraine du Nord-Est: Les Répercussions de la Division Linguistique du Département de la Moselle," *Mosella,* 5 (October–December 1975), 51–58.)

JOHANN HEINRICH VON THÜNEN
1783–1850

Von Thünen was not a professional scholar, but rather the landlord of an estate in the German province of Mecklenburg. He did attend several universities in Germany. A contemporary of von Humboldt and Ritter, he apparently never met them, and yet his contribution to geography has been very great. He was concerned with maximizing the agricultural profit from his extensive landholdings. This financial concern and his own curiosity led him to create the model of land use referred to as the "isolated state." Modern location theory in agricultural geography is based on von Thünen's model, and he is widely regarded as the originator of spatial models.

influenced (see box, "Cultural Integration: The Example of Cattle Among the Dasanetch").

Selected Cultural Influences

One potent cultural force at work in shaping the agricultural map is traditional dietary preference. The Germanic European fondness for bovine-derived dairy products, for example, helps explain the presence of commercial dairy belts in Europe, North America, and Australia, as well as their absence in Mediterranean and Latin American countries, where people are not as partial to such milk products.

Coffee and tea consumption in the world also display some striking regional patterns from one country to another, as Figure 3.16 reveals. Notable in this pattern is the contrast between the preference for coffee in the United States and the British fondness for tea. In light of this contrast in beverage preference, it is hardly surprising that tropical highland plantations in the Western Hemisphere, nearer the United States, concentrate on coffee production, while in the Eastern Hemisphere similar hill plantations in the tropical areas in former British colonies such as India produce tea. The Dutch, like Americans, drink more coffee than tea, and during their rule of the East Indies, the name of their tropical island of Java became almost synonymous with coffee. In fact, most dictionaries still list *java* as a slang word for coffee, commemorating the traditional major highland plantation crop of the mountainous, formerly Dutch island.

Even so seemingly passive a trait as population density can influence the type of agriculture, particularly insofar as land-use intensity is concerned. One theory holds that increased population density in areas where traditional subsistence farming is practiced necessarily forces intensification. Diversified selection gives way to stabilizing selection as the local farmers systematically discard the more extensive strategies to focus upon those that provide greater yield per unit of land. In this manner, the population increase is accommodated. The resultant farming system may be riskier, since it offers fewer options and possesses greater potential for catastrophic environmental modification, but it does yield more food, at least in the short run. Certain geographers reject this theory, believing instead that population density increases *following* innovations that lead to greater land-use intensity.

The von Thünen Model

An even more significant force influencing commercial agriculture is transportation cost. A century and a half ago, the German scholar-farmer Johann Heinrich von Thünen developed a European-oriented agricultural

---

CULTURAL INTEGRATION: THE EXAMPLE OF CATTLE AMONG THE DASANETCH

The Dasanetch are a herding people living close to Lake Rudolf in East Africa, where the borders of Ethiopia, Kenya, and Sudan meet. For them, cattle are more than mere domestic animals from which they derive milk, meat, blood, and skins. Instead, cattle occupy a central position in their society, serving religious and social roles in addition to the economic function. Dasanetch men identify closely with their cattle and sometimes even assume the personal name of a favorite ox. Cattle themes appear frequently in the song, dance, myth, and ritual of the Dasanetch. Cattle are also an

essential aspect of the unmarried woman's dowry and serve as a medium of exchange. "Cattle are therefore central in the organization and functioning of Dasanetch society," bearing utilitarian, subjective, and monetary values. In this way, agriculture, religion, and society are thoroughly integrated.

Derived from data in Claudia J. Carr, *Pastoralism in Crisis: The Dasanetch and Their Ethiopian Lands* (University of Chicago, Dept. of Geography, Research Paper No. 180, 1977), pp. 99–100.

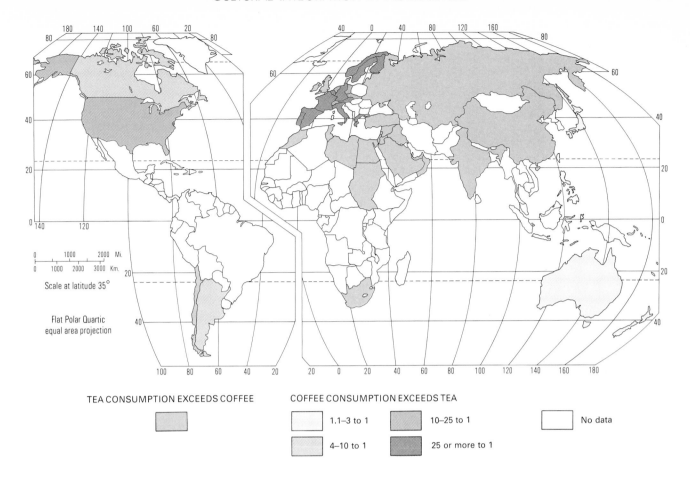

TEA CONSUMPTION EXCEEDS COFFEE

COFFEE CONSUMPTION EXCEEDS TEA

1.1–3 to 1

4–10 to 1

10–25 to 1

25 or more to 1

No data

FIGURE 3.16
Coffee and tea consumption. In recent years, coffee preference has diffused rapidly, at the expense of tea, but regional differences persist. What cultural factors might explain this pattern? (Sources: United Nations, *Statistical Yearbook*, 1976, 1983–1984; see also Norman Berdichevsky, "A Cultural Geography of Coffee and Tea Preferences," *Proceedings, Association of American Geographers*, 8 (1976), 25.)

location theory based upon the cost of transporting farm produce to market (see biographical sketch). That is, he believed distance from the market was the main determinant both of the type and the intensity of agriculture.

As was mentioned briefly in Chapter 1, von Thünen tested his theory by creating a core/periphery land-use model. He proposed an "isolated state" that had no trade connections to the outside world; possessed only one market, located centrally in the state; and had uniform soil, climate, and level terrain throughout. He further assumed that all farmers the same linear distance from the market had equal access to it and that all farmers sought to maximize their profits and produced solely for market.

Figure 3.17 is a modified version of von Thünen's model, the isolated state. Improvements in transportation since the 1820s, when he wrote his work, render obsolete certain of his conclusions, such as the finding that bulky products would be produced near the market. The resultant revised model, in common with the original, reveals a series of concentric zones, each occupied by a different type of agriculture, located at progressively greater distances from the central market. For any given crop, the *intensity* of cultivation, that is, the amount of labor and capital applied to the farming system, would decline with increasing distance from the market, since nearby farmers would have minimal transport costs and could invest almost all of their resources in labor, equipment, and supplies to augment production. With increasing distance from market, farmers would invest progressively less in production per unit of land because they would have to spend progressively more on transporting produce to market. Moreover, highly perishable products such as milk, fresh fruit, and garden

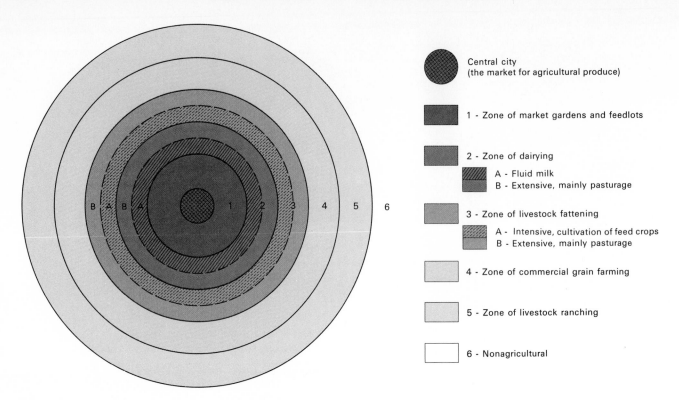

Central city
(the market for agricultural produce)

1 - Zone of market gardens and feedlots

2 - Zone of dairying
A - Fluid milk
B - Extensive, mainly pasturage

3 - Zone of livestock fattening
A - Intensive, cultivation of feed crops
B - Extensive, mainly pasturage

4 - Zone of commercial grain farming

5 - Zone of livestock ranching

6 - Nonagricultural

FIGURE 3.17
This simple model, modified from von Thünen, shows the hypothetical distribution of types of commercial agriculture in an "isolated state." It is based on the following assumptions: (1) Only one market (the central city) is available to farmers; (2) all farmers are market-oriented, producing goods for sale rather than for personal subsistence; (3) all aspects of the physical environment are uniform throughout the area; (4) all points the same distance from the central city have equal access to transportation to the city; (5) all farmers behave in an economically rational manner by maximizing their profits; and (6) the dietary preferences of the population are those of Germanic Europeans. These factors are held constant so that we may see the effect of transportation costs and differing distances from the market. The more intensive forms of agriculture, such as market gardening, are located nearest the market, while the least intensive form (livestock ranching) is most remote. Compare this model to the real-world pattern of agricultural types in Uruguay, South America, shown in Figure 3.18.

vegetables would need to be produced near market, whereas peripheral farmers would have to produce nonperishable products or convert perishable items into a more durable form, such as cheese or dried fruit.

Although it is by no means implicit in von Thünen's original theory, our modified concentric zone model describes a situation in which highly capital-intensive forms of commercial agriculture, such as market gardening and feedlots, are located nearest to market (Figure 3.17). The increasingly distant, successive, concentric belts are occupied by progressively less intensive types of agriculture, represented by dairying, livestock fattening, commercial grain farming, and ranching. In no small part, the greater intensity near the market is the result of higher land values and taxes there, which require farmers to maximize production and income per unit of land.

How well does this modified model describe reality? As we would expect, the real world is far more complicated. Models are not meant to depict reality, but instead to simplify conditions for some specific explanatory purpose. Still, on a world scale, we can see that intensive commercial types of agriculture tend to occur most commonly near the huge urban markets of northwestern Europe and the eastern United States (Figure 3.2). An even closer match can be observed if a smaller area is concerned, as in the South American nation of Uruguay (Figure 3.18). At the local scale, as represented by individual farm villages, the concentric zonation is often quite striking (Figure 3.19).

Nor is evidence of the validity of von Thünen's model lacking in the underdeveloped countries of the world. Geographer Ronald J. Horvath made a detailed study of the African region centering on the Ethiopian capital city of Addis Ababa. While noting disruptions caused by ethnic and environmental contrasts, Professor Horvath found "remarkable parallels between Thünen's crop theory and the agriculture around Addis Ababa." Similarly, German geographer Ursula Ewald applied the model to the

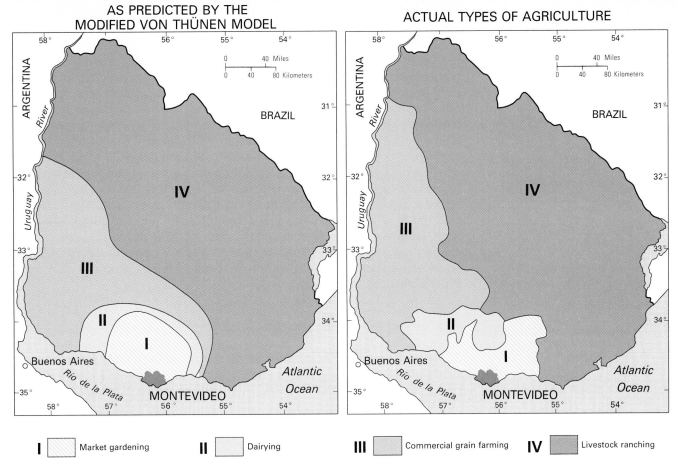

AS PREDICTED BY THE MODIFIED VON THÜNEN MODEL

ACTUAL TYPES OF AGRICULTURE

I ☐ Market gardening   II ☐ Dairying   III ☐ Commercial grain farming   IV ☐ Livestock ranching

FIGURE 3.18
Ideal and actual distribution of types of agriculture in Uruguay. This South American country possesses some attributes of von Thünen's isolated state, in that it is largely a plains area dominated by one city. In what ways does the spatial pattern of Uruguayan agriculture conform to von Thünen's model? How is it different? What might cause the anomalies? (For the answers, see Ernst Griffin, "Testing the von Thünen Theory in Uruguay," *Geographical Review*, 63 (1973), 500–516; the figure is derived from maps on page 510).

farming patterns of colonial Mexico during the period of Spanish rule, concluding that even this culturally and environmentally diverse land provided "an excellent illustration of von Thünen's principles on spatial zonation in agriculture."

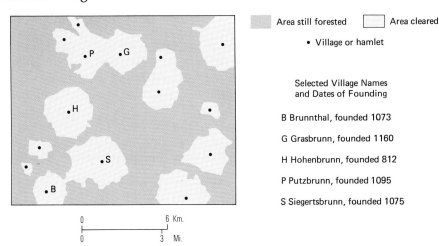

☐ Area still forested   ☐ Area cleared

• Village or hamlet

Selected Village Names and Dates of Founding

B Brunnthal, founded 1073

G Grasbrunn, founded 1160

H Hohenbrunn, founded 812

P Putzbrunn, founded 1095

S Siegertsbrunn, founded 1075

FIGURE 3.19
Von Thünen's core/periphery land-use principles can be applied on various scales. This pattern of agricultural clearings and surviving forest, near Munich in Bavaria, West Germany, reveals von Thünen's concentric zones at a local level. The village-dwelling settlers, beginning over 1100 years ago, cleared the forest in roughly circular areas closest to their villages, leaving the outlying areas wooded as range for their hogs. In this way, the most intensive land use—raising crops—was found nearest to the village, while the less intensive herding of livestock occupied peripheral lands. (Adapted from Terry G. Jordan, *The European Culture Area: A Systematic Geography,* 2nd ed., New York: Harper & Row, 1988, p. 55.)

AUGUST MEITZEN
1822–1910

Geographers studying the agricultural landscape owe an enormous debt to the German scholar August Meitzen, widely acknowledged as the founder of rural settlement geography. Meitzen held the position of Prussian Special Commissioner for Land Consolidation, concerned with redrawing property lines so as to reduce farm fragmentation. In this capacity, he traveled over much of the German country-side, in the process becoming intimately familiar with the agrarian landscape. Not content to study only the field and cadastral patterns, he also gave detailed considera-tion to village types (see Chapter 2) and folk architec-ture (see Chapter 7).

Although not a profes-sional geographer, he attended the first annual national meeting of German geographers in 1881 and read a paper on rural house types. Meitzen, not an academician, was nevertheless named honorary professor at the Uni-versity of Berlin for many years.

His classic work, which provided a scholarly founda-tion for the study of agricul-tural landscapes, was pub-lished in four volumes in 1895. Published only in German, this work's English title is *Settle-ment and Agrarian Character of the West and East Ger-mans, of the Celts, Romans, Finns, and Slavs.* Meitzen, more than any other scholar, was responsible for introducing the theme of cultural land-scape into geography, and it was he who first proposed that landscape, particularly the relic forms, possessed diagnos-tic potential.

■ AGRICULTURAL LANDSCAPES

A great part of the world's land area is cultivated or pastured. In this huge area, the visible imprint of humankind might best be called the **agricul-tural landscape** (see biographical sketch of August Meitzen). The agricul-tural imprint on the land often varies even over short distances, telling us much about local cultures and subcultures. Although this agricultural landscape changes constantly, it also remains in many respects a window on the past. Archaic features abound. For this reason, the rural landscape can teach us a great deal about the cultural heritage of its occupants.

We have already discussed, in Chapter 2, some aspects of the agricul-tural landscape, in particular the rural settlement forms. We saw the dif-ferent ways farming people situate their dwellings in various cultures. In Chapter 7, which deals with folk geography, we will consider traditional rural architecture, another element in the agricultural landscape. In this chapter, we will confine our attention to a third aspect of the rural land-scape: the patterns of fields and properties created as people occupy land for the purpose of farming.

Traditional Survey, Cadastral, and Field Patterns

A **cadastral pattern** is one describing property ownership lines, while a field pattern reflects the way a farmer subdivides his land for agricultural use. Both can be much influenced by **survey patterns,** the lines laid out by surveyors prior to the settlement of an area. There are three major regional contrasts in survey, cadastral, and field patterns: (1) *unit-block* versus *fragmented land-holding*; (2) regular, geometric survey versus irregular or unsurveyed property lines; and (3) private versus communal landowner-ship.

Fragmented farms are the rule rather than the exception in non-Com-munist portions of the Old World. Under this system, farmers live in farm villages or hamlets. Their small landholdings are splintered into many separate fields that lie at varying distances and directions from the settle-ment. It is not uncommon for a farm to be divided into 100 pieces. Some farmers may even own several hundred separate, tiny parcels of land. The individual plots may be roughly rectangular in shape, as in the Orient and southern Europe, or they may lie in long, narrow strips. The latter pattern is most common in western, northern, and eastern Europe, where farmers traditionally worked with a bulky, large plow that was difficult to turn (see Figure 3.20). The origins of the fragmented farm system go back to an early period of peasant communalism. One of its initial justifications was a desire for peasant equality. Each farmer in the village was to have land of varying soil composition and terrain. Distance of travel from the village was to be equalized. From the rice paddies of Japan and India to the pastures and fields of western Europe, the fragmented holding remains a prominent feature of the cultural landscape. Almost everywhere they are found, fragmented holdings display irregular property lines. If surveying was ever done in these areas, it occurred in dim antiquity and did not produce regular geometric shapes. The property lines seem a hopeless jumble to the outsider visiting such settlements.

Unit-block farms, by contrast, are those in which all of the farmer's property is contained in a single, contiguous piece of land. Such landhold-ings are typical mainly of the overseas area of European settlement, partic-ularly the Americas, Australia, New Zealand, and South Africa. Most

FIGURE 3.20
Fragmented landholdings lie around a French farm village. The numerous fields and plots belonging to one individual farmer are shaded. Such fragmented farms are common in many parts of Europe and Asia. What advantages and disadvantages does this system have? (After Albert Demangeon, *La France,* Vol. 6 of *Géographie Universelle,* Paris: Armand Colin, 1946.)

Buildings

Holdings of one farmer

Garden, vineyards, and orchards

often, they display the imprint of regular geometric land survey. The checkerboard of farms and fields in the rectangular survey areas of the United States is a good example of this cadastral pattern (refer to Figure 2.28d).

The American rectangular survey system was developed after the Revolutionary War as an orderly method for parceling out federally owned land for sale to pioneers. It imposed a rigid, square, graph-paper pattern on much of the American countryside, geometry triumphant over physical geography. All lines are oriented to the cardinal directions. The basic unit of the system is the "section," a square of land 1 mile (1.6 kilometers) on each side and thus 640 acres (259 hectares) in area (Figure 3.21). Land was often bought and sold in half-sections or quarter-sections. Larger squares, measuring 6 miles (9.7 kilometers) on each side, or 36 square miles (93.25 square kilometers) of land, are called townships, and also serve as political administrative subdistricts within counties. Roads follow section and township lines, adding to the square aspect of the American agricultural landscape. Canada adopted an almost identical rectangular survey system, which is particularly evident in the Prairie Provinces (Figure 3.22). Traces of more ancient rectangular survey systems can be seen in some European and Asian landscapes. Examples include the Roman *centuriation* pattern, which left visual evidence in parts of the long-vanished empire, and the Japanese *jori* rectangular survey system, dating from the seventh century.

Equally striking in appearance are *long-lot* farms, where the landholding consists of a long, narrow unit-block stretching back from a road, river, or canal (Figure 3.23). Rather than occurring singly, long-lots are found lined up in rows, allowing this cadastral-survey pattern to dominate entire districts. Long-lots occur widely in the hills and marshes of central and western Europe, in parts of Brazil and Argentina, along the rivers of French-settled Québec and southern Louisiana, and in parts of Texas and northern New Mexico (Figure 3.24). The reason for elongating these unit-block farms lay in the desire to provide each farmer with access to transportation facilities, either roads or rivers. In French America, long-lots appear in rows along streams, since water transport was the chief means of movement in colonial times. In the hill lands of central Europe, a road along the valley floor provides the focus, and long-lots reach back from the road to the adjacent ridgecrests.

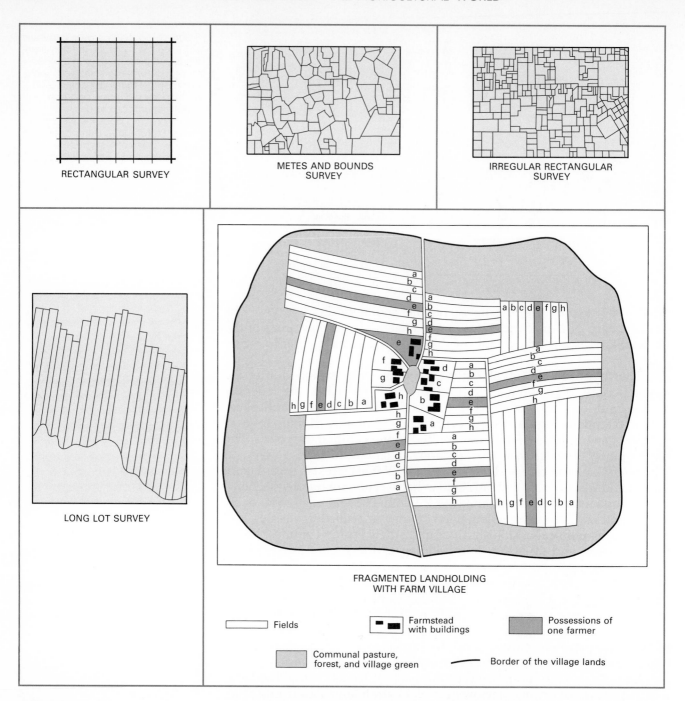

RECTANGULAR SURVEY

METES AND BOUNDS SURVEY

IRREGULAR RECTANGULAR SURVEY

LONG LOT SURVEY

FRAGMENTED LANDHOLDING WITH FARM VILLAGE

☐ Fields

■■ Farmstead with buildings

▨ Possessions of one farmer

▨ Communal pasture, forest, and village green

— Border of the village lands

FIGURE 3.21
Some types of original land division.

Some unit-block farms have irregular shapes rather than the rectangular or long-lot patterns. Most of these result from *metes and bounds surveying,* a type that makes much use of natural features such as trees, boulders, and streams. Much of the eastern United States was surveyed under the metes and bounds system, with the result that farms there are much more irregular in outline than those where rectangular survey was imposed. The juncture of the two systems of survey is quite apparent from an airplane (Figure 3.25).

Field and cadastral patterns often vary greatly in accordance with the type of agriculture. In areas where shifting cultivation is practiced the pattern is one of scattered, irregularly shaped clearings that look like

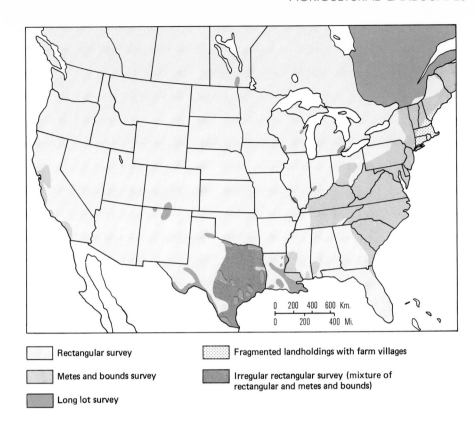

FIGURE 3.22
Original land survey patterns in the United States and southern Canada. The cadastral patterns still retain the imprint of the various original survey types. What impact on rural life might the different patterns have?

Rectangular survey

Metes and bounds survey

Long lot survey

Fragmented landholdings with farm villages

Irregular rectangular survey (mixture of rectangular and metes and bounds)

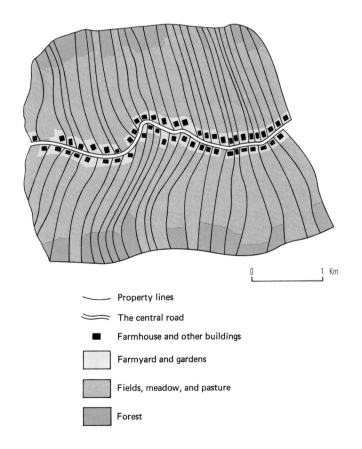

Property lines

The central road

Farmhouse and other buildings

Farmyard and gardens

Fields, meadow, and pasture

Forest

FIGURE 3.23
A long-lot settlement pattern in the hills of central Germany. Each property consists of an elongated unit-block of land stretching back from the road in the valley to an adjacent ridgecrest, part of which remains wooded.

FIGURE 3.24
Aerial view of riverine long-lot farms in French-settled southern Louisiana. Each farm consists of a narrow strip of land stretching back at right angles from the stream. The farmsteads are located at the front of the lot, near the banks and levees. (Photo courtesy of Professor Sam B. Hilliard, Louisiana State University.)

islands in a sea of forest. In commercial dairying and ranching regions, unit-block holdings cover the land. Other types of farming, such as paddy rice farming and grape growing, lend themselves well to fragmented holdings.

Land Reform and Consolidation

In many parts of the world, particularly in Eurasia, major changes in cadastral and field patterns have occurred in the last century. In non-Communist areas, considerable progress has been made in consolidating fragmented holdings into farms that are either unit-blocks or at least less fragmented than they were prior to consolidation (Figure 3.26).

Even more radical changes have occurred in most Communist countries. Large collective and state farms have replaced privately owned ones, and huge fields worked by large groups of laborers have taken the place of tiny individually worked parcels (Figure 3.27). Collective farms are owned either by the government or by a group of farmers, with proceeds or profits divided among the members. State farms are government property and are worked by groups of hired laborers.

Fencing and Hedging

Property and field borders are often, but not always, marked by fences or hedges, heightening the visibility of these lines in the agricultural landscape. Open-field areas, where the dominance of crop raising and the careful tending of livestock make fences unnecessary, are still the rule in India, Japan, much of western Europe, and some other Old World areas,

ORIGINAL SURVEY LINES

PROPERTY LINES, ABOUT 1955
(Those which follow original survey
lines are shown by thicker lines)

FIELD AND WOODLOT BORDERS,
ABOUT 1955

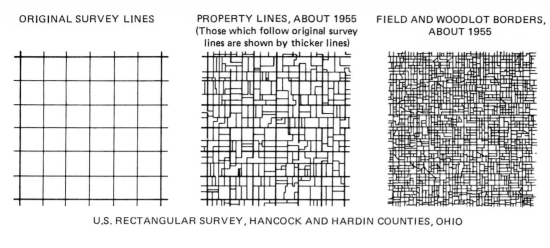

U.S. RECTANGULAR SURVEY, HANCOCK AND HARDIN COUNTIES, OHIO

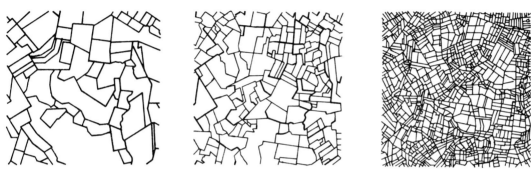

METES AND BOUNDS SURVEY, UNION AND MADISON COUNTIES, OHIO

FIGURE 3.25
Two contrasting original survey patterns, rectangular and metes and bounds, were used in an area of west-central Ohio. Note the impact these survey patterns have had on cadastral and field patterns. What other features of the cultural landscape might be influenced by these patterns? (After Norman J. W. Thrower, *Original Survey and Land Subdivision*, Chicago: Rand McNally, 1966, pp. 40, 63, 84.)

but much of the remainder of the world's agricultural lands are enclosed.

Where present, fences and hedges add a distinctive touch to the cultural landscape (Figure 3.28). Different cultures have their own methods and ways of enclosing land, so that fences and hedges often can be linked to particular groups. Fences in different parts of the world consist of substances as diverse as steel wire, logs, poles, split rails, brush, rock, and earth. Those who have visited rural New England, western Ireland, or Yucatán may retain as a visual memory the mile upon mile of stone fence that typify those landscapes. Barbed wire fences swept across the American countryside a century ago, but some remnants of older types can still be seen. In Appalachia, the traditional split rail zigzag fence of pioneer times survives here and there, and pine jack leg fences remain in evidence in Rocky Mountain states such as Montana. Like most visible features of culture, fence types can serve as indicators of cultural diffusion.

The hedge is, in effect, a living fence. Few who have visited the mazelike hedgerow country of Brittany and Normandy in France or large areas of Great Britain and Ireland fail to perceive these living fences as a major aspect of the rural landscape. To walk or drive the roads of hedgerow country is to experience a unique feeling of confinement quite different from the openness of barbed wire or open-field landscapes.

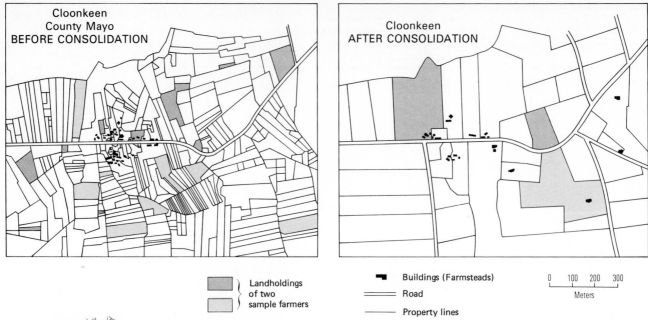

Cloonkeen
County Mayo
BEFORE CONSOLIDATION

Cloonkeen
AFTER CONSOLIDATION

} Landholdings
   of two
} sample farmers

■ Buildings (Farmsteads)
═══ Road
─── Property lines

0 100 200 300
Meters

FIGURE 3.26
Land consolidation in an Irish farm hamlet. The consolidation, carried out in 1909, greatly reduced fragmentation of holdings and produced unit-block farms for some inhabitants. Note that the consolidation caused the breakup of the hamlet and its replacement by isolated farmsteads. What advantages does the new cadastral pattern have over the old one? In what ways might the new be less advantageous than the old? (After James H. Johnson, ''Studies of Irish Rural Settlement,'' *Geographical Review*, 48 (1958), 564.)

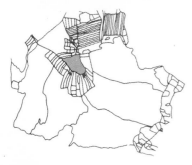

■ Village

─── Property and field borders

FIGURE 3.27
A village in Czechoslovakia before and after Communist collectivization. Six large blocks of land were set aside as the collective lands. Farmers were allowed to retain some small plots as private landholdings, and these cadastral lines were unchanged. But the greater part of the village farmlands was collectivized and the pattern greatly simplified (After R. Urban, ''Die Strukturwandlung der tschechischen Landwirtschaft,'' *Zeitschrift für Ostforschung*, 1953, pp. 130–137, with modifications.)

FIGURE 3.28
A jack leg fence in Wyoming. It is made of lengths of lodgepole pine—a common fencing material for farmers in the area. (Photo by Terry G. Jordan, 1987.)

◼ CONCLUSION

We have seen that the ancient and honored form of livelihood called agriculture varies markedly from place to place, displaying the same tendency for spatial variation that we observed earlier for population. We expressed these regional patterns as 11 agricultural regions, ranging from traditional subsistence hand-labor farming systems of tropical rain forests to the highly mechanized cash grain operations of midlatitude wheat belts.

All of these diverse systems are rooted ultimately in the ancient innovations of plant and animal domestication, ideas that diffused from multiple points of origin to occupy their present distributions. Subsequently, countless other agricultural innovations arose, diffused across agricultural space by expansion and relocation, collided with barriers, and reached their present distributions.

Cultural ecology is implicit in the tilling of the soil and grazing of natural vegetation. Humankind cannot engage in agriculture, even on the most primitive level, without developing an adaptive strategy and deliberately modifying the physical environment. The results, as we saw, include deforestation, soil erosion, and the expansion of deserts. By the same token, and because agriculturists work in such direct contact with the land, they are influenced in some measure by the physical environments in which they live and work. We observed the role of climatic advantage and disadvantage and the invitation of level terrain to large-scale mechanized farming as examples of this environmental influence.

Cultural integration taught us to look for cause-and-effect connections between agriculture and other cultural features. In particular, in the von Thünen model we saw the influence of transportation costs and nearness to market on types of farming.

We found the agricultural landscape particularly rich in spatial variations. The ways of dividing land for agricultural use proved to be diverse, ranging from large, unit-block farms to tiny, fragmented ones. These spatial contrasts, added to the differences in rural settlement forms discussed in Chapter 2, reveal a highly varied agricultural landscape.

Suggested Readings

T. P. Bayliss-Smith. *The Ecology of Agricultural Systems.* New York: Cambridge University Press (Cambridge Topics in Geography), 1982.

Harm J. de Blij. *Wine: A Geographical Appreciation.* Totowa, N.J.: Barnes & Noble, 1983.

Helmut Blume. *Geography of Sugar Cane: Environmental, Structural and Economic Aspects of Cane Sugar Production.* Berlin: Albert Bartens, 1985.

Leonard W. Bowden. *Diffusion of the Decision to Irrigate.* Chicago: University of Chicago, Dept. of Geography, Research Paper No. 97, 1965.

I. R. Bowler. "Agricultural Geography," *Progress in Human Geography,* 9 (1985), 255–263; 10 (1986), 249–257; 11 (1987), 425–432; 12 (1988), 538–548.

D. Briggs and F. Courtney. *Agriculture and Environment: The Physical Geography of Temperate Agricultural Systems.* London: Longman, 1987.

Karl W. Butzer. *Early Hydraulic Civilization in Egypt: A Study in Cultural Ecology.* Chicago: University of Chicago Press, 1976.

Roland Chardon. "Sugar Plantations in the Dominican Republic," *Geographical Review,* 74 (1984), 441–454.

Michael Chisholm. *Rural Settlement and Land Use: Essay in Location,* 3rd ed. London: Methuen, 1979.

M. D. Dennett, J. Elston, and C. B. Speed. "Climate and Cropping Systems in West Africa," *Geoforum,* 12 (1981), 193–202.

Michael R. Dove. *Swidden Agriculture in Indonesia: The Subsistence Strategies of the Kalimantan Kantú.* Amsterdam: Mouton, 1985.

D. M. Epstein and A. Valmari. "Reindeer Herding and Ecology in Finnish Lapland," *GeoJournal,* 8 (1984), 159–169.

Ursula Ewald. "The von Thünen Principle and Agricultural Zonation in Colonial Mexico," *Journal of Historical Geography,* 3 (1977), 123–133.

Colin S. Freestone. *The South-East Asian Village: A Geographic, Social and Economic Study.* London: George Philip, 1974.

Andrew Gilg. *An Introduction to Rural Geography.* London: Edward Arnold, 1985.

Howard F. Gregor. *Geography of Agriculture: Themes in Research.* Englewood Cliffs, N.J.: Prentice-Hall, 1970.

David Grigg. "The Agricultural Regions of the World: Review and Reflections," *Economic Geography,* 45 (1969), 95–132.

David B. Grigg. *An Introduction to Agricultural Geography.* London: Hutchinson, 1984.

Lawrence S. Grossman. *Peasants, Subsistence Ecology, and Development in the Highlands of Papua New Guinea.* Princeton, N.J.: Princeton University Press, 1984.

Gerry A. Hale. "The Origin, Nature, and Distribution of Agricultural Terracing," *Pacific Viewpoint,* 3 (1961), 1–40.

S. Helmfrid (ed.). "Morphogenesis of the Agrarian Cultural Landscape," *Geografiska Annaler,* 43 (1961), 1–328.

Leslie Hewes. *The Suitcase Farming Frontier, A Study in the Historical Geography of the Central Great Plains.* Lincoln: University of Nebraska Press, 1973.

Keith Hoggart and Henry Buller. *Rural Development: A Geographical Perspective.* New York: Barnes & Noble, 1987.

Ronald J. Horvath. "Von Thünen's Isolated State and the Area Around Addis Ababa, Ethiopia," *Annals of the Association of American Geographers,* 59 (1969), 308–323.

Brian W. Ilbery. *Agricultural Geography: A Social and Economic Analysis.* New York: Oxford University Press, 1985.

Erich Isaac. *Geography of Domestication.* Englewood Cliffs, N.J.: Prentice-Hall, 1970.

Carl L. Johannessen. "The Domestication Processes in Trees Reproduced by Seed: The Pejibaye Palm in Costa Rica," *Geographical Review,* 56 (1966), 363–376.

Harley E. Johansen. "Diffusion of Strip Cropping in Southwestern Wisconsin," *Annals of the Association of American Geographers,* 61 (1971), 671–683.

Douglas L. Johnson. *The Nature of Nomadism: A Comparative Study of Pastoral Migrations in Southwestern Asia and Northern Africa.* Chicago: University of Chicago, Dept. of Geography, Research Paper No. 118, 1969.

Hildegard Binder Johnson. *Order Upon the Land: The U.S. Rectangular Land Survey and the Upper Mississippi Country.* New York: Oxford University Press, 1976.

Terry G. Jordan. *Trails to Texas: Southern Roots of Western Cattle Ranching.* Lincoln: University of Nebraska Press, 1981.

H. G. Kariel. "A Proposed Classification of Diet," *Annals of the Association of American Geographers,* 56 (1966), 68–79.

Fritz L. Kramer. "Eduard Hahn and the End of the 'Three Stages of Man'," *Geographical Review,* 57 (1967), 73–89.

Anthony Leeds and Andrew P. Vayda (eds.). *Man, Culture, and Animals: The Role of Animals in Human Ecological Adjustments.* Washington, D.C.: American Association for the Advancement of Science, Publication No. 78, 1965.

Eugene Cotton Mather and John Hart. "Fences and Farms," *Geographical Review,* 44 (1954), 201–223.

Alan Mayhew. *Rural Settlement and Farming in Germany.* New York: Barnes & Noble, 1973.

William R. Mead. "The Study of Field Boundaries," *Geographische Zeitschrift,* 54 (1966), 101–117.

Mark Overton. "The Diffusion of Agricultural Innovations in Early Modern England: Turnips and Clover in Norfolk and Suffolk, 1580–1740," *Transactions of the Institute of British Geographers,* 10 (1985), 205–221.

Michael Pacione (ed.). *Progress in Rural Geography.* Totowa, N.J.: Barnes & Noble, 1983.

Clifton W. Pannell. "Recent Chinese Agriculture," *Geographical Review,* 75 (1985), 170–185.

Mushtaqur Rahman. "Ecology of Karez Irrigation: A Case of Pakistan." *GeoJournal,* 5 (1981), 7–15.

H. F. Raup. "The Fence in the Cultural Landscape," *Western Folklore,* 6 (1947), 1–12.

H. A. Reitsma. "Agricultural Changes in the American-Canadian Border Zone, 1954–1978," *Political Geography Quarterly,* 7 (1988), 23–38.

Jonathan D. Rigg. "The Role of the Environment in Limiting the Adoption of New Rice Technology in Northeastern Thailand," *Transactions of the Institute of British Geographers,* 10 (1985), 481–494.

Brain K. Roberts. *Rural Settlement in Britain.* Hamden, Conn.: Archon Books, 1977.

John Rutherford. *Rice Dominant Land Settlement in Japan.* Sydney, Australia: Dept. of Geography, University of Sydney, 1984.

Je-Hun Ryu. "Oral Tradition, Genealogy and Korean Village Morphology," *Journal of Cultural Geography,* 6, No. 1 (1985), 41–50.

Thomas F. Saarinen. *Perception of Drought Hazard on the Great Plains.* Chicago: University of Chicago, Dept. of Geography, Research Paper No. 106, 1966.

Carl O. Sauer. *Agricultural Origins and Dispersals.* New York: American Geographical Society, 1952.

Louis Seig. "The Spread of Tobacco: A Study in Cultural Diffusion," *Professional Geographer,* 15 (January 1963), 17–21.

Joseph E. Spencer and R. J. Horvath. "How does an Agricultural Region Originate?" *Annals of the Association of American Geographers,* 53 (1963), 74–92.

Dan Stanislawski. *Landscapes of Bacchus: The Vine in Portugal.* Austin: University of Texas Press, 1970.

R. Suppiah. "Four types of Relationships Between Rainfall and Paddy Production in Sri Lanka," *GeoJournal,* 10 (1985), 109–118.

Dorothy Sylvester. *The Rural Landscapes of the Welsh Borderland: A Study in Historical Geography.* New York: Macmillan, 1969.

Leslie Symons. *Agricultural Geography,* 2nd ed. Boulder, Colo.: Westview Press, 1979.

J. R. Tarrant. *Agricultural Geography.* Newton Abbot, U.K.: David & Charles, 1974.

Colin Thomas (ed.). *Rural Landscapes and Communities.* Blackrock, County Dublin: Irish Academic Press, 1986.

Johann Heinrich von Thünen. *Von Thünen's Isolated State: An English Edition of Der Isolierte Staat.* Translated by Carla M. Wartenberg. Elmsford, N.Y.: Pergamon Press, 1966.

B. L. Turner, II, and Stephen B. Brush (eds.). *Comparative Farming Systems.* New York: Guilford, 1987.

B. L. Turner, II, Robert Q. Hanham, and Anthony V. Portararo. "Population Pressure and Agricultural Intensity," *Annals of the Association of American Geographers,* 67 (1977), 384–396.

Harald Uhlig and Cay Lienau (eds.). *Types of Field Patterns, Basic Material for the Terminology of the Agricultural Landscape,* Vol. I. Giessen, West Germany: W. Schmitz, 1967.

Donald E. Vermeer. "Collision of Climate, Cattle, and Culture in Mauritania During the 1970's," *Geographical Review,* 71 (1981), 281–297.

Ingolf Vogeler. *The Myth of the Family Farm: Agribusiness Dominance of United States Agriculture.* Boulder, Colo.: Westview Press, 1981.

Iain Wallace. "Towards a Geography of Agribusiness," *Progress in Human Geography,* 9 (1985), 491–514.

Bret Wallach. "The Potato Landscape: Aroostook County, Maine," *Landscape*, 23, No. 1 (1979), 15–22.

Derwent S. Whittlesey. "Major Agricultural Regions of the Earth," *Annals of the Association of American Geographers*, 26 (1936), 199–240.

Gene C. Wilken. *Good Farmers: Traditional Agricultural and Resource Management in Mexico and Central America*. Berkeley: University of California Press, 1987.

Joseph S. Wood. "Village and Community in Early Colonial New England," *Journal of Historical Geography*, 8 (1982), 333–346.

Chapter 4

Political Patterns

POLITICAL CULTURE REGIONS

    Formal Culture Regions in Political
      Geography
    Functional Culture Regions in Political
      Geography
    Insurgent States
    Multinational Political Bodies

DIFFUSION OF POLITICAL INNOVATIONS

    Nation-Building as Expansion and
      Relocation Diffusion
    Diffusion of Political Ideas and
      Ideologies

POLITICAL ECOLOGY

    Folk Fortresses
    Landform Patterns
    Environment and the Balance of Power

**CULTURAL INTEGRATION IN POLITICAL
GEOGRAPHY**

    Religion and Language
    Population Distribution
    Ideology
    Common Historical Experiences
    Economy

POLITICAL LANDSCAPES

    Imprint of the Legal Code
    Physical Properties of Boundaries
    The Impress of Central Authority
    Nationalism and Ideology in the
      Landscape

CONCLUSION

From boundaries to voting patterns, from separatism to the formation of multinational organizations, politics is inherently spatial, or geographical. Political geography, accordingly, involves the study of a great range of subjects, from the political expression of the subjective, humanistic sense of place to the functional division and organization of territory in different environments and under varying cultural conditions.

Traditionally, political geographers concentrated mainly on the spatial development of the independent state, on theories of the international power balance, and on the possibilities of world conquest. Why does a nation develop in the first place? What factors in the environment and culture make it stronger or weaker, historically stable like France or unstable like Lebanon? What strategic advantages might one national territory have over another? How do these matters relate to the physical environmental configurations of the world? These aspects of political geography,

121

particularly as related to international matters, are collectively known as **geopolitics.**

Today, political geography involves much more than the independent state and the world power balance. Spatial differences of a political nature take many other forms and appear on a variety of scales, from small voting precincts to the mountain domain of a guerrilla force. Jean Gottmann, a famous and much-honored political geographer, feels that ten topics, all of which involve spatial aspects of politics, define this subdiscipline. Political geography, he wrote recently, consists of (1) the study of boundaries; (2) the strategic use of topographic and other natural features; (3) the balance of power in the world; (4) the distribution of territory, population, and resources within and among states; (5) the study of voting patterns and electoral districting; (6) the concept of territoriality and its significance; (7) jurisdiction over maritime space; (8) the provincial spatial structure within states, with particular attention to sectionalism, the sense of place, and separatism; (9) the spatial analysis of local governmental systems; and (10) spatial factors in conflict resolution. It is significant, for example, that political geographers have become involved in the redistricting process that follows each census of the United States. In 1972, geographer Richard Morrill was called upon to direct reapportionment of legislative and congressional districts in the state of Washington, and he subsequently published several works on the subject. We will attempt to sample most or all of the ten topics in the present chapter, using the now-familiar themes of region, diffusion, ecology, integration, and landscape.

POLITICAL CULTURE REGIONS

Political geographers are interested in both formal and functional culture regions. The self-governing state and its political subdivisions constitute functional regions, and we can devise formal regions in studying such topics as voting patterns and legal systems. We will begin by considering formal culture regions in political geography and how they can be used to help understand the political structure of culture.

Formal Culture Regions in Political Geography

Since political attitudes and even government itself are cultural attributes, they can be categorized into formal culture regions (Figure 4.1). Perhaps most rewarding to the cultural geographer are regions based on voting behavior.

Voting Patterns.   A free vote of the people on some controversial topic can be one of the purest expressions of culture. Election returns can provide data on the distribution of cultural attitudes toward such topics as race relations, food taboos, and separatism. For example, the vote for Alabamian George Wallace in the United States presidential election of 1968 was the political expression of the Lower Southern culture region (compare Figures 4.2 and 1.6). This vote suggested that the culture and society of the old Confederacy was still intact over a century after the American Civil War, though many changes have occurred in the South since then.

We need not look to nationwide or sectional voting patterns to find important spatial variations in voting, to detect formal culture regions.

FIGURE 4.1
Under Swiss democracy all adult citizens take part in regional parliamentary sessions. This open-air meeting is in Glarus.

There are many local examples within your own state, county, or city. California provides some excellent examples, on both the state and local levels. As early as the 1850s, the people of northern and southern California differed noticeably in voting behavior, and these differences have persisted to the present. The north, settled largely by people of Midwestern and New England background, acquired a liberal political image, while southern California, peopled from the Upper and Lower South, as well as Mexico, became a conservative stronghold. Geographers Stanley D. Brunn and Robert M. Pierce, using multivariate statistical analysis, identified these political culture regions, and their findings are shown in Figure 4.3.

Party Membership.   Political party membership presents another vivid aspect of regionalism, not just in democratic societies, but also in Communist and certain other totalitarian states. In the Soviet Union, for example,

FIGURE 4.2
Two recent political expressions of the Lower Southern culture region (see Figure 1.6). Goldwater, the conservative Republican presidential candidate in 1964, found his major support in the Lower South, as did independent populist candidate George Wallace in 1968. What might explain the differences between the two maps, as for example in South Carolina? The similarities? (Adapted from Stanley D. Brunn, *Geography and Politics in America,* New York: Harper & Row, 1974, pp. 279, 281.)

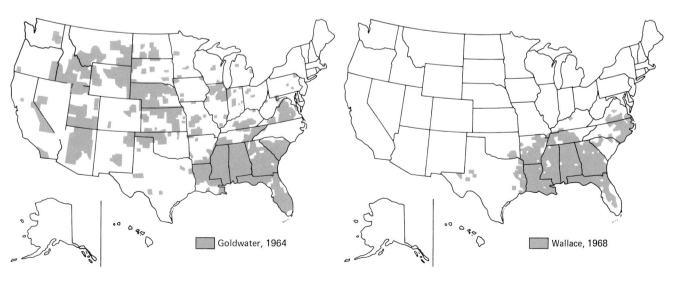

Goldwater, 1964

Wallace, 1968

Consistently
liberal counties

Consistently
conservative
counties

FIGURE 4.3
Liberal and conservative strongholds
in California, as revealed by recent
voting patterns. Most of the south,
anchored in Los Angeles and San
Diego, is a conservative region, while
San Francisco is the center of a
northern liberal region. What factors
might explain this contrast?
(Adapted from Robert M. Pierce and
Stanley D. Brunn, "The Classification
and Regionalization of California
Politics," *California Geographer,* 15
(1975), 22.)

membership in the Communist party varies greatly from one district to
another, inviting geographical analysis (Figure 4.4). To understand such
formal regions, one must consider patterns of language, religion, ethnicity,
demography, and economy.

Legal Systems.   Another interesting political facet of culture is found in
bodies of law, or legal systems, most of which were originally confined to
particular ethnic groups. Some legal systems are of ancient origin, and
often we can trace migrations that occurred long ago by studying these
traditions. The Moors, for example, left behind them in Spain many
Islamic laws pertaining to irrigation and water rights. Overlapping of legal
systems is common, and confusion often results when different cultures
each impose their own body of laws on an area. For example, Spanish
settlers implanted their largely Roman legal system in Texas in the eighteenth century. Then, in the 1800s, Anglo-American settlers seized political control of the province and superimposed their system of English
common law, retaining some Hispanic laws. The mixture was confusing
enough to assure employment for generations of lawyers, but confusing or
not, the laws of Texas provide an index of the diffusion of Spanish and
British cultures. A similar blending of English common law and Roman
law is found in Québec, Louisiana, and the Philippines.

FIGURE 4.4
Communist Party (CPSU) membership per thousand population in the Soviet Union. In the
European (western) part of the country, a core/periphery pattern is evident. Most of the
peripheries are inhabited by non-Russian ethnic minorities. Lowest percentages are
among Muslims in the southern border area. Compare this map to Figures 5.3, 5.8, and
6.1. Many persons regard party membership as essential to their careers. (Source: *The
USSR: A Spatial Perspective,* Washington, D.C.: Office of the Geographer, U.S. Department
of State and Center for International Research, U.S. Bureau of the Census, 1987.)

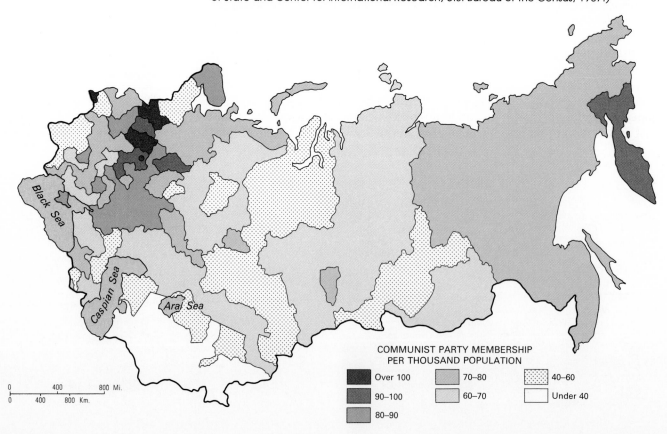

COMMUNIST PARTY MEMBERSHIP
PER THOUSAND POPULATION

Over 100   70–80   40–60

90–100   60–70   Under 40

80–90

Functional Culture Regions in Political Geography

The functional culture region is rather different from the formal type. It involves a region organized to function in some way, a region that may well be heterogeneous in its cultural makeup.

Independent States. The independent state is such a culture region, organized to function politically. This organization, this functioning, makes the independent state a functional rather than a formal region.

The state is, at present, the dominant political type of functional culture region — the principal device by which the Earth is divided politically — and every indication is that it will remain so. The independent state can give tangible expression to one of the most basic human needs: to belong to a group that controls its own piece of earth, its own territory. This need is sometimes called the **territorial imperative** or **territoriality** (see box, "The Territorial Imperative"). Geographers and other scholars cannot agree whether territoriality, this seeming compulsion to possess and defend a homeland, is instinctive — a part of our animal behavior — or learned — a culturally based trait. Geographer Robert Sack, for example, believes that territoriality is not a human instinct, but instead a cultural strategy that uses power to control area and communicate that control, thereby subjecting the inhabitants and acquiring resources. He warns against uncritical borrowing of concepts from students of animal behavior and points out, for example, that the precise marking of borders is a concept originally unique to Western culture.

Whether instinctive or learned, territoriality takes many forms. It can be discovered in loyalty to homestead, neighborhood, hometown, province, or nation. Think of your own territorial attachments and allegiances. Even in the mobile American culture, attachments to neighborhood, town, baseball or football team, university and high school can be detected. These loyalties are territorial, rooted deeply in people's psychological makeup, and if such allegiances are found in such a migratory people as Americans, imagine the territorial attachments of less mobile peoples in other countries. Try to comprehend the feelings of a peasant in India whose great-great-grandfather may have tilled the same land he now tills, whose ancestral memories layer the countryside, filling each landmark with a mythic depth. If you can do that, you can also understand the

---

THE TERRITORIAL IMPERATIVE

Zoologists have for some time recognized that animal behavior in many species is in part motivated by a territorial instinct, a need to possess and defend a home area as individuals or as members of a group. Territory provides a sense of identity to these animals and satisfies a basic need for belonging. Such an instinct is found in animals as diverse as the mockingbird, lemur, crab, and prairie dog. For these animals and others, the attachment to territory is genetic, a need perhaps even stronger than the sex drive.

Robert Ardrey, in his book *The Territorial Imperative*, says that humans are territorial animals, motivated by the same instinct that affects mockingbirds and prairie dogs. In other words, the political organization of territory into states, provinces, countries, and the like is the product of animal instinct — as are nationalism, patriotism, and the desire to defend territory against invaders. On the smallest scale, the territorial imperative finds human expression in the home-stead and family. Then it ranges upward through clan and tribe, through neighborhood, district, and province, to reach humankind's ultimate territorial creation — the independent state. The territory involved may be a family's suburban yard, the domain of a street gang in the ghettos of New York City, the hilly refuge of a Stone Age tribe in New Guinea, or the expanses of an empire. In Ardrey's words, "The dog barking at you from behind his master's fence acts for a motive indistinguishable from that of his master when the fence was built."

Is human territorialism learned or instinctual? Ardrey argues for instinct, but many social scientists do not agree. The question is still being debated.

Based on Robert Ardrey, *The Territorial Imperative: A Personal Inquiry into the Animal Origins of Property and Nations.* New York: Atheneum, 1966.

powerful emotions that are unleashed when such a person's attachment to the land is threatened. Clearly, territoriality is an essential ingredient in developing the sense of place that so fascinates humanistic geographers.

The independent state is perhaps the most advanced expression of human territoriality. Thousands of years of human organization lie behind it, beginning in prehistoric times with the small, loosely organized territories of hunting bands. Today, political geographers study independent states in order to learn how and why each came to occupy a particular area. They are also interested in each state's spatial and ecological stability; in its chances for long-term survival. They explore the character of a national territory as well as the bonds that cause a nation's people to feel like and function as a group.

Distribution of National Territory.   Many factors help determine the fate of independent states. Not the least of such influences is the state's shape. The more compact a nation's territory, the more cohesive it is likely to be. Theoretically, the most desirable shape for a nation is circular or hexagonal. These two geometric forms maximize compactness, allow short communication lines within a country, and minimize the amount of border to be defended. Of course, no states actually enjoy this ideal degree of compactness, although some—such as France, Poland, Zaïre, and Brazil—come close to it (see Figure 4.5).

Any one of several unfavorable territorial distributions can inhibit national cohesiveness. Particularly damaging to a state's stability are **enclaves** or **exclaves.** An enclave is a district surrounded by a state but not ruled by it. It can be either self-governing or a part of another state (Figure 4.5). In either case, its presence can be an actual or potential menace to the surrounding state. For instance, the independent black African state of Lesotho is completely surrounded by the Republic of South Africa. Yet mountainous Lesotho may some day become a base of operations for black nationalist guerrillas who wish to destroy the surrounding republic's white supremacist government. Closely related and potentially just as disruptive is the *pene-enclave,* an intrusive piece of territory with only the smallest of outlets free of the surrounding state (Figure 4.6).

Exclaves are pieces of national territory separated from the main body

FIGURE 4.5
These differences in the distribution of national territory, drawn from Europe, Africa, and South America, show wide contrasts in territorial form. Poland and, to a lesser extent, Zaire approach the ideal hexagonal shape, but West Germany is elongated and has an exclave in West Berlin. The Republic of South Africa has a foreign enclave, Lesotho. Chile must overcome extreme elongation. What problems can arise from elongation, enclaves, and exclaves? How might these problems be overcome?

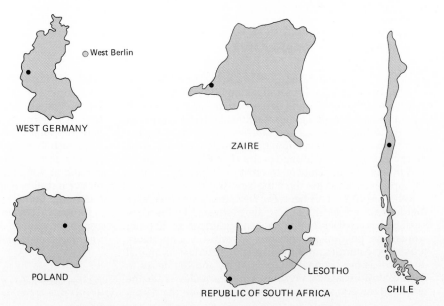

WEST BERLIN

WEST GERMANY

ZAIRE

POLAND

REPUBLIC OF SOUTH AFRICA

LESOTHO

CHILE

• Capital city (in South Africa, function divided between several cities)

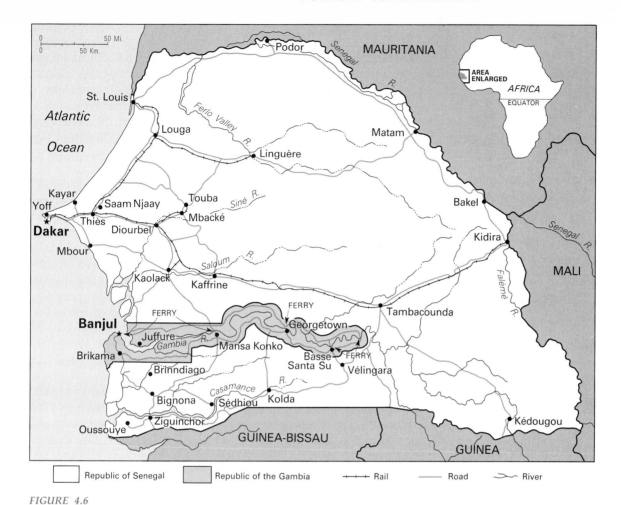

| Republic of Senegal | Republic of the Gambia | ┼─┼ Rail | ── Road | ⌇ River |

FIGURE 4.6
The shoestring Republic of the Gambia is a pene-enclave virtually surrounded by Senegal, but with an outlet to the sea. Separation of the two states is a legacy of the era of colonialism, when Britain ruled the Gambia and France held Senegal. The territorial awkwardness led to confederation in 1982 as Senegambia, which merged transportation, communications, and defense, while preserving the sovereignty of the two countries. Complete unification could eventually occur. In this manner, the two independent states have partially mitigated the effects of an enclave problem. (Derived from Michael and Aubine Kirtley, "Senegambia—A Now and Future Nation," *National Geographic*, 168 (1985), 277).

of a country by the territory of another. Alaska is an exclave of the United States. Exclaves are particularly undesirable if a hostile power holds the intervening territory, for defense of such an isolated area is always difficult and may stretch national resources to the breaking point. Moreover, an exclave's population, isolated from their fellow countrymen, may develop separatist feelings, causing additional problems. Pakistan provides a good recent example of the national instability created by exclaves. Pakistan was created in 1947 as two main bodies of territory separated from each other by almost 1000 miles (1600 kilometers) of northern India. West Pakistan had the capital and most of the territory, but East Pakistan was home to most of the people. West Pakistan hoarded most of the nation's wealth, exploiting East Pakistan's resources and giving little in return. Ethnic differences between the peoples of the two sectors further complicated matters. In 1973, a quarter of a century after its founding, Pakistan disintegrated. The Indian army intervened, and West Pakistan found itself unable to defend its distant exclave, which seceded to become the independent nation of Bangladesh.

Even when a national territory is one piece, instability can develop if the shape of the state is awkward. Narrow "shoestring" nation-states, such as Chile, the Gambia, and Norway, can be difficult to administer, as can island nations such as Indonesia, consisting of many separate islands (Figures 4.5 and 4.6). In these situations, transportation and communications are often difficult, causing administrative problems. The West Indies Federation, a short-lived union of islands in the Caribbean, disintegrated in part because the sea encouraged islanders to develop local rather than national allegiances.

Boundaries.   The boundaries that define political territories are of different types. Until fairly recent times, many boundaries were not sharp, clearly defined lines, but instead zones or *frontiers.* Another term for such frontier zones is **march** or **marchland.** Today, about the nearest equivalent to the marchland is the **buffer state,** an independent but small and weak country lying between two powerful, potentially belligerent states. The Peoples' Republic of Mongolia, for example, is a buffer state between the Soviet Union and China; Nepal occupies a similar position between India and China. If the buffer state falls under the domination of one or the other powerful neighbor, it becomes a **satellite state** and loses much of its independence.

Most modern boundaries are lines rather than zones, and we can distinguish several types. **Natural boundaries** follow some feature of the natural landscape, such as a river or mountain ridge. **Ethnographic boundaries** are based on some culture trait, in particular language or religion, and **geometric boundaries** are regular, often perfectly straight lines drawn without regard for physical or cultural features. The United States-Canada boundary west of the Lake of the Woods is a geometric border. So are most county and state borders in the western United States and Canada. Some boundaries are of mixed type, composites of two or more of the types listed. Some others are arrived at by historic accident and correspond to none of these types.

Another way of classifying boundaries is genetic. **Antecedent boundaries** are those determined prior to settlement — the western part of the United States-Canada boundary is, once again, a good example. **Subsequent boundaries,** by contrast, follow settlement and are often decided by the fortunes of war. The United States-Mexico boundary is subsequent, and when established, it severed established Spanish-speaking settlements from their traditional ties with Mexico. In Africa, the subsequent borders imposed by European colonial powers in their contest to dominate the continent survived into the independence period, causing problems for the present states because the boundaries lack a cultural basis, crossing tribal/ethnic lines and lumping disparate peoples into individual states. **Relic boundaries** are those that no longer exist but may still be evidenced by local cultural contrasts (see Figure 4.24).

Capital Cities.   The capital of the nation is often also the largest in population and has the greatest concentration of economic and cultural functions. We call such dominant capitals **primate cities.** Moscow, Paris, and Mexico City are all primate capitals. Sometimes, the capital city has been moved from the original location; several factors might prompt such a relocation. Territorial loss has been one cause. For example, Turkey's capital was moved in 1923 from coastal Istanbul to Ankara in the interior, partly in response to Turkey's continued loss of its Balkan territories. Economic and cultural factors can also influence the movement of a capital. For instance, a capital might be moved closer to a border in order to be near the main routes of commerce and cultural exchange. The result is a **head-link capital.** St. Petersburg, now Leningrad, lies on the northwestern edge of Russia. For two centuries (1703–1918), it replaced Moscow as the Russian capital because the czars wanted more contacts with Europe. In the same way, independent states that are conquered and become colonies sometimes move their capitals to the port cities nearest the ruling country, only to return them to the traditional location after they regain independence.

In certain cases, a country's political headquarters are moved nearer to its expanding frontier, creating a **forward-thrust capital.** A modern example is Brasilia, present capital of Brazil. Traditionally, Brazil's population clung to the nation's elongated seacoast. Rio de Janeiro, a world-famous port city, was the capital. Brazil's leaders, realizing the resource wealth of their country's vast interior, were determined to break the ocean's hold on the Brazilian people, and at a spot in the interior wilderness, they built from scratch a capital city. Brasilia was meant to symbolize their nation's new interior-directed, continental attitude. Throwing cost aside and employing the most modern architecture, they attempted to create a new national ego for a whole country. However, the experiment was not totally successful. Even government employees were reluctant to move away from their nation's maritime core area.

Spatial Organization of Territory.   Independent states differ greatly in the way their territory is organized for purposes of administration. Political geographers recognize two basic types: the **unitary state** and the **federal state.** Unitary states are characterized by power being concentrated in the central government, with little or no provincial authority. All major decisions are made in the central government, and policies are applied uniformly through the national territory. France and China are both unitary states, even though one is democratic and the other totalitarian. A federal state, by contrast, is a more geographically expressive political system. It acknowledges the existence of regional cultural differences and provides the mechanism by which the different regions can perpetuate their individual characters. Power is diffused and the central government surrenders much authority to the individual provinces. The United States, Canada, Australia, and Switzerland are all federal states, though with varying degrees of federalism. The trend in the United States, particularly since the defeat of the Confederacy in the Civil War, has been toward a more unitary, less federal government, with fewer states' rights. In Canada, on the other hand, increasing federalism has resulted from French-Canadian demands for Québec's autonomy. Core/periphery contrasts and tensions tend to be less severe in federal than in unitary states.

Whether federal or unitary, a state functions through some system of political subdivisions, normally on several different levels. In federal systems, these subdivisions sometimes overlap in authority, with confusing results. For example, the Indian reservation in the United States occupies a unique and ambiguous place in the federal system of political subdivisions. These semiautonomous enclaves are legally sanctioned political territories that only indigenous Americans can possess. While not sovereign, they do have certain self-government rights that conflict with other local authority. Reservations do not fit neatly into the American political system of states, counties, townships, precincts, and incorporated municipalities. They add to the confusion that so often typifies federal systems.

The boundaries and size of political subdivisions are sometimes redrawn to decrease overlap of authority or to produce units of optimum size. Some planners in the United States, for example, suggest that counties are too small and should be consolidated. Most American counties were drawn small enough that a farmer in the most distant reaches could journey on horseback to the county seat, transact business, and return home in one day. In the modern era of rapid transportation, it is argued, the county has become an obsolete, overly small administrative subdivision. Along these lines, England recently redrew many of its county borders, some of which were many centuries old, to increase administrative efficiency.

Centrifugal and Centripetal Forces.   The spatial organization of territory, degree of compactness, type of boundaries, and capital all can influence an independent state's stability. However, stronger forces are also at work, and the human factor often makes or breaks a state. Political geographers have long recognized that the most viable independent states, the states least troubled by internal discord, are those that developed and retained a strong feeling of group solidarity among their populations. Group identity is the key; the size and shape of a state can operate to its advantage only when its population possesses such cohesiveness.

Political geographers refer to factors that promote national unity and solidarity as **centripetal forces.** Whatever disrupts internal order and encourages destruction of the state is called a **centrifugal force.** Many nations have one principal centripetal force that, more than any other single factor, provides fuel for nationalistic sentiment. Such a unifying force, which stands out above all others in any given state, is referred to as the **raison d'être**—the "reason for being."

In spite of the ascendant position of the independent state in the present-day map of political culture regions, challenges to its dominance do exist. Through much of the world, subnational groups desiring autonomy have been increasing and growing stronger in the latter half of the twentieth century (see box, "How Many Independent States Should There Be?"). Even so stable an independent state as France must now cope with autonomist or separatist feelings of Bretons, Corsicans, Basques, and certain other minorities. Another challenge to the stability of the independent state can come from revolutionary groups desiring not its dismemberment, but instead an overthrow of the existing ideology and power structure. Separatism and revolution are capable of producing a type of functional culture region called an insurgent state.

HOW MANY INDEPENDENT STATES SHOULD THERE BE?

"If territory is regarded as space to which identity is attached by a distinctive group who hold or covet . . . and who desire to have full control of it, . . . there is still a fundamental question that must be answered. Should all groups with distinct territoriality-based identities have the right to . . . independence? If the answer is 'yes', then should we encourage the 'Balkanization' of the world? . . . If the answer is 'no', then should we simply accept the status quo and demand . . . that no further partitioning of territory into national units should occur? Or should we hope for ever-increasing supranational regional identities, with the possibility that citizens of the constituent states will attain new identities . . . that might weaken and eventually replace existing state identities? . . . Here we return to the dilemma of how and at what scale to define nation."

From David B. Knight, "Identity and Territory: Geographical Perspectives on Nationalism and Regionalism," *Annals of the Association of American Geographers,* 72 (1982), 526.

Insurgent States

The **insurgent state,** a product of guerrilla warfare, in recent years has commanded more attention from political geographers. If successful, guerrilla war passes through roughly three stages, each of which has particular territorial traits and can be treated as a functional political region. Indeed, when geographers discuss the development of insurgent states, they are really dealing with the emergence of independent states from within the body of old ones. In fact, guerrillas themselves must become good geographers, keenly aware of both the physical and the cultural environment. They are usually not as well armed as their adversaries. Therefore, if they do not know the land they are moving across, they will be trapped and destroyed. Just as important, if they cannot tap the basic stresses and strains in the cultural groups they wish to win over, they are bound to lose.

The raison d'être of insurgencies lies in deep dissatisfaction with the existing order and the belief that needed changes can be accomplished only by force. The dissidents need not be numerous, but they require the sympathy and support of a sizable segment of the population. The first stage of insurgency is mobile warfare, in which small guerrilla bands are unable to seize permanent control over territory and are constantly on the move to avoid capture. These bands confine their operations to specific, carefully chosen regions, usually in mountains or other inaccessible lands where the guerrillas can easily conceal themselves. At the same time, this chosen area should be largely self-sufficient economically, discontented politically, and located near key military objectives, such as cities and transport lines.

In the second stage, the guerrillas become strong enough to establish permanent bases that they continuously control (see Figure 4.7). These bases form the core area of the evolving insurgent state. The insurgent movement adds political administration to its functions and forms a government. The command base becomes a "capital." The ideas on which the insurgency is based are disseminated to the local people. In this way the guerrillas publicize the raison d'être of the state. The base area expands outward into surrounding areas and guerrillas are dispatched to establish new bases in other suitable regions. As a result, the insurgent state has bases scattered throughout the country. Such fragmentation, although necessary, often produces the same weakness that plagues territorially fragmented independent states. Communication between the bases is difficult, and there is real danger that each base will become a separate insurgent state, more and more out of touch with the leadership and goals of the original revolution.

In the final stage of a successful insurgency, the revolutionary forces abandon guerrilla tactics and engage in conventional warfare. In effect, the rival governments are now military equals competing for territory. At this stage, the guerrillas make major efforts to enlist the support of all dissident elements in the country and to portray the revolution as inevitably successful. The insurgents may carry out promised reforms in lands they already control in order to set up attractive models.

The sequence of insurgency described here has typically been carried out in the rural areas of agrarian states or colonies. In industrial societies, the scene of activity is more likely to be urban areas. However, much of the same basic sequence applies to urban guerrilla warfare. Examples of urban-based insurgencies include the revolt of Jews in the Warsaw ghetto during the German occupation of Poland and, more recently, the Irish Republican Army's ongoing activities in the cities of Northern Ireland.

FIGURE 4.7
Burma is a state plagued by multiple guerrilla insurgencies in its eastern hills and mountains. Various peripheral ethnic groups maintain armies and strive for autonomy within the Burmese state, while the Communists seek an overthrow of the central government. To do so, they will eventually have to venture down into the densely populated Burmese central plains. Clearly, the situation in Burma contains a core/periphery component, one that is further complicated by the lucrative production of illegal drugs in the ethnic and Communist areas. (Source: *National Geographic,* 166 (1984), 100.)

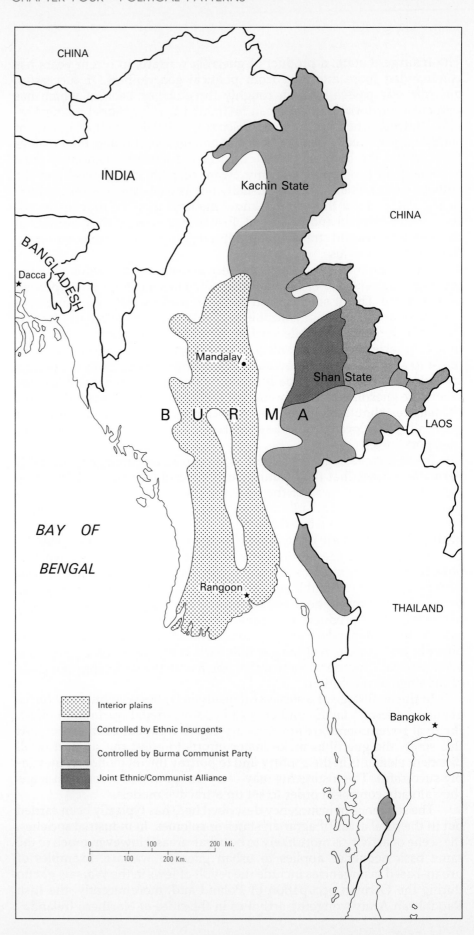

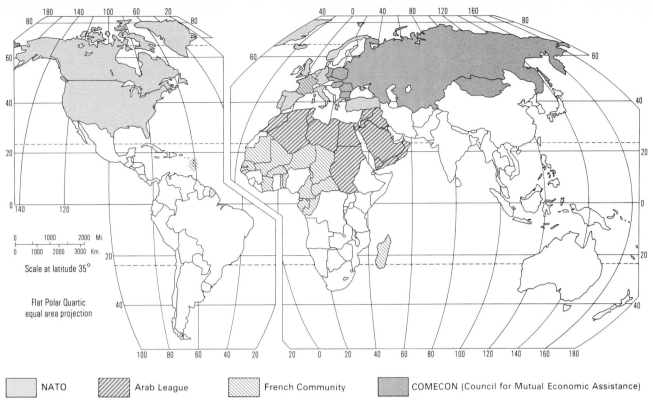

NATO   Arab League   French Community   COMECON (Council for Mutual Economic Assistance)

FIGURE 4.8
Some multinational political organizations.

For us, the central point of insurgencies is that the leaders are geographically conscious at every stage of their campaign. Conditions of the physical environment and patterns of local cultures and economies have the same vital role in the success or failure of insurgent states that they have in the stability of independent states.

Multinational Political Bodies

The third major type of political functional culture region, in addition to independent and insurgent states and their subdivisions, is the **supranational organization.** These represent a second major threat to the supremacy of the independent state. For many centuries, self-governing states have formed international associations of one kind or another for purposes of trade, military assistance, or mutual security (Figure 4.8). Many of the city states of ancient Greece, for example, formed leagues and associations.

In the twentieth century, multinational organizations have grown in number and importance. Increasingly, independent states seem willing to give up some of their sovereignty in return for economic advantage, protection, or similar benefit. Some of these, such as the British Commonwealth or the French Community, are the relics of former colonial empires. Some others, including the North Atlantic Treaty Organization (NATO), are largely military in function. The Common Market, established to create a tariff-free zone in western Europe, may eventually achieve some measure of political union among its member nations. The Council for Mutual Economic Assistance (COMECON) constitutes a Russian-dominated economic empire in Eurasia. Still other multinational organizations are ethnic in concept, as for example the Arab League, which links most Arabic-speaking nations.

The extent to which individual states have given up sovereignty to belong to these multinational bodies varies from one organization to another. Most have sacrificed very little independence. NATO membership, for example, has not prevented fellow members Greece and Turkey from engaging in military confrontation with one another, just as Arab League members Morocco and Algeria have fought border skirmishes.

The most ambitious international undertaking is the United Nations, a multinational body that claims all but a very few of the world's independent states as members. In this sense, it has achieved greater success than its ill-fated predecessor, the League of Nations.

Are these multinational organizations forerunners of political union on a large scale? It is too early to tell, but most likely the answer is no. Certainly, if the "territorial imperative" is instinctual in humans rather than learned, there can be little hope for world political unity.

■ DIFFUSION OF POLITICAL INNOVATIONS

Political ideas and institutions spread from place to place by means of cultural diffusion. Indeed, independent and insurgent states normally develop by means of different types of cultural diffusion. Moreover, political boundaries can act as barriers to the spread of ideas or knowledge, thereby retarding diffusion (see box, "Political Boundaries as Barriers to Cultural Diffusion"). Clearly, the diffusionary concepts outlined in Chapter 1 can be applied to political geography.

Nation-Building as Expansion and Relocation Diffusion

Some states and nations have sprung full-grown into the world, but most diffused outward from a small nucleus called a **core area**, annexing adjacent lands, often over many centuries. Generally, such core areas have, like the Nile River Valley of Egypt, some particularly attractive set of resources for human life and culture (Figure 4.9). Larger numbers of people cluster there than in surrounding districts, particularly if the area has some measure of natural defense against aggressive neighboring political entities. This denser population, in turn, may produce enough wealth to

---

POLITICAL BOUNDARIES AS BARRIERS TO CULTURAL DIFFUSION

Political boundaries can strongly affect how we look at the world. For instance, geographers have shown that a political boundary can be a strong barrier against the flow of information from one area to another. A study of schoolchildren in Dals Ed, in Sweden, and Halden, just across the border in Norway, shows that the children can easily recall place-names in their own country but not those of the neighboring country. Although language differences between Sweden and Norway are slight, the border puts a powerful barrier between schoolchildren only miles apart.

When the children of Dals Ed and Halden drew mental maps of both countries, each group showed a marked preference for its own national locations. On the Swedish maps, areas of desirability sloped gently away from Swedish places that the children were familiar with. The nearby Norwegian border looked like a geological fault line. Preference suddenly dropped away.

A partial explanation for this is that the children on each side of the border are open to quite different sources of information. The Swedish geographer T. Lundén has analyzed textbooks on both sides of the border and has demonstrated clearly how the geographic content in them differs, always offering the readers more information about *us* than about *them*.

Can you think of any boundaries that might have changed how you think about the world? Are they national boundaries? Or have state or even local boundaries sometimes acted as barriers to the free flow of information to you or to others outside?

Adapted from Peter Gould and Rodney White, *Mental Maps* (Baltimore: Penguin, 1974), pp. 143–146.

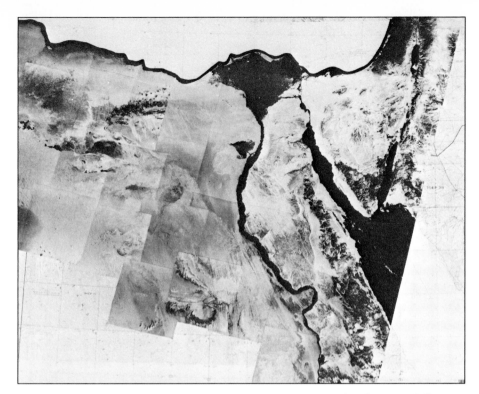

FIGURE 4.9
The Nile River Valley, clearly visible
on this satellite photograph, has long
served as the political core area for
Egypt. Its densely populated,
irrigated farmland stands in marked
contrast to the barren deserts on
either side.

support a large army, which then provides the base for further diffusion
from the core area. Finally, the core area requires an organized government headed by ambitious and able leaders bent on enlarging their territory.

During this diffusionary state-building process, the core area typically remains the state's single most important district, housing the capital
city and the cultural and economic heart of the nation. The core area can
thus be regarded as the node of a functional culture region. France expanded to its present size from a small core area around the capital city of
Paris. China diffused from a nucleus in the northeast, and the Soviet
Union originated in the small principality of Moscow, as Figure 4.10
shows. At the end of this process, the core area may remain roughly at the
center of the national territory, or if diffusion occurred mainly in one
direction, it may lie at the edge of the nation. For example, the United
States grew westward from a core between Massachusetts and Virginia on
the Atlantic coastal plain, a peripheral area that still has the national
capital, the densest population, and the greatest concentration of industry.
Clearly, the diffusion of independent states in this manner produces the
core/periphery configuration, described in Chapter 1 as being typical of
both functional and formal culture regions. Implicit are the domination of
the periphery by the core and a certain amount of friction between the
two. Peripheral areas generally display pronounced, self-conscious regionalism, and occasionally are the settings for secession movements.

Even so, nations that diffused from core areas are as a rule more stable
than those created all at once to fill a political void. The absence of a core
area, to which citizens can look as the national heartland, can leave a
state's national identity blurred and makes it easier for various provinces
to develop strong local or even foreign allegiances. Belgium, West Germany, and Zaïre are examples of states without political core areas.

Potentially, states with multiple, competing core areas are the least
stable of all. This situation often develops when two or more independent

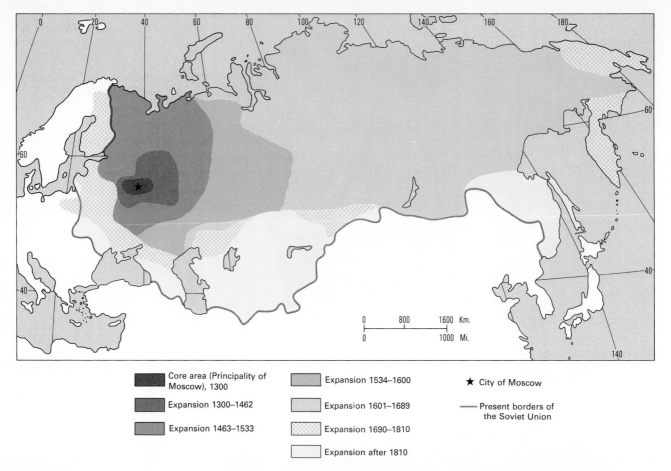

Core area (Principality of Moscow), 1300

Expansion 1300–1462

Expansion 1463–1533

Expansion 1534–1600

Expansion 1601–1689

Expansion 1690–1810

Expansion after 1810

★ City of Moscow

——— Present borders of the Soviet Union

FIGURE 4.10
Note the territorial development of the Russian state from a core area. Can you think of reasons why expansion to the east was greater than to the west? What environmental goals might have motivated Russian expansion?

states are united. The main threat is that one of the competing cores will form the center of a separatist movement and dissolve the state. In the Republic of South Africa, the province of Transvaal competes with the Cape Province, centered in Cape Town. This rivalry reflects the forced union of these areas after the Boer War in the early twentieth century. In Spain, Castile and Aragon united in 1479, but the union is still shaky — in part because the old core areas of the two states, represented by the cities of Madrid and Barcelona, continue to compete for political control and to symbolize two cultures, the Castilian and Catalonian.

Diffusion of Political Ideas and Ideologies

Instances of political ideas and ideologies carried by relocation diffusion are very numerous. Empires are typically built in this way. The presence of "British-type" governments and English common law in Australia and New Zealand, on the opposite side of the world from Britain, is explained by relocation diffusion accomplished in the nineteenth century by settlers from Great Britain. Similarly, the establishment of the Republic of Texas (1836–1845) with an "American-type" government can be attributed to immigrants from the South, as can the subsequent union of Texas and the United States. The Boers of coastal South Africa, people of Dutch descent whose government had been taken over by the British Empire, migrated to the interior in the nineteenth century and established new self-ruling Boer states.

Relocation diffusion is not always the result of mass migrations, however. Small groups or even individual migrants with political ideas can accomplish the same political diffusion, although it is harder for small groups and they do not always succeed. For example, "Ché" Guevara was sent by the Communist government of Cuba to the South American nation of Bolivia, where he unsuccessfully tried to organize a Communist guerrilla movement.

Even more impressively, European colonial powers implanted much of their culture in wide areas of Africa, Asia, and Latin America, without ever sending large numbers of settlers. Colonialism, employing a relative handful of traders, missionaries, soldiers, and administrators, was perhaps the most successful vehicle ever employed for cultural diffusion. Through it, much of the world was at least superficially Europeanized. Even after the colonial empires collapsed, many cultural features imported from Europe survived. Thus India retains English as the language of the educated elite, boasts universities modeled after those of Britain, enjoys a rail network created by the British, and preserves the political unity originally fashioned by the English colonialists.

Contagious expansion diffusion frequently operates in the political sphere. It can be seen in the spread of political independence in Africa, in voting patterns and approval of women's suffrage in the United States, and in many other cases. In 1914, only two African states—Liberia and Ethiopia—were fully independent of European colonial or white minority rule. Ethiopia later fell temporarily under Italian control. Influenced by developments in India and Pakistan, the Arabs of North Africa began a movement for independence. Their movement began to gain momentum in the 1950s and swept southward across most of the continent between 1960 and 1965, as Figure 4.11 shows. Since 1970, African independence

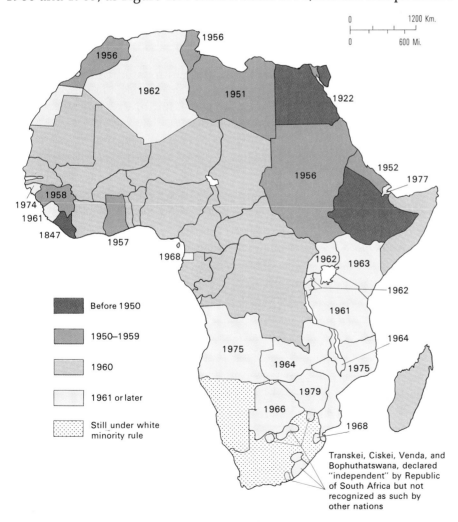

FIGURE 4.11
Independence from European colonial rule (or white minority rule) has diffused through most of Africa. Independence for Africans was an idea first implanted in the northeastern and western reaches of the continent. Since 1959, independence has spread rapidly to the south.

has spread into all remaining colonies. Only the white minority rule of South Africa now bars the path of continued diffusion of this political idea southward to the Cape of Good Hope. No colonies ruled from Europe exist in present-day Africa. A less-welcomed political idea—military coup— has seemingly followed the same route of contagious diffusion in Africa. The majority of the newly independent African states are now ruled by armed forces.

Barriers of various types can halt or slow the diffusion of political ideas. The spread of independence in Africa in the 1950s and 1960s was very rapid because most European powers had grown disenchanted with colonialism and viewed their African colonies more as burdens than assets. In effect, then, few barriers were thrown in the path of African independence. Portugal, by contrast, clung tenaciously to its African colonies until a change in government in Lisbon reversed a 500-year-old policy and the colonies were quickly freed. However, white minority rule in southern Africa, controlled by African-born people of European ancestry, is proving to be much more of a barrier to black self-government than was European colonial rule. Even so, the Republic of South Africa, the last white-minority-ruled bastion, is having to cope with the contagious diffusion of the self-rule idea, an idea already implanted in the minds of its restive black majority. Time will tell whether white minority rule was a permeable or absorbing barrier to this diffusion, or whether white rule is swept away altogether by military force. In fact, permeability is already evident. The Republic of South Africa recently granted a quasi-independence to several Bantu native reservations within the country (see Figure 4.11).

American politics abound with examples of cultural diffusion. A classic case is the spread of suffrage for women, a movement that began in the interior West just after the Civil War and culminated in 1920 with the ratification of a constitutional amendment (see Figure 4.12). Opposition to women's suffrage was strongest in the Deep South, a region where more recently the greatest resistance to ratification of the E.R.A. was found.

FIGURE 4.12
The diffusion of suffrage for women in the United States, 1870–1920, and the Equal Rights Amendment, 1972–1983. The suffrage movement began in the West and diffused steadily for five decades, finally gaining national acceptance through a constitutional amendment in 1920. Both the suffrage movement and the equal rights for women campaign failed to gain approval in the Lower South. Compare this map to Figure 1.6. What were the barriers to diffusion in the Lower South? A half-century later, the states failing to ratify the Equal Rights Amendment lay mostly in the same area. Why did certain western states which were centers of suffrage innovation fail, generations later, to ratify the E.R.A.? The E.R.A. movement did not succeed, in contrast to the earlier suffrage movement. (Adapted in part from C. Paulin and J. K. Wright, Atlas of the Historical Geography of the United States, New York: American Geographical Society and the Carnegie Institute, 1932.)

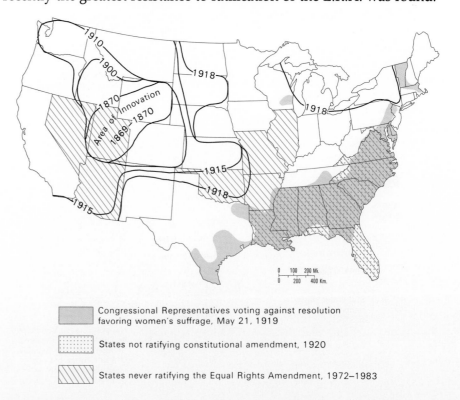

Congressional Representatives voting against resolution favoring women's suffrage, May 21, 1919

States not ratifying constitutional amendment, 1920

States never ratifying the Equal Rights Amendment, 1972–1983

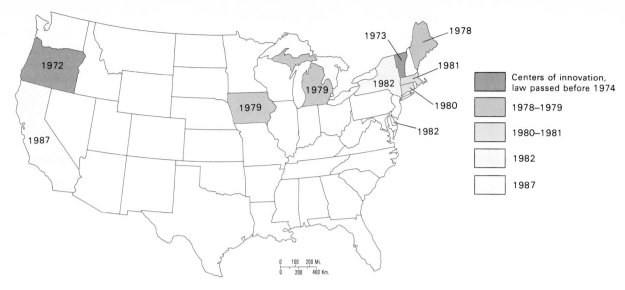

FIGURE 4.13
The diffusion of state laws requiring deposit or return beverage containers. Two states, one on the Pacific and the other far away in New England, were the innovation centers. The movement seems to be meeting major barriers to further diffusion, and the California law of 1987 is far weaker than earlier ones. What barriers might lie in the path of diffusion?

On the local and state levels, political scientists have long recognized the "friends and neighbors" voting effect. This principle is based on the fact that support for particular candidates is generally strongest in their home districts and weakens with distance. The "friends and neighbors" effect is contagious diffusion resulting from interpersonal communication within a small area. However, the growing importance of mass media has allowed candidates to reach a larger audience, which makes "friends and neighbors" diffusion outdated in many elections.

Federal statutes permit, to some degree, laws to be adopted in the individual functional subdivisions. In the United States and Canada, for example, each state and province enjoys broad law-giving powers, vested in the legislative bodies of these subdivisions. The result is often a patchwork legal pattern that reveals the processes of cultural diffusion at work. A good present-day example is provided by the movement to reduce littering by requiring beverage manufacturers to market their products in reusable or deposit containers (Figure 4.13). While it is too soon to tell, we may be viewing in this case an innovation in an early stage of diffusion.

▮ POLITICAL ECOLOGY

Political culture regions do not exist, nor do political ideas diffuse, in an environmental vacuum. Spatial variations and the spread of political phenomena often can be linked to terrain, soils, climate, vegetation, and other facets of the physical environment. Conversely, established political authority can be a powerful instrument of environmental modification, providing the framework for organized alteration of the landscape. This established authority enacts and enforces laws that allow large populations to have a great impact on the environment, for better or worse. Thus political entities influence and are influenced by the physical surroundings.

The political geographer's view of humankind's relationship to the land has changed over the years. In the early part of the twentieth century, the concept of environmental determinism prevailed among English and American political geographers. The writings of the English geographer Vaughan Cornish are representative of the period. In his classic work *The Great Capitals,* first published in 1923, Cornish argued that the existence of western Europe's oceanic colonial empires was "easily explained" on physical environmental grounds. The indented coastline of Europe, he pointed out, offered many natural harbors. Moreover, European countries on the Atlantic coast enjoyed the shortest sailing distances to the main trade areas of the world and stood at the gateway to the easiest routes to the interior of Eurasia via the plains of northern Europe and the Mediterranean Sea. As Cornish saw it, the insularity of the British provided an extra spur to seamanship. Maritime empires, then, were seen as the inevitable result of good natural harbors, short sea routes, and access to the Eurasian interior.

We must be cautious in accepting such environmentalist pronouncements. We might ask why England remained a backward, underdeveloped country even as late as the 1600s and why the "inevitable" maritime empire was so long in coming. What is there in the environmentalist argument that would explain the subsequent collapse of the British Empire? Did sailing distances change and harbors disappear? In the decades following 1940, political geographers adopted a less rigid viewpoint when considering how the physical environment affects political features. Possibilists acknowledge that environmental forces influence political life, but they deny that these forces are the only influence. We should approach the study of such physical influences as the folk fortress with this view in mind.

Folk Fortresses

Before modern air and missile warfare was developed, a state's survival was enhanced by some sort of natural protection, such as surrounding mountain ranges, deserts, or seas; bordering marshes or dense forests; or outward-facing escarpments. Political geographers called natural strongholds **folk fortresses.** The folk fortress might shield an entire state or only its core area. In either case, a folk fortress was a valuable asset. Surrounding seas sheltered the British Isles from invasion for the last 900 years. In Egypt, desert wastelands on east and west insulated the fertile, well-watered Nile Valley core. The Netherlands was traditionally protected by low-lying wetlands, which also threatened the country itself with floods. In the same way, Russia's core area was shielded for centuries by dense forests, expansive marshes, bitter winters, and vast distances.

States without any sort of natural defense have often been hard-pressed to maintain their independence. Korea, a land bridge leading from China to Japan, has repeatedly attracted invaders from both directions. Only rarely has Korea achieved unity and full independence. Poland, which lies on the open plains of northern Europe, has been overrun and partitioned many times by hostile neighbors. Yet, interestingly, these two peoples have fiercely maintained their national and cultural identities.

Landform Patterns

Closely related to the concept of the folk fortress is the distribution of landforms. Ideally, a state should have rugged mountains and hills around its edges and plains in the interior (see box, "Terrain and Political Geography"). Such a pattern not only facilitates defense but also provides a natural unit of enclosed plains as the basis for a cohesive state.

TERRAIN AND POLITICAL GEOGRAPHY

The Bavarian town of Berchtesgaden is known today mainly because Adolf Hitler and some other high Nazi officials had resort homes nearby. To the political geographer, Berchtesgaden has another significance: It is an example of the political importance of terrain.

Berchtesgaden is situated in the Bavarian Alps, in the midst of a wreath of high mountains. In the era before modern transportation and communication, these mountains isolated and sheltered the valley. It was shielded from both cold winter winds and invading armies.

In this setting, Berchtesgaden developed as an independent principality ruled by a religious order. For seven centuries, from 1156 to 1803, Berchtesgaden maintained its independence. The borders of the principality, which followed the surrounding mountain ridges, scarcely changed at all during this long period. Even after Berchtesgaden lost its independence and was annexed by Bavaria and Germany, most of its mountain-marked border survived as part of the international boundary between Germany and Austria. In this way, terrain and the political pattern often are linked.

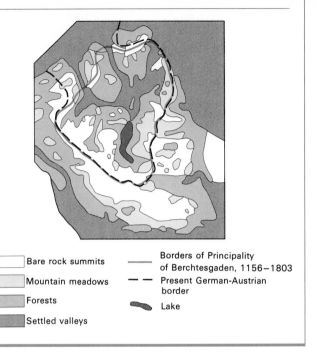

☐ Bare rock summits

☐ Mountain meadows

☐ Forests

☐ Settled valleys

—— Borders of Principality of Berchtesgaden, 1156–1803

- - - Present German-Austrian border

◠ Lake

Few countries enjoy entirely satisfactory landform patterns, although France — centered on the plains of the Paris basin and flanked by bordering mountains and hills such as the Alps, Pyrenees, Ardennes, and Jura Mountains — comes very close to the ideal. Figure 4.14 shows how France is sheltered. Mountain-ridge borders are also desirable, because they stand out on the landscape and cross thinly populated country. Rivers, by contrast, are much less suitable as borders. They often change course and generally flow through densely settled valleys, creating all sorts of potentially provocative situations for the nations on either bank.

An undesirable arrangement of physical features may disrupt a state's internal unity. A mountain range, a desert, or some other barrier cutting through the middle of the state's territory forms perhaps the worst pattern imaginable. Such barriers can disrupt communications within the state and often isolate one part of a population from another. Separatist sentiments grow more easily when shielded by environmental barriers. In addition, internal mountain ranges provide excellent potential guerrilla bases where insurgents can live in relative safety. Peru, which straddles the Andes with fringes of territory in the Amazon basin and the Pacific coastal lowlands, faces such a problem. So does Spain, which consists of a number of plains areas separated by hills and mountains. Both Peru and Spain have problems of internal unity, partly because of their unfavorable physical settings. It is interesting to note that Portugal is the only area in the Iberian Peninsula to escape Castilian Spanish rule. It may owe its freedom in part to the thinly populated hills and mountains separating it from Spain.

For nation-states, perhaps the best borders of all have proved to be those marked by seacoasts. Islands, and the small continent that hosts Australia, have been excellent natural barriers to expansive or acquisitive neighbors. Among others, Iceland, Sri Lanka and the Malagasy Republic have benefited from their island locations. However, island nations are not totally free from attacks by neighbors, as the histories of Hawaii, Cuba, and the Philippines show. In addition, disputes still arise among nations

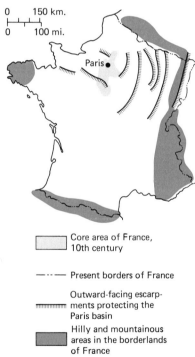

0   150 km.

0   100 mi.

Paris ●

☐ Core area of France, 10th century

- · - · - Present borders of France

▥▥▥ Outward-facing escarpments protecting the Paris basin

▨ Hilly and mountainous areas in the borderlands of France

FIGURE 4.14

The French distribution of landforms is linked to the protection of such terrain features as ridges, hills, and mountains. Sheltering, outward-facing escarpments formed a folk fortress protecting the core area and capital of the French state until as recently as World War I. Hill districts and mountain ranges have lent stability to French boundaries in the south and southeast.

**HALFORD J.
MACKINDER**
1861-1947

Mackinder developed a fascination for spatial patterns and maps at a young age. At school in England, he was caned by a teacher for drawing maps instead of writing Latin exercises. His interest in geography persisted, and in 1887 he became one of Oxford University's first lecturers in geography.

Much influenced by the scientific geography found in nineteenth-century German universities, Mackinder introduced many of the German concepts into England. Previously, the Royal Geographical Society of London had been interested mainly in exploration rather than in analytical studies and theories. Mackinder's famous heartland theory was first proposed in a scholarly address to the society in 1904 and was later enlarged to book form. He served as a member of Parliament for 12 years, and after World War 1 he helped redraw the boundaries of Europe. In 1945, he was awarded the Royal Geographical Society's highest honor, the Patron's Medal. His influence on analytical political geography has been very great indeed. (For more on Mackinder and his work, see W. H. Parker, *Mackinder: Geography as an Aid to Statecraft*. Oxford: Clarendon Press, 1982, and Brian W. Blouet, *Halford Mackinder: A Biography*. College Station: Texas A&M University Press, 1987.)

about the placement of borders in adjacent ocean areas. Icelanders argued bitterly with the United Kingdom and other nations about fishing rights in the ocean near Iceland. Peninsular location provides some of the same advantages for such countries as Italy, India, and Turkey, although peninsulas are usually harder to defend than are islands.

Expanding states often regard coastlines as the logical limits to their territorial growth, even if they belong to other states. This was true of the United States' drive to the Pacific Ocean in the first half of the nineteenth century, an expansion justified by the doctrine of **manifest destiny.** This doctrine was based on the belief that the Pacific shoreline was the logical and predestined western border for the United States. A somewhat similar doctrine has long led Russia to seek expansion in the direction of the Mediterranean Sea and Indian Ocean.

Environment and the Balance of Power

Discussions of environmental influence, manifest destiny, and the outward probings of the Russian state lead naturally to one of the earliest geopolitical theories, the so-called **heartland theory** of Halford J. Mackinder (see biographical sketch). As early as 1904, Mackinder was concerned with the balance of power in the world and in particular with the possibility of world conquest. His theory was heavily tinged with environmental determinism.

Mackinder thought that the continent of Eurasia would be the most likely base from which a successful campaign for world conquest could be launched. Eurasia dwarfs all other continents in size and natural resources and is home to almost four-fifths of the human race. In examining this huge landmass—this "world island," as he called it—Mackinder discerned two environmental regions. The **heartland,** or interior, of Eurasia was isolated from the sea. The coastland fringes along the Atlantic Ocean, Mediterranean Sea, Indian Ocean, and Pacific Ocean—that is, the maritime lands, oriented to the sea—were walled off from much of the heartland by mountain ranges (see Figure 4.15). Of these two areas, Mackinder judged the heartland to be potentially better as a base for world conquest, mainly because it was immune to sea power. A navy was the main strength of the coastland countries, especially England. The coastlands, however, were not invulnerable to infantry and cavalry thrusts from the heartland. For this reason, in Mackinder's view, a unified heartland power could with impunity probe into the coastlands, eventually conquering the maritime countries and annexing their navies. This sea power could then be turned against the outlying continents and islands until the entire world was subject to the heartland.

Mackinder felt that the initial unification of the heartland could best be achieved from the East European plain, which is the most densely populated and economically productive part of the heartland. Mackinder proposed, in effect, that

> Who rules the East European plain rules the heartland.
> Who rules the heartland rules Eurasia.
> Who rules Eurasia rules the world.

By 1904, the Russian state had largely accomplished the first step, having spread over six centuries from a small core area in the East European plain to most of the heartland (look again at Figure 4.8). The rise of a Communist regime and consequent fears of Soviet-inspired "world revolution" brought considerable attention to the heartland theory after 1917.

The recent abortive Soviet invasion of Afghanistan could be viewed as their latest attempt to extend control over one of the few remaining parts of the heartland.

The heartland theory has several fallacies. In particular, it neglects the consequences of air power and overestimates the potential of the thinly settled Eurasian interior, which consists largely of frozen tundra and parched desert. In past decades, Mackinder's ideas were probably more important for the people they influenced, including Adolf Hitler, than for their overall validity. In the final analysis, the greatest value of the heartland theory was its stimulation of controversy and thought among scholars.

One result of this ferment was Nicholas Spykman's **rimland theory,** proposed in 1944 in his book *The Geography of the Peace.* Although Spykman shared Mackinder's belief that Eurasia was the key to world conquest, he placed greater value on the coastlands, which he called the **rimland.** Spykman felt that the huge population of the rimland, amounting to about two-thirds of the human race, coupled with the area's sizable mineral and agricultural resources, made these coastal lands far more important than the thinly populated and environmentally harsh heartland. He stressed that land power was no monopoly of the heartland, that

FIGURE 4.15
The huge interior of the Eurasian continent, isolated from maritime influences and partially walled off by mountain ranges and frozen Arctic seas, stands in marked contrast to the ocean-fringed rimland. The theories of Mackinder and Spykman are based on this environmental contrast. Abortive interventions recently by the United States in Vietnam and by the Soviet Union in Afghanistan indicate that heartland and rimland survive in superpower foreign policies. (After Mackinder and Spykman, with modifications.)

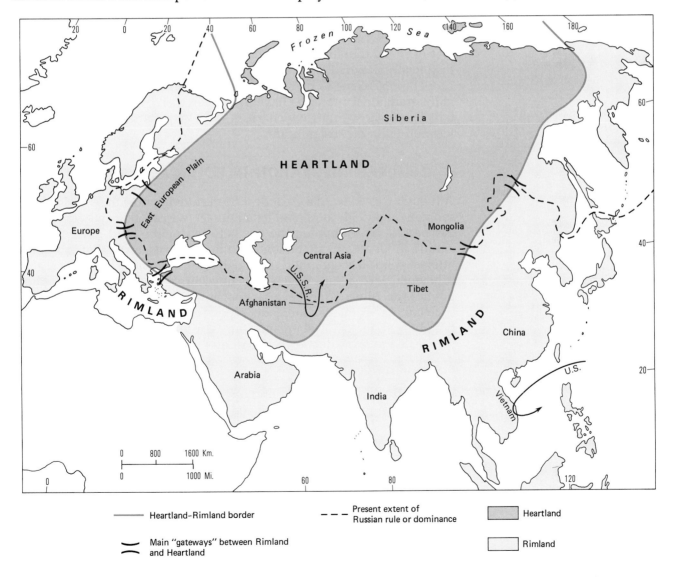

Heartland–Rimland border

Main "gateways" between Rimland and Heartland

Present extent of Russian rule or dominance

Heartland

Rimland

the masses of the rimland could invade the interior of Eurasia through any number of natural gateways. Spykman concluded that

> Who rules the rimland rules Eurasia.
> Who rules Eurasia rules the world.

Fortunately, in Spykman's view, the rimland is one of the most thoroughly fragmented political zones in the world. Its great potential for power is diffused among numerous independent states. Spykman felt that both the United States and the Soviet Union could maintain their independence by keeping the rimland divided politically. He saw the German and Japanese thrust prior to and during World War II as a serious attempt to unify the rimland.

Much of American foreign policy since 1946 has been based on the Mackinder and Spykman theories, aimed at keeping the rimland divided and the rimland states either pro-West or neutral. In the "domino theory," "containment" policy, and other common phrases of America's postwar foreign policy, we can hear the echoes of both Mackinder's and Spykman's pronouncements. American military involvement in Korea, Vietnam, and western Europe were all intended to prevent rimland areas from falling under Communist rule. Events have suggested, however, that Americans have neither the need nor the will to police the rimland.

Theories of Soviet world conquest have splintered on the rocks of Chinese, Vietnamese, Afghan, and European nationalism. Spykman's fear of rimland unification has proven illusory among nations that have historically shown little inclination to work together. In fact, warfare, not cooperation, seems to be the normal order within the rimland area. Finally, traditional strategies have been overtaken by technology, particularly by missile warfare, which has in some ways rendered environmental location militarily insignificant.

CULTURAL INTEGRATION IN POLITICAL GEOGRAPHY

Although we can learn a great deal from studying how the physical environment and political phenomena interact, we can gain an even broader perspective by examining the ties between politics and other facets of culture in an area. State building, voting patterns, and other topics that interest political geographers, although often influenced by physical environmental factors, are largely explained in cultural terms. In addition, political decisions often have far-reaching effects on the distribution of such cultural elements as religion, type of economy, land use, and migration. Indeed, the political organization of territory, both past and present, is revealed to some degree in almost every facet of culture.

Religion and Language

Political stability is closely bound up with the spatial distribution of religions and languages. In fact, religion and language are perhaps the most potent forces in the modern independent state. If the whole population in a country speaks the same tongue and adheres to the same faith, national unity is fostered and a **nation-state** is said to exist. Indeed, language or religion provides the raison d'être for many states, such as Denmark, Greece, and Japan. In contrast, instability frequently develops when two or more sizable religious or linguistic groups share citizenship in a single state. Such differences have promoted historic and recent conflicts in areas as diverse as India, Lebanon, Ireland, Canada, Israel-Palestine, and

Guyana (Figure 4.16). Some states and empires have collapsed under these divisive pressures. Examples from this political obituary list include the Austro-Hungarian Empire and the Turkish Ottoman Empire.

When religious and linguistic diversity are combined in the same state, the situation becomes even more critical, especially if languages and religions display similar spatial variations, thus reinforcing one another. Precisely such a problem plagued the island nation of Cyprus in the eastern Mediterranean. The struggle there pitted Greek-speaking Christians against Turkish-speaking Muslims, with the Christians constituting about four-fifths of the total population. War broke out between these factions on several occasions during Cyprus's brief existence as a unified state, and the nations of Greece and Turkey became involved. Turkish invasion and population relocations added to the bitter hatred between Greek and Turkish Cypriots. In 1983 dominantly Turkish northern Cyprus declared independence. In nearby Lebanon, an Arab nation, Christians and Muslims have very nearly succeeded in partitioning the territory of the state.

The last two to three decades have witnessed a notable resurgence of ethnic separatism, usually based in language or religion, particularly in industrialized states. Europe is the scene of a great many such conflicts. Geographers still do not fully understand the causes of these movements, but perhaps they are reactions against cultural homogenization—against the overly large scale of our political units that renders individual voices inaudible, or against the uneven economic development that places the affected provinces in an unfavorable position. Significantly, the ethnic uprisings almost always coincide with peripheral rather than core locations within states. The combination of minority ethnic status, peripheral location, and regional economic distress apparently bears great potential for producing political separatism. Examples of states facing the problem of peripheral ethnic resurgence are Spain, where Basques, Catalonians,

+ Roman Catholic residence   • Protestant residence   ▨ Nonresidential land

FIGURE 4.16
When bitterly opposed religious groups occupy the same political unit, and particularly when the groups are highly segregated residentially, political instability can result. This map shows residential segregation of Catholics and Protestants in a section of Belfast, Northern Ireland, about 1958. What administrative problems might a pattern such as this present to the authorities? Would the pattern likely be more, or less, segregated today? (After F. W. Boal, "Territoriality on the Shankill-Falls Divide, Belfast," *Irish Geography*, 6 (1969), 37.)

and Galicians seek independence or autonomy; France, faced with unrest in its Basque, Breton, Catalonian, Corsican, and German regions; India, which battles Sikh religious secessionists on its northwestern border; Italy, faced with demands for autonomy by its German-speaking element adjacent to Austria; China, confronted by ethnic separatists in Tibet; and the U.S.S.R., where Estonians, Lithuanians, Latvians, and certain other groups are restive. In nations where free elections are held, the peripheral ethnic groups often have their own political parties, and voting patterns record the symptoms of such internal discord. Even in the nations where linguistic and religious differences have not produced separatist sentiments, the voting map often duplicates the pattern of language and religion (see Figure 6.15).

Population Distribution

How a population is distributed over a national territory can also influence political stability. A clustering of people in the interior of the state, with a sparser population in border regions, is considered desirable. Such a pattern tends to create a feeling of community within the state and keeps contacts with residents of foreign areas at a minimum. The least advantageous population distribution is a concentration of people around the country's borders, leaving a thinly settled core. This pattern tends to retard contacts with the interior and to encourage closer ties with people across the borders in other states. People living near borders may in fact establish international contacts stronger than those binding them to their own state. However, with modern advances in communications, population distribution is much less important today, although it may still be influential.

Favorable population distribution characterizes such states as Egypt, where 95 percent of the people occupy about 3.5 percent of the land constituting the Nile Valley core area (see Figure 4.17). In Chile, a clustering of population in the central region partly compensates for the country's unwieldy shape. Unfavorable distributions appear in the concentrations of people around the edges of Canada, Brazil, Australia, and Spain. As already noted, Brazil has tried to change this situation by actively encouraging its people to move to the interior.

Ideology

Ideally, there should be no great differences in political and economic philosophy within a state. To maintain a strong state, people should be

FIGURE 4.17
Population distributions within independent states vary widely. Spain has an unfavorable distribution of people. Most Spaniards are clustered around the edges of the state, even though the capital is centrally located. The fact that Portugal is independent of Spain is partly a consequence of the coastal concentration of the Iberian population. Egypt, by contrast, has the overwhelming majority of its people concentrated in one central corridor, the Nile Valley and delta. What difficulties might this population distribution cause if Egypt were successful in uniting with countries to the east and west—as for example, union with Libya to the west?

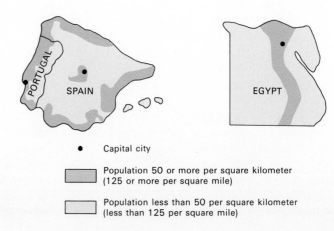

•   Capital city

Population 50 or more per square kilometer
(125 or more per square mile)

Population less than 50 per square kilometer
(less than 125 per square mile)

fairly united in their approval of democracy, republic, monarchy, theocracy, or dictatorship; of free enterprise, socialism, or communism. In free societies, voting patterns can reflect regional differences in political and economic philosophy. For example, France, Italy, Portugal, and some other democratic countries contain certain districts that regularly vote Communist. Figure 4.18 shows a recent Portuguese voting pattern suggesting Communist sectionalism. If major rival political-economic factions divide a state, and if each draws support from one or more regions, the resulting struggle for control can lead to secession, civil war, and destruction of the state.

The United States was very nearly destroyed by such a civil war in the 1860s, when advocates of slavery and weak central government seceded and established the southern Confederacy. Although the South collapsed and was forced to rejoin the union—a victory for those in favor of abolition and a strong central government—the rift was very long in healing.

Common Historical Experiences

National unity gets much of its strength from past experiences shared by the population. Ideally, a people should feel that their state exists because they or their ancestors willfully established it and defended it against alien enemies. The common memory of a war of independence, struggles against invaders, and the deeds of national heroes all serve the cause of group cohesiveness and, consequently, national unity. These memories, even if historically inaccurate, tend to emphasize a people's heroic struggle for independence. Even defeats and long periods of subjugation may well be the glue that binds a people together. The French, for instance, are well aware of recent and ancient struggles against German and English invasions and oppression. They learn in early childhood about the legendary anti-English exploits of their great national heroine, Jeanne d'Arc.

Economy

The cultural factors discussed in the preceding sections all influence the stability of political states, but equally important influences flow in the opposite direction, leaving a political imprint on other facets of culture. Laws and governmental policies can have far-reaching effects on a nation's cultural patterns. This political influence is evident in the distribution of economic features. For example, the United States-Canada border in the Great Plains crosses an area of environmental and cultural sameness. The land and people on both sides of the boundary are very similar. Yet the presence of the border, representing two different bodies of law and regulations, has fostered differences in agricultural practices. In the United States, an act passed in the 1950s encourages sheep raising by guaranteeing an incentive price for wool. No such law was passed in Canada. As a result, sheep are far more numerous on the American side of the border, while Canadian farmers rely more on hogs. Figure 4.19 illustrates the difference.

As an exercise to test the concepts presented concerning the independent state in the preceding sections on culture region, cultural ecology, and cultural integration, turn now to Figure 4.20. Read the caption carefully before proceeding to your analysis.

Less than 10%

10–30%

More than 30%

FIGURE 4.18
Portugal: Communist votes as a percentage of the total, 1976. When democracy was restored to Portugal in the mid-1970s, free elections showed Communist strength to be greatest in the southern half of the nation, duplicating the pattern of some other cultural features. For example, the Moorish imprint is much more apparent in the south, and landownership by farmers is much less common there. Why might the Communists have the greatest appeal there?

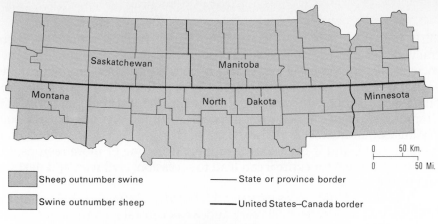

FIGURE 4.19

The political impact on economy can be revealed in the choice of livestock—in this case, the border area between the United States and Canada. Sheep are more numerous than swine on the United States side of the boundary, in part because of government-backed price incentives for wool. What other factors might account for this contrast? (Based on data in Hendrik J. Reitsma, "Crop and Livestock Production in the Vicinity of the United States–Canada Border," *Professional Geographer*, 23 (1971), 220–221.)

Saskatchewan	Manitoba
Montana	North Dakota	Minnesota

0   50 Km.
0   50 Mi.

☐ Sheep outnumber swine
☐ Swine outnumber sheep
— State or province border
━ United States–Canada border

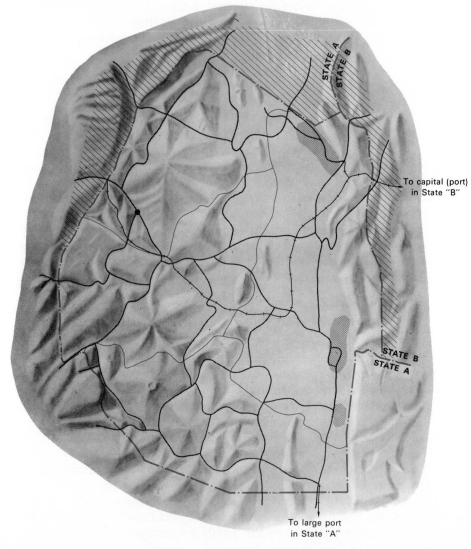

STATE A
STATE B

To capital (port)
in State "B"

STATE B
STATE A

To large port
in State "A"

——— Political district borders
—·—·— International boundaries
+—+—+ Railroads
——— Main roads
● National capital

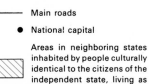 Areas in neighboring states inhabited by people culturally identical to the citizens of the independent state, living as ethnic minorities

▨ Rugged mountains and hills

▨ Plains

▨ Major areas of cropland

0   10   20   50 Km.
0   10   20   30 Mi.

FIGURE 4.20

This is a map, derived from satellite imagery, of an existing independent state, a member of the United Nations. Its population, numbering about 660,000, belongs almost entirely to a single ethnic-linguistic group. No great internal splits in ideology or religion exist, and common historical experiences, some so remote as to lie in folklore and oral tradition, bind the population. Livestock raising is the most widespread form of livelihood. Large independent neighbor state A, with a population of 27 million and a land area of 471,000 square miles (1,220,000 square kilometers), and large independent neighbor state B, with 14 million inhabitants and 302,000 square miles (782,000 square kilometers) of territory, have been bitterly hostile toward one another, and A is the more powerful of the two. A recent treaty between A and B promises at least temporary peace, though A continues to support a guerrilla movement aimed at overthrowing the Marxist government of B.

Using this information and that contained on the map, evaluate the internal stability of this state and speculate concerning its external relationships and viability. Give consideration to shape, size, terrain, borders, transport, neighbors, ethnic-linguistic features, economy, and other characteristics, applying the themes of culture region, cultural ecology, and cultural integration. Is this a buffer state? A satellite state? If the latter, which neighbor likely dominates it? Finally, after completing your evaluation, use an atlas to find the state. (The name of the state, as a check of your work, is contained in a source citation at the end of the Suggested Readings section of this chapter.)

▓ POLITICAL LANDSCAPES

The cultural landscape reveals the imprint of politics in diverse ways. Nationalism, political ideology, the legal code, and authority can all be highly visible, as can the boundaries separating independent states. All of these, collectively, constitute the political landscape.

Imprint of the Legal Code

Many laws find their way into the cultural landscape. Among the most noticeable are those that regulate the land-surveying system, because the law often requires that land be divided into specific geometric patterns. In most of the United States, as was discussed Chapter 3, a rigid rectangular system was imposed on the land, producing a distinctive checkerboard appearance that is striking from the air. In Canada, the laws of the French-speaking province of Québec encourage land survey in long, narrow parcels, but English-speaking provinces, such as Ontario, adopted a rectangular system. As a result, the political border between Québec and Ontario can be spotted easily from the air.

Even legal decisions made long ago by vanished governments can remain imprinted on the landscape. For example, Denmark ruled the provinces of Schleswig and Holstein, now held by West Germany, until the 1860s. During that period, Danish laws broke up farm villages and dispersed the rural population in isolated farmsteads. At the same time, many fragmented landholdings were combined into unit-block farms. In nearby German-ruled provinces, different laws prevailed, and the population and property lines remained unchanged. Today, even though Germany has ruled Schleswig-Holstein for over a century, the old border is still clearly visible in the settlement landscape.

Legal imprint can also be seen in the cultural landscape of urban areas. In Rio de Janeiro, height restrictions on buildings have been enforced for a long time. The result is a waterfront lined with buildings of uniform height. By contrast, most American cities have no height restrictions, allowing skyscrapers to dominate the central city. The consequence is a jagged skyline, like that of San Francisco or New York City (see Figure 4.21).

Physical Properties of Boundaries

Perhaps no more purely human creation exists than a demarcated political boundary. These features vary greatly in the degree to which they stand out in the landscape. On one extreme are highly visible boundaries marked by walls, cleared strips, and barbed-wire barriers. The famous Berlin Wall, first erected in 1961, is an excellent example (see Figure 4.22). As a general rule, political borders are most visible where tight restrictions limit the movement of people and goods between neighboring states. Sometimes such boundaries are even lined with pillboxes, tank traps, and other obvious defensive installations. At the opposite end of the spectrum are international borders, such as that between the United States and Canada, that are unfortified, thinly policed, and very nearly invisible. But even undefended borders of this type are usually marked by regularly spaced boundary pillars or cairns and by customs houses and colorfully striped guardhouses at crossing points.

Moreover, the visible aspect of international borders is surprisingly durable, sometimes persisting centuries or even millennia after the bound-

FIGURE 4.21
Legal height restrictions, or their absence, can greatly influence urban landscapes. New York City lacks such controls and its skyline is punctuated by spectacular skyscrapers. In Rio de Janeiro, by contrast, height restrictions allow the natural environment to provide the "highrises."

ary becomes relic. Ruins of boundary defenses, some dating from ancient times, are common in certain areas. Hadrian's Wall in England marks the northern border during one stage of Roman occupation and parallels the modern border between England and Scotland. The Great Wall of China and the elaborate concrete and steel installations of France's Maginot Line are two other reminders of boundaries of the past (see Figure 4.23). In far more subtle ways, too, long defunct international political borders can continue to be reflected in the cultural landscape, occasionally in quite baffling ways (Figure 4.24).

A quite different type of boundary, marking the territorial limits of urban street gangs, is also evident in the central areas of many American cities. The principal device used by these teenaged gangs to mark their "turf" is graffiti. Geographers David Ley and Roman Cybriwsky studied this phenomenon in Philadelphia. They found that borders were marked by externally directed, aggressive epithets, taunts, and obscenities, placed there for the benefit of neighboring gangs. A street gang of white youths, for example, plastered its border with a black gang with slogans like "White Power," "Do Not Enter [District]21-W, — ," and similar graffiti painted on walls. The gang's "core area," its "home corner," contains internally supportive graffiti, such as "Fairmount Rules" or a roster of gang members. Thus a perceptive observer can map the gang territories on the basis of these political landscape features.

The Impress of Central Authority

The attempt to impose centralized government appears in many facets of the landscape. Railroad and highway patterns focused on the national core area, and radiating like the spokes of a wheel to reach the hinterlands of the state, are good indicators of central authority. In Germany, the rail network was developed largely before unification of the country in 1871. As a result, no focal point stands out. On the other hand, the superhighway system of autobahns, encouraged by Hitler as a symbol of national unity and power, tied the various parts of the Reich to such focal points as Berlin and the Ruhr industrial district.

Central authority backed by military power tends to produce a landscape in which the rural population is dispersed and the cities are without defense installations. Clustered farm villages and walled towns can be physical signs of an absence of central authority, of a need to provide defense on the local level. In England, where effective central government has prevailed for a thousand years, few cities retain their former walls, and the villages have shrunk as farmers dispersed into the countryside. However, in central Europe, which remained politically fragmented until very recent times, numerous town walls can still be seen, and the farmers remain concentrated in farm villages. To be sure, other factors also helped shape these contrasts between Britain and mainland Europe, but the different concentration of authority definitely played an important role. In the same way, the inability of the former government in South Vietnam to protect effectively the rural areas from the insurgent Viet Cong caused many farm folk to move to "fortified hamlets," enclosed with barbed wire, creating an altered rural settlement landscape.

The visibility of provincial borders within a nation can also reflect the central government's strength and stability. Stable, secure nations, such as the United States, often permit considerable display of provincial borders. Most state boundaries within the United States are marked with signboards or other features announcing the crossing. In contrast, insecure countries, where sectionalism threatens national unity, often suppress such signs of provincial borders.

Some of the most visible central governments are those that have recently taken power. They try to assure their survival by saturating the landscape with evidence of their existence. The Greek military leaders who took power in 1967 soon placed placards with the risen-phoenix symbol of their government in every town, village, and hamlet. They supplemented the placards with countless slogans painted on signs, spelled out in white rocks on hillsides, and commemorated in changed street names. These visible symbols of the government were just as quickly removed when the military junta fell from power in 1974.

FIGURE 4.22
The Berlin Wall divides a city that was once whole. The brick and barbed wire visually mark the limits of political control. Are political boundaries visible in your area?

FIGURE 4.23
The Great Wall of China is likely the most spectacular political landscape ever created and one of the few features made by humans that is visible from outer space. Fifteen hundred miles (2400 kilometers) long, the wall was constructed over many centuries by the Chinese in an ultimately unsuccessful attempt to protect their northern boundary from adjacent tribes of nomadic herders. The closest modern equivalent is perhaps the Berlin Wall. (Photo by Terry G. Jordan, 1983.)

FIGURE 4.24
Roofing material contrasts along a relic border, about 1800. In the 1500s, the present boundary between the Swiss cantons of Baselland and Aargau formed the Swiss/Hapsburg Austrian border. Can we detect surviving traces of that long defunct international border? Well, the old boundary remains today the line between Protestant (in Baselland) and Catholic majorities (in Aargau), continues to function as a cantonal border, and, at least into the nineteenth century, could be detected in the cultural landscape in such unlikely features as the choice of roofing material. How might political states have influenced the way roofs were built? (Source: D. Opferkuch, *Der Einfluss einer Binnengrenze auf die Kulturlandschaft,* Basel: Basler Beitrage zur Geographie, No. 21, 1977.)

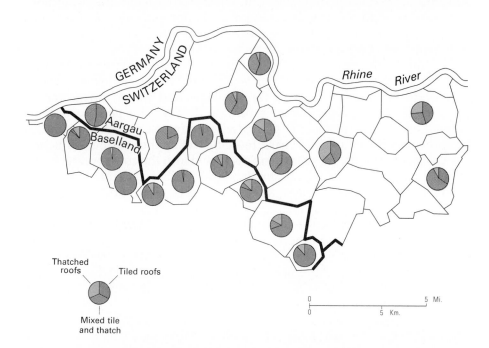

Nationalism and Ideology in the Landscape

The cultural landscape is rich in symbolism and visual metaphor, and political messages are often conveyed through such means with an intensity that varies greatly from one country to another. In the United States, flags and eagles convey clear messages to citizen and visitor alike. Statues of national heroes or heroines and of symbolic figures such as the goddess of liberty or mother Russia form important parts of the political landscape, as do assorted monuments (Figure 4.25). The elaborate use of national colors or, in the case of Communist countries, ideological color, can be very powerful visually, and symbols such as the swastika, hammer and sickle, or rising sun possess great potency.

FIGURE 4.25
This statue of the parish priest Father Miguel Hidalgo y Costilla stands before the church in the town of Dolores Hidalgo, Guanajuato state, Mexico, where he instigated the Mexican war of independence from Spain in 1810. Captured and executed the following year, Hidalgo is venerated as a martyr-hero in Mexico. His statue is, therefore, a component of Mexico's political landscape. (Photo by Terry G. Jordan, 1986.)

Ideology can be promoted by slogans affixed to billboards or structures. More importantly, political ideology can be impressed upon entire national landscapes. The two Germanies provide a fine example. While perhaps the most striking feature of the political landscape there is the heavily fortified, cleared death strip along the Iron Curtain border separating the two German states, an aerial view quickly also reveals that the farmland on the German Democratic Republic (Communist) side of the line is little divided, forming huge collectives with very large fields, while on the German Federal Republic (western) side, the cropland is fragmented into tiny, privately owned fields. In Germany, two very different ideologies produce two highly distinctive landscapes.

■ CONCLUSION

Political spatial variations—from local voting patterns to the spatial arrangement of international power blocs—add yet another dimension to the complex human mosaic. In particular, independent and insurgent political states function as vital culture regions. They help shape many other facets of culture. Political culture regions constantly change as political innovations ebb and flow across their surfaces. Political phenomena as varied as guerrilla movements, women's suffrage, and territorial expansion of nations move along the paths of diffusion.

Cultural ecology helps us understand the links between systems of power and the physical environment. States do not exist in an environmental vacuum. The spatial pattern of landforms, hydrogeography, and vegetation are frequently reflected in boundaries, core areas, folk fortresses, and global strategies. Although the environment molds the political state, the state also molds the environment. Governments can act as agents of destruction or conservation.

The cultural integration approach underscores the relationships between politics and other facets of culture. Harmony and stability within nations often depend on relative cultural homogeneity of the population. This is so critical that leaders sometimes seek to impose homogeneity by force. The integration of politics and culture is also revealed in the economy. A map of agricultural contrasts in the border zone between the United States and Canada illustrates this point.

Finally, politics leaves an imprint on the cultural landscape. The imprint is often overlooked, as in the patterns of survey systems or highways. Occasionally the imprint is brutal, as in the Berlin Wall. Frequently it is overt, as in the billboards and banners of totalitarian regimes.

Suggested Readings

Anouar Abdel-Malek. "Geopolitics and National Movements: An Essay on the Dialectics of Imperialism," in Richard Peet (ed.), *Radical Geography: Alternative Viewpoints on Contemporary Social Issues.* Chicago: Maaroufa Press, 1977.

John A. Agnew. *Place and Politics: The Geographical Mediation of State and Society.* Winchester, Mass.: Allen & Unwin, 1987.

J. Clark Archer and Peter J. Taylor. *Section and Party: A Political Geography of American Presidential Elections, from Andrew Jackson to Ronald Reagan.* New York: Wiley, 1981.

Michael Bateman and Raymond Riley (eds). *The Geography of Defense.* New York: Barnes & Noble, 1987.

Mark Blacksell. *Post-War Europe: A Political Geography.* Boulder, Colo.: Westview Press, 1977.

Harm J. de Blij and Martin Ira Glassner. *Systematic Political Geography,* 3rd ed. Toronto: Wiley, 1980.

Frederick W. Boal and J. Neville H. Douglas (eds.). *Integration and Division: Geographical Perspectives on the Northern Ireland Problem.* London and Orlando, Fla.: Academic Press, 1982.

Stanley D. Brunn. "A World of Peace and Military Landscapes," *Journal of Geography,* 86 (1987), 253–262.

Alan D. Burnett and Peter J. Taylor (eds.). *Political Studies from Spatial Perspectives.* New York: Wiley, 1981.

R. J. Harrison Church. "West African Boundaries and the Cultural Landscape," *Regio Basiliensis,* 22 (1981), 258–267.

P. J. Cooke. "Recent Theories of Political Regionalism," *International Journal of Urban and Regional Research,* 8 (1984), 549–572.

Vaughan Cornish. *The Great Capitals: An Historical Geography.* London: Methuen, 1923.

Kevin R. Cox. *Location and Public Problems: A Political Geography of the Contemporary World.* Chicago: Maaroufa Press, 1979.

Alastair Drysdale and Gerald H. Blake. *The Middle East and North Africa: A Political Geography.* New York: Oxford University Press, 1985.

Ernest S. Easterly, III. "Global Patterns of Legal Systems," *Geographical Review,* 67 (1977), 209–220.

John R. Gold. "Territoriality and Human Spatial Behaviour," *Progress in Human Geography,* 6 (1982), 44–67.

Jean Gottmann. "The Basic Problem of Political Geography: The Organization of Space and the Search for Stability," *Tijdschrift voor Economische en Sociale Geografie,* 73 (1982), 340–349.

Jean Gottmann (ed.). *Center and Periphery: Spatial Variation in Politics.* Beverly Hills, Calif.: Sage, 1980.

Jean Gottmann. *The Significance of Territory.* Charlottesville: University of Virginia Press, 1973.

George W. Hoffman. "Regional Policies and Regional Consciousness in Europe's Multinational Societies" *Geoforum,* 8 (1977), 121–129.

Rex Honey. "Political Geography: A Behavioral Framework," *Geographical Perspectives,* 37 (Spring 1976), 3–11.

John W. House. *Frontier on the Rio Grande: A Political Geography of Development and Social Deprivation.* New York: Oxford University Press, 1982.

Ronald J. Johnston. "The Changing Geography of Voting in the United States, 1946–1980," *Transactions of the Institute of British Geographers,* 7 (1982), 187–204.

Ronald J. Johnston and Peter J. Taylor. "Political Geography: A Politics of Places Within Places," *Parliamentary Affairs,* 39 (1986), 135–149.

Nurit Kliot and Stanley Waterman (eds.). *Pluralism and Political Geography: People, Territory and the State.* New York: St. Martin's Press, 1983.

David B. Knight. "Impress of Authority and Ideology on Landscape: A Review of Some Unanswered Questions," *Tijdschrift voor Economische en Sociale Geografie,* 63 (1971), 383–387.

David Ley and Roman Cybriwsky. "Urban Graffiti as Territorial Markers," *Annals of the Association of American Geographers,* 64 (1974), 491–505.

William S. Logan. "The Changing Landscape Significance of the Victoria-South Australia Boundary," *Annals of the Association of American Geographers,* 58 (1968), 128–154.

Robert W. McColl. "The Insurgent State: Territorial Base of Revolution," *Annals of the Association of American Geographers,* 59 (1969), 613–631.

Halford J. Mackinder. "The Geographical Pivot of History," *Geographical Journal,* 23 (1904), 421–437.

Richard L. Morrill. *Political Redistricting and Geographic Theory.* Washington, D.C.: Association of American Geographers, Resource Publications, 1981.

Richard Muir and Ronan Paddison. *Politics, Geography, and Behaviour.* London and New York: Methuen, 1981.

John O'Loughlin. "The Identification and Evaluation of Racial Gerrymandering," *Annals of the Association of American Geographers,* 72 (1982), 165–184.

John O'Loughlin. "Political Geography," *Progress in Human Geography,* 10 (1986), 69–83; 11 (1987), 247–263; 12 (1988), 121–137.

Patrick O'Sullivan. *Geopolitics.* New York: St. Martin's Press, 1986.

Patrick O'Sullivan and Jesse W. Miller, Jr. *The Geography of Warfare.* New York: St. Martin's Press, 1983.

Michael Pacione (ed.). *Progress in Political Geography.* London: Croom Helm, 1985.

Geoffrey Parker. *Western Geopolitical Thought in the Twentieth Century.* New York: St. Martin's Press, 1985.

David Pepper and Alan Jenkins (eds.). *The Geography of Peace and War.* New York: Basil Blackwell, 1985.

Political Geography Quarterly. The only English-language journal devoted exclusively to political geography. Published in the United Kingdom by Butterworth Scientific Ltd., Sevenoaks, Kent. Volume I appeared in 1982.

J. Douglas Porteous. "Home: The Territorial Core," *Geographical Review,* 66 (1976), 383–390.

J. R. V. Prescott. *Political Frontiers and Boundaries.* Winchester, Mass.: Allen & Unwin, 1987.

Robert D. Sack. *Human Territoriality: Its Theory and History.* Cambridge: Cambridge University Press (Studies in Historical Geography, No 7), 1986.

A.-L. Sanguin. "The Quebec Question and the Political Geography of Canada," *GeoJournal,* 8 (1984), 99–107.

J. R. Short. "Political Geography," *Progress in Human Geography,* 7 (1983), 122–125.

Nicholas J. Spykman. *The Geography of the Peace.* New York: Harcourt Brace, 1944.

Glen V. Stephenson. "Cultural Regionalism and the Unitary State Idea in Belgium," *Geographical Review,* 62 (1972), 501–523.

Studies in Comparative International Development. This international journal devoted all four numbers of Volume 22 (1987–1988) and part of Volume 23 (1988–1989) to "Geography and National & International Issues."

Imre Sutton. "Sovereign States and the Changing Definition of the Indian Reservation," *Geographical Review,* 66 (1976), 281–295.

Will D. Swearingen. "Geopolitical Origins of the Iran-Iraq War," *Geographical Review,* 78 (1988), 405–416.

Peter J. Taylor. *Political Geography: World Economy, Nation-State and Locality.* London: Longman Scientific & Technical Publication, 1986.

Peter J. Taylor and John House (eds.). *Political Geography: Recent Advances and Future Directions.* London: Croom Helm, 1984.

Peter J. Taylor and R. J. Johnston. *Geography of Elections.* London: Croom Helm, 1979.

Derwent Whittlesey. "The Impress of Effective Central Authority Upon the Landscape," *Annals of the Association of American Geographers,* 25 (1935), 85–97.

Colin H. Williams. "Ethnic Separatism in Western Europe," *Tijdschrift voor Economische en Sociale Geografie,* 71 (1980), 142–158.

Colin H. Williams. "Ideology and the Interpretation of Minority Cultures," *Political Geography Quarterly,* 3 (1984), 105–125.

Colin H. Williams and Anthony D. Smith. "The National Construction of Social Space," *Progress in Human Geography,* 7 (1983), 502–518.

Wilbur Zelinsky. "The Changing Face of Nationalism in the American Landscape," *Canadian Geographer,* 30 (1986), 171–175.

Wilbur Zelinsky. "O Say, Can You See? Nationalistic Emblems in the Landscape," *Winterthur Portfolio,* 19 (1984), 277–286.

The source for Figure 4.20 is "Experimental Satellite Image Map of Swaziland," Provisional Edition, published by the Regional Centre for Services in Surveying and Mapping, Nairobi, Kenya, and the United Kingdom Directorate of Overseas Surveys, Tolworth, Surrey, for the Surveyor General, Ministry of Works, Power and Communications, Mbabane, Swaziland, 1981.

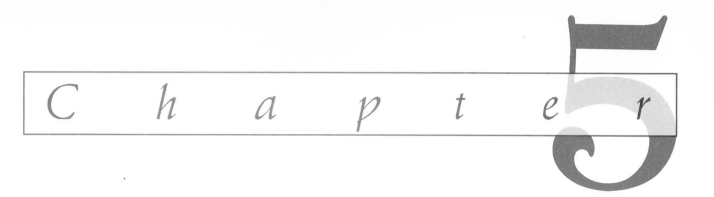

The Babel of Languages

LINGUISTIC CULTURE REGIONS

   Language Families
   English Dialects in the United States

LINGUISTIC DIFFUSION

   Indo-European Diffusion
   Malayo-Polynesian Diffusion
   Searching for the Primordial Tongue
   Diffusion and Linguistic Decline

LINGUISTIC ECOLOGY

   The Environment and Vocabulary
   The Environment: Provider of Refuge
   The Environment: Guide for Migration

LINGUISTIC CULTURAL INTEGRATION

   Empire Building and the Spread of
   Language

Language and Conquest
Language and Nationalism
Processes of Decline
Language and Religion
Economics and Language
The French-Canadians: An Illustration
   of Linguistic Cultural Integration

LINGUISTIC LANDSCAPES

   Toponyms
   Generic Toponyms of the United States
   Toponyms and Cultures of the Past
   Toponyms and Environmental
      Modification

CONCLUSION

Every time you go to a dance, ride a bus, or listen to a radio talk show, you probably automatically make some pretty good guesses about the origins of the people you hear. You base many of these guesses on how they talk. To do so, you unconsciously take a number of factors into account: accent, pronunciation, stress, inflection, and word choice. We can often distinguish out-of-towner from local resident, black from white, suburbanite from city dweller, immigrant from native-born, and one neighborhood from another.

   For geographers, language is particularly important, because speech is so basic an aspect of culture and of creating a sense of place. It is a major means by which cultural elements pass from one generation to the next. Thus language is one of the principal means of preserving a way of life, since it operates as a culturally agreed-upon system of symbolic communication. Nearly every cultural group and subgroup has its own distinctive speech, if not a separate language, then at least a **dialect**—a local or regional variant that is distinct, yet mutually intelligible to speakers of other dialects of the same language. For this reason, geographers often use language and dialect to identify different cultures. Because language is essential to communication, it influences the sort of political, social, and economic institutions we create. As a result, economic and religious systems frequently follow patterns of language distribution, and political borders quite often parallel language boundaries. Environmental features such as mountains, plains, and bodies of water can also affect the distribution of languages, and language can color perception of the physical environment. In short, human linguistic patterns form a highly varied mosaic whose design both affects and is affected by many elements of culture and the physical environment.

■ LINGUISTIC CULTURE REGIONS

Many different kinds of culture regions can be devised on the basis of speech. They can range from those that reflect the distribution of individual words to those that reveal the broad range of differences in vocabulary, grammar, and pronunciation among separate dialects and languages.

The borders of word usage or pronunciation are called **isoglosses.** No two words, phrases, or pronunciations have exactly the same spatial distribution; that is, no two isoglosses are duplicates. Figure 5.1 provides an

FIGURE 5.1
Many words have been adopted from Spanish into English in the western and southern parts of Texas. Note that the isogloss for each "loanword" is slightly different from every other one but that the result is a typical "bundle" of isoglosses, dividing Texas into two dialect regions. (Source: E. B. Atwood, *The Regional Vocabulary of Texas,* Austin: University of Texas Press, 1962.)

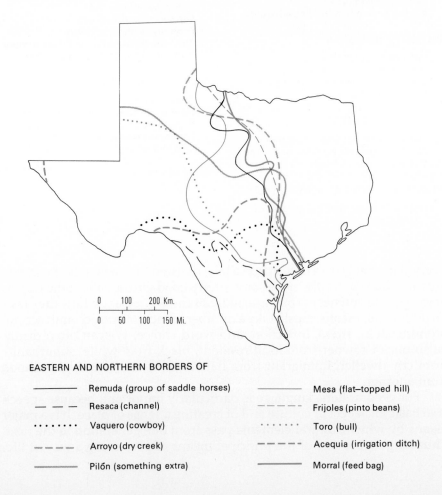

```
0     100    200 Km.
0   50    100   150 Mi.
```

EASTERN AND NORTHERN BORDERS OF

―――――― Remuda (group of saddle horses)   ―――――― Mesa (flat–topped hill)

― ― ― Resaca (channel)   ― ― ― ― Frijoles (pinto beans)

· · · · · · · Vaquero (cowboy)   · · · · · · Toro (bull)

― · ― · ― Arroyo (dry creek)   ― · · ― · · Acequia (irrigation ditch)

―――――― Pilón (something extra)   ―――――― Morral (feed bag)

example of how isoglosses crisscross one another. Geographers commonly devise multitrait linguistic culture regions, seeking borders where numerous features of speech change. Isoglosses often cluster together, and these "bundles" serve as the most satisfactory dividing lines among dialects and among languages. Using this approach, the cultural geographer can prepare maps of the German-language culture region, the Southern dialect region of American English, and so on.

Few, if any, borders between languages are sharp, in keeping with the general character of cultural borders. Rather than a dividing line, the geographer usually encounters a core/periphery pattern, in which dominance of the language diminishes away from the center of the region, through an outlying zone of bilingualism, or spatial mixing of speakers of two different languages. Linguistic "islands," separated from the main body of a language, often further complicate the drawing of borders (Figure 5.2). Similarly, dialect terms often overlap considerably, making it difficult to draw isoglosses. Indeed, linguistic geographers often disagree about how many dialects are present in an area and where isoglosses should be drawn. One scholar surveys the speech of the American South and detects two major dialects; another equally qualified linguist surveys the same vocabulary evidence in the same area and concludes that only one dialect, containing four subdialects, exists. Still another expert asks, in all seriousness, "Do dialect borders exist?" You should be aware, then,

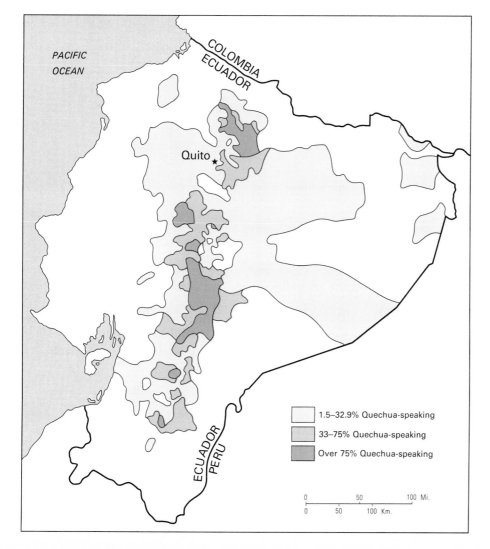

FIGURE 5.2
The formal culture region of Quechua, the main Indian language of Ecuador in South America, 1950. The core/periphery configuration typical of formal regions is evident. Urban populations are excluded. Does the distribution of Quechua, mapped in this manner, suggest whether the language is advancing or retreating? (Source: Gregory Knapp, *Geografía Quichua de la Sierra del Ecuador,* Quito: Ediciones Abya Yala, 1987, pp. 53–57).

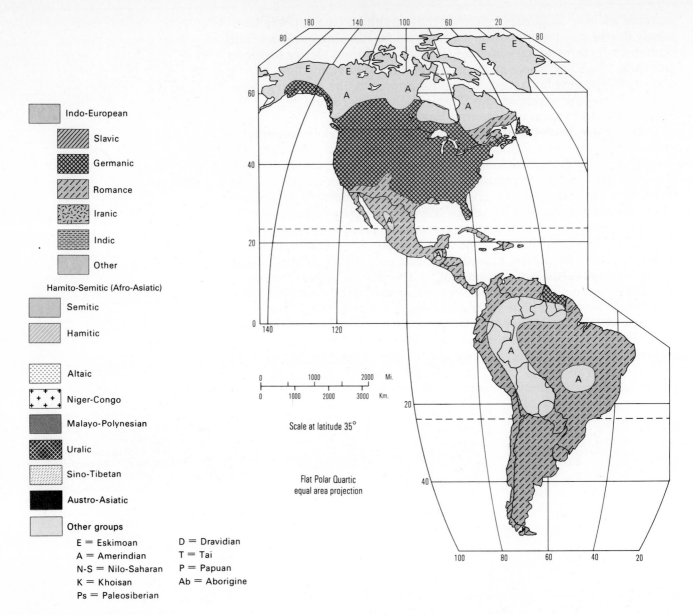

Indo-European
- Slavic
- Germanic
- Romance
- Iranic
- Indic
- Other

Hamito-Semitic (Afro-Asiatic)
- Semitic
- Hamitic

- Altaic
- Niger-Congo
- Malayo-Polynesian
- Uralic
- Sino-Tibetan
- Austro-Asiatic
- Other groups

E = Eskimoan   D = Dravidian
A = Amerindian   T = Tai
N-S = Nilo-Saharan P = Papuan
K = Khoisan   Ab = Aborigine
Ps = Paleosiberian

0   1000   2000   Mi.
0 1000 2000 3000 Km.

Scale at latitude 35°

Flat Polar Quartic
equal area projection

FIGURE 5.3
This map shows the major linguistic culture areas of the world. Although there are hundreds of languages and thousands of dialects in the world, they can be grouped into a few linguistic families. Note particularly the broad extent of the Indo-European language family. English-speaking Americans share Indo-European language roots with a wide variety of other cultural groups.

that linguistic borders shown on maps, like most cultural boundaries, are often arbitrarily drawn, oversimplified, and potentially misleading. They are, at best, generalizations.

In spite of these shortcomings, the linguistic culture region is a convenient and necessary device to facilitate the spatial study of language. One of the most useful types of culture region depicts **language families.**

Language Families

Certainly, the mosaic of languages across the globe reflects the long, turbulent history of humankind. Look at Figure 5.3, showing world language distribution. As you can see, the linguistic pattern looks like a crazy quilt. In reality, of course, the distribution is far more complex than this, encompassing literally thousands of dialects and languages, each spoken in its own distinct area. Some order can be brought to this seeming chaos only if we recognize that most individual languages belong to families,

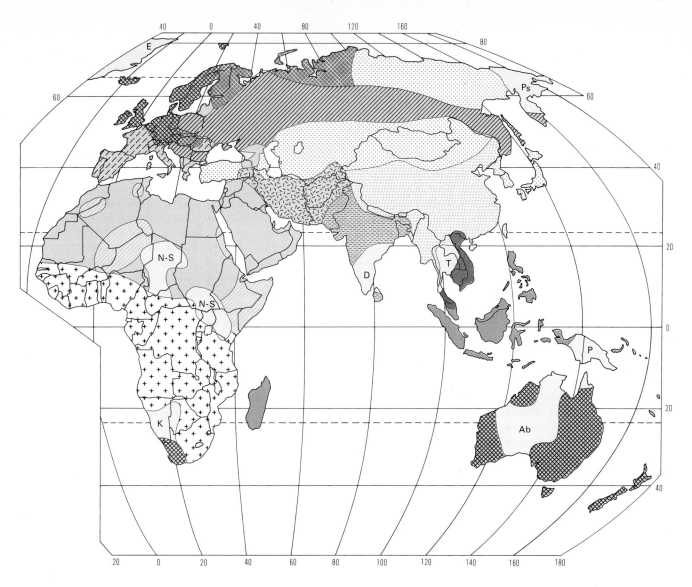

each consisting of related tongues derived from a common ancestral speech.

The Indo-European Language Family.   The largest and most widespread language family is the *Indo-European*, which is dominant in Europe, the Soviet Union, North and South America, Australia, and parts of southwestern Asia and India. Subgroups such as Romance (Italic), Slavic, Germanic, Indic, Celtic, and Iranic are part of the Indo-European family, and they in turn are subdivided into individual languages. For example, English is a Germanic Indo-European language. Eight Indo-European tongues are among the top 12 languages in the world, ranked by number of speakers (Table 5.1).

If we compare the vocabularies of various Indo-European tongues, we can readily see the kinship of these languages. For example, the English word *mother* is similar to the Polish *matka*, the Greek *meter*, the Spanish *madre*, the Armenian *mair*, the Avestan (spoken in Iran) *matar*, and the

TABLE 5.1
The Leading Languages (Those with over 100 Million Total Speakers)

Language	Family	Millions of Speakers	Main Areas Where Spoken
Chinese (Mandarin)	Sino-Tibetan	806	China, Taiwan, Singapore
English	Indo-European	426	British Isles, Anglo-America, Australia, New Zealand, South Africa, Philippines, former British colonies in tropical Asia and Africa
Hindi	Indo-European	313	northern India
Spanish	Indo-European	308	Spain, Latin America, southwestern United States
Russian	Indo-European	210	Soviet Union
Arabic	Hamito-Semitic	182	Middle East, North Africa
Bengali	Indo-European	175	Bangladesh, eastern India
Portuguese	Indo-European	166	Portugal, Brazil, southern Africa
Indonesian	Malayo-Polynesian	132	Indonesia
Japanese	Altaic	123	Japan
German	Indo-European	118	Germany, Austria, Switzerland, Luxembourg, eastern France, northern Italy
French	Indo-European	115	France, Belgium, Switzerland, Québec, New Brunswick, and as a language of the educated elite (and official language) in most former French and Belgian colonies

Sinhalese (spoken in Sri Lanka) *mava*. Such similarities in vocabulary suggest that these languages had a common ancestral tongue.

The Hamito-Semitic Family.   A second language family, unrelated to the Indo-European, is the *Hamito-Semitic*, also called Afro-Asiatic, consisting of two major subdivisions, Hamitic and Semitic. These originated in southwestern Asia before recorded time, and the ancient Babylonians, Assyrians, Phoenicians, and Hebrews were Semites. The Semitic languages cover the area from the Arabian peninsula and the Tigris-Euphrates river valley in the Fertile Crescent of Iraq westward through Syria and North Africa to the Atlantic Ocean. Despite the considerable size of this domain, there are fewer speakers of the Semitic languages than of the other major language families, mainly because most of the areas Semites inhabit are sparsely populated deserts.

Arabic is by far the most widespread Semitic language and has the greatest number of speakers, about 182 million. Although many different dialects of Arabic are spoken, the written form is standard.

Hebrew also is a Semitic tongue, closely related to Arabic. For many centuries, Hebrew was a "dead" language, used only in religious ceremonies by millions of Jews scattered around the world. With the creation of the state of Israel in 1947, a common language was needed to unite the immigrant Jews, who spoke the languages of many different countries. Hebrew was revived and made the official national language of what otherwise would have been a **polyglot,** or multilanguage, state. However, Hebrew had lain dormant for 2000 years. It had to be modernized. To make the transition to the twentieth century, words had to be coined for *telephone, airplane, rifle,* and the like.

Migrants from southwestern Arabia brought Semitic speech to Ethiopia about 3000 years ago. There, in the isolation of the East African mountain highlands, it gradually evolved into Amharic, a third major Semitic tongue, today claiming 12 million speakers.

Smaller numbers of linguistically related people who speak Hamitic languages share North and East Africa with the Semites. These tongues originated in Asia but today are spoken almost exclusively in Africa, by the Berbers of Morocco and Algeria, the Tuaregs of the Sahara, and the Cushites of East Africa. The Hamitic speech area was formerly much larger than it is now. It once covered the lands of the ancient Egyptians, but it was greatly reduced and fragmented by the expansion of Arabic over a thousand years ago.

Niger-Congo Languages. Most of Africa south of the Sahara Desert is dominated by the *Niger-Congo* language family, spoken by about 190 million people. The greater part of the Niger-Congo culture region belongs to the Bantu subgroup, which includes Swahili, the **lingua franca** of East Africa. Both Niger-Congo and its Bantu constituent are highly fragmented into a great many different languages and dialects.

Altaic Family. Flanking the Slavic Indo-Europeans on north and south in Asia are the speakers of *Altaic* languages, including Turkic, Mongolic, and several other subgroups. Most linguistic geographers now also list Korean and Japanese among the Altaic family. In this new classification, Japanese, with 123 million speakers, ranks as the largest member language. The Altaic homeland lies largely in the inhospitable deserts, tundras, and coniferous forests of northern and central Asia.

Uralic Family. Also occupying tundra and grassland areas adjacent to the Slavs are the *Uralic* languages. Finnish and Hungarian are the two most important Uralic tongues, and both enjoy the status of official legal languages in their respective countries.

Sino-Tibetan Family. Dominated numerically and spatially by Chinese, *Sino-Tibetan* is one of the major language families of the world. The Sino-Tibetan speech area extends throughout most of China and Southeast Asia. Chinese itself is spoken in a variety of dialects by perhaps 800 million people in China and in scattered locales from Singapore to San Francisco. Mandarin (or Han) Chinese, originally spoken only in northeastern China, has now been adopted as the official form of speech for the People's

HANS KURATH
1891–

Though a native of Austria, Professor Kurath is best known for his studies of the linguistic geography of the eastern United States, some of which are listed among the readings at the end of this chapter. He immigrated to America in 1907 and was educated at the University of Texas and the University of Chicago. Most of his academic career was spent at Brown University, where he served as professor of Germanics and linguistics, and at the University of Michigan, where he was professor of English until retiring in 1961. Cultural geographers have profited greatly from Kurath's seminal works on American English dialects, works rich in maps of vocabulary and pronunciation usages. His research provided the original basis for the map, Figure 5.4. Much honored and widely respected, Dr. Kurath holds honorary doctorates from the universities of Chicago and Wisconsin and has, for a quarter-century, been professor emeritus at Michigan.

Republic of China. Other Sino-Tibetan languages include Burmese and Tibetan, which border the Chinese speech area on the south and west.

Austro-Asiatic Languages.   In Southeast Asia, the Vietnamese, Cambodians, and lesser tribal peoples of Malaya and parts of India, totaling 70 million persons, constitute the *Austro-Asiatic* family. These seem to occupy a remnant peripheral domain, and have been encroached upon by Sino-Tibetan, Indo-European, and Tai.

Malayo-Polynesian Languages.   One of the most remarkable language families in terms of distribution is the *Malayo-Polynesian*, also referred to as Austronesian. Representatives of this group live mainly on tropical islands stretching from Madagascar, off the east coast of Africa, through Indonesia and the Pacific Islands, to Hawaii and Easter Island. This east-west, or longitudinal, span is more than half the distance around the world. The language area also covers a north-south, or latitudinal, range from Hawaii and Taiwan in the north to New Zealand in the south. By far the largest single language in this family is Indonesian, with over 130 million speakers (Table 5.1).

Other Language Families and Groups.   Occupying refuge areas after retreat before rival groups are remnant language families such as *Khoisan,* found in the Kalahari desert of southwestern Africa and characterized by distinctive clicking sounds; *Dravidian,* spoken by the numerous darker-skinned peoples of southern India and adjacent northern Sri Lanka; *Tai;* Australian *Aborigine; Papuan; Nilo-Saharan; Paleosiberian; Eskimoan;* and a variety of *Amerindian* families.

English Dialects in the United States

Most of the people in the United States speak English, yet American English is hardly uniform from region to region. At least three major dialects, corresponding to the three major culture regions, had developed in the eastern United States by the time of the American Revolution: the Northern, Midland, and Southern dialects (compare Figures 5.4 and 1.6) (see biographical sketch of Hans Kurath). As the three subcultures expanded westward, their dialects spread and fragmented. Nevertheless,

TABLE 5.2
Three Major Dialects of American English, as Indicated by Vocabulary Samples

Meaning	Northern Dialect	Midland Dialect	Southern Dialect
Food eaten between meals	bite	piece	snack
Dragonfly	darning needle	snake feeder, snake doctor	mosquito hawk, skeeter hawk
Fence built of stone	stone wall	stone fence	rock fence
Cottage cheese	Dutch cheese, pot cheese	smear cheese	curds, clabber cheese
Beans eaten in the pod	string beans	green beans	snap beans
Worm in ground	angleworm	fish worm, redworm	earthworm

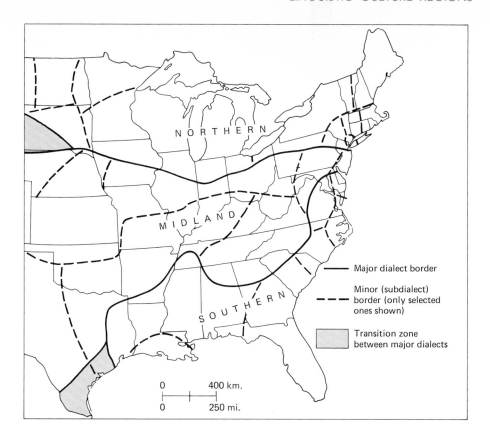

FIGURE 5.4
One classification of dialects of American English in the eastern United States. These correspond to three culture regions described in Chapter 1: New England, Middle Atlantic, and Lower South. Compare this map to Figure 1.6. (After Kurath; Allen; Wood; and E. B. Atwood, *The Regional Vocabulary of Texas*, Austin: University of Texas Press, 1962.)

the dialects retained much of their basic character even beyond the Mississippi River, although mixing occurred. The three dialects have distinctive vocabularies and pronunciations, as Table 5.2 suggests. Even so, it is often difficult to draw the dialect boundaries, even east of the Mississippi (see Figure 5.5).

Today, many of the regional words are becoming old-fashioned, and American English is becoming standardized into a midwestern form of the Midland dialect. Even so, new words that display regional variations are still being coined. For instance, the following terms are all used to describe a controlled-access divided highway: *freeway, turnpike, parkway, thruway, expressway,* and *interstate.* Of these, *parkway* and *turnpike* seem to be mainly northeastern and midwestern words, whereas *freeway* is the California word. In England, *motorway* is the preferred term.

Many members of America's black minority speak their own distinctive form of English. Black English, once dismissed by linguists as no more than inferior substandard English, is in reality a blend of the Southern dialect of English and a variety of African languages. This subdialect, which seems to have developed from the early plantation **pidgin** English (see the section on "Economics and Language" later in this chapter) of the slaves, is spoken by perhaps 80 percent of America's black population. The structures of Black English, with their African heritage, can be heard in the speech of black ghetto dwellers who have yet to make their compromises with the mainstream culture in America. The use of undifferentiated pronouns ("Me help you?"); the lack of pronoun differentiation between genders ("He a nice little girl"); the "he"/"she" pronoun possessive ("Ray sister she got a new doll baby"); "been" in special sentence structures ("I been wash the car"); and many other features of Black English separate it from standard speech. There are numerous local variants of Black English.

FIGURE 5.5
Some Midland and Southern words in the South. Each dot represents one person interviewed who gave the response indicated. If you were drawing the isoglosses for these words, where exactly would you place them? If these two maps were your only evidence, where would you draw the Midland-Southern dialect border? These are common problems for the linguistic geographer, and they illustrate how artificial dialect maps are. (Sources: Wood, pp. 325, 337–339; Kurath, *Word Geography;* Allen; E. Bagby Atwood, *The Regional Vocabulary of Texas,* Austin: University of Texas Press, 1962, pp. 196, 199.)

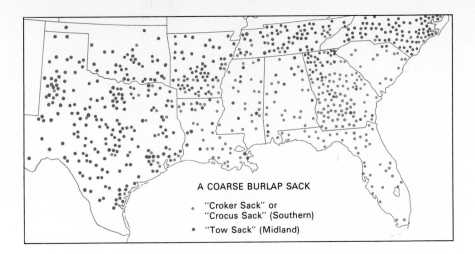

A COARSE BURLAP SACK

• "Croker Sack" or "Crocus Sack" (Southern)

• "Tow Sack" (Midland)

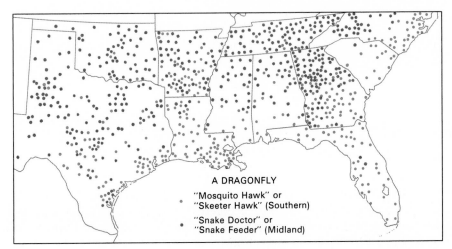

A DRAGONFLY

"Mosquito Hawk" or "Skeeter Hawk" (Southern)

"Snake Doctor" or "Snake Feeder" (Midland)

In the American school system, such dialect forms are usually considered mistakes—evidence of the verbal inability or impoverishment of blacks—rather than as part of the proper grammar of a separate linguistic group. In the same way, linguists have often been unwilling to admit the contributions that blacks and other minorities have made to American speech. Black English seems to have been a repressed but innovative linguistic force that probably produced some of the evident differences between Southern and Northern white dialects.

■ LINGUISTIC DIFFUSION

All types of cultural diffusion help interpret the linguistic map. Relocation diffusion has been extremely important, and languages spread as groups, in whole or part, migrated from one area to another. Some individual tongues or entire language families are no longer spoken in the regions where they originated, and in certain other cases the linguistic hearth is peripheral to the present distribution (compare Figures 5.3 and 5.6).

Indo-European Diffusion

Diffusion is certainly evident in the distribution of the far-flung Indo-European language family. Using words as clues, geographers and lin-

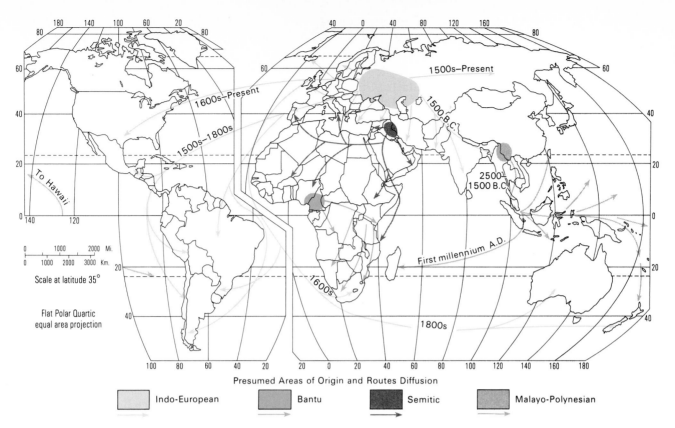

FIGURE 5.6
Linguistic hearths and diffusions are shown here. Indo-European, Bantu, Semitic, and Malayo-Polynesian languages spread from relatively small hearth areas to occupy expansive linguistic domains. Until about A.D. 1500, the Malayo-Polynesian family was the most widespread linguistic group, but Indo-European tongues have explosively expanded across the world since that time. What do the different patterns and routes of diffusion tell you about the transportation technologies of the four language groups?

guists have concluded that the earliest speakers of the original Indo-European language probably lived in interior Eurasia or eastern Europe 5000 or more years ago. Figure 5.6 shows how these speakers then spread west and south. As they lost contact with one another, different Indo-European groups gradually developed variant forms of the language. Today's widespread distribution of Indo-European languages is partly the result of political empire building and the resulting migrations. The Romance languages, which are derived from Latin, owe their broad distribution to the empires of the Romans, Spaniards, and Portuguese; English spread with the creation of the British Empire.

In such cases, relocation, expansion, and hierarchical diffusion were not mutually exclusive. Relocation diffusion often involved a relatively small number of speakers, a conquering elite who came to rule an alien people. The language of the conqueror, implanted by relocation diffusion, often gained wider acceptance through expansion diffusion. Typically, the conqueror's language spread hierarchically—adopted first by the more important and influential persons and by city folk. The diffusion of Latin with Roman conquests frequently occurred in this manner, as did Spanish in Latin America.

Occasionally such circumstances resulted in a linguistic blend. French was introduced into England by the Norman conquerors in 1066 and became the speech of the ruling class. In time, Norman French merged with the Anglo-Saxon speech of the conquered people to form the English language. Perhaps a third of all English words are of French origin.

Not infrequently, the process of linguistic diffusion was reversed, particularly when a conqueror or immigrant group lost its dominance over the native speakers. Swedish was implanted in coastal Finland by Swedish soldiers and settlers during a brief period of political greatness centuries ago. Now Swedish retreats steadily before Finnish there through the device of contagious expansion diffusion.

Malayo-Polynesian Diffusion

One of the most impressive examples of linguistic diffusion is revealed in the spatial evolution of the Malayo-Polynesian languages. From a presumed hearth 5000 years ago in the interior of Southeast Asia, completely outside the present Malayo-Polynesian culture region, speakers of this language family initially spread southward into the Malay Peninsula. Then, in a process lasting perhaps several millenia and requiring remarkable navigational skills, they migrated through the islands of Indonesia and sailed in tiny boats across uncharted, vast expanses of water to New Zealand, Easter Island, Hawaii, and Madagascar.

Perhaps most remarkable of all was the diffusionary achievement of the Polynesian people, who occupy the eastern part of the Malayo-Polynesian culture region. Polynesians occupy a triangular-shaped realm consisting of hundreds of Pacific islands, with New Zealand, Easter Island, and Hawaii at the three apexes (Figure 5.7). Most incredible of all was the Polynesians' watery leap of 2500 miles (4000 kilometers) from the South Pacific to Hawaii, a migration in outrigger canoes against prevailing winds and currents into a new hemisphere with different navigational stars. No humans had previously found the isolated Hawaiian Islands, and the Polynesian sailors had no way of knowing ahead of time that land existed in that quarter of the Pacific.

The relocation diffusion that produced the remarkable present distribution of the Polynesian people has long been the subject of controversy. How, when, and by what means could so relatively primitive a people have achieved the diffusion? What skills were required? Several decades ago, two cultural geographers, John Webb and Gerard Ward, in company with a computer scientist, attempted to answer these questions, thereby solving a problem of prehistoric diffusion. Their method, both unusual and rewarding, involved the development of a computer model, into which was built data on winds, ocean currents, vessel traits and capabilities, island visibility, day of departure, possible voyage duration, and the like. Both drift voyages, in which the boat simply floats with the winds and currents, and navigated voyages were considered. Over 100,000 voyage simulations were run through the computer.

The authors concluded, on the basis of these experiments, that the Polynesian triangle had been entered from the west, from the direction of the ancient Malayo-Polynesian hearth area, by way of western insular chains in a process of "island hopping," that is, migrating from one island to another visible in the distance. The core of eastern Polynesia was likely reached in navigated voyages, but once attained, drift voyages could easily explain much internal diffusion. A peripheral region, an "outer arc from Hawaii through Easter Island to New Zealand" was attainable only by means of "intentionally navigated" voyages, feats that must be ranked among the greatest human achievements of all time.

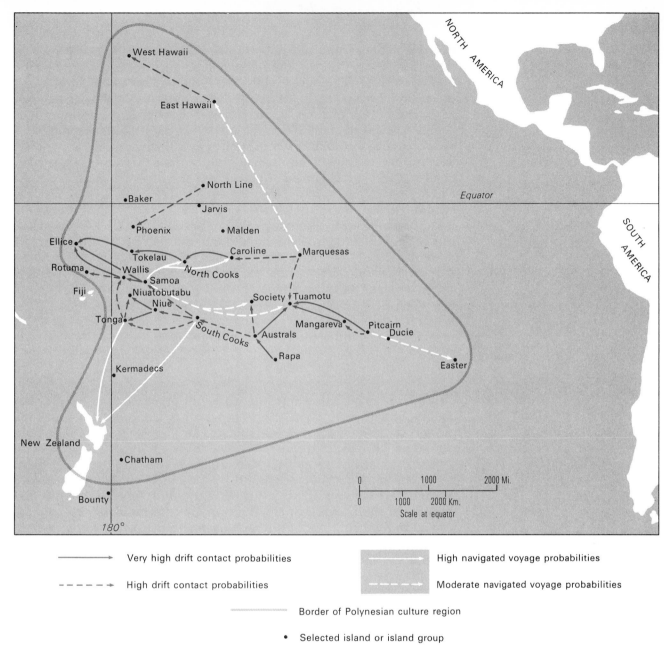

FIGURE 5.7
Probabilities of selected Polynesian drift and navigation voyages in the Pacific Ocean, based upon a computer model. According to this model, the outer arc of Polynesia, represented by Hawaii, Easter Island, and New Zealand, could have been reached only by navigated voyages. (Adapted from Levison, Ward, and Webb, *Settlement of Polynesia,* pp. 5, 33, 35, 43, 61.)

Note that in this application of the geographer's spatial skills, Webb and Ward employed the themes of culture region (present distribution of Polynesians) and cultural ecology (currents, winds, visibility of islands) to help describe and explain the workings of a third theme, cultural diffusion. Again, as suggested in Chapter 1, the five themes unite rather than divide cultural geography.

Searching for the Primordial Tongue

Using techniques that remain controversial, linguists are probing even more deeply into the origin and diffusion of languages, seeking still more elusive prehistoric tongues. Evidence is building that an ancestral speech called *Nostratic,* spoken in the Middle East 12,000 to 20,000 years ago, was ancestral to nine modern language families, including Indo-European, Uralic, Altaic, and Hamito-Semitic. A 500-word Nostratic dictionary has been compiled, containing words such as *kuni* ("wife," "woman"), which became, for example, the ancient Indo-European *gwen* (and modern English *queen*), the archaic Altaic *küni,* and the old Hamito-Semitic *KwVn.* Contemporary with Nostratic were several other ancient tongues, including *Dene-Caucasian,* which reputedly gave rise to Sino-Tibetan and to one form of early American Indian speech called Na-Dene. These pioneering scholars are now attempting to establish a kinship among Nostratic, Dene-Caucasian, and other ancient languages in order to find the primorial tongue, the single original speech from which they presume all modern languages are ultimately derived. They seek nothing less than the linguistic hearth area where complex speech first arose and from which it diffused. The study of language thus bears the potential to unravel the origin and spread of civilization.

Diffusion and Linguistic Decline

Cultural diffusion has as much to do with the retreat and death of languages as with their spread. The geographer Charles Withers listed a number of basic processes by which minority linguistic areas shrink and perish, two of which involve relocation diffusion. In his *clearance model,* decline is caused by a significant emigration of speakers to places outside the linguistic refuge area, leaving behind a much smaller population to perpetuate the tongue. Rural-to-urban migration, so prevalent in the modern era, is often involved, since **linguistic refuge areas** are generally located in the countryside. Withers's *changeover model,* by contrast, describes the reduced viability caused by a sizable immigration into the refuge area of an alien population. The intrusion by Anglo-Americans into the Spanish-speaking highlands of northern New Mexico provides an example. There, recreational and retirement development of various kinds has introduced an ever-larger English-speaking population. Sometimes such changeovers occur as a deliberate government action to dilute troublesome minorities, as in Soviet-ruled Latvia, where almost half of the population is now Russian-speaking.

▨ LINGUISTIC ECOLOGY

The theme of cultural ecology contributes greatly to the geographical study of languages. The following section, from the viewpoint of the possibilist, suggests some ways that the physical environment influences vocabulary and the distribution of language.

The Environment and Vocabulary

Humankind's relationship to the land has played a strong role in the development of linguistic differences (see box, "An English Speaker Walks in the Desert"). The environment even affects vocabulary. For

AN ENGLISH SPEAKER WALKS IN THE DESERT

Our individual languages evolve in particular physical environmental surroundings. When their speakers try to cope with a very different ecological setting, they find the vocabulary inadequate. Very revealing are the remarks of an American humanist, describing his walk across the desert of Sonora and Arizona:

I know no desert language.
I struggle with a tongue forged on another continent, with words spawned in green forests under gray, soggy skies.

Quote from Charles Bowden, "A Desert Tale: Cherishing the Hidden Waters," *Texas Humanist,* 6 (July–August 1984), 6.

example, the Spanish language, derived from Castile, a land rimmed by hills and high mountains, is especially rich in words describing rough terrain, allowing speakers of this tongue to distinguish even subtle differences in the shape and configuration of mountains, as Table 5.3 reveals. Similarly, Scottish Gaelic possesses a rich vocabulary to describe types of rough terrain — a common attribute of the Celtic languages, spoken by hill peoples. In the Romanian tongue, words relating to mountainous features tend to be keyed to use of that terrain for livestock herding. English, by

TABLE 5.3
Some Spanish Words Describing Mountains and Hills

Spanish Word	English Meaning
Candelas	literally "candles"; a collection of *peñas*
Ceja	steep-sided breaks or escarpment separating two plains of different elevation
Cejita	a low escarpment
Cerrillo or *cerrito*	a small *cerro;* a hill
Cerro	a single eminence, intermediate in size between English *hill* and *mountain*
Chiquito	literally "small," describing minor secondary fringing elevations at the base of and parallel to a *sierra* or *cordillera*
Cordillera	a mass of mountains, as distinguished from a single mountain summit
Cuchilla	literally "knife"; the comblike secondary crests that project at right angles from the sides of a *sierra*
Cumbre	the highest elevation or peak within a *sierra* or *cordillera;* a summit
Eminencia	a mountainous or hilly protuberance
Loma	a hill in the midst of a plain
Lomita	a small hill in the midst of a plain
Mesa	literally "table"; a flat-topped eminence
Montaña	equivalent to English *mountain*
Pelado	a barren, treeless mountain
Pelon	a bare conical eminence
Peloncilla	a small *pelon*
Peña	a needlelike eminence
Picacho	a peaked or pointed eminence
Pico	a summit point, English *peak*
Sandia	literally "watermelon"; an oblong, rounded eminence
Sierra	an elongated mountain mass with a serrated crest
Teta	a solitary, conical mountain in the shape of woman's breast
Tinaja	a solitary, hemispherical mountain shaped like an inverted bowl

Source: Robert T. Hill, "Descriptive Topographic Terms of Spanish America," *National Geographic Magazine,* 7 (1896), 292–297.

contrast, developed in coastal plains and marshes, and our language is as a consequence very poor in words describing mountainous terrain. The Eskimoan tongue has many different words for "seal," depending on whether the seal is old or young, on land or in the water. This reflects the seal's importance to the Eskimos' livelihood. Eskimoan also has many words for "snow," each describing a different type, and at least 12 unrelated terms for various winds. Similarly, in the rural South, from Virginia to Texas, there are many terms to describe and distinguish streams: *river, creek, branch, fork, prong, run, bayou,* and *slough.* This indicates that the area is a well-watered land with a dense network of streams.

Clearly, then, language serves adaptive strategy, at least in traditional societies. Vocabularies are highly developed for those features of the environment that involve livelihood. Without such detailed vocabularies, it would be difficult to communicate sophisticated information relevant to the adaptive strategy.

The Environment: Provider of Refuge

One of the most obvious environmental influences on language is the protection and isolation offered by inhospitable environments. Such areas often provide hard-pressed, outnumbered linguistic groups refuge from aggressive neighbors. Rugged hill and mountain areas, excessively cold or dry climates, impenetrable forests, islands, and extensive marshes and swamps can all offer refuge to minority language groups. For one thing, unpleasant environments rarely attract conquerors. Also, mountains tend to isolate the inhabitants of one valley from those in adjacent ones, retarding the contacts that might lead to linguistic diffusion.

Examples of these linguistic refuge areas are numerous. The rugged Caucasus Mountains and nearby ranges in the borderlands between the Soviet Union, Iran, and Turkey are populated by a large variety of peoples (see Figure 5.8). They form a living museum of declining and dying linguistic stocks (see Figure 5.9). Similarly, the Alps, Himalayas, and highlands of Mexico are linguistic **shatter belts**, and the American Indian tongue Quechua clings to a refuge in the Andes Mountains of South America. The Dhofar, a mountain tribe in the back country of Oman in Arabia, preserves Hamitic speech, a family otherwise vanished from Asia. Bitterly cold tundra climates of the far north have sheltered certain Uralic, Altaic, and Eskimoan peoples, and the dry desert has shielded Khoisan speakers from Bantu invaders. In short, hostile environments protect linguistic groups who are willing and able to endure the hardships they offer.

Even in the United States, we can find linguistic refuge areas. For instance, the Cajuns, living in the marshy bayou areas of Louisiana, have clung to a form of French despite a heavy dose of Americanization in recent decades. Unquestionably, their isolation has helped them hang on to their old linguistic identity, a holdover from the time when Louisiana was French territory. The Cajuns had earlier sought this refuge when expelled from Nova Scotia in Canada in the 1700s. Remnants of the African Gullah survive in the Sea Islands, off the coast of South Carolina and Georgia. Still, environmental isolation can no longer be the vital linguistic force it once was. It becomes harder and harder to discover spots on the earth so isolated that they remain little touched by outside influences. Today, inhospitable lands may offer linguistic refuge but it is no longer certain that they will in the future. Even an island situated in the middle of the vast Pacific Ocean can offer no reliable refuge in an age of airplanes. Similarly, marshes and forests will provide refuge only if they

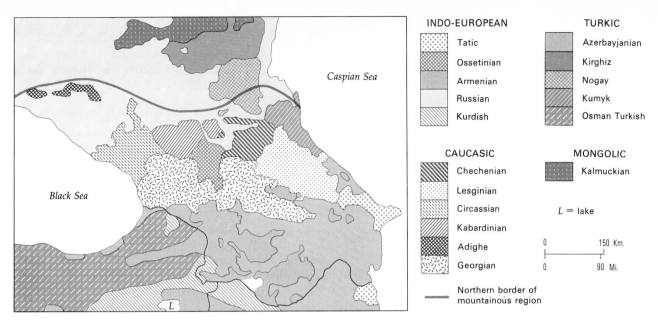

INDO-EUROPEAN
- Tatic
- Ossetinian
- Armenian
- Russian
- Kurdish

CAUCASIC
- Chechenian
- Lesginian
- Circassian
- Kabardinian
- Adighe
- Georgian

TURKIC
- Azerbayjanian
- Kirghiz
- Nogay
- Kumyk
- Osman Turkish

MONGOLIC
- Kalmuckian

L = lake

0 ————— 150 Km.
0 ————— 90 Mi.

——— Northern border of mountainous region

Caspian Sea

Black Sea

FIGURE 5.8
The environment is a linguistic refuge in the Caucasus Mountains. The rugged mountainous region between the Black and Caspian seas, on the border between the Soviet Union, Turkey, and Iran, is peopled by a great variety of linguistic groups, representing three major language families. Mountain areas are often linguistic shatter zones, because the rough terrain provides refuge and isolation. (After C. S. Coon, *The Races of Europe,* New York: Macmillan, 1954, with modifications.)

are not drained and cleared by farmers who want new farmlands. The reality of the world is no longer isolation but interaction.

The Environment: Guide for Migration

Migrating people often were attracted to new lands that seemed environmentally similar to their homelands, in order to be able to pursue the

FIGURE 5.9
The Georgians are one of the ethnic groups whose language and culture are sheltered by the Caucasus Mountains. Even the sweeping political changes within the Soviet Union have not caused the disappearance of this language. The Georgians occupy one of the 15 separate linguistic republics within the Soviet Union, the Georgian Soviet Socialist Republic.

adaptive strategies already known to them. Germanic Indo-Europeans sought familiar temperate zones in America, New Zealand, and Australia. Semitic peoples rarely spread outside arid and semiarid climates. Ancestors of the modern Hungarians, a Uralic linguistic stock, left the grasslands of inner Eurasia in the tenth century and found a new home in the grassy Alföld, one of the few prairie areas of Europe.

Environmental barriers and natural routeways have often guided linguistic groups in certain paths. The wide distribution of the Malayo-Polynesian language group cannot be fully understood without studying prevailing winds and water currents in the Pacific and Indian oceans. Migrating Indo-Europeans entering the Indian subcontinent through low mountain passes in the northwest were deflected by the Himalayas and the barren Deccan Plateau into the rich Ganges-Indus river plain. Even today in parts of India, according to Charles Bennett, the Indo-European/Dravidian "language boundary seems to approximate an ecological boundary" between the water-retentive black soils of the plains and the thinner, reddish Deccan soils.

Because such physical barriers as mountain ridges can retard groups from migrating from one area to another, they frequently serve as linguistic borders. In parts of the Alps, speakers of German and Italian live on opposite sides of a major ridge. The mountain rim along the northern edge of the Fertile Crescent in the Middle East forms the border between Semitic and Indo-European tongues. Linguistic borders that follow such physical features generally tend to be stable, and they often endure for thousands of years. Language borders that cross plains and major routes of communication are frequently unstable.

■ LINGUISTIC CULTURAL INTEGRATION

Language is intertwined with all aspects of culture. The theme of cultural integration permits us to probe some of these complex links between speech and other cultural phenomena. In particular, this section focuses on the links between language and politics, economics, and religion.

Empire Building and the Spread of Language

The expansion of European and American power across the globe in the last four centuries has affected the linguistic patterns of millions of people. The United Kingdom, France, the Netherlands, Belgium, Portugal, Spain, the United States, and Japan all controlled overseas empires. This empire building superimposed Indo-European tongues on the map of the tropics and subtropics. The areas most affected were Asia, Africa, and the Malayo-Polynesian island world. In South America as well, two alien tongues — Spanish and Portuguese — were imposed on most of an entire continent.

Even though the imperial nations have given up part or all of their colonial empires, the languages they transplanted overseas have survived. As a result, English still has a foothold in much of Africa, the Indian subcontinent, the Philippines, and certain areas of the Pacific islands. French persists in the former French and Belgian colonies, especially in north, west, and central Africa, Madagascar, and Polynesia. In some of these areas, English and French are still the languages of the educated political elite and enjoy a role as languages of government, commerce, and higher education. In fact, they often enjoy official legal status. The colonial tongues function in such settings as link languages, helping hold together states in which the native languages are multiple and divisive.

In South America, two expanding empires—Spain and Portugal—clashed in the fifteenth century. Their compromise had far-reaching linguistic consequences. In 1494, Spain and Portugal signed the Treaty of Tordesillas. Under this treaty, Spain received control over all colonial lands west of a certain meridian (mapped in Figure 5.10), and Portugal gained control over the lands east of the line. In this way, Brazil eventually became a Portuguese-speaking land, in contrast to most of the rest of South America, where Spanish prevailed.

Language and Conquest

Conquering armies have often carried their own languages with them. After Christian forces conquered the Moors in Iberia, Arabic disappeared from southern Spain and Portugal, though many Arabic loanwords survived to become part of modern Spanish and Portuguese. Conquests have often uprooted entire ethnic groups from ancestral homelands and forced them to settle elsewhere, carrying their languages with them. For example, 10 million German-speaking residents were evacuated and expelled from the eastern provinces of Germany during and after World War II. This area was then recolonized by Polish- and Russian-speaking settlers. As a result, some 50,000 square miles (130,000 square kilometers) of territory quickly changed from Germanic to Slavic speech.

Language can even more directly be a weapon of conquest. The imposition of a foreign language is a powerful way to break a people's self-esteem, national or cultural pride, and identity. One typical strategy of control is to forbid the use of native languages in the conquered country's educational system. Japan took this course in Korea after it annexed the peninsula in 1910; the United States did the same thing after its conquest of the Philippines in the late 1890s.

The linguistic history of the United States is a running tale of the suppression and destruction of non-English languages. One of the early tricks slavers learned was to mix captured blacks from different African language areas in the same ship. This practice cut down the ability of the slaves to communicate with one another and thereby lessened the possibility of coordinated slave revolts. The result seems to have been the early acceptance of Africanized English as the speech of American blacks. Almost up to the present day, American Indians have been subjected to linguistic assaults from the dominant culture (see box, "Conquering the Indian with Words"). Large numbers of Indian children have traditionally been taken from their families and placed in special boarding schools, often hundreds of miles from their homes. In these schools, run by the white-controlled Bureau of Indian Affairs, the Indian children have in the past been forbidden on pain of punishment to speak their own languages.

Language and Nationalism

Speech and nationality became increasingly synonymous after the early 1800s. As a result, political boundaries often coincide with linguistic borders, as Figure 5.11 shows. One of the principal tasks of many central governments in the past two centuries has been to produce and promote a standardized form of the nationally dominant language and award it a

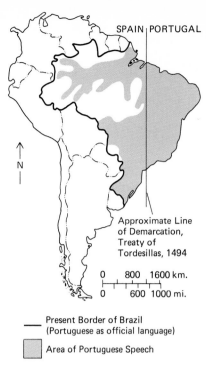

SPAIN | PORTUGAL

N

Approximate Line of Demarcation, Treaty of Tordesillas, 1494

0   800   1600 km.

0   600   1000 mi.

―――― Present Border of Brazil (Portuguese as official language)

▢ Area of Portuguese Speech

FIGURE 5.10
This map depicts the mesh of language and politics in South America. The Treaty of Tordesillas, cosigned by Spain and Portugal in 1494, established the political basis for the present linguistic pattern in South America. Portugal was awarded the eastern part of the continent, and Spain the west. The Portuguese language was implanted in Portuguese territory, and today it has diffused westward from its source.

CONQUERING THE INDIAN WITH WORDS

Wilfred Pelletier, an Odawa Indian, was born on Manitoulin Island, Ontario, Canada. He remembers what problems language caused him when, as a child, he first had to leave the Indian reservation and enter the English-speaking world that surrounded and dominated it:

Many of us as children . . . were not even permitted to speak our own language. Of course, we still tried to speak our own language, but we were punished for it. Four or five years ago they were still stripping the kids of their clothes up around Kenora and beating them for speaking their own language. It is probably still happening in many other institutions today. I was punished several times for speaking Indian not only on the school grounds but off the school grounds and on the street, and I lived across from the school. Almost in front of my own door my first language was forbidden me, and yet when I went into the house my parents spoke Indian.

Our language is so important to us as a people. Our language and our language structure related to our whole way of life. How beautiful that picture language is where they only tell you the beginning and the end, and you fill in everything, and they allow you to feel how you want to feel. Here we manipulate and twist things around and get

you to hate a guy. The Indian doesn't do that. He'll just say that some guy got into an accident, and he won't give you any details. From there on you just explore as far as you want to. You'll say: "What happened?" and he'll tell you a little more. "Did he go through the windshield?" "Yep." He only answers questions. All of the in-between you fill in for yourself as you see it. We are losing that feeling when we lose our language at school. We are taught English, not Indian, as our first language. And that changes our relationship with our parents. All of a sudden we begin saying to our parents "you're stupid." We have begun to equate literacy [in English] with learning, and this is the first step down. It is we who are going down and not our parents, and because of that separation we are going down lower and lower on the rung because it is we who are rejecting our parents; they are not rejecting us. The parents know that, but they are unable to do anything about it. And we take on the values, and the history of somebody else.

From Wilfred Pelletier, "Childhood in an Indian Village," in Satu Repo (ed.), *This Book Is About Schools*, pp. 23–24. Copyright © 1969 by Pantheon Books, a Division of Random House, Inc. With permission.

favored legal status. Italian, Greek, Norwegian, and many other national tongues underwent such a process, allowing political geography to achieve a powerful linguistic effect. Minority languages and nonstandard dialects declined as a result in these countries, increasing the correlation between political and linguistic borders.

An unofficial suppression of minority languages has occurred in the United States. As late as 1910, one out of every four Americans could speak some language other than English with the skill of a native. This was a result of the mass immigrations from Germany, Polish-speaking lands, Italy, Russia, China, and many other foreign areas. Much of this linguistic diversity has given way to English, partly because these imported languages lacked legal status. Only the Spanish-speaking population experienced any long-term success in preserving their speech in the United States. They achieved this, however, at the price of discrimination and lower socioeconomic status. Linguistically, the United States has been not a melting pot, but rather a destroyer.

The Soviet Union took, superficially at least, a different approach to its large number of diverse linguistic minorities. The boundaries of many political subdivisions within the country are based on language. The 15 largest linguistic groups occupy separate republics, equivalent to states within the United States. Ukrainian speakers live in the Ukrainian Soviet Socialist Republic, the speakers of Lettish in the Latvian Soviet Socialist Republic, and so on. Smaller linguistic groups, although not granted full republican status, are recognized politically in subdivisions that include Autonomous Soviet Socialist Republics, autonomous *oblasts*, and national *okrugs*. Although the Soviet system is designed to preserve linguistic distinctiveness, it seems to have masked a campaign of Russianization. All schools in the Soviet Union require years of instruction in Russian, and the best jobs generally require fluency in that language.

Processes of Decline

Once empires have been built, conquest achieved, and nationalism established, precisely how does the language of the victorious and dominant group advance? How are the vanquished linguistically assimilated? Various processes of cultural integration help explain the decline and extinction of minority languages, even in their refuges. Charles Withers proposed two such processes, which he labeled the *social morale* and the *economic development models.* The former is the process by which a linguistic minority, over time, loses pride in and voluntarily abandons its speech. An educational system using solely the majority language in a country produces bilingualism and fosters illiteracy in the minority tongue. Depriving the language of legal or churchly status conveys the same message—that the minority way of speech is inferior and its use socially degrading. Denying the language access to the printed and broadcast media can hasten the process, but even permitting such access generally does not reverse social demoralization. In the United States, the social morale model has been the principal one at work in destroying minority languages.

In the economic development model, new modes of production and adaptive strategies, particularly industrialization accompanied by urbanization, can break up the social structure needed to perpetuate a language.

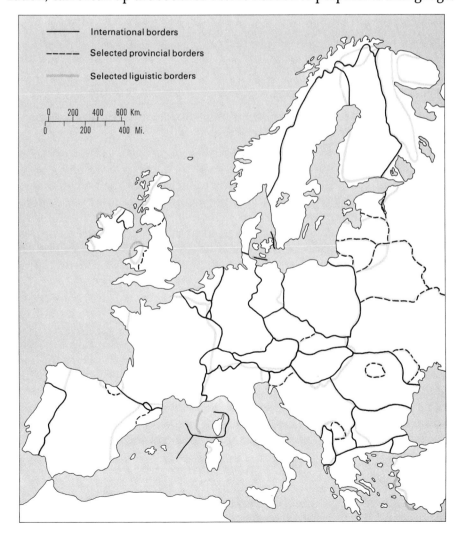

FIGURE 5.11
This map presents political borders and language borders in Europe. Note the close correspondence between the two types of borders today. Why are linguistic and political borders more similar in eastern Europe than in the western part?

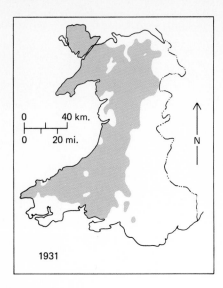
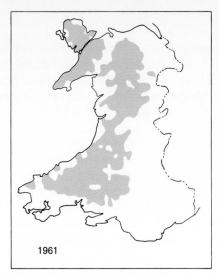
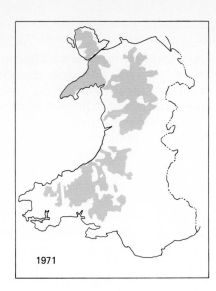

80% or more of the population
(over three years of age)
able to speak Welsh

FIGURE 5.12
Retreat of the Welsh language in the mid-twentieth century. Welsh is a Celtic Indo-European language spoken in the region of Wales. For centuries the Welsh have been dominated by English-speaking people in the United Kingdom. As a result the language is dying. Between 1931 and 1961 the number of Welsh speakers declined from 909,000 to 656,000, by 1971 to 542,000 and by 1981 to 508,000. Meanwhile, the district known as the *Bro Gymraeg,* where Welsh is spoken, shrank and began to fragment. English is penetrating along the coast and valleys, causing Welsh to retreat into the hilliest terrain. (Based on data in D. Trevor Williams, ''A Linguistic Map of Wales According to the 1931 Census, with Some Observations on Its Historical and Geographical Setting,'' *Geographical Journal,* 89 (1937), 146–151; Emrys Jones and Ieuan Griffiths, ''A Linguistic Map of Wales, 1961,'' *Geographical Journal,* 129 (1963), 192–196; and E. G. Bowen and H. Carter, ''The Distribution of the Welsh Language in 1971; An Analysis,'' *Geography,* 60 (1975), 1–5.)

The transition from subsistence farming to factory laboring, even if made within the linguistic region, can be quite destructive to minority tongues, particularly if the language of the work place is not that of the farm. Geographer Keith Buchanan has referred to the decline of the Celtic languages as a ''liquidation'' carried out by the ruling English in order to produce a loyal, obedient work force for the mines and factories (Figure 5.12).

Language and Religion

Language and religion are often closely associated, expanding and contracting together. Perhaps Arabic provides the best example of this cultural link. It spread from a core area on the Arabian peninsula with the Islamic faith. Had it not been for the evangelical fervor of the Muslims, Arabic would not have diffused so widely. The other Semitic languages also correspond to particular religious groups. Hebrew-speaking people are of the Jewish faith, and the Amharic speakers in Ethiopia are Coptic Christians. Indeed, we can attribute the preservation and revival of Hebrew to the tenacity of the Jewish faith.

Certain languages have even acquired a religious status. Latin survived mainly as the ceremonial language of the Roman Catholic Church and Vatican City. In non-Arabic Muslim lands, such as Iran, Arabic is still used in religious ceremony. Even in English, the seventeenth-century language of the King James Bible, replete with *thee, thou,* and various second-person singular verb forms, survives in spoken prayers.

Great religious books can also shape languages by providing them with a standard form. Luther's translation of the Bible led to the standardization of the German language, and the Koran is the model for written Arabic. The appearance of a hymnal and the Bible in the Welsh language greatly aided the survival of that Celtic tongue.

Economics and Language

Economic forces also help transform linguistic maps. Languages often migrate along transportation routes. Railroads and highways usually spread the languages of the cultural groups who build them, sometimes spelling doom for the speech of technologically less advanced peoples whose lands are suddenly opened to outside contacts. The Trans-Siberian Railroad, built around the turn of the century, spread the Russian language eastward to the Pacific Ocean, and the Alaska Highway through Canada carried English into Amerindian refuges. At present, the construction of highways into Brazil's remote Amazonian interior threatens the Indian languages of that region.

Livelihood also helps shape vocabulary. The Bedouin, Arabic nomads who rely upon the camel for many of life's necessities, have 160 different words for that domestic animal. In this manner they are able to be precise and concise when describing the age, color, bloodline, sex, and other characteristics of the camel.

In other cases, languages may develop or expand largely because of commercial needs. When groups from different linguistic backgrounds transact business, pidgin languages often result. These consist of relatively few words, some borrowed from each language group involved. The word *pidgin* derives from a Chinese pronunciation of the English word *business.* Because England was so widely involved in trade during its colonial era, many pidgin languages are simplified forms of English. In other commercial situations, one existing language is elevated to the status of **lingua franca,** or language of communication and commerce, over a wide area where it is not a mother tongue. The Bantu tongue Swahili enjoys this status in much of East Africa.

The French Canadians: An Illustration of Linguistic Cultural Integration

The theme of cultural integration in relation to language is well illustrated by the French-speaking Canadians. Concentrated in the province of Québec and numbering over 6 million, these *Canadiens* are descended from French colonists who arrived in the 1600s and 1700s. From 1760 to 1867, they lived under English rule; and since 1867, Québec has been part of Anglo-dominated Canada. Throughout the period of English rule, the French Canadians maintained their language and culture, successfully resisting assimilation. In 1980 about half of the French-speaking population of Québec voted in favor of seeking sovereignty for their province. Speakers of English began leaving Québec at an accelerated rate in the 1970s.

The French language survived in large part because of religious factors. Its survival is an excellent example of the integration of speech and faith within a culture. Most other Canadians are Protestant. The French

Canadians are Roman Catholics, and the Church provided social cohesion, a cultural rallying point. French language and culture were preserved in the numerous rural Catholic churches and church schools of Québec.

In time, the linguistic and religious solidarity of the French Canadians found a political expression centered in their attachment to the province of Québec. For many decades, government of the province was dominated by English-speaking administrators, but a political awakening allowed the *Canadiens* to gain political control of Québec. As a result, the province is politically different from the rest of Canada, and in some ways it now resembles a state within a state. The laws of Québec retain a dominantly French influence, but the remainder of Canada adheres to English common law. The provincial flag, adopted in 1948, preserves the old *fleur-de-lis* symbol of the French kings. French is the sole legal language in Québec, and most *Canadiens* cannot speak any other language. French is used in newspapers, schools, churches, radio, television, court proceedings, and legislative gatherings. All visible use of English, on signs, was until very recently illegal, though the Canadian Supreme Court recently struck down some provisions of the French-only law. The province even has its own distinctive land-survey pattern, derived from French colonial times and preserved in provincial law. The political expression of the Québec French has periodically led to demands for independence.

The economic expression of French Canada has historically been class division between English and French. People who spoke English came to occupy an economic upper class, dominating managerial and other high positions. To a remarkable degree, the wealth of the province was in the hands of the English. Even the old French fur-trapping interests, which dated back to the early 1600s, came under English and Scottish ownership. Moreover, the French Canadians were slower to be absorbed into the industrial life of the cities, and many remained in the rural areas until recent times. The traditional economic role of the *Canadiens* as second-class citizens now lies largely in the past, because the longtime English dominance of Québec's economy is rapidly fading. Perhaps economic equality will weaken *Canadiens'* desire for political independence.

Thus language, religion, politics, and economics are closely interwoven in Canada. Such integration is typical of culture regions.

■ LINGUISTIC LANDSCAPES

The cultural landscape, the visible human-made landscape, bears the imprint of language in various ways. Figure 5.13 shows several examples of linguistic landscapes. Road signs, billboards, graffiti, placards, and other publicly displayed writing not only reveal the locally dominant language, but also can be a visual index to bilingualism and other facets of linguistic geography (Figure 5.14). Furthermore, Johanna Drucker points out, "As we observe words in the landscape, they charge and activate the environment, sometimes undermining, sometimes reinforcing our perceptions." Messages, both overt and subtle, are sent by language in the landscape.

Toponyms

Most revealing, perhaps, are the names people place on the land, the names they have given to settlements, terrain features, streams, and various other aspects of their surroundings. These place-names, or **toponyms,** often directly reflect the spatial patterns of language, dialect,

FIGURE 5.13
Linguistic landscapes are conveyed not just by language, but also by alphabet. For those, like Americans, who are visually accustomed to the Latin alphabet, the linguistic landscapes of Japan, where characters and syllabaries were both traditionally used in writing, and Israel, which employs the unique Hebrew alphabet, appear quite exotic. Some visitors experience an emotion akin to fright or panic when confronted with such alien linguistic landscapes.

FIGURE 5.14
Bilingualism in the cultural landscape of New Brunswick, the only legally bilingual Canadian province. (Photo by Terry G. Jordan, 1984.)

and national origin. Toponyms become part of the cultural landscape when they are placed on the signs and placards that dot the countryside. As you drive through English-speaking portions of North America, you read highway signs such as "Huntsville City Limits," "Harrisburg 25," "Ohio River," "Newfound Gap, Elevation 5048," or "Entering Cape Hatteras National Seashore." For the linguistic geographer such toponyms often provide an excellent visible index to the distribution of cultural traits.

Many place-names consist of two parts — the **generic** and the specific. For example, in the American place-names we listed above — Huntsville, Harrisburg, Ohio River, Newfound Gap, and Cape Hatteras — the specific names are *Hunts, Harris, Ohio, Newfound,* and *Hatteras.* The generic parts, which tell what kind of place is being described, are *ville, burg, river, gap,* and *cape.*

Generic toponyms are of greater potential value to the cultural geographer than are specific names since they appear again and again throughout a culture region. There are literally thousands of generic place-names, and every culture or subculture has its own distinctive set of them. They can be particularly valuable in tracing the spread of a culture, and they often aid in the reconstruction of culture regions of the past. Sometimes they provide information about changes that people once wrought in their physical surroundings. We will look at each of these ways cultural geographers use generic toponyms.

Generic Toponyms of the United States

The three previously mentioned dialects of the eastern United States (Figure 5.4) — Northern, Midland, and Southern — illustrate the value of generic toponyms in cultural geographical detective work. For example, New Englanders, speakers of the Northern dialect, frequently used the term *center* in the name of the town or hamlet near the center of a township. Outlying settlements then bore the prefix *east, west, north,* or *south* with the specific name of the township as the suffix. Thus in Randolph Township, Orange County, Vermont, we find settlements named Randolph Center, South Randolph, East Randolph, and North Randolph. These generic usages and duplications are peculiar to New England, and we can locate colonies founded by New Englanders as they migrated from their homelands by looking for such place-names in other parts of the country. Westward from New England — through upstate New York, Ontario, and into the upper Midwest — we can observe a trail of "Centers" and name duplications that clearly indicate their path of migration and settlement (Figure 5.15). Thus we can see the toponymic evidence of New England in areas as far afield as Walworth County, Wisconsin — where Troy, Troy Center, and East Troy are clustered. Other generic place-names identified with the Northern dialect are *brook, notch,* and *corners.* The trace of New England even reaches the Pacific shore, where "center" and "corners" suffixes abound in the Seattle area. Similarly, we can identify Midland areas by such terms as *gap, cove, hollow, knob* (a low, rounded hill), and *burgh,* as in Stone Gap, Cades Cove, Stillhouse Hollow, Bald Knob, and Pittsburgh. We can recognize Southern speech by such names as *bayou, gully,* and *store* (for rural hamlets), as in Cypress Bayou, Gum Gully, and Halls Store.

Toponyms and Cultures of the Past

Place-names often survive long after the culture that produced them has vanished from an area. Such place-names preserve traces of the past. One

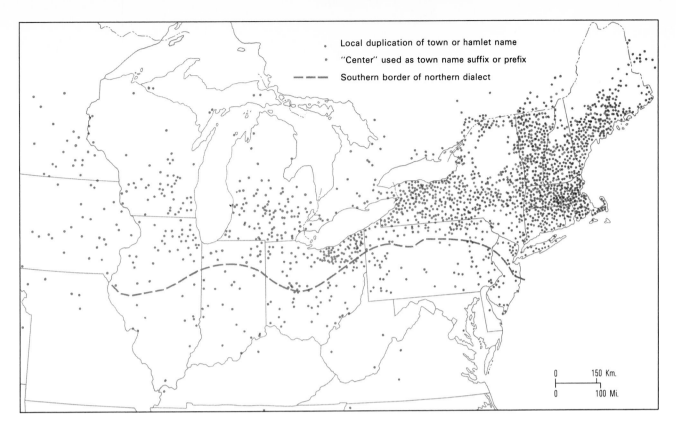

.   Local duplication of town or hamlet name
•   "Center" used as town name suffix or prefix
– – –   Southern border of northern dialect

0   150 Km.

0   100 Mi.

FIGURE 5.15
The migration of New Englanders and the spread of the Northern dialect is revealed by generic place-names. Two of the most typical place-name characteristics in New England are the use of *Center* in the names of the principal town in a township and the tendency to duplicate the names of settlements within townships by adding the prefixes *East, West, North,* and *South* to the town name. As the concentration of such place-names suggests, Massachusetts, the first New England colony, is where these two New England traits originated. Note how these traits moved westward with New England settlers, but thinned out rapidly to the south, in areas not colonized by New Englanders. Some names on this map come from nineteenth-century atlases and are no longer in use.

need look no further than the numerous Indian place-names of the United States for an example (see box, "Amerindian Names on the Land").

In general, this study of archaic names has greater value in the Old World, where many movements of peoples occurred before history was recorded. East of the Elbe and Saale rivers, in what is today the German Democratic Republic, the suffixes *ow, in,* and *zig* (as in Teterow, Berlin, and Leipzig) are very common in the names of villages, towns, and cities. Each of these suffixes is of Slavic rather than Germanic origin and their distribution describes quite accurately the region peopled by Slavic tribes as late as A.D. 800, even though the Slavic languages have since disappeared from most of East Germany (see Figure 5.16). Similarly, the common occurrence of the suffix *weiler,* as in Eschweiler, in the names of German villages south of the Danube and west of the Rhine, reminds us of former Roman rule and the use of Latin. *Weiler,* which means "hamlet," derives from the Latin *villare,* meaning "country estate." Look back to Figure 1.7.

Further south, in Spain, seven centuries of Moorish rule left behind a great many Arabic place-names, as Figure 5.17 shows. An example is the prefix *guada* on river names (as in Guadalquivir and Guadalupe), a corruption of the Arabic *wadi,* meaning "river" or "stream." Thus Guadalquivir, corrupted from Wadi al Kabir, means "the great river." The frequent occurrence of Arabic names in any particular region or province of Spain points to the strong Moorish influence in that area.

AMERINDIAN NAMES ON THE LAND

From one part of the country to another, from Walla Walla to Waxahachie, from Kissimmee to Kalamazoo, our map is dotted with all kinds of Indian names. They are on the lips of our people every day. They constitute an integral part of the flavor of American life and culture. Even the names of twenty-seven of the fifty states of the union are Indian in origin. . . .

"These place names represent various types of linguistic treatment. Often the English-speaking settlers merely took over, more or less accurately, the name given to a place by the Indians themselves. Frequently such names were descriptive of the landscape or of the life about it. Mackinac Island [is] a shortening of *Michilimackinac*, 'great turtle.' Mississippi is simply 'big river.' . . . The name *Chicago* has several interpretations, the most likely being 'garlic field,' the final *-o* serving really as a locative suffix. Occasionally Indian names were given to places by white settlers who were familiar with one or another of the various Indian languages. This

was the case with Negaunee, 'high place,' in Michigan, named by Peter White, and a number of Michigan counties have Indian names coined by Henry Rowe Schoolcraft.

"Many times in the course of our name giving, the Indian name was translated into its English equivalent. As the survey of place names in South Dakota puts it, 'When a creek is called White Thunder, Blue Dog, or American Horse, the Indian influence is obvious, since these adjectives are not those which a white man would use with these nouns. Four Horns, Greasy Horn, and Dog Ear are other examples.' The survey neglected to mention Stinking Water and Stinking Bear creeks, both of which are further convincing and delightful illustrations of this same process. . . .'"

From *American English*, 2nd ed., by Albert H. Marckwardt, revised by J. L. Dillard. Copyright © 1958, 1980, by Oxford University Press, Inc. Reprinted by permission.

New Zealand, too, offers some intriguing examples of the subtle messages that can be conveyed by archaic toponyms. The native Polynesian people of New Zealand, the Maori, are today confined mainly to refuge areas, not unlike the Amerindians. Cultural geographer Hong-key Yoon has observed that the survival rate of Maori names for towns varies according to size. The four largest New Zealand cities all have European names. Next lowest in the urban hierarchy are 20 regional centers, with 10,000 to 100,000 population, and 40 percent of these have Maori names, while almost 60 percent of the small towns, with fewer than 10,000 inhabitants, bear Maori toponyms. Similarly, only 20 percent of New Zealand's provinces have Maori names, but 56 percent of the counties do. What interpretation might the cultural geographer derive from this difference in scale?

FIGURE 5.16
Twelve hundred years ago, the area along the Saale River near the city of Halle in the German Democratic Republic was a linguistic border zone between speakers of German, on the west, and Slavic languages to the east. Today German is spoken throughout the area, and no Slavic people remain, a situation that has existed for about a thousand years. Even so, the ancient language border is still revealed in the landscape by the distribution of generic place-names of towns and villages. Names bearing the Slavic generic suffixes *itz, zig,* or *in* remain dominant east of the Saale, while the German generic suffixes *dorf, ingen, rode, leben, stadt, beck, burg, berg, heim, hausen, tal, born,* and *münde* prevail in the west. If you were drawing the Germanic-Slavic language border of A.D. 800 on this basis, where would you place it? What other evidence might you seek? (Source: Terry G. Jordan, *The European Culture Area: A Systematic Geography*, 2nd ed., New York: Harper & Row, 1988, p. 98.)

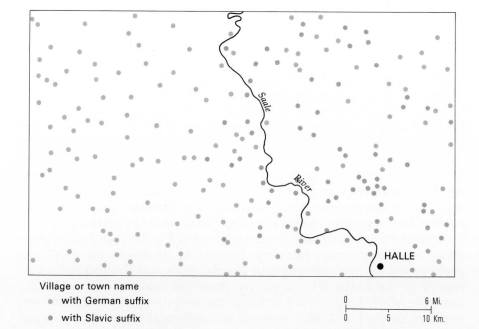

Village or town name
- with German suffix
- with Slavic suffix

0   6 Mi.

0   5   10 Km.

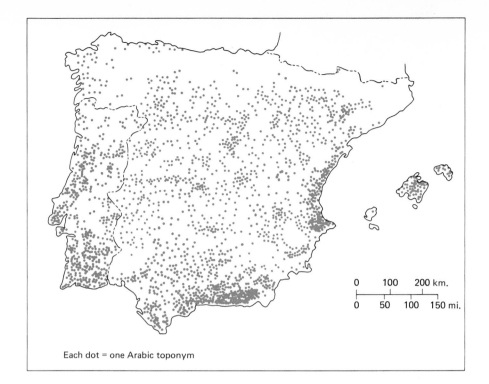

Each dot = one Arabic toponym

FIGURE 5.17
Arabic, a Semitic language, spread into the Iberian Peninsula by relocation diffusion, accompanying the Moorish Islamic military conquest, and subsequently spread by hierarchical diffusion to much of the indigenous population. A reconquest by Catholic Romance speakers subsequently rooted out Arabic in Iberia, but a reminder of the Semitic language survives still in the toponyms. Using this map, speculate concerning the direction of the Moorish invasion and retreat, the duration of Moorish rule in different parts of Iberia, and the main centers of former Moorish power. (Adapted from James M. Houston, *The Western Mediterranean World*, New York: Praeger, 1967.)

Toponyms and Environmental Modification

Generic place-names also inform us about humankind's alteration of the environment in prehistoric or poorly documented times. From about A.D. 800 to 1300, Germanic peoples cleared forests in lands from England eastward into present-day Poland, an activity well commemorated in toponyms. These names sometimes even indicate how the clearing was accomplished. In Germany, the generic suffixes *roth* and *reuth,* as Neuroth and Bayreuth, mean "rooted out" or "grubbed out" and refer to the practice of digging out roots after cutting down the trees. In England, the suffix *ley* or *leigh,* as in Woodley, means "clearing" or "open place" in the forest. *Brind, brunn,* and *brand,* in European place-names such as Brindley and Branderoda, reveal that clearing was done with fire (see Figure 3.19).

In the eastern woodlands of the United States, agricultural Indians cleared considerable forest areas before the coming of the white man. Their abandoned grass-covered fields survived, and white settlers preserved a record of the Indian deforestation by placing such generic names on the land as *prairie*, which refers to grassy areas. Over 200 of these generic terms appear in wooded eastern Texas alone, suggesting the wide extent of Indian forest-clearing activities.

◼ CONCLUSION

Language is an essential part of culture that can be studied using the five themes of cultural geography. Its families, dialects, vocabulary, pronunciation, and toponyms display distinct spatial variations that can be shown on maps. The differences from one place to another find expression as linguistic culture regions.

Languages ebb and flow across geographic areas through the processes of diffusion. Expansion and relocation diffusion, both hierarchic and contagious, are apparent in the movement of language, and all the concepts of cultural diffusion can be applied to language.

Language and physical environment interact in a linguistic ecology. The Malayo-Polynesian people rode the prevailing winds and ocean currents to carry their speech and toponyms across the vast Pacific and Indian oceans. Some linguistic groups found refuge in areas of difficult terrain, such as mountain ranges. Environment is present in vocabulary, and the secrets of ancient environmental alteration are sometimes revealed in toponyms.

The study of linguistic cultural integration clearly shows that language is causally related to other elements of culture. In fact, language is the basis for the expression of all other elements of culture, so the geography of languages is closely bound to the geographies of religion, politics, and economy. Certain tongues have advanced with empire-building armies; others share the evangelical diffusion of religious faiths; still others serve the purposes of commerce and trade. Although we may try to isolate language, it is firmly enmeshed in the cultural whole.

We can see language in the landscapes created by literate societies. The visible alphabet, public signs, and generic toponyms create a linguistic landscape that can accentuate the alien appearance of lands where we cannot understand the speech, comprehend the alphabet, or decipher the toponyms.

Although language allows us to express our culture, religion provides the basis for many of our cultural attitudes. Even where religion is no longer actively practiced, it provides much of the underlying philosophy of the culture. Values and beliefs grow out of religious heritage. The next chapter examines religion from the viewpoint of the cultural geographer.

Suggested Readings

Harold B. Allen. *The Linguistic Atlas of the Upper Midwest.* 3 vols. Minneapolis: University of Minnesota Press, 1973–1976.

F. A. Barrett. "The Relative Decline of the French Language in Canada: A Preliminary Report," *Geography,* 60 (1975), 125–129.

Robert W. Bastian. "Generic Place-Names and the Northern-Midland Dialect Boundary in the Midwest," *Names,* 25 (1977), 228–236.

Charles J. Bennett. "The Morphology of Language Boundaries: Indo-Aryan and Dravidian in Peninsular India," in David E. Sopher (ed.), *An Exploration of India: Geographical Perspectives on Society and Culture.* Ithaca, N.Y.: Cornell University Press, 1980, pp. 234–251.

Keith Buchanan. "Economic Growth and Cultural Liquidation: The Case of the Celtic Nations," in Richard Peet (ed.), *Radical Geography: Alternative Viewpoints on Contemporary Social Issues.* Chicago: Maaroufa Press, 1977, pp. 125–143.

Meredith F. Burrill. "Toponymic Generics," *Names,* 4 (1956), 129–137, 226–240.

Donald G. Cartwright. "Changes in the Patterns of Contact Between Anglophones and Francophones in Quebec," *GeoJournal,* 8 (1984), 109–122.

Donald G. Cartwright and Colin H. Williams. "Bilingual Districts as an Instrument in Canadian Language Policy," *Transactions of the Institute of British Geographers,* 7 (1982), 474–493.

Craig M. Carver. *American Regional Dialects: A Word Geography.* Ann Arbor: University of Michigan Press, 1986.

Frederick C. Cassidy (ed.). *Dictionary of American Regional English.* Cambridge, Mass.: Belknap Press of Harvard University Press. Volume 1 of this ambitious multivolume effort, covering words beginning with A–C, appeared in

1985. When complete, it will constitute an invaluable resource for word geographers.

C. M. Delgado de Carvalho. "The Geography of Languages," in Philip L. Wagner and Marvin W. Mikesell (eds.), *Readings in Cultural Geography.* Chicago: University of Chicago Press, 1962, pp. 75–93.

Johanna Drucker. "Language in the Landscape," *Landscape,* 28, No. 1 (1984), 7–13.

J. S. Dugdale. *The Linguistic Map of Europe.* London: Hutchinson University Library, 1969.

Ashok K. Dutt, Chandrakanta Khan, and Chandralekha Sangwan. "Spatial Pattern of Languages in India: A Culture-Historical Analysis," *GeoJournal,* 10 (1985), 51–74.

Matti Kaups. "Finnish Place Names in Minnesota: A Study in Cultural Transfer," *Geographical Review,* 56 (1966), 377–397.

Kevin C. Kearns. "Resuscitation of the Irish Gaeltacht," *Geographical Review,* 64 (1974), 83–110.

John Kirk, Stewart F. Sanderson, and John D. A. Widdowson (eds.). *Studies in Linguistic Geography.* London: Croom Helm, 1985.

Hans Kurath. *Word Geography of the Eastern United States.* Ann Arbor: University of Michigan Press, 1949.

Hans Kurath and Raven I. McDavid, Jr. *The Pronunciation of English in the Atlantic States.* Ann Arbor: University of Michigan Press, 1961.

Michael Levison, R. Gerard Ward, and John W. Webb. *The Settlement of Polynesia: A Computer Simulation.* Minneapolis: University of Minnesota Press, 1973.

Ivan Lind. "Geography and Place Names," in Philip L. Wagner and Marvin W. Mikesell (eds.), *Readings in Cultural Geography.* Chicago: University of Chicago Press, 1962, pp. 118–128.

Raven I. McDavid. "Linguistic Geography and Toponymic Research," *Names,* 6 (1958), 65–73.

E. Wallace McMullen. "The Term 'Prairie' in the United States," *Names,* 5 (1957), 27–46.

Ian Matley. "Perceptions of Mountain Environments as Reflected in the Names of Landforms in the Scottish Highlands, Norway and Romania," in Breandán S. MacAodha (ed.), *Topothesia.* Galway, Ireland: Dept. of Geography, University College, 1982, pp. 25–39.

Allen G. Noble and Ramesh C. Dhussa. "The Linguistic Geography of Dumka, Bihar, India," *Journal of Cultural Geography,* 3 (Spring–Summer 1983), 73–81.

James J. Parsons. "Hillside Letters in the Western Landscape," *Landscape,* 30, No. 1 (1988), 15–33.

G. H. Pirie. "Ethno-Linguistic Zoning in South African Black Townships," *Area,* 16 (1984), 291–298.

W. T. R. Pryce. "Migration and the Evolution of Culture Areas: Cultural and Linguistic Frontiers in North-East Wales, 1750 and 1851," *Transactions, Institute of British Geographers,* 65 (1975), 79–108.

H. F. Raup. "Names of Ohio's Streams," *Names,* 5 (1957), 162–168.

George R. Stewart. *Names on the Land: A Historical Account of Place-Naming in the United States.* Boston: Houghton Mifflin, 1958.

Peter Trudgill. "Linguistic Geography and Geographical Linguistics," *Progress in Geography: International Reviews of Current Research,* 7 (1975), 227–252.

Peter Trudgill. *On Dialect: Social and Geographical Perspectives.* Oxford: Basil Blackwell, 1983.

Philip L. Wagner. "Remarks on the Geography of Language," *Geographical Review,* 48 (1958), 86–97.

Leo Waibel. "Place Names as an Aid in the Reconstruction of the Original Vegetation of Cuba," *Geographical Review,* 33 (1943), 376–396.

Robert C. West. "The Term 'Bayou' in the United States: A Study in the Geography of Place Names," *Annals of the Association of American Geographers,* 44 (1954), 63–74.

Colin H. Williams and C. J. Thomas. "Linguistic Decline and Nationalist Resurgence in Wales," in Glyn Williams (ed.), *Social and Cultural Change in Contemporary Wales.* London: Routledge & Kegan Paul, 1978, Chapter 12.

Charles W. J. Withers. *Gaelic in Scotland, 1698–1981: The Geographical History of a Language.* Edinburgh: Donald, 1984.

Ronald Wixman. *Language Aspects of Ethnic Patterns and Processes in the North Caucasus,* University of Chicago, Dept. of Geography Research Paper No. 191, 1980.

Gordon R. Wood. *Vocabulary Change: A Study of Variation in Regional Words in Eight of the Southern States.* Carbondale and Edwardsville: Southern Illinois University Press, 1971.

Hong-key Yoon. "Maori and Pakeha Place Names for Cultural Features in New Zealand." In *Maori Mind, Maori Land: Essays on the Cultural Geography of the Maori People from an Outsider's Perspective.* Bern, Switzerland: Peter Lang, 1986, pp. 98–122.

Wilbur Zelinsky, "Generic Terms in the Place Names of the Northeastern United States," *Annals of the Association of American Geographers,* 45 (1955), 319–349.

Religious Realms

RELIGIOUS CULTURE REGIONS

> **Christianity**
> **Islam**
> **Judaism**
> **Hinduism**
> **Buddhism**
> **Animism**
> **Secularized Areas**

RELIGIOUS DIFFUSION

> **The Semitic Religious Hearth**
> **The Indus-Ganges Hearth**
> **Barriers and Distance Decay**

RELIGIOUS ECOLOGY

> **The Environment and Monotheism**
> **Religion and Environmental**
> ** Modification**
> **Religion and Environmental Perception**

CULTURAL INTEGRATION IN RELIGION

> **Religion and Economy**
> **Religion and Political Geography**

RELIGIOUS LANDSCAPES

> **Religious Structures**
> **Landscapes of the Dead**
> **Religion and Rural Settlement Patterns**
> **Religious Names on the Land**

CONCLUSION

Your first reaction to a chapter on the geography of religions may well be: "What does geography have to do with religious faith?" You might be inclined to award the study of religion in its entirety to philosophers and theologians—after all, the word *theology* means literally "the study of God," while the exact original Greek meaning of *geography* is "description of the earth." Still, **religion** is part of culture. It involves a set of beliefs and practices, a social system, through which people seek mental and physical harmony with the powers of the universe, through which we attempt to influence the awesome forces of nature, life, and death. As such, religion has been an essential attribute of culture, and the geographer would be foolish to ignore it. For some cultural groups, religion is little more than a protective buffer between humans and the mysterious, potentially de-structive forces of nature. Others have, over centuries, developed highly articulated systems of belief with elaborate moral codes.

The appropriateness of the study of religion in cultural geography will be revealed through our five themes. Religion differs from one place to another, producing variations that can be mapped as culture regions. These spatial variations were produced by cultural diffusion and reflect a complex interplay among religion, the environment, and other aspects of culture. In turn, the spatial pattern of religion is visibly imprinted on the cultural landscape. Religion is an essential hue in the human mosaic.

■ RELIGIOUS CULTURE REGIONS

Both functional and formal religious culture regions abound. The functional partitioning of the Earth into networks of parishes and larger church administrative units covers most inhabited areas. The smallest such unit, the congregation, is a functional social unit with spatial dimensions and constraints. Perhaps the most basic spatial act by religious groups is the functional designation of **sacred space,** including areas and sites recognized as worthy of devotion, loyalty, fear, or esteem. By virtue of their sacredness, these special religious regions can be avoided by the faithful, sought out by pilgrims, or barred to members of other religions. Often sacred space contains the site of supposed supernatural events or is viewed as the abode of gods. Conflict can result if two religions venerate the same space, as in Jerusalem, where the Muslim Dome of the Rock, the site of Muhammad's ascent to heaven, stands above the Wailing Wall, the remnant of a great Jewish temple. Cemeteries are generally regarded as a type of sacred space.

We can devise all kinds of formal culture regions based on religion. One might, for instance, define culture regions on the basis of a single religious trait. An example would be a map of all areas where **monotheism,** the worship of a single god, is prevalent. Much of the world is in such a culture region, since monotheism is typical of a number of major religions. We may choose instead to set up religious culture regions based on a combination of traits. The most basic kind of multitrait formal religious culture region depicts the spatial distribution of generally acknowledged religious groups, such as Christians, Jews, Muslims, and Hindus. Figure 6.1 reveals the worldwide patterns of such groups. On a different scale, a similar map, Figure 6.2, shows areal variation in dominance by the leading Christian **denominations** in the United States and Canada. The boundaries of formal religious culture regions such as these, like most cultural borders, are rarely sharp. Persons of different faiths live in the same province or town, and individuals can belong to a number of different religious sects in a lifetime.

There are two major categories of religion, both of which are further divided into various groups, sects, and denominations. The first category includes **universalizing religions,** those that actively seek new members and have as a goal the conversion of all humankind. Universalizing religions instruct their faithful to spread the Word to all the Earth, using one method or another to convert the heathen.

Contrasted to universalizing religions are **ethnic religions,** each of which is identified with some particular ethnic or tribal group and does not seek converts. Universalizing religions grow out of ethnic religions—the evolution of Christianity from its parent Judaism is the primary example. This change usually occurs within an ethnic religion when a charismatic leader or reformer emerges whose revelations are so profound and whose personality is so dynamic that persons beyond the immediate cultural

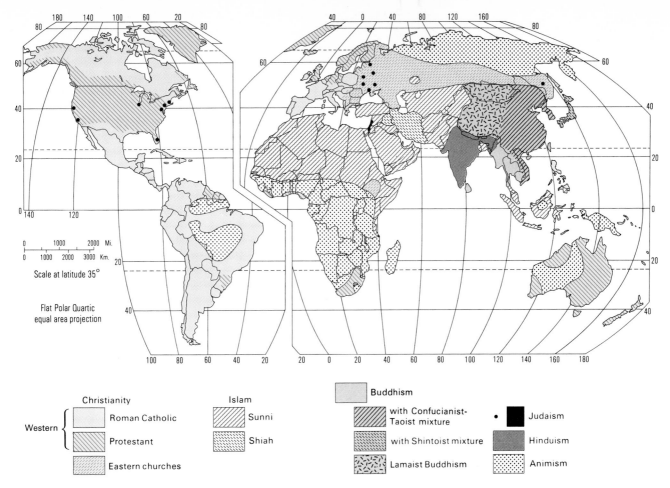

FIGURE 6.1
The world distribution of major religions.

group are attracted. Once the evangelical spirit of such a universalizing religion is spent, a fragmentation and reversion to ethnic status sometimes occurs.

Christianity

Christianity is the largest universalizing religion, both in area and number of adherents, with about 1.7 billion people (32 percent of humanity), though it has long been fragmented into separate churches (Figure 6.1). The single greatest division is between Western and Eastern Christianity, each of which is further subdivided. Belonging to the Eastern group are the *Coptic* Church, originally the nationalistic religion of Christian Egyptians and still today a minority faith there, as well as being the dominant church among the highland people of Ethiopia; the *Maronites*, Semitic descendants of seventh-century heretics who retreated to a mountain refuge in Lebanon; the *Nestorians*, who live in the mountains of Kurdistan and in India's Kerala State; and *Eastern Orthodoxy*, originally centered in Greek-speaking areas and focused upon the city of Constantinople (currently Istanbul). After converting many Slavic groups, Eastern Orthodoxy also split into a variety of national sects, such as Russian, Greek, and Serbian Orthodoxy.

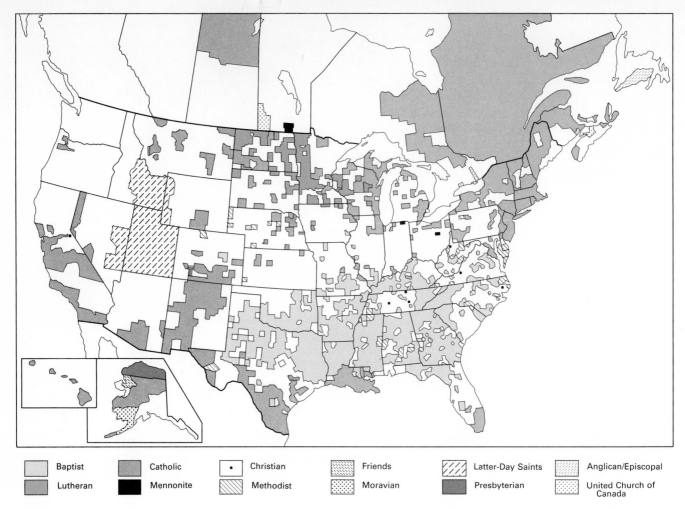

Baptist | Catholic | • Christian | Friends | //// Latter-Day Saints | Anglican/Episcopal

Lutheran | Mennonite | Methodist | Moravian | Presbyterian | United Church of Canada

FIGURE 6.2
Leading Christian denominations in the United States and Canada are shown by counties, or, for Canada, census districts. In the shaded areas, the church or denomination indicated claimed 50% or more of the total church membership. The most striking features of the map are the "Baptist belt" through the South, a Lutheran zone in the upper Midwest, Mormon (Latter-Day Saints) dominance centered in Utah, and the zone of mixing in the Midland area from Pennsylvania through Nebraska and Kansas. The Roman Catholic presence is probably exaggerated in some areas, especially the West, because of the church's more inclusive membership criteria. Can you explain the religious pattern in Louisiana, Florida, and Illinois? Why are individual denominations less likely to dominate areas in western parts of the continent? (Redrawn and simplified from Quinn, Anderson, Bradley, Goetting, and Shriver, *Churches and Church Membership in the United States 1980,* Atlanta: Glenmary Research Center, 1982. Copyright © 1982 by the National Council of the Churches of Christ in the U.S.A. and the *National Atlas of Canada,* 4th ed., Toronto: Macmillan, 1974.)

Western Christianity splintered also, most notably in the Protestant breakaway of the 1400s and 1500s. Since then, the Roman Catholic Church has remained strongly unified, but Protestantism, from its beginnings, tended to divide into a rich array of sects. The denominational map of the United States and Canada vividly reflects the fragmented nature of Western Christianity and the resulting complex pattern of religious culture regions (Figure 6.2). Numerous faiths imported from Europe were later augmented by Christian sects developed in America. The American frontier was a breeding ground for new religious groups, as individualistic pioneer sentiment found expression in splinter Protestant denominations. In numerous parts of the country, a relatively small community may contain the churches of half a dozen religious groupings, with individual families sometimes split along religious lines.

As a result of this local fragmentation and mixing, the religious map of the United States displays less regionalization of faiths than is found in much of the rest of Christendom. Still, we can find some patterns in Figure 6.2. In a broad "Bible Belt" across the South, Baptist and other conservative fundamentalist denominations are dominant, and Utah is at the core of a Mormon realm. A Lutheran belt stretches from Wisconsin westward through Minnesota and the Dakotas, and Roman Catholicism dominates southern Louisiana, the southwestern borderland, and the heavily industrialized areas of the Northeast. The Midwest is a thoroughly mixed zone, though Methodism is generally the largest single faith.

In a recent study in American religious geography, Roger W. Stump found a twentieth-century trend toward Protestant denominational-regional divergence. Baptists in the South, Lutherans in the upper Midwest, and Mormons in the West each dominate their respective regions more thoroughly today than at the turn of the century. Each of the three denominations is conservative and has a long-standing, strong infrastructure. In an age when many social scientists proclaim that Americans are becoming homogenized, with a national culture supplanting traditional regional cultures, Stump's findings reassure us that the ancient message of geography, "different place, different people," remains true. At the same time, we need to be aware that certain denominations, in particular Methodism, are very important on a national scale but are dominant in only a small number of counties.

Another way of mapping formal religious regions in the United States is to cut across denominational lines, grouping churches and sects by philosophy, ideology, intensity, and local diversity. Geographer James R. Shortridge used such an approach, and Figure 6.3 shows some of the

FIGURE 6.3
Some regional religious types in the United States. These regions were devised by measuring (1) the relative degree of liberalism and conservatism, (2) the strength of religious belief or commitment, and (3) the degree of religious diversity within an area. The classification crosses denominational lines to some extent. For example, Southern Baptists are considered "conservative," while Northern Baptists are "liberal." Compare the Southern "Bible Belt" of intense, conservative Protestantism with the Lower Southern culture region shown in Figure 1.6. Geographer James R. Shortridge prepared this map using the same data as in Figure 6.2, correcting some of the omissions and exaggerations and reorganizing denominational groupings. (Derived in part from James R. Shortridge, "A New Reorganization of American Religion," *Journal for the Scientific Study of Religion,* 16 (1977), 146–147. Canadian areas were added by Jordan, without statistical basis.)

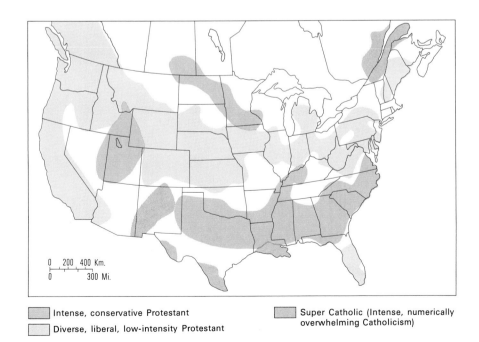

0   200   400 Km.
0   300 Mi.

☐ Intense, conservative Protestant

☐ Diverse, liberal, low-intensity Protestant

☐ Super Catholic (Intense, numerically overwhelming Catholicism)

results he obtained. Dr. Shortridge divided the individual churches into "liberal" and "conservative" categories. Some Baptist, Methodist, and Lutheran sects, for example, were judged to be liberal, while others, such as the Lutheran Church-Missouri Synod, the Southern Baptist, and the Free Methodist, were placed in the conservative category. Measurements were made to determine how many churches were present in each county and how strong religious belief or commitment was. The results revealed a Lower Southern "Bible Belt" of intense, conservative Protestantism; a northern belt of diverse, liberal, low-intensity Protestantism; and several "Super Catholic" areas, where the Roman Catholic Church was overwhelmingly dominant.

Not just denominational traits, religious ideology, intensity, and diversity vary spatially. Geographer Stump also found that regional variations in religious behavior extend "into the very motivations of religious participation," reflecting the variable cultural importance of religion. In the Bible Belt, for example, the great importance of religion leads to "the expectation that higher-status individuals will actively support and participate in religious institutions."

Islam

Islam, another great monotheistic, universalizing faith, claims perhaps as many as 820 million followers, centered mainly in the great desert belt of Asia and northern Africa, but extending as far east as Indonesia and the Philippines. Although not as severely fragmented as Christianity, Islam too has split into separate groups. Two major sects prevail. The *Shiite* Muslims, 11 percent of the Islamic total, form the majority in Iran, Iraq, and Bahrain. Substantial Shiite groups also live in Afghanistan, Pakistan, North Yemen, Kuwait, Turkey, India, and Lebanon. A fundamentalist

FIGURE 6.4
Muslims in Senegal, Africa, stop in the street to mark a time of prayer. Each man has unrolled his prayer rug and faces Mecca. This ritual is repeated several times a day throughout the Islamic world.

revival is occurring among the Shiites, under Iranian leadership, producing religious and political tension. *Sunni* Muslims form most of the remaining majority within Islam (see Figure 6.4). Their strength is greatest in the Arabic-speaking lands, a reflection of the fact that Islam arose in Arabia, though non-Arabic Indonesia now contains the world's largest Sunni Islamic concentration, and other large clusters occur in Indo-European Bangladesh and Pakistan. The Shiite group, by contrast, is strongest among Indo-European groups.

Judaism

Judaism, another monotheistic faith, is the parent of Christianity and closely related to Islam, as well. The Hebrew prophets and leaders, such as Moses, are recognized in all three religions. In contrast to the other monotheistic faiths, Judaism does not actively seek new converts and has remained an ethnic religion through most of its existence. It has split into a variety of subgroups, partly as a result of the dispersal of the Jews in Roman times and the subsequent loss of contact among the various colonies. Jews, scattered to many parts of the Roman Empire, became a minority group wherever they were found. In later times, they spread through much of Europe, North Africa, and even southern Arabia. Those Jews who resided in the Mediterranean lands were called the *Sephardim,* while those in central and eastern Europe were known as the *Ashkenazim.* The late nineteenth and early twentieth centuries witnessed large-scale Jewish migration from Europe to America. The disaster that befell European Judaism during the Nazi years involved the systematic murder of perhaps a third of the entire Jewish population of the world, mainly Ashkenazim. Europe ceased to be the primary homeland of Judaism as many of the survivors fled overseas, mainly to Israel and America.

Judaism has close to 14 million adherents throughout the world. At present, almost half of the world's Jewish population lives in the United States; another 30 percent in Europe and the western Soviet Union; and 20 percent in Asia, mainly Israel. The large majority of American Jews settled in cities and towns rather than rural areas. Most Jews in the larger urban centers, such as New York City, are descendants of Ashkenazim from eastern Europe, especially Poland and Russia, who immigrated between 1880 and 1915. Those found in towns and small cities of the Midwest and the South immigrated largely from Germany in the period before 1880.

Hinduism

Hinduism, a religion closely tied to India and its ancient culture, claims about 650 million adherents. A decidedly **polytheistic** religion, involving the worship of hundreds of deities, Hinduism is also linked to the *caste system,* a rigid segregation of people according to ancestry and occupation; *ahimsa,* the veneration of all forms of life, involving noninjury to all sentient creatures; and a belief in reincarnation.

The faith straddles a major linguistic divide, including both Indic Indo-Europeans and Dravidians. The skin color of the Hindu population ranges from dark to light, and the faith takes many local forms. No standard set of beliefs prevails, and some Hindus eat fish, venerate military prowess, or even practice monotheism. These internal contrasts suggest, correctly, that Hinduism was once a universalizing religion, but it long since reverted to the status of a regional, biethnic faith. Also suggestive of

FIGURE 6.5
Kamakura's praying Buddha in Japan attracts many pilgrims and tourists. Compare the style, setting, and size with statues used in Christian religions. Such an overwhelming presence in the landscape is one way by which religion contributes to the sense of place.

former missionary activity is an outlier of Hinduism on the distant Indonesian island of Bali.

Buddhism

Buddhism is the most widespread religion of the Orient, dominating a culture region stretching from Sri Lanka to Japan and from Mongolia to Vietnam. It began in India as a reform movement within Hinduism, much as Christianity did within Judaism, based in the teachings of Prince Siddhartha, the Buddha (Figure 6.5). He promoted the four "noble truths": life is full of suffering; desire is the cause of this suffering; cessation of suffering comes with the quelling of desire; and an "Eight-Fold Path" of proper personal conduct and meditation permits the individual to overcome desire. The resultant state of escape and peace is known as Nirvana.

In the process of its spread, particularly in China and Japan, Buddhism fused with native ethnic religions such as Confucianism, Taoism, and Shintoism to form composite faiths. Southern Buddhism, dominant in Sri Lanka and mainland Southeast Asia, retains the greatest similarity to the religion's original form, while a special variation known as Lamaism prevails in Tibet and Mongolia. Buddhism's tendency to merge with native religions, particularly in China, makes it difficult to determine the number of its adherents. Estimates range from 300 million to 800 million people. While Buddhism in China has become enmeshed with local faiths to become part of an ethnic religion, elsewhere it retains a decidedly universalizing character. Along with Christianity and Islam, Buddhism remains one of the three great universalizing religions in the world.

Buddhism has won some converts in the United States, making inroads mainly among well-educated young intellectuals. Perhaps the most popular form of Buddhism in America is Zen, derived from Japan and ultimately from China. The essence of Zen Buddhism is acquiring a new way of looking at life and things generally. Zen Buddhists seek to realize the nature of things, the nature of being, and their oneness with the universe. In their search they try to break from the everyday, logical thought processes that, as they see it, shackle and confine the human mind.

Animism

Tribal peoples who do not adhere to any of the world's major ethnic or universalizing religions are usually referred to collectively as **animists.** Animists, currently numbering about 28 million, believe that certain inanimate objects possess spirits or souls. These animistic spirits live in rocks and rivers, mountain peaks and heavenly bodies, forests and swamps. Each tribe has its own characteristic form of animism and has vested a particular set of objects with spirits. Usually a tribal religious figure serves as an intermediary between the people and the spirits. To some other animists, the objects in question do not actually possess spirits, but rather are valued because they have a particular potency to serve as a link between a person and the omnipresent god. It is easy but deceptive to classify such systems of belief as primitive or simple, but they can be extraordinarily complex.

Animism is in retreat almost everywhere. It survives in remote areas where tribal peoples have found refuge, such as interior Africa, the Amazon Basin, and the mountains of New Guinea. Not surprisingly, many of these are the same places we identified as linguistic refuge areas in Chapter 5. As we will see later, many animistic beliefs survive in universalizing religions.

Secularized Areas

In some parts of the world, especially in urban and industrial areas, traditional religions are declining. Secularization—the discarding of religious faith—is taking place in lands as different as India, the Netherlands, and the Soviet Union (Figure 6.8). Typically, secularization displays a vivid regionalization on a variety of scales. Areas of surviving religious vitality lie alongside secularized districts, in a disorderly jumble (Figures 6.6, 6.7). Such patterns once again reveal the inherent spatial variety of humankind and invite analysis by the cultural geographer. In some instances, the retreat from organized religion has resulted from a government's active hostility toward a particular faith or religion in general. In other cases, we can attribute the decline to the failure of religions oriented to the needs of rural folk to adapt to the urban scene.

For many Americans, religion today plays a minimal role in their daily lives. To some extent, this change is reflected in the way churches are built. Unlike the great cathedrals of Europe's past and the churches in Québec or Mexico today, churches in the United States are almost never built at the functional center of a city. Instead, they are usually constructed on peripheral sites where land values are lower or in the suburbs where fragmenting urban congregations have moved in large numbers. This suggests that our lives, like our cities, revolve around business and commerce, not religious activities.

Quasi-religions, or systems of belief similar to religions but lacking worship services, often fill the emotional vacuum produced by secularization. Perhaps the most widespread quasi-religion is communism, which

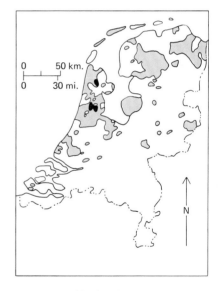

 20–50% of population reporting no religious affiliation, 1960

50–80% of population reporting no religious affiliation, 1960

FIGURE 6.6
Secularization in the Netherlands is mapped for 1960. The deepest inroads against traditional religion have been made in the northern part of the Netherlands, formerly a Calvinist Protestant stronghold. In the Catholic south, which is less urbanized and industrialized, few have defected from the Christian faith.

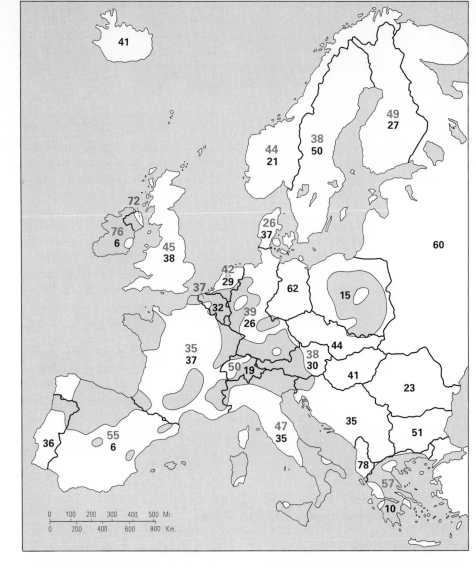

Secularized areas

Regions of surviving
Christian vitality

45   % Believing in afterlife

41   % Atheist, nonreligious,
          and nonpracticing

owes much to the Judeo-Christian world from which it sprang. The Communist image of a victorious proletariat parallels the Christian belief that "the meek shall inherit the earth," and both Communists and Christians value sexual morality and hard work. A quasi-religion can also take a nationalistic form, as in Nazi Germany. In Israel, Judaism may be evolving toward quasi-religious nationalism.

■ RELIGIOUS DIFFUSION

The distribution of religions and denominations is the product of innovation and cultural diffusion. To a quite remarkable degree, the origin of the major religions was concentrated spatially, occurring in two principal Asian hearth areas.

The Semitic Religious Hearth

All three of the great monotheistic faiths — Christianity, Judaism, and Islam — arose among Semitic-speaking peoples in or on the margins of the deserts of southwestern Asia, in the Middle East (Figure 6.8). Judaism, the oldest of the three, originated 4000 years ago, probably along the southern edge of the Fertile Crescent. Only later did its followers acquire dominion over the lands between the Mediterranean and the Jordan River—the territorial base of modern Israel. Christianity, child of Judaism, originated in this "Promised Land" about halfway through the temporal existence of Judaism. Seven centuries later, the Semitic hearth once again gave birth to a major faith when Islam arose in western Arabia.

Religions spread by both relocation and expansion diffusion. As you recall, the latter can be divided into hierarchical and contagious subtypes. In hierarchical diffusion, ideas are implanted at the top of a society, leapfrogging across the map to take root in cities, bypassing smaller villages and rural areas. The use of missionaries, by contrast, involves relocation diffusion.

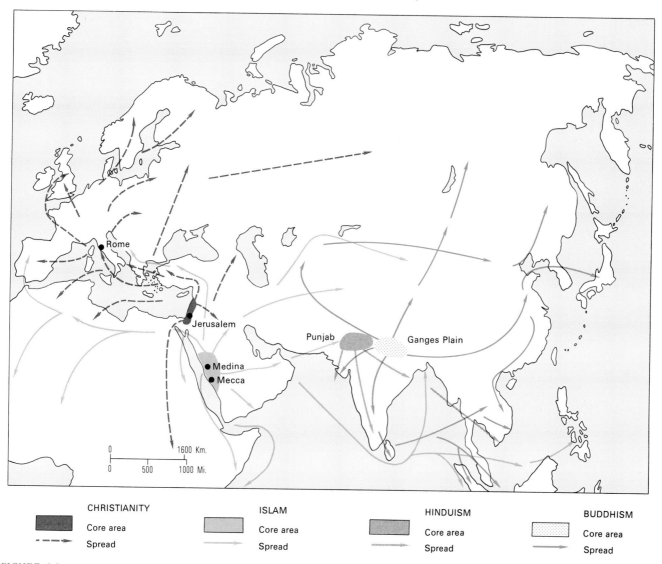

FIGURE 6.8

The origin and diffusion of four major religions in Eurasia. Christianity and Islam, the two great universalizing monotheistic faiths, arose in Semitic southwestern Asia and spread widely through the Old World. Hinduism and Buddhism both originated in the northern reaches of the Indian subcontinent and spread through southeastern Eurasia.

Obviously, universalizing faiths are more likely to diffuse than ethnic religions, and it is not surprising that the spread of monotheism was accomplished largely by Christianity and Islam, rather than Judaism. From Semitic southwestern Asia, both of the universalizing monotheistic faiths diffused widely. Christians, observing the admonition in the Gospel of Matthew, "Go ye therefore and teach all nations, baptizing them in the

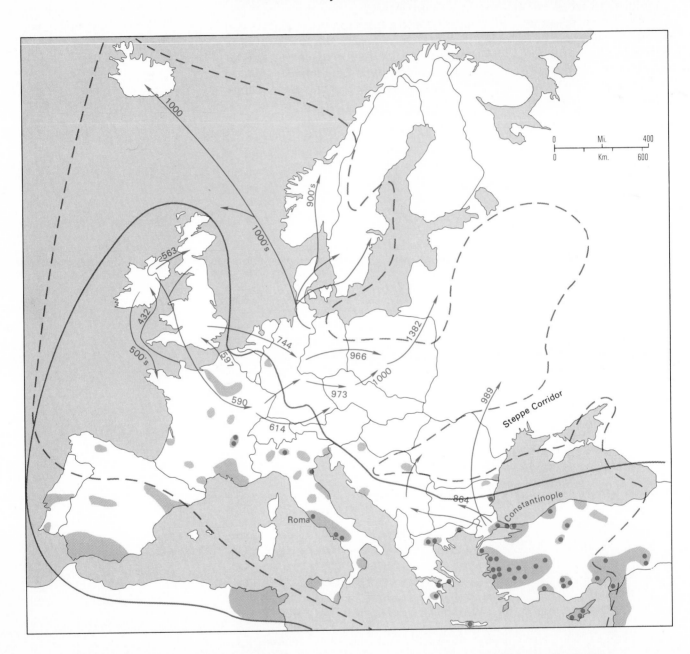

- ●   Christian congregations of the first and second centuries

- ▨   Christianized areas by the year 300

---------   Limit of Christianity, A.D. 700

– – – –   Limit of Christianity, A.D. 1050

FIGURE 6.9
The diffusion of Christianity in Europe, first to eleventh centuries. In what way do the patterns for the first and second centuries and for the year 300 suggest hierarchical expansion diffusion? Compare to Figure 1.10. Who were the "knowers" (converts) and who were the laggards at this stage? What barriers to diffusion might account for the uneven advance by the year 1050? Why did retreat occur in some areas?

name of the Father, and of the Son, and of the Holy Ghost, teaching them to observe all things whatsoever I have commanded you," initially spread through the Roman Empire, using the splendid system of imperial roads to diffuse the faith. In its early centuries of spread, Christianity displayed a spatial distribution that clearly reflected hierarchical expansion diffusion (Figure 6.9). The early congregations were in cities and towns, temporarily producing a pattern of Christianized urban centers and pagan rural areas. Indeed, traces of this process remain in our language. The Latin word *pagus*, "countryside," is the root of both *pagan* and *peasant*, suggesting the ancient heathen connotation of rurality.

Once implanted in this manner, Christianity spread further by means of contagious diffusion. When applied to religion, this method of spread is called **contact conversion** and is the result of everyday association between believers and nonbelievers. Of course, the scattered urban clusters of early Christianity were created by relocation diffusion, as missionaries such as the apostle Paul moved from town to town bearing the news of the emerging faith. In later centuries, Christian missionaries often used the technique of converting kings or tribal leaders, setting in motion additional hierarchical diffusion. The Russians and Poles were converted in this manner. Some Christian expansion was militaristic, as in the reconquest of Iberia and the invasion of Latin America. This process involves a mixture of contagious expansion and relocation diffusion.

The Islamic faith also spread from its Semitic hearth area in a militaristic manner. Obeying the command in their holy book, the Koran, that they "do battle against them until there be no more seduction from the truth and the only worship be that of Allah," the Arabs exploded westward across North Africa in a wave of religious and linguistic conquest. The Turks, once converted, carried out similar Islamic conquests. In a different sort of diffusion, Muslim missionaries followed trade routes eastward to implant Islam in the Philippines, Indonesia, and the interior of China. Tropical Africa is the current major scene of Islamic expansion, an effort that has produced competition with Christians for the remaining animists.

The Indus-Ganges Hearth

The second great religious hearth area lay in the plains fringing the northern edge of the Indian subcontinent. This lowland, drained by the Ganges and Indus rivers, gave birth to Hinduism and Buddhism. The earliest faith to derive from this hearth was Hinduism, at least 4000 years old. Its origin lay in the Punjab, from where Hinduism diffused to dominate the subcontinent. Missionaries later carried the faith, in its universalizing phase, to overseas areas, but most of these convert regions were subsequently lost.

Buddhism began in the foothills bordering the Ganges Plain about 500 B.C., branching off from Hinduism (Figure 6.8). For centuries it remained confined to the Indian subcontinent, but missionaries later carried Buddhism to China (100 B.C.–A.D. 200), Korea and Japan (A.D. 300–500), Southeast Asia (A.D. 400–600), Tibet (A.D. 700), and Mongolia (A.D. 1500). Like Christianity, Buddhism developed many regional forms and eventually died out in its area of origin, reabsorbed into Hinduism.

Barriers and Distance Decay

Religious ideas move in the manner of all innovation waves. They weaken with increasing distance from their places of origin and with the passage of time. Barriers often retard or halt their spread. Similarly, religion itself can act as a barrier to the spread of nonreligious innovations. Religious taboos occasionally function as absorbing barriers, preventing diffusion of foods and practices that violate the taboo. In this way, cigarette smoking, an innovation introduced into the United States mainly during World War I, has been unable to penetrate Mormon communities in Utah. Similarly, the relocation diffusion of a religious doctrine encounters an absorbing barrier if laws are passed to forbid immigration by the doctrine's believers. More commonly, barriers are of the permeable type, allowing part of the innovation wave to diffuse through it, but weakening it and retarding its spread. The partial acceptance of Christianity by various Indian groups in Latin America and the western United States, serving in some instances as a camouflage beneath which many aspects of the tribal religions survive, is an example. A permeable barrier can also be seen in the commercial cultivation of tobacco by certain Pennsylvania farmers who belong to sects that forbid smoking.

The attempt to introduce Christianity into China provides a good example of barriers to diffusion, barriers not just of a religious nature, but also a linguistic one. Unlike Buddhism, for which Chinese culture presented a permeable barrier to diffusion (see box, "Buddhism in China: Passing a Permeable Barrier"), Christianity faced there, in effect, an absorbing barrier. When Catholic and Protestant missionaries reached China from Europe and the United States in the nineteenth century, they expected to find fertile ground for conversion—millions of people ready to receive the word of God. However, they had crossed the boundaries of a culture region thousands of years old, in which the basic social ideas left little opening for Christianity. For instance, the missionaries were left in a quandary about how to translate *sin* into Chinese for no equivalent concept existed in the Chinese language. They tried a word meaning "not good"; a Chinese negative particle, the equivalent of the word *not*; and a word carrying the idea of something abhorrent or corrupt. Finally, they settled on the word *tsui,* borrowed from popular Buddhist sects. It meant to do something wrong and was tied to a newly developing Buddhist idea of keeping personal internal ledgers of merit and demerit. Even *tsui,*

BUDDHISM IN CHINA: PASSING A PERMEABLE BARRIER

The diffusion of Buddhism into China profoundly changed society and culture. Yet China also fundamentally modified Buddhism. In short, Chinese culture presented a permeable barrier to the diffusion of Buddhism.

A few examples will illustrate what happened. Early Chinese translations quickly changed the relatively high position Buddhism had granted women. The "husband supports his wife" became, in Chinese, "The husband controls his wife." "The wife comforts her husband" became "The wife reveres her husband." In addition, the Chinese cult of the family was soon interwoven with Buddhist observances. A typical inscription from a Buddhist temple of the fourth century might read: "We respectfully make and present this holy image in honor of the Buddhas, Bodhisattvas, and pray that all living creatures may attain salvation, and particularly that the souls of our ancestors and relatives may find repose and release."

Among the Chinese masses, Buddhism fused with other popular cults. The Buddhist heavens and hells of India, for instance, were retained, but given a Chinese bureaucratic structure. Over time, Chinese artists transformed the Indian sculptural ideal, the half-naked ascetic, into the potbellied, earthy "happy Buddha" that can be bought in gift shops today.

Such merging of religions is a common occurrence when adherents of one faith attempt to supplant a traditional religion. In this way, spatial variation develops even within the same religious faith, and each culture or subculture places its own distinctive mark on the belief system.

From Arthur F. Wright, *Buddhism in Chinese History* (Palo Alto, Calif.: Stanford University Press, 1959).

though, could not solve the problem. Centuries before, the Chinese had settled to their own satisfaction the question of what is basic human nature. As they saw the matter, humans were basically good. Evil desires represented merely a deviation from that natural state. People only had to shrug them off and they would return to the basic nature that they share with heaven. Consequently, the idea of "original sin" left the Chinese baffled. The Christian image of humankind as flawed, of a gap between creator and created, of the Fall and the impossibility of returning to god-hood, was culturally incomprehensible to the Chinese. Other aspects of Christianity added to the cultural gap. How could the fall from grace come from too much knowledge, a commodity highly prized in China? What was wrong with a giant snake in the garden of Eden to a people whose art was filled with reptilian dragons, the imperial symbol? Even an adequate word for Jehovah, the personalized, single god of the West, was lacking.

In short, many concepts of Christianity fell on rocky soil in China. Moreover, Westerners first appeared neither as conquerors nor as superior beings, but as crude barbarians. The thought that they would have anything to offer in the realm of ideas did not occur to the Chinese, secure in their own civilization. Only in the early twentieth century, as China's social structure crumbled under Western assault, did a significant, though still small, number of Chinese convert to Christianity. Many of these were "rice Christians," poor Chinese who were willing to become Christians for the rice the missionaries could give them. For the geographer, this is a good example of an attempted relocation diffusion of a major religion that did not work because of absorbing cultural barriers.

■ RELIGIOUS ECOLOGY

One of the main functions of many religions is the maintenance of a harmonious relationship between a people and their physical environment. That is, religion is at least perceived by its adherents to be part of the adaptive strategy, and for that reason physical environmental factors, particularly natural hazards and disasters, have exerted a particularly powerful influence on the development of various religions. Environmental influence is most readily apparent in the tribal animistic faiths. In fact, an animistic religion's principal goal is to mediate between the people and the spirit-infested forces of nature. Animistic ceremonies and even the rites of great religions often are intended to bring rain, quiet earthquakes, end plagues, or in some other way manipulate environmental forces by placating the spirits believed responsible for these events (see box, "How to Intercede with the Cloud People").

Sometimes the link between religion and natural hazard is even visual. The great pre-Columbian temple pyramid at Cholula, near Puebla in central Mexico, strikingly mimics the shape of the awesome nearby volcano Popocatépetl, towering to the menacing height of nearly 18,000 feet (5,500 meters). Catholic missionaries retained the sacred status of the Cholula pyramid, though not its imagined volcano-appeasing attribute, by erecting a church atop it.

While the physical environment's influence on the major religions is less pronounced than in animistic faiths, it is still evident. Animistic nature-spirits lie behind certain practices found in the great religions, such as the previously described **geomancy** of Chinese and Korean Buddhism, by which environmentally auspicious sites are chosen for houses, villages,

HOW TO INTERCEDE WITH THE CLOUD PEOPLE

The following songs or prayers derived from animistic groups are typical pleas aimed at influencing environmental conditions. From the Pueblo Indians of the Sia Pueblo, near Bernalillo, New Mexico, a plea for rain:

> White floating clouds
> Clouds like the plains
> Come and water the earth.
> Sun embrace the earth
> That she may be fruitful.
> Moon, lion of the north,
> Bear of the west,
> Badger of the south,
> Wolf of the east,
> Eagle of the heavens,
> Shrew of the earth,
> Elder war hero,
> Warriors of the six mountains of the world,
> Intercede with the cloud people for us.

From the Haida Indians of coastal British Columbia, Canada, a plea for fair weather:

> O good Sun,
> Look thou down upon us;
> Shine, shine on us, O Sun,
> Gather up the clouds, wet, black, under thy arms—
> That the rains may cease to fall.
> Because thy friends are all here on the beach
> Ready to go fishing—
> Ready for the hunt.
> Therefore look kindly on us, O Good Sun.

Reprinted from *American Indian Poetry: An Anthology of Songs and Chants,* edited by George W. Cronyn, with the permission of Liveright Publishing Corporation. Copyright 1934 Liveright Publishing Corporation. Copyright renewed 1962 by George W. Cronyn.

temples, and graves. In the same category is the veneration of rivers, mountains, rocks, and forests. For instance, the River Ganges is holy to the Hindus (see Figure 6.10), and the Jordan River has a special meaning to Christians. In the same category is the veneration of high places—for example, Mount Fujiyama, sacred in Japanese Shintoism, and holy volcanoes in Mexico. Rocks and stones sometimes retain holy status. The famous Black Stone at Mecca has a special significance for Muslims (see Figure 6.11), who believe that this stone was sent down from heaven by Allah. In fact, it is probably a meteorite. Trees and forests have an honored position in certain major religions. In some areas, Christians use evergreen trees in Christmas celebrations and plant evergreens in cemeteries as symbols of everlasting life—both are relics of the pre-Christian tree worship that covered much of heavily forested northern Europe. We can also

FIGURE 6.10
Hindus bathe in the River Ganges in Varanasi (Benares), India. Hindus regard this as a holy river. Many travel to Varanasi to cremate relatives along the banks of the river, and millions come for religious festivals.

see the survival of animistic worship of the heavenly bodies in the placement of the Christian day of worship on Sun-day and the celebration of Christmas near the winter solstice. Perhaps the widespread sacred or semisacred status of cattle is related to the former worship of the moon. This phenomenon, most notable in Hinduism, also appears elsewhere in the Old World. Scholars have suggested that the crescent shape of cattle horns led early humans to associate these animals with the crescent moon. Indeed, humans may have originally domesticated cattle because of this animal's sacred quality.

Even today, environmental stress can evoke a religious response not so different from that of animistic cults. Local ministers and priests often attempt to alter unfavorable weather conditions with special services, and there are few churchgoing people in the Great Plains of the United States who have not prayed for rain in dry years. In northeastern China, repeated plagues of crop-destroying locusts gave rise over the centuries to a number of "locust cults," complete with temples. Almost 900 such temples were built, providing a place of worship for the locust and locust-gods (see Figure 6.12). Suitable sacrifices and rituals were developed in an effort to avert the periodic infestations.

FIGURE 6.11
This small building, the *kaaba*, houses the sacred Black Stone in Mecca, Saudi Arabia. Pilgrims come from afar to this site, for they believe the stone was sent down from heaven by Allah, the Islamic god.

The Environment and Monotheism

On a much broader scale, some geographers have sought to explain the origins of monotheism by environmental factors. The three major monotheistic faiths—Christianity, Islam, and Judaism—all have their roots among the desert dwellers of the Middle East. Lamaism, the most nearly monotheistic form of Buddhism, flourishes in the deserts of Tibet and Mongolia. In all of these cases, the people involved (Hebrews, Arabs, Tibetans, Mongolians) were once nomadic herders (see Chapter 3), wandering from place to place in the desert with flocks and herds of livestock. The geographer Ellen Churchill Semple argued in the early twentieth century that such desert-dwelling peoples "receive from the immense monotony of their environment the impression of unity" (see biographical sketch). Semple believed that the unobstructed view of the stars and planets provided by the clear desert skies allowed the herders to see that the heavenly bodies moved across the sky in an orderly, repeated progression. This revelation supposedly suggested to the desert stargazers that a single guiding hand was responsible for the orderly system. Semple, in the classic style of environmental determinism, concluded that desert dwellers "gravitate inevitably into monotheism."

Other possibilistic rather than deterministic explanations have been proposed for the origins of monotheism. Some cultural geographers feel that we should look at the social structure of nomadic herding people for answers. Desert nomads are organized into tribes and clans ruled by a male chieftain who has dictatorial powers over the members of the group. It is possible that the all-powerful male deity of Middle Eastern monotheism is simply a theological reflection of the all-powerful, secular, male chieftain. Significantly, female deities are usually associated with farming societies, probably because women represent fertility and are the original domesticators of plants, while male deities are linked with herding or hunting peoples.

Other geographers have noted that these nomadic peoples lived on the edges of larger, more established culture regions. New ideas, these scholars feel, have a tendency to develop at the borders, not at the core or the regions where older structures and ideas are firmly entrenched. The fact is, however, that we do not know enough about early monotheism to say with certainty why or even where it arose. We are not even certain that the first monotheists were desert nomads, and we do know that some desert dwellers were polytheistic.

Religion and Environmental Modification

Just as the physical environment can influence religious belief and practice, so the religious outlook of a people can help determine the extent to which they will modify their environment. In the words of Professor Lynn White, "Human ecology is deeply conditioned by beliefs about our nature and destiny—that is, by religion." In some faiths, human power over natural forces is assumed. The Maori people of New Zealand, for example, believe that humans represent one of six aspects of creation, the others being forest/animals, crops, wild food, sea/fish, and wind/storms. People rule over all of these except the latter, in the Maori world view.

The Judeo-Christian religious tradition also teaches that humans have dominion over nature, but goes further to promote a teleological

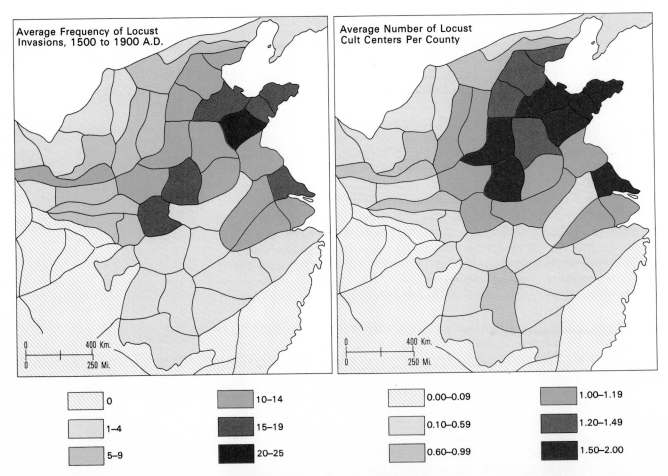

FIGURE 6.12

The frequency of locust infestations and the number of "locust cults" in China are shown here. These cults arose as an adaptive strategy in response to an environmental hazard. The worship of locusts was grafted onto the Buddhist-Confucianist-Taoist composite religion of China. (Redrawn with permission from Shin-Yi Hsu, "The Cultural Ecology of the Locust Cult in Traditional China," *Annals of the Association of American Geographers*, 59 (1969), 734, 745.)

view. Teleology is the doctrine that the Earth was created especially for human beings, who are separate from and superior to the natural world. This view is implicit in God's message to Noah after the Flood, promising that "every moving thing that lives shall be food for you, and as I gave you the green plants, I give you everything." The same theme is repeated in the Psalms, where Jews and Christians are told that "the heavens are the Lord's heavens, but the earth he has given to the sons of men." Within the teleological view is the belief that humans are not part of nature, but are separate, forming one member of a God-nature-human trinity.

Believing that the Earth was given to humans for their use, Christian thinkers in medieval Europe adopted the view that humans were God's helpers in finishing the task of creation. These theologians believed that human modifications of the environment were God's work. Small wonder that the medieval period in Europe witnessed an unprecedented expansion of agricultural acreage, involving the large-scale destruction of woodlands and drainage of marshes. Nor is it surprising that Christian monastic orders, such as the Cistercian and Benedictine Fathers, supervised many of these projects, directing the clearing of forests and the establishment of new agricultural colonies.

Christianity, according to Professor White's view, destroyed classical antiquity's feeling for the holiness of natural things. Subsequently, he argues, scientific advances permitted the Judeo-Christian West to modify the environment at an unprecedented rate and on a massive scale. This marriage of technology and teleology is, White proposes, the root of our modern ecological crisis. By contrast, the great religions of the Orient and many animistic tribal faiths contain teachings and beliefs that are protective of nature (see box, "The Yanoama World View"). In Hinduism, for example, geographer Deryck O. Lodrick found that the doctrine of ahimsa had resulted in the establishment of numerous animal homes, refuges, and hospitals, particularly in the northwestern part of India. The hospitals, or *pinjrapoles,* were closely linked to the Hindu Jain sect. People are part of and at harmony with nature. Such religions do not threaten the ecological balance, says Professor White.

Geographer Yi-Fu Tuan disagrees. He points to a discrepancy between the stated ideals of religions and reality. Even though China enjoys an "old tradition of forest care" based in its composite religion, the Chinese woodlands have been systematically destroyed through the millennia. Nor are the Oriental and tribal religions consistently protective of the environment. Buddhism, for example, protects temple trees but demands huge quantities of wood for cremations. Animistic shifting cultivators sometimes make offerings to appease the woodland spirits before destroying huge acreages of forest with machete and fire. Civilization itself, argues Tuan, is the exercise of human power over nature. Religion can resist but not overcome that exercise. Also, if people are assumed to be part of nature, then one might conclude that no stewardship of the land by humankind seems logical, since we and all our works are "natural."

Other ecologists point out, too, that the Judeo-Christian tradition is not lacking in concern for environmental protection. In the Book of Leviticus, for example, farmers are instructed by God to let the land lie fallow one year in seven and not to gather food from wild plants in that "sabbath of the land." Robin W. Doughty, a cultural geographer, suggests that "Western Christian thought is too rich and complex to be characterized as hostile toward nature," though he feels that Protestantism, "in which worldly success symbolizes individual predestination," may be more conducive to "ecological intemperance."

ELLEN CHURCHILL SEMPLE
1863–1932

Born in Louisville, Kentucky, of a well-to-do family, Semple received a master's degree in history from Vassar and then went to Germany to study. At that time, few women attended universities in Germany, and some claim she had to listen to geography lectures from outside the classroom door. When she returned to America, she brought some of the ideas of German geography. She wrote eloquently and voluminously on environmental determinism. Best known, perhaps, is her book *Influences of Geographic Environment,* published in 1911. Among the ideas presented in her works is the theory that religions are largely the product of the physical environment. Her books gained a very wide readership, both among professional geographers and educated laypersons. She was on the geography faculties at the University of Chicago and Clark University for many years and was a well-known personality in geography. In selecting Semple as president in 1921, the Association of American Geographers became the first national professional academic organization in the United States to place a woman in its highest honorific position.

THE YANOAMA WORLD VIEW

Persons of Judeo-Christian religious heritage need to be reminded that most other cultures do not perceive humans, God, and nature as a trinity of distinct entities. The world view of the Yanoama, an animistic Indian tribe of the Brazilian-Venezuelan borderland, is instructive.

Religion impinges on all aspects of life, without the conceptual distinction between *man, nature,* and the *divine* that characterizes Judeo-Christianity. No omnipotent God exists. There is no material world surrounding the Yanoama and existing independently of them, no world that they view as capable of being dominated and turned to satisfy their own needs. . . . Mysteriously, man can share a common life with an animal, or even with some natural phenomenon, such as the wind or thunder. People not only live now in intimate association with the monkeys, tapirs, deer, and birds of the forest, but also have been—or might be—these very creatures.

There is an easy transmutability among the Yanoama between what [we] commonly define as different realms: the human, natural, and divine. . . . Thus, adult males share spirits, or souls, with other creatures. Among these, the harpy eagle and the jaguar are particularly prevalent. The alter egos of females are associated spiritually with totally different creatures, such as butterflies.

Religion and Environmental Perception

Religion can also influence the way people perceive their physical environment. Nowhere is this more evident than in the perception of environmental hazards such as floods, storms, and droughts. Hinduism and Buddhism teach followers to accept such hazards without struggle, to regard them as natural and unavoidable. Christians are more likely to view storm, flood, or drought as unusual and preventable. As a result, they will generally take steps to overcome the hazard. Sometimes, however, Christians see natural disasters as divine punishment for their sins, in which case worshipers feel they can prevent future disasters by repenting.

Within a single major religion, people's relationship with the land can vary from one sect to another. We have already discussed the overall Judeo-Christian view of the God-nature-human trinity. A study conducted in several small southwestern settlements in the United States by Florence Kluckhohn suggests that individual religious groups see this trinity differently. The large majority (72 percent) of Spanish-American Catholics interviewed felt that humans are subject to nature. Most Mormons (55 percent) saw humans in harmony with nature, a relationship preserved by proper living and hard work. The most common response from Protestant Anglo-Texans (48 percent) held that humans control nature and can overcome environmental hazards. Two-thirds of the Zuni and Navaho Indians, most of whom cling to animism, favored the view of humans in harmony with natural forces. Similarly, a study by John Sims and Duane Baumann revealed that residents of Alabama, where intense, conservative Protestantism prevails, were more likely to react to a tornado threat fatalistically, relying on God to see them through, while Illinoisans, as adherents of a liberal, low-intensity Protestantism, felt in control of their own destinies and took more measures to protect themselves. Perhaps partly as a result, the mortality rate in tornadoes is markedly lower in the Midwest than in the South.

■ CULTURAL INTEGRATION IN RELIGION

While the interaction between religious belief and the environment can shape both religions and the land, religious faith is similarly intertwined with other aspects of culture. Spatial variations in religious belief influence and are influenced by social, economic, demographic, and political patterns in countless ways. Religions and languages often travel together, and religious belief is sometimes at the root of nationalism. Notice, for example, the high degree of spatial correlation between Christianity and the Indo-European languages. Belief systems can interfere with the demographic transition, as in many Islamic areas, and can even influence urban structure. In the economic sphere, religion can guide commerce; determine which crops and livestock are raised by farmers, and what foods and beverages people consume; and even help decide the type of employment a person has.

see prof. notes

Religion and Economy

People make their livings in many different ways, and these forms of livelihood vary greatly from one area to another. Religion is partially responsible for these variations. Try to place yourself in the position of the Hindu street sweeper of Calcutta, whose religion discourages him from aspiring to any higher position in life. Try to imagine what job you might get if your town suddenly attracted religious pilgrims from all over the country. Consider the possible economic effect of religious-based food taboos on the agriculture of your area. In these ways and many more, religion and economics are bound together (see box, "A Marriage of Religion and Economy"). This relationship is evident in agriculture.

Religion and Agriculture. Within some religions, certain plants and livestock, as well as the products derived from them, are in great demand because of their roles in religious ceremonies and traditions. When this is the case, the plants or animals tend to spread with the faith. For example, in some Christian sects in Europe and the United States, celebrants drink from a cup of wine that symbolizes the blood of Christ during the sacrament of Holy Communion. The demand for wine created by this ritual aided the diffusion of grape growing from the sunny lands of the Mediterranean to newly Christianized districts beyond the Alps in late Roman and early medieval times. When you drink German Rhine wine, you are benefiting from this diffusion, because the vineyards of the Rhine were the

Religion + grapes
diffusion of grapes

A MARRIAGE OF RELIGION AND ECONOMY: THE CARGO CULTS OF MELANESIA

Cultural integration is perhaps nowhere more startlingly revealed than in the so-called cargo cults of the western Pacific tropical islands, the area known as Melanesia. There, a religion has arisen based on the hoped-for arrival of Western material goods delivered in American cargo-laden ships. Saviorlike Americans will bring the cargo to the islands. Dr. Kal Muller tells of one such cult on the New Hebridean island of Tanna:

> On the volcano's rim looms a blood-red cross. Nearby, men with "U.S.A." daubed on their bodies shoulder make-believe rifles of bamboo. Soldiers of Christ? Hardly. On the New Hebridean island of Tanna, both cross and marchers herald a hoped-for messiah of material riches — a savior cryptically called John Frum.
>
> Some followers of the mythical Frum consider him a beneficent spirit; others see him as a god come to earth, or as the "king of America." All believe he will someday

usher in a prosperous, work-free millennium of unlimited "cargo" — pidgin English for Western material goods. . . .

> In 1942, World War II reached Tanna's shores. U.S. troops landed on nearby islands, bringing food, arms, prefabricated houses, jobs, and legions of jeeps. . . . But with the war's end, the cargo disappeared, and islanders . . . turned to mock military drills in the hope of luring GIs — and cargo-laden Liberty ships — back to Tanna. . . .
>
> Although Frum fails to materialize — as has been the case for [nearly a half-century] — his followers remain devout, often attributing his absence to their own shortcomings or to governmental intervention.

From Kal Muller, "Tanna Awaits the Coming of John Frum," *National Geographic Magazine,* 145 (1974), 707, 714.

creation of monks who arrived from the south between the sixth and ninth centuries (Figure 6.13; see also box, ''Wine and Religion in Germany''). For the same reason, Catholic missionaries introduced the cultivated grape to California. In fact, wine was associated with religious worship even before Christianity arose. Vineyard keeping and wine making spread westward across the Mediterranean lands in prehistoric times in association with worship of the god Dionysus.

Religion also can often explain the absence of individual crops or domestic animals in an area. The environmentally similar lands of Spain and Morocco, separated only by the Strait of Gibraltar, show the agricultural impact of food taboos. On the Spanish, Roman Catholic side of the strait, pigs are common, but they are not found in Muslim Morocco on the

food TAboos
pork - Muslim Taboo Alcohol

FIGURE 6.13
A label from a bottle of German Rhine wine depicting a religious connection with the vineyards. The word *Liebfraumilch* means ''the milk of the Holy Virgin.''

WINE AND RELIGION IN GERMANY

Even back into prehistoric times in Europe, wine has been linked to religion. In early Christian times, vineyards were introduced into southwestern Germany by Roman monks, who desired ceremonial wine for the holy sacrament. This close attachment of church to wine in Germany left vestiges discernible even today. Among these vestiges are the religious names given to many individual vineyards, names that in turn appear on the wine bottle labels. Some are listed below. Certain generic wine names also reveal the link to religion. One of the most famous of these is *Liebfraumilch*, a mild, semisweet blend from German Rheinhessen. The name means ''milk of the Holy Virgin.''

Derived from Hugh Johnson, *The World Atlas of Wine* (New York: Simon & Schuster, 1971), pp. 140–166. Copyright Mitchell Beazley Publishers Ltd. 1971, 1985.

German Wine District	Town or Village	Name of Vineyard	(Translation)
Rheingau	Rüdesheim	Mönchspfad	(''Monks' Path'')
Rheingau	Rüdesheim	Magdalenenkreuz	(''Cross of Mary Magdalen'')
Rheingau	Oestrich	Gottesthal	(''God's Valley'')
Rheinpfalz	Forst	Jesuitengarten	(''Jesuits' Garden'')
Rheinpfalz	Forst	Mariengarten	(''Virgin Mary's Garden'')
Rheinpfalz	Deidesheim	Paradiesgarten	(''Garden of Paradise'')
Rheinpfalz	Deidesheim	Herrgottsacker	(''Lord God's Field'')
Mosel	Graach	Himmelreich	(''Heaven'')
Mosel	Klüsserath	Bruderschaft	([Monastic] ''Brotherhood'')
Nahe	Bad Kreuznach	Mönchberg	(''Monks' Hill'')
Nahe	Niederhausen	Pfaffenstein	(''Priest's Rock'')
Nahe	Bad Kreuznach	Kapellenpfad	(''Chapel Path'')
Saar	Wiltingen	Klosterberg	(''Monastery Hill'')

African side. The Islamic avoidance of pork underlies this contrast. Figure 6.14 maps the pork taboo. Judaism also has restrictions against pork and other meats, as is stated in the following passage from the Book of Leviticus:

> These shall ye not eat, of them that chew the cud, or of them that divide the hoof: as the camel, because he cheweth the cud, but divideth not the hoof; he is unclean unto you. And the coney, because he cheweth the cud, but divideth not the hoof; he is unclean unto you. And the hare, because he cheweth the cud, but divideth not the hoof; he is unclean unto you. And the swine, though he divide the hoof, and be cloven-footed, yet he cheweth not the cud, he is unclean unto you.

Scholars have attempted to explain the Islamic and Judaic pork taboos in various ways. Some have suggested that these two cultures were primarily concerned with the danger of intestinal parasites (trichinosis), or that they considered pigs unclean. However, it is unlikely that the cause-and-effect relationship between poorly cooked pork and intestinal parasites could have been detected prior to the days of modern medical technology. Other scholars have suggested a theory based on economy and ecology, after observing that pork avoidance is characteristic of the monotheistic faiths that arose among desert nomads. The proponents of this view believe that nomadic herding originated on the borders of the great farming areas of the ancient Middle East, near the Tigris, Euphrates, Nile,

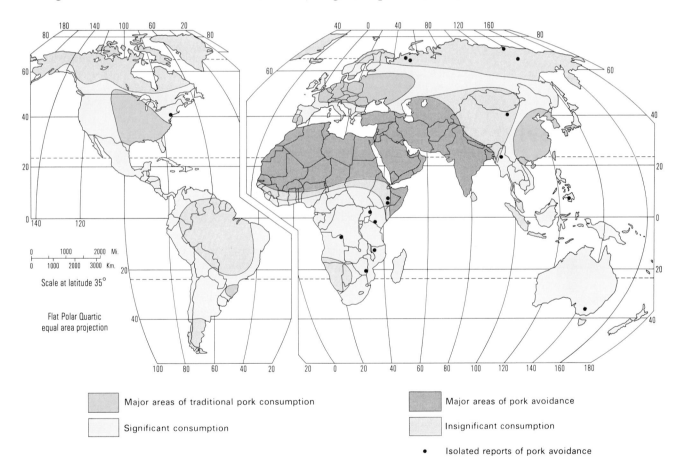

Major areas of traditional pork consumption

Significant consumption

Major areas of pork avoidance

Insignificant consumption

• Isolated reports of pork avoidance

FIGURE 6.14
Consumption and avoidance of pork are influenced by religion. Some religions and churches—such as Islam, Judaism, and Seventh-Day Adventism—prohibit the eating of pork. Cultural groups with a traditional fondness for pork include central Europeans, Chinese, and Polynesians. How can you explain the pattern in North America? (Based in part on Simoons.)

and other rivers. Population pressures forced people to settle farther and farther from the river banks, so that eventually some groups lost access to irrigation waters. As we saw in Chapter 3, these people were forced to abandon most crop farming and turn to animal husbandry. The poor quality of the range required them to wander from place to place in the desert, in nomadic fashion, seeking forage for their livestock. Pigs, valuable animals to the sedentary farmers of the river valleys, could not travel long distances, and there was little for them to eat in the desert. As a result, the nomad relied instead on sheep, goats, horses, camels, and, in some areas, cattle. Since environmental conditions prevented the nomads from owning pigs, they may have declared pork undesirable in a "sour grapes" reaction. In time, this declaration may have found religious expression as a taboo. Ages later, as a final "revenge" in the seventh century A.D., the Muslim nomads imposed their religion, complete with the pork taboo, on the farming people of the river valleys.

Muslims are also not permitted any alcoholic beverages. The Koran states: "O ye who have believed, wine, games of chance, idols, and divining arrows are nothing but an infamy of Satan's handiwork. Avoid them so that ye may succeed." Christians, however, have failed to reach a consensus on this taboo. Some Christian denominations prohibit all consumption of alcohol, in the belief that it is detrimental to health, welfare, and behavior, while others, as described above, even use wine in religious ceremonies. In the United States, such groups as the Baptists, Methodists, Mormons, and Seventh-Day Adventists support prohibition, while Roman Catholics, Lutherans, and several other churches tolerate alcohol. The economic imprint of these different attitudes can be seen in a map of "wet" and "dry" areas in the United States. Texas provides an excellent example, since it is religiously diverse and by law allows each community to decide in local-option elections whether alcohol may be sold or served (Figure 6.15). Almost without exception, Catholic and Lutheran areas in Texas are "wet," while Baptist and Methodist counties are "dry."

Religion and Fishing.   Food taboos also strongly affect the fishing industry. Practices such as the traditional Roman Catholic avoidance of meat on Friday greatly stimulated fishing, since fish became the standard Friday fare in Catholic areas. Indeed, the Christian tradition has always honored fishermen. We can perhaps trace this back to the apostle Peter, a fisherman by profession. The fish was an early symbol of Christianity, initially exceeding the cross in importance. Use of this symbol stimulated the fishing industry, particularly in Catholic countries, and a lively trade in shipping preserved fish from coast to interior developed.

Other cultures place religious taboos on fish consumption and produce an opposite economic result. Most Hindus will not eat fish. India regularly suffers food shortages and dietary deficiencies while the nearby ocean teems with protein-rich fish. Among Christians, the Seventh-Day Adventists have a finless fish taboo and also will not eat pork. When missionaries of this church converted the population of Pitcairn Island in the South Pacific to their faith, the island's economic self-sufficiency collapsed, because the people had previously depended heavily on pork and finless fish in their diet.

Religious Tourism: The Pilgrim Trade.   For many religious groups, sites of particular importance to the faith have become the goal of **pilgrimages** (see Figure 6.16). Journeys to these places often involve the movement of large numbers of people. Pilgrimages are typical of both ethnic and uni-

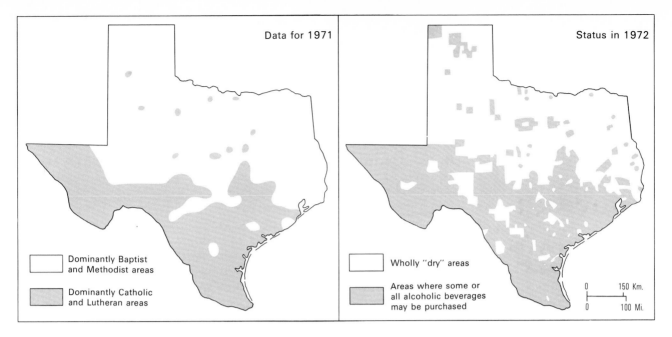

FIGURE 6.15

The distributions of religion and alcohol sales in Texas show a spatial correlation. Catholic and Lutheran areas generally choose to be "wet," and Baptist-Methodist areas retain prohibition. Both the Baptist and Methodist churches have traditionally taken a stand against alcoholic beverages. (From *38th Annual Report of the Texas Alcoholic Beverage Commission,* Austin, 1972, p. 49; and *Churches and Church Membership in the United States: 1971,* National Council of the Churches of Christ in the U.S.A., 1974.)

versalizing religions. They are particularly significant to followers of Islam, Hinduism, Shintoism, and Roman Catholicism.

The sites vary in character. Some have been the setting for miracles; some are the source regions of religions or areas where the founders of the faith lived and worked; others contain sacred physical features such as

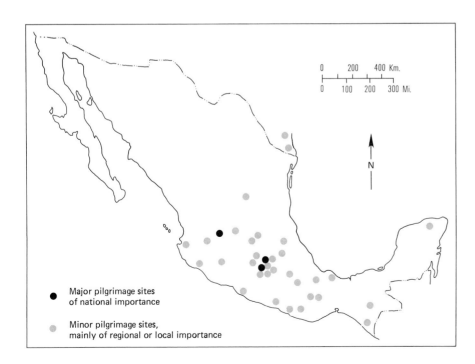

FIGURE 6.16

This map displays the distribution of religious pilgrimage shrines in Mexico and south Texas. These shrines vary greatly in importance and age. Some date from pre-Christian times, and others have arisen in recent years. Pilgrimages are a facet of religious life in most Roman Catholic countries, including Mexico. The concentration of sites in central Mexico corresponds to an area of greatest population density. What kinds of major religious sites are located in the rest of North America and in your own region? (Redrawn with modifications from Mary Lee Nolan, "The Mexican Pilgrimage Tradition," *Pioneer America,* 5, 2, (July 1973), 16.)

rivers and mountain peaks; and still others are believed to house gods or are religious administrative centers where leaders of the church reside. Examples include the Arabian cities of Mecca and Medina in Islam; Rome and the French town of Lourdes in Roman Catholicism; the Indian city of Varanasi on the holy Ganges River, a goal of Hindu pilgrims; and Ise, the hearth of Shintoism in Japan. The distribution of pilgrimage shrines in Mexico is shown in Figure 6.16.

Religion provides the stimulus for pilgrimage by offering those who participate the reward of soul purification or the attainment of some desired objective in their lives. Pilgrims often come from great distances to see major shrines. Other sites, of lesser significance, draw pilgrims only from local districts or provinces. Pilgrimages can have tremendous economic impact, since the movement of pilgrims amounts to a form of tourism. In some favored localities, the pilgrim trade provides the only significant source of revenue for the community. Lourdes, a town of 18,000 in the south of France, attracts between 4 and 5 million pilgrims each year, many seeking miraculous cures at the famous grotto where the Virgin Mary supposedly appeared. Not surprisingly, among French cities, Lourdes ranks second only to Paris in number of hotels, although most of these are small. Mecca, a small city of 367,000 residents, attracted 1,950,000 Muslim pilgrims in 1982 from every corner of the Islamic culture region, as is shown in Figure 6.17. By land, sea, and air, the faithful come to this hearth of Islam, a city closed to all non-Muslims. As you might expect, such massive pilgrimages have a major impact on the development of transportation routes and carriers. To facilitate the pilgrimage to Mecca and Medina, steamships connect the Arabian port of Jidda with overseas Muslim areas in East Africa, Indonesia, Malaysia, and other lands. Char-

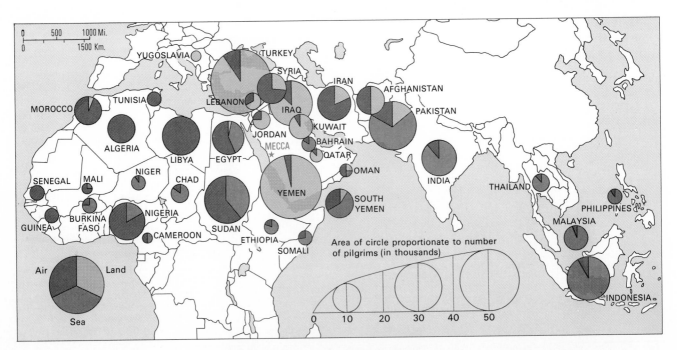

FIGURE 6.17
The pilgrimage of foreign Muslims to Mecca, 1968. In 1968, 375,000 Muslim pilgrims converged on the holy city of Mecca, in spite of the blockage of the Suez Canal that resulted from the Arab-Israeli war of the previous year. Saudi Arabians, in whose nation Mecca is situated, are not shown. (After Russell King, ''The Pilgrimage to Mecca: Some Historical and Geographical Aspects,'' *Erdkunde,* 26 (1972), 70.)

tered and scheduled airline service is also available to Mecca pilgrims. In medieval Europe, many roads and bridges were built to accommodate pilgrims. Monks often helped maintain these routes and established shelters at regular intervals as way stations. Some of these hospices still survive, as at the summit of St. Gotthard Pass in the Swiss Alps.

Religion and Profession.   Often religion and employment are closely connected. In Hinduism, persons in each caste traditionally had a pre-scribed economic role to play. To follow any occupation other than that dictated by caste was a violation of moral obligations. In southern India alone, over 2000 castes and subcastes developed, most with rigidly deter-mined occupational requirements. The caste system apparently originated about 1500 B.C., when Indo-Europeans invaded and conquered northern India. These conquerors formed a light-skinned, elite upper class, while the vanquished native population was kept by law in a subservient posi-tion. From this segregation of conqueror and native grew the caste system. More recently, however, this system has been made illegal, and a total correspondence between caste and occupation no longer exists. However, the caste system has by no means disappeared in rural India, where the greater part of the population lives, although it has waned in urban areas.

In medieval Europe, Christians were generally restricted from lend-ing money for interest. Jews, outcasts in Christian Europe, found most professions closed to them by law. As a result, while most of the Jewish population remained in poverty, individual Jews found an economic niche as moneylenders. They then used this occupation as a capitalist foothold from which they developed skills as retailers, and in time some became important businessmen.

Religion and Political Geography

Americans, accustomed by their heritage to the doctrine of separation of church and state, are usually unaware how closely religion and politics are intertwined in much of the world. Religious practices and traits often change abruptly at political boundaries, as along parts of the Franco-Belgian border in western Europe (Figure 6.18), and political parties are often identified with religious denominations.

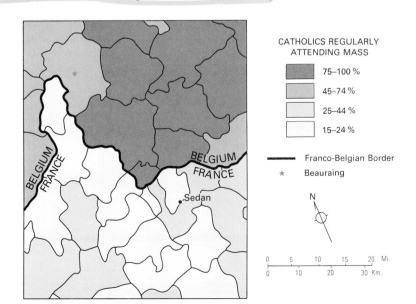

CATHOLICS REGULARLY
ATTENDING MASS

75–100 %
45–74 %
25–44 %
15–24 %

——— Franco-Belgian Border
★ Beauraing

FIGURE 6.18
Attendance at mass along the Franco-Belgian border, about 1950. The people on both sides of the boundary speak French and share many other cultural traits; yet Catholicism remains a vital force only on the Belgian side. The political border has become a religious border. Beauraing is a major Catholic pilgrimage site, lying on the Belgian side of the border. What developments in the respective countries might help explain this striking pattern? (Adapted from Fernand Boulard, *An Introduction to Religious Sociology,* trans. M. J. Jackson, London: Darton, Longman and Todd, 1960. Copyright 1960 by Darton, Longman and Todd Limited, London, and is used by permission of the publishers.)

In some nations, religion has been the rallying point for nationalistic sentiment and has even provided a justification for national existence. In 1947, when Britain granted independence to her colonial holdings in India, the area split to form a Hindu state (India) and a Muslim state (Pakistan). Those who created this division felt that the two religious groups could not coexist peacefully within the same state. Time has since shown that Hindus and Muslims have difficulty living together on the same subcontinent, even in separate states. However, the sizable Muslim population left in India has lived rather peacefully in the dominantly Hindu state in the last three decades. Israel and the Republic of Ireland are two other nations based on religion. In Israel, automatic citizenship is available only to Jews. In cases where religion is an important basis of nationalism, a **state church** is often created. Such a church is recognized by law as the only one in the state, and the government controls both church and state. In Norway, for example, the constitution establishes the Lutheran faith as the state church, and pastors and officials are appointed government employees.

In still other cases, the church is actively involved in governing countries. Such a government is known as a **theocracy** (see box, "The Mormon Region"). The head of the church is often also the head of state. Vatican City, ruled by the Pope, is a fully independent state occupying parts of Rome. Similar to theocracies, but less rigid, are countries where the secular ruler is the nominal head of the state church, as was true of prerevolutionary Russia. Until 1974, Greek Orthodox bishops were actively involved in the government of Cyprus. The danger for the church in such a situation is that the religion may fall with the government.

The presence of two hostile religious groups within the same country can lead to disruption, and perhaps even civil war. States currently threatened by religious divisions include Cyprus, where Turkish Muslims, with

THE MORMON REGION: A CASE STUDY IN CULTURAL INTEGRATION

An excellent example of the interworkings of religion, politics, economy, and population is provided by the Mormon culture region in the Great Basin of the American West. Established by members of the Church of Jesus Christ of Latter-day Saints in 1847, the Mormon culture region spread from the Salt Lake City area to encompass Utah and parts of all bordering states. The population was originally derived from New York and New England, but later immigrants came from Europe and other areas.

Initially, and through most of the nineteenth century, a theocratic government ruled in the Mormon culture region, giving a political expression to the faith. The church leader, Brigham Young, was also the territorial governor of Utah. Repeated efforts were made to create the state of Deseret, to be part of the United States but still under church administration. While the power of the United States government was finally employed to destroy the Mormon theocracy, the tie between church and government remained strong for many years.

In the economic sphere, the church leadership exerted an immense influence on development of the Great Basin area. A goal of economic self-sufficiency was proclaimed. Everything needed in Deseret was to be produced there. Artisans possessing necessary craft skills were actively recruited in

Europe and elsewhere. Agricultural colonies were established in southern Utah, the "Mormon Dixie," to produce cotton and other warm-climate crops that did not grow in the colder Salt Lake area. Most facets of the economy were directly or indirectly controlled by the church, even to the point of ownership in some cases. To a remarkable degree, the plan of economic self-sufficiency succeeded, and through organized hard labor the desert of the Great Basin was made to produce abundantly.

The church also profoundly influenced the population geography of the Great Basin. Indeed, the very settlement of the area was undertaken as a result of a decision by church leaders to migrate from Illinois. After colonization of the Salt Lake area, new colonies were founded, also under church direction. Sites for the new colonies were chosen by the church, and even the selection of colonists was made by the religious leaders. From a very early time, the Mormon church has encouraged large families, thereby further influencing the population distribution of the Great Basin.

In this way, an integration of religion, politics, economy, and demography developed in the Great Basin. To this day, the Mormon culture region retains the distinctive imprints of this interplay.

Turkey's help, seceded in 1983 from the dominantly Greek Orthodox state to form an independent nation; Lebanon, where Christians and Muslims are fighting a civil war; the United Kingdom, which has sought unsuccessfully to reconcile warring Catholics and Protestants in Northern Ireland; and the Philippines, where Catholics are at war with a Muslim minority on the island of Mindanao.

In some nations, political parties are linked to particular church groups. As a result, voting returns often duplicate the religious map. Such ties are particularly common in Europe, where political parties have names like Catholic People's Party or Christian Democrats. It is common in these countries for churchgoers to be advised from the pulpit on how they should vote. Even in countries like the United States, where legal separation of church and state is maintained, voting patterns often correspond to religion.

RELIGIOUS LANDSCAPES

Because religion is so vital an aspect of culture, its visible impress, reflecting the role played by religious motives in the human transformation of the landscape, can be quite striking. In some regions, the religious aspect offers the dominant visible evidence of culture, producing what we might call sacred landscapes. At the opposite extreme are areas almost purely secular in appearance. Religions, then, differ greatly in visibility, but even those least apparent to the eye normally leave some mark on the countryside. The content of religious landscapes is varied, ranging from houses of worship to cemeteries, wayside shrines, and place-names. Moreover, religion can help shape other landscape features such as settlement patterns.

Religious Structures

The most obvious religious contributions to the landscape are the buildings erected to house divinities or to shelter worshipers. These structures vary greatly in size, function, style of architecture, construction material, and degree of ornateness (see Figure 6.19). To Roman Catholics, for example, the church building is literally the house of God, and the altar is the focus of vitally important ritual. Partly for these reasons, Catholic churches are typically large, elaborately decorated, and visually imposing. In many towns and villages, the Catholic house of worship is the focal point of the settlement, exceeding all other structures in size and grandeur. To many Protestants, particularly the traditional "chapel-goers" of British background, including Methodists and Baptists, the church building is, by contrast, simply a place to assemble for worship. God visits the church but does not live there. The result is an unsanctified, smaller, less ornate structure. The simpler church buildings of these Protestants appeal less to the senses and more to the personal faith. For this reason, their traditional structures are typically not designed for comfort, beauty, or high visibility, but instead appear deliberately humble (Figure 6.19).

The building materials chosen for a religious structure often demonstrate the value a religion places on its visibility in the landscape. Sects that wish to call attention to their sacred structures typically build them of different materials than those used in the construction of houses and other nonreligious buildings. In some parts of Europe, for example, churches are built of stone, while secular structures in the same communities are made of brick or wood. In Islam, mosques are normally the most imposing items

FIGURE 6.19
Traditional religious architecture takes varied forms. St. Basil's Church on Red Square in Moscow reflects a highly ornate Russian landscape presence, while the plain board chapel in rural Georgia, in the American South, demonstrates an opposite tendency favoring visual simplicity on the part of British-derived Protestants. The domed mosques and minarets of Islam, in turn, offer still another very distinctive visual religious presence. (Moscow and Georgia photos by Terry G. Jordan, 1981, 1988.)

in the urban landscape, while the visibility of Jewish synagogues varies greatly. Hinduism has produced large numbers of visually striking temples for its multiplicity of gods, but much worship is practiced in private households.

Religious structures can also become mere façades. In rural areas and secularized regions, churches are often abandoned and taken over by very different functions. Along the United States-Canada border west of the Great Lakes, some former churches are now used as granaries, clinics, American Legion halls, garages, and apartments. In the Soviet Union, many have been converted into museums. What appear to be functioning religious landscapes are, in fact, relic.

Paralleling this contrast in church styles are attitudes toward wayside shrines and similar manifestations of faith. Catholic culture regions typically abound with shrines, crucifixes, crosses, and assorted visual reminders of religion, as do some Eastern Orthodox Christian areas. One of the writers of this textbook vividly recalls driving along a mountain road in southern Bavaria on a summer night many years ago, when suddenly the headlights illuminated a realistic, life-sized crucifix in a shrine bordering the pavement. Instinctively, his foot went to the brake, and it was several seconds before he could adjust to the reality of this German Catholic religious landscape (Figure 6.20). Protestant areas, by contrast, are bare of such symbols and do not startle the night driver. Their landscapes do, however, occasionally display such features as signboards advising the traveler to "Get Right With God," a common sight in the southern United States. A billboard on the interstate highway near Montgomery, Alabama, advises the traveler: "Go to Church or the Devil will get you."

Most tribal ethnic religions do not stand out in the cultural landscape. Animistic groups regard many objects as sacred, but these items are commonplace and would not reveal their religious significance to the eyes of an outsider. Tribal religions often do not have separate houses of worship.

Landscapes of the Dead

Religions differ greatly in the type of tribute they award to the dead. This variation appears in the cultural landscape. Hindus and Buddhists cremate their dead. Having no cemeteries, their dead leave no obvious mark on the land (Figure 6.21). In the same way, the few remaining Zoroastrians, called Parsees, who preserve a once-widespread Middle Eastern

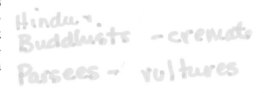

FIGURE 6.20
A wayside shrine in rural Germany. Such shrines are a highly visible part of the religious landscape in some Christian areas. (Photo by Terry G. Jordan, 1978.)

FIGURE 6.21
Hindus burn the bodies of their dead in funeral pyres on the bank of the holy River Ganges in the pilgrimage city of Varanasi, India.

faith now confined to parts of India, have traditionally left their dead exposed to be devoured by vultures. In Egypt, on the other hand, spectacular pyramids and other tombs were built to house dead leaders. These monuments were generally placed on land not suitable for crop farming. Christians and Muslims, as well as Chinese who practice the composite Confucianist-Buddhist religion, typically bury their dead, setting aside land for that purpose and erecting monuments to the deceased kin (see Figure 6.22). In parts of pre-Communist China, as much as 10 percent of the land in some districts was covered by cemeteries and ancestral shrines, greatly reducing the acreage available for agriculture.

Traditionally, Chinese grave sites were geomantically chosen for their *Feng Shui,* literally "wind and water," the perfect combination of tangible and intangible elements that would leave the dead in harmony with their surroundings (Figure 6.23). It is believed that if the *Feng Shui* of a grave site is wrong, the dead will be restless and their descendants will suffer. Ideally, for a grave site in China, the configuration of the earth should be perfect—neither featureless and flat, nor steep and rugged. The active and passive forces of Chinese cosmology, *Yin* and *Yang,* should correctly surround the site. As Chuen-yan David Lai, a Canadian geographer, has written: "The *Yang* energy is expressed as a lofty mountain range, symbolically called the 'Azure Dragon,' and the *Yin* energy as a lower ridge called the 'White Tiger.' The most auspicious model of *Feng Shui* topography is a secluded spot where these two energies converge, interact vigorously, and are kept together in abundance and in harmony by surrounding mountains and streams."

Cemeteries often preserve truly ancient cultural traits, for people as a rule are reluctant to change practices relating to the dead. The traditional rural cemetery of the southern United States provides a case in point. All grass is chopped from the southern cemetery, exposing the bare earth, and freshwater mussel shells are placed atop elongated grave mounds. Rose bushes and cedars are planted through the cemetery. Recent research suggests that the use of roses may be derived from the worship of the ancient, pre-Christian mother goddess of the Mediterranean lands. The rose was a symbol of this great goddess, who could restore life to the dead. Similarly, the cedar evergreen is an age-old Mediterranean and Germanic symbol of death and eternal life, and the use of shell decoration apparently derives from a pagan custom in West Africa, the source of southern slaves. While the present Christian population of the South is unaware of the origins of their cemetery symbolism, it seems likely that their landscape of the dead contains animistic elements thousands of years old.

Religion and Rural Settlement Patterns

As we saw in Chapter 2, most farming peoples live either in clustered villages or in dispersed farmsteads separated from one another. Religion often helps determine which of these patterns will prevail. In the United States and Canada, many highly cohesive religious groups have traditionally formed village settlements, in contrast to the more typical American pattern of dispersed farmsteads. The farm village tradition in Anglo-America was introduced by the Puritans of New England and later perpetuated by Mennonites in Canada, Mormons in the Great Basin of the American West, and the Amana colonists in Iowa. The large majority of utopian communities, so common on the American frontier, also utilized

FIGURE 6.22
A striking landscape of the dead has been created in the Sahara Desert by the Nubian peoples of the Sudan. The burials are mounded and covered with hundreds of small rounded rocks. A very different landscape is seen in the French cemeteries of southern Louisiana, including New Orlelans, where the dead rest in aboveground crypts. (New Orleans photo by Terry G. Jordan, 1978.)

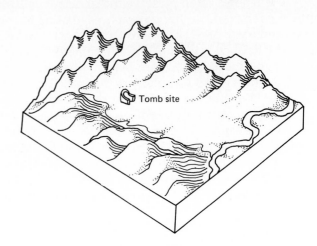

FIGURE 6.23
The model shows an ideal tomb site according to the Chinese principles of *Feng Shui*. The tall mountain range represents the spirit of the "Azure Dragon," a figure of active Yang energy. The lower hills symbolize the "White Tiger," a figure of the complementary passive Yin energy. The winding stream represents wealth. (After Chuen-yan David Lai, "A Feng Shui Model as a Location Index," *Annals of the Association of American Geographers*, 64 (1974), 506–513.)

the farm village pattern. These sects, religious and utopian alike, typically placed a high value on group interaction and mutual support, and they felt that the clustered village was necessary to provide the daily contacts essential to the practice and perpetuation of their faiths.

If the sect weakened and declined, or if factionalism developed, the clustered farm settlements often broke up. In Colonial New England, where some Puritan settlements had developed as villages, the power of church leaders in Boston waned after about 1700, and the Puritan movement began to fragment. Thereafter the farm villages gave way to scattered farmsteads, for religious individualism and scattered farmsteads had replaced the cohesive, village-based theocracy.

Religious Names on the Land

"St.-Jean," "St.-Aubert," "St.-Damase-des-Aulnaies," "Ste. Perpétue de L'Islet," "St.-Pamphile," "St.-Adalbert," "Ste.-Lucie," "St.-Fabien-de-Panet," "St.-Juste-de-Bretenières," "Ste.-Camille-de-Bellechasse" — so read the town-name placards as one drives from the St. Lawrence River south on Highway 24 in Québec, paralleling the Maine border (Figure 6.24). All this saintliness is merely a part of the French Canadian religious landscape, as Figure 6.25 shows. The point is that religion often inspires the names people place on the land. Within Christianity, the use of saints' names for settlements is very common in Roman Catholic and Greek Orthodox areas, especially in overseas colonial lands settled by Catholics, such as Latin America and French Canada. In areas of the Old World that were settled long before the advent of Christianity, saints' names were often grafted onto pre-Christian names, as in Alcazar de San Juan, in Spain, which combines Arabic and Christian elements.

Toponyms in Protestant regions display less religious influence, but some imprint can usually be found. In the southern United States, for example, the word *chapel* as a prefix or suffix, as in Chapel Hill and Ward's Chapel, is very common in the names of rural hamlets. Names like this accurately convey the image of the humble, rural Protestant churches that are so common in the South.

FIGURE 6.24
Religious toponyms permeate the cultural landscape of French Catholic Québec in Canada, helping create a special sense of place. (Photo by Terry G. Jordan, 1984.)

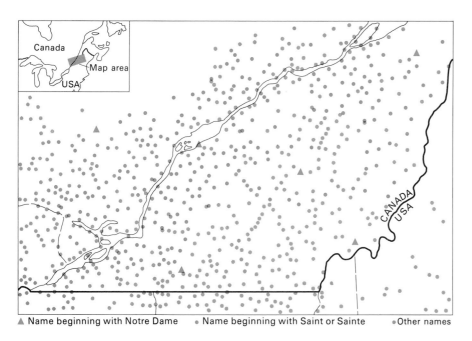

▲ Name beginning with Notre Dame   • Name beginning with Saint or Sainte   •Other names

FIGURE 6.25
Religious place-names dot the map of French Canada. In the French Canadian province of Québec, the dominant Roman Catholic religion finds an expression in the names given to towns and villages. Saintly names are dominant in the areas of purest French settlement. Nearer the United States-Canadian border, in townships settled by English-speaking people, religious place-names are rare. On this basis, where exactly would you draw the French Catholic/English Protestant border at the time of initial settlement? Is that border still in the same location today?

◼ CONCLUSION

Religion is firmly interwoven in the fabric of culture, a bright hue in the human mosaic, for religions and individual religious elements vary greatly from one area to another. Several major religions and many minor ones form a variety of culture regions. We illustrated some of these spatial variations with maps.

Such religious spatial variation led us to ask how these distributions came to be, a question best answered through the methods of cultural diffusion. Some religions, universalizing denominations, actively encourage their own diffusion. Most Christian churches, for example, send out missionaries to "spread the word." Other religions erect barriers to expansion diffusion by restricting membership to one particular ethnic group. Jews, for instance, do not seek converts. The spatial diffusion of religious ideas often parallels and accompanies other, nonreligious elements of culture, such as language, crops, and political systems.

The theme of cultural ecology reveals some fundamental ties between religion and the physical environment. One major function of many religious systems, particularly the animistic faiths, is to appease and placate the forces of nature and to achieve harmony between the people and the physical environment. Religions differ in their outlook on environmental modification by humans. Some religious groups view such alterations as an affront to the gods. We need to face the question of whether the Christian ecological outlook is leading us to environmental disaster.

Religion is culturally integrated — that is, systemically related to economy and politics, among other things. Everything from tourism to nationalism can have a religious component. This further strengthens the view of culture as a functioning whole.

The cultural landscape abounds with expressions of religious belief. Places of worship — temples, churches, and shrines — differ in appearance, distinctiveness, prominence, and frequency of occurrence from one religious culture region to another. These buildings provide a visual index to the various faiths. Cemeteries and religious place-names also add a special effect to the landscape that tells us about the religious character of the population.

Suggested Readings

Surinder M. Bhardwaj. *Hindu Places of Pilgrimage in India.* Berkeley and Los Angeles: University of California Press, 1973.

Michael E. Bonine. "Islam and Commerce: Waqf and the Bazaar of Yazd, Iran," *Erdkunde,* 41 (1987), 182–196.

Stanley D. Brunn and James O. Wheeler. "Notes on the Geography of Religious Town Names in the United States," *Names: Journal of the American Name Society,* 14, No. 4 (1966), 197–202.

Manfred Büttner. "Religion and Geography," *Numen,* 21 (1974), 163–196.

Joseph Chamic. *Religion and Fertility: Arab Christian-Muslim Differentials.* New York: Cambridge University Press, 1981.

John I. Clarke. "Islamic Populations: Limited Demographic Transition," *Geography,* 70 (1985), 118–128.

Daniel Doeppers. "The Evolution of the Geography of Religious Adherence in the Philippines Before 1898," *Journal of Historical Geography,* 2 (1976), 95–110.

R. A. Donkin. *The Cistercians: Studies in the Geography of Medieval England and Wales.* Toronto: Pontifical Institute of Mediaeval Studies, 1978.

Robin W. Doughty. "Environmental Theology: Trends and Prospects in Christian Thought," *Progress in Human Geography,* 5 (1981), 234–248.

L. Alan Eyre. "Biblical Symbolism and the Role of Fantasy Geography Among the Rastafarians of Jamaica," *Journal of Geography,* 84 (1985), 144–148.

Isma'il R. al-Fārūqi and David E. Sopher. *Historical Atlas of the Religions of the World.* New York: Macmillan, 1974.

Richard H. Foster, Jr. "Changing Uses of Rural Churches: Examples from Minnesota and Manitoba," *Yearbook of the Association of Pacific Coast Geographers,* 45 (1983), 55–70.

Richard V. Francaviglia. *The Mormon Landscape.* New York: AMS Press, 1978.

Robert H. Fuson. "The Orientation of Mayan Ceremonial Centers," *Annals of the Association of American Geographers,* 59 (1969), 494–511.

John D. Gay. *The Geography of Religion in England.* London: Gerald Duckworth, 1971.

Clarence J. Glacken. *Traces on the Rhodian Shore.* Berkeley: University of California Press, 1967.

Peter L. Halvorson and William M. Newman. *Atlas of Religious Change in America, 1952–1971.* Washington, D.C.: Glenmary Research Center, 1978; and their accompanying volume, *Patterns in Pluralism: A Portrait of American Religion.* Washington, D.C.: Glenmary Research Center, 1980.

Manfred Hannemann. *The Diffusion of the Reformation in Southwestern Germany, 1518–1534.* Chicago: University of Chicago, Dept. of Geography, Research Paper No. 167, 1975.

Charles A. Heatwole. "The Unchurched in the Southeast, 1980," *Southeastern Geographer,* 25 (1985), 1–15.

Sara Hershkowitz. "Residential Segregation by Religion: A Conceptual Framework," *Tijdschrift voor Economische en Sociale Geografie,* 78 (1987), 44–52.

Richard H. Jackson. "Religion and Landscape in the Mormon Cultural Region," in K. W. Butzer (ed.), *Dimensions of Human Geography.* Chicago: University of Chicago, Dept. of Geography, Research Paper No. 186, 1978, pp. 100–127.

Richard H. Jackson and Roger Henrie. "Perception of Sacred Space," *Journal of Cultural Geography,* 3 (Spring–Summer 1983), 94–107.

Terry G. Jordan. "Forest Folk, Prairie Folk: Rural Religious Cultures in North Texas," *Southwestern Historical Quarterly,* 80 (1976), 135–162.

Terry G. Jordan. *Texas Graveyards: A Cultural Legacy.* Austin: University of Texas Press, 1982.

Jeanne Kay and Craig J. Brown. "Mormon Beliefs About Land and Natural Resources, 1847–1877," *Journal of Historical Geography,* 11 (1985), 253–267.

Florence R. Kluckhohn et al. *Variations in Value Orientations.* Evanston, Ill.: Row, Peterson, 1961.

Gregory J. Levine. "On the Geography of Religion," *Transactions of the Institute of British Geographers,* 11 (1986), 428–440.

David N. Livingstone. "Environmental Theology: Prospect in Retrospect," *Progress in Human Geography,* 7 (1983), 133–140.

Deryck O. Lodrick. *Sacred Cows, Sacred Places: Origins and Survivals of Animal Homes in India.* Berkeley and Los Angeles: University of California Press, 1981.

Emanuel Maier. "Torah as Movable Territory," *Annals of the Association of American Geographers,* 65 (1975), 18–23.

Joseph T. Manyo. "Italian-American Yard Shrines," *Journal of Cultural Geography,* 4 (1983), 119–125.

Donald W. Meinig. "The Mormon Culture Region: Strategies and Patterns in the Geography of the American West, 1847–1964," *Annals of the Association of American Geographers,* 55 (1965), 191–220.

William M. Newman and Peter L. Halvorson. "American Jews: Patterns of Geographic Distribution and Change, 1952–1971," *Journal for the Scientific Study of Religion,* 18 (1979), 183–193.

Hans-Jürgen Nitz. "The Church as Colonist: The Benedictine Abbey of Lorsch and Planned Waldhufen Colonization in the Odenwald," *Journal of Historical Geography,* 9 (1983), 105–126.

Mary Lee Nolan. "Irish Pilgrimage: The Different Tradition," *Annals of the Association of American Geographers,* 73 (1983), 421–438.

Mary Lee Nolan and Sidney Nolan. *Religious Pilgrimage in Modern Western Europe.* Chapel Hill: University of North Carolina Press, 1989.

Ellen Churchill Semple. *Influences of Geographical Environment.* New York: Henry Holt, 1911.

Yosseph Shilhav. "Principles for the Location of Synagogues: Symbolism and Functionalism in a Spatial Context," *Professional Geographer,* 35 (1983), 324–329.

James R. Shortridge. "Patterns of Religion in the United States," *Geographical Review*, 66 (1976), 420–434.

James R. Shortridge. "The Pattern of American Catholicism," *Journal of Geography*, 77 (1978), 56–60.

Frederick J. Simoons. *Eat Not This Flesh: Food Avoidances in the Old World*. Madison: University of Wisconsin Press, 1961.

Paul Simpson-Housley. "Hutterian Religious Ideology, Environmental Perception, and Attitudes Toward Agriculture," *Journal of Geography*, 77 (1978), 145–148.

John H. Sims and Duane D. Baumann. "The Tornado Threat: Coping Styles of the North and South," *Science*, 176 (1972), 1386–1392.

Rana P. B. Singh. "Distribution of Castes and Search for a New Theory of Caste Ranking: Case of the Saran Plain," *National Geographical Journal of India*, 21 (March 1975), 20–46.

David E. Sopher. *The Geography of Religions*. Englewood Cliffs, N.J.: Prentice-Hall, 1967.

David E. Sopher. "Geography and Religions," *Progress in Human Geography*, 5 (1981), 510–524.

David Spring and Eileen Spring (eds.). *Ecology and Religion in History*. New York: Harper & Row, 1974.

Dan Stanislawski. "Dionysus Westward: Early Religion and the Economic Geography of Wine," *Geographical Review*, 65 (1975), 427–444.

Roger W. Stump (ed.). "The Geography of Religion." Special issue, *Journal of Cultural Geography*, 7, No. 1 (Fall–Winter 1986), 1–140.

Roger W. Stump. "Regional Divergence in Religious Affiliation in the United States," *Sociological Analysis*, 45 (1984), 283–299.

Roger W. Stump. "Regional Migration and Religious Commitment in the United States," *Journal for the Scientific Study of Religion*, 23 (1984), 292–303.

Roger W. Stump. "Regional Variations in Denominational Switching Among White Protestants," *Professional Geographer*, 39 (1987), 438–449.

H. Tanaka. "Geographical Expression of Buddhist Pilgrim Places on Shikoku Island, Japan," *Canadian Geographer*, 21 (1977), 111–133.

Yi-Fu Tuan. "Discrepancies Between Environmental Attitude and Behavior: Examples from Europe and China," *Canadian Geographer*, 12 (1968), 176–191.

Yi-Fu Tuan. "Sacred Space: Explorations of an Idea," in Karl W. Butzer (ed.), *Dimensions of Human Geography: Essays on Some Familiar and Neglected Themes*. Chicago: University of Chicago, Dept. of Geography, Research Paper No. 186, 1978, pp. 84–99.

Stephen W. Tweedie, "Viewing the Bible Belt," *Journal of Popular Culture*, 11 (1978), 865–876.

Ingolf Vogeler. "The Roman Catholic Culture Region of Central Minnesota," *Pioneer America*, 8 (1976), 71–83.

S. Waterman and B. A. Kosmin. "The Distribution of Jews in the United Kingdom," *Geography*, 71 (1986), 60–65.

Lynn White, Jr. "The Historical Roots of our Ecologic Crisis," *Science*, 155, 3767 (March 10, 1967), 1203–1207.

Hong-key Yoon. *Maori Mind, Maori Land: Essays on the Cultural Geography of the Maori People from an Outsider's Perspective*. Bern, Switzerland: Peter Lang, 1986.

Wilbur Zelinsky. "An Approach to the Religious Geography of the United States: Patterns of Church Membership in 1952," *Annals of the Association of American Geographers*, 51 (1961), 139–167.

Chapter 7

Folk Geography

FOLK CULTURE REGIONS

    **Material Folk Culture Regions in
      Eastern North America**
    Folklore Regions

FOLK CULTURAL DIFFUSION

    Diffusion of Religious Folk Songs
    Diffusion of the Agricultural Fair
    The "Beaverslide" Hay Stacker
    **The Blowgun: Diffusion or Independent
      Invention?**

FOLK ECOLOGY

    Folk Foods: The Example of Geophagy
    Folk Medicine and the Environment
    **Folk Culture and Environmental
      Perception**

CULTURAL INTEGRATION IN FOLK
GEOGRAPHY

    **The Mountain Moonshine Whiskey
      Industry**
    The Bluegrass Country Music Industry

FOLK ARCHITECTURE IN THE CULTURAL
LANDSCAPE

    Traditional Building Materials
    Floorplan and Layout
    Other Characteristics
    Folk Housing in Eastern North America

CONCLUSION

Students of culture, geographers included, recognize two major classes of cultural groups: the **popular,** consisting of large masses of people who conform to and prescribe ever-changing norms, and the **folk,** made up of people who retain the traditional. The word *folk* conjures up many images for citizens of the urban, industrialized world. It describes a rural people who live in an old-fashioned way—a people holding to a simpler life-style little influenced by the industrial revolution, modern technology, and the flight to the cities. Many disillusioned American urban young people were seeking this lost, simpler way of life when they "dropped out" and moved to rural communes in the late 1960s and early 1970s.

Closely related to the concept of folk are the concepts of folk culture, folklore, folklife, and folk geography. A **folk culture** is a small, isolated, cohesive, conservative, nearly self-sufficient group that is homogeneous in custom and race, with a strong family or clan structure and highly developed rituals. Order is maintained through sanctions based in the religion or family, and interpersonal relationships are strong. Tradition is

subsistance

FIGURE 7.1
The Amish in the United States retain
many aspects of folk culture in their
everyday lives.

paramount, and change comes infrequently and slowly. There is relatively little division of labor into specialized duties. Rather, each person is expected to perform a great variety of tasks, though duties may differ between the sexes. Most goods are handmade, and a subsistence economy prevails. Individualism is generally weakly developed in folk cultures, as are social classes. Unaltered folk cultures no longer exist in industrialized countries such as the United States and Canada. Perhaps the nearest modern equivalent in Anglo-America is the Amish, a German-American farming sect that largely renounces the products and labor-saving devices of the industrial age (Figure 7.1). In Amish areas, horse-drawn buggies still serve as a local transportation device, and the faithful are not permitted to own automobiles. The Amish's central religious concept of *demut*, "humility," clearly reflects the weakness of individualism and social class so typical of folk cultures, and there is a corresponding strength of Amish group identity. Rarely do the Amish marry outside their sect. The religion, a variety of the Mennonite faith, provides the principal mechanism for maintaining order.

By contrast, a **popular culture** (the subject of Chapter 8) is a large, heterogeneous group, often highly individualistic and constantly changing. Interpersonal relationships tend to be impersonal, and a pronounced division of labor exists, leading to the establishment of many specialized professions. Secular institutions of control such as the police and army take the place of religion and family in maintaining order, and a money-based economy prevails. Because of these contrasts, "popular" may be viewed as clearly different from "folk." The popular is replacing the folk in

delimited.

industrialized countries and in many developing nations. Folk-made objects give way to their popular equivalent, usually because the popular item is more quickly or cheaply produced, is easier or time-saving to use, or lends more prestige to the owner.

Typically, bearers of folk culture combine folk and nonfolk elements in their lives. The proportion of folk to nonfolk characteristics in an individual's cultural makeup varies from one person to another, but most of us display at least some folk traits. Are children's games such as "London Bridge" part of your heritage? Have you ever chanted the ancient count-out phrase "eenie, meenie, miney, moe"? Have you consulted an astrologer or placed a horseshoe over a door for good luck? If so, then you retain some folk elements in your cultural makeup.

Folklife refers to the totality of the folk culture, including both material and nonmaterial elements. **Material culture** includes all objects or "things" made and used by members of a cultural group: tools, utensils, buildings, furniture, clothing, artwork, musical instruments, vehicles, and other physical objects. Material elements are visible. By contrast, **nonmaterial culture,** including **folklore,** can be defined as oral, including the wide range of tales, songs, lore, beliefs, superstitions, and customs that is passed from generation to generation as part of an oral or written tradition. Folk dialects, religions, and world views can also be regarded as aspects of nonmaterial culture.

Cultural geographers adopt the folklife approach in their study of folk groups, although emphasis traditionally has been placed on the material aspects of culture, particularly folk architecture. **Folk geography,** a term coined by the cultural geographer Eugene Wilhelm, may be defined as the study of the spatial patterns and ecology of folklife. Folk geography is an integral, growing branch of cultural geography, and our five themes are well suited to it.

▮ FOLK CULTURE REGIONS

As a rule, elements of folklife exhibit major variations from place to place and minor variations through time, while popular culture displays less difference from region to region but changes rapidly through time. The natural divisions of folklife, then, are spatial—that is, geographic. For this reason, the theme of culture region is well suited to the study of folklife.

good diferentiation between popular c. y folk c.

Formal regions of folklife can be delimited on the basis of material or nonmaterial elements. Cultural geographers have tended to emphasize material culture in most of their studies, but recently some have turned to nonmaterial topics.

Material Folk Culture Regions in Eastern North America

Figure 7.2 shows the material folk culture regions of the eastern United States and Canada. Not surprisingly, these regions bear a resemblance to the traditional rural culture regions shown in Chapter 1 (Figure 1.6), since material folk culture is obviously a major component of rural cultural geography. Many artifacts were considered in devising the map—everything from dolls and outdoor ovens to tombstones, bean pots, homemade boats, folk architecture, and blackbird pies. Using this evidence, we can identify eight folk regions in eastern North America: the North, Mid-Atlantic, Midwest, Upland South, Lowland South, Acadiana, French Canada, and Upper Canada. As popular culture spread during the last

FIGURE 7.2
Material folk culture regions of the
eastern United States. Compare this
map with Figure 1.6. (In part after
Glassie, *Pattern in the Material Folk
Culture of the Eastern United States*,
p. 39.)

century or so, folk culture retreated and very nearly vanished in much of
the area included in the study. Nevertheless, we can find interesting
remnants of folk culture in all of the regions.

The Mid-Atlantic folk region, also called the Pennsylvania culture
region, is the smallest of the eight but possibly the most important, since
through relocation diffusion it exerted influence on the Midwest, Upper
Canada, and the Upland South. Encompassing the greater part of Pennsylvania, the southern half of New Jersey, northern Maryland, and most of
Delaware, the Mid-Atlantic region reveals a material folk culture that
combines continental European and British contributions. From the
German-language areas of central Europe came such diverse material
items as the well-known "Pennsylvania" barn, distinguished by an overhanging, upper-level "forebay" on one eave side; elaborate and brightly
colored birth and baptismal certificates; the "long rifle" made famous by
the likes of Daniel Boone; and a type of pottery decoration called *sgraffito*,
made by pouring a thin layer of liquid clay over unfired red pottery and
then scratching designs through the clay layer to expose the red color
underneath (Figure 7.3). From Scandinavia came notched-log construction, relics of which survive even in the suburban environs of Philadelphia.

The material folk culture of the North is more purely English in origin,
reflecting the background of the early Puritan settlers of New England.
Typically English are such folk items as tombstones adorned with a
winged death's head and the village greens, or "commons," that lie at the
core of many villages and towns (Figure 7.4). Beans baked with molasses,
salt pork, and onions in a large pot set in a stone-lined pit are a typical
northern folk food, particularly in New England. The folk region is
an extensive one, reaching from the Canadian Maritime Provinces to
Wisconsin.

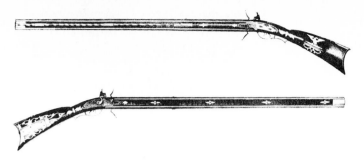

FIGURE 7.3
The photograph on the left shows three examples of sgraffito pottery. On the right is a double-barrel superposed long rifle from the period following the Revolutionary War. The building is a typical Pennsylvania barn, complete with projecting forebay and German hex signs. All three of these items are derived from the German-language areas of Europe. (Barn photo by Terry G. Jordan, 1980.)

In the Lowland South, centered in the coastal plains of the Atlantic and the Gulf of Mexico, the material folk culture reflects a mixture of British and African influences. Among the distinctive material items of this culture region are the African-style head kerchiefs worn by black women; the mule-powered syrup mill in which cane or sorghum is crushed; the banjo, an important instrument in the folk music of the region; the scraped-earth cemetery, from which all grass is laboriously chopped to expose the bare ground; and the typically British fireplace and exterior chimney.

The material folk culture of the Upland South is derived from both the Mid-Atlantic and the Lowland South, although the former region seems to have been its most important source. Both British and continental European influences are strong here. The Applachian and Ozark highlands, which form eastern and western centers of the Upland South, provided the shelter and isolation that permitted a greater survival of material folk culture, as did the hills of central Texas. Abundant notched-log structures, split-rail fences, whiskey stills, and tobacco barns are among the material folk items surviving in the Upland South. Perhaps for this reason, students of folklife have long been attracted to the Upland South, and many of the examples presented in this chapter will be drawn from this culture region.

The Midwest, a narrow, wedge-shaped material folk culture region, is a complex patchwork of Mid-Atlantic, Northern, and Upland Southern influences, to which were added a host of items derived directly from Europe. As such, it might be regarded as the most thoroughly "American" region of the eastern United States, more closely akin to the West than the East. The Midwest has long been a progressive farming area, where the products and methods of the industrial age were quickly adopted, with the

FIGURE 7.4
A variation of the winged death's head tombstone found in upstate New York.

FIGURE 7.5
French folk fences in Europe (left) and Québec (right) illustrate both the French Canadian folk culture and the process of cultural diffusion. (Source: Jean Brunhes, *Human Geography,* London: George G. Harrap & Co., Ltd., 1955, Figures 71 and 72.)

result that popular culture has almost entirely replaced the earlier folk forms in many areas. Here and there in the Midwest, however, you may still glimpse a large Pennsylvania barn type, an Upland Southern log house, a German half-timbered structure, or a typical New England town meeting hall.

French Canada was settled in the seventeenth century by migrants, mainly from northern France. The highly distinctive French Canadian material folk culture, centered in Québec, is revealed in features as diverse as traditional house architecture (see Figure 7.28); fence types (Figure 7.5); grist windmills with sturdy stone towers; *pétanque,* a bowling game played with small metal balls; and maple sugar pies. Some items were adopted by the French from Indian tribes of the St. Lawrence Valley, as for example the snowshoe, which has for three centuries been manufactured by folk artisans of ash wood and strips of cowhide. In some respects, Acadiana, or the traditional Gallic area of southern Louisiana, can be regarded as an outlier of French Canada, largely because the resident "Cajuns" (Acadiens) came from Acadia, along the Bay of Fundy in Nova Scotia. However, Cajun interaction with the Lowland South and Louisiana Indians, in the context of a swampy, subtropical seacoast and delta, produced a very distinctive folk culture, recognized particularly in its foods (such as gumbo) and music.

Upper Canada, occupying the southern part of the province of Ontario, is similar to the Midwest in that it is a folk region where different cultural traditions mixed. Perhaps the major shaping influences came from the Mid-Atlantic and the North, particularly Pennsylvania, the Maritime Provinces, and upstate New York. Adding diversity were numerous settlers coming directly from Europe. In this way, Pennsylvania log construction and barns, Northern folk foods, and a host of other items of material folk culture were implanted in Ontario. Curiously, very few features of French Canadian material folk culture penetrated Upper Canada, in spite of the proximity of the two regions.

Folklore Regions

Nonmaterial folk culture displays regional contrasts in much the same manner as material folk culture does. Increasingly, folk geographers have become concerned with nonmaterial phenomena, such as folktales, dance, music, myths, legends, and proverbs. In general, nonmaterial culture closely corresponds spatially to material culture regions. The North, Lowland South, Mid-Atlantic, and other American folk regions can usually also be recognized through a study of nonmaterial folk culture.

Folk music provides an excellent basis for delimiting formal regions of nonmaterial items of culture. Alan Lomax, an expert on the English-language folk songs of North America, recognized four folk-song culture regions in the United States: the Northern, Southern, Western, and Black song families (Figure 7.6). The Northern tradition, characterized by unaccompanied solo singing in hard, open-voiced, clear tones with unison on the refrains, is based largely in British ballads and has not deviated greatly from the English prototype. In the Southern folk-song tradition, by contrast, unison singing is rare and the solo is high-pitched and nasal. Combining English and Scotch-Irish (as the Ulster Protestant Irish are called in the United States) elements, the Southern style features ballads that are more guilt-ridden and violent than those of the North. The Western style, according to Lomax, is simply a blend of the Southern and Northern traditions. The Black folk-song family contains both African and British elements, featuring polyrhythmic songs of labor and worship with instrumental accompaniment, chorus group singing, clapping, swaying of the body, and a strong, surging beat. Black and Southern styles coexist across much of the coastal plain South, each still closely linked to its respective racial group. In addition to the folk-music regions delimited by Lomax, we can recognize a Mexican-American and a French-Canadian region, each displaying distinctive instrumentation, melodies, and motifs. Some of the French-Canadian fur trader songs, such as "Alouette, gentille Alouette,"

FIGURE 7.6
Folk-song culture regions of the eastern United States and Canada. Compare this map to Figures 1.6 and 7.2. Folk music is rarely used as a criterion for devising culture regions, but is well suited to this purpose. (Modified from Alan Lomax, *The Folk Songs of North America in the English Language,* New York: Doubleday, 1960, frontispiece.)

FIGURE 7.7
Switzerland: Where do newborn children come from? When you were little and asked your parents where babies come from, did you get the old runaround about storks or some other equally absurd answer? If so, don't judge them too harshly, for they were only perpetuating an old folk custom of deception. This map of Switzerland reveals that different provinces and districts are characterized by distinctive evasive answers to this age-old question. The map provides us with another example of how nonmaterial folk culture can provide an index to culture regions. Where exactly would you draw the boundaries of the culture regions on this map? How many culture regions would you designate? Cultural geographers always face the same difficult decisions in delimiting culture regions. Most French-speaking Swiss parents prefer the cabbage-pumpkin explanation, German-Swiss children are more likely to hear the stork story, and Italian-Swiss youngsters are usually told that their siblings come by purchase from the store. (After Elsbeth Liebl, "Herkunft der Kinder," in Paul Geiger et al., *Atlas der Schweizerischen Volkskunde,* Basel: Schweizerische Gesellschaft für Volkskunde, Vol. 2, part 4, 1950, plates 202–205.)

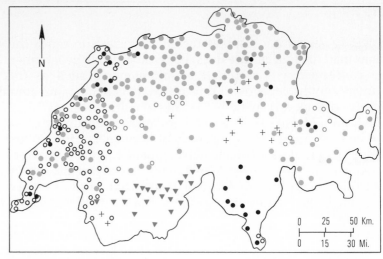

- ● Purchased at store
- ▼ Monks of the forest or hermits
- + Church, chapel, or monastery
- ○ Cabbage or pumpkin
- ○ Hollow tree or log
- ● Stork

have spread to the North American population at large. The music of traditional Mexican mariachi street bands is commonly heard on radio stations in the southwestern states.

Many other facets of folklore can be categorized into culture regions. Figure 7.7 depicts an example from the rich folklore of Switzerland, a meeting ground of German, French, Italian, and Rhaeto-Romanic peoples. The great *Atlas der schweizerischen Volkskunde* (Atlas of Swiss Folklore), perhaps the best of its kind in the world, contains hundreds of maps of value to the folk geographer in formulating culture regions.

FOLK CULTURAL DIFFUSION

Folk culture, both material and nonmaterial, spreads by the same processes of diffusion as do other types and elements of culture. The material folk culture regions described earlier in this chapter (Figure 7.2) were produced mainly by relocation diffusion, as different groups of settlers moved west from major source areas and implanted their folk cultures in new lands (Figure 7.8; see also box, "A Transatlantic Fish Story"). If, however, expansion diffusion is the process by which items of folk culture spread, then the movement across areas is often very slow. In part this is due to the weakly developed social stratification within folk cultures, a feature that tends to retard hierarchical diffusion, and in part it is the consequence of inherent conservatism and resistance to change. Certainly, an essential difference between folk and popular culture (see Chapter 8) is the speed by which expansion diffusion occurs.

Diffusion of Religious Folk Songs

An example of the slow progress of expansion diffusion in a folk setting can be seen in the spread of Anglo-American religious folk songs in the United States (Figure 7.9). From an eighteenth-century core area based mainly in the New England, or Northern, culture, these white spiritual

FIGURE 7.8
Diffusion of folk cultures through eastern North America. The material folk culture regions shown in Figure 7.2 were produced by ideas carried along the routes of diffusion shown here. In large part, folk culture was spread by relocation diffusion, as settlers moved west. What factors might have caused the currents of diffusion to flow as they did? (In part after Glassie, *Pattern in the Material Folk Culture of the Eastern United States*, pp. 37, 38, with modifications.)

Major source areas

Route of diffusion

0   200   400 Km.
0   100   200   300 Mi.

songs spread southwest into the Upland South and finally into the Lowland South, where such songs retain their greatest acceptance today. In the meantime, religious folk songs largely disappeared from the Northern source regions, possibly because of the rapid urbanization and popularization of culture in that area. The white spiritual movement began as an expression of protest against the entrenched Protestant establishment. Simple folk melodies were the main musical device of the spirituals, and they spread rapidly by means of outdoor "revivals" or "camp meetings."

A TRANSATLANTIC FISH STORY

Cultural diffusion is often revealed by comparing folktales in different regions. The following tale, presented in a much-abridged form, occurs both in Celtic Wales on the island of Great Britain and among people of British extraction in the Ozark Mountains of Missouri and Arkansas. It apparently spread by relocation diffusion to America and halfway across the continent, changing somewhat in the process.

Ozark Mountain Version

A man living up the Meramec River
caught a yellow catfish using only
his hands
he took it home and put it in a rain
barrel
the fish turned into a woman
she became a fish again
he put it back in barrel
and took it back to the river

Welsh Version

A man living
on the River Towey
caught a salmon
from a small boat with a rod
the fish spoke Welsh and English,
                                          and
turned into a naked girl with a
                              fish-hook in her lip
she became the man's wife

Adapted from E. Joan Wilson Miller, "The Ozark Culture Region as Revealed by Traditional Materials," *Annals of the Association of American Geographers*, 58 (1968), 59.

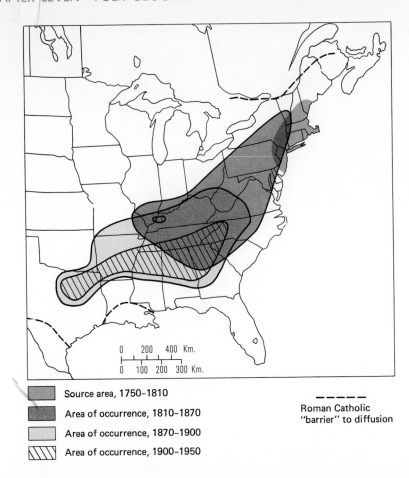

FIGURE 7.9
Spatial diffusion of Anglo-American religious folk songs, 1750–1950. These songs, white spirituals, spread by expansion diffusion from New England to the South, eventually disappearing from the source region. (After George P. Jackson, "Some Factors in the Diffusion of American Religious Folksongs," *Journal of American Folklore,* 65 (1952), 365–369.)

Source area, 1750–1810

Area of occurrence, 1810–1870

Area of occurrence, 1870–1900

Area of occurrence, 1900–1950

Roman Catholic "barrier" to diffusion

Non-English-speaking peoples and non-Protestants were little influenced by the spiritual movement, for language and religion proved effective barriers to diffusion. The French Canadians and Louisiana French were not affected by the movement.

Diffusion of the Agricultural Fair

Another element of folk culture that originated in the Northern region and spread west and southwest by expansion diffusion was the American agricultural fair, a custom rooted in medieval European folk tradition. According to folk geographer Fred Kniffen (see biographical sketch), the first American agricultural fair was held in Pittsfield, Massachusetts, in 1810, and the idea quickly gained favor throughout western New England and the adjacent Hudson Valley (Figure 7.10). From that source region it diffused westward into the American heartland, the Midwest, where it gained its widest acceptance. Normally promoted by agricultural societies, the fairs were originally educational in purpose, and farmers could learn about improved methods and breeds. Soon an entertainment function was added, represented by a racetrack and midway, and competition for prizes for superior agricultural products became common. By the early twentieth century, the agricultural fair had diffused through most of the United States, though farmers in culture regions such as the Upland South and Lowland South did not accept it as readily or fully as did the Midwesterners. The spread of the agricultural fair followed a more northerly route than that of white spiritual songs, although the source areas of the two were almost identical.

The "Beaverslide" Hay Stacker

The American West, too, produced folk innovations, though the traditional cultures of that region have been less thoroughly researched than those of the eastern states and provinces. A good example is the so-called *beaverslide hay stacker*, an item of traditional material culture recently studied by geographer John A. Alwin. Because of his work and the relatively recent origin of the device, we know more about its diffusion than is typical of folk culture. The stacker is a 30-odd foot (10 meters) tall, derricklike structure, used to raise hay to the top of a stack, employing horsepower to pull a basket up an inclined surface (Figure 7.11). Alwin found that the beaverslide originated in 1907 in Montana's Big Hole Valley and its use subsequently spread to at least eight nearby states and across the international border into three Canadian provinces (Figure 7.12). The map of its distribution raises some basic cultural geographical questions and suggests the manner in which items of folk culture are dispersed.

The Blowgun: Diffusion or Independent Invention?

Often the past diffusion of an item of folk culture is not clearly known or understood, presenting folk geographers with a problem of interpretation.

★ First agricultural fair, Pittsfield, Mass., 1810

• Fairs by 1820

· New fairs by 1858

· New fairs by 1912

FIGURE 7.10
Diffusion of the American agricultural fair, 1810–1910. Both the agricultural fair and the white spiritual arose in the same general area. Compare the diffusion of the fair and the spiritual. What differences can you detect in the routes of diffusion? Why might these differences have developed? (After Fred B. Kniffen, "The American Agricultural Fair," *Annals of the Association of American Geographers,* 41 (1951), 45, 47, 51.)

FRED B. KNIFFEN
1900–

A native of Michigan, Fred Kniffen is of New England ancestry and spent much of his boyhood in the transplanted New England folk culture of the upper Midwest. At the University of California, Berkeley, Kniffen studied under the famous cultural geographer Carl O. Sauer and the renowned anthropologist Alfred Kroeber. This combination of geography and anthropology in his doctoral degree work provided the basis of Kniffen's interest and expertise in folk geography. He is acknowledged as the founder and kindly "father figure" of American folk geography. His circle of influence is wide.

From 1929 to the present, Dr. Kniffen has been associated with the Department of Geography and Anthropology at Louisiana State University, Baton Rouge, where he is presently professor emeritus. He has authored some 125 titles, and his range of interest has been great. In his list of publications are works on folk houses, agricultural fairs, covered bridges, outdoor folk ovens, log construction, and other fascinating items of material culture. His 1936 article on the folk houses of Louisiana is regarded as a classic, seminal work, and his 1968 book *Louisiana: Its Land and People* has been widely praised. Dr. Kniffen has received many honors and tributes, most notably the honorary presidency of the Association of American Geographers in 1966–1967, an Honors Award from the same group in 1978, and membership in Phi Beta Kappa.

An example is provided by the blowgun, a long, hollow tube through which a projectile is blown by the force of the breath. The cultural geographer Stephen C. Jett mapped the distribution of this hunting weapon and found it among folk societies in both the Old and New Worlds, all the way from the island of Madagascar off the African coast to the Amazonian jungles of South America, over halfway around the world (Figure 7.13). Apparently the blowgun was first invented by Malaysian peoples, probably on the island of Borneo in the East Indies. It became the principal hunting weapon of this folk society and was diffused with the Malayo-Polynesian linguistic group through much of the equatorial island belt of the Eastern Hemisphere. How do we account for its presence among Amerindian groups in the Western Hemisphere? Was it independently invented by the Amerindians? Was it brought by relocation diffusion in pre-Columbian times to the Americas? Or did it spread to the New World only after the European discovery of America? The answers to these questions are not known, but the problem presented is one common to cultural geography, and particularly to folk geography, since the nonliterate condition of most folk cultures precludes written records that might reveal diffusion.

If you choose to believe that the blowgun had a single origin and spread to America, then you must explain the wide gaps where it is not found in the South Pacific island world and Africa, which lie between the two zones of occurrence. If you choose instead to support the independent invention theory, then you have to accept the proposition that an identical device was invented two times, in very different folk cultures. The study of cultural diffusion often presents such problems.

Indeed, the issue of independent invention versus diffusion has been one of the most perplexing for cultural geographers. Clearly, independent invention is possible, even, as we have seen, in a folk setting. Carl O.

FIGURE 7.11
Three beaverslide hay stackers stand in the broad meadows of the Big Hole Valley in southwestern Montana, the place of origin of this device. (Photo by Terry G. Jordan, 1987.)

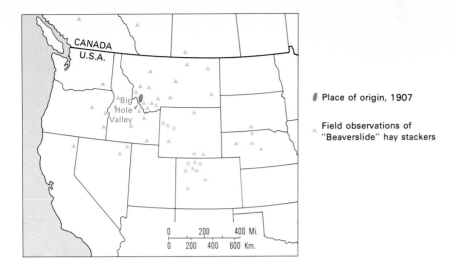

FIGURE 7.12
Past and present distribution of the "Beaverslide" hay stacker. Why was the diffusion greatest in an eastward direction? What barriers might have prevented dispersal into Utah and to the Pacific shore? Why did the international boundary not serve as a barrier? Take an atlas showing natural routeways and draw arrows on this figure showing the most likely paths of diffusion from the place of origin. Then refer to Alwin's article and read how the diffusion actually occurred. The Mormons have their own distinctive type of hay stacker (for their distribution, see Figures 1.6 and 6.2). (From John A. Alwin, "Montana's Beaverslide Hay Stacker," *Journal of Cultural Geography*, 3 (Fall–Winter 1982), 47, Bowling Green State University and including data provided by Charles F. Gritzner and field data gathered by Terry G. Jordan in 1987.)

Sauer's proposal that the domestication of plants occurred independently in the two hemispheres (see Chapter 3) helped free cultural geographers from their traditional view that each element of culture had a single origin. Certain rules of thumb can be employed in any given situation to help resolve the issue. For example, if it were found that one or more *nonfunctional* features of blowguns, such as a decorative motif, occurred both in South America and the East Indies, then the logical conclusion would be that cultural diffusion explained the distribution of blowguns.

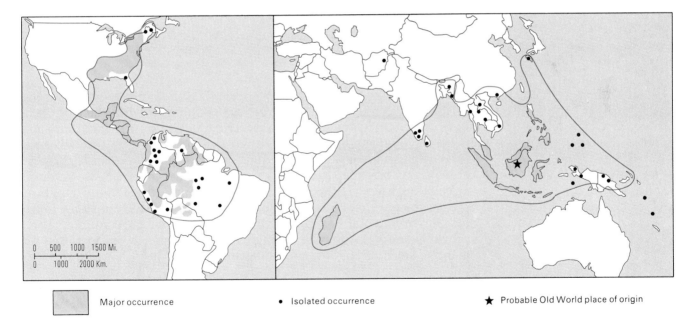

FIGURE 7.13
Former distribution of the blowgun among American Indians, South Asians, Africans, and Pacific Islanders. The blowgun occurred among folk cultures in two widely separated areas of the world. Was this the result of independent invention or cultural diffusion? What kinds of data might one seek to answer this question? Compare and contrast the occurrence in the Indian and Pacific ocean lands to the distribution of the Malayo-Polynesian languages (Figures 5.3). (Sources: Stephen C. Jett, "The Development and Distribution of the Blowgun," *Annals of the Association of American Geographers*, 60 (1970), 668, 674, and more recent data provided by Professor Jett.)

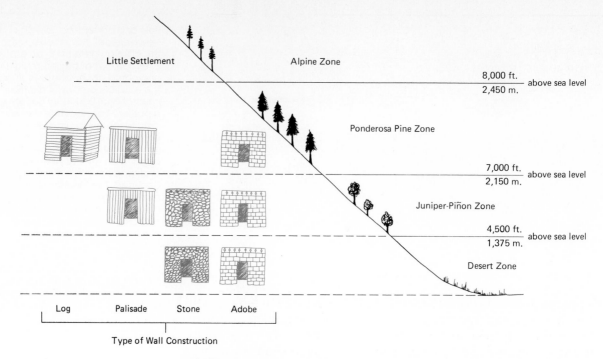

FIGURE 7.14

The ecology of folk architecture in northern New Mexico. Buildings erected by people belonging to folk groups consist of materials available. So it is among the Hispanic and Indian folk of northern New Mexico, where the type of wall construction changes with elevation above sea level, reflecting in part the progression of microenvironments encountered at different heights. (Adapted from Charles F. Gritzner, "Construction Materials in a Folk Housing Tradition: Considerations Governing Their Selection in New Mexico," *Pioneer America,* 6 (January 1974), 26.)

◼ FOLK ECOLOGY

Cultural ecology is an especially appropriate theme in folk geography, because folk groups enjoy a very close relationship with their physical environment. This closeness is largely explained by the fact that such people live on the land, gaining their livelihood directly through such primary activities as farming, herding, hunting, gathering, and fishing. A great many facets of folk culture relate at least indirectly to the local ecology and involve adaptive strategies. The languages of folk groups bear the vocabularies required to exploit the habitat, their religions act to mitigate environmental hazards, their folk tales honor great hunters, their proverbs offer wisdom concerning the weather and the proper time for planting, and their traditional architecture reflects the local building materials and climate (Figure 7.14).

Indeed, one is tempted, when dealing with folk groups, to conclude that culture is synonymous with adaptation—that folkways all exist to facilitate the adjustment to physical environment. Equally easy is the path of environmental determinism, believing that folk cultures will inevitably be guided along similar courses in similar ecological settings. But folk culture is more than merely an adaptive system, and a great variety of folk cultures can exist in any particular physical environment. While folk cultures may be more sensitive than popular cultures to the qualities of the soil, climate, and terrain, it does not follow that they are enslaved and wholly shaped by their physical surroundings, nor is it necessarily true

geophagy

that folk groups are in close harmony with their environment, for often soil erosion, deforestation, and overkill of wild animals can be attributed to traditional rural folk. Even so, we must always keep the cultural ecological context in mind when seeking to interpret folk culture, for otherwise we overlook a quite fundamental possibilistic explanatory mainspring.

Folk Foods: The Example of Geophagy

Most folk groups consume natural foods derived directly from the land either through husbandry of domesticated plants and animals or through hunting and gathering of wild species. The large majority of people in such societies are directly involved in food production and are therefore intimately in contact with the land. Each folk group has its own distinctive selection of foods and means of food preparation.

Perhaps no food habit intertwines environment and culture more closely than **geophagy,** the deliberate eating of earth. While found among many different cultures, dirt eating is most common in black Africa and among Americans of African ancestry. Certain kinds of clay are the preferred earth material for geophagy. In the African source regions of this folk custom, clays are consumed for a variety of reasons (Figure 7.15). Some African earth eaters feel that the clay is an effective treatment for

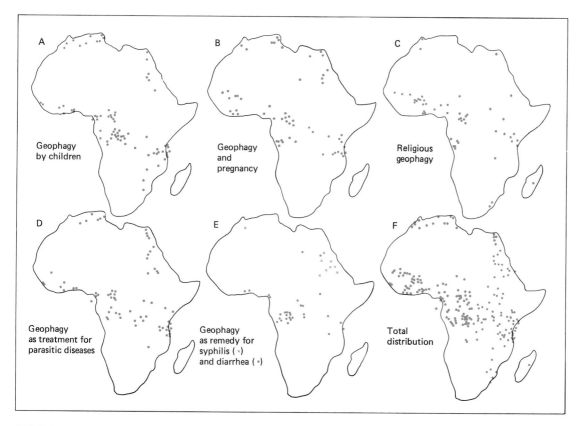

FIGURE 7.15
Geophagy in Africa. Clay eating is a widespread folk custom in Africa, especially in the West African region where many of the slaves brought to America originated. African geophagy is associated by its practitioners with both health and religion. (After John M. Hunter, "Geophagy in Africa and in the United States: A Culture-Nutrition Hypothesis," *Geographical Review*, 63 (1973), 172; and Sture Lagercrantz and B. Anell, "Geographical Customs," *Studia Ethnographica Upsalensia*, 17 (1958), 24–84.)

certain diseases and parasites, while others believe it provides needed nutrients for pregnant women and growing children. Some consume clay as part of religious ceremonies. In Holmes County, Mississippi, an intensive study made by cultural geographer Donald E. Vermeer and health expert Dennis A. Frate found that geophagy is confined mainly to pregnant black women and to black children under the age of five. By way of comparison, 28 percent of pregnant black women and 7 percent of pregnant whites in the county consume clay. The average intake is about 50 grams per day. The preferred clays, obtained from digs or highway cuts in the upland section of the county, are fine-textured and grit-free, light gray or whitish in color, and sour in taste. The clay is heated in a pan on a stove for several hours; some add salt and vinegar before baking. Geophagy in Holmes County is apparently unrelated to dietary deficiencies or intestinal parasites. Rather, it is best regarded as a folk custom that persists for cultural reasons.

Geophagy is deeply rooted in Afro-American folk culture and has survived in spite of persistent attempts to abolish it. In slavery times, some white masters put mouthlocks on the blacks to prevent geophagy, and local health officials today generally oppose it. In Alabama, the consumption level is so great that the Highway Department has posted signs forbidding digging at road cuts because of the damage it causes. Often southern rural blacks send packages of geophagical clays to kinfolk in northern or western cities.

The barrier preventing a wider diffusion of geophagy in America seems to be the social stigma attached to the practice. Yet it is a permeable barrier: Many persons who do not eat clay will consume commercial, store-bought starch, which is perceived as a more respectable substitute. In addition to the 28 percent of pregnant black women in Holmes County who consume clay, another 19 percent eat box starch, as do an additional 10 percent of the pregnant whites.

Folk Medicine and the Environment

In geophagy we find an intimate tie between folk culture and the environment, but close links are also typical of folk medicine. It is common in folk societies to treat diseases and disorders with drugs and medicines derived from the root, bark, blossom, or fruit of plants. In the United States, folk medicine is best preserved in the Upland South, particularly southern Appalachia; on some Indian reservations; and in the Mexican borderland. Many of the folk cures have proven effectiveness.

The outlook of the Upland Southerner toward cures is well expressed in the comments of an eastern Tennessee mountaineer root digger who, in an interview with cultural geographer Edward T. Price, said that "the good Lord has put these yerbs here for man to make hisself well with. They is a yerb, could we but find it, to cure every illness." Root digging has been popularized to the extent that much of the produce of the Appalachians is now funneled to dealers, who serve a larger market outside the folk culture (Figure 7.16), but root digging remains at heart a folk enterprise, carried on in the old ways and requiring the traditionally thorough knowledge of the plant environment.

Along the Texas-Mexico border, on both sides of the Rio Grande, folk medicine is still widely practiced by *curanderos,* or "curers." Over 400 medicines are derived from both wild and domestic plants growing in the border region, perpetuating a tradition rooted in sixteenth-century Indian and Spanish sources. The local folk medicine is based on the belief that

FIGURE 7.16
An Appalachian root digger holding ginseng.

health and welfare depend on harmony between the natural and supernatural; disease and misfortune are thought to involve some disharmony.
The *curandero*, through the use of counseling and botanical medicines,
strives to restore harmony. In recent years, fewer border folk have sought
herbal remedies for infections, sprains, or broken bones, choosing instead
to go to doctors and hospitals, but *curanderos* are treating more cancer,
diabetes, and hypertension than previously. The thriving *curandero* business along the Rio Grande is best viewed as a persistent folk element in a
culture undergoing considerable change and popularization. Some *curanderos* have responded to change by becoming virtual paramedics and
employing antibiotics in some cures.

Folk Culture and Environmental Perception

An intimate knowledge of the environment, then, provides food and
medicines for people in a folk culture. It is not surprising, in view of this
close association with the land, that members of such groups, when migrating, seek lands similar to those they leave behind (Figure 7.17). They
function best in environments like those their ancestors have occupied for

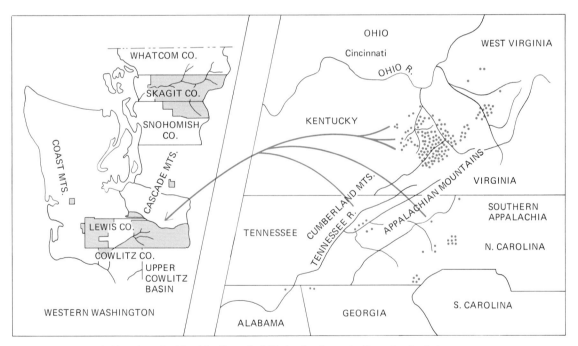

  •   Appalachian place of origin of families or individuals migrating to the Upper Cowlitz Basin

       Settlement areas of Appalachian hill folk in Washington state

FIGURE 7.17
The relocation diffusion of Appalachian hill folk to western Washington. Each dot
represents the former home of an individual or family that migrated to the upper Cowlitz
River basin in the Cascade Mountains of Washington State between 1884 and 1937.
Some 3000 descendants of these migrants lived in the Cowiltz area by 1940. What does
the high degree of clustering of the sources of the migrants and subsequent clustering in
Washington suggest about the processes of folk migrations? How should we interpret their
choices of familiar terrain and vegetation for a new home? Why might members of a folk
society choose a similar land? (After Woodrow R. Clevinger, "The Appalachian
Mountaineers in the Upper Cowlitz Basin," *Pacific Northwest Quarterly*, 29 (1938), 120;
and Woodrow R. Clevinger, "Southern Appalachian Highlanders in Western Washington,"
Pacific Northwest Quarterly, 33 (1942), 4, with modifications.)

centuries, because the lore of the land passed down to them relates to one particular locale.

When overpopulation or some other "push" factor causes folk groups to seek a new homeland, they are often "pulled" to places that are similar in terrain, soils, vegetation, and wildlife. A good example can be seen in the migrations of southern highland folk from the mountains of Appalachia in the century between 1830 and 1930. As the Appalachians filled up, many highlanders began looking elsewhere for similar areas to pioneer. In their migrations, they normally moved in clan or extended-family groups. Initially they found an environmental twin of the Appalachians in the Ozark-Ouachita Mountains of Missouri and Arkansas. Somewhat later, others sought out the hollows, coves, and gaps of the central Texas hill country. The final migration of Appalachian hill folk brought some 15,000 members of this culture to the Cascade and coastal mountain ranges of Washington State between 1880 and 1930 (Figure 7.17). The role of environmental perception and clan ties in directing these migrations can be seen in the following remarks by a Kentucky mountaineer, recorded by W. R. Clevinger in 1937: "I've been figurin' fer a right smart time about leavin' fer Washington. I hear there's a good mountin country out thar where a man can still hunt, git work in mills and loggin', and git a piece of land right cheap. Some of my kin out thar have writ back, wantin' me to jine 'em."

People so close to nature are also sensitive to what they perceive as very subtle environmental qualities. Nowhere is this sensitivity more evident than in the practice of "planting by the signs," found among folk farmers in the United States and elsewhere (see box, "Planting by the Signs of the Zodiac"). Reliance on the movement and appearance of planets, stars, and the moon might seem absurd to the managers of huge, corporation-owned farms, but these beliefs and practices are still widespread among the members of folk cultures.

All in all, folk groups are much more observant of their local physical environment than are most people in the popular culture. They strive for harmony with nature, though they do not always achieve it, and often

---

PLANTING BY THE SIGNS OF THE ZODIAC

Each day of a month is said to be dominated by one of the signs of the zodiac. Every sign appears at least once a month, holding sway for two or three days at a time. The signs were long ago assigned traits, such as masculine or feminine; fiery, airy, earthy, or watery; barren or fruitful.

Many rural folk in America, and elsewhere as well, use the signs as indicators of the proper planting time. The following are some "rules" for farming "by the signs," collected from interviews in rural north Georgia and from various other sources. They illustrate the intimate ties between people and the physical environment so typical in folk cultures:

Planting is best done in the fruitful signs of Scorpio, Pisces, Taurus, or Cancer.

Plow, till, and cultivate in Aries.

Always set plants out in a water or earth sign [Taurus, Cancer, Virgo, Scorpio, Capricorn, or Pisces].

Graft just before the sap starts to flow, while the moon is in its first or second quarter, and while it is passing through fruitful, watery sign, or Capricorn. Never graft or plant on Sunday as this is a barren, hot day.

Plant flowers in Libra, which is an airy sign that also represents beauty.

Corn planted in Leo will have a hard, round stalk and small ears.

Crops planted in Taurus and Cancer will stand drought.

Don't plant potatoes in the feet [Pisces]. If you do, they will develop little nubs like toes all over the main potato.

Plant all things which yield above ground during the increase or growing of the moon, and all things which yield below the ground (root crops) when the moon is decreasing or darkening.

Never plant on the first day of the new moon, or on a day when the moon changes quarters.

ascribe animistic religious sanctity to the forces of the environment and to particular parts of their habitat. Some members of the popular culture, from Henry David Thoreau to disenchanted American youth of the 1970s, have lamented the loss of closeness to nature that accompanied the rise of nonfolk culture, and they have sought to recapture that intimacy by withdrawing to rural retreats. To reestablish the close ties, they, like folk groups, will have to depend on nature for their day-to-day livelihood, a risk and sacrifice that relatively few are able or willing to take or make. Such intimacy is the product of centuries of trial and error and, once lost, is not easily regained.

■ CULTURAL INTEGRATION IN FOLK GEOGRAPHY

In reading the discussion of culture regions, diffusion, and ecology, you perhaps got the impression that folk groups are completely self-sufficient and totally segregated from the popular culture. Rarely is that true. Few folk cultures are so isolated and remote as to escape altogether from interaction with the larger world. The theme of cultural integration will allow us to see how groups can retain their folk character and yet be in almost daily contact with popular cultures — that is, how folk groups are integrated into the nonfolk world. There is a lively exchange constantly under way between the folk and the popular cultures. Perhaps most commonly, the folk absorb ideas filtering down from the popular culture, but occasionally elements of the folk culture penetrate the popular society. Even peasants innovate, despite the relatively unchanging character of folk society, and these innovations and ideas can spread to other classes of society. Two examples from the culture of the Appalachian hill folk of the southern United States will illustrate the integration of folk and popular, showing the impact that these two cultures can have on each other. These examples are mountain "moonshining" and "country" music.

The Mountain Moonshine Whiskey Industry

Corn whiskey has been manufactured since the earliest days of Anglo-American pioneering in the southern Appalachians in the eighteenth century. Very likely its origins lie still further back, in the Scottish folk tradition of making whiskey from barley. The word *whiskey* is itself of Celtic origin, probably from the Scottish Gaelic *uisge beatha* ("water of life"), and the techniques of making the beverage were likely diffused to America and to the Appalachians with the Scotch-Irish, a people of Scottish origin who came from Northern Ireland. Home manufacture of whiskey has prevailed in many Appalachian hill settlements for 200 years and is a deep-rooted folk custom (Figure 7.18). Whiskey making withstood the prohibitionist attitudes of the great nineteenth-century religious revival, and even though many mountaineers are devout Baptists or Methodists, they continue to defy the antiliquor teachings of these and other Protestant churches. The mountain folk were more than willing to vote their areas legally "dry," but they were not prepared to give up distilling and drinking hard liquor. Much like the geophagy of southern blacks, corn whiskey among the mountain whites is very persistent in the folk diet.

Traditionally, corn liquor was intended mainly for consumption within the family, not for market. In other words, the manufacture of "white lightning" was still purely in the folk tradition. Gradually over the years, however, some Appalachian moonshine began finding its way to

FIGURE 7.18
An Appalachian whiskey still.

market. Whiskey provided the best opportunity for the hill folk to participate in the money economy of the country, since its manufacture converted a bulky grain crop of low cash value into a beverage that was compact and of high value per unit of weight. As early as 1791, the United States federal government had begun taxing manufacturers of whiskey, but from the beginning the mountaineers found ways to avoid the tax. Stills were concealed in remote coves and hollows to escape detection by the federal revenue collectors; if the stills were discovered and destroyed, new ones in different locations soon replaced them. The revenuers proved no more successful in abolishing the making of whiskey than the churches had been. In effect, the mountain folk accepted the markets offered by the popular culture but rejected its legal and political institutions.

The mountain people proved more than capable of evading the law. By the 1950s, some 25,000 gallons of white lightning were reaching the market each week from the counties of eastern Tennessee alone (Figure 7.19). In spite of numerous raids by the federal authorities, production

FIGURE 7.19
Approximate number and location of illegal stills captured monthly in eastern Tennessee in the mid-1950s. The rugged Smoky Mountains and Cumberland Plateau offer more abundant hiding places for stills than does the ridge and valley region. What might account for the clustering in two main areas? (After Loyal Durand, Jr., "Mountain Moonshining in East Tennessee," *Geographical Review*, 46 (1956), 171.)

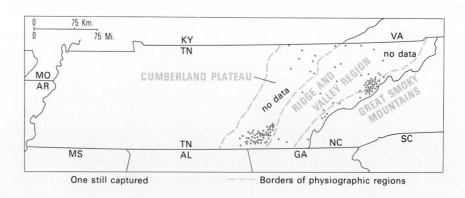

continued unabated. Even today, a substantial amount of illicit whiskey reaches market from southern Appalachia. This production, coupled with that of the legal, taxpaying whiskey manufacturers of Kentucky and Tennessee, represents an impressive survival of a folk industry in a popular society.

Interaction with the popular culture in the production of illegal whiskey led to other kinds of contact, providing still more examples of cultural integration. To market the produce, after about 1930 at least, fast vehicles were required in order to outrun the law. The result was a ''folk automobile,'' a souped-up jalopy quite humble in appearance but capable of very high speeds. Some claim that the mountaineer's whiskey-running automobile was the forerunner of the basic American stock car and that stock car racing is simply a recreational form of the traditional flight from revenuers (Figure 7.20). The Ford flathead V-8 of the 1930s and 1940s owed much of its commercial success in the South to the fact that it was the easiest and best engine to modify for these purposes. Thus, stock car racing is another result of the interplay between folk and popular cultures.

The Bluegrass Country Music Industry

Country music is derived, to a great degree, from the folk ballads of the English and Scotch-Irish who settled the southern Appalachians in colonial times. Some experts have even hypothesized that the use of the fiddle (violin) to produce the shrill sounds so typical of mountain music is an effort to recapture the sound of the Celtic Scottish bagpipe. Gradually, Appalachian folk music absorbed influences of the American social experience, becoming a composite of Old World and New World folk traditions. Like whiskey making, Appalachian music long remained confined to the traditional society that had developed it. As folk music, it gave expression to a unique life-style and a particular land, while dealing with

FIGURE 7.20
Stock car racing in the American South may be a product of interaction between folk and popular culture.

such universal themes as love and hate, happiness and sorrow, comedy and tragedy.

Entry of country music into the popular culture began about the time of World War I and was facilitated by the invention and diffusion of the radio. Popularization brought changes to country music. The number of tunes and songs, which had been relatively small and slow to increase in the folk society, exploded in a few decades into tens of thousands. Performers in crowded, noisy night spots soon resorted to electrical amplification to achieve the needed volume, producing such curious folk-popular mixtures as the electric guitar. The themes of lyrics were addressed to life in the popular rather than the folk culture. But at its core, country music remained folk.

Bluegrass, one of many styles of country music, emerged in the 1930s during the process of popularization of Appalachian folk music. It was developed by Bill Monroe, a Kentuckian. The unique bluegrass sound is achieved by the joining of a lead banjo, of African origin, with a fiddle, guitar, mandolin, and string bass. In many ways, bluegrass remains faithful to its folk origins. Only nonelectric instruments are used, and the high-pitched, emotional vocal sound clearly reveals derivation from Scottish church singing. The acceptance of bluegrass music remains greatest in its Appalachian core area in Kentucky, Tennessee, Virginia, and North Carolina (Figure 7.21). Most bluegrass performers are drawn from this core area, and the music retains a strong identification with Appalachian places, both in the titles and lyrics of songs and in the names of performing groups. Thus we find such songs as "Hills of Roane County" (Tennessee) performed by such groups as the Clinch Mountain Boys.

The nineteenth-century migration of Appalachian hill folk to Missouri, Arkansas, Texas, and Oklahoma, coupled with the Depression-era movement of "Okies" and "Arkies" to the Central Valley of California, provided natural areas for bluegrass expansion in the mid-twentieth century. The distribution of bluegrass music festivals, mapped by cultural geographer George O. Carney, accurately reflects these migrations (Figure 7.21).

Thus, music of the folk tradition has been modified, popularized, and spread by means of technology that is part of the popular culture. Such music provides yet another example of the interaction of cultural forces that underlies the cultural integration theme.

FIGURE 7.21
The geography of bluegrass country music. The southern Appalachian core area of bluegrass music is clearly revealed by the location of major performers; the distribution of festivals indicates both the popularization of this style of country music and the migration of Appalachian people to other states. How many of the festival sites are in hill or mountain areas? What barriers, if any, might prevent the continued diffusion of bluegrass? (After George O. Carney, "Bluegrass Grows All Around: The Spatial Dimensions of a Country Music Style," *Journal of Geography*, 73 (April 1974), 37, 46.)

• Home of professional bluegrass music performer, 1972

. Bluegrass music festivals held, 1972

BUILDING A FOLK HOUSE: A GEORGIA LOG CABIN

Folk houses are built without architects, often by communal labor. Here is a description of a log cabin "raising":

> Most of 'em we built was log houses, and we'd pitch in and in a couple a' days we'd have a man a house built. Ever'body 'd just go in and help a man. Wasn't countin' on gettin' a dime out of it. 'Course they'd have a big supper, and when we got done we always had somethin' at th' end — some kinda big party 'r dance in th' house 'fore they ever moved in. . . .
>
> You take fifty men and it didn't take but a little bit t' build a dadblame house. It went up fast. Some done th' notchin'. Some done th' layin' up. Some carryin' th' logs. Some peelin' th' logs. They 'uz always a job fer every bunch, and ever'body 'uz on their job and they kep' ever'thing goin', y' know. God, it didn't take long t' build a *big* house. Puttin' down th' floorin' was th' biggest job in it.

"Building a Folk House: A Georgia Log Cabin," from *Foxfire 2* by Eliot Wigginton. Copyright © 1973 by The Southern Highlands. Literary Fund, Inc., and Brooks Eliot Wigginton. Reprinted by permission of Doubleday & Company, Inc.

◼ FOLK ARCHITECTURE IN THE CULTURAL LANDSCAPE

Every folk culture produces its own distinctive landscape, and one of the most obvious and visible aspects of the folk landscape is the architecture. The products of **folk architecture** are derived not from the drafting tables of professional architects, but from the collective memory of a traditional people. These buildings, whether dwellings, barns, churches, mills, or inns, are not based on blueprints, but on mental images that change little from one generation to the next. In this sense, we can speak of an "architecture without architects" (see box, "Building a Folk House"). Folk buildings are extensions of a people and their region. They help provide the unique character or essence of each district or province and are a highly visible aspect of the human mosaic. Do not look to folk architecture for refined artistic genius or spectacular, revolutionary design (see box, "The Cultural Ecology of a Folk House"). Seek in it instead the traditional, the

---

THE CULTURAL ECOLOGY OF A FOLK HOUSE

Folk houses, as a rule, are beautifully suited to their physical environment. Centuries of trial and error taught their builders how to construct dwellings that provide comfort and protection from the extremes and hazards of the local weather. Nowhere are these attributes of folk architecture better displayed than on Lan Yü (Orchid Island), located in the Pacific Ocean 40 miles off the coast of Taiwan.

The Malayo-Polynesian inhabitants of Lan Yü, the Yami, build their folk houses mostly below ground level, in stone-lined pits, for protection from hurricanes. The sketch shows a cross section of a Yami house. A strongly reinforced, streamlined roof projects partly above ground level, exposing a section of an elongated slope to the brunt of the hurricane winds. The force of the storm wind presses down on the roof and slides by, keeping it in place. To escape the midday heat when no storms are blowing, each Yami builds a "cool tower" above ground level. These are easily replaced when hurricanes blow them away.

Adapted with permission from Chang Shuhua, "The Gentle Yamis of Orchid Island," *National Geographic Magazine*, 151 (January 1977), 107.

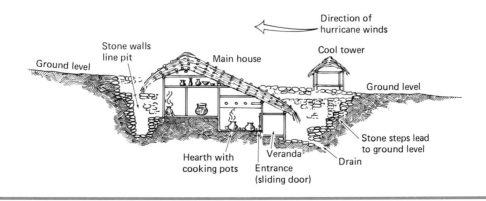

geomorphology

conservative, and the functional. Expect from it a simple beauty, a harmony with the physical environment, a visible expression of folk culture.

The house, or dwelling, is the most basic structure erected by people, regardless of their culture. For most persons in nearly all folk cultures, a house is the single most important thing they will ever build. Folk cultures as a rule are rural and agricultural. For these reasons, it seems appropriate to focus on traditional farmstead architecture, and particularly on the folk house, in this treatment of the cultural landscape.

Traditional Building Materials

One way we can classify folk houses and farmsteads is by the type of building material used in construction (see Figure 7.14). A hallmark of folk building is the use of locally available raw materials, causing the structures to blend nicely with the natural landscape. Farm dwellings range from massive houses of stone, endowed with as much permanency as humans can give to a structure, to temporary brush and thatch huts. Figure 7.22 maps the traditional building materials used in rural folk architecture in different parts of the world. Environmental conditions, particularly climate, vegetation, and geomorphology, strongly influence the choice of construction materials (Figure 7.23).

Shifting cultivators of the tropical rain forests typically build houses of poles and leaves, while sedentary subsistence farming peoples of the

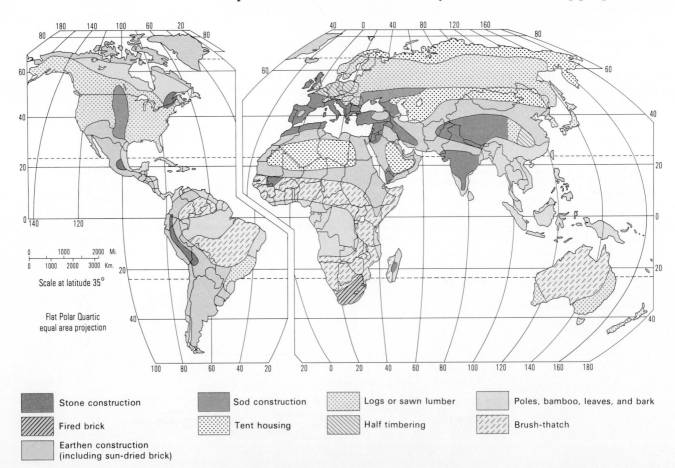

Stone construction

Fired brick

Earthen construction (including sun-dried brick)

Sod construction

Tent housing

Logs or sawn lumber

Half timbering

Poles, bamboo, leaves, and bark

Brush-thatch

FIGURE 7.22
Traditional building materials in rural areas vary from the relative permanence of stone to cloth tents. What factors might explain this pattern?

adjacent highlands and the oases and river valleys of the Old World desert zone rely principally on earthen construction, in the form of sun-dried (adobe) bricks or pounded earth. In some more prosperous regions, kiln-baked bricks are available. Herders and farmers of the semiarid, tropical savanna grasslands, particularly in Africa, construct thatched houses from coarse grasses and thorn bushes. Mediterranean farmers, most of whom live in rocky, deforested lands, use stones as their principal building material, as do some rural residents of interior India and the Andean highlands of South America. Entire landscapes of stone, including walls, roofs, terraces, streets, and fences, lend an air of permanence to the cultural landscapes of these regions.

In middle and higher latitudes, in areas where timber remains abundant, farm folk traditionally built their houses of sawn lumber or unmilled logs (see Figure 1.17). The log cabin of the United States and its frame successors fit in this category, as do the folk houses of northern Europe and most of the Soviet Union. In some partially deforested temperate regions, including lands as diverse as central Europe and parts of China, farmers once built half-timbered houses, raising a framework of hardwood beams and filling the interstices with some other material. Sod or turf houses are typical of some prairie and tundra areas, such as the Russian steppes and, in pioneer times, the American Great Plains. Nomadic herders generally live in portable tents made of skins or wool.

Floorplan and Layout

Another way to classify traditional farmsteads is on the basis of the floorplan and layout. One style is the *unit farmstead*, in which people, farm

FIGURE 7.23
The building materials of folk architecture vary from the cloth tents of central Asian nomads to the thatch-roofed huts of peasants in northeastern Mexico and the half-timbering of a traditional Norman French house in Québec province, Canada. (Mexican and Canadian photos by Terry G. Jordan, 1986 and 1984.)

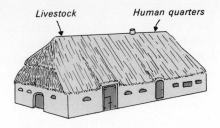

Livestock   Human quarters

Switzerland   Northern Germany

FIGURE 7.24
Two examples of unit farmsteads from Europe. The northern German folk structure is single story, with people and livestock occupying different ends separated by an open hearth. The Swiss chalet is multistory; the ground floor houses livestock and the upper stories are for people.

animals, and storage facilities are all under one roof in a single structure (Figure 7.24). Such houses, in their simplest form, are rectangular and single-storied. People and livestock occupy different ends of the structure. Often not even a dividing wall separates human and animal quarters. More complex unit farmsteads are multistoried and arranged so that people and livestock live on different levels. Unit farmsteads of both types are widely distributed in Europe.

More common are farmsteads in which the house, barn, and stalls occupy separate buildings. The *courtyard farmstead* is a common type within this category (see Figure 7.25). The various structures of the courtyard farmstead cluster around an enclosed yard. This type appears in several seemingly unrelated culture regions, such as the Inca-settled portions of the Andes Mountains, the hills of central Germany, and eastern China. Courtyard farmsteads have a wide distribution in part because they offer both privacy and protection.

In most countries where Germanic Europeans immigrated and settled, including Anglo-America, Australia, and New Zealand, the *strewn farmstead* prevails. The various farm buildings, instead of being linked together around a central courtyard, are spaced apart from one another in no consistent pattern. Strewn farmsteads are especially common in zones of wooden construction, where the danger of fire is greatest. Spacing the buildings reduces the danger that fire will spread from one building to another. Since they are poorly suited to defense, they are often associated with rural regions of greater than average tranquility.

Other Characteristics

Material composition, floorplan, and layout are all important ingredients of folk architecture, but there are numerous other characteristics that can

German Frankish farmstead, Central Europe
(half-timbering, multistory house)

Inca *Marca* farmstead, Peru and Bolivia
(stone construction, single story)

Adobe wall, thatched at top for protection from weather

Chinese farmstead, Szechwan province
(adobe brick, thatched roof, single story)

FIGURE 7.25
These three multistructure courtyard farmsteads come from widely divergent cultures. What could account for the similarity? Is it a case of cultural diffusion? Or did the obvious advantages of the courtyard farmstead for defense and privacy lead to its independent invention by folk societies in Germany, South America, and China?

be used to classify farmsteads and dwellings. The form or shape of the roof, the placement of the chimney, and even such details as the number and location of doors and windows can be important classifying criteria. Professor Estyn Evans (see biographical sketch), the noted expert on Irish folk geography, considered roof form and chimney placement, among other traits, in devising an informal classification of Irish folk houses (Figure 7.26). He discerned three major folk-housing culture regions, as determined by chimney and roof, on the small island of Ireland. If floor-plan and material composition had been included, additional culture regions would have been identified, based on local architectural features such as the bed outshot of far north Ireland, the mud wall constructions of the interior counties, and the off-center door found in several districts (Figure 7.26).

Folk Housing in Eastern North America

In the United States and Canada, folk architecture is largely a relict form in the cultural landscape. Popular culture, with its mass-produced, commercially built houses, has so overwhelmed the folk tradition that few if any folk houses are being built today, but many survive in the landscape, reminders of the rich American legacy in folk architecture.

Geographers recognize five major folk architecture regions in eastern North America, three of which are in the United States (Figure 7.27). The

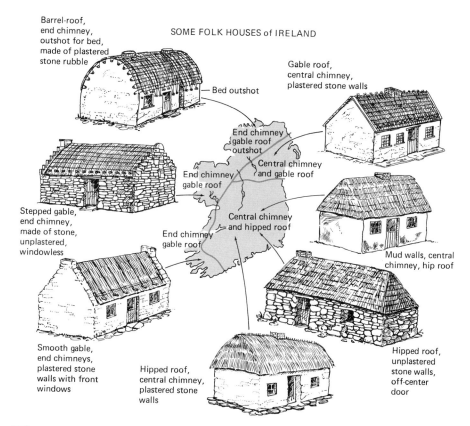

SOME FOLK HOUSES of IRELAND

Barrel-roof, end chimney, outshot for bed, made of plastered stone rubble

Gable roof, central chimney, plastered stone walls

Bed outshot

End chimney gable roof outshot

Central chimney and gable roof

End chimney gable roof

Stepped gable, end chimney, made of stone, unplastered, windowless

End chimney gable roof

Central chimney and hipped roof

Mud walls, central chimney, hip roof

Smooth gable, end chimneys, plastered stone walls with front windows

Hipped roof, central chimney, plastered stone walls

Hipped roof, unplastered stone walls, off-center door

FIGURE 7.26
Some folk houses of Ireland. The Irish houses, while basically similar, differ in roof form, chimney placement, location of windows, material composition, and floorplan. Some are unit farmsteads, such as the barrel-roofed type, in which people lived in one end and the livestock in the other. What architectural features do all these houses have in common? The western coastal fringe of Ireland is the windiest part of the country. What effect might wind have had on roof form? (After various publications of E. Estyn Evans.)

FIGURE 7.27
Eastern American folk architecture culture regions. Compare this map to Figure 1.6. For examples of folk houses typical of some of these regions, see Figure 7.28. (After Kniffen, 1965, in part, with modifications.)

names given to the architectural regions in the eastern United States should by now be familiar to you: New England, Midland, and Lowland South. You have encountered similar terms and regions in Chapters 1 and 5, as well as earlier in this chapter.

The New England folk houses are of wooden frame construction and often shingled siding covering the exterior walls. Among the oldest New England types, dating to colonial times, are the one-room *English cottage*, characterized by a steep roof and interior, gable end chimney; and the "large" house, a huge dwelling of two-and-a-half stories built around a central chimney. The latter's floorplan consists of four full-sized rooms on each story. The addition of a one-and-a-half story shed on the rear of a New England "large" produced the *saltbox house*, so named because the roof profile has a longer slope at the rear, duplicating the shape of an old-fashioned salt container (Figure 7.28). The New England "large" and "saltbox" are massive houses, well suited to the extremely cold New England winters, when most work must be done indoors (Figure 7.29). Somewhat later, New England folk developed the smaller *Cape Cod house*, similar to the earlier central-chimney saltbox and large houses but only one-and-a-half stories tall. Still later came the *upright and wing house*, essentially one-story and two-story houses facing different directions and joined together as one dwelling. The upright and wing type is common in the upper Midwest and reappears with frequency in western Washington and Oregon. Because of the cold climate, New England farmhouses are often structurally connected to the barn, so that it is unnecessary to go out of doors to reach the stabled animals.

Lowland Southern folk houses, like those of New England, are generally of wooden frame construction, though some half-timbering occurs. They differ, however, in their smaller size, front porches, and high foundations, all of which reflect a warmer climate. Many have exterior rather than interior chimneys, to minimize the heat retention in this hot, subtropical zone. The *tidewater raised cottage* consists of two full-sized rooms, side by side, with rear shed rooms and a front porch, all raised high above

Some New England Folk Houses

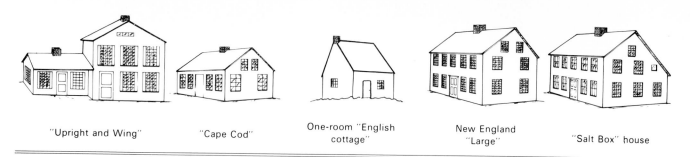

"Upright and Wing"   "Cape Cod"   One-room "English cottage"   New England "Large"   "Salt Box" house

Some Lower Southern Folk Houses

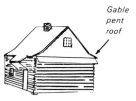

"Shotgun" house   Tidewater raised cottage   Louisiana "Creole" house

Some Midland Folk Houses

Gable pent roof

Single-pen log house   "Cumberland" house   Log "Saddlebag" house, front view   "Dogtrot" house   German "Continental" 3-room log house

Some Canadian Folk Houses

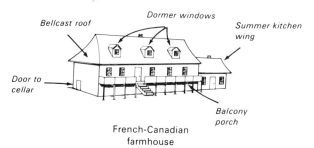

Bellcast roof   Dormer windows   Summer kitchen wing

Door to cellar

Balcony porch

French-Canadian farmhouse   British-Canadian "Ontario" farmhouse

FIGURE 7.28
Examples of American folk houses. Each of the five folk architecture regions in eastern North America (Figure 7.27) has characteristic house types. In floorplan, many of these are derived from the British Isles. What similarities can you detect between these American types and the Irish types shown in Figure 7.26? What differences? (After Kniffen, Glassie, T. Lewis, and George Gauthier-Larouche, *Évolution de la maison rurale traditionnelle dans la région de Québec*, Québec: Presses de l'Université Laval, 1975.)

FIGURE 7.29
A New England folk house and New England generic place name, in the Western Reserve area of northeastern Ohio. The cultural landscape of this section of Ohio bears the unmistakable imprint of the Northern, or New England, folk culture. The folk house is a "New England large" (see Figure 7.28), and the "Center" suffix is also a good indicator of New England's influence, as is the "Classical Revival" Mediterranean prefix, Mantua, derived from Mantova, Italy. See Figures 5.15 and 8.10. (Photo by Terry G. Jordan, 1977.)

ground level on a brick superstructure to escape periodic floodwaters. Louisiana *Creole houses* are often of half-timbered rather than frame construction, and they have a central chimney and a distinctive roof style consisting of two unbroken slopes covering the two main rooms, shed rooms, and porch. The *shotgun house* has gables facing the front and rear rather than the sides, and it is two or more rooms plus a porch in length but only one room wide. Its name derives from the folk saying that you can fire a shotgun through the entire length of the house without hitting anything, since the doors are all lined up in a row. According to John M. Vlach, a scholar of American folklife, the shotgun is an African folk house, brought initially by slaves to Haiti in the West Indies and later, about 1800, from Haiti to Louisiana.

The most distinguishing trait of Midland folk architecture is log construction, formed by laying logs horizontally and notching them together to form the walls. Introduced by Germans, Swedes, and Finns in the Delaware Valley and southeastern Pennsylvania in the 1600s and 1700s, log construction remained confined largely to the Midland architectural zone. The simplest folk house is the log *single-pen house,* or one-room dwelling (Figure 7.28). The addition of a second log room to the chimney end of a single-pen house forms the *saddlebag house,* a type common in the Ohio Valley. Adding a room to the gable end opposite from the chimney produces the *Cumberland house,* a common folk house of middle Tennessee and some other Upland Southern regions. Also of Midland affiliation is the *dogtrot* house, in which an open breezeway separates the two main rooms (Figure 7.30). The dogtrot exemplifies many of the adaptive attributes common in folk architecture. It represented the easiest way to enlarge from one log room to two, in part because the splicing of log walls is difficult (and labor minimization is an adaptive virtue, particularly on the frontier), and the plan accommodated the cooling summer breezes of the oppressive Upland Southern summer. From a different European tradition comes the German *continental* house, distinguished by an asymmetrical division into three parts—living room, bed chamber, and kitchen;

story-and-a-half height; off-center door; central hearth; a large, rectangular pen measuring about 20 by 30 feet (6 by 9 meters); and a cellar (Figure 7.28).

Canada also offers a variety of traditional folk houses (Figure 7.27). In French-speaking Québec, one of the common types consists of a main story atop a cellar, with attic rooms beneath curved, bell-shaped, or *bell-cast* roof (Figure 7.28). A balcony-porch with railing extends across the front, sheltered by the overhanging eaves. Attached to one side of this French-Canadian folk house is a summer kitchen that is sealed off during the long, cold winter. Often the folk houses of Québec are built of stone. To the west, in the British-Canadian region, one type of folk house occurs so frequently that it is known as the *Ontario farmhouse.* One-and-a-half stories in height, the Ontario farmhouse is usually built of brick and has a distinctive gabled front dormer window (Figure 7.28).

Now, using these sketches (Figure 7-28) and descriptions of eastern North American folk houses, try to identify the four illustrated in Figure 7.31. Enumerate the form elements that led to your decision.

Many other folk-built structures are part of the landscape and have been studied by cultural geographers. A rich literature exists, for example, on folk barns, covered bridges, grist windmills, traditional fences, and folk churches. The preceding material on folk houses should be regarded as only an introduction to and small sample of the kinds of landscape features studied by folk geographers.

CONCLUSION

Folk geographers study traditional cultures and are interested in both material and nonmaterial aspects of folklife. Because folk culture displays major variations from one place to another, the device of culture region is a useful starting point for the study of traditional life-styles. We saw how, by employing the theme of culture region, we could bring spatial order to the myriad of folk traits that survive, in vestige at least, in the United States.

The study of cultural diffusion allowed us to see how, even in conservative, change-resistant folk societies, innovations and traits spread across geographical space, how a Welsh folktale reaches Missouri or a New England agricultural fair reaches the Pacific Coast. Our study of the blowgun presented us with the kind of spatial problem that leads to speculation concerning diffusion versus independent invention. We also suggested that many problems remain to be solved, that the study of folklife is still wide open to imaginative scholars of the future.

By using the theme of cultural ecology, we explored the fundamental, almost religious tie that binds folk groups to the land. We glimpsed and began to appreciate the intimate knowledge, far surpassing that of the popular culture, that folk groups have of their physical surroundings.

The study of cultural integration revealed the many connections and causal relationships that exist between folk and popular cultures. We saw how elements of folk culture can penetrate and influence the popular realm and the kinds of changes they undergo in the process.

Through our study of folk architecture, we saw an example of the visible imprint of folk groups on the cultural landscape. The folk house, perhaps the most basic type of structure ever built, served as our guide to the incredibly varied landscapes created by folk groups. We learned that even in industrialized, urbanized societies like that of the United States,

FIGURE 7.30
A dogtrot house, typical of the Midland region. The distinguishing feature is the open-air passageway, or dogtrot, between the two main rooms. The house is located in central Texas. (Photo by Terry G. Jordan, 1970.)

(a)

(b)

(c)

(d)

FIGURE 7.31
Four folk houses in North America. Using the sketches in Figure 7.28 and the related section of the text, determine the regional affiliation and type of each. The answers are provided at the end of the "Suggested Readings" section in this chapter. (All photos by Terry G. Jordan.)

the folk architecture, in relict form, remains clearly imprinted on the land.

In America, the study of folk culture, particularly material folk culture, is still in its infancy. It needs the diligent research of a new generation of cultural geographers, folklorists, anthropologists, and archaeologists; of psychologists, sociologists, linguists, and historians. For those who are intrigued by the study of folklife, the future offers an abundance of needed research and fieldwork. It promises the rich satisfaction that comes from discovery, personal contacts with folk groups, and the recording and preservation of endangered traditional customs and objects.

Suggested Readings

Robert W. Bastian. "Indiana Folk Architecture: A Lower Midwestern Index," *Pioneer America,* 9, No. 2 (1977), 115–136.

Jan H. Brunvand (ed.). *The Study of American Folklore: An Introduction,* 2nd ed. New York: Norton, 1978.

Ronald H. Buchanan. "Geography and Folk Life," *Folk Life*, 1 (1963), 5–15.

George O. Carney. "T for Texas, T for Tennessee: The Origins of American Country Music Notables," *Journal of Geography*, 78 (1979), 218–225.

George O. Carney. "The Shotgun House in Oklahoma," *Journal of Cultural Geography*, 4 (1983), 57–71.

Peter M. Ennals. "Nineteenth-Century Barns in Southern Ontario," *Canadian Geographer*, 16 (1972), 256–270.

Robert F. Ensminger. "A Search for the Origin of the Pennsylvania Barn," *Pennsylvania Folklife*, 30, No. 2 (1980–1981), 50–59.

E. Estyn Evans. "The Cultural Geographer and Folklife Research," in Richard M. Dorson (ed.), *Folklore and Folklife: An Introduction.* Chicago: University of Chicago Press, 1972, pp. 517–532.

E. Estyn Evans. "The Ecology of Peasant Life in Western Europe," in William L. Thomas (ed.), *Man's Role in Changing the Face of the Earth.* Chicago: University of Chicago Press, 1956, pp. 217–239.

E. Estyn Evans. *Irish Folk Ways.* London: Routledge & Kegan Paul, 1957.

Joseph W. Glass. *The Pennsylvania Culture Region: A View from the Barn.* Ann Arbor, Mich.: UMI Research Press, 1986.

Henry Glassie. *Pattern in the Material Folk Culture of the Eastern United States.* Philadelphia: University of Pennsylvania Press, 1968.

Charles F. Gritzner. "Log Housing in New Mexico," *Pioneer America*, 3, No. 2 (1971), 54–62.

Lee C. Hopple. "Spatial Organization of the Southeastern Pennsylvania Plain Dutch Group Culture Region to 1975," *Pennsylvania Folklife*, 29, No. 1 (1979), 13–26.

Stephen C. Jett and Virginia E. Spencer. *Navajo Architecture: Forms, History, Distributions.* Tucson: University of Arizona Press, 1981.

Terry G. Jordan. *American Log Buildings: An Old World Heritage.* Chapel Hill: University of North Carolina Press, 1985.

Terry G. Jordan. "The Texan Appalachia," *Annals of the Association of American Geographers*, 60 (1970), 409–427.

Terry G. Jordan and Matti Kaups. "Folk Architecture in Cultural and Ecological Context," *Geographical Review*, 77 (1987), 52–75.

Clarissa T. Kimber. "Plants in the Folk Medicine of the Texas-Mexico Borderlands," *Proceedings, Association of American Geographers*, 5 (1973), 130–133.

Ronald G. Knapp. *China's Traditional Rural Architecture: A Cultural Geography of the Common House.* Honolulu: University of Hawaii Press, 1986.

Fred B. Kniffen. "American Cultural Geography and Folklife," in Don Yoder (ed.), *American Folklife.* Austin: University of Texas Press, 1976, pp. 51–70.

Fred B. Kniffen. "Folk-Housing: Key to Diffusion," *Annals of the Association of American Geographers*, 55 (1965), 549–577.

Victor A. Konrad and Michael Chaney. "Madawaska Twin Barn," *Journal of Cultural Geography*, 3 (Fall–Winter 1982), 64–75.

Peirce F. Lewis. "Common Houses, Cultural Spoor," *Landscape*, 19:2 (January 1975), 1–22.

Thomas R. Lewis. "To Planters of Moderate Means: The Cottage as a Dominant Folk House in Connecticut before 1900," *Proceedings, New England-St. Lawrence Valley Geographical Society*, 10 (1980), 23–27.

Christopher Lornell and W. Theodore Mealor, Jr. "Traditions and Research Opportunities in Folk Geography," *Professional Geographer*, 35 (1983), 51–56.

Material Culture: Journal of the Pioneer America Society. Published three times annually, this leading periodical specializes in the subject of traditional American material culture. Volume 1 was published in 1969, and prior to 1984 the journal was called *Pioneer America.*

E. Cotton Mather and Pradyumna P. Karan. "Geography of Folk Art in India," in Allen G. Noble and Ashok K. Dutt (eds.), *India: Cultural Patterns and Processes.* Boulder, Colo.: Westview Press, 1982, pp. 165–194.

Gwyn I. Meirion-Jones. *The Vernacular Architecture of Brittany: An Essay in Historical Geography.* Edinburgh: Donald, 1982.

E. Joan Wilson Miller. "The Ozark Culture Region as Revealed by Traditional Materials," *Annals of the Association of American Geographers,* 58 (1968), 51–77.

Milton Newton. "Cultural Preadaptation and the Upland South," *Geoscience and Man,* 5 (1974), 143–154.

Milton Newton and Linda Pulliam-di Napoli. "Log Houses as Public Occasions: A Historical Theory," *Annals of the Association of American Geographers,* 67 (1977), 360–383.

Allen G. Noble. *Wood, Brick, and Stone: The North American Settlement Landscape.* 2 vols. Amherst: University of Massachusetts Press, 1984.

Campbell W. Pennington. *The Tarahumar of Mexico: Their Environment and Material Culture.* Salt Lake City: University of Utah Press, 1963.

Richard Pillsbury. "Pattern in the Folk and Vernacular House Forms of the Pennsylvania Culture Region," *Pioneer America,* 9 (1977), 12–31.

Richard Pillsbury. "The Pennsylvania Culture Area: A Reappraisal," *North American Culture,* 3, No. 2 (1987), 37–54.

Edward T. Price. "Root Digging in the Appalachians: The Geography of Botanical Drugs," *Geographical Review,* 50 (1960), 1–20.

Amos Rapoport. *House Form and Culture.* Englewood Cliffs, N.J.: Prentice-Hall, 1969.

Ellen Churchill Semple. "The Anglo-Saxons of the Kentucky Mountains: A Study in Anthropogeography," *Geographical Journal,* 17 (1901), 588–623.

Karl A. Sinnhuber. "On the Relations of Folklore and Geography," *Folk-lore,* 68 (1957), 385–404.

Peter Smith. *Houses of the Welsh Countryside: A Study in Historical Geography.* London: Royal Commission on Ancient and Historical Monuments in Wales, 1975.

Dorothy Sylvester. *The Rural Landscape of the Welsh Borderland: A Study in Historical Geography.* London: Macmillan, 1969.

Roger T. Trindell. "American Folklore Studies and Geography," *Southern Folklore Quarterly,* 34 (1970), 1–11.

Donald E. Vermeer and Dennis A. Frate. "Geophagy in a Mississippi County," *Annals of the Association of American Geographers,* 65 (1975), 414–424.

Peter O. Wacker. "Folk Architecture as an Indicator of Culture Areas and Culture Diffusion: Dutch Barns and Barracks in New Jersey," *Pioneer America,* 5 (July 1973), 37–47.

Peter O. Wacker. "Traditional House and Barn Types in New Jersey: Keys to Acculturation, Past Cultureographic Regions, and Settlement History," *Geoscience and Man,* 5 (1974), 163–176.

John M. Wagstaff. "Traditional Houses in Modern Greece," *Geography,* 50 (1965), 58–64.

Eugene J. Wilhelm, Jr. "Field Work in Folklife: Meeting Ground of Geography and Folklore," *Keystone Folklore Quarterly,* 13 (1968), 241–247.

Eugene J. Wilhelm, Jr. "The Mullein: Plant Piscicide of the Mountain Folk Culture," *Geographical Review,* 64 (1974), 235–252.

Hubert G. H. Wilhelm. "The Pennsylvania-Dutch Barn in Southeastern Ohio," *Geoscience and Man,* 5 (1974), 155–162.

John J. Winberry. "The Log House in Mexico," *Annals of the Association of American Geographers,* 64 (1974), 54–69.

Key to Figure 7.31: (a) French-Canadian farmhouse, Port Joli, Québec. (b) New England "large" house, near Fredericton, New Brunswick. (c) Shotgun house, Alleyton, Texas. (d) Cape Cod cottage, upstate New York.

Chapter 8

Popular Culture

"change"
placelessness

good examples of
Barriers to diffusion

POPULAR CULTURE REGIONS

    Food and Drink
    Formal Culture Regions in American
      Sport
    Vernacular Culture Regions

CULTURAL DIFFUSION IN POPULAR
CULTURE

    Diffusion of Classical Place-Names
    Diffusion of the Rodeo
    International Diffusion
    Communications Barriers

THE ECOLOGY OF POPULAR CULTURE

    Environmental Influence
    Impact on the Environment

CULTURAL INTEGRATION IN POPULAR
CULTURE

    The Impact of Communications Media
    Why Football Fever?

LANDSCAPES OF POPULAR CULTURE

    American Front Yards
    Elitist and Amenity Landscapes
    Landscapes of Consumption
    The American Scene

CONCLUSION

What do Big Macs, symphony orchestras, neatly manicured suburban grass lawns, collegiate basketball games, and the latest clothing fashion, hairstyles, and makeup fashions have in common? How are they, in turn, linked to fraternity house Frisbee tossing, a can of beer from a Milwaukee brewery, rock music, or a rodeo? The answer is that all are aspects of the **popular culture** (Figure 8.1).

The preceding chapter dealt with folk culture. We suggested there that folk and popular could be regarded as contrasting cultural alternatives, describing popular culture as constantly changing, based in large, heterogeneous groups of people concentrated mainly in urban areas. Popular material goods are mass-produced by machines in factories, and a money economy prevails. Relationships between individuals are more numerous but less personal than in folk cultures, and the family structure is weaker. People are more mobile, less attached to place and environment. A distinct division of labor, reflected in myriad, highly specialized professions and jobs, characterizes the earning of a livelihood, and consid-

261

erable leisure time is available to most people. Secular institutions of control, such as the police, army, and courts, take the place of family and church in maintaining order.

If there is a single hallmark of popular culture, it is *change*. Words such as *growth, progress, fad,* and *trend* crop up frequently in newspapers and conversations. So pervasive is change that some persons are unable to cope with it, leading them to an insecurity expressed in the term *future shock*. In a humorous debunking of popular culture and his own inability to change quickly enough, *Dallas Morning News* columnist John Anders recalled some years ago that he "danced the Twist when others had moved on to the Swim, wore Old Spice after the rest of the guys had graduated to English Leather, donned corduroy during the burlap frenzy, and ate Big Boy Hamburgers while my peers moved into Quiche Lorraine. . . ." As you can tell, the whole bunch of them is now out of date.

If all these characteristics seem rather commonplace and "normal" it should not be surprising. You are, after all, firmly enmeshed in the popular culture, or else you would not be attending college or reading a book. The large majority of people in Europe, the United States, Canada, and other "developed" countries now belong to the popular rather than the folk culture. Industrialization, urbanization, the rise of formal education, and the resultant increase in leisure time have all contributed to the spread of popular culture and the consequent retreat of folklife. We and our recent ancestors abandoned the hidebound, secure, stable, traditional folk culture to embrace with enthusiasm the free, open, dynamic life-style offered by popular culture. Tradition and superstition gave way to change and knowledge; science challenged religion for dominance in our daily lives. We profited greatly in material terms through this transition.

In reality, all of culture presents a continuum, on which folk and popular represent extreme forms. All sorts of gradations between the two are possible. Disadvantages, as well as the previously mentioned benefits, become apparent as one moves toward the popular end of the continuum. We forfeited much in discarding folkways, as Chapter 7 suggested. Certainly, it would not be proper to regard popular culture as somehow superior to folk culture. With popularization, we weakened both family structure and interpersonal relationships. One prominent cultural geographer, Fred B. Kniffen (see biographical sketch in Chapter 7), who has lived in both folk and popular settings, feels that of all the elements of popular culture and the age of technology, "only two would I dislike to give up: inside plumbing and medical advances."

Cultural geographers could hardly ignore the impressive triumph and ascendant position of popular culture in the Western world. While geographers, as we have seen, do not neglect folk studies, they devote an increasing proportion of their energies to the study and understanding of the spatial characteristics of popular culture. It is true that popular culture varies less areally than does folk culture. Edward Relph went so far as to propose that North American popular culture produces a profound "placelessness," a spatial standardization that diminishes and demeans the human spirit. Even so, regional patterns can be detected, even on the local scale. The popular culture of New England or Québec is different in many ways from that of California, western Canada, or the South (Figure 8.2). The geographer wants to know what these spatial variations are and how they came to be. Moreover, the sense of place, however trivialized or stereotyped, attains representation in the advertising, music, cinema, and art of popular culture. These images, too, interest the cultural geographer.

FIGURE 8.1
Popular culture is reflected in every aspect of life, from the fast foods we eat to the clothes we wear and the recreational activities that occupy our leisure time. Rarely are these manifestations place-specific, since popular culture tends to produce "placelessness." The man standing by the street sign could be almost anywhere in the English-speaking world. (He happens to be in Melbourne, Australia.)

■ POPULAR CULTURE REGIONS

The theme of culture regions facilitates a description of the place images and spatial variations of popular culture. We have chosen three examples as illustrations—food and drink, sports, and vernacular regions.

Food and Drink

Pronounced regional differences can be noted in our choices of beverages and food. In beer consumption, for example, the highest levels occur in the upper Midwest, Northeast, mountain West, and Texas, while least is sold in the Lower South and Utah (Figure 8.2). Whiskey made from corn, both of legal and illegal manufacture, has been a traditional southern alcoholic beverage, while Californians place more importance on wine.

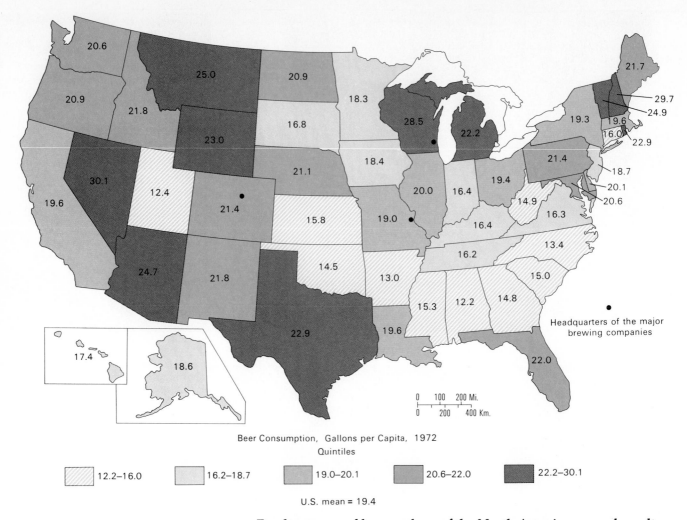

Beer Consumption, Gallons per Capita, 1972
Quintiles

| 12.2–16.0 | 16.2–18.7 | 19.0–20.1 | 20.6–22.0 | 22.2–30.1 |

U.S. mean = 19.4

FIGURE 8.2
THe cultural geography of commercial beer consumption. Looking at Figures 6.2 and 9.2 may help explain the regional pattern displayed on this map. Over one-quarter of all Americans claim at least partial German ancestry, and their distribution could help explain the pattern. What other causal factors might be at work? The regional pattern of wine or hard liquor consumption differs from that of beer. (Adapted from John F. Rooney, Jr., and Paul L. Butt, ''Beer, Bourbon and Boone's Farm: A Geographical Examination of Alcoholic Drink in the United States,'' *Journal of Popular Culture,* 11 (1978), 832–856.)

Foods consumed by members of the North American popular culture also vary from place to place. In the South, barbecued pork and beef, fried chicken, and hamburgers enjoy far greater than average popularity, while more pizza is consumed in the North, the focus of Italian immigration. Indeed, pizza reached the southern states only in the mid-1950s.

The so-called fast foods might seem to epitomize popular culture, yet the importance of such restaurants varies greatly within the United States, revealing a pattern somewhat similar to that for beer consumption (Figure 8.3). In general, states where fast-food sales form a larger-than-average proportion of total restaurant business also have below-average beer sales. How might these two traits be related?

Formal Culture Regions in American Sport

Abundant leisure is a hallmark of popular culture, and Americans devote much of that time to watching or participating in sports. Few aspects of popular culture are as widely publicized as our games, both amateur and professional. From Little League through high school, college, olympic, and professional contests and leagues, athletics receive almost daily attention from many members of the popular culture. In fact, the rise of competitive spectator sports parallels closely the development of popular culture in North America and Europe. The further we withdrew from our folk tradition, the more important organized games became for us. It is no

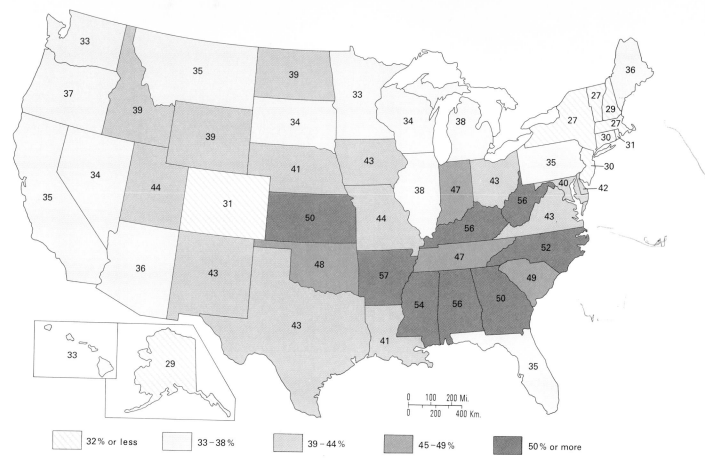

32% or less   33–38%   39–44%   45–49%   50% or more

accident that the nineteenth century, which witnessed the industrialization and resultant popularization of our culture, also gave us football, ice hockey, baseball, soccer, and basketball—our major spectator sports. While our folk ancestors played a variety of games, these were limited mainly to children or helped hone skills needed in everyday life; relatively little time or attention was devoted to them. Certainly, the concept of professional athletes and admission-paying spectators is unique to the popular culture and is not to be found in folk cultures. Hard as it may be for us to realize, our folk ancestors knew nothing even remotely like our Super Bowl, World Series, Stanley Cup, or N.C.A.A. tournaments (Figure 8.4).

As commercial spectator sports spread through North America, distinct regional contrasts developed. "Hotbeds" of football arose in some regions, basketball became a winter mania in certain areas, baseball came to rule supreme in some states, and ice hockey ascended to reign in still other provinces. Participant sports reveal similar regionalization. Skiing, tennis, bowling, and golf vary greatly in popularity from one region to another.

Geographer John F. Rooney, an expert on the spatial aspects of American sport, has found pronounced regional differences, some of which are summarized in Figure 8.5. He discovered, for example, that most leading states in the production of football players for the major professional and college teams, both in terms of total numbers and on a per capita basis, were grouped together in clusters, in rather confined areas of the country (Figure 8.5). The top five states in per capita production of National Football League players are Texas, Louisiana, Mississippi, Alabama, and Georgia, all in a contiguous belt across the Deep South (Figure 8.5). Texas also

FIGURE 8.3
Fast-food sales as a share of total restaurant sales, by state, 1987. What might account for the spatial variation in this aspect of popular culture? Does the pattern bear any similarity to the map of traditional and folk cultures shown in Figures 1.6 and 7.2? The national average was 38 percent. What does this suggest about the *convergence hypothesis,* which holds that regional cultures in America are collapsing into a national culture? Compare this map to Figure 8.2. (From "20th Annual Restaurant Growth Index," *Restaurant Business,* 86, no. 14 (September 20, 1987), 188.)

FIGURE 8.4
Football arose with popular culture in North America and has become an important leisure-time activity for the masses and an opportunity to demonstrate opulence by the wealthy few, as manifested in this private box at the Superdome in New Orleans.

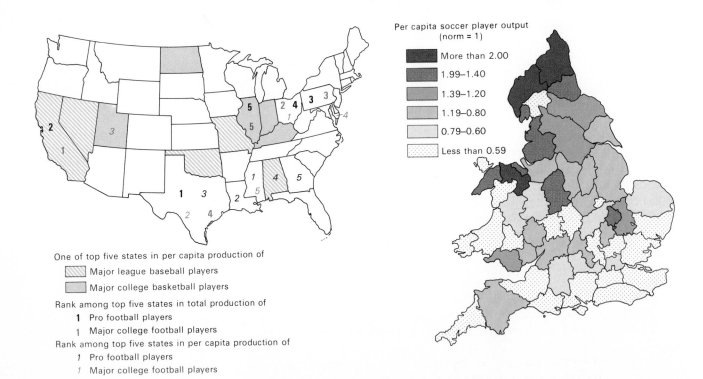

Per capita soccer player output
(norm = 1)

- More than 2.00
- 1.99–1.40
- 1.39–1.20
- 1.19–0.80
- 0.79–0.60
- Less than 0.59

One of top five states in per capita production of

- Major league baseball players
- Major college basketball players

Rank among top five states in total production of

1 Pro football players
1 Major college football players

Rank among top five states in per capita production of

1 Pro football players
1 Major college football players

FIGURE 8.5
Major source regions of American athletes playing football, baseball, and basketball by state, and of English and Welsh professional soccer players by county. What cultural or environmental factors might explain these patterns? (After data in John F. Rooney, Jr., "Up From the Mines and Out From the Prairies: Some Geographical Implications of Football in the United States," *Geographical Review,* 59 (1969), 483; and John F. Rooney, Jr., *A Geography of American Sport,* Reading, Mass.: Addison-Wesley, 1974, 118, 152, 179; and John Bale, "The Football (County) League," *Geographical Magazine,* 50 (1977–1978), 488. Reproduction from the *Geographical Magazine,* London.)

ranks among the top five states in per capita production of major college football players and in total production of both college and pro "gridders." Ohio, Pennsylvania, Illinois, and California also rank high as contributing states. Significantly, some populous states, such as New York, do not rank high as producers of football players. New York, second ranking in population, is not among the top ten states in production of professional football players. Neighboring Pennsylvania, by contrast, is the fourth most populous state and ranks third as a producer of pro players. Oklahoma, not among the leading states in per capita production of college and pro players, draws heavily upon high schools in neighboring Texas to man traditionally excellent football teams at the University of Oklahoma. Clearly, football's appeal and intensity vary regionally. One writer facetiously described football in the East as a cultural exercise, in the West as tourism, in the North as cannibalism, and in the South as religion.

The highest per capita production of major college basketball players is concentrated in an Ohio Valley cluster of three states: Indiana, Kentucky, and Illinois (Figure 8.5). As we might expect, colleges and universities in these three states are more often known as basketball rather than football powers. Major league baseball players, on a per capita basis, are drawn mainly from California, Nevada, Oklahoma, Missouri, and Alabama (Figure 8.5).

The regionalization evident in men's athletics is also evident in the leading women's intercollegiate sports. The Midwest is a basketball area, the Northeast is ruled by field hockey, tennis is the major sport in the South, and softball and volleyball share distinction as popular women's games in the West (Figures 8.6 and 8.7).

FIGURE 8.6
Basketball reigns supreme in some parts of North America, and women's basketball is especially popular in the South.

FIGURE 8.7
The geography of girls' high school sports in the United States. Letters indicate the most popular female high school sport in each state, while shadings show the percentage of girls participating in all organized sports. What might explain the very high percentages in the northern plains area and the low percentages in the South? Compare the distribution to that shown in Figure 4.12. (After Barbara G. Shortridge, *Atlas of American Women*, New York: Macmillan, 1987, pp. 70, 71.)

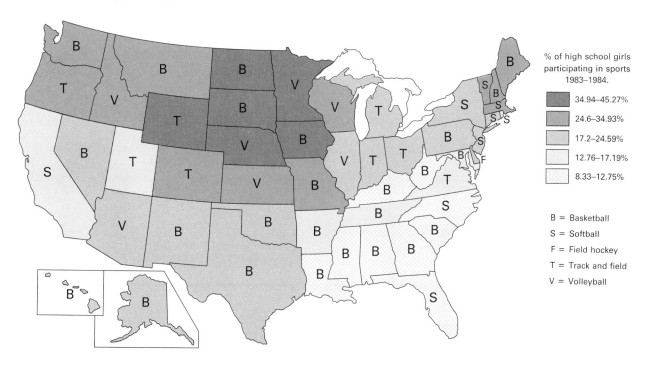

% of high school girls participating in sports 1983–1984.

- 34.94–45.27%
- 24.6–34.93%
- 17.2–24.59%
- 12.76–17.19%
- 8.33–12.75%

B = Basketball
S = Softball
F = Field hockey
T = Track and field
V = Volleyball

American sport, then, displays marked areal variations, and we can best reveal these contrasts in formal culture regions. A quite different application of the culture region theme to the study of popular culture is seen in vernacular regions.

Vernacular Culture Regions

"Exciting Green Country," proclaims a brochure published by Green Country, Inc., and the Oklahoma Tourism and Recreation Commission, "where a blend of natural beauty, ideal climate and frontier heritage offers visitors a memorable vacation experience." News media based in Tulsa repeatedly drum "Green Country" into the minds of local Oklahomans; billboard advertisements and businesses with "Green Country" as part of their name spread the same message: Northeastern Oklahoma *is* Green Country (Figure 8.8).

Green Country is but one example of hundreds of **vernacular regions** in America. A vernacular region may be defined as one perceived to exist by its inhabitants, one existing as part of the popular culture. Rather than being the intellectual creation of the professional geographer, a vernacular region is the product of the spatial perception of the population at large. Rather than being a formal region based on carefully chosen criteria, a vernacular region is a composite of the mental maps of the people. Such regions vary greatly in size, from small districts covering only part of a city or town to huge, multistate areas. Like most other geographical regions, they often overlap and usually have poorly defined borders.

FIGURE 8.8
"Green Country," a popular culture vernacular region, includes all of northeastern Oklahoma and manifests itself in promotional billboards and business names in the town of Tahlequah. Once the proud capital of the Cherokee Indian Nation, Tahlequah is today merely a small town in Green Country. Promotional regions such as this are becoming increasingly common in America. For more detail, see R. Todd Zdorkowski and George O. Carney, "This Land is My Land: Oklahoma's Changing Vernacular Regions," *Journal of Cultural Geography*, 5, No. 2 (1985), 97–106, especially 101. (Photos by John A. Milbauer, 1989.)

Almost every part of the industrialized Western world offers examples of vernacular regions based in the popular culture. Figure 8.9 shows some province-sized popular regions in North America. Geographer Wilbur Zelinsky (see biographical sketch) compiled these regions by determining the most common provincial name appearing in the white pages of urban telephone directories. One curious feature of the map is the sizable, populous district in New York, Ontario, eastern Ohio, and western Pennsylvania where no affiliation to province is perceived. Using a quite different source of information, geographer Joseph Brownell in 1960 sought to delimit the popular "Midwest" (Figure 8.10). Professor Brownell, in this pioneering study, sent out questionnaires to postal employees in the midsection of the United States, from the Appalachians to the Rockies. He asked each employee whether, in his or her opinion, the community lay in the "Midwest." The results revealed a core area in which the residents looked upon themselves as Midwesterners. A similar survey done 20 years later, using student respondents, yielded an almost identical result (Figure 8.10).

Vernacular regions exist on many different scales. A resident of Alabama's "Black Belt," for example, might also claim to reside in "Dixie" and "the South" (see Figure 1.8). Regardless of size or origin, vernacular regions of America are perceptual in character. They exist because members of the popular or folk culture perceive them. As befits an element of popular culture, the vernacular region is often perpetuated by the mass media, especially radio and television. In fact, many are initially diffused through the media.

■ CULTURAL DIFFUSION IN POPULAR CULTURE

Culture regions, as you know by now, imply cultural diffusion. The same processes of cultural diffusion described in previous chapters permit the spread of items and ideas of popular culture, but hierarchical diffusion seems to play a greater role in popular culture, perhaps because popular society is highly stratified into classes, unlike folk culture. For example, the spread of McDonald's restaurants in the United States, beginning in 1955, was almost exclusively hierarchical, bearing little relation to the nearness of existing restaurants.

Diffusion also progresses much more rapidly in popular culture, and time-distance decay is considerably weaker. In ancient times, thousands of years were normally required for innovations to complete their areal spread, and even as recently as the early nineteenth century, the normal time span was still measured in decades. In the popular culture, modern transportation and communications networks now permit cultural diffusion to occur within weeks or even days. The propensity for change makes diffusion extremely important in the popular culture. It may also be true that the availability of devices permitting rapid diffusion is one of the major causes of change in the popular culture (see box, "Popular Culture Comes to Hunza").

Geographer Wilbur Zelinsky, in his book *The Cultural Geography of the United States,* described a personal experience with the lightninglike diffusion of a classic item of popular material culture, the hula hoop. "In August, 1958," he wrote, "I drove from Santa Monica, California to Detroit at an average rate of about 400 miles per day; and display windows in almost every drugstore and variety store along the way were being hastily

WILBUR ZELINSKY
1921 –

Wilbur Zelinsky, professor at Pennsylvania State University, is one of America's most prominent cultural geographers. An Illinoisan by birth, but a "Northeasterner by choice and conviction," Dr. Zelinsky received his education at the University of California at Berkeley, where he was a student of the famous geographer Carl O. Sauer. His doctorate was awarded in 1953.

As the frequent references in this chapter to his work will attest, Dr. Zelinsky has made numerous important geographical studies of American popular culture, ranging the gamut from the diffusion of classical place-names to the spatial patterns of personal given names. One of his most ambitious and imaginative projects was a provocative assessment of the impact of increasingly powerful personal preference on the spatial character of American society (see the box entitled "Personal Preference and the Changing Map of American Society" in this chapter). In 1973, Profession Zelinsky published his widely acclaimed book *The Cultural Geography of the United States.* In addition to his research in popular culture, Dr. Zelinsky has made substantial contributions in the fields of population and folk geography.

In 1966, Professor Zelinsky received the Award for Meritorious Contributions to the Field of Geography, presented by the Association of American Geographers. He served as president of the association in 1972–1973.

How will this affect the Amish

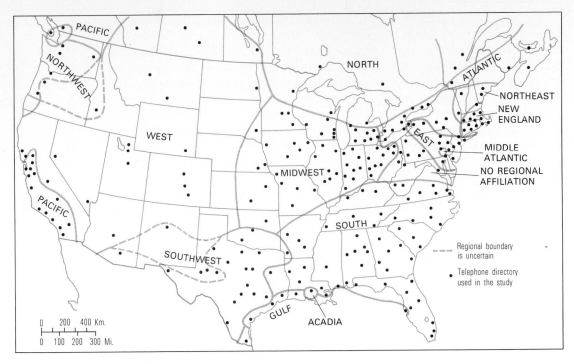

FIGURE 8.9
Some vernacular regions in North America. Cultural geographer Wilbur Zelinsky mapped these regions on the basis of business names in the white pages of metropolitan telephone directories. Why are "West" names more widespread than those containing "East"? What might account for the areas where no region name is perceived? (Adapted with permission from Wilbur Zelinsky, "North America's Vernacular Regions," *Annals of the Association of American Geographers,* 70 (1980), 14.)

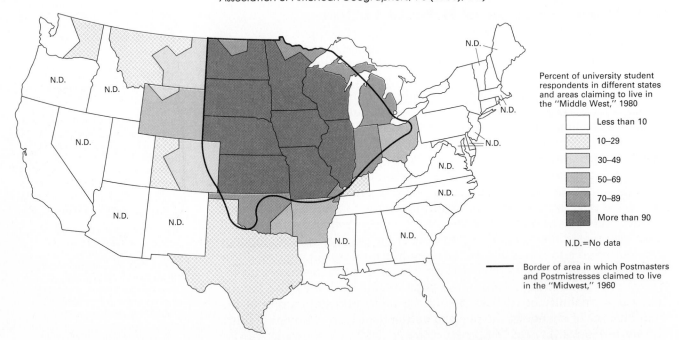

Percent of university student respondents in different states and areas claiming to live in the "Middle West," 1980

	Less than 10
	10–29
	30–49
	50–69
	70–89
	More than 90

N.D.=No data

Border of area in which Postmasters and Postmistresses claimed to live in the "Midwest," 1960

FIGURE 8.10
The vernacular "Middle West" or "Midwest." Two surveys, taken a generation apart and using two quite different groups of respondents, yielded quite similar results. What might account for the differences between this map and Figure 8.9, which utilized still another data base? (Sources: James R. Shortridge, "The Vernacular Middle West," *Annals of the Association of American Geographers,* 75 (1985), 50; and Joseph W. Brownell, "The Cultural Midwest," *Journal of Geography,* 59 (1960), 83; see also James R. Shortridge, "The Emergence of 'Middle West' as an American Regional Label," *Annals of the Association of American Geographers,* 74 (1984), 209–220.)

POPULAR CULTURE COMES TO HUNZA

Popular culture often diffuses along modern transport facilities, such as highways, causing folk culture to retreat. Below, a resident of Hunza, a previously isolated valley in the Karakorum Mountains of Pakistan, describes what happened when a highway was built through his home district:

> Hunza is not the same since the Karakorum Highway invaded our quiet lives. Before, no one even locked their doors. Theft was unheard of. Before, the social pressure to be honest was strong. Besides, there was little money to steal. Now everyone chases after money . . . or ruins their health eating canned food from Karachi. Every year there is more crime. Only 10 years ago we had no jail or police! But the saddest part is that Hunza people are forgetting their own culture. We used to share everything. We passed the winters by dancing all day for hours on end. Our life was communal and that was enough.

From Michael Winn, "Hunza: Shangri-La of Islam," *Aramco World Magazine,* 34 (January–February 1983), 33, 36.

stocked with hula hoops just off the delivery trucks from Southern California. A national television program the week before had roused instant cravings. It was an eerie sensation, surfing along a pseudo-innovation wave."

Diffusion of Classical Place-Names

A much earlier cultural diffusion, also studied by Professor Zelinsky, provides us an even more detailed look at the spread of popular culture and the different types of diffusion. This example involves the origin and spread of classical town-names in the United States. If you have traveled much in the United States, particularly in the North and Midwest, you have no doubt encountered town, county, and township names such as Rome, Athens, Syracuse, Troy, Corinth, Arcadia, Euclid, or Homer (Figures 8.11 and 7.29). If you live in the United States, these may not have seemed unusual to you, because they are so common, but is it not strange that in a country with no direct ties to ancient Greece and Rome, so many names of this type appear? They are a product of the so-called Classic Revival, based in the view that America is the latter-day successor to the glories of the Greco-Roman world. This view, which arose with the independence of the United States, persisted through the nineteenth century. Because of it, Americans adopted a neoclassical architecture for public buildings, Latin mottoes and inscriptions (for example, *E Pluribus Unum*), and even Latin and Greek personal names such as Horace, Virgil, and Ulysses. American popular culture took on a decidedly Greco-Roman flavor. The use of place-names derived from Greece and Rome was merely one aspect of this Classic Revival.

Central New York state was the hearth area where the innovation of classical town-names first appeared in the 1780s. The cities of that region bear witness to the innovation—Syracuse, Ithaca, Utica, Troy, Rome, and others. In the decades that followed, on through the nineteenth century, classical names diffused over much of the United States, most commonly in a "classical belt" stretching westward from New York state to central Nebraska and Kansas (see Figure 8.12). Some 1500 such names are still in use.

More important, the spread of classical place-names illustrates many of the types and principles of cultural diffusion. Contagious expansion diffusion is suggested by the compact clusters of classical names that occur here and there, as in southern Iowa. The implantation of one or several classical names apparently influenced founders of nearby communities to adopt similar names for their settlements. Relocation diffusion is also

FIGURE 8.11
The influence of the Classic Revival, one of the earliest manifestations of American popular culture, can be seen in the toponyms of upstate New York, where cities and towns bear names such as Syracuse, Rome, Troy, and Ithaca, conjuring up images of the classical Roman and Greek world. Ithaca, a Greek island and town in the Ionian Sea, was notable as the home of Odysseus, the hero of Homer's *Odyssey*.

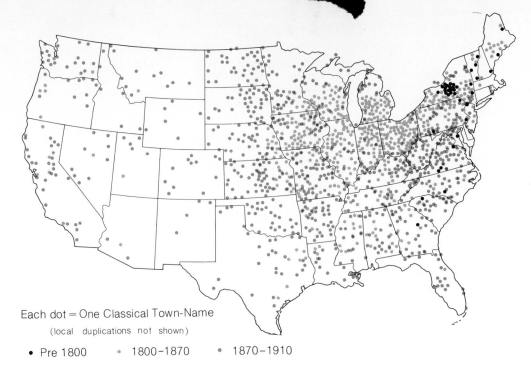

Each dot = One Classical Town-Name

(local duplications not shown)

• Pre 1800   • 1800–1870   • 1870–1910

FIGURE 8.12
Diffusion of classical town-names in the United States, 1780–1910. From a hearth area in upstate New York in the 1780s, classical names diffused across much of America. What might explain the uneven distribution of such names? Do classical town-names occur in your home area? If so, who implanted them there? (After Wilbur Zelinsky, "Classical Town Names in the United States: The Historical Geography of an American Idea," *Geographical Review,* 57 (1967), 480, 490, 491.)

apparent, for it is no accident that the density of classical names is greatest along the pathway leading from central New York, the route of thousands of westward-moving settlers. Utica, New York, for example, has name-sakes in Ohio, Indiana, Michigan, Illinois, Kansas, and Nebraska—all perpetuating the name of an ancient Phoenician-Roman city in North Africa.

The spread of classical names also suggests hierarchical expansion diffusion. For example, some such names appeared in southern Maine after 1800, east of the core area in central New York. Relocation diffusion is not likely in this instance, since the flow of migrants was westward, and Maine is too remote from central New York to have been affected by contagious diffusion. In all probability, the idea reached Maine through written communications between elite, educated individuals—a perfect example of hierarchical diffusion.

The Canadian-United States boundary between New York and Ontario acted as an absorbing barrier to the diffusion of classical town-names. Canadians, still under British rule as late as 1867, did not envision their country as a latter-day Greece or Rome and were thus not attracted to classical place-names. To cross into Canada at Niagara or Detroit is to leave "Greece" and "Rome" behind.

Diffusion of the Rodeo

FIGURE 8.13
Commercial rodeos, such as the Frontier Days rodeo in Cheyenne, Wyoming, developed from informal cowboy contests, a folk tradition in the American West.

From the Classic Revival to the rodeo may seem a quantum jump, yet popular culture is so diverse as to include both. The American commercial rodeo provides another good example of cultural diffusion (Figure 8.13). Like so many elements of popular culture, the modern rodeo had its origins in folk tradition. Rodeos began simply as roundups of cattle in the Spanish livestock ranching system in northern Mexico and the American Southwest. In fact, the word *rodeo* is derived from the Spanish *rodear*, "to surround" or "to round up."

When Anglo-Americans adopted certain Mexican cowboy skills in the nineteenth century, the foundation for riding and roping contests was laid. Cowboys from adjacent ranches began holding contests at roundup time. No prizes were awarded, and these competitive tests of skills remained folk in character initially. After the Civil War, some cowboy contests on the Great Plains were formalized, with prizes awarded (Figure 8.14). Still, no admission was charged, preserving much of the folk aspect of the event.

The transition to commercial rodeo, with admission tickets and grandstands, came quickly as an outgrowth of the formal cowboy contests. One such contest, at North Platte, Nebraska, in 1882, led to the inclusion of some rodeo events in a "Wild West Show" at Omaha in 1883. These shows, which moved by railroad from town to town in the manner of circuses, were probably the most potent agent of early rodeo diffusion. Within a decade of the Omaha affair, commercial rodeos were being held independently of Wild West shows at several towns, apparently first at

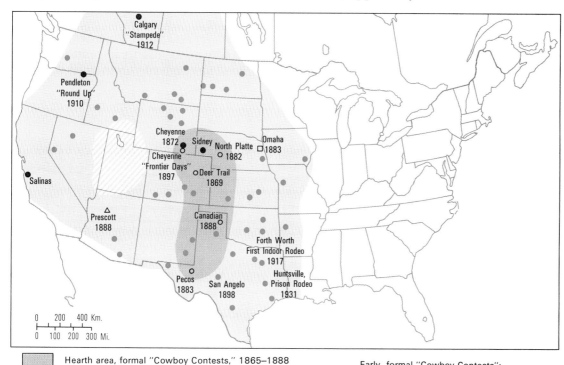

Hearth area, formal "Cowboy Contests," 1865–1888

Major rodeo interest today

Minor importance

● Major rodeo, of national fame (and date of founding)

● Major rodeo, of regional importance

o Early, formal "Cowboy Contests"; prizes, but no admission charged.

□ Earliest "Wild West Show" to include some rodeo events.

△ First commercial rodeo, admission charged.

FIGURE 8.14
Origin and diffusion of the American commercial rodeo. Derived originally from folk culture, rodeos evolved through formal "cowboy contests" and "Wild West shows" to emerge, in the late 1880s and 1890s, in their present popular culture form. The border between the United States and Canada proved no barrier to the diffusion, though Canadian rodeo, like Canadian football, differs in some respects from the American type. See also Kristine Fredriksson, *American Rodeo from Buffalo Bill to Big Business* (College Station: Texas A&M University Press, 1984).

Prescott, Arizona, in 1888. The spread was extremely rapid, as is typical of cultural diffusion in the popular culture. By the turn of the century, commercial rodeos were being performed in much of the West. At Cheyenne, Wyoming, the famous Frontier Days rodeo was first held in 1897. By the time of World War I, the rodeo had also become an institution in provinces of western Canada, where the Calgary Stampede began in 1912.

Today, rodeos are held in almost every community of any size in the western United States. For example, the state of Oklahoma's calendar of events for the period April through September 1977 listed no fewer than 98 rodeos scheduled. Racial and sexual lines have been crossed by the rodeo in culturally diverse Oklahoma, producing such events as the Creek Nation All Indian Rodeo at Okmulgee, the All Girls Rodeo at Duncan, and the All Black Rodeo at Wewoka. In Texas and some other states, rodeo competition has become an official high school sport.

The diffusion of the commercial rodeo has carried it even into New York's Madison Square Garden. Professional rodeos are now held in 36 states and three Canadian provinces. Its major acceptance in the popular culture is found west of the Mississippi and Missouri rivers (Figure 8.14).

Barriers to the diffusion of commercial rodeo were encountered at the border of Mexico, south of which bullfighting occupies a dominant position, and in the Mormon culture region centered in Utah. Nor, except in California, did rodeo popularity penetrate the Cascade and coastal mountain ranges to reach the Pacific shore. However, a uniquely Mexican form of rodeo, the *charreada*, is growing rapidly in popularity in central Mexico today. As we might expect, the greatest strength of commercial rodeo in the United States lies in the beef cattle areas.

International Diffusion

Cultural diffusion, even among folk cultures, has never respected international borders, but in popular culture, innovations are diffused between countries and continents as rapidly as jet airplanes and satellite-beamed television programs. As a result, the popular cultures of North America and western Europe have become rather similar and are constantly in contact with one another. Country-western music is now heard in Northern Ireland's pubs, Levi-clad Yugoslavs in small towns flock to American-made movies, Americans wait in line to hear touring British rock musicians, Rocky Mountain ski resorts are built in Alpine-Swiss architecture, and the latest Paris clothes fashions appear in American department stores. Fast-food franchises of McDonald's and Kentucky Fried Chicken diffuse even to mainland China and Communist eastern Europe, while motel chains such as Holiday Inn improbably leap the same, formerly absorbing barriers to take root in Poland and other unlikely countries. Even in many underdeveloped countries, acceptance of Western popular culture occurs among a socioeconomic elite, so that the visitor to a provincial town in India may find a thriving local Lions Club. The international diffusion of popular culture has been so successful that many people now share aspects of a global culture.

Not all international diffusions of popular culture are so trivial or innocuous. The recreational and addictive use of illegal drugs has become an important aspect of North American and European popular culture. Many of these products come from foreign areas and reach the United States by long, difficult, clandestine routes of diffusion. Cocaine as well as opium (and its derivative heroin) are produced mainly in tropical areas, particularly in the highlands of southeast Asia and South America, reaching market by relocation diffusion (Figure 8.15).

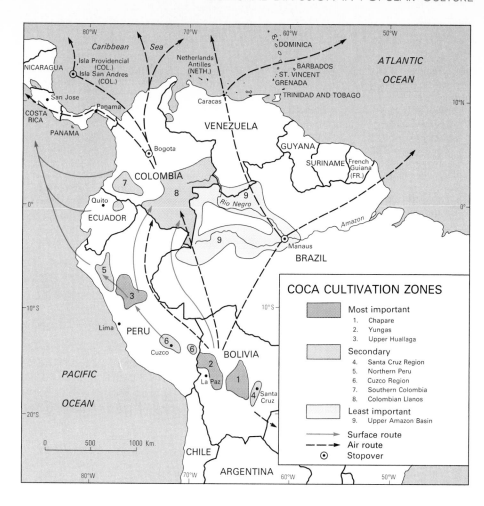

FIGURE 8.15
Cultivation source areas of coca (*Erythroxylum coca*) and relocation diffusion routes of trafficking of its derivative, the drug cocaine. Like it or not, cocaine is part of American popular culture, just as unrefined coca belongs to Andean and Amazonian folk culture. It moves illegally along many shifting paths of diffusion, overcoming various barriers to reach market. Colombia provides about 75 percent of the cocaine that reaches the United States, Peru 10 percent, and Bolivia 10 percent. (Source: Based in large part on Tim Hudson, "South American High: A Geography of Cocaine," *The American Geographical Society's Focus*, 35, No. 1 (1985), 22, 24, 27.)

Communications Barriers

While the communications media have the potential to allow almost instant diffusion over very large areas, spread can be greatly retarded if access to the media is denied (see box, "The Geography of 'Rock and Roll'"). An issue of *Billboard*, a magazine devoted largely to popular music, described such a barrier to diffusion. In the May 14, 1977, issue, record company executive Seymour Stein complained that radio stations and disk jockeys were refusing to play "punk rock" records, denying the style an equal opportunity for exposure. Stein claimed that punk devotees were concentrated in New York City, Los Angeles, Boston, and London, where many young people had found the style reflective of their feelings and frustrations. Without access to radio stations, punk rock could diffuse from these centers only through live concerts and the record sales they generated. The publishers of *Billboard* noted that "punk rock is but one of a number of musical forms which have had problems breaking through nationally out of regional footholds," for *pachanga*, *ska*, pop/gospel, "women's music," and more recently *reggae* experienced similar difficulties. All eventually overcame these barriers, but to control the programming of radio and television is to control much of the diffusionary apparatus in popular culture. The diffusion of innovations ultimately depends upon the flow of information.

Newspapers, though potent agents of diffusion in popular culture, also act as selective barriers, often reinforcing the effect of political boundaries. For example, between 21 and 48 percent of all news published in

THE GEOGRAPHY OF "ROCK AND ROLL"

Diffusion occurs rapidly in popular culture. A style of music, "rock and roll," arose in the early 1950s, achieved its maximum diffusion within a decade, then gave way to other music forms. Its chief personality, Elvis Presley, was only 42 years old at the time of his death in 1977, yet the heyday of rock and roll had ended a decade and a half before he died.

The hearth of rock and roll, about 1952 or 1953, was the "Upper Delta" country along the Mississippi River, centered on Memphis, Tennessee. Elvis, Little Richard, Fats Domino, Chuck Berry, and Jerry Lee Lewis, the chief practitioners of rock and roll, all worked in the Upper Delta. The style developed as a blending of black "rhythm and blues" and hill southern white "rockabilly," a fast-tempo country and western style. Diffusion was achieved both through the radio and sales of inexpensive 45 r.p.m. records, coupled with live concerts. The spread occurred most rapidly between 1955 and 1958; after 1963, rock and roll was in decline.

Barriers were encountered in the diffusion. Parental opposition to the music and lyrics as "degraded" led to the banning of rock and roll on radio stations in some cities. The barriers proved to be permeable — explicit sexual references, so common in rhythm and blues and vintage rock and roll, were softened. "Roll with me, Henry" became the less suggestive "Dance with me, Henry."

Hierarchical diffusion was clearly evident. Early adopters were inquisitive, gregarious young people, trendsetters in their generation. From them acceptance spread down through lower hierarchies until the hard core of nonaccepters remained. Similar trendsetters abandoned rock and roll for other rock styles after about 1963, and the major musical phenomenon of the 1950s went into decline. The influence of rock and roll is seen in later styles, but in its pure form it is rarely performed today.

Adapted from Richard V. Francaviglia, "Diffusion and Popular Culture: Comments on the Spatial Aspects of Rock Music," in David A. Lanegran and Risa Palm (eds.), *An Invitation to Geography* (New York: McGraw-Hill, 1973), pp. 87–96; and from research by Larry Ford.

Canadian newspapers is of foreign origin, mainly involving the flow northward of United States news, while only about 12 percent of all news appearing in papers in the United States comes from foreign areas. One might conclude from this discrepancy that Americans are a more provincial people than Canadians.

■ THE ECOLOGY OF POPULAR CULTURE

Because popular culture is largely the product of industrialization and the rise of technology, it is less directly tied to the physical environment than is folk culture. Gone is the intimate association between people and land known by our folk ancestors. Gone, too, is our direct vulnerability to many environmental forces, though our security is more apparent than real. The adaptive strategies pursued by people functioning within popular cultures have enormous potential for producing ecological disasters, as the recent concern over atmospheric ozone depletion suggests. Also, because popular culture encourages little intimate contact with and knowledge of the physical world, our environmental perceptions can become quite distorted. Such considerations indicate that the theme of cultural ecology is quite relevant to the study of popular culture.

Environmental Influence

Even though technology has removed us from close touch with nature and reduced many environmental hazards, our physical surroundings can still exert an influence. Indeed, some natural hazards are actually intensified by popular culture. For example, our urbanized society has chosen to locate many millions of city dwellers astride the major earthquake zone in California, producing the potential for a catastrophe of much greater proportion than a folk culture would face in that area. Similarly, our popular demand for seaside residence has greatly increased the number of dwellings susceptible to hurricane destruction along the Gulf Coast, magnifying the eventual damage. Also, epidemic diseases can spread more rapidly along our modern transportation networks, which were intended to carry only passengers and commodities.

The environmental influence on popular culture can be seen in more frivolous ways, as well. Our previous example of American sports provides some suggestion, at least, of environmental influence. Is the greater popularity of basketball and the higher per capita production of players in the North partly a result of colder winters there? Presumably the cold weather might make basketball, a traditional indoor sport, more desirable for spectators. Does cold weather likewise favor bowling and ice hockey, perhaps explaining their greater popularity in northern states and Canada? Surely it is not mere chance that the five major college football bowl games—Cotton, Rose, Fiesta, Orange, and Sugar—are all played in Sun Belt states on the southern border of the United States, or that until 1982 the professional Super Bowl had never been played outside the Sun Belt.

Even in these instances, though, climatic influence is waning. Huge covered stadiums now make it possible to play football and baseball indoors, and artificial wave-making machines permit surfboarding in the Arizona desert (Figure 8.16). Migrating northerners bring their interest in ice hockey to the South, where the game is played in refrigerated arenas while outside temperatures soar into the nineties. These examples suggest that the popular way of life has become a high-energy culture. Even the devices of diffusion in the popular culture require large amounts of electricity and gasoline, and countless labor-saving machines add to the seemingly insatiable need for fossil fuels and other energy supplies. Recently, we have witnessed a sharp rise in energy costs. Should these costs continue to rise, we might conceivably reach a point where many aspects of the popular culture could no longer be maintained.

FIGURE 8.16
Surfing, once tied to beach locations, can now be practiced in places like the desert, where artificial wave-making machines have been installed. This scene is in Tempe, Arizona, hundreds of miles from the nearest coast.

Impact on the Environment

Popular culture makes some heavy demands on the physical environment. This is true even in the realm of recreation. Since World War II, leisure time and related recreational activities have increased greatly in the United States, Canada, Europe, and other developed countries. Much leisure time is now spent by members of the popular culture in some space-consuming activity in areas outside the cities. The demand for "wilderness" recreation zones has risen sharply in the last quarter-century, and no end to the increase seems at hand (Figure 8.17).

Hikers, campers, hunters, fishers, bikers, dune buggy and snowmobile enthusiasts, weekend cottagers, surfers, spelunkers, mountain climbers, boaters, sightseers, and others are making unprecedented demands on the open country. Such a massive presence of people in our open areas cannot help damaging the physical environment. National parks now suffer from traffic jams, residential congestion, litter, and noise pollution—very much like the urban areas (Figure 8.18). A recent study by geographer Jeanne Kay and her students in Utah revealed substantial environmental damage by off-road recreational vehicles, including "soil loss and long-term soil deterioration." In less congested wilderness districts, as few as several hundred hikers a month can beat down trails to the extent that vegetation is altered, erosion encouraged, and wildlife diminished. Even the best-intentioned, conservation-minded visitors do some damage. One of the paradoxes of the modern age and popular culture seems to be that the more we cluster in cities and suburbs, the greater our impact on open areas. We carry our popular culture with us when we vacation in such regions.

Some countries have reacted to the recreational tourist boom merely by making natural areas ever more accessible, ever more crowded and damaged. Others, including the United States, have now drawn a distinction between national park tourism and wilderness areas. Access to many wild districts is now greatly restricted, in hopes that they can be saved from the damage that necessarily accompanies recreational activity. In

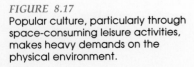
FIGURE 8.17
Popular culture, particularly through space-consuming leisure activities, makes heavy demands on the physical environment.

FIGURE 8.18
Popular culture might be better called "litter culture," as this scene after an outdoor rock concert suggests.

some national parks, access by private automobile and camper pickup is restricted, but for the greater part of the countryside, the recreational assault on the environment continues.

CULTURAL INTEGRATION IN POPULAR CULTURE

The interaction of popular culture and physical environment, while significant, is overshadowed in importance by the internal workings of the culture. The most potent forces shaping any element of popular culture are other elements of the same popular culture. Thus we turn to the theme of cultural integration to increase our understanding of cause-and-effect relationships.

The Impact of Communications Media

The impact of the communications media provides an excellent example of cultural integration. Geographer Ronald F. Abler concluded that our modern communications system, a product of the industrialized popular culture, is the most potent force for spatial change that people presently command. It was long assumed that the overall effect of efficient, rapid communications, particularly radio and television, was to homogenize popular culture and reduce the differences between places. Indeed, impressive evidence can be marshaled to support this **convergence hypothesis.** Geographer Wilbur Zelinsky, for example, found by comparing the given names of persons in various regions of the eastern United States for 1790 and 1968 that a more pronounced regionalization existed in the eighteenth century than today (see box, "The Geography of Personal Given Names"). The personal names bestowed on children by the present generation of parents vary less from place to place than did those of our

THE GEOGRAPHY OF PERSONAL GIVEN NAMES

Does your given name give you a geographical label? Within the popular culture of America, can we identify regions on the basis of the names parents choose for their children? Maybe, according to cultural geographer Wilbur Zelinsky, who published the first geographical study of personal names in America. His findings, however, also give some support to the **convergence hypothesis** (see Glossary).

Regionalization is suggested by the following selection of given names, belonging to students who completed graduate degrees at universities in one region of America during the period 1960–1975: Ruzelle, Dailis, Norence, Lenola, La-Verta, Pearlean, Jessyetene, Homoizelle, Jamesetta, Fedies, Jearl, Zerline, Christella, Vernice, and Bevelyn. Imaginative and out of the ordinary? Indeed they are! Did you correctly

identify them as names of students at black universities in the American South? Do compound names like Billy Joe, Eddie Mae, Mary Alice, Donna Jean, and John Henry similarly remind you of the South? How about the use of initials instead of names, such as J. B., J. D., and C. L.?

While the trend in American popular culture may be toward less regional diversity in personal names, some contrasts apparently remain. The American South, both black and white, provides evidence to support this conclusion.

Inspired by Wilbur Zelinsky, "Cultural Variation in Personal Name Patterns in the Eastern United States," *Annals of the Association of American Geographers*, 60 (1970), 743–796. Black personal names are from thesis directories at Prairie View A&M and Texas Southern universities in Texas.

ancestors two centuries ago. Similarly, daily exposure to the Midland dialect favored by national television and radio announcers is causing the decline of other dialects, presenting the rather dreary prospect that our grandchildren may all speak the English of Tom Brokaw and other newscasters. The possible end product of the convergence would be a national or even planetary culture.

Professors Abler and Zelinsky, however, both suggest that the media have a potential for reinforcing or even promoting regional cultural differences. Popular culture, to a degree previously unknown, through leisure, wealth, and rapid communications, allows the individual personality to come to the forefront (see box, "Personal Preference and the Changing Map of American Society"). Increasingly, free exercise of individual preferences, with each person "doing his own thing," is creating a new spatial order in countries such as the United States and Canada. The number of special-interest groups and publications has exploded in recent decades. Many radio stations now cater to very special clienteles, as do almost countless magazines and clubs. For example, the number of black-oriented radio stations in the United States increased from only 32 in 1956 to 130 in 1970 and 226 by 1987.

The media, in effect, are helping to create new subcultures and to sustain some traditional ones. They are assisting the rise of consciousness and even militance along ethnic, racial, age, and sexual lines by putting persons of similar backgrounds, interests, preferences, or beliefs into frequent contact with one another. Will such subcultures segregate spatially? Will regionalization within the popular culture be the end product? It is really too early to tell for certain, since the massive impact of special-interest media "narrowcasting," to use Professor Abler's term, is too recent to have produced a final result, but there are suggestions that the media are, indeed, helping to create a spatially diverse popular culture. Hints of this trend are seen in the segregated communities where only older people live, as in Sun City, Arizona; or in the concentration of people favoring "swinging singles" and gay life-styles in certain districts within cities such as San Francisco and Dallas (Figure 8.19).

Planetary culture, then, may well be illusory. Popular culture, under the shaping influence of special-interest communications media, may be drifting toward a regionalization as pronounced as any found in folk culture. In any case, the media are unquestionably fostering and strengthening subcultural identities.

PERSONAL PREFERENCE AND THE CHANGING MAP OF AMERICAN SOCIETY

"Take a large human population. After it has been stirred and seasoned well for two centuries, relax traditional social and economic constraints. Give many of its individual members enough leisure time and money so that they can do pretty much what they wish to please themselves. Add several dashes of new social and technological forces; let the mixture simmer for a couple of decades; then ask: what sorts of choices will be made by the millions of participants in such a macro-experiment? What things will how many persons do, and *where* will they do them?

"The ingredients for this recipe are, of course, to be found in the United States. . . . Our nation has witnessed the attainment of a degree of affluence and freedom of attitude and action, of a range of individual and social options, on the part of a quite massive fraction of its total adult population that is unprecedented in human history, yet may be predictive of things to come in other highly advanced countries. . . . The increasingly free exercise of individual preferences as to values, pleasures, self-improvement, social and physical habitat, and general life-style in an individualistic, affluent national community may have begun to alter the spatial attributes of society and culture in the United States to a significant extent.

"This notion happens to be imbedded in an even more fundamental proposition, namely, that we are now engaged in a process of deep, perhaps revolutionary, structural change in human society, the causes and consequences of which are still unclear. The geographer has been accustomed to seeking the sources for a real diversity in human activities in three sets of factors . . . : the laws of economic behavior; the still dimly apprehended laws of socio-cultural behavior; and the opportunities of constraints of an exceedingly complicated physical environment. Perhaps we can no longer afford to ignore a fourth major set of less familiar factors: the differences in personality structure . . . among a growing number of human beings in quest of self-fulfillment. . . .

"Are the newly emergent, often vicarious communities of self-selected individuals superior, or even acceptable, replacements for the confining, womblike certitudes of traditional local societies? Are we trudging down the road to utopia or dystopia? May not individual alienation or the burden of constant choice be too stiff a price to pay for the intoxication of almost limitless mobility and personal experimentation? Putting it boldly: Is what we are winning worth what we are losing?"

Excerpted, with minor changes, from Wilbur Zelinsky, "Selfward Bound? Personal Preference Patterns and the Changing Map of American Society," *Economic Geography*, 50 (1974), 144, 176, with permission.

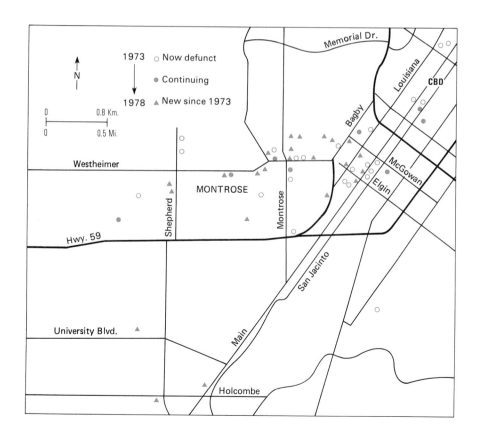

FIGURE 8.19
Distribution of gay bars in the city of Houston, 1973 and 1978. Neighborhoods devoted to one or another sexual preference flourish in the popular culture of North America. Some of these are both residential and recreational, as in the "swinging singles" apartment districts. In Houston, Texas, bars patronized by male homosexuals are tightly clustered in one part of the city, clearly revealing a "geography." (Redrawn from Barbara A. Weightman, "Gay Bars as Private Places," *Landscape*, 24, 1 (1980), 10.)

Why Football Fever?

The cultural integration theme may also permit us to understand better some of the spatial patterns presented earlier in the discussion of culture regions. For example, some of the differences among places in American sport may be explained in part by other elements of culture. "Football fever" is a case in point.

Why do certain districts exceed others in football interest and per capita player production? Part of the answer, as suggested earlier, may lie in the realm of cultural ecology, but even more important causal forces are likely to be found in other elements of the popular culture. The four major football "hotbeds," according to Professor Rooney, are (1) western Pennsylvania, eastern Ohio, and northern West Virginia; (2) parts of Texas and western Oklahoma; (3) northern Utah and portions of adjacent states; and (4) southern Mississippi. Interestingly, the Pennsylvania-Ohio-West Virginia region, which seems to be the original American football "hotbed," corresponds well to a zone of heavy industry, particularly steelmaking. Are such blue-collar workers the hard-core supporters of football? If so, it is more than appropriate that the professional team located in the core of this region is nicknamed the "Steelers." Other "blue-collar" type nicknames for sports teams around the country, such as "Packers," "Brewers," "Boilermakers," and "Mariners," imply a working-class clientele.

Texas football fever apparently originated among oil-field roughnecks, another blue-collar group, and the support of high school football in that state seems even today to be most fanatical in oil towns. Texas professional teams are owned by oil-rich families, and the Houston franchise is nicknamed "Oilers." It is possible, as Dr. Rooney suggests, that roughnecks coming from the Pennsylvania oil fields implanted football fever in Texas. These examples would suggest that there is a tie between one's interest in football and one's type of employment, at least in some areas.

Northern Utah, on the other hand, presents a quite different situation. There football fever rages in a largely nonindustrial region, among affluent, well-educated people. The key seems to be the local dominance of the Mormon faith, which places great emphasis on physical fitness and group-team cooperation. Southern Mississippi is a rural, thinly populated region with many poor people and blacks. The reasons for its prominence as a producer of football players are not clear, but they are likely cultural.

■ LANDSCAPES OF POPULAR CULTURE

Landscape mirrors culture. We are what we see and what we build for others to see. Popular culture permeates the landscape of countries such as the United States and Canada, including everything from mass-produced suburban houses to golf courses and neon-lighted "strips." So overwhelming is the presence of the popular culture in most American settlement landscapes that an observer must often search diligently to find visual fragments of the older folk cultures. The popular landscape is in continual flux, for change is a hallmark of popular culture.

American Front Yards

As an example of the popular cultural landscape and the changes that occur in it, let us consider a truly American institution: the front yard

(Figure 8.20). A dwelling set back from the street, with the nonfunctional intervening space covered by an expanse of grassy lawn, has since the early 1800s been one of the most pervasive symbols of the urban and suburban Anglo-American popular landscape. Homeowners who neglect to tend these lawns properly, or who put the space into some functional use such as vegetable gardening, invite the animosity and contempt of their neighbors, not to mention the lowering of property value. For most of us, the grass-covered front yard is so universally accepted that we assume it to be a part of the natural order of things in suburbia.

Anglos migrating west in the nineteenth century brought the front lawn with them, even into the desert areas of the American Southwest, where irrigation was necessary to maintain the grass. The desert became dotted with green suburban oases. In cities such as Tucson, the Anglo dwellings flanked by lawns stood in marked contrast to the older Hispano houses, which either lacked yards altogether or had bare-earth areas. Geographer Melvin E. Hecht has studied the popular culture yard landscape that resulted from the Anglo-Hispano contact, and he has documented the decline of the grass lawn tradition. Increasingly, Anglo southwesterners are turning to "desert front" yards, where grass is replaced by gravel, crushed rock, desert plants, paving, or undisturbed desert (Figure 8.20). A few innovators among the Anglos adopted such yards even in the early part of this century, but the rapid rise of the desert front yard began in the 1950s, spurred by a new wave of urban immigrants who found the desert beautiful rather than repulsive. In the manner of typical hierarchical diffusion, acceptance occurred earliest in the higher-priced subdivisions and spread gradually to the middle-class districts. Professor Hecht found that fully one-half of all houses built in Tucson between 1965 and 1975 had desert front yards. Some of these are covered with gravel dyed green, a simulation of the lawn and a classic example of a permeable barrier in cultural diffusion, but most represent complete departures from the older custom. Hecht concluded that the decline of the lawn tradition heralded the emergence of a new, distinct popular culture region, one which reflected an appreciation of Arizona's natural setting and Hispanic heritage. Desert fronts have since diffused to become part of the popular cultural landscape in neighboring states and even beyond. It is perhaps symptomatic of the visual excesses of popular culture that desert fronts are now appearing in high-rainfall states such as Florida, where plastic sheets have to be installed under the gravel layer to prevent grass and weeds from emerging.

FIGURE 8.20
The grass-covered front yard and the more recently developed "desert front" are both elements of the landscape of popular culture. (Desert front photo, El Paso, by Terry G. Jordan, 1980.)

Elitist and Amenity Landscapes

A distinctive aspect of popular, as opposed to folk, culture is the development of social classes. A small elite group consisting of persons of wealth, education, and taste occupies the top position in popular cultures. The important geographical fact about such people is that because of their wealth, desire to be around similar people, distinctive tastes, and hedonistic life-styles, they can and do create distinctive cultural landscapes, often over fairly large areas.

Daniel W. Gade, a cultural geographer, coined the term *elitist space* to describe such landscapes, using the French Riviera as an example (Figure 8.21). In that district of stunning natural beauty and idyllic climate, the French elite have applied "refined taste to create an aesthetically pleasing cultural landscape" characterized by preservation of old buildings and town cores, a sense of proportion, and respect for scale. Building codes and height restrictions are rigorously enforced. Land values, in response, have risen, making the Riviera ever more elitist, far removed from the folk culture and poverty that prevailed there before 1850. Farmers and fishermen have almost disappeared from the region, though one need but drive a short distance, to Toulon, to find a "scruffy and proletarian port." It seems, then, that the different social classes generated within popular culture become geographically segregated, each producing a distinctive cultural landscape.

America, too, offers elitist landscapes. An excellent example is the *gentleman farm,* an agricultural unit operated for pleasure rather than profit (Figure 8.22). Typically, gentleman farms are owned by affluent city people as an avocation, and such farms help to create or maintain a high social standing for those who own them. Some rural landscapes in America now contain many such gentleman farms; perhaps most notable among these areas are the inner Bluegrass Basin of north-central Kentucky, the Virginia Piedmont west of Washington, D.C., Long Island in

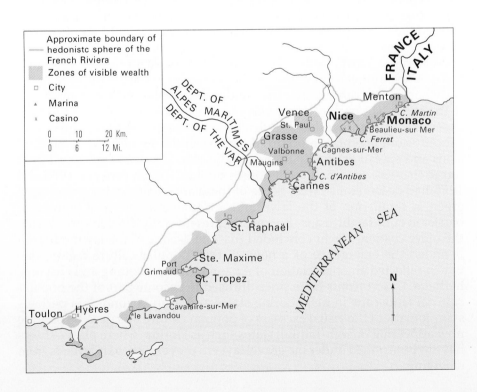

FIGURE 8.21
The distribution of elitist or hedonistic cultural landscape on the French Riviera. What forces in the popular culture generate such landscapes? (Adapted from Daniel W. Gade, "The French Riviera as Elitist Space," *Journal of Cultural Geography,* 3 (Fall–Winter 1982), 22.)

FIGURE 8.22
Gentleman farm in the Kentucky Bluegrass region near Lexington. The photo reveals some typical landscape features, such as board fences and imposing mansions. (Photo courtesy of Professor Karl B. Raitz.)

New York, and parts of southeastern Pennsylvania. Gentleman farmers engage in such activities as breeding fine cattle, racing horses, or hunting foxes.

Geographer Karl Raitz made a study of gentleman farms in the Kentucky Bluegrass Basin, where the concentration is so great that they constitute a dominant feature of the cultural landscape (Figure 8.23). The result is an idyllic scene, a rural landscape created more for appearance than for function. Professor Raitz provided a list of visual indicators of Kentucky gentleman farms: wooden fences, either painted white or creosoted black, a type costing upwards of $7000 per mile to build; an elaborate entrance gate; a fine hand-painted sign giving the name of the farm and owner; a network of surfaced, well-maintained driveways and pasture roads; and a large elegant house, visible in the distance from the public highway through a lawnlike parkland dotted with clumps of trees and perhaps a pond or two. So attractive are these estates to the eye that tourists cruise the rural lanes to view them, convinced they are seeing the "real" rural America, or at least rural America as it ought to be.

Closely related to elitist space are *amenity landscapes*, to use a phrase coined by geographer Richard D. Hecock. He had in mind areas such as the Minnesota North Woods lake country, where, in one area he sampled, fully 40 percent of all dwellings were not permanent residences, but instead weekend cottages or vacation homes. These are often rustic or even humble in appearance, in contrast to what we find in elitist landscapes, but such amenities reflect the luxury and leisure typical of popular culture.

Landscapes of Consumption

Not all popular landscapes are elitist or amenity-related, of course. The eye-catching, ubiquitous commercial "strips" along urban arterial streets provide a case in point. Geographer Robert Sack has used the term "landscape of consumption," very appropriate for such places. In an Illinois

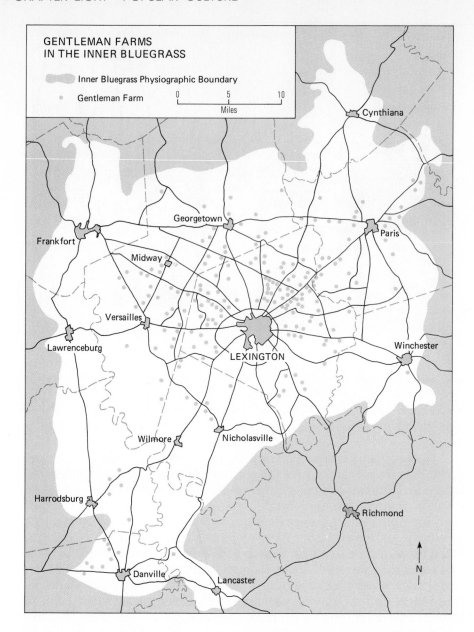

GENTLEMAN FARMS
IN THE INNER BLUEGRASS

░░ Inner Bluegrass Physiographic Boundary

· Gentleman Farm

0   5   10
Miles

Cynthiana

Georgetown

Frankfort

Paris

Midway

Versailles

Lawrenceburg

Winchester

LEXINGTON

Wilmore

Nicholasville

Harrodsburg

Richmond

Danville

Lancaster

N

FIGURE 8.23
The gentleman farm is an elitist landscape feature in central Kentucky. Why might a concentration have developed there? How does such a landscape differ from one that might be produced by a folk culture? (After Raitz, p. 44.)

college town, two other cultural geographers, John A. Jakle and Richard L. Mattson, made a study of the evolution of such a strip, covering the period 1919–1979. During that 60-year span, the street under study changed from single-family residential to a commercial focus (Figure 8.24). The researchers suggested a five-stage model of strip evolution, beginning (stage 1) with the single-family residential period. In stage 2, the introduction of gasoline stations forms the vanguard of commercialization; while in stage 3 other businesses join the growing number of filling stations, multiunit housing becomes common, and absentee ownership increases. Stage 4 is clearly dominated by the commercial function; businesses catering to the drive-in trade proliferate and residential use declines sharply. Income levels of the remaining inhabitants are low. In stage 5 the residential function of the street disappears and a totally commercial landscape prevails. Business properties expand in order that off-street parking can be provided, and often a public outcry against the ugliness of the strip is

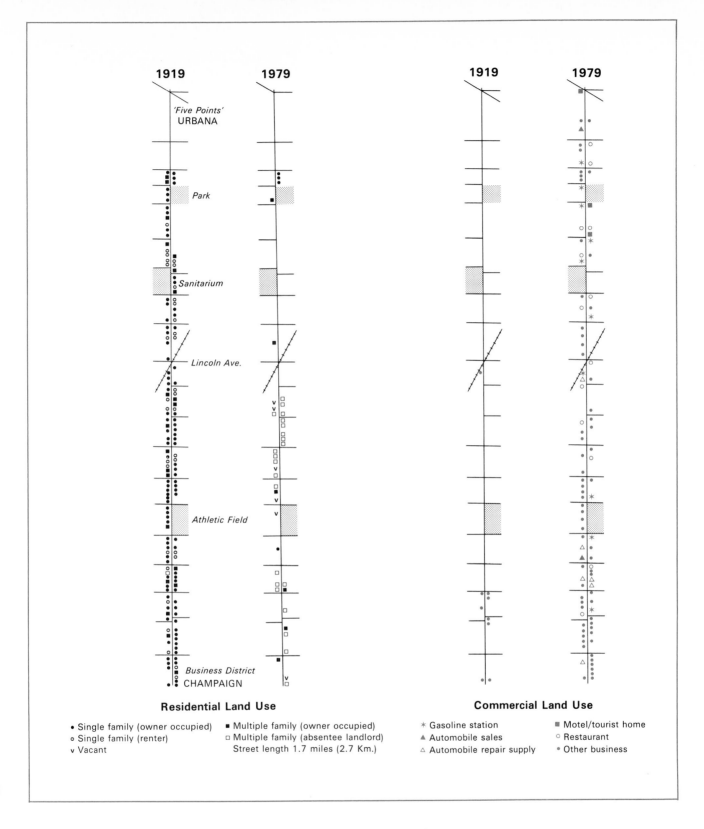

Residential Land Use

- • Single family (owner occupied)
- ○ Single family (renter)
- v Vacant
- ■ Multiple family (owner occupied)
- □ Multiple family (absentee landlord)

Street length 1.7 miles (2.7 Km.)

Commercial Land Use

- ✱ Gasoline station
- ▲ Automobile sales
- △ Automobile repair supply
- ■ Motel/tourist home
- ○ Restaurant
- • Other business

raised. Such places not only represent popular aesthetic values, but perhaps also reveal social and cultural problems that need redress. On the other hand, they may be a needed antidote to the plastic artificiality of overly sanitized elitist landscapes.

FIGURE 8.24
The evolution of a commercial strip in Champaign-Urbana, Illinois, 1919–1979. (Adapted from Jakle and Mattson, pp. 14, 20.)

The American Scene

Front yards, gentleman farms, weekend cottages, and commercial strips are but several features of the American popular landscape. One very perceptive and sensitive cultural geographer, David Lowenthal, attempted a broader analysis, an overall evaluation of the visible impact of popular culture in the American countryside. In an article entitled "The American Scene," Professor Lowenthal lists the main characteristics of popular landscape in the United States. Among these are the "cult of bigness"; the tolerance of present ugliness to achieve a supposedly glorious future; zoolike enclaves of historical artifacts, either genuine or fake; emphasis on individual features at the expense of aggregates, producing a "casual chaos"; and the preeminence of function over form.

The fondness for massive structures is reflected in structures such as the Empire State Building, the Pentagon, the San Francisco-Oakland Bay Bridge, or Salt Lake City's Mormon Temple (Figure 8.25). Americans have dotted their cultural landscape with the world's largest of this or that,

cult of bigness

FIGURE 8.25
The landscape of American popular culture is characterized by massive structures, such as the Mormon Temple in Salt Lake City, and by functionality, well exemplified by the unsightly oil derrick on the Oklahoma State Capitol grounds.

perhaps in an effort to match the grand scale of the physical environment, which offers such superlatives as the Grand Canyon, the redwoods, and the Yellowstone geysers. Americans apparently admire these structures more for their size than their beauty.

Americans, says Professor Lowenthal, tend to regard their cultural landscape as unfinished. Because of this, they are "predisposed to accept present structures that are makeshift, flimsy, and transient," resembling, in Lowenthal's view, "throwaway stage sets." Similarly, the hardships of pioneer life perhaps preconditioned Americans to value function more highly than beauty. A shopping center, junk car lot, or mobile home park may seem ugly to the passerby, but so long as it is functional it seems to give no serious cause for complaint (Figure 8.26). For many years, the state capital grounds in Oklahoma City were adorned with little more than oil derricks, standing above busy pumps drawing wealth from the Sooner soil — an extreme but revealing view of the American landscape (Figure 8.25).

Individual landscape features, says Lowenthal, take precedence over groupings. Five buildings or houses in a row may display five different architectural styles, and rarely is an attempt made to erect assemblages of structures that "belong" together. "Places are only collections of heterogeneous buildings." To be worthy, each structure must be unique and eye-catching, and architects in the popular culture vie with one another in producing attention-grabbing edifices. Each fast-food chain seems to require its own outlandish style of structure to facilitate instant visual recognition by potential customers.

The past, reflected in archaic landscape relics, has traditionally been confined by Americans to zoolike "historylands," often enclosed by imposing wire-link fences and open only during certain seasons or hours. If the desired bit of visual history has perished, Americans do not hesitate to rebuild it from scratch, undisturbed by the lack of authenticity, as for example at Jamestown, Virginia. Normally the history zoos are segregated and sanitized to the extent that people no longer live in them. Europeans incorporate historic buildings into their functioning landscape; Americans keep them at arm's length.

FIGURE 8.26
Trailer park inhabitants live in a makeshift part of our functional environment.

Lowenthal, a resident both of the United Kingdom and the United States, sees the American landscape partially with the eyes of a visitor. People who create the landscape and live in it fulltime are likely to perceive it differently, in a less elitist way, than do visitors. For example, geographer Yi-Fu Tuan suggests that a commercial strip of stores, hamburger joints, filling stations, and used-car lots may appear as visual blight to an outsider, but the owners or operators of the businesses are very proud of them and of their role in the community. Hard work and hopes color their perceptions of the popular landscape. Similarly, what is an unsightly sprawl of suburban houses to the passerby may be a beautiful realization of a desire for home ownership to the inhabitant.

America, then, has a distinctive popular cultural landscape. Some perceive it to be ugly and dismaying. Others see it as dynamic and reflective of a self-confident, future-oriented people, and still others, perhaps even the majority, simply take it for granted and pay little heed.

CONCLUSION

Geographers clearly have a role to play in the study of popular culture. The examples we have presented, drawn mainly from North America, reveal that our five themes permit a distinctly geographical approach to the subject. Cultural regions reveal spatial contrasts; diffusion allows us to glimpse the movement of elements of popular culture through geographic space; ecology and integration explain some of the processes and factors involved in the development of spatial diversity; and landscape makes us more aware of the diverse visible impact of popular culture. Hopefully, too, this chapter and the one preceding have broadened your perspective concerning the popular culture life-style you now pursue. If you are a typical member of the popular culture, your way of life is an extreme one — as extreme as that of the self-sufficient farmers who belong to folk culture.

Suggested Readings

Ronald F. Abler. "Monoculture or Miniculture? The Impact of Communication Media on Culture in Space," in David A. Lanegran and Risa Palm (eds.), *An Invitation to Geography.* New York: McGraw-Hill, 1973, pp. 186–195.

John Bale. *Sport and Place: A Geography of Sport in England, Scotland, and Wales.* Lincoln: University of Nebraska Press, 1983.

Donald J. Ballas and Margaret J. King. "Cultural Geography and Popular Culture: Proposal for a Creative Merger," *Journal of Cultural Geography,* 2 (1981), 154–163.

Peter Blake. *God's Own Junkyard: The Planned Deterioration of America's Landscape,* 2nd ed. New York: Holt, Rinehart and Winston, 1979.

R. W. Butler. "The Geography of Rock: 1954–1970," *Ontario Geography,* 24 (1984), 1–33.

Alvar W. Carlson. "Cultural Geography and Popular Culture," *Journal of Popular Culture,* 9 (1975), 482–483.

Alvar W. Carlson, "The Contributions of Cultural Geographers to the Study of Popular Culture," *Journal of Popular Culture,* 11 (1978), 830–831.

George O. Carney. "From Down Home to Uptown: The Diffusion of Country-Music Radio Stations in the United States," *Journal of Geography,* 76 (1977), 104–110.

George O. Carney (ed.). *The Sounds of People and Places: Readings in the Geography of American Folk and Popular Music.* Lanham and New York: University Press of America, 1987.

Laurence W. Carstensen, Jr. "The Burger Kingdom: Growth and Diffusion of McDonald's Restaurants in the United States, 1955–1978," *Geographical Perspectives,* 58 (1986), 1–8.

James R. Curtis. "McDonald's Abroad: Outposts of American Culture," *Journal of Geography,* 81 (1982), 14–20.

James R. Curtis and Richard F. Rose. "The 'Miami Sound': A Contemporary Latin Form of Place-Specific Music," *Journal of Cultural Geography,* 4, No. 1 (1983), 110–118.

James Duncan. "Landscape Taste as a Symbol of Group Identity: A Westchester County Village," *Geographical Review,* 63 (1973), 334–355.

Larry R. Ford and Floyd M. Henderson. "The Image of Place in American Popular Music: 1890–1970," *Places,* 1 (1974), 31–37.

Richard V. Francaviglia. "Diffusion and Popular Culture: Comments on the Spatial Aspects of Rock Music," in David A. Lanegran and Risa Palm (eds.), *An Invitation to Geography.* New York: McGraw-Hill, 1973, pp. 87–96.

Daniel W. Gade. "The French Riviera as Elitist Space," *Journal of Cultural Geography,* 3 (1982), 19–28.

Ernst C. Griffin and Larry R. Ford. "Tijuana: Landscape of a Culture Hybrid," *Geographical Review,* 66 (1976), 435–447.

Charles F. Gritzner. "Geomythography (Geographic Myths as Popular Culture)," in Mark Gordon and Jack Nachbar (eds.), *Currents of Warm Life: Popular Culture in American Higher Education.* Bowling Green, Ohio: Bowling Green University Popular Press, 1980, pp. 118–122.

Melvin E. Hecht. "The Decline of the Grass Lawn Tradition in Tucson," *Landscape,* 19 (June 1975), 3–10.

Richard D. Hecock. "Changes in the Amenity Landscape: The Case of Some Northern Minnesota Townships," *North American Culture,* 3, No. 1 (1987), 53–66.

Richard P. Horwitz. *The Strip: An American Place.* Lincoln: University of Nebraska Press, 1985.

M. Thomas Inge (ed.). *Handbook of American Popular Culture.* 3 vols. Westport, Conn.: Greenwood Press, 1978–1981.

John A. Jakle. "Motel by the Roadside: America's Room for the Night," *Journal of Cultural Geography,* 1 (Fall–Winter 1980), 34–49.

John A. Jakle. "Roadside Restaurants and Place-Product-Packaging," *Journal of Cultural Geography,* 3 (1982), 76–93.

John A. Jakle and Richard L. Mattson. "The Evolution of a Commercial Strip," *Journal of Cultural Geography,* 1 (Spring–Summer 1981), 12–25.

Journal of Popular Culture. An interdisciplinary journal published by the Popular Culture Association and Bowling Green State University. Volume 1 appeared in 1967. See in particular Volume 11, No. 4 (Spring 1978), a special issue on cultural geography and popular culture.

Herbert G. Kariel and Lynn A. Rosenvall. "United States News Flows to Canadian Newspapers," *American Review of Canadian Studies,* 13 (1983), 44–64.

Jeanne Kay et al. "Evaluating Environmental Impacts of Off-Road Vehicles," *Journal of Geography,* 80 (1981), 10–18.

Fred B. Kniffen. "Milestones and Stumbling Blocks," *Pioneer America,* 7 (January 1975), 1–8.

David Lowenthal. "The American Scene," *Geographical Review,"* 58 (1968), 61–88.

David Lowenthal. "The Bicentennial Landscape: A Mirror Held Up to the Past," *Geographical Review,* 67 (1977), 253–267.

Richard Pillsbury. "Carolina Thunder: A Geography of Southern Stock Car Racing," *Journal of Geography,* 73 (January 1974), 39–47.

Karl B. Raitz. "Gentleman Farms in Kentucky's Inner Bluegrass," *Southeastern Geographer,* 15 (1975), 33–46.

Karl B. Raitz. "Place, Space and Environment in America's Leisure Landscapes," *Journal of Cultural Geography,* 8 (Fall–Winter 1987), 49–62.

Edward Relph. *Place and Placelessness.* London: Pion, 1976.

Michael Roark. "Fast Foods: American Food Regions," *North American Culture,* 2, No. 1 (1985), 24–36.

John F. Rooney, Jr. *A Geography of American Sport.* Reading, Mass.: Addison-Wesley, 1974.

John F. Rooney, Jr. "Up From the Mines and Out From the Prairies: Some Geographical Implications of Football in the United States," *Geographical Review,* 59 (1969), 471–492.

Robert D. Sack. "The Consumer's World: Place as Context," *Annals of the Association of American Geographers,* 78 (1988), 642–664.

Keith A. Sculle. "The Vernacular Gasoline Station: Examples from Illinois and Wisconsin," *Journal of Cultural Geography,* 1 (Spring–Summer 1981), 56–74.

James R. Shortridge. "Changing Usage of Four American Regional Labels," *Annals of the Association of American Geographers,* 77 (1987), 325–336.

Neil L. Shumsky and Larry M. Springer. "San Francisco's Zone of Prostitution, 1880–1934," *Journal of Historical Geography,* 7 (1981), 71–89.

Sport Place: An International Journal of Sports Geography deals with this important aspect of popular culture. Published by Black Oak Press, Stillwater, Oklahoma. Volume 1 appeared in 1987.

Stephen W. Tweedie. "Viewing the Bible Belt," *Journal of Popular Culture,* 11 (1978), 865–876.

Norman R. Yetman and D. Stanley Eitzen. "Some Social and Demographic Correlates of Football Productivity," *Geographical Review,* 63 (1973), 553–557.

Wilbur Zelinsky. "Classical Town Names in the United States: The Historical Geography of An American Idea," *Geographical Review,* 57 (1967), 463–495.

Wilbur Zelinsky. *The Cultural Geography of the United States.* Englewood Cliffs, N.J.: Prentice-Hall, 1973.

Wilbur Zelinsky. "Cultural Variation in Personal Name Patterns in the Eastern United States," *Annals of the Association of American Geographers,* 60 (1970), 743–769.

Wilbur Zelinsky. "North America's Vernacular Regions," *Annals of the Association of American Geographers,* 70 (198), 1–16.

Wilbur Zelinsky. "Selfward Bound? Personal Preference Patterns and the Changing Map of American Society," *Economic Geography,* 50 (1974), 144–179.

Leo E. Zonn (ed.). *Place Images in the Media: A Geographical Appraisal.* Totowa, N.J.: Rowman & Littlefield, 1989.

Chapter 9

Ethnic Geography

ETHNIC REGIONS

  Ethnic Culture Regions in Rural North
    America
  Urban Ethnic Neighborhoods and
    Ghettos
  Canadian/American Ethnic Contrasts

**CULTURAL DIFFUSION AND ETHNIC
GROUPS**

  Ethnic Migration
  Diffusion of Ethnic Traits
  The Factor of Geographical Isolation
  Cultural Rebound

CULTURAL ECOLOGY AND ETHNICITY

  Selecting a Site

CULTURAL INTEGRATION AND ETHNICITY

  Ethnicity and Business Activity
  Ethnicity and Type of Employment
  Ethnicity and Farming Practices

NORTH AMERICA'S ETHNIC LANDSCAPES

  The Finnish Sauna in Rural America
  Settlement Patterns
  Traditional Architecture
  Exterior Wall Murals

CONCLUSION

A fine statue of the American national hero Paul Revere, mounted on his trusty horse, towers over a pedestrian mall near the Old North Church in Boston. Close by is the Revere home, carefully and lovingly preserved. As American as apple pie, you may say, a shrine to national independence. But what language are the elderly women speaking as they sit on benches near the statue and go about their knitting? Certainly it is not good Yankee English, by the sound of it. The same tongue dominates conversation in a nearby barbershop. Can it be Italian? Indeed it is. Closer inspection reveals Italian family names on almost every business establishment in Revere's neighborhood, like Giuffre's Fish Market, Italian pizza parlors, an Italian-dominated outdoor vegetable market, a Sons of Italy lodge hall, and Italian-American women leaning out of upper-story windows on opposite sides of the street to converse, Naples-style. Revere, himself of French ethnic extraction, would be astounded. Boston's North End is Italian! A pilgrimage to the site where the American Revolution began has become a trip to Little Italy.

The small midwestern town of Wilber, settled by Bohemian immigrants beginning about 1865, claims to be "The Czech Capital of Nebraska" and invited visitors to attend in 1990 the twenty-ninth "Annual Czech Festival of Nebraska Czechs, Incorporated, of Wilber, Nebraska." Celebrants are attracted by promises of eating Czech foods like *koláče*, *jaternice*, poppyseed cake, and *jelita*; seeing Czech folk dancing; purchasing glassware, "colored Czech postcards and souvenirs" imported from Czechoslovakia, or handicraft items made by Nebraska Czechs (and bearing an official seal and trademark to prove authenticity). "Czech Foods, Czech Refreshments, Czech Bands," proclaim the festival leaflets, and "breathtaking pageants of old world history" as well. "Many shops are decorated in the Czech motif and music can be heard on the streets during most hours of the day. Many items of Czech heritage . . . are sold. Czech baking and meat items are offered daily by local merchants who use authentic recipes." Thousands of visitors from the United States, Canada, and overseas attend the festival each year. Indeed, the visitor to the state of Nebraska can see much of "Europe" without ever leaving this American heartland, for besides the Wilber festival, Nebraska offers "Swedish Days" at the town of Holdrege in May, "Danish Days" at Minden in June, "German Heritage Days" at McCook in April, "Czech Festival" at Clarkson in June, "Swedish Festival" at Stromsburg in June, and "St. Patrick's Day Celebration" at O'Neill in March, in addition to five Indian tribal "pow wows" and assorted additional European ethnic festivals.

In 1893, the famous American historian Frederick Jackson Turner claimed that "the frontier promoted the formation of a composite nationality for the American people; . . . immigrants were Americanized, liberated, and fused into a mixed race. . . ." For generations we have been taught that America is a **melting pot** in which various ethnic groups were blended to produce something homogeneously American. How then do we explain the Italians at Paul Revere's feet, the incorporated Czechs of Wilber, and thousands of similar ethnic enclaves? The fact is that Turner was wrong about the formation of a composite nationality. The United States, Canada, and many other countries retain, in both urban and rural areas, an ethnic crazy-quilt pattern, and ethnic groups remain an important aspect of the human mosaic.

What exactly is an **ethnic group**? Much controversy has surrounded attempts to formulate an accepted definition. *Ethnic* is derived from the Greek word *ethnos,* meaning a "people" or "nation," but that definition is too broad for our use. To narrow it down, we can define an ethnic group as an involuntary one possessing a common ancestry, regional origin, and cultural tradition, with a strong feeling of belonging and cohesiveness, living as a minority in a larger society, or **host culture.** The main problem encountered in defining *ethnic* is that different groups base their identities on different traits. For some, such as the Amish, it is primarily religion; for the Swiss-Americans it is ancestral nationality; for the blacks it is principally race; for the German-Americans it is ancestral language; for the French-Canadians it is mother tongue; for the Cuban-Americans it is perhaps mainly anticommunism; for the Appalachian southerners it is folk culture. Indeed, no two ethnic groups establish their identities in exactly the same way. In this sense, we can see that ethnic identity is very similar to nationalism, discussed in Chapter 4. Just as states often have a *raison d'être*—a reason for being, a basic unifying force—so do ethnic groups. Just as the main unifying force differs from one country to another, so it differs from one ethnic group to another.

Ethnic groups are the keepers of distinctive cultural traditions and the focal point of various kinds of social interaction. They can provide not only group identity, but also friendships, marriage partners, recreational facilities, business success, and a political power base. They offer the cultural security and reinforcement so essential for minorities, but they can also give rise to suspicion, friction, distrust, clannishness, and even violence. Ethnicity, in America at least, produces one of the brighter hues in the human mosaic.

This is not to say that North American ethnic minorities have remained unchanged by their host culture. **Acculturation** occurs, meaning that the ethnic group changes sufficiently to be able to function within the host society. On the other hand, **assimilation** implies a complete blending with the host culture, involving the loss of many distinctive ethnic traits and the acceptance of others by the hybridized host culture. For example, the American host culture now includes descendants of colonial and many postcolonial Germans, Scots, Irish, French, Swedes, and Welsh settlers, who possessed ethnicity upon arriving in North America. Some of their traits became typical of the entire host culture, but lost ethnicity through assimilation. Intermarriage is perhaps the most effective assimilatory device. Many students of American culture have long assumed that all ethnic groups would be assimilated, but it is increasingly clear that relatively few have been. In fact, the past quarter-century has witnessed a resurgence of ethnic identity, both in the United States and Canada. In Europe, too, ethnic minorities in countries as diverse as France, the United Kingdom, and Spain have raised demands for cultural autonomy, as we saw in Chapter 4.

Ethnic geography is the study of the spatial and ecological aspects of ethnicity. Ethnic groups are highly territorial in organization and often practice distinctive adaptive strategies. They occupy clearly defined areas, whether rural or urban, and place is an essential aspect of ethnicity. An ethnic group, no less than a political state, cannot exist without its own territory. In other words, the study of ethnicity has built-in geographical dimension, and ethnic geography is the result. Cultural differences from one place to another can often be explained in terms of ethnicity.

The beginnings of the academic subdiscipline of ethnic geography lie in the period during and just after World War I, when numerous ethnic groups in Europe were clamoring for political self-determination. American and European geographical journals during that period contained numerous articles on ethnic patterns. German cultural geographers in the 1930s continued this interest in ethnic groups, but unfortunately much of their work served the purposes of Nazi propaganda. A few American geographers devoted attention to ethnic studies through the thirties, forties, and fifties, but it was not until the mid-1960s that ethnic geography began to grow and thrive as a subdiscipline, a rise that coincided with and resulted from increasing ethnic awareness in the United States and Canada (see biographical sketch of Walter M. Kollmorgen).

■ ETHNIC REGIONS

Our five themes of cultural geography are well adapted to the study of ethnic groups. Since such groups typically occupy compact, clearly definable territories, culture region is a particularly appropriate theme. Ethnic regions exist in almost every country, from Australia to Brazil, Sweden to Vietnam. In the present chapter, we will emphasize the ethnic groups in the United States and Canada because they offer particularly abundant examples, both urban and rural, but you should be aware that the phenomenon of ethnicity is almost universal.

WALTER M. KOLLMORGEN
1907–

Dr. Kollmorgen, Professor Emeritus of Geography at the University of Kansas and noted agricultural geographer, made some early contributions to the study of American ethnic groups. Beginning in the late 1930s, he undertook research on the farming practices of ethnic minorities in the United States—in particular, the Germans in Alabama and Pennsylvania, the German Swiss in Tennessee, the French in Louisiana, and other ethnic minorities located mainly in the American South. Professor Kollmorgen's detailed statistical comparisons of ethnic and nonethnic farmers provided geographers with the first conclusive evidence of ethnic distinctiveness in agriculture and established a model of rigorous scholarship for later ethnic geographical studies.

Like so many geographers, Professor Kollmorgen received the inspiration for his research while traveling through the countryside and carefully observing what he saw. In the 1930s, he made numerous tours through the southern Appalachians. Intrigued by the visual contrasts he saw between the settlement areas of Germans and non-Germans, Kollmorgen decided to make a comparative study.

Kollmorgen was honored for meritorious contributions by the Association of American Geographers in 1953 and 1962, and served as honorary president of that organization in 1968.

These ethnic culture regions can be detected and mapped by surname counts, linguistic data, field interviews, and national origin responses in censuses (Figure 9.1). Regardless of the mapping method, ethnicity is revealed to be an inherently geographical phenomenon, integrally linked to place. Indeed, much ethnic identity is in fact place identity. Ethnic culture regions can be both cause and effect in explaining ethnic persistence or the lack of it.

Ethnic Culture Regions in Rural North America

In the eighteenth and nineteenth centuries, massive numbers of non-English European peoples migrated to North America, constituting the greatest migration of all time. A great many of these immigrants settled in rural areas, forming thousands of ethnic farming communities. The bulk of the rural settlers were German and Scandinavian, with lesser numbers of Dutch, Catholic Irish, Swiss, Poles, Ukrainians, Czechs, and other groups. Most chose the agricultural lands of Pennsylvania, the Midwest, and the Canadian Prairie Provinces. The South, with the exception of southern Louisiana, central Texas, and parts of Missouri, was not greatly

FIGURE 9.1
The Louisiana French ethnic province, as mapped by two different methods. The 1939 map was compiled by sampling the surnames in telephone directories. The ten most common names in each directory were determined and the percentage of these ten that was of French origin was recorded. When no telephone directories were available, surnames on mailboxes were used. Look through the telephone directory for your hometown. What are the ten most common family names? What ethnic background do the names reveal? What distortions or inaccuracies might result from using only telephone directories to enumerate ethnic groups? The 1970 map is based on the U.S. census data for the white population's "mother tongue," defined by the Bureau of the Census as the language spoken in the home during the respondent's childhood. (After Peveril Meigs, 3rd, "An Ethno-Telephonic Survey of French Louisiana," *Annals of the Association of American Geographers*, 31 (1941), 245; and a map produced by James P. Allen of the Department of Geography, California State University, Northridge, for distribution at the 1978 meeting of the Association of American Geographers at New Orleans.)

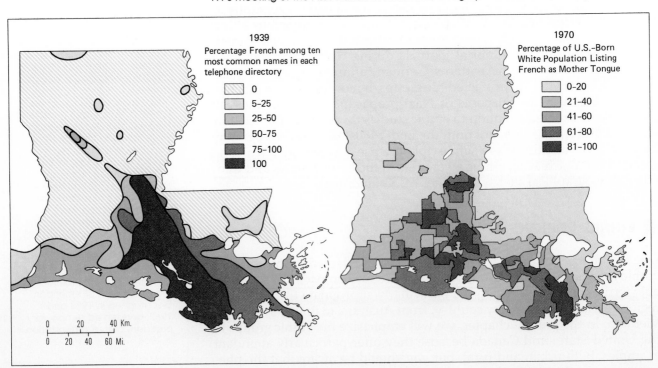

1939
Percentage French among ten most common names in each telephone directory

- [hatched] 0
- 5–25
- 25–50
- 50–75
- 75–100
- 100

1970
Percentage of U.S.–Born White Population Listing French as Mother Tongue

- 0–20
- 21–40
- 41–60
- 61–80
- 81–100

0   20   40 Km.
0   20   40   60 Mi.

influenced by this migration. By the end of the nineteenth century, successive waves of immigrants had established colonies, representing almost every linguistic area of Europe, throughout much of the American countryside.

The rural ethnic settlement areas of the United States and Canada can be divided into two categories: **ethnic provinces** and **ethnic islands.** The difference is in size, both in terms of area and population. Ethnic provinces cover large areas, usually including all or part of several states and containing hundreds of thousands or even millions of people, while ethnic islands are small dots in the countryside, typically occupying an area smaller than a county and housing anywhere from several hundred to several thousand people.

Only a few ethnic provinces can be found in North America (Figure 9.2). They include the expansive Hispanic borderland of the American Southwest, French Canada, French Louisiana, and the Afro-American or Black Belt of the American South. These districts, in most cases, are large enough in area and population to retard acculturation. Ethnic provinces can be weakened by emigration, as has occurred in the black South, or strengthened by continued immigration, as in the Hispanic American borderland. In fact, the influx of over one million Mexicans each year represents the greatest ethnic immigration presently under way in North America and is permitting the Mexican ethnic province in the United States to expand northward.

FIGURE 9.2
Ethnic provinces and ethnic islands in the United States and southern Canada. An ethnic province is a large area dominated by a single ethnic group. The Hispanic-American borderland has no sharp boundary, but is spreading north as immigration from Mexico continues. At present, French Canada is probably the purest and most powerful ethnic province; by contrast, French Louisiana is probably the weakest and most subject to acculturation. The Black Belt has been greatly weakened in the last half-century by out-migration. (Radio data from Broadcasting/Cablecasting Yearbook 1987; French radio station data exclude the province of Québec.)

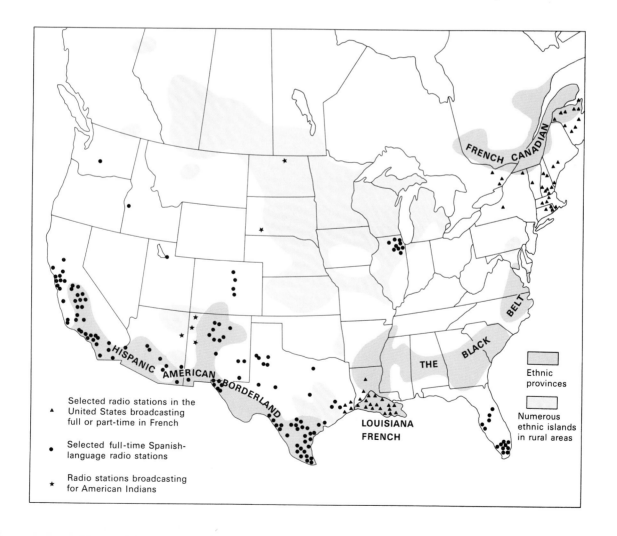

Ethnic islands are much more numerous. Large areas of rural North America have many ethnic islands, as Figure 9.2 suggests. Figure 9.3 provides some Midwestern examples of ethnic islands, revealing the crazy-quilt pattern typical of much of the American heartland. Germans, the largest single group in American ethnic islands, are clustered principally in southeastern Pennsylvania and in Wisconsin, with lesser concentrations in Minnesota, Illinois, Missouri, Texas, Kansas, and several other states. Scandinavians, primarily Swedes and Norwegians, came mainly to Minnesota, the eastern Dakotas, and western Wisconsin. Ukrainians were drawn mainly to the Canadian Prairie Provinces (Figure 9.4). The other Slavic groups, consisting mostly of Poles and Czechs, did not establish as many large rural clusters as did the Germans and Scandinavians, but they are found scattered about the Midwest and Texas.

Ethnic islands develop because, in the words of geographer Alice Rechlin, "a minority group will tend to utilize space in such a way as to minimize the interaction distance between group members," facilitating contacts within the ethnic community and minimizing exposure to the outside world. The ideal shape of such an ethnic island is circular or hexagonal, and many do approximate that configuration (Figure 9.5). People are drawn to rural places where others of the same ethnic background are found. Ethnic islands survive from one generation to the next because most land is inherited. In addition, the sale of land is typically confined within the ethnic group, helping preserve the identity of the island. A social stigma is often attached to the sale of land to outsiders. Even so, the smaller size of ethnic islands makes their populations more susceptible to acculturation.

FIGURE 9.3
Ethnic islands in the rural American heartland are illustrated in the distribution of ethnic groups in a small portion of western Wisconsin and southeastern Minnesota during the 1940s. Although not all parts of the United States display this many ethnic islands, it is typical of much of the Midwest. Are ethnic islands found in your home area? How are they distinctive? (After G. W. Hill, "The People of Wisconsin According to Ethnic Stocks, 1940," *Wisconsin's Changing Population,* Madison: Bulletin of the University of Wisconsin, Serial no. 2642, October 1942; and Douglas Marshall, "Minnesota's People," *Minneapolis Tribune* (August 28, 1949), Part 4, p. 1; with modifications.)

Legend:
- Irish
- Norwegian
- Swiss-German
- German
- Swedish
- Polish
- C Czech
- D Dutch
- English
- Danish
- French
- Old-stock Anglo-American
- — — County boundary

0   15   30 Km.
0   10   20 Mi.

Urban Ethnic Neighborhoods and Ghettos

Ethnic culture regions are also typical of the cities of North America. An ethnic quarter is an area within a city where members of an ethnic group are concentrated. Such quarters became typical in the United States and Canada after about 1840, coinciding with the urbanization and industrialization of North America. Instead of dispersing through the residential areas of the city, the ethnic groups clustered together in separate districts of the city. The ethnic groups involved were, to a degree, derived from different parts of Europe than were the immigrants to rural areas. While Germany and Scandinavia supplied most of the rural settlers, the cities drew much more heavily on Ireland and eastern and southern Europe. Catholic Irish, Italians, Poles, and East European Jews became the main urban ethnic groups, though lesser numbers of virtually every nationality in Europe came to the cities of North America. In the United States, these

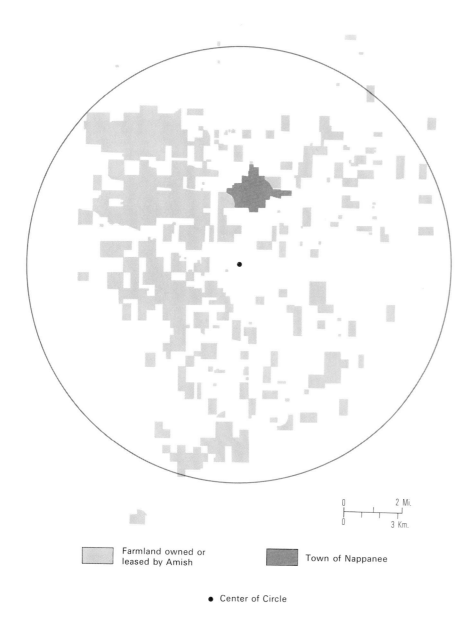

FIGURE 9.4
In a Ukrainian ethnic island near Edmonton in Alberta province, Canada. The church is Uniate (or "Greek Catholic"), an Eastern Orthodox Christian group that acknowledges the supremacy of the Roman pope. About 60 percent of Canadian Ukrainians belong to that denomination. Ukrainians settled particularly in the transition zone between prairie and woodland in western Canada, a setting similar to their European homeland. (Photo by Terry G. Jordan, 1987.)

░ Farmland owned or leased by Amish	▓ Town of Nappanee

● Center of Circle

FIGURE 9.5
The Amish ethnic island at Nappanee, Indiana, about 1975. A roughly circular configuration is evident, suggesting the ideal shape of such ethnic enclaves. What factors might have acted to prevent the island from attaining a perfectly circular shape? Does this appear to be a pattern reflecting areal growth, stagnation, or retreat? (Derived from Alice T. M. Rechlin, *Spatial Behavior of the Old Order Amish of Nappanee, Indiana*, Michigan Geographical Publication No. 18, 1976, p. 40.)

groups were later joined by French Canadians, southern blacks, Puerto Ricans, Filipinos, Chinese, Appalachian whites, Amerindians, Cubans, and other groups not of European birth.

America was not the first society to have urban ethnic segregation. Rather, distinct ethnic quarters have long been a part of urban history. In cities built by conquerors during periods of empire expansion, the native people often were forced to live in specific districts. Sometimes walls were built around such quarters to set them off from the rest of the city. Roman cities had distinct Christian neighborhoods; Islamic cities had Christian quarters; and Christian cities have long had Jewish quarters. Still, cities in the United States and Canada are perhaps more ethnically diverse than any others in the world. The census in 1870 showed that the populations of New York, Chicago, and San Francisco were about 45 percent foreign-born. Even after legislation was passed in the 1920s to close the door to European and Asian immigrants, large numbers of southern blacks, Appalachian whites, Puerto Ricans, and Mexicans migrated to North American cities. Figures 9.6 and 9.7 show concentrations of ethnic groups in Cleveland and Winnipeg. The removal of biased anti-Asian immigration restrictions in the United States in the 1960s led to a large influx of Asians, particularly from Korea, the Philippines, India, and Vietnam. By 1980, some 3.5 million persons of Asian birth or ancestry lived in the United States, most concentrated in urban areas. Canada also has a large Asian population.

It maybe — the ethnic people who will be the ones who "pull it off" in the future.

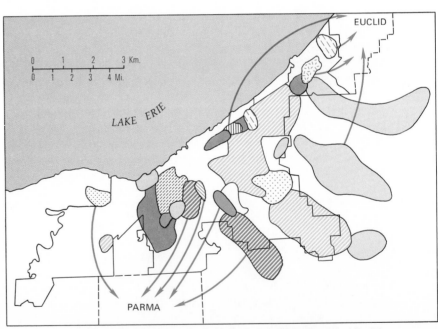

Arrows indicate movements to mixed-ethnic suburbs in Parma and Euclid.

———— Cleveland city limits   — — — — Parma and Euclid city limits

Blacks	Italians	Slovenes
Croats	Lithuanians	Ukrainians
Czechs	Poles	Appalachian whites
Hungarians	Slovaks	Spanish surnamed

FIGURE 9.6
Ethnic neighborhoods in the Cleveland area, 1960s. What similarities and differences are revealed by comparing this map with the one of Winnipeg (Figure 9.7)? Compare both to the model shown in Figure 9.8 and see if you can detect the outlying clusters. Note the movement to suburbs (After Allen G. Noble and Albert J. Korsok, *Ohio—An American Heartland*, Bulletin 65, State of Ohio, Division of Geological Survey, Columbus, 1975, p. 176, with modifications.)

1961

Asian	
Italian	
Mixed Italian and Asian	
Ukrainian	
Polish	
Mixed Ukrainian and Polish	
French	

N

FIGURE 9.7
Selected ethnic neighborhoods in Winnipeg, Manitoba, 1961. What similarities and contrasts in ethnic concentration does this Canadian city reveal in comparison with Cleveland (Figure 9.6)? (From Peter Matwijiw, "Ethnicity and Urban Residence: Winnipeg, 1941–71," *Canadian Geographer*, 23 (1979), 50.)

The heritage of these ethnic quarters continues to play an important role in urban affairs. In the 1970s, the offspring of Irish immigrants zealously guarded their ethnic turf in South Boston against blacks. Japanese in San Francisco fought against a redevelopment plan that would have replaced neighborhood housing with hotels and convention centers. In East Los Angeles, the residents of a Mexican-American community attempted, but failed, to incorporate their neighborhood so that they could achieve self-rule, and a similar movement in South Tucson, Arizona, succeeded.

An **ethnic neighborhood** is a voluntary community where people of like origin reside by choice. Such neighborhoods are, in the words of Peter Matwijiw, an Australian geographer, "the results of preferences shown by different ethnic groups . . . toward maintaining group cohesiveness." The benefits of an ethnic neighborhood are many: common use of language, nearby kin, stores and services specially tailored to a certain group's tastes, presence of factories relying on ethnically based division of labor, and institutions important to the group—such as churches and lodges—that remain viable only when a number of people live close enough to participate frequently in their activities (see box, "Leaving an Ethnic Neighborhood").

There is a difference between a **ghetto** and an ethnic neighborhood. The term *ghetto* has traditionally been used to describe an area within the city where a certain ethnic group is forced to live. In medieval Europe, often ghettos were walled and set off from the rest of the city by a gate that was locked at sundown, thereby physically reinforcing the segregation of certain groups such as the Jews. Use of the term today should be reserved for areas of residential segregation where an ethnic group lives because it has very little choice in the matter—options are limited or nonexistent. In other words, a ghetto is an involuntary community.

Whether an ethnic group lives in a ghetto or voluntarily forms its own neighborhood usually depends on how discriminatory the majority society is. For example, because American society discriminates more against blacks and Asians than Italians, a black ghetto or Chinatown is more likely

LEAVING AN ETHNIC NEIGHBORHOOD

Here is one account of what it felt like to a young Chinese girl to move from San Francisco's Chinatown to a white neighborhood in the late 1930s.

When I was three and a half my family moved out of Chinatown to the Mission District. . . . I was very conscious that Chinatown was a long way from the Mission District and I was coming from another world. . . . When my parents would talk about the outside being a bad place, they would refer sort of generally to "the whites out there," they always called them *sai yen*. To me, of course, that meant the whites right around us. It meant the bar downstairs where there was an Irish tavern, Cavanaugh's, that we could hear coming up through the floor every night. We'd hear this crashing, singing, people being thrown around down there, they would have brawls and they would pee on our doorstep. Every other day we would go down there with a bucket to wash it off. But at the same time my parents kept reminding us that "the whites out there," the same people who would vomit and pee on our doorstep, were the people who had the power to take our home away from us. We had to do a little placating of them. Every Easter, every Christmas, every

American holiday, I would be sent on a little tour of all the local businesses. I would go to the bakery across the street, the barbershop down the street, the realty company, and the bar. I would deliver a little cake to each one. We wanted to be known as that nice Chinese family upstairs or down the street, you know, whom you wouldn't ever want to hurt in any way. My family was very aware that they were embattled Chinese in a white district, that they had spent many years finding that place to live, and that at any moment they would be asked to leave. And somehow a quality I sensed out of all this, about being Chinese, was a vulnerability. At any moment you could be thrown out. So you had to watch your step and you had to be very clever, you had to placate, you had to maneuver. And no matter what happened, you did not get openly angry, because if you did, you would have lost your dignity. No matter what they did you had to be stronger than they, you had to outlast them.

From Victor G. Nee and Brett de Bary Nee, *Longtime Californ': A Documentary Study of an American Chinatown* (New York: Pantheon, 1973), pp. 162–166. Copyright © 1973 by Pantheon, a Division of Random House, Inc. With permission.

to exist than an Italian ghetto. This was revealed in a study of Cleveland, Ohio, by John F. Kain. The Cleveland blacks are confined to a ghetto by discriminatory housing practices and are much more highly segregated residentially than are white ethnic groups (Figure 9.6). Italians, Poles, Jews, Appalachian folk, and other white ethnic groups in Cleveland occupy neighborhoods rather than ghettos and are more likely to disperse to the suburbs than are blacks. Even so, the American urban blacks are in a far superior position to the city-dwelling blacks of the Republic of South Africa. There, the mandatory racial segregation act of 1923, with subsequent amendments, has created distinct ethnic quarters. The only blacks allowed by law to reside in white neighborhoods of Johannesburg, for example, are domestic live-in servants, and even their numbers have declined in recent decades, in part because they are not allowed to have their families with them.

Although an ethnic neighborhood or ghetto may seem homogeneous to outsiders, it is a diverse area. A typical ethnic urban area has four different sectors: the core, middle, fringe, and outlying cluster (Figure 9.8).

④

FIGURE 9.8
Zones within an ethnic quarter are depicted in this diagram. A typical immigrant might first settle in the ghetto core. Gradually in a series of short moves the immigrant progresses to the middle area, the fringe, and at last to an outlying cluster. Many members of the ethnic community remain behind.

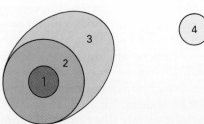

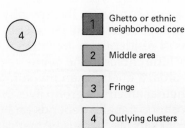

1 Ghetto or ethnic neighborhood core

2 Middle area

3 Fringe

4 Outlying clusters

FIGURE 9.9
A scene in the Chicano ethnic core of Los Angeles. Such districts serve as "ports of entry" for immigrants newly arrived from Mexico and Central America.

The core is the original area dominated by the ethnic group, normally on the edge of the central business district. Here, housing is oldest, and, as a result, deteriorating. Rents are generally low. Often residences have been broken up into small apartments, rooming houses, or transient hotels. The core is usually the **port of entry** for migrants new to the city. It is populated by a large number of single men who have come to the city without their families. Generally the new migrants lack skills and information about jobs, making this an area of high unemployment (Figure 9.9).

If core-area residents land a steady job, they may seek more permanent dwellings—a flat or a larger apartment in the middle zone, with higher rents and more available space. Here you would likely find families instead of only single men. The fringe area is the transition between ghetto and neighborhood. Here, homes come at premium prices. The nonethnic residents who surround the ghetto fear the group's expansion and try to contain it by economic barriers. Those group members who can afford the higher rents are more skilled and better educated than the rest of their ethnic group. Because some of them live on the fringe out of choice rather than necessity, it probably can be called a neighborhood instead of a ghetto.

Some ethnic areas lack the fringe. Often it cannot develop because nearby tightly knit ethnic groups strongly resist expansion into their territories. In this case, outlying clusters take over the fringe's role, but a new emotional element also enters the picture. Some group members, having achieved a degree of economic success, want to remove themselves, literally and symbolically, from their ghetto past. Consequently, as the outlying cluster develops, it often becomes a desirable goal for those who are still trapped in the ghetto core. For example, San Francisco has two distinct areas of Chinese settlement outside of Chinatown, the original ethnic ghetto. These began to develop in the late 1940s, when federal law made it illegal to restrict ethnic groups from living in FHA-financed housing. Gradually, the Chinese bought homes in areas outside Chinatown. As more and more Chinese moved to these fringe areas, true ethnic neighborhoods emerged, complete with shops, services, and restaurants.

The organization of the ethnic area into these four zones relates to the **immigrant's ladder,** a metaphor for the way new migrants supposedly enter society at the bottom and climb progressively higher and higher in status. The bottom rungs of the ladder are in the ghetto core; the middle rungs, in the ethnic fringe or outlying cluster. Typically, earlier-arrived ethnic groups eventually abandon poorer residential areas altogether and are replaced by newcomers of different ethnic backgrounds. We can see this historic process in action in the succession of groups that dominated certain neighborhoods and then passed on to more desirable areas. Boston's West End was mainly an Irish area in the nineteenth century. As the twentieth century began, the Irish were replaced in this deteriorating neighborhood by the Jews, who in turn were replaced in the late 1930s by Poles and Italians. The list of groups that passed through Chicago's Adams area from the nineteenth century to the present provides an almost complete history of American migratory patterns. First came the Germans and Irish, who were succeeded by the Greeks, Poles, French Canadians, Czechs, and Russian Jews, who were soon hard-pressed by the Italians. They in turn were challenged by Chicanos and a small group of Puerto Ricans. Blacks, who have played such a great role in urban migration, were the only major group absent from this list. As a rule, the tendency to leave an ethnic neighborhood and settle in a mixed residential area increases as acculturation progresses. The more acculturated the person, the less likely he or she is to live in an ethnic neighborhood.

TABLE 9.1
The Largest National Origin Groups in the United States and Canada

	United States, 1980			Canada, 1981	
Origin Group	Number Wholly or Partially of this Ancestry	As Percentage of Total Population	Origin Group	Number Descended on Male Line from this Group	As Percentage of Total Population
English	49,598,035	26%	French	6,439,100	27%
German	49,224,146	26%	English	6,109,253	25%
Irish	40,165,702	21%	Scottish	1,415,200	6%
African	20,964,729	11%	Irish	1,151,955	5%
French	12,892,246	7%	German	1,142,365	5%
Italian	12,183,692	6%	Italian	741,970	3%
Scottish	10,048,816	5%	Ukrainian	529,615	2%
Polish	8,228,037	4%	Amerindian	436,580	2%
Mexican	7,692,619	4%	Dutch	408,235	2%
Amerindian and Eskimo	6,715,819	4%	Jewish	264,020	1%
Dutch	6,304,499	3%	Polish	254,485	1%
Swedish	4,345,392	2%	Hungarian	116,395	<1%

Sources: U.S. Census, 1980; Census of Canada, 1981.

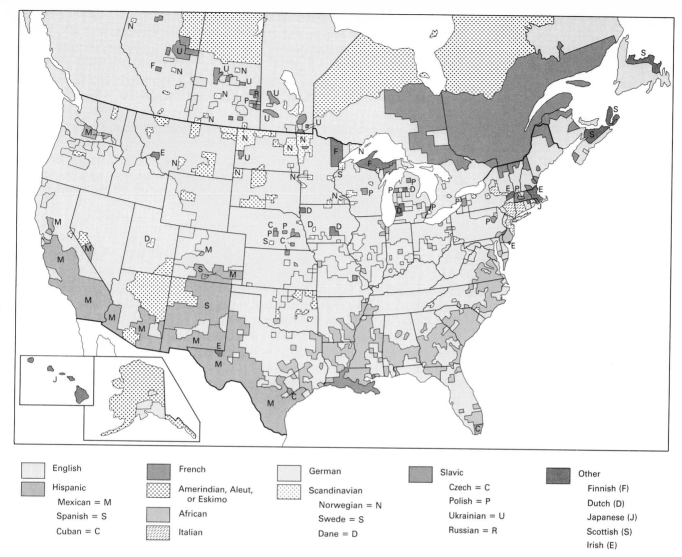

English		French		German		Slavic		Other	
Hispanic		Amerindian, Aleut, or Eskimo		Scandinavian		Czech = C		Finnish (F)	
Mexican = M		African		Norwegian = N		Polish = P		Dutch (D)	
Spanish = S		Italian		Swede = S		Ukrainian = U		Japanese (J)	
Cuban = C				Dane = D		Russian = R		Scottish (S)	
								Irish (E)	

FIGURE 9.10
Ethnic and national origin groups in North America. A striking feature is the German dominance of the northern states. The Black Belt, French Canadian, Louisiana French, and Hispanic ethnic provinces are highly visible, as are some ethnic islands. The U.S. data are for 1980 and show the largest national-origin group by county (except for a few Indian reservations); the Canadian pattern was derived from census data and regional studies. (Sources: Allen and Turner, *We the People,* p. 210; Dawson, *Group Settlement,* p. iv; Censuses of Canada, 1961 and 1981 (data on mother tongue and national origin); Andrew H. Clark, "Old World Origins and Religious Adherence in Nova Scotia," *Geographical Review,* 50 (1960), 320; Howard and Tamara Palmer, *Peoples of Alberta,* Saskatoon: Western Producer Prairie Books, 1985.)

Canadian/American Ethnic Contrasts

It is important to recognize that Canada and the United States have rather different ethnic makeups, both urban and rural (Table 9.1). No small part of the reason that these two countries remain apart as independent states is that their populations have strikingly different origins. The British-derived host culture is of about the same proportion in both, but the ethnic components differ greatly. Both the United States and Canadian censuses permit a rather detailed analysis of national origin, in terms of total numbers and geographical distribution (Figure 9.10). Certainly the most obvious differences involve the German, French, Irish, and African origin groups.

National origin need not imply ethnicity, and often does not. Most persons in the United States who claim German origin, for example, are not German-Americans. Rather, they have been much acculturated and often assimilated, becoming part of the host culture. The massive absorption of Germans into the mainspring culture of the United States has been a major factor in shaping a national character distinct from that of Canada (Figure 9.10).

■ CULTURAL DIFFUSION AND ETHNIC GROUPS

Glancing at the maps of North American ethnic provinces, islands, and neighborhoods, you might conclude that the complex spatial pattern is the result of pure chance. In reality, though, orderly concepts and processes are linked to the ethnic mosaic, which we may refer to as *dominant personality*, *emigrant letters*, and *chain migration*. These all fit quite well the mechanism of relocation diffusion.

Ethnic Migration

Most voluntary migrations are begun by a **dominant personality.** This individual is a forceful, ambitious type, a natural leader, who perceives emigration as a solution to economic, social, political, or religious problems in the homeland, and, by the force of his or her personality, convinces others to migrate. It is usually possible in retrospect to point to the activities of one such dominant personality and conclude that, had it not been for that person, the migration in question would not have occurred or would have been inconsequential.

The main device used by dominant personalities to promote migrations is the **emigrant letter.** After choosing a settlement site, the dominant personality exerts influence by writing letters back to the homeland, extolling the virtues of the new country and urging friends and relatives to follow. In such letters, positive aspects of the adopted country are stressed and the negative are downgraded or omitted altogether, with the result that the new homeland is made to sound like a second Garden of Eden (see box, "An Emigrant Letter from an American Land of Milk and Honey"). If the emigrant has the chance to make a return visit to his or her native place, then no letter is necessary, since the information about the new land can be conveyed in person. In either case, other people are induced to follow in a **chain migration.** Once begun, such migrations tend to snowball. Those who follow the dominant personality in turn influence others to do the same. Friends and relatives are most susceptible to this kind of influence. The number of emigrant letters rapidly increases, and among the secondary migrants are other forceful personalities who also wield persuasive powers. Chain migration, then, describes the tendency of people to move in clusters, leaving certain small districts in the homeland to settle similarly confined colonial areas overseas. It is a natural and expected result of dominant personalities and their use of emigrant letters (Figure 9.11). In this manner, people from several parishes in rural Germany can be responsible for occupying a township or small district in the United States or Canada. Typically neighbors in the new homeland had been neighbors in the Old World. The influence of dominant personalities spreads most easily among people they know, and the decision to emigrate spreads by contagious diffusion through a population. Chain migration has continued to function in the most recent mass immigration to the United States —the twentieth-century influx of Mexicans. Work by the geographer Richard C. Jones revealed that different parts of the southwestern

AN EMIGRANT LETTER FROM AN AMERICAN LAND OF MILK AND HONEY

The following excerpts are from a letter written in 1832 by the first German settler in Texas to a friend back in Germany. The letter was eventually published in a German newspaper and prompted a large chain migration from northwestern Germany to Texas.

Each married immigrant who wishes to engage in farming receives a *league* of land, and a single person gets one-quarter of a *league*. . . . A *league* of land contains 4,440 acres of land, including hills and valleys, woods and meadows with creeks flowing through. . . . He must pay in installments a fee of $160 for surveying . . . and must take an oath of citizenship. After one year he becomes a citizen of Mexico. . . . A father of a family . . . receives on his arrival a land grant that is virtually a count's estate, and within a short time the land will be worth $700 to $800. . . . The expenses for the land need not be paid immediately. Many obtain the money by raising cattle. . . . Farmers who own 700 head of cattle are common hereabouts. . . . Europeans are especially welcome in the colony, and I was given an excellent *league* of land, upon which I built my home. . . .

The land here is hilly, covered partly with forest and partly with natural prairies. There are various types of trees. The climate is similar to that of Sicily. . . . There is no real winter, and the coldest months are almost like March in Germany. Bees, birds, and butterflies stay all through the winter season. . . . The soil requires no fertilizer. . . . The main crops are tobacco, rice, indigo, sweet potatoes, melons of special goodness, watermelons, wheat, rye, and vegetables of all kinds. Peaches are found in abundance growing wild in the forest, as are mulber-

ries, . . . walnuts, plums, persimmons as sweet as honey, and wine grapes in great quantity. . . . There is much . . . wild game, and hunting and fishing are free. The prairies are filled with the most lovely flowers. There are many snakes here, . . . but each farmer knows how to protect himself against them. . . . The more children you have, the better, for you will need them as field laborers. . . . Mosquitos and gnats are common only near the coast. Formerly there were no taxes at all, and now we have only community taxes. Each year you need work barely three months to make a living. . . .

There is freedom of religion here, . . . and English is the prevailing language. . . . Up the river there is much silver to be found, but Indians still live there.

. . . All Germans who come to the colony will be given land at once. When you arrive at San Felipe, ask for Friedrich Ernst of Mill Creek. It is thirty miles from there to my place, and you will find me without any difficulty. . . . For my friends and former countrymen, I have built a shelter on my estate where they can stay while selecting their *league* of land.

Your friend,
Fritz Ernst

Translated, adapted, and rearranged from Hermann Achenbach, *Tagebuch meiner Reise nach den Nordamerikanischen Freistaaten, oder: Das neue Kanaan* [Diary of My Trip to the North American Free States, or The New Canaan] (Düsseldorf: G. H. Beyer and J. Wolf, 1835), pp. 132–135; and Detlef Dunt, *Reise nach Texas, nebst Nachrichten von diesem Lande; für Deutsche, welche nach Amerika zu gehen beabsichtigen* [A Trip to Texas, Together with News of That Country, for Germans Who Plan to Come to America] (Bremen: Carl W. Wiehe, 1834), pp. 4–16.

United States draw upon different source regions in Mexico in the immigration of undocumented workers (Figure 9.12).

Diffusion of Ethnic Traits

As ethnic groups migrated from Europe and elsewhere to North America, they had the potential to introduce, by relocation diffusion, all of the traits of their Old World culture or subculture. Conceivably they could have perpetuated every facet of their ancestral way of life, both material and nonmaterial. Had they done so, then a visit to a North American ethnic province, island, or neighborhood would indeed be a visit to Europe, Africa, or Asia.

However, the ethnic immigrants did not reproduce their Old World cultures overseas. Only selected traits were successfully introduced, and others underwent considerable modification before becoming established in the new homeland. In other words, absorbing barriers prevented the diffusion of many Old World traits to America, and permeable barriers caused changes in many other traits, greatly simplifying the migrant cultures.

When an ethnic group migrates into a new environmental and cultural setting, the members have four choices. They may retain traditional ways, borrow alien ways from the groups they encounter in the New World, invent new techniques better suited to the adopted homeland, or

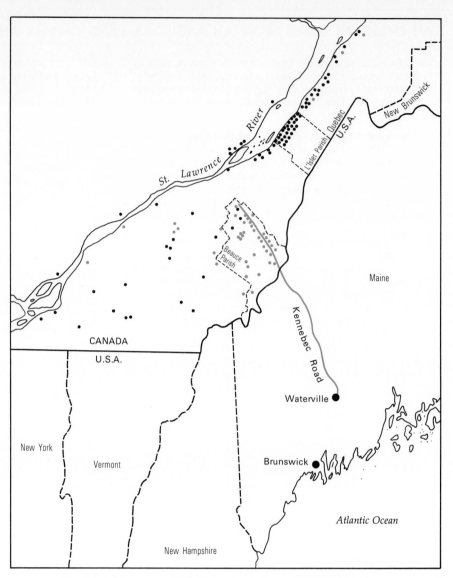

FIGURE 9.11
Ethnic chain migration from French Canada to the United States. Ethnic islands and urban neighborhoods typically result from chain migration. One of the more significant ethnic migrations of the last century has been the movement of French Canadians to the factory towns of New England, a migration accomplished by numerous small clusters of people. This map shows the clustered sources of French Canadians who migrated to the towns of Brunswick and Waterville in Maine in the 1880–1925 period. The parish of Beauce supplied most of the Waterville French, while L'Islet Parish was the leading source of Brunswick French. Try to reconstruct in your own mind the sequence of events which might have led to this clustering of migration source and destination. If you were migrating to a foreign country, would you seek out people of your own nationality who had preceded you there? (After James P. Allen, "Migration Fields of French Canadian Immigrants to Southern Maine," *Geographical Review*, 62 (1972), 377. See also James P. Allen, "Franco-Americans in Maine: A Geographical Perspective," *Acadiensis*, 4 (1974), 32–66.)

● Birthplace of ten immigrants to Brunswick, Maine, 1880–1900

● Birthplace of one immigrant to Waterville, Maine, 1890–1925

modify traditional or alien ways as they see fit. Most immigrant ethnic groups resort to all four devices, in varying degrees. The displacement of a group and relocation in a new homeland can have widely differing results. Perhaps most commonly, the relocation weakens tradition and upsets an age-old balance, causing a rapid discarding of Old World traits and accelerated borrowing, invention, and modification—in short, acculturation.

The Factor of Geographical Isolation

The degree of isolation of an ethnic group in the new homeland helps determine if traditional traits will be retained, modified, or abandoned. If the new settlement area is remote and contacts with outsiders are few, diffusion of traits from the Old World is more likely. Because contacts with alien groups are rare, little borrowing of traits can occur. Isolated ethnic groups often preserve in archaic form cultural elements that disappear from their former homeland; that is, they may, in some respects, change

FIGURE 9.12
Sources by state and county of
undocumented Mexican nationals
apprehended by the Immigration
and Naturalization Service in South
Texas and southern California. A
weighted index was employed to
assign values to the different
Mexican states. Why are certain
areas greater contributors than
others? How might such clustered or
channelized migration sources
influence the ethnic cultures in the
two extremities of the Hispanic
borderland? Might it help explain
Hispanic cultural contrasts between
southern California and South Texas?
For answers, see the sources listed
below. (Derived from Richard C.
Jones, "Channelization of
Undocumented Mexican Migrants to
the U.S.," *Economic Geography*, 58
(1982), 165–166; and Richard C.
Jones, "Micro Source Regions of
Mexican Undocumented Migration,"
National Geographic Research, 4
(1988), 17.)

less than their kinfolk back in the homeland. Language and dialects offer some good examples of this preservation of the archaic. The Polish dialect spoken by descendants of immigrants who came from the province of Silesia to south-central Texas in the 1850s, although infiltrated with English words, is closer to mid-nineteenth-century Silesian Polish than is the speech found today in Silesia itself, prompting Polish linguists to come halfway around the world to Texas to learn more about the spoken Polish of the previous century. Similarly, Germans living in ethnic islands in the Balkan region of southeastern Europe preserve archaic South German dialects better than in Germany itself, and some Elizabethan-age English usages are more common in southern Appalachia than in England.

The effect of isolation on cultural diffusion can be seen in Figure 9.13. The Newfoundland Irish are the most isolated of the three groups included. Note that they have introduced and preserved more Old World ways than either of the other two groups. As a rule, the earlier an ethnic community was established, the more likely its members were to introduce Old World ways. As the decades passed, particularly in the nineteenth century, transportation and communcation systems were rapidly improved, breaking down isolation.

Cultural Rebound

Cultural diffusion in ethnic settlements is often delayed by a temporary barrier imposed by the struggle for survival and related difficulties during the early years of pioneering in the new homeland. Years later, after the immigrants establish a more comfortable existence, they often revert to homeland ways, a process we can call **cultural rebound.** Figure 9.13

FIGURE 9.13

Diffusion of selected Old World culture traits to three ethnic farm colonies in North America. Note the interesting similarities and differences between the three settlement areas. The Cape Shore Irish were very isolated and the Hill Country Germans moderately so, but the Petersborough Irish had frequent contacts with non-Irish Catholics. The two Irish colonies were in climates colder than that of Ireland, while the Texas Germans found their new homeland warmer and drier than Germany. The Irish, from a deforested country, moved to densely wooded colonies, while the Germans found timber only slightly more abundant in the new homeland. What effects might these contrasts have had on the diffusion and retention of Old World traits? (After John J. Mannion, *Irish Settlements in Eastern Canada: A Study of Cultural Transfer,* University of Toronto, Department of Geography, Research Publication No. 12, 1974, pp. 166–167; and Terry G. Jordan, *German Seed in Texas Soil: Immigrant Farmers in Nineteenth-Century Texas,* Austin: University of Texas Press, 1966, pp. 118–191.)

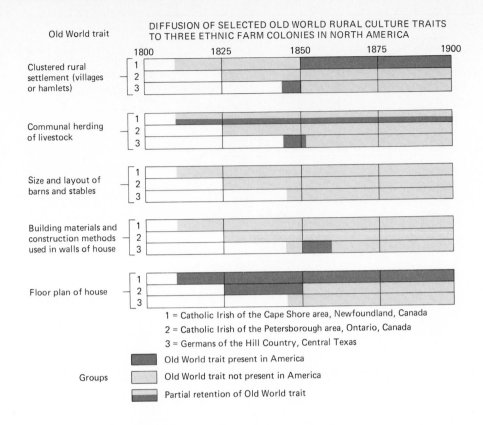

DIFFUSION OF SELECTED OLD WORLD RURAL CULTURE TRAITS TO THREE ETHNIC FARM COLONIES IN NORTH AMERICA

1 = Catholic Irish of the Cape Shore area, Newfoundland, Canada
2 = Catholic Irish of the Petersborough area, Ontario, Canada
3 = Germans of the Hill Country, Central Texas

Old World trait present in America
Old World trait not present in America
Partial retention of Old World trait

illustrates two examples of cultural rebound, or belated cultural diffusion. The Newfoundland Irish, who had lived in clustered clan hamlets in Ireland, initially established scattered farmsteads in America, probably because they were generally not blood kin of the other Irish in their neighborhoods. After several generations, however, natural population increase and intermarriage produced extended families and clans, and the Irish clan hamlet reappeared. In Texas, German settlers built crude log cabins in the Anglo-American style to serve as temporary houses until they could get their farms established. After a few years, when the most difficult pioneering was behind, they reverted to the typically German half-timbered construction in building their homes.

■ CULTURAL ECOLOGY AND ETHNICITY

Ethnicity is closely tied to ecology and cultural adaptation. To generalize, we can say that indigenous ethnic groups — those residing in their ancient homelands and acquiring minority ethnic status by being annexed into a larger political state and society — usually base much of their cultural distinctiveness on adaptive traits. The American Indian certainly falls in this category, as do the Australian Aborigines, New Zealand Maori, and Scandinavian Lapps. In other words, the adaptive strategies of these indigenous groups provide an ample basis for their ethnic status and distinctiveness. Immigrant ethnic groups, by contrast, often jettison much or all of their Old World adaptive strategy to accept ways that better assure viability in their new environmental settings. They seek to retain their ethnic identity in nonadaptive aspects of culture, such as traditional music, games, and clubs.

Selecting a Site

In the eighteenth and nineteenth centuries, many factors influenced ethnic immigrants as they chose settlement sites for colonies in the North American countryside. Some immigrants were prompted by a desire to find lands ecologically similar to those they left behind in the old country. When this occurred, the settlers were ecologically preadapted to success in the new home. **Preadaptation** involves a complex of adaptive traits possessed by a group in advance of migration that gives them survival ability and competitive advantage in occupying the new environment. In such cases, the adaptive strategy can reinforce ethnicity among immigrant minorities.

The state of Wisconsin, dotted with scores of ethnic islands, provides some fine examples of preadapted immigrant groups who sought environments resembling their homelands. Particularly revealing are the choices of settlement site made by Finns, Icelanders, English, and Cornish who came to Wisconsin (Figure 9.14). The Finns, coming from a cold, thin-soiled, glaciated, lake-studded, coniferous forest zone in Europe, chose to settle the North Woods of Wisconsin, a land very similar in almost every respect to the one from which they had departed. Icelanders, from a bleak, remote island in the North Atlantic, located their only Wisconsin colony on Washington Island, an isolated outpost surrounded by the waters of Lake Michigan. The English, accustomed to good farmland, generally founded ethnic islands in the better agricultural districts of southern and southwestern Wisconsin. Many of the English were Cornish miners from the Celtic highlands of western Great Britain, and they sought out the lead-mining communities of southwestern Wisconsin, where they continued their traditional occupations. On a broader scale, thousands of ethnic Germans from wheat-growing communities on the open steppe grass-

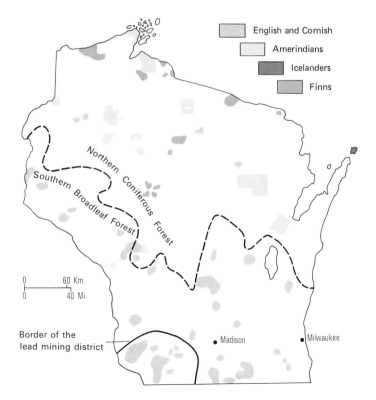

FIGURE 9.14
The ecology of selected ethnic islands in Wisconsin. Notice that Finnish settlements are concentrated in the infertile North Woods section, as are the Amerindian reservations. The Finns went there by choice, the Indians survived there because few whites were interested in such land. The English, by contrast, are found more often in the better farmland south of the border of the North Woods. Some of the English were miners from Cornwall, and they were drawn to the lead-mining country of southwestern Wisconsin, where they could practice the profession already known to them. Icelanders, an island people, chose an island as their settlement site in Wisconsin. (After G. W. Hill, "The People of Wisconsin According to Ethnic Stocks, 1940," *Wisconsin's Changing Population,* Madison: Bulletin of the University of Wisconsin, Serial No. 2642, October 1942.)

lands of south Russia, the so-called Russian-Germans, chose to settle the prairies of the American and Canadian Great Plains, where they established fine wheat farms not unlike those of their east European homeland.

However, most immigrant groups coming to North America chose settlement sites different in important environmental respects from those of their former homelands, often because they desired better lands that would facilitate economic advancement or because they had to take what was available at the time of their arrival. For them, a largely new adaptive strategy was required, and preadaptation played little or no role. The numerous Norwegians who settled the fertile prairie plains of interior North America provide an example of a group occupying a land very different from the one they had known in Europe. Some immigrant groups developed a reputation as very good judges of soil fertility in America. Germans and Czechs, in particular, are reputed to have chosen consistently the best farmland, a choice that helped them become prosperous and superior farmers. Geographer Russel L. Gerlach, researching the German communities of the Ozarks, found that while Appalachian southern settlers in that region chose easy-to-work sandy and bottomland soil, Germans often chose superior soils that were harder to work. In Lawrence County, Missouri, for example, the Germans were relative latecomers but still got some of the best land when they selected dark-soiled prairie lands that had been avoided by earlier Anglo-American settlers. In Gerlach's words, "A map showing the distribution of Germans in the Ozarks can also be a map of the better soils in the region." A similar ability to select choice soils can be detected among the Czechs in Texas, the state containing the largest rural Czech population in the United States. Figure 9.15 reveals, to a quite remarkable degree, that the Czech farming communities in Texas are concentrated in prairie regions underlain by dark, fertile soils. By contrast, Anglo-Texans tended to avoid open prairies as farming sites, and no other group was as drawn to this ecological niche as the Czechs.

As a general rule, members of immigrant ethnic groups in the rural areas of North America tended to perceive their new environments as being more like the European lands they had abandoned than was actually the case. Their peceptions of the new country emphasized the similarities and downgraded the differences. Perhaps the seeking for similarity was a symptom of homesickness or an unwillingness to admit that migration had brought them to a largely alien land. Perhaps growing to adulthood in a particular kind of physical environment retards one's ability to perceive a different setting accurately.

Whatever the reason, the distorted perception occasionally caused problems for ethnic farming groups. Sometimes crops that had thrived in the old homeland were not well suited to the particular American setting. A period of trial and error was often necessary to come to terms with the New World environment. In a few instances, the misperception was of such magnitude that economic disaster resulted and the ethnic island had to be abandoned.

◼ CULTURAL INTEGRATION AND ETHNICITY

The complicated spatial pattern of ethnic islands, provinces, ghettos, and neighborhoods is related to a variety of other cultural geographical phenomena. Ethnicity can play a role in deciding what people buy, how they vote, how they make a living, where they do their shopping, how they spend their free time, or whom they choose as their marriage partners. In

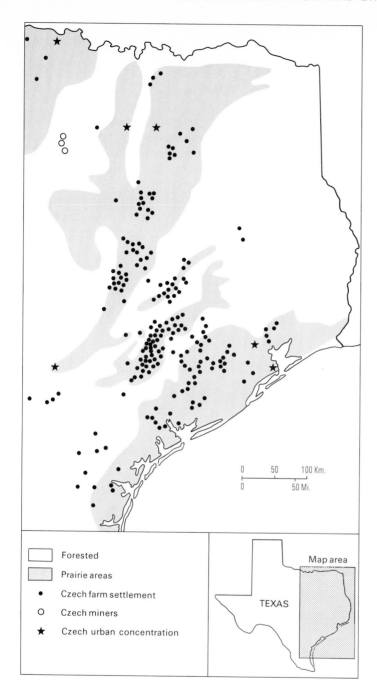

FIGURE 9.15
The cultural ecology of Czech farm settlements in Texas. Note the tendency of Czechs to settle in prairie regions. The prairie grasses were underlain by rich soils that have supported a prosperous Czech farming class for well over a century. (After Henry R. Maresh, "The Czechs in Texas," *Southwestern Historical Quarterly*, 50 (1946–47), 236–240 and map.)

other words, ethnicity is causally related to many other facets of culture, and therefore we can profitably apply the theme of cultural integration to the geographic study of ethnic groups. To illustrate how ethnicity is integrated into the cultural fabric of North America, we will use three economic examples.

Geographer Hansgeorg Schlichtmann speaks of economic *performance,* meaning "the way of the success in making a living and accumulating wealth," noting that inter-ethnic differences in performance have frequently been observed. He adds that ethnic groups exhibit contrasts in economic orientation, ranging from those seeking self-sufficiency through a diversified agricultural economy to those specializing in particular products for market, and in economic success. We have chosen both rural and urban examples, involving contrasts in choice of employment, types of business activity, and farming practices to illustrate the integration of ethnicity and economy.

Ethnicity and Business Activity

Differential ethnic preferences give rise to distinct patterns of purchasing goods and services. This in turn is reflected in the types of businesses and services available in different ethnic settlement areas in a city.

The geographer Keith D. Harries made a detailed study of businesses in the Los Angeles urban area, comparing Anglo-American, black, and Mexican-American neighborhoods (Figure 9.16). He found that an East Los Angeles Mexican-American neighborhood has unusually large numbers of food stores, eating and drinking places, personal services, and repair shops. This Mexican area has, in fact, three times as many food stores as the Anglo neighborhoods. In large part, this is due to the domi-

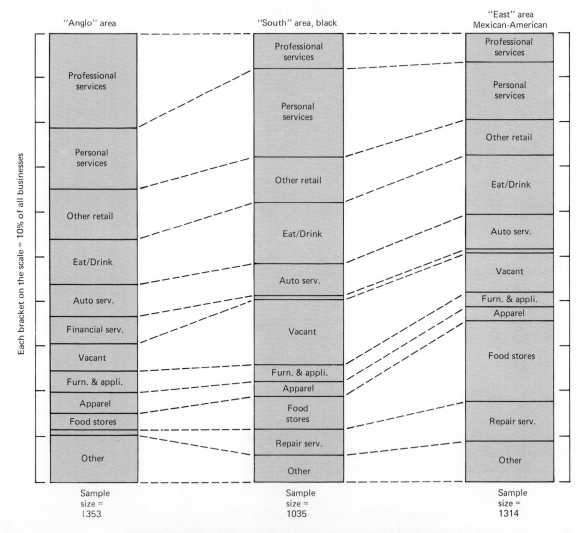

FIGURE 9.16
"Professional services" include such persons as doctors and lawyers, while "personal services" are represented by businesses like barbershops and shoeshine parlors. Do such differences exist between ethnic neighborhoods in your city? (After Keith D. Harries, "Ethnic Variations in Los Angeles Business Patterns," *Annals of the Association of American Geographers*, 61 (1971), 739.)

nance of small corner grocery stores and the fragmentation of food sales among several kinds of stores, such as *tortillerias.* The large number of eating and drinking places is related to the Mexican custom of gathering in *cantinas* (bars), where much of the social life is centered. The large number of small barbershops provides one reason why personal service establishments rank so high.

Black south Los Angeles ranks highest in personal service businesses, and vacant stores rank second. Eating and drinking places there are the third most numerous. In contrast to the Mexican eastern part of town, the south has relatively few bars but a large number of liquor stores and liquor departments in food and drugstores. Secondhand shops are very common, but there are no antique or jewelry stores and only one book-stationery shop. A distinctive black personal service enterprise, the shoe-shine parlor, is found only in south Los Angeles.

The Anglo neighborhoods, more affluent on the average than either the Mexican or black areas, rank very high in professional and financial service establishments, such as doctors, lawyers, and banks. These services are much less common in the non-Anglo neighborhoods. Furniture, jewelry, antique, and apparel stores are more numerous among the Anglos, as are full-scale restaurants. In short, Dr. Harries found major differences among the three ethnic areas. Though due in part to economic rather than ethnic contrasts, these differences are also related to dietary and social customs. The contrasts observed by Dr. Harries in the urban scene can also be found in rural and small town areas. An example can be taken from a study by the geographer Elaine M. Bjorklund of an ethnic island in southwestern Michigan. The area was settled in the mid-nineteenth century by Dutch Calvinists (Figure 9.17). Their descendants adhered to a strict moral code and tended to regard the non-Dutch Reformed world outside their ethnic island as sinful and inferior. The Calvinist Reformed Church was clearly the key to their ethnicity, since the Dutch language died out in the area. The impact of the Calvinist code of behavior on business activity in this Dutch ethnic island could be seen in various ways. There were, as recently as 1960, no taverns, dance halls, or movie theaters except in the city of Holland, and no business activity was permitted on Sunday. In most towns and villages, businesses are still restricted to grocery stores, and filling stations. Since Calvinists believe that leisure and idleness are evil, most present-day farmers work at second jobs during slack seasons in the agricultural year.

Ethnicity and Type of Employment

Closely related to type of business is type of employment. In many urban ethnic neighborhoods, individual groups gravitated early to particular kinds of jobs. These job identities were never rigid, and they were stronger in the decades immediately following immigration than they are today, due to advancing acculturation, but some notable examples can be found. In some cases, the identification of ethnic groups and job types was sufficiently strong to produce stereotyped images in the American popular mind, such as Irish policemen, Italian grocers and restaurant owners, and Jewish retailers.

The contrast in ethnic activity in the restaurant trade is quite striking. Certain groups have been highly successful in marketing versions of their traditional cuisines to the population at large. In particular, the Chinese,

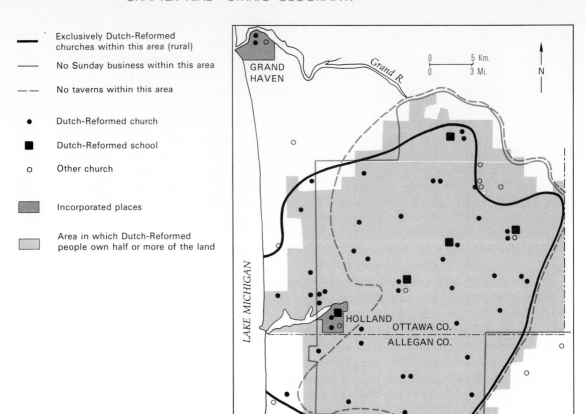

FIGURE 9.17
The impact of ethnicity in southwestern Michigan, about 1960. An ethnic island of Dutch Reformed (Calvinist) immigrants was established here in the 1840s, and has survived to the present. The Calvinists kept taverns, movie theaters, non-Calvinist churches, and Sunday business activity out of their area. What other economic activities might be influenced by strict religious groups such as the Calvinists? (After Elaine M. Bjorklund, "Ideology and Culture Exemplified in Southwestern Michigan," Annals of the Association of American Geographers, 54 (1964), 235.)

Mexicans, and Italians have succeeded in this venture (Figure 9.18). Each dominates a restaurant region in North America that is far larger than their ethnic provinces, islands, or neighborhoods.

In Boston, the Irish once provided most of the laborers in the warehouse and terminal facilities near the central business district, the Italians dominated the distribution and marketing of fresh foods, the Germans gravitated to the sewing machine and port supply trades, and the Jews found employment in merchandising and the manufacture of ready-made clothing. Italians in the northeastern United States still control the terrazzo and ceramic tile unions, and Czechs dominate the pearl button industry. In many cases, these ethnic job identities were related to occupational skills developed in the European homeland. A recent example is the immigration of Basques from Spain to serve as professional *jai alai* players in the cities of southern Florida, where this ancient Basque ball game has become a major medium of legal gambling. An older example, also provided by Basques, involved their concentration in sheep ranching areas of the American west, where they found employment as herders, a skill well developed in the Basques' European homeland.

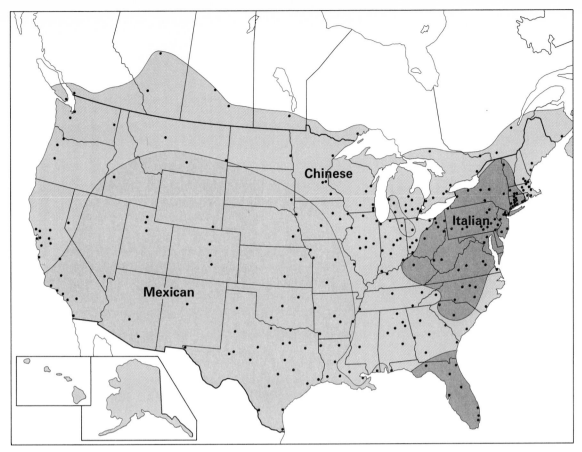

• Telephone directory consulted.

FIGURE 9.18
Dominant ethnic restaurant cuisine in North America, about 1980. In each region, the cuisine indicated is the leading type of ethnic restaurant. Why do Mexican foodways balloon northward faster than the main diffusion of these people? Why does Italian cuisine prevail so far south of the major concentration of Italian-Americans? All ethnic cuisines were considered in compiling the map, based on telephone yellow page listings. (After Wilbur Zelinsky, "The Roving Palate: North America's Ethnic Restaurant Cuisines," *Geoforum*, 16 (1985), 66.)

Ethnicity and Farming Practices

Even within the same occupation, different ethnic groups can retain distinctiveness. For example, there has long been a popular belief in the United States that farmers of German ethnic origin are superior to Anglo-Americans as tillers of the soil. As early as 1789, Benjamin Rush, describing the Pennsylvania Germans, enumerated 16 ways "in which they differ from most of the other farmers" of that state. Similar remarks can be found in accounts dealing with German ethnic islands in other parts of America.

A number of cultural geographers have tested the claim of German agricultural distinctiveness in the United States (Table 9.2). One such study focused on the Hill Country of central Texas in the nineteenth century. Germans who settled there farmed the land more intensively, derived more income from their land, and were more likely to be landowners than were the Anglos. German-owned sheep yielded 24 percent more wool per capita, and German poultry laid 15 percent more eggs than their Anglo livestock counterparts, due to better feeding and care.

TABLE 9.2
German-American and Anglo-American Farmers Compared

	Texas Hill Country 1860–1880		Cullman County, Alabama, 1930		Missouri Ozarks, 1972	
	Germans	Anglos	Germans	Anglos	Germans	Non-Germans
Percentage owning land	96%	75%	91%	46%	88%	80%
Percentage owning slaves	0%	11%	—	—	—	—
Percentage of cropland in small grains	25%	10%	—	—	15%	3½%
Percentage of cropland in cotton and corn	52%	60%	73%	89%	—	—
Average farm size, acres	557	323	60	45	180	162
Average cropland, acres	33	33	23	23	103	79
Average value of farm produce	$233	$176	$1341	$1032	—	—
Average number of cattle owned	55	52	3.4	2.2	—	—

Sources: Terry G. Jordan, *German Seed in Texas Soil* (Austin: University of Texas Press, 1966); Russel Gerlach, *Immigrants in the Ozarks: A Study in Ethnic Geography* (Columbia: University of Missouri Press, 1976); Walter M. Kollmorgen, *The German Settlement in Cullman County, Alabama: An Agricultural Island in the Cotton Belt* (Washington, D.C.: U.S. Department of Agriculture; Bureau of Agricultural Economics, 1941).

Perhaps the major reason for these differences was that Anglo farmers, for several centuries, had been faced with a superabundance of land on the frontier, which blunted the traditional European "land hunger" and permitted large landholdings, thus making intensive land use and soil conservation unnecessary. The Germans, newly arrived from Europe, retained the more intensive European system. This explanation received added support from a study of colonial Pennsylvania by geographer James T. Lemon. He found that the farming practices of the Germans, English, and Scotch-Irish — all recently arrived from Europe — did not differ in any significant way.

Germans in the South still retained their agricultural superiority in the 1930s, according to a study by Professor Walter M. Kollmorgen, a pioneer in the field of ethnic geography (see earlier biographical sketch). His research on a German ethnic island in Alabama revealed that the German-Americans there practiced a more diversified agriculture, had higher incomes, and were more often landowners than Anglos (Table 9.2). "Agricultural practices in the county," he concluded, "represent to a considerable extent a projection of patterns introduced by the Germans and the non-Germans."

An even more recent study, by Russel L. Gerlach, revealed that in the 1970s farmers of German descent living in the Missouri Ozarks remained distinct in many respects from non-Germans (Table 9.2). They had larger farms, had more acreage under cultivation, and were more likely to be landowners. It seems, then, that German-Americans continue even to the present day to farm differently from their non-German neighbors. They are, indeed, superior agriculturists, at least when compared to old-stock Anglo-Americans.

Similar differences along ethnic lines can be detected in present-day Canada. In a recent study of southern Manitoba, geographers D. Todd and J. S. Brierley compared the rural economies in German Mennonite, Slavic, British, French, and Dutch communities there. After detecting contrasts among these groups in type of agriculture, level of education, and kinds of nonfarm employment, Todd and Brierley concluded that fundamental functional linkages between ethnicity and the regional economic structure exist.

NORTH AMERICA'S ETHNIC LANDSCAPES

Ethnicity is often, or even generally, visible, and we can properly speak of ethnic landscapes. Ethnic groups frequently differ in styles of traditional architecture, in the patterns of surveying the land, in the distribution of houses and other buildings, and in the degree to which they "humanize" the land. In particular, many rural areas of the United States and Canada bear an ethnic imprint on the cultural landscape. Frequently this is a relict landscape: visible features produced by previous generations and surviving to the present. Other ethnic landscape elements are apparently still being produced today. Often the imprint is subtle, discernible only to those who pause and look closely; sometimes it is quite striking, flaunted as an "ethnic flag" and immediately visible, even to the untrained eye. Persistence, change, and degree of subtlety in the ethnic landscape can provide valuable evidence of acculturation and the level of group pride (see box, "The Face of the Fox").

The Finnish Sauna in Rural America

A good example of ethnicity in the cultural landscape of America is provided by the *sauna*. In Finland, these small steam bathhouses normally built of logs are seen at almost every farmstead. The Finns find it refreshing in cold weather to take a steam bath in the superheated sauna, often followed by an undressed romp in the snow. The European sauna is an important element in the cultural landscape of Finland.

When Finns came to America, they brought the preference for the sauna with them. The cultural geographers Matti Kaups and Cotton Mather made a study of this Finnish landscape feature in Minnesota and Michigan (Figure 9.19). They found the sauna to be an excellent visual indicator of Finnish-American ethnic islands. In one sample area, an al-

---

THE FACE OF THE FOX: INDIAN AND NON-INDIAN LANDSCAPES IN IOWA

America's Indian reservations have distinctive landscapes. Below is one non-Indian visitor's reaction to the Fox Indian countryside, surrounded by Anglo-American farmland in central Iowa:

> One fall day I chanced to drive through the Iowa countryside, the landscape wrought by white Iowa farmers: rolling hills stretched out, and impressed upon the hills were rectangular shapes, sharp and precise, each shape its own color. An Iowa farmer looking out upon his handiwork must have sensed, it seemed to me, his enormous power and must have felt great pride. Here and there, along a river or on some steep slope, nature was allowed to hold forth — trees and grass and brush — but not to encroach. Then I drove onto the roads of the Fox community. Immediately nature leapt up: the terrain was formed of hills and bluffs and streams; trees were seen in any direction in small and large clusters and covering whole hills, and some reached high. In the spaces that remained, grass and weeds and brush threatened to reach as high. Growth was beneath me, around me on all sides, and overhead.
>
> There, I recognized, was the difference. Passing through the countryside of white Iowa, one senses, as the Iowa farmer must sense, that he stands on top of what he sees, and a relationship is compellingly conveyed: man and his works. Entering the Fox community, one senses, as a Fox must sense, that he is enveloped.

If a Fox Indian were to provide a similar impression of a nearby Anglo cultural landscape, how might he or she express it? Would the Indian likely have a high opinion of massive transformation of the natural landscape?

Quoted from Frederick O. Gearing, *The Face of the Fox* (Chicago: Aldine, 1970), p. 47.

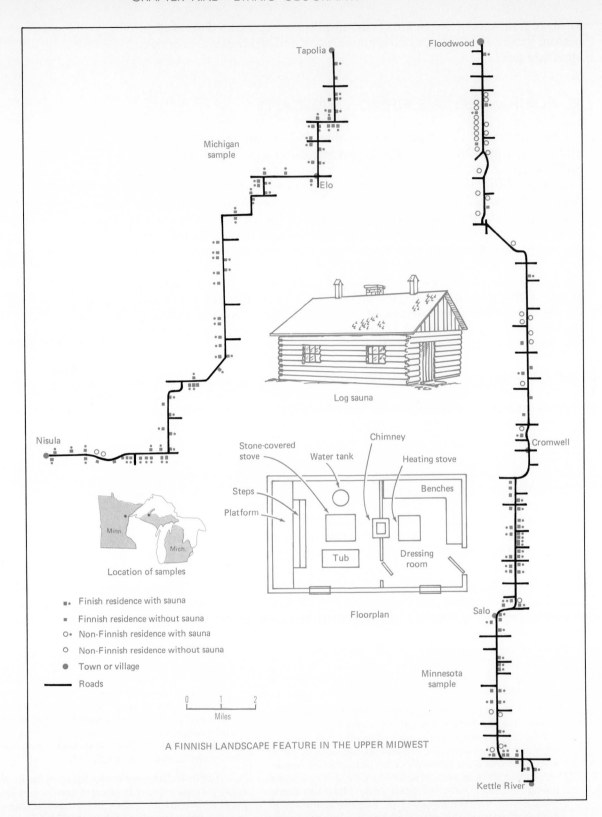

Tapolia

Floodwood

Michigan
sample

Elo

Nisula

Cromwell

Log sauna

Stone-covered
stove

Chimney

Water tank

Heating stove

Steps

Benches

Platform

Tub

Dressing
room

Floorplan

Salo

Location of samples

Minnesota
sample

Minn.

Mich.

■• Finish residence with sauna

■ Finnish residence without sauna

○• Non-Finnish residence with sauna

○ Non-Finnish residence without sauna

● Town or village

━━ Roads

0   1   2
Miles

A FINNISH LANDSCAPE FEATURE IN THE UPPER MIDWEST

Kettle River

FIGURE 9.19

A Finnish landscape feature in the upper Midwest. In two traverses through Finnish ethnic islands in northern Minnesota and Michigan, two geographers found that the *sauna,* a small steam bathhouse, was an almost unfailing visual sign of Finnish settlement. In this way, ethnicity is imprinted on the cultural landscape. (After Cotton Mather and Matti Kaups, "The Finnish Sauna: A Cultural Index to Settlement," *Annals of the Association of American Geographers,* 53 (1963), 495, 499.)

most purely Finnish rural district in the Upper Peninsula of Michigan, Kaups and Mather found that 88 percent of all Finnish-American residences had a sauna out behind. In an area of greater ethnic mixture in northern Minnesota, 77 percent of Finnish houses had saunas adjacent, as contrasted to only 6 percent of non-Finnish residences in the same district.

Settlement Patterns

Even within the constraints of a governmentally imposed survey system, some ethnic groups were able to produce their own distinctive settlement patterns. Often this was accomplished even where a rigid checkerboard survey was present.

In the Missouri Ozarks, for example, Germans and non-Germans alike settled a region of rectangular survey. In a close look at present-day settlement maps, Russel L. Gerlach found that rather different patterns have developed. German-American farmsteads are much less frequently situated on public roads than are non-German houses (Figure 9.20). Farmhouses lie in many cases a half-mile from the nearest public road. To be precise, over three-quarters of all non-German farmhouses are within a hundred yards of public roads, as contrasted to just over half of the German-owned houses.

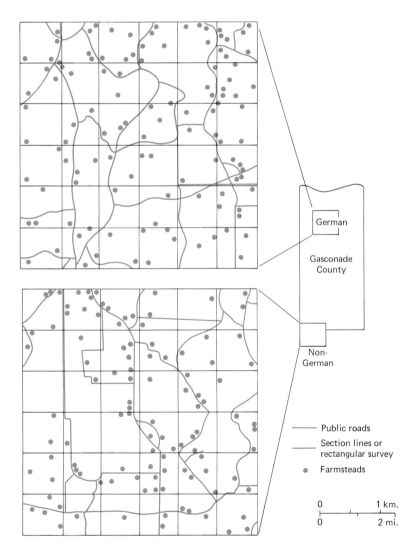

German

Gasconade
County

Non-
German

—— Public roads

—— Section lines or
rectangular survey

• Farmsteads

0   1 km.
├───┼───┤
0   2 mi.

FIGURE 9.20
Distribution of farmsteads in German and non-German rural parts of Gasconade County, Missouri, 1970. Both areas have identical survey systems and similar road patterns, yet the German farmers generally situate their houses farther from the public roads than do non-Germans. Can you think of any reasons why the German-Americans are distinctive in this way? (After Russel L. Gerlach, *Immigrants in the Ozarks: A Study in Ethnic Geography,* Columbia: University of Missouri Press, 1976, p. 71.)

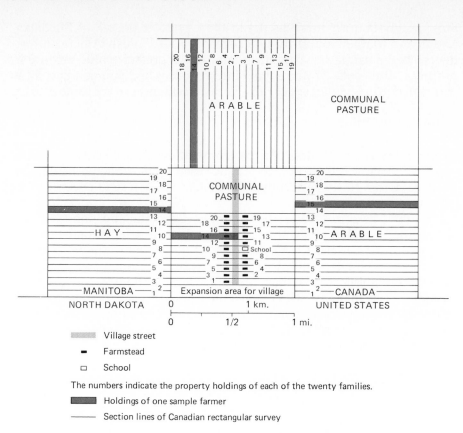

FIGURE 9.21
A Mennonite street village in Manitoba, Canada. The Mennonites, a German-speaking religious sect from Russia, settled this area in 1875. Accustomed to living in such farm villages (see Chapter 2) in Russia, the Mennonites created similar settlements in Canada. The fragmentation of landholdings and communal pasture are also Old World customs. The Mennonites created this village, named Neuhorst, in spite of the Canadian rectangular survey system, which encouraged scattered farmsteads and unit-block holdings. While many such villages later disappeared, some survive as part of the Mennonite ethnic landscape. From a distance, these surviving villages are revealed by long rows of cottonwood trees which line the central street. What advantages would clustered village settlement offer to an ethnic group? What disadvantages? (After John Warkentin, "Mennonite Agricultural Settlements of Southern Manitoba," *Geographical Review,* 49 (1959), 359.)

The numbers indicate the property holdings of each of the twenty families.

Similarly, some Russian-German Mennonite colonists in the prairie provinces of Canada were able to create clustered street villages in a rectangular survey area, in marked contrast to their non-Mennonite neighbors (Figure 9.21). Mennonites duplicated the villages they had known in Russia, while other farmers in the area lived out on their land in dispersed farmsteads. Numerous other rural ethnic groups, in both Canada and the United States, settled in clustered farm villages. Apparently the cohesive bond of ethnicity encouraged these immigrants to live in clustered communities, where they could be in close daily contact with people of their own kind. In most cases, however, the villages later broke up as acculturation progressed, and the farmers moved out to build homes on their farmlands.

Traditional Architecture

The architecture of houses and outbuildings in rural areas in many instances provides a visual index of ethnicity. Most often, the distinctive structures are old and survive as relicts in the landscape. Typically, they represent folk architecture (see Chapter 7). In ethnic islands, at least, it is uncommon for folk architectural styles and building methods to be employed after the foreign-born generation dies off, but the early structures are so well built that some persist in the landscape.

As you travel about North America, you can see this ethnic architecture in diverse landscapes: Southeastern Pennsylvania offers the massive "Dutch" barns, built of stone and equipped with a *forebay,* an overhang on one side of the second story of the barn; the Mexican borderland is dotted with adobe structures; the French St. Lawrence Valley is lined with neat stone farmhouses of a distinctive style (see Chapter 7); Pueblo Indian communities of northern New Mexico display spectacular "apartment" dwellings built of mud bricks; and scattered German ethnic islands reveal aged half-timbered houses. In some cases, the similarity between structures in the Old and New Worlds is quite striking, extending to minor details of construction (Figure 9.22).

Even if Old World architecture styles are not present, it is still often possible to discern architectural differences between ethnic and nonethnic areas. For example, while purely American in style, German-owned farmhouses in the Missouri Ozarks are on the average larger, older, in better condition, and more often equipped with lightning rods than are non-German homes, according to Gerlach's survey.

Exterior Wall Murals

The visible ethnic imprint also extends to landscape elements other than buildings and settlement forms. A fine example is the Mexican-American exterior wall mural, a highly visible, brightly colored ethnic "flag" that reflects rising Hispanic pride and, often, political or social expression (Figure 9.23). Mural painting began to appear in Mexican ethnic neighborhoods in the southwestern United States in the 1960s, according to geographer Daniel D. Arreola, and its roots can be traced both to Spain and to pre-Columbian Mexico. A wide variety of wall surfaces offer the

FIGURE 9.22
A striking example of architectural transferral from Europe to America. The top illustration shows a folk house in the Opole district of Poland, the bottom a dwelling built in south-central Texas by a Polish immigrant from the Opole area. The architectural style is that of Upper Silesia. (Photos by T. Lindsay Baker, Associate Curator, Panhandle-Plains Historical Museum, Canyon, Texas. Used with permission. See also Baker's book, *The First Polish Americans: Silesian Settlements in Texas,* College Station: Texas A&M University Press, 1979.)

FIGURE 9.23
Mexican-American wall mural, San Diego, California, which bears an obvious ideological-political message and helps create a special sense of place in the Mexican *barrio* of the city. Can you identify the persons and events depicted in the mural? (Photo by Terry G. Jordan, 1987.)

opportunity for this ethnic expression, from apartment house and store exteriors to bridge abutments. The subjects also cover a wide range, from religious motifs to political ideology, from statements concerning historic wrongs to urban zoning disputes. Often they are quite specific to the site, incorporating well-known elements of the local landscape, and thus heightening the sense of place and ethnic "turf." Inscriptions can be either in Spanish or English, but many Mexican murals do not contain a written message, relying instead on the sharpness of image and vividness of color to make an impression. There is some suggestion that Chicano mural painting has begun a decline toward relic status, after a heyday in the 1970s, but such murals remain a highly visible aspect of many American urban ethnic landscapes.

■ CONCLUSION

Through the theme of culture region, we saw how ethnic groups, whether rural or urban, tend to cluster spatially. In fact, we could say that spatial identity is a prerequisite of ethnicity, so that the study of ethnic groups is inherently geographic. Cultural diffusion allowed us to see the selective process by which immigrating ethnic groups introduced only some of their Old World traits while abandoning or modifying others and adopting some new traits. Cultural ecology taught us that migrating ethnic groups often look for familiar physical environments in choosing new homes and tend, as a rule, to perceive greater similarity between their old and new homelands than is actually the case. The imprint of ethnicity on economic activity was revealed through the theme of cultural integration. Examples of the visual aspects of ethnicity, some obvious and some quite subtle, became evident in our discussion of the cultural landscape.

The melting pot, in North America and elsewhere, has apparently not reached a high enough "temperature" to dissolve ethnic minorities into a homogeneous mixture. Maybe it never will. There are "lumps" in the stew. By adopting the viewpoint of the cultural geographer, we have been able to look at many spatial facets of ethnicity, decipher some of the reasons why the ethnic mosaic has come to be, and interpret the cultural imprint of ethnic groups.

Suggested Readings

James P. Allen and Eugene J. Turner. *We the People: An Atlas of America's Ethnic Diversity.* New York: Macmillan, 1987. An award-winning geographical portrayal in full color of national origin groups in the United States, based on the 1980 census.

Kay J. Anderson. "The Idea of Chinatown: The Power of Place and Institutional Practice in the Making of a Racial Category," *Annals of the Association of American Geographers,* 77 (1987), 580–598.

Daniel D. Arreola. "The Chinese Role in Creating the Early Cultural Landscape of the Sacramento-San Joaquin Delta," *California Geographer,* 15 (1975), 1–15.

Daniel D. Arreola. "Mexican American Exterior Murals," *Geographical Review,* 74 (1984), 409–424.

Daniel D. Arreola. "Mexican American Housescapes," *Geographical Review,* 78 (1988), 299–315.

Bradley H. Baltensperger. "Agricultural Change Among Great Plains Russian Germans," *Annals of the Association of American Geographers,* 73 (1983), 75–88.

Bruce Bigelow. "Marital Assimilation of Polish-Catholic Americans: A Case Study in Syracuse, N.Y., 1940–1970," *Professional Geographer,* 32 (1980), 431–438.

T. D. Boswell and T. C. Jones. "A Regionalization of Mexican-Americans in the United States," *Geographical Review,* 70 (1980), 88–98.

William A. Bowen. "American Ethnic Regions, 1880," *Proceedings of the Association of American Geographers,* 8 (1976), 44–46.

Colin Clarke, David Ley, and Ceri Peach (eds.). *Geography and Ethnic Pluralism.* Winchester, Mass.: Allen & Unwin, 1984.

John W. Cole and Eric R. Wolf. *The Hidden Frontier: Ecology and Ethnicity in an Alpine Valley.* New York and London: Academic Press, 1974.

Harold F. Creveling. "Mapping Cultural Groups in an American Industrial City," *Economic Geography,* 31 (1955), 364–371.

G. A. Davis and O. F. Donaldson. *Blacks in the United States: A Geographic Perspective.* Boston: Houghton Mifflin, 1975.

C. A. Dawson. *Group Settlement: Ethnic Communities in Western Canada.* Toronto: Macmillan, 1936.

Jacqueline Desbarats. "Indochinese Resettlement in the United States," *Annals of the Association of American Geographers,* 75 (1985), 522–538.

Robert L. Franklin. "Ethnicity and an Emerging Indochinese Commercial District in Orange County," *Yearbook of the Association of Pacific Coast Geographers,* 45 (1983), 85–99.

Russel L. Gerlach. *Settlement Patterns in Missouri: A Study of Population Origins, with a Wall Map.* Columbia: University of Missouri Press, 1986.

Wsevolod W. Isajiw. "Definitions of Ethnicity," *Ethnicity,* 1 (1974), 111–124.

John A. Jakle and James O. Wheeler. "The Changing Residential Structure of the Dutch Population in Kalamazoo, Michigan," *Annals of the Association of American Geographers,* 59 (1969), 441–460.

Hildegard Binder Johnson. "The Location of German Immigrants in the MIddle West," *Annals of the Association of American Geographers,* 41 (1951), 1–41.

Philip N. Jones. "Colored Minorities in Birmingham, England," *Annals of the Association of American Geographers,* 66 (1976), 89–103.

Richard C. Jones. *Patterns of Undocumented Migration: Mexico and the United States.* Totowa, N.J.: Rowman and Allanheld, 1984.

Terry G. Jordan. "Population Origin Groups in Rural Texas," *Annals of the Association of American Geographers,* 60 (1970), 404–405 and colored fold map.

Terry G. Jordan. "Preadaptation and European Colonization in Rural North America," *Annals of the Association of American Geographers,* 79 (1989), in press.

John F. Kain. "Race, Ethnicity, and Residential Location." *Discussion Paper No. D75-3, Department of City and Regional Planning,* Harvard University. Cambridge, Mass., 1975.

Jeanne Kay. "The Ecological Basis of Menominee Ethnobotany," *Journal of Cultural Geography,* 2, No. 2 (1982), 1–12.

Walter M. Kollmorgen. "A Reconnaissance of Some Cultural-Agricultural Islands in the South," *Economic Geography,* 17 (1941), 409–430; 19 (1943), 109–117.

Leszek A. Kosínski. "Changes in the Ethnic Structure in East-Central Europe, 1930–1960," *Geographical Review,* 59 (1969), 388–402.

Trevor R. Lee. *Race and Residence: The Concentration and Dispersal of Immigrants in London.* Oxford: Clarendon Press, 1977.

John Lehr. "The Log Buildings of Ukrainian Settlers in Western Canada," *Prairie Forum,* 2 (1980), 183–196.

James T. Lemon. "The Agricultural Practices of National Groups in Eighteenth-Century Southeastern Pennsylvania," *Geographical Review,* 56 (1966), 467–496.

Dean R. Louder and Eric Waddell (eds.). *Du continent perdu à l'archipel retrouvé: Le Québec et l'Amerique française.* Québec: Travaux du Département de Géographie de l'Université Laval, No. 6, 1983. A superb geographical portrayal of ethnic French in the United States and Canada.

Jesse O. McKee (ed.). *Ethnicity in Contemporary America: A Geographical Appraisal.* Dubuque, Iowa: Kendall/Hunt, 1985.

Sallie A. Marston. "Neighborhood and Politics: Irish Ethnicity in Nineteenth Century Lowell, Massachusetts," *Annals of the Association of American Geographers,* 78 (1988), 414–432.

Hugh Millward. *Regional Patterns of Ethnicity in Nova Scotia: A Geographical Study.* Halifax: International Education Centre, St. Mary's University, 1981.

Richard L. Nostrand. "The Hispanic-American Borderland: Delimitation of an American Culture Region," *Annals of the Association of American Geographers,* 60 (1970), 638–661.

Robert Ostergren. *A Community Transplanted: The Trans-Atlantic Experience of a Swedish Immigrant Settlement in the Upper Middle West, 1835–1915.* Madison: University of Wisconsin Press, 1988.

Risa Palm. "Ethnic Segmentation of Real Estate Agent Practice in the Urban Housing Market," *Annals of the Association of American Geographers,* 75 (1985), 58–68.

"The Peoples of China," Map Supplement, *National Geographic Magazine,* Vol. 158 (July 1980). A splendid color map showing China's ethnic mosaic.

Edward T. Price. "The Melungeons: A Mixed-Blood Strain of the Southern Appalachians," *Geographical Review,* 41 (1951), 256–271.

Thomas L. Purvis. "The Pennsylvania Dutch and the German-American Diaspora in 1790," *Journal of Cultural Geography,* 6, No. 2 (1986), 81–99.

Karl B. Raitz. "Ethnic Maps of North America," *Geographical Review,* 68 (1978), 335–350. A valuable listing of maps that reveal ethnic distributions.

Karl B. Raitz. "Themes in the Cultural Geography of European Ethnic Groups in the United States," *Geographical Review,* 69 (1979), 77–94.

Thomas E. Ross and Tyrel G. Moore (eds.). *A Cultural Geography of North American Indians.* Boulder, Colo.: Westview Press, 1987.

Hansgeorg Schlichtmann. "Ethnic Themes in Geographical Research on Western Canada," *Canadian Ethnic Studies,* 9 (1977), 9–41.

Stephan Thernstrom (ed.). *Harvard Encyclopedia of American Ethnic Groups.* Cambridge, Mass.: Harvard University Press, 1980.

D. Todd and J. S. Brierley. "Ethnicity and the Rural Economy: Illustrations from Southern Manitoba," *Canadian Geographer,* 21 (1977), 237–249.

Cécyle Trépanier. "The Catholic Church in French Louisiana: An Ethnic Institution?" *Journal of Cultural Geography,* 7, No. 1 (1986), 59–75.

Ingolf Vogeler. "Ethnicity, Religion, and Farm Land Transfers in Western Wisconsin," *Ecumene,* 7 (1975), 6–13.

David Ward. "The Ethnic Ghetto in the United States: Past and Present," *Transactions of the Institute of British Geographers,* 7 (1982), 257–275.

Colin H. Williams. "Ethnic Resurgence in the Periphery," *Area,* 11 (1979), 279–283.

M. D. Winsberg. "Ethnic Segregation and Concentration in Chicago Suburbs," *Urban Geography.* 7 (1986), 135–145.

10

The City in Time and Space

CULTURE REGION

ORIGIN AND DIFFUSION OF THE CITY

Urban Hearth Areas
The Diffusion of the City from Hearth Areas

EVOLUTION OF URBAN LANDSCAPES

The Greek City
Roman Cities
Urban Decline in the Dark Ages
The Medieval City
The Renaissance and Baroque Periods
The Industrial City and Urbanization
Megalopolis
The Landscape of Non-Western Cities

Three Urban Models: Indigenous, Colonial, and Emerging Cities
The Indigenous City
The Colonial City
The Emerging City

THE ECOLOGY OF URBAN LOCATION

Site and Situation
Defensive Sites
Trade-Route Sites

CULTURAL INTEGRATION IN URBAN GEOGRAPHY

CONCLUSION

If the 2 million years humankind has spent on Earth were compared to a 24-hour day, then only in the last half-hour have there been settlements of more than a hundred people. Only a few minutes have elapsed since towns and cities first emerged, and large-scale urbanization has been going on for less than 60 seconds. Yet such has been the impact of those "minutes" on humans that the very word we use for society's total cultural complex — *civilization* — is inextricably connected with the city. *Civitas,* the Latin root word for "civilization," was first applied to settled areas of the Roman empire. Later it came to mean a specific town or city within an area. "To civilize" in Western terms means literally "to citify."

Furthermore, urbanization of the last 200 years has strengthened the links among culture, society, and the city. An "urban explosion" has gone hand in hand with the industrial revolution. Cities have grown at unprecedented rates, and the ways of the countryside are increasingly replaced by

FIGURE 10.1
Urbanization, one of the most important forces affecting the world, is the cause of pressing problems in many countries. Shown here are scenes from the business district in Calcutta (upper left), squatter settlements in Rio de Janeiro (upper right), and the residential district of Bombay (bottom). For further discussion of non-Western cities, see the section "The Landscape of Non-Western Cities."

urban life-styles. The cultural geography of the world will change dramatically as we become a predominantly urban people. Recent United Nations estimates demonstrate that the world's urban population more than doubled since 1950 and might well double again by the year 2000. By then, over 50 percent of the Earth's population will live in some sort of city.

This is the first of two chapters on urban cultural geography. In this chapter, we will consider the overall patterns of urbanization, learn how urbanization began and progressed through time, and discuss the differing forms of Western and non-Western cities. In addition, we will examine some of the external factors influencing city location. In the following chapter, the emphasis will be on the internal aspects of the city, cultural regions, diffusion, ecology, integration, and landscape.

■ CULTURE REGION

The culture region theme can be applied to the topic of world urbanization at several levels. First, if we were to take a general outline map of the world and shade in each country according to its **urbanized population**—the percentage of the nation's population living in towns and cities—there would be striking differences between countries; while some would have close to 90 percent of their population in cities, others would have less than 20 percent. Consequently, we could speak of culture regions based on varying rates of urbanization, of a world pattern of "urban" versus "rural" countries. Also, if we looked more closely at each individual country, we could delimit formal and functional culture regions within each nation, separating urban and rural domains. Each of these points is elaborated upon below.

Past editions of this book began this chapter with a detailed world map placing each country into a category based on its percentage of urbanized population. Because these data are not comparable, however, they tend to hinder rather than help accurate generalizations about world urbanization patterns. The problem is that there is no agreed-upon international definition of what constitutes a city, so the criteria used to calculate a country's urbanized population vary greatly from nation to nation, and mapping these data reinforces a myth of comparability. There is probably more to be learned from examining how different countries think about their urbanized population than by invalidly comparing data. To illustrate, the Indian government defines an urban center as 5000 inhabitants, with an adult male population employed predominantly in nonagricultural work. In contrast, the United States Census Bureau defines a city as a densely populated area of 2500 people or more, and South Africa counts as a city any settlement of 500 or more people. Furthermore, some countries change and revise their definitions of urban settlements to suit specific purposes; China-watchers were baffled in 1983 when that country's urban population swelled by an incredible 13 percent in one year, only to learn that China had simply revised its census definitions for urban settlements with criteria that vary from province to province. The point, then, is that an international comparison of urbanized population data can be made only with explicit qualifications that emphasize the varying definitions of the term *city*.

Nonetheless, several valid generalizations can be made about the spectrum of differences in the world's urbanized population. First, there is a close link between urbanized population and the more-developed world. Put differently, highly industrialized countries have higher rates of urbanized population than do less-developed countries. For example, the United Nations estimates that in 1990, 73 percent of the population in the more-developed countries will live in cities, while only 34 percent will be urban in the less-developed countries—a point highlighted by the contrast between North America (74 percent) and Europe (73 percent) on the one hand, and Africa (33 percent) and South Asia (30 percent) on the other. The second generalization, which is closely tied to the first, is that Third World and less-developed countries are urbanizing rapidly, and that over the next decade the proportion of urban to rural population will change dramatically. In other words, an urban explosion is taking place in the less-developed world, caused by massive migration away from the country as people flock to cities in search of a better life. This urban migration, however, should not be compared to the familiar images from the past of farm-to-city relocation during Europe or America's industrializing period; city migration in the less-developed countries today is often driven by desperation, as rural supply systems collapse, and urban migrants today cannot always find employment in the city. Unemployment rates in Third World cities are disturbingly high, often over 50 percent for newcomers to the city. Consequently, one of the world's ongoing crises will be this radical restructuring of population and culture as people in the less-developed countries move into the cities.

We can also apply the culture region theme at the intranational scale to better understand this dynamic urbanization process, and this application can be made in various ways. To begin with, if we took a fairly typical less-developed African country such as Ethiopia, we could conceptualize two distinct culture regions, the urban and the rural, with less than 20 percent of the population in cities. The cultural patterns of the urbanities in the capital, Addis Ababa, contrast dramatically with the tribal and kinship-based cultural fabric of rural peoples. Furthermore, a map of social and economic indicators—such as income, education, literacy, and fertility—would show striking differences between urban and rural regions. One might be tempted to characterize urban-rural distinctions within Third World countries as differences between "haves" and "have-nots," just as we do between the developed and less-developed world. This difference, or cultural gradient, which we might think of as the "pull" force, gives us some sense of why there is such widespread migration to the city, particularly when we add "push" forces from the countryside, such as famine, political disruption, and land alienation.

Urban growth in these countries comes from two sources: first, quite obviously, the migration of people to the cities, and, second, from the higher natural population growth rates of these recent migrants. Because urban employment is unreliable, many migrants continue having large numbers of children to construct a more extensive family support system; with a larger family, the chances of someone getting work are increased. The demographic transition to smaller families seems to come only later when a certain dimension of security is assured. Often this results when women enter the work force.

While this massive rural-to-city migration affects just about all urban centers in the developing world, the most publicized and visible cases are the extraordinarily large settlements we call world cities—those having over 5 million in population. Table 10.1 displays the world's 20 largest cities based on a recent study, and we see that over half of these are in what we might call the Third, or developing, World. This is a major change from the case 30 years ago when the list would have been dominated by Western, industrialized cities. While projecting the growth of these large cities is

TABLE 10.1
The World's 20 Largest Metropolitan Areas*

Rank	Metropolitan Area	Country	Size (in millions)	Average Annual % Growth
1	Tokyo/Yokohama	Japan	28.7	1.09
2	Mexico City	Mexico	19.4	3.73
3	New York	U.S.A.	17.4	0.42
4	São Paulo	Brazil	17.2	3.81
5	Osaka/Kobe/Kyoto	Japan	16.8	0.65
6	Seoul	South Korea	15.8	3.73
7	Moscow	Soviet Union	13.1	0.97
8	Bombay	India	12.9	3.65
9	Calcutta	India	12.8	1.92
10	Buenos Aires	Argentina	12.4	1.73
11	Los Angeles	U.S.A.	11.5	1.82
12	London	England	11.0	−0.12
13	Cairo	Egypt	11.0	2.84
14	Rio de Janeiro	Brazil	11.0	2.44
15	Paris	France	10.0	0.45
16	Jakarta	Indonesia	9.9	4.24
17	Delhi/New Delhi	India	9.8	4.38
18	Manila	Philippines	9.2	3.29
19	Shanghai	China	9.2	1.49
20	Tehran	Iran	8.1	4.47

*Data as of January 1, 1989.

Source: Prepared by Richard L. Forstall for Rand McNally and Company's *The International Atlas,* 1989. Used by permission.

subject to a number of qualifications that will be discussed shortly, most urbanists agree that by the year 2000, the list will be even more dominated by the Third World because its cities are growing far faster than are Japanese, North American, and European cities. For example, some futurists expect Mexico City to top 30 million by the turn of the century — others suggest a population close to 50 million is possible — and Sao Paulo could challenge Tokyo at 25 million because the latter city has nowhere to grow.

Projections for future growth must be qualified by two considerations. First, Third World cities will continue to explode in size only if economic development expands; if it stagnates because of political or resource problems, city growth would probably slow, although urban migration might actually increase if rural economics deteriorate. For example, the uncertainty about Mexico City's growth is linked to that country's economic growth and, more specifically, to Mexico's oil industry, which is, of course, a function of the international context. Second, because these world cities are plagued by transportation, housing, and employment problems, some countries are trying desperately to control and regulate urban migration; therefore, the failure or success of these policies will influence city size in the year 2000. China, for example, closely regulates urban growth. Accurate population projections, then, are evasive because they depend on variables that range from international economies to national and local policies.

The target for much urban migration is what are called **primate cities,** those settlements that dominate the economic, political, and cultural life of a country, and, as a result of rapid growth, expand their primacy or dominance. Once again, Mexico City is an excellent example because that settlement far exceeds Guadalajara, the second-largest city in Mexico in size and importance. While many developing countries are dominated by a primate city, which was often a former center or capital of colonial power, urban primacy is not unique to Third World countries: Think of the way London and Paris dominate their respective countries. Although there are some advantages to having one city as the focus of all activities, there are also numerous problems, such as the way these cities tend to inhibit development in other parts of the country.

In summary, we are fast becoming a predominantly urban world, where most people will live in cities and the Earth's cultural geography will be dominated by urban society. We will next investigate the rise and evolution of the earliest settlements to gain more insight into the phenomenon of urbanization.

■ ORIGIN AND DIFFUSION OF THE CITY

As we seek explanations for the origin of cities, we see a relationship between areas of early agriculture, permanent village settlement, the development of new social forms, and urban life. The first cities resulted from a long and complicated transition that took thousands of years.

Early people were nomadic hunters and gatherers, constantly moving in their search for sustenance. Through time, campsites became semi-permanent as these hunters and gatherers became increasingly efficient in gathering resources, often occupying the same sites for months, seasons, and years at a time. As the quantities of domesticated plants and animals increased (see Chapter 3), settlements became even more permanent. In the Near East, which is where the first cities appeared, a network of permanent agricultural villages developed about 10,000 years ago.

These farming villages were modest in size, rarely with more than 200 people, and were probably organized on a kinship basis. Jarmo, one of the earliest villages, located in present-day Iraq, had 25 permanent dwellings clustered together in a compound centered around grain storage facilities. Even though the people did not have plows, agriculture was based on cultivating local grains, which was the earliest form of wheat and barley cultivation. It is thought that domestic dogs, goats, and sheep were used for meat; food supplies were augmented by hunting and gathering.

Although small farming villages like Jarmo are found predating cities in different parts of the world, it is wrong to assume that a simple quantitative change took place whereby villages slowly grew into towns, then into cities. Instead, major qualitative changes nurtured true urban life.

The two crucial elements behind this change were the generation of an agricultural surplus and the development of a stratified social system. Surplus food, which can be defined as a food supply larger than the everyday needs of the agricultural labor force, is a necessary prerequisite for supporting nonfarmers — that is, people who work at administrative, military, or handicraft tasks. Social stratification, where there are distinct differences between elite and lower classes, facilitates the collection, storage, and distribution of resources through well-defined channels of authority that can exercise control over goods and people. At some point, early settlements grew by gaining advantage over their neighbors, so they were able to dominate their region by controlling access to vital resources. This might have been done through pure military force. Or, possibly, power could have been expanded by forcing tribute to a religious figurehead, such as a god-king. Or perhaps a settlement's sphere of power expanded simply because it controlled a needed resource, such as water, and others had to assume secondary roles to gain access to this resource.

In the search for understanding the transition from village to city life, some scholars prefer to construct models for the development of urban life based on one single factor as the "trigger" behind the change. Four of these models are discussed below.

The **hydraulic civilization** model sees the development of large-scale irrigation systems as the prime mover. Higher crop yields resulted from irrigated agriculture, and, in turn, this food surplus could support the development of a large nonfarming population. A strong, centralized government, backed by an urban-based military, expanded power into the surrounding areas. Those farmers who resisted the new authority were denied water. Continued reinforcement of the power elite came from the need for organizational coordination to assure continued operation of the irrigation system.

Because of irrigation, a surplus was created that was able to support nonfarmers. Class distinctions were reinforced by power differences as well, and labor specialization developed. Some people were farmers, some worked on the irrigation system, others became artisans creating the implements needed to maintain the system, while others became administrative workers in the direct employ of the power elite's court.

Some writers have also used this model to explain the decline of urban-based civilizations. If there is disruption in the political system, a breakdown of power, then the irrigation facilities might not be maintained. Canals silt up, water supplies are lost through dam breakages, and, as the irrigation system loses effectiveness, the urban-rural support system breaks down, leading to reduced agricultural output and subsequent population stress.

Although the hydraulic model fits several areas where cities first arose—namely, China, Egypt, and Mesopotamia—it cannot be applied to all urban hearths. In Mesoamerica, for example, an urban civilization blossomed without widespread irrigated agriculture. This model also begs the question of how or why a culture might first develop an irrigation system.

Other writers have suggested what we might call the **innovation model,** where one group gains advantage over others by exploiting new technology or a new resource base. A new trait, such as irrigated agriculture or a plow, might be invented by one group, and this could lead to increased agricultural yields. An expanded food supply might also come from domestication of a new animal or crop, or by moving into a productive yet previously unoccupied ecological niche. In Mesopotamia, the first farming villages were on the hillsides above the river floodplain. Some writers argue that the first groups to move into the floodplain quickly developed a more productive agricultural system than their neighbors who remained on the river valley flanks. A surplus food supply was generated in the floodplain that could support nonfarmers—people who could specialize in the kinds of occupations necessary to support city life. Perhaps some specialized in the making of agricultural tools that in turn could be traded to surrounding villages.

This model assumes a certain degree of inventiveness. Some critics feel that humans invent new technologies or new tools, or move into new areas, only when they must. In other words, "necessity is the mother of invention." Consequently, these critics seek explanations as to *why* new areas were occupied or new systems innovated.

One explanation is the **environmental stress model.** Although this model has numerous variations, all concern changes in the physical environment leading either to further innovations or to one group controlling resources at the expense of others. Some scholars believe that a change in climate has been a major factor behind invention and movement. They argue that original crop domestication took place in Mesopotamia under conditions that were wetter and cooler than those that currently exist in the area. Then, beginning about 10,000 years ago, the climate became warmer and drier; early hillside farmers moved down from the valley flanks to draw upon river water for irrigation. Of course, this was a gradual process, taking hundreds of years, but the result was that those groups first able to adapt to the new climatic conditions monopolized the floodplain resource base.

But supporting evidence is not convincing. There is no question that our climate has become increasingly warmer in the last 10,000 years; however, it does not automatically follow that precipitation has lessened with warmer temperatures. In some parts of the world, rainfall has actually increased as the climate warmed. We must await more precise supporting data from Mesopotamia before giving serious consideration to this particular variation of the stress model.

However, there are other kinds of environmental stress that can be considered, such as the effect that human activities might have on a fragile ecosystem. Activities such as cultivation or grazing might lead to soil depletion or erosion, thereby depriving a group of its agricultural resource base. Some writers suggest that increased population from an initial innovation might stress the existing resource base. Once again, those groups that can successfully adapt to changing conditions ascend to positions of power, able to dominate their less innovative neighbors, and able to build upon surplus and trade in a way leading to population growth, dense settlement, and stratified society.

Implicit in the previously mentioned models is the extension of political power by one group over others, so it is not surprising that some writers place major emphasis on **coercion and warfare** as the trigger behind the rise of cities. They argue that competition among groups for scarce resources such as land or water leads to conflict, and that the group most able to dominate others will control the resources. By controlling resources, the dominant group can demand allegiance and tribute.

Proponents of this model suggest that a town is the most easily defended settlement. It can be surrounded by walls and fortifications, and wealth, be it grain or gold, can be stored in a central place and guarded against intruders. Urban dwellers can easily be pressed into service in defense of their city, for surrender or defeat will have dire consequences for all. A clustered settlement, then, might be an effective adaptation to pervasive conflict; once people are clustered together, the extension of power over these city people is relatively easy.

Critics of this model note that cities have developed in areas where warfare was not common or widespread. In fact, some scholars maintain that warfare became widespread only *after* the rise of cities. Others argue that cooperation—not conflict—is a necessary prerequisite for interaction of towns and villages.

Obviously, then, all single-factor models have their limitations when it comes to explaining the qualitative change from agricultural villages to true cities. A wiser course is to accept the idea that multiple factors are responsible for changes leading to urban life. For example, in an area such as Mesopotamia, it appears that an initial advantage may have gone to those groups first exploiting the unoccupied river bottoms. They may have experimented with primitive watering systems on the hillsides; with vast amounts of river water available, invention of a sophisticated irrigation system may have resulted. This would have consolidated power in the hands of one or two groups, and they may have extended control over the hinterland through coercion and warfare. Yet, at a later stage, sedimentation may have reduced the effectiveness of irrigation. Food shortages may have resulted, thus weakening the political system, and a change of power or demise of the settlement could result. Then, those settlements best able to adapt to the new conditions might rise to dominance. So the cycle would repeat itself.

In summation, it is probably unwise to think that one single-factor model can explain the rise of cities in all areas of the prehistoric world. Instead, we must appreciate the complexities of the transition period from agricultural village to true city; what explains this change in one area may not apply in another.

Urban Hearth Areas

The first cities appeared in distinct regions such as Mesopotamia, the Nile valley, Pakistan's Indus River valley, the Yellow River valley (or Huang Ho) of China, and Mesoamerica. These are called the **urban hearth areas** (see box, "Cahokia"). Figure 10.2 gives the general dates for the emergence of urban life in each region.

It is generally agreed that the first cities arose in Mesopotamia, the river valley of the Tigris and Euphrates in what is now Iraq. These cities, small by current standards, covered one-half to two square miles (1.28 to 5.12 square kilometers) and embraced populations that rarely exceeded 30,000. Nevertheless, with such a population concentrated in such a small area, the densities within these cities could easily reach 10,000 people per square mile (4000 per square kilometer). This is comparable to many contemporary cities. Detroit, for example, has a population density of

---

CAHOKIA: AN EARLY URBAN CENTER ON THE MISSISSIPPI

Cahokia, a pre-Columbian urban center on the Mississippi, shows that not all early cities were found in the five urban hearth areas mentioned in the text. Instead, Cahokia illustrates the process of independent city origin and can be taken as an example of events duplicated in hundreds of areas around the world.

The Cahokia settlement is an aggregation of mounds and living structures dating from about A.D. 100, located in the American Bottoms region of the Mississippi valley, close to St. Louis. It is the largest of 10 large population centers and some 50 smaller farming villages that flourished between 900 and 1500 A.D.

How did this city arise? Archaeologists maintain that the city resulted from a complicated feedback process that involved population growth and an increase in agricultural productivity. In the late eighth century, the hoe replaced a less effective digging stick and a new variety of maize diffused into the American Bottoms region better suited to environmental conditions of the warm river valley.

Peak population came centuries later, probably between 1150 and 1250, when Cahokia may have approached a pop-

ulation of 40,000. Archaeological evidence suggests that houses were mainly of pole-and-thatch construction and varied in size according to the status of the occupants. The settlement also contained many ceremonial structures, most notably large earthen mounds similar to the pyramids of Mesoamerican cities. Close to the largest mound was an enclosed area of large public structures that reminds one of the citadel areas of Mesopotamian cities.

Cahokia flourished because it was an ideally located central place, situated on fertile agricultural lands, with access to local and long-distance trade moving through the network of sloughs and rivers. Scholars who have investigated the site believe that Cahokia declined in importance around 1250. Perhaps this was due to exhaustion of local resources, perhaps because its trade hinterland was eclipsed by the growing strength of other Mississippi River cultures. Whatever the reason, further investigation is bound to shed light on the complicated processes that lead to the rise and fall of cities.

Adapted from Melvin Fowler, "A Pre-Columbian Urban Center on the Mississippi," *Scientific American* (August 1975), 93–102.

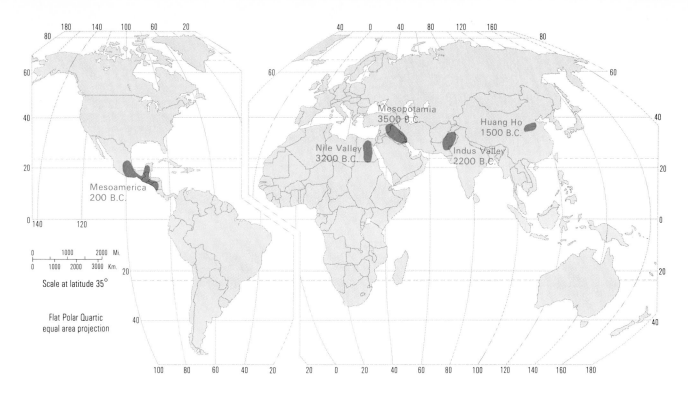

FIGURE 10.2
The world's first cities arose in five urban hearth areas. The dates are conservative figures for the rise of urban life in each area; some scholars would, for example, suggest urban life in Mesopotamia existed by 5000 B.C. New discoveries are constantly being made that suggest that urban life appeared earlier in each of the hearth areas. Note, however, that the latest date is in Mesoamerica.

roughly 12,000 per square mile (4500 per square kilometer). Congestion and crowdedness have apparently been urban problems since the first cities were formed.

If we were to look at the landscape of the Mesopotamian cities, we would first see that most of the urban population was contained within a wall, which provided both physical protection and a symbolic boundary for the inhabitants (see Figure 10.3). Beyond the wall, directly outside the main gates, we might find a few clusters of houses—the first suburbs. These would probably house visitors to the city. Within the wall, the central part of the city would be dominated by the citadel, the seat of the power elite. Here we would find three important buildings that symbolized the functions of the early cities: the *ziggurat* or temple, the palace, and the granary.

The temple made up the religious core of the ancient Mesopotamian city. This precedent was repeated in different forms—the pyramid, the dome, the cathedral—right up to our own age. Over time, the Mesopotamian ziggurat developed from a temple complex open to believers into an imposing structure mounted on a raised platform, overseen by priestly guardians, and often closed to the general population. The well-known Tower of Babel was a gigantic ziggurat rising 200 feet (61.5 meters). The immense scale of these later temples evidently was meant to reflect the power that lay menacingly behind them. Because the urban power structure almost always based its rule on religion, the palace, the actual seat of power, was usually close to the temple. The granary, too, was enclosed in the citadel, which suggests that this storehouse for the agricultural surplus of the population was often guarded from the population itself.

Inside the walled and guarded citadel, in a city within a city, lived the ruler and the court, as well as their military forces. Even today, the Pentagon, the Kremlin, and similar sites prove that the citadel persists in contemporary cities. Before 2000 B.C., within the citadels, the streets were

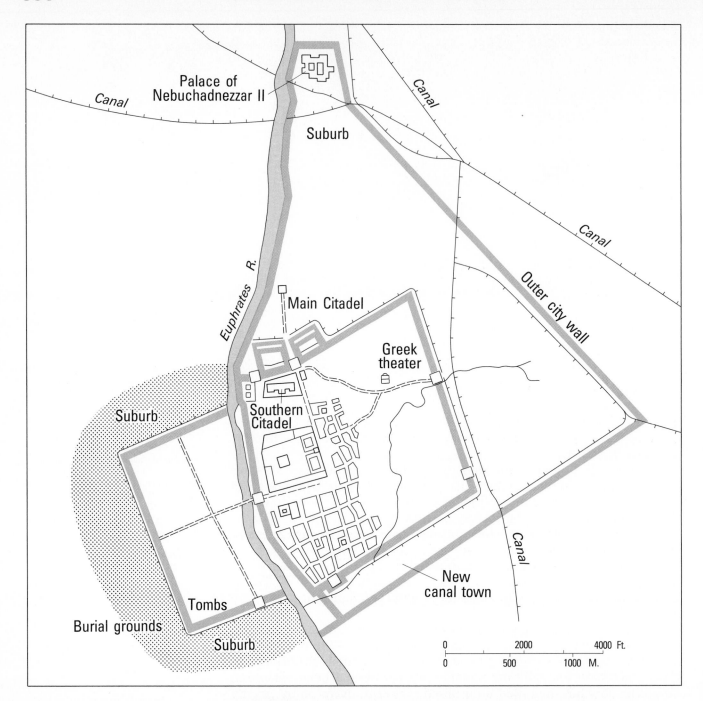

FIGURE 10.3
This map of Babylon illustrates the urban morphology of early Mesopotamian cities. Note the citadel in the inner city, which was the center of the ruling elite, characterized by the ziggurat, main temple, palace, and granary. Beyond that lay the residential areas, which are incompletely shown in this reconstruction; we can assume they extended out to the inner walls and occupied both sides of the river. Suburbs grew outside the major gates and were occupied by people not allowed to spend the night in the city, such as traders and noncitizens. (After map in the *New Encyclopaedia Britannica,* vol. 2, Chicago: Encyclopaedia Britannica, Inc., 1984, p. 555.)

paved, drains and running water were provided, private sleeping quarters were built, bathtubs and water closets were installed, and spacious villas were constructed. But the privileges of the ruling class did not extend to the city as a whole.

Outside the citadel, and covering most of the city, lay the cramped residential quarters of the masses. Houses were one or two stories tall, were composed of clay brick, and contained three or four rooms. They fronted on narrow streets that were unsurfaced and without drainage and that served as the community dump. Excavations at Ur, one of the earliest Mesopotamian cities, show that the level of garbage rose so high that new entrances had to be cut into the second stories of the houses. The only open spaces were the small market squares dotting the city. Here artisans clustered to trade their goods; here food was distributed; and here the military herded the urban population to hear the latest edict from their rulers. Just inside the walls of the city were the first ghettos. There, the lowest classes lived in huts of mud and reed rather than houses of fired clay.

Cities found in the other hearth areas demonstrate essentially the same spatial characteristics. Usually they were walled, with a citadel monopolizing the central place. Streets were crooked and narrow, with tightly clustered dwellings of one or two stories lining them. The poor lived on the outskirts, nearest the wall, where they were most vulnerable during times of attack. Yet there were some differences among hearth areas. For example, the early cities of the Nile were not walled, which suggests that a regional power structure kept individual cities from warring with one another.

The most important differences are found in the Mesoamerican hearth area (see box, "City Planning in the New World: Teotihuacán"). Here, cities were less dense and covered large areas (see Figure 10.4). Furthermore, these cities arose without benefit of the technological advances found in the other hearth areas, most notably the wheel, the plow, metallurgy, and draft animals. However, the domestication of maize compensated for these shortcomings. Maize is a grain that yields several crops a year without irrigation in the tropical climate, and it can be cultivated without heavy plows or pack animals. Probably most striking is the relatively recent (200 B.C.) date of urban life in Central America. All other urban hearth areas arose by at least 1500 B.C. Did the Mesoamerican cities arise later because they lacked technological innovations? Or did they evolve only after Old World urbanites had crossed the oceans and planted the seeds of city life? This question opens the door to a discussion of how cities have spread across the face of the Earth.

CITY PLANNING IN THE NEW WORLD: TEOTIHUACÁN

Teotihuacán was a Mesoamerican city created by a society that had no metal tools, had not invented the wheel, and had no pack animals. At its height, Teotihuacán covered 8 square miles (20 square kilometers), which made it larger than imperial Rome. Its central religious monument, the Temple of the Sun, was as broad at its base as the great pyramid of Cheops in Egypt. Its population may have reached 100,000.

Strategically located astride a valley that was the gateway to the lowlands of Mexico, Teotihuacán flourished for 500 years as a great urban commercial center. Yet it was more than that. It was the Mecca of the New World, a religious and cultural capital that probably housed pilgrims from as far away as Guatemala. Not a trace of fortification has ever been unearthed. Perhaps most startling, Teotihuacán was a totally planned city. Its two great pyramids, its citadel, its hundred lesser religious structures and its 4000 other dwellings were laid out according to an exact design. Its streets (and many of its buildings) were organized on an exact grid aligned with the city center. Even the shape of the river that divided the city was changed to fit the grid pattern.

Planning for the construction of Teotihuacán's major temples must have been an incredible undertaking. The Temple of the Sun, for instance, rises to a height of 215 feet and has a base of 725 square feet. These dimensions meant that it took about one million tons of sun-baked mud bricks to build the temple. When the Spaniards conquered Mexico in the sixteenth century, they were amazed to find Teotihuacán's ruined temples. Local inhabitants claimed that the temples had been built by giants. They showed the Spaniards the bones of giant elephants (which had lived there in prehistoric times) to prove their point.

But the small as well as the large was cleverly conceived in Teotihuacán. Houses were apparently planned for maximum space and privacy. Apartments were constructed around central patios, and each patio designed to give dwellers light and air, as well as an efficient drainage system. In a Teotihuacán housing complex, a person could indeed have lived in relative comfort.

FIGURE 10.4
Monumental and ceremonial architecture, as seen here in the Mayan city of Chichen Itza, often dominated the morphology and landscape of hearth area cities, and reinforced ruling class power.

The Diffusion of the City from Hearth Areas

Although urban life originated at specific places in the world, cities are now found everywhere—North America, Africa, Southeast Asia, Latin America, Australia. How did city life come to these regions? While many of these cities resulted from European colonialism in the last two centuries, let us first discuss the diffusion of cities before this period. There are two possibilities. The first is that cities evolved spontaneously as native peoples created new technologies and social institutions. A second hypothesis is that the preconditions for urban life are too specific for most cultures to invent without contact with other urban areas; therefore they must have learned these traits through contact with city dwellers. This arrangement emphasizes the diffusion of ideas and techniques necessary for city life.

Diffusionists strongly suggest that the complicated array of ideas and techniques that gave rise to the first cities in Mesopotamia was shared with other people, in both the Nile and the Indus river valleys, who were on the verge of the urban transformation. There is no question that these three civilizations had contact with one another. Archaeological evidence documents trade ties. Soapstone objects manufactured in Tepe Yahyā, 500 miles (800 kilometers) to the east of Mesopotamia, have been uncovered in the ruins of both Mesopotamian and Indus Valley cities, which are separated by thousands of miles. Indus Valley writing and seals have also been found in Mesopotamian urban sites. Although diffusionists use this artifactual evidence to argue that the idea of the city was spread from hearth to hearth, an alternative view is that trading took place only after these cities were well established.

But what about the cities of Mesoamerica? Did they evolve in isolation, or did they have cultural contact across the oceans with the urban dwellers of Asia and Africa? This topic is controversial, yet some evidence strongly suggests that Japanese fishers visited the coasts of North and South America before the rise of urban cultures in Mesoamerica. Contact with Mediterranean cultures is another possibility. In voyages on replicas of ancient seagoing rafts across both the Atlantic and Pacific oceans, the anthropologist Thor Heyerdahl has shown that there may have been a wide variety of contacts between continents. He maintains that the symbol of his transatlantic expedition—the sun god Ra—was common to both Mesoamerican and North African civilizations. Further discoveries may well show the extent of sharing among the urban civilizations of Asia and Africa and strengthen the diffusionist argument. Until then, the controversy continues.

Nonetheless, there is little doubt that the diffusion process has been responsible for the dispersal of the city in historical times. This is because the city has commonly been used as the vehicle for imperial expansion. The sociologist Gideon Sjoberg, in his book *The Preindustrial City*, states: "The extension of the power group's domain, notably through empire-building, is the primary mechanism for introducing city life into generally non-urbanized territories." Typically, urban life is carried outward in waves of conquest as the borders of an empire expand. Initially, the military controls newly won lands and sets up collection points for local resources, which are then shipped back into the heart of the empire and used for its economy. As the surrounding countryside is increasingly pacified, the new settlements lose some of their military atmosphere and begin to show the social diversity of a city. Artisans, merchants, and bureaucrats increase in number. Families appear. The native people are slowly assimilated into the settlement as workers and may eventually dominate the city. Finally, the process repeats itself as the empire pushes farther outward: first a military camp, then a collection point for resources, then a full-fledged city expressing true division of labor and social diversity.

Examples of imperial city-building dot history. Alexander the Great, in the course of his conquests, ordered his architects to establish at least 70 cities. The Roman Empire, a power expanding from a single urban center, built literally thousands of cities, changing the rural faces of Europe, North Africa, and Asia Minor in the process. In other times, the Persians, the Maurya Empire of India, the Han civilization of China, the Greeks, and others performed the same city-spreading task. In more recent times, European empires have used the resources of cities to expand and consolidate their power in colonies in the Americas, Africa, and Asia. England, France, and Spain contained the key hearth areas; North America's first cities were simply military outposts of a sort.

Think of the westward expansion of North American cultures launched from the eastern coast. First, military posts were built to control and administer frontier lands. These became central points for trade with and exploitation of the surrounding areas. Other kinds of activities clustered around the original forts. The new settlements had all the diversity necessary to call them cities. Such was the case with Detroit, Pittsburgh, Chicago, San Francisco, and many other American cities. As the American nation spread, so did cities.

This sort of expansion diffusion is, then, a major process in dispersing urban life over the surface of the Earth. Figure 10.5 shows some of the routes the city took in this diffusion process.

By Empires see map.

■ EVOLUTION OF URBAN LANDSCAPES

Understanding urban landscapes necessitates an appreciation of urban processes both past and present. The patterns we see today in the city, such as building form, architecture, street plans, and land use, are a composite of past and present cultures; they reflect the needs, ideas, technology, and institutions of human occupance. This section, then, will exam-

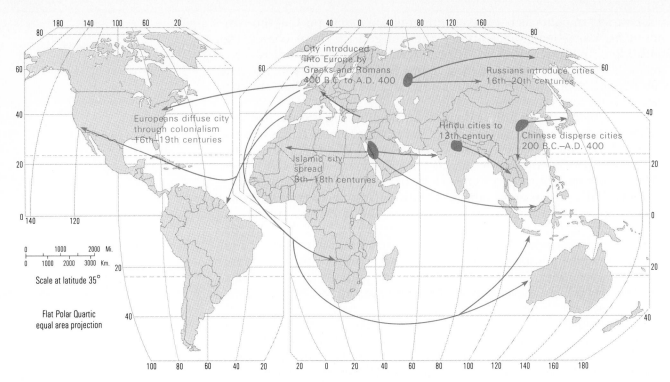

FIGURE 10.5
This map illustrates how cities have spread with the expansion of certain empires.

ine major stages in the evolution of urban landscapes in both Western and non-Western cities.

Two concepts underlie our examination of urban landscapes. The first is **urban morphology,** or the physical form of the city, which consists of street patterns, building sizes and shapes, architecture, and density. The second concept is **functional zonation.** This refers to the pattern of land uses within a city, or the existence of areas with differing functions, such as residential, commercial, or governmental. Functional zonation is also concerned with social patterns—whether an area is occupied by the power elite or by low-status persons, by Jews or by Christians, by high-income persons or by low. Both concepts are central to understanding the cultural landscape of cities, because both make statements about how cultures occupy and shape space (see Figure 10.6).

FIGURE 10.6
This photo of San Francisco shows us how the concepts of urban morphology and functional zonation can be used in examining cities. In the foreground, close to the shoreline, are older brick factories that have been converted for the tourist trade associated with the Fisherman's Wharf area. The residential areas exhibit two morphological characteristics: high-rises on the hills to the right, and blocks of low-rise apartments in the middle ground. Finally, the skyscrapers of the central business district show up in the background.

We will begin our study of urban landscapes with Western cities, examining the evolution of urban patterns from Greek times to the post-industrial. Following that will be a discussion of non-Western cities.

The Greek City

Western civilization and the Western city both trace their immediate roots back to ancient Greece. City life diffused to Greece from the Near East. By 600 B.C., there were over 500 towns and cities on the Greek mainland and surrounding islands. As Greek civilization expanded, cities spread with it throughout the Mediterranean — to the north shore of Africa, to Spain, to southern France, and to Italy. These cities were of modest size, rarely containing more than 5000 inhabitants. Athens, however, may have reached 300,000 in the fifth century B.C. (This figure, however, includes perhaps 100,000 slaves, the labor power behind Greek society.)

Greek cities had two distinctive functional zones — the *acropolis* and the *agora.* In many ways, the acropolis was similar to the citadel of Mesopotamian cities. Here were the temples of worship, the storehouse of valuables, and the seat of power. The acropolis also served as a place of retreat in time of siege (see Figure 10.7). If the acropolis was the domain of the power structure, the agora was the province of the citizens. As originally conceived, the agora was a place for public meetings, education, social interaction, and judicial matters. In other words, it was the civic center, the hub of democratic life for Greek men (women were excluded from political life). During the classical period, commercial activities were not considered fitting for the agora, but later it became the major marketplace of the city — without losing its atmosphere of a social club. In Latin countries, the social function of the agora has carried over to the plaza, with its open space surrounded by cafés and restaurants.

Early Greek cities were messy, despite their outstanding public buildings and temples. Narrow muddy streets littered with garbage became obstacle courses for pedestrians. Private housing was often crude at best, miserable at worst. The earlier Greek cities probably were not planned but rather grew spontaneously, without benefit of formal guidelines. Yet the

FIGURE 10.7
Part of the historic core of Athens, the Acropolis dominates the contemporary city and reminds us that many cities throughout the world have been centered on fortified places that, through time, have become more symbolic than functional. Compare this landscape with other defensive acropolis sites.

Greeks, concerned as they were with aesthetics and humankind's total environment, may have been the first to formulate the principles of city planning. Many of the later Greek colonial cities around the Mediterranean clearly were planned. For instance, Greek cities in Italy were built on a checkerboard pattern, with streets of uniform width and city blocks of relatively uniform dimensions. However, it seems unlikely that the Greeks were the only ancient people to approach city building this way, for it does not seem possible that all the earlier cities in Mesopotamia, the Nile, China, and the Indus evolved without some degree of planning. For example, the street pattern of Indus cities was a gridiron, with straight streets meeting at right angles. Such a pattern required some degree of planning. Nevertheless, Greek cities were held up as models of urban planning during the later Renaissance period (A.D. 1500–1700) and stimulated artists and engineers of the sixteenth century to think about a totally planned environment. This topic is discussed later in this section.

Roman Cities

By 200 B.C., the focus for the Western city had shifted from Greece to Rome. The Romans adopted many urban traits from the Greeks, as well as from the Etruscans, a civilization of northern Italy that the Romans had conquered. As the Roman Empire expanded, city life was diffused into France, Germany, England, interior Spain, the Alpine countries, and parts of eastern Europe. The military camp, or *castra,* was the basis for many of these new settlements. In England, the Roman trail of city building can be found by looking for the suffixes *-caster* and *-chester*—as in Lancaster or Winchester, cities originally founded as Roman camps. Figure 10.8 shows the diffusion of urban life into Europe as the Greek and Roman frontiers advanced.

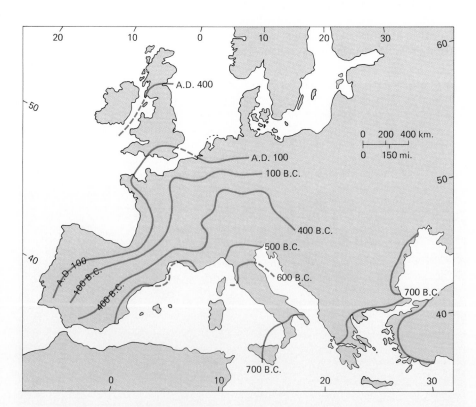

FIGURE 10.8
The early spread of urban development moved in waves across Europe. The nucleus of city life was well established in the Greek lands by 700 B.C. In the centuries that followed, urbanization diffused west and north until it finally reached the British Isles. (Reproduced by permission from an article by Norman J. G. Pounds in the *Annals of the Association of American Geographers,* 59, 1969.)

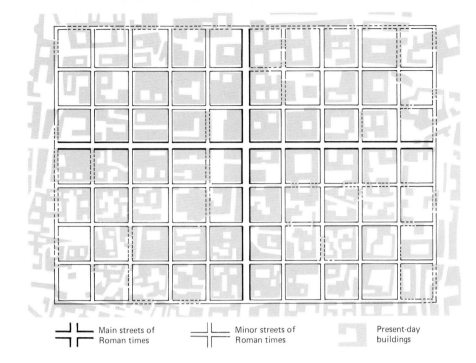

FIGURE 10.9
The Roman grid street pattern still survives in Pavia, Italy, and the original city site is still used. Many of the straight streets from Roman times remain in use twenty centuries after they were first built. The dotted lines indicate the Roman streets that do not exist today. Beyond the Roman core the streets developed in irregular patterns.

The landscape of these Roman cities shared several traits with its Greek predecessors. The gridiron street pattern, used in later Greek cities, was fundamental to Roman cities. This can still be seen in the heart of such Italian cities as Verona and Pavia (see Figure 10.9). These straight streets and right-angle intersections make a striking contrast to the curved, wandering lanes of the later medieval quarters or the streets of Rome itself. At the intersection of a city's two major thoroughfares was the *forum*, a zone combining elements of the Greek acropolis and agora. Here were not only the temples of worship, administrative buildings, and warehouses, but also the libraries, schools, and marketplaces that served the common people.

Clustered around the forum were the palaces of the power elite. For comfort, the West had nothing like these palaces and suburban villas of the wealthy until the twentieth century. They were sanitary, well heated in winter, and spacious—marvels of domestic architecture.

Despite the architectural accomplishments of the Roman engineers, the Roman masses lived in squalid conditions. While the homes of the rich spread horizontally across the landscape, the homes of the poor rose vertically. They lived in shoddy apartment houses, often four or five stories high, called *insula*. These tenements seem to be the first Western example of high-density dwellings. With this Roman "invention," two now common human urban types arrived on the scene—the land speculator and the slum landlord. The elaborate system of aqueducts and underground sewers did not extend to the poor. The result, probably a low in urban sanitation, was that the garbage of perhaps a million Romans was thrown into open pits around the city. Thus, even in its best days, Rome's population was continually at the mercy of plagues.

Rome's most important legacy probably was not its architectural engineering feats, although they remain landmarks in European cities to this day (see Figure 10.10), but rather that the Romans developed a lasting method for choosing the site of a city. They consistently chose sites with transportation in mind. That is, the Roman Empire was held together by a

FIGURE 10.10
The Colosseum in Rome was an important center of activity, where crowds of 60,000 were entertained by mock battles, circuses, gladiators fighting, and sports events. Most large Roman cities had similar structures. Today, most cities have stadiums and coliseums that continue the tradition of public spectacles started by the Romans.

complicated system of roads and highways, linking towns and cities. In choosing a site for a new settlement, access was a major consideration. In contrast, other cultures placed primary emphasis on defensive locations; hence their settlements might have been located in inaccessible places such as marshes or islands or on hilltops. The significance of Roman location was that even though urban life declined dramatically with the collapse of the empire, numerous old Roman sites — such as Paris, London, and Vienna — were refounded centuries later on the same spots because they offered unquestioned advantages of access to the surrounding countryside.

Urban Decline in the Dark Ages

With the decline of the Roman Empire (by A.D. 400), urban life also declined. Historians attribute the fall of Rome to internal decay, the invasion of the Germanic "barbarians," and other factors. Cities were sapped of their vitality. The highway system that linked them fell into disrepair, so that cities could no longer exchange goods and ideas. When Roman cities were invaded by wandering tribes, they could no longer count on outside military support as the administrative structure of the empire collapsed. Isolated from one another, they lost vital functions. Within 200 years, many of the cities founded by the Romans withered totally away. Yet there were exceptions. Cities of the Mediterranean survived because they established trade with the Byzantine civilization centered in Constantinople. After the eighth century, some cities — particularly those in Spain — were infused with new vigor by the Moorish Empire, which spread across the Mediterranean from northern Africa. But the cities of northern regions were unable to survive. Cities became small villages. Where thousands had formerly thrived, a few hundred eked out a subsistence living from agriculture.

The Medieval City

The medieval period, lasting roughly from A.D. 1000 to 1500, was a time of renewed urban expansion in Europe and a period that deeply influenced the future structure of urban life. Urban life spread beyond the borders of the former Roman Empire, into the north and east of Europe, as the Germanic and Slavic peoples expanded their empires. In only four centuries, 2500 new German "cities" were founded. Most cities of present-day Europe were founded during this period. While many were on old Roman sites, others were new.

The major functions of the medieval city are expressed in five symbols—the fortress, the charter, the wall, the market, and the cathedral. The fortress expresses the importance of defense. Usually the cities were clustered around a fortified place. The importance of this role is expressed today in many place-names. This is demonstrated by cities in Germanic lands ending in -burg, such as Salzburg or Würzburg; in France with -bourg, as in Strasbourg; and in English with -burgh, as in Edinburgh. Each suffix has the same meaning—a fortified castle. The terms burgher and bourgeoisie, which now refer to the middle class, originally referred to a citizen of the medieval city (see Figure 10.11).

The charter was a governmental decree from a regional power, usually a feudal lord, granting political autonomy to the town. This act had several important implications. It freed the population from feudal restrictions, made the city responsible for its own defense and government, and allowed it to coin money. Thus city life became even freer than life on rural feudal estates. These rights and responsibilities contributed to the development of urban social, economic, and intellectual life and, in turn, to the development of civilization.

The wall was important for defense, but it was more important as a symbol of the sharp distinction between country and city. Within the wall, most inhabitants were, by charter, free; outside, most were serfs. "City air sets a man free" went the medieval proverb. Indeed, even though the medieval city had feudal characteristics, it generally was a community of citizens able to move about with little restriction, free to buy and sell property and goods. A city of "free" citizens, not based on a vast pool of slave labor, was a first in the history of the Western city.

At the wall's gates the division between city residents and nonresidents was sharpest. Here, goods entering the city were inspected and taxed. Here, nonresidents were issued permits for entry and undesirables were excluded. And here, at sunset, the gates were closed, shutting out the

FIGURE 10.11
Rothenburg, West Germany, shown here, still typifies the West European medieval city. Houses are built of stone (or, in some cases, are half-timbered), with residences above street-level stores and shops, and are clustered together, with little open space in yards or gardens. This probably resulted from the fact that the city was enclosed by a defensive wall that restricted outward growth. Church towers rise above the city, reminding the population of the important role played by these religious institutions.

rural world until sunrise. Often nonresidents were required to leave the city at dusk and seek accommodations outside the wall. As a result, suburbs—called **faubourgs,** meaning "beyond the fortress"—sprang up. In time, these communities demanded to be included in the true city. If their petition was accepted, the walls would be expanded to encompass the former suburb. By this process, the medieval cities grew, much as modern cities annex their sprawling suburbs. Then, in the sixteenth century, the increasing use of gunpowder and the invention of accurate artillery made the building of elaborate permanent fortifications a necessity. The wall lost its "mobility." Even so, within the walls the medieval city was never a giant. At its widest point, it was probably no more than half a mile from the city center to the wall, easy walking distance even for citizens of a modern industrial city.

Another key zone was the marketplace. It symbolized the important role of the medieval city in economic activities (see box, "The Greatest City in the World: Hangchow"). The city depended on the countryside for its food and produce, which were traded in the market. The market also was a center for long-distance trade, which linked city to city. Textiles, salt, ore, and other raw materials were bought and sold in the marketplace. Usually the market "square" became the focus for guild houses and the residences of wealthy merchants, so that it was the heart of the commercial zone. One important aspect of the medieval market is still found in Europe. Even today, open-air markets are held at least one day a week, and many European housewives do their shopping there. In some cities, the strength of the market tradition has inhibited development of suburban supermar-

THE GREATEST CITY IN THE WORLD: HANGCHOW

The Chinese city Hangchow, wrote the Italian Marco Polo, "is the greatest city . . . in the world, where so many pleasures may be found that one fancies himself to be in Paradise." According to a contemporary Chinese account, in the markets of thirteenth-century Hangchow one could buy "beauty products (ointments and perfumes, eyebrow-black, false hair), pet cats and fish for feeding them with, . . . bath wraps, fishing tackle, . . . chessmen, oiled paper for windows, fumigating powder against mosquitoes," and other merchandise unobtainable elsewhere in China (or probably anywhere else on earth). In addition, one could visit any of 15 big specialized markets—including the principal pig market, which was right in the center of town—or the scores of smaller markets for products ranging from flowers and oranges to pearls and precious stones.

Indeed, to the European visitor, Hangchow was a wonder that his medieval city had not prepared him for. As French historian Jacques Gernet comments, "The largest city of Europe, with a population of several tens of thousands, were nothing but petty market towns in comparison with the 'provisional capital' of China." Its vast ramparts were pierced by five gateways for canals that carried boats loaded with products from all over the country. Its great thoroughfares (the largest 60 yards or 56 meters wide and 3 miles or 5 kilometers long) terminated at the ramparts in 13 monumental gates. It had a population of about 1 million people, which made it "the biggest urban concentration in the world at the time."

Visually, the city had a modern urban look. An unbroken line of dwellings stretched as far as the eye could see. As one of its inhabitants wrote, "The city of Hangchow is large . . . and overpopulated. The houses are high and built close to each other. Their beams touch and their porches are continuous. There is not an inch of unoccupied ground anywhere." Yet almost all the streets of Hangchow were paved, and the level of public cleanliness was probably higher than anywhere in the Western urban world before our own time. The authorities in Hangchow jealously guarded the purity of the water in its giant artificial lake. They realized something that nineteenth-century Europeans had not yet grasped: Polluted water leads to epidemics. "The townspeople who drink no other water but this," wrote a city official, "run the risk of epidemics [if it becomes impure]."

The population was so large (and space so tight) that it spilled beyond the ramparts into giant suburbs. It seems fitting to end this description of thirteenth-century Hangchow with the awestruck words of Oderic de Pordenone, another visitor from medieval Europe, on seeing these suburbs: "At each of [Hangchow's] gates . . . are cities larger than Venice or Padua might be, so that one will go about one of those suburbs for six or eight days and yet will seem to have travelled but a little way."

Adapted from Jacques Gernet, *Daily Life in China* (New York: Macmillan Publishing Company, 1962). Reprinted with permission of the publisher. Copyright © 1962 by George Allen & Unwin, Ltd.

kets. Residents seem to prefer the activity and human contact of a market in the city's heart to modern decentralized shopping facilities.

The medieval town's crowning glory was usually the cathedral, a dominating architectural symbol of the important role of the church. Often the cathedral and the marketplace were in close proximity, indicating close ties between religion and commerce. More important, the church was often the prevailing political force in medieval towns.

The morphology and landscape of the medieval city are extremely important concerns for contemporary urban life. For example, the streets were typically narrow wandering lanes, rarely more than 15 feet (4½ meters) wide. The narrowness of the streets in these medieval cores constrains twentieth-century automobile use. To illustrate, in 141 West German cities, 77 percent of the streets are too narrow for safe and efficient two-way traffic. Similar problems plague other cities, and as a result many towns, such as Vienna, Salzburg, and Munich, have excluded auto traffic from the old areas, turning them into pedestrian zones where cars may enter only during certain hours (see Figure 10.12).

Many central-city buildings are also remnants of this period. These structures were originally built three stories high, with the bottom floor reserved for work space and the upper floors for dwelling and storage. This is still a common pattern. Many European shop owners and artisans live above their workplaces. However, many of the medieval buildings are hardly adequate for twentieth-century use. They are cramped by modern standards—as anyone who has seen a medieval suit of armor knows, people were physically smaller then—and they lack adequate heating and plumbing. Of course physical deterioration is also a problem. These factors have turned some inner-city medieval quarters into modern low-rent districts. As a result, most are occupied by lower-income people who are often retired and on fixed pensions. A move to a modern apartment would be too expensive for these people, so they put up with the hardships of life in a fourteenth-century dwelling.

In summary, there are three important points about the role of the medieval period in the evolution of the Western city: (1) This was the period when most European cities were founded; (2) many of the traditions of Western urban life were begun then; and (3) the medieval landscape is still with us, giving a visible history of the city and physically constraining twentieth-century activities.

The Renaissance and Baroque Periods

During the Renaissance (1500–1600) and baroque (1600–1800) periods, the form and function of the European city changed significantly. Absolute monarchs arose to preside over a unified nation-state. The burghers, or rising middle class, of the cities slowly gave up their freedoms to join with the king in pursuit of economic gain. City size increased rapidly because the bureaucracies of regional power structures came to dominate cities and because trade patterns expanded with the beginnings of European imperial conquest. A new concern with city planning and military technology also acted to remold and constrain the physical form of the city (see Figure 10.13).

Cities and the surrounding countryside began to combine into nation-states, ruled by all-powerful monarchs. One city, the national capital, rose to prominence in most countries. Provincial cities were subjected to its tastes, and power was centralized in its precincts. The first office buildings, those structures that came to stretch from Washington, D.C., to

FIGURE 10.12
The typical narrow, winding street pattern of the medieval period still persists in Heidelberg, West Germany. Besides the pedestrian-scale inner city, we see other typical medieval features, such as residences located above street-level shops, churches, and, barely visible in the background, the hilltop fortress.

FIGURE 10.13
The townscape of Salzburg, Austria, illustrates two important periods of urban development. In the foreground is tightly compacted housing of the medieval period, while the middle ground is made up of churches, the cathedral, and the university of the Baroque period. In the background is the fortress, built in the medieval period and elaborated in the Baroque.

Moscow, were built to house a growing new government bureaucracy. Most important, the capital city was restructured to reflect the power of the central government and to ensure its control over the urban masses.

Hand in hand with these developments went a new interest in city planning. This concern grew from a revival of all things classical, including Greek and Roman urban planning; from a new philosophical emphasis on humankind's earthly home; and from new aesthetic concepts that gave urban planners a foundation to work from. Most of these planning measures were meant to benefit the privileged classes. Rulers considered the city a stage on which to act out their destinies, and if the city was a stage, it could be rearranged at will. Typical of the time was the infatuation with wide, grandiose boulevards. The rich could ride along them in carriages, and the army could march along them in an impressive display of power. Other features of the baroque city were large open squares, palaces, and public buildings. Statues were everywhere. This environment was strikingly different from the dark, closed world of the medieval quarters, where the middle classes still resided. The spacious new aristocratic sections often were created at the expense of the middle class, whose homes were demolished to make way for a new palace or boulevard.

Although the height of baroque planning was between 1600 and 1800, this autocratic spirit also carried into the nineteenth century, as is illustrated in Paris. There, Napoléon III had Baron Haussmann build a system of boulevards designed to control the populace. Cobblestone streets were carefully paved so that there would be no loose ammunition available for rioting Parisians. Streets were straightened and widened and cul-de-sacs were broken down to give the army—should the people arise—space to maneuver, with ordered sight lines for its artillery. Whole neighborhoods were torn down to build wide avenues. Thousands were displaced as their apartment buildings were demolished. They had to seek new shelter on their own, and many ended up in the congested working-class sections of east and north Paris. These areas are still overcrowded, and much of the blame can be assigned to the baroque planners.

In these developments, we can see the coming of the modern city. The masses of city dwellers were sacrificed to the traffic pattern. Neighborhoods were overwhelmed by the straight line. In our own times, the highway has replaced the avenue as the yardstick of the urban planner, but the results have been the same—the wholesale destruction of inner-city neighborhoods.

The new military technology aggravated the problems of congestion and high density within the city. Extensive urban fortifications were needed as a defense against artillery bombardment. These fortifications could not easily be extended outward to encompass new urban growth. Instead, new stories were added to medieval buildings. As a result, population densities increased within the walls, and urban overcrowding became a reality. The walls also threatened the independent financial status of the city. They were so expensive to erect that without outside aid, urban bankruptcy always remained a possibility. Moreover, the wall was no longer the simple dividing line between city and countryside that it had been in medieval times. The area outside the walls became a military no-man's-land, a dangerous space subject to artillery fire in time of war. People who settled there did so at their own risk, because the military reserved the right to torch all structures in time of war to deprive the enemy of shelter and cover. Figure 10.14 contrasts the morphology or physical form of typical medieval and baroque cities. In particular, note the differences in the street patterns and fortifications.

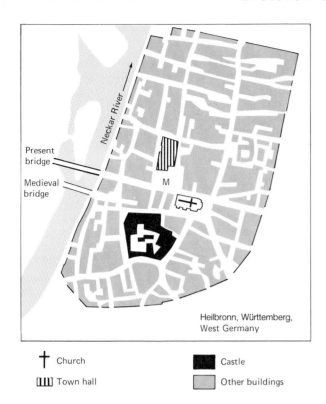

† Church

[III] Town hall

■ Castle

▨ Other buildings

□ River and water fortifications

M – Marketplace

Heilbronn, Württemberg, West Germany

Saarlouis in the Saarland, West Germany

Today, the Renaissance and baroque urban landscapes offer mixed blessings to the city dweller. The boulevards help traffic circulation in some cases and hinder it in others, depending on whether the boulevard system is linked together. Most boulevards were built as disjointed entities. The palaces and mansions of the period still dominate the central part of many cities. Most of these structures are now museums, government buildings, or banks and other financial institutions. The spacious gardens, meant for the private pleasure of aristocrats, are now usually open to the public and offer the inner-city resident much-appreciated open space. Figures 10.15 and 10.16 show typical modern-day use of the baroque landscape.

FIGURE 10.14
Contrasts in medieval and baroque city urban morphology can be seen in two West German cities. Heilbronn developed in medieval times around a castle-fortress. The church, town hall, marketplace, and fortress were clustered at the center of the town, surrounded by an irregular street pattern. Saarlouis was founded in 1681 by Louis XIV of France, and exhibits the typical Baroque concern with symmetry, boulevards, squares, and elaborate water fortifications.

FIGURE 10.15
The boulevard was a favorite of Baroque planners: a ceremonial street that often led to public buildings and monuments was lined with upper-income housing and trees, and offered public space for the wealthy. Unfortunately, these boulevards were often created at the expense of thousands of those less well off who were displaced as older housing was destroyed by the boulevard builders, as was the case in Paris, shown here. Has this happened in your city as freeways have been built?

FIGURE 10.16
An important part of the Baroque consciousness was expressed in the planned garden, as shown here in Versailles, France. Although gardens were originally the province of the aristocracy, today most of them are open to the public and serve as much-needed open space for urban populations.

Renaissance and baroque planning had a profound effect on many American cities, as well as European cities. For example, Washington, D.C., was originally designed by a French planner during the height of the baroque period. Although the original plan has been compromised somewhat, its intent is still visible in the wide boulevards, open spaces, public buildings, and monuments of the city. Other examples of the baroque spirit can be found in such cities as Philadelphia; Williamsburg, Virginia; and Columbia, South Carolina.

The Industrial City and Urbanization

The function, structure, and landscape of the Western city have changed dramatically since the industrial revolution. Furthermore, the industrial city has profoundly altered the fabric of society itself. It has given the world its first societies with urban majorities, where more people live in cities than in the countryside. All indications are that this trend will continue.

Up to the industrial period, the rate of urbanization in Western countries was relatively low. For example, in 1600, urban dwellers made up only 2 percent of the German, French, and English populations; the Netherlands and Italy were 13 percent urban dwellers. However, as millions of people migrated to the cities during the past 200 years, the rate of urbanization skyrocketed. By 1800, England was 20 percent urbanized, and it became the world's first urban society around 1870. By the 1890 census, 60 percent of its people lived in cities. The United States was 3 percent urbanized in 1800, 40 percent in 1900, 51 percent in 1920 (when it became an urban country), and now has about 75 percent of its population in towns and cities. The link between urbanization and industrialization is clear, because the United States industrialized later than England.

Western cities often grew too fast, without planning or guidelines, and at the expense of the working class (see box, "Living Conditions in the Industrial Age: London 1849"). The industrial revolution and the triumph of capitalism turned the city from a public institution into private property—spoils to be divided with an eye to maximum profits. New urban symbols—the factory, the railroad, and the slum—appeared with the emergence of the commercial city. The old marketplace was replaced by the merchants' exchange, the bank, and finally the stock market. Bisected by the railroad and captured by the land speculator, the city fragmented. Overall planning for the efficient use of land disappeared. Instead, a new philosophy emerged, **laissez-faire utilitarianism.** Lewis Mumford, in his book *The City in History,* defines this as a belief that divine providence ruled over economic activity and ensured the maximum public good through the unregulated efforts of every private, self-seeking individual.

One expression of this new philosophy was a changed attitude toward land and the buildings on that land. Once raw materials such as coal and iron ore could be brought to the city by rail, factories began to cluster together to share the benefits of **agglomeration**—that is, to share labor, transportation costs, and utility costs and to take advantage of financial institutions found in the city. Industry concentrated in the city itself, around labor, the commercial marketplace, and capital. Land use intensified drastically. In medieval Europe, land was leased for long periods (99 to 999 years) and was rarely sold. After the seventeenth century, land came to be treated as a commodity. With the increased competition for land in the industrial period, land transactions and speculation became an everyday part of the city. Land parcels became the property of the

---

LIVING CONDITIONS IN THE INDUSTRIAL AGE: LONDON 1849

Henry Mayhew was a journalist who spent part of his life investigating poverty, labor, and living conditions in nineteenth-century England. In *London Labour and the London Poor,* he has left us a classic account of life in industrial England. The summer of 1849, when Mayhew started his work, was a period of particular tension in England, because a cholera plague was sweeping the country. Within three months, 13,000 people were estimated to have died of the disease in London alone. Mayhew visited the cholera areas, which were mainly the districts where the laborers and unemployed poor lived. At the time, the way cholera spread was still being debated, but Mayhew's conclusions seem clear. "So well-known are the locations of fever and disease," he wrote, "that London would almost admit of being mapped out pathologically, and divided into its morbid districts and deadly cantons." Here is part of his account of his trip to one of the "deadly cantons":

We then journeyed on to London-street, down which the tidal ditch continues its course. In No. 1 of this street the cholera first appeared seventeen years ago, and spread up it with fearful virulence; but this year it appeared at the opposite end, and ran down it with like severity. As we passed along the reeking banks of the sewer the sun shone upon a narrow slip of the water. In the bright light it appeared the colour of strong green tea, and positively looked as solid as black marble in the shadow—indeed, it was more like watery mud than muddy water; and yet we were assured this was the only water the wretched inhabitants had to drink. As we gazed in horror at it, we saw drains and sewers emptying their filthy contents into it; we saw a whole tier of doorless privies in the open road, common to men and women, built over it; we heard bucket after bucket of filth splash into it, and the limbs of the vagrant boys bathing in it seemed by pure force of contrast, white as Parian marble. . . .

In this wretched place we were taken to a house where an infant lay dead of the cholera. We asked if they *really did* drink the water? The answer was, "They were obliged to drink the ditch, without they could beg a pailful or thieve a pailful of water." [It was not uncommon for the poor to go from house to house in wealthier sections begging for water.] But have you spoken to your landlord about having it laid on for you? "Yes sir; and he says he will do it, and do it, but we know him better than to believe him."

owner, who had no obligations toward society in deciding how to use them. The historic urban core was often destroyed, the older city replaced. The result was a chaotic mosaic of mixed land uses: factories directly next to housing; slum tenements next to public buildings; open spaces and parks violated by railroad tracks. A planned attempt to bring order to the city came only in the twentieth century with the concept of zoning. Yet even this idea was rooted in some of the same forces — profit, bigotry, and individualism — that had already made the industrial city unresponsive to the needs of most of its inhabitants (see box, "The Origins of Zoning in America: Race and Wealth").

Laissez-faire industrialism in the "age of invention" did surprisingly little for the human fodder that fueled its shops and plants. If the wholesale distribution of such utilities as gas and water is excluded, the industrial city made no improvements in human living standards beyond what had already been available in the seventeenth-century city. Moreover, the industrial city took environmental necessities from the new working class. In their slum dwellings, direct sunlight was seldom available, and open spaces were nonexistent (see Figure 10.17). In Liverpool, for instance, one-sixth of the population reportedly lived in "underground cellars." Vast tenement areas quickly grew to accommodate new migrants from the countryside. Large families commonly shared a single room. A study from the middle of the nineteenth century in Manchester, England, showed that there was but one toilet for every 212 people. Running water was usually available only on the ground floors of apartment buildings. Sometimes a whole neighborhood depended on a corner well and pump that already was polluted by the runoff from outhouses. Disease was pervasive, and mortality rates ran high. In 1893, the life expectancy of a male worker in Manchester was 28 years; his country cousin might live until 52. The death rate in New York City in 1880 was 25 per thousand, whereas it was half that in the rural counties of the state. The infant mortality rate per

THE ORIGINS OF ZONING IN AMERICA: RACE AND WEALTH

"The standard zoning ordinance of American cities was originally conceived from a union of two fears — fear of the Chinese and fear of skyscrapers. In California a wave of racial prejudice had swept over the state after Chinese settlers were imported to build the railroads and work in the mines [in the mid-nineteenth century]. Ingenious lawyers in San Francisco found that the old common law of nuisance could be applied for indirect discrimination against the Chinese in situations where the constitution of the state forbade direct discrimination. Chinese laundries of the 1880s had become social centers for Chinese servants who lived outside the Chinatown ghetto. To whites they represented only clusters of 'undesirables' in the residential areas where Chinese were living singly among them as house servants. By declaring the laundries nuisances and fire hazards, San Francisco hoped to exclude Chinese from most sections of the city. . . . Such nuisance-zone statutes spread down the Pacific coast. . . .

"[Meanwhile,] in New York [City] the Fifth Avenue Association, a group composed of men who owned or leased the city's most expensive retail land, demanded that the city protect their luxury blocks from encroachment by the new tall buildings of the garment district. . . . The Fifth Avenue Association feared that the ensuing decades would see the [skyscraper] lofts invading their best properties, bringing with them [lower-class] lunch-hour crowds and a blockade of wagons, trucks, and carts. In short, they feared that skyscraper lofts, low-paid help, and traffic congestion would drive their middle-class and wealthy customers from the Avenue."

The combination of West Coast racism plus the fears of wealthy New York merchants resulted in the New York Zoning Law of 1916, a prototype zoning statute for the nation. These were the roots of the first American attempts to deal coherently with urban growth. Not surprisingly, the zoning law was no sooner passed than it was seized on in the South and elsewhere "as a way to extend [the] laws and practices of racial segregation. . . . A land or structure limitation . . . became a financial, racial, and ethnic limitation by pricing certain groups out of particular suburbs. Italians were held at bay in Boston, Poles in Detroit, blacks in Chicago and St. Louis, Jews in New York."

Abridged and adapted from Sam Bass Warner, Jr., *Urban Wilderness* (New York: Harper & Row, 1972), pp. 28–32, 117–118. Copyright © 1972 by Sam Bass Warner, Jr.

FIGURE 10.17
This etching of Birmingham, England, gives us a sense of the nineteenth-century industrial city; factories and working-class housing are close together, and the only open space is provided by the cemetery in the foreground. Many North American cities developed with similar traits.

thousand live births rose from 180 in 1850 to 240 in 1870. Legislation correcting such ills came only in the latter part of the century, and only after the 1890 census did the mortality rates in the United States once again head downward.

But not all city dwellers had to live in the industrial landscape. New transportation modes—particularly the electric trolley, perfected in the 1880s—triggered a suburban explosion. The middle class left the central city in large numbers, now that they had a cheap and efficient means of travel, and they created a haven of large homes, spacious lots, and tree-lined streets on the outskirts of the city. The social differences between central city and suburbs became significant, because only the wealthy could afford suburban dwellings. The central city was left for the working class. The influx of European immigrants to American cities in the last decades of the nineteenth century coincided with the middle-class flight to the suburbs—and, in part, triggered it. Areas that had seen middle-class families move to the suburbs often saw large numbers of blue-collar migrants move into the city's old residential core. The middle-class houses were broken up into small apartments, so that where one family had lived previously, now five or six immigrant families resided (see box, "Reviving Old Neighborhoods: German Village, Columbus, Ohio").

Megalopolis

In the nineteenth century, cities grew at unprecedented rates because of the concentration of people and commerce. Movement away from the central city quickened in the last decades of the century. The inner city became increasingly dominated by commerce and the working class. By the turn of the century, the change in the industrial city was so apparent that H. G. Wells wrote:

> *Many of the railroad begotten "giant cities" will reach their maximum in the coming century and in all probability are destined to such a process of dissection and diffusion as to amount almost to obliteration. . . . These coming cities will not be, in the old sense, cities at all; they will present a new and entirely different phase of human distribution.*

REVIVING OLD NEIGHBORHOODS: GERMAN VILLAGE, COLUMBUS, OHIO

During the past decade, historic preservation has become a significant force in halting inner-city decay. Yet, as with all urban issues, preservation is deeply intertwined with complicated community issues, as is illustrated by this case study of a historic district in the center of Columbus, Ohio.

Settled by German immigrants between 1820 and 1860, the German Village population reached 10,000 in 1872 and manifested all the aspects of a typical nineteenth-century ethnic community. But by 1920, hastened in part by the anti-German feelings of World War I, both the quality of life and the ethnic nature of the Village had declined drastically. Physical deterioration of the small red-brick cottages was widespread; much of the land was zoned for commercial or industrial land use. By the mid-1950s, German Village exhibited the classic symptoms of urban blight: overcrowding, poor sanitary conditions, an excess of renter-occupied housing, and a low-income population. In 1956 the city of Columbus made plans for widespread redevelopment and clearance.

Talk of restoration as an alternative to renewal began and a few property owners renovated their buildings as an example. As a result of intensive promotional efforts, a German Village society was formed in 1960 and soon afterward the mayor established a commission to review building permits and recommend legislation needed to protect and restore the Village. Boundaries for a historic district were established the following year, and the area was rezoned from industrial to residential. Private investment increased as the threat of redevelopment ended. A "certificate of appropriateness" became a prerequisite to apply for a building permit, and a restoration manual was issued describing "appropriate" construction. Over 600 certificates had been issued in 1967.

The housing market changed drastically as well-off, well-educated young professionals moved in. Living in "the Village" gave identity in a sprawling city and today the area is one of the most prestigious districts in Columbus.

But many see German Village as a classic case of **gentrification**—the displacement of poor people by higher-income groups as older buildings are renovated. However, a survey by Ford and Fusch of low-income residents in surrounding neighborhoods found these people felt far more positively toward the German Village development than previously imagined. One of the major factors was that they felt German Village had been instrumental in changing the city's view of inner-city neighborhoods, which, not insignificantly, had led to more financial support for central-city areas. While it is true that low-income people may be forced from the core of a historic district, perhaps this dislocation is a small price to pay for increased stability in surrounding neighborhoods.

Adapted from Larry R. Ford, "Saving the Cities: Urban Preservation in America," *Focus,* 30:1 (September–October 1979).

Wells was right, because a new form of city has emerged in the twentieth century. It is the dispersed and decentralized city, brought about by new forms of transportation—the auto, truck, bus, airplane, and pipeline—and new methods of communication—radio, television, FAX, and airmail. With decentralization, instead of being concentrated in dense, compact areas, the new cities sprawl until they merge with their neighbors. One metropolitan area blends into another, until supercities are created that stretch for hundreds of miles.

The prototype of this new form is found on the eastern seaboard of the United States, stretching from Boston in the north to Washington, D.C., in the south. Some call it the supercity of Boswash. The geographer Jean Gottmann coined the term **megalopolis** to describe it. This term is now used worldwide in reference to giant metropolitan regions. Aside from Boswash, there are Chipitts, stretching from Chicago to Pittsburgh; Ciloubustonis, consisting of Cincinnati, Louisville, Columbus, Dayton, and Indianapolis; and San-San, the California supercity that someday may reach from San Diego to San Francisco. Canada's megalopolis, the Golden Horseshoe, wraps around the west end of Lake Ontario. In Europe, the Ruhr area in Germany, most of the Netherlands, the Midlands of England, and the Po Valley of northern Italy could qualify as megalopolises. Other highly industrialized, highly urbanized countries, such as Japan, have new supercities.

The characteristics that these urban regions share are high population densities, extending over hundreds of square miles or kilometers; concentrations of numerous older cities; transportation links formed by freeway, railroad, air routes, and rapid transit; and an extremely high proportion of the nation's wealth, commerce, and political power. As noted, the prototype is in the northeastern section of the United States, from New Hampshire to Virginia. Here, 20 percent of the American population lives on 2 percent of the land area, at a density of almost 600 persons per square mile (240 per square kilometer). No other state outside this area's core has a density higher than 300 per square mile (120 per square kilometer). The high level of urbanization in this area reflects the advantages of an early start. The area itself is not particularly well endowed with natural resources and from early times has specialized in trading, manufacturing, and services. As the resources of the interior were opened up to them, these cities grew until they formed what Jean Gottmann calls "the financial and managerial Main Street of the modern world."

The megalopolitan form has major drawbacks because problems come on a giant scale with such an immense concentration of people and activities. Common problems in these supercities are congestion, high land prices, overcrowding, financial insolvency, deteriorating inner cores, a poor and disenfranchised population in contrast to the affluent in the suburbs, and air and water pollution. Unfortunately, solutions to these problems will not soon be found, for another characteristic of megalopolitan areas is political fragmentation. Because most of the problems are regionwide, they go beyond the legal jurisdiction of the smaller towns and counties. Often they cross state borders. Solutions will come only with increased cooperation among all political units and the formation of regional agencies. Until then, the megalopolis will continue to grow, and its problems will increase.

Now that we have examined the evolution of the Western city, let us look at the development of non-Western cities.

The Landscape of Non-Western Cities

Most of the world's population lives in non-Western countries, and it is in these areas that we see the greatest potential for dramatic change in urban patterns. This change is mainly a function of high natural population growth coupled with enormous rates of migration from countryside to cities. Recent growth in these non-Western cities has been staggering. In 1950, only 4 of the 15 largest cities of the world were in non-Western countries; the latest census shows that most of the largest 20 cities are non-Western (see Table 10.1). Accompanying this rapid growth are serious economic, political, and social problems. In this section, we will examine these non-Western cities in order to gain better understanding of the urban landscape, processes, and problems.

But first, we must think about terminology. Up to now, we have simply differentiated between Western and non-Western cities. However, such a simplistic dichotomy has limitations because Western culture has profoundly influenced urban life throughout the world, first through colonialism and presently through capitalistic industrialism. Many African cities, for example, were founded as colonial outposts of the French or British empires. Their form and function articulate ties to Europe, and even through the period of independence, the Western influence remains strong; references to these cities as "non-Western" therefore involves some hesitation and qualification.

However, it would be equally wrong to overlook completely local cultural influences. Even though many of these cities have been strongly stamped by Western culture, they may not automatically follow the same developmental paths taken by Western cities. Local political, economic, and social forces—what we call the "cultural context"—affect these cities in ways vastly different from the Western experience. Therefore, even though non-Western cities may face some of the same problems as Western cities, such as traffic congestion, housing shortages, and inadequate public services, their solutions may differ considerably. In fact, these cultural influences are so strong that it is difficult to generalize about non-Western cities as a single category. More detailed studies use a finer cultural scale so that conclusions take into consideration these local and regional influences and explicate the similarities — and differences — between, say, West Africa cities and those of the north, or the contrasts between the cities of China and those of Southeast Asia. This is the task of the cultural geographer.

So the following is admittedly a broad-brush treatment of a complex topic. References listed at the end of the chapter will guide the student interested in learning more about this complicated theme.

Three Urban Models: Indigenous, Colonial, and Emerging Cities

The preceding section on the evolving landscape of Western cities was able to delimit specific evolutionary periods, such as medieval and industrial. This is more difficult to do with non-Western cities because local influences have been so important and city histories are so varied. Instead, we will generalize about non-Western cities by using three models representing idealized or hypothetical stages that a typical non-Western city might experience.

The first model is that of the **indigenous city,** referring to one created by purely local forces, removed, say, from the influences of the West. Examples would be early Islamic cities in Africa developed in the eleventh century, or the precolonial cities of Mexico and Central America.

The second model is that of the **colonial city.** This refers both to those cities founded by colonialism and to those precolonial or indigenous cities whose existing structure was deeply influenced by Western colonialism. Cities in this category are far more common and widespread than indigenous cities.

The third model is that of the **emerging city.** This is the city of the present — the urban settlements of those nations that we call "emerging," "Third World," or "less-developed countries."

Although each model will be discussed in turn, implying that cities have experienced each of the three stages, this might convey a faulty impression. Some cities in the world were untouched by historical European colonialism. Kabul, Afghanistan, is an example. On the other hand, there are also a few cities today that might still qualify as colonial cities, such as Hong Kong. And still other cities are products of only the last decades; that is, they have been developed to meet contemporary needs, so they have not been either indigenous or colonial cities. They are true "emerging" centers: Brasilia, the relatively new capital of Brazil, is an obvious example.

The Indigenous City

Indigenous cities developed without contact with Western influences. Most of them predate European colonialism; a very few, as mentioned earlier, may have been untouched by the landscape and structure of the later colonial period.

If we were to examine the worldwide distribution of precolonial indigenous cities, we would see urban centers in the New World restricted to

Mexico, Central America, and the Andean highlands. In Africa, there would be small cities in the west, a band of Islamic empires in the north, and some more small cities in the eastern highlands, again associated with Islamic empires. Most of the continent would be without citylike settlements until the European colonial period. Asia would have the largest number of indigenous cities, reaching from the Near East, across present-day Pakistan and India, to China and Japan. The least number of cities within the continent would be found in southwest Asia.

The landscape and structure of the indigenous city are very similar to those already described in the section on the Western medieval city. In fact, some would argue that cities could be generalized into a **preindustrial city** model, suggesting that cities in both Western and non-Western countries were essentially the same in form and function before the industrial period. The major proponent of this argument is the sociologist Gideon Sjoberg, who first formulated and presented generalizations on the preindustrial city. The fact that his terminology is not used as a major classification or stage in this text does not imply rejection of his concepts. Indeed, much information on both medieval and indigenous cities has been drawn from his works.

Let us examine some of the landscape characteristics of the indigenous city. Street patterns are narrow and winding, built for cart and food traffic, but also expressing the slow, unplanned development of the city through time. Land use is mixed, particularly when compared to the colonial and emerging city. Residences and workplaces generally occupy the same one- or two-story structures, often with the shop closest to the street and residences either in back rooms or on the upper floor.

Like the medieval city, there is some occupational and ethnic clustering. For example, all silver merchants might be found on one street, gold workers on another. But many activities do not have permanent locations. We call these **floating activities;** goods are sold from pushcarts plying the streets, or from a regular spot on the marketplace. (Another less fortunate floating activity is common in contemporary emerging cities: the thousands of homeless urban dwellers living on the streets. The street people in modern Calcutta are legendary.)

Ethnic groups may dominate certain areas. Sometimes this is formalized into "quarters" that form semiautonomous villages within the city. For example, it was common in an Islamic city to have one quarter for Jews, another for Christians. Foreign traders and merchants were also usually restricted to certain areas of the city.

The central part of the city is dominated by the marketplace or bazaar, religious buildings, monuments, government buildings, and the homes of the elite. As a consequence, the city demonstrates a much higher density in the center than on the outer edges. As one moves away from the core, one generally finds decreasing wealth and social status. The disadvantaged are found close to the city's edges. Groups of recent urban migrants might be found there, or neighborhoods of unassimilated ethnic groups.

This model of the city's social structure, with the elite at the center and the disadvantaged on the outskirts, is usually referred to as the preindustrial model, because it was first generalized and presented in Sjoberg's works. This scheme describes not only non-Western indigenous cities, but also North American urban social patterns up until the time that the railroad and electric streetcar facilitated suburbanization in the second half of the nineteenth century.

Few cities today would fit the indigenous model. Most were profoundly altered by European colonialism, so let us now turn to a model of colonial cities.

The Colonial City

A colonial city, by definition, is an administrative and commercial outpost for an external power. As we look at the landscape of the colonial city, we will see expressions of these two functions. Another important characteristic is the separation of colonial and indigenous activities.

When colonial cities were built near indigenous cities, the Europeans would either weld their city onto the existing settlement or, in a few extreme cases, build a totally new city nearby. The British built New Delhi across from original Delhi, and today the two still illustrate the contrast between colonial and indigenous cities. In old Delhi, gross density is 213 persons per acre; in New Delhi, 13 persons per acre. This contrast results from the very difficult urban morphology. New Delhi has wide streets, gardens surround the spacious houses of administrative staff, and parks and squares ring government buildings. All of this reminds one of the baroque period in Western urban development. And well it should. Remember that much European colonialism was coincidental with the baroque era; therefore, it is not surprising that colonial cities express these planning ideas. Old Delhi, on the other hand, is medieval in character, with narrow, winding streets, little open space, and cramped residences (see Figure 10.18).

As the baroque was used in Europe to express the power of the elite, so it was used in colonial cities. Grandiose boulevards were often cut through native residential quarters, large monumental buildings demonstrated the presence of the new power structure, and the Europeans were housed in elaborate residences that constantly reminded locals of their new masters (see Figure 10.19). Architecture and urban planning have long been used by power structures to reinforce their status and control.

When new colonial cities were founded, they were often based on a standardized plan. For example, all Spanish cities in the New World were constructed according to the Laws of the Indies, drafted in 1573. The document explicitly outlined how colonial cities were to be constructed. Law 114, quoted in Vance, *This Scene of Man*, stated:

> From the plaza the four principal streets are to diverge, one from the middle of each of its sides and two streets are to meet at each of its corners. The four corners of the plaza are to face the four (cardinal) points of the compass, because thus the streets diverging from the plaza will not be directly exposed to the four principal winds, which would cause much inconvenience.

The laws go on to say that this gridiron street plan should be centered on a church and central plaza and that all individual lots should be walled. Smaller plazas were to dot the neighborhoods, occupied by parish churches or monasteries, so that religious teaching would be evenly spread across the new city. In many ways, the formal guidelines for Spanish colonial cities duplicate the planning rules used by the Romans.

France and England also used the gridiron street plan as the basis for many of their colonial cities. It is found in former colonial towns across both Africa and Asia. Remember also that the United States spread colonial towns across the country during the westward movement. As in other colonial cities, the rectangular gridiron plan was often used, demonstrating that a simple, orderly street plan, fitting for the military, which so often initiated early colonial settlement, could be easily extended and was extremely effective for colonial town planning.

Another important characteristic of the colonial city is that the landscape expresses a greater degree of functional zonation than precolonial indigenous cities. Unlike the earlier city, colonial settlements would have distinct districts dominated by one particular land use. A commercial

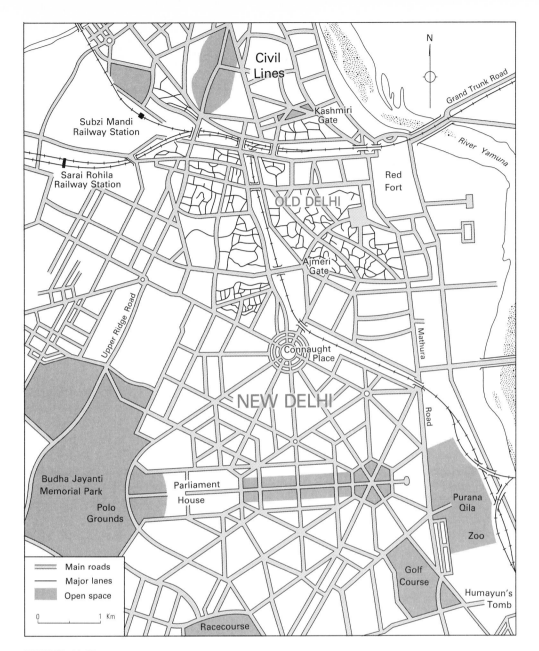

FIGURE 10.18
This map of Delhi, India, shows the contrast between the morphology and landscape of the indigenous city, Delhi, and the British colonial addition, New Delhi. Note the straight, symmetrical ceremonial boulevards and open space in the colonial city, expressions of Baroque planning in the colonial age; then compare that with the morphology of Old Delhi. (After David Drakalis-Smith, *The Third World City*, London: Methuen, 1987, p. 20, with modifications.)

district would have warehouses, docks, and small factories; the administrative section would have government buildings, the governor's mansion, banks, insurance firms, and monuments. Very often a retail district would grow close to the colonial residential area, complete with shops and stores. This would be quite different from the mosaic of land uses found in the indigenous city, where the marketplace, the carts, and the dispersed houses of the merchants served local retail needs.

In summation, several themes make up the colonial city model. First, if a colonial city was built close to an existing city, the two would be very different in form and function. This difference is not just physical; the

FIGURE 10.19
Monuments, parks, and palaces—
often designed by European
planners—are found in many former
colonial cities, such as La Paz, Bolivia,
and contrast with the densely
populated residential areas that
surround the central city.

cities would be socially separate as well. Colonialism, after all, is by definition a power structure controlling another culture, so this class distinction
pervades all aspects of the city. An extreme contemporary example might
be Cape Town, South Africa, which, through the policy of apartheid,
continues a colonial tradition. Second, colonial cities were often built to a
standardized plan and frequently used the gridiron street pattern. Last, the
colonial city demonstrated much more functional zonation than did indigenous cities. This resulted both from the administrative and commercial
goals of the city and from the social distance between native and colonial
cultures.

The Emerging City

With the end of colonialism and the movement toward political and economic independence, non-Western countries entered a period of rapid,
sometimes tumultuous change, and cities have often been the focal point
of change. Millions of people have migrated to cities in search of a better
life. Economic activities clustered in and around cities have often changed
their orientation from external to local markets. As well, political and
social unrest has been centered in the cities. So the emerging city model is a
fluid one; it is still in the process of forming, and the end results cannot be
predicted accurately.

Some scholars think that non-Western cities will duplicate the
changes experienced by Western cities as the latter underwent industrialization. Though there are similarities, the differences are much greater.
William Hance has written on the differences between contemporary
African urbanization and that experienced earlier in Europe, and most of
his conclusions can be extended beyond Africa to include emerging cities
in Asia and Latin America.

First, Hance notes that population growth is more rapid in African
cities than it was in Europe. This results not only from a high natural
increase, but mainly from an extremely high rate of migration to the cities.
And although the people flock to the cities in search of jobs, Hance points
out that there is less of a correlation between economic growth and urbanization than there was in Europe. Cities increase in size not because there
are jobs to lure workers, but rather because conditions in the countryside
are so bad. People leave in hopes that urban life will offer a slight improve-

ment. This results in high urban unemployment. Often 25 percent of the labor force is without work. In Europe during the nineteen century, workers could migrate to the New World to find work or land. No such safety valve exists today in the emerging countries; the city is the last hope.

Hance goes on to point out that emerging cities have weaker ties with their domestic hinterlands than did European cities. They are dependent on the outside world for raw materials. This means that the local countryside is excluded from the kind of development that could offer employment to rural populations. A vicious circle must be broken: People will leave the countryside for cities until jobs are available; yet it will be difficult to develop rural employment as long as economic activities continue to cluster around cities.

The combination of high numbers of immigrants coupled with widespread unemployment leads to overwhelming pressure for low-rent housing. Governments have rarely been able to meet these needs through housing projects, so one of the most common folk solutions has been construction of illegal housing or squatter settlements. In Lima, Peru, the **barriadas** house fully a quarter of the urban population; in Caracas, Venezuela, about 35 percent. Similar figures are found in emerging cities in Africa and Asia (see Figure 10.20).

FIGURE 10.20
Migration to cities has been so rapid that often illegal squatter settlements have been the only solution to housing problems. The top photograph is from the Persian Gulf, the bottom from Manila.

These squatter settlements usually begin as collections of crude shacks constructed from scrap materials, and gradually they become increasingly elaborate and permanent. Paths and walkways link houses, vegetable gardens spring up, and often water and electricity are bootlegged into the area so that a common tap or outlet serves a number of houses. At later stages, economic activities such as handicrafts or small-scale artisan activities take place in the squatter settlements.

Governments treat squatter settlements in various ways. Some bulldoze them down periodically, not simply because they are illegal, but also to discourage migration to the city. Their reasoning is that if squatter settlements are destroyed, fewer migrants will come to the city, knowing that any housing solution they find will only be temporary. On the other hand, some city governments turn their backs on the squatter settlements, viewing them as satisfactory solutions to the problem of low-cost urban housing. Zambia has what is called a "site and service" scheme where a settlement is laid out and prospective residents are given about $50 in order to buy basic materials needed for a crude house. Usually this includes concrete for the floor and a corrugated iron roof. After that, the occupants are on their own. The government knows that housing will be improved as the dweller finds work and has a regular paycheck.

Regardless of official policy, be it to destroy or condone, squatter settlements are an important part of the emerging city landscape. They occupy vacant land both on the outskirts and in the city center; downtown parks are often covered by squatters' houses. More frequently they spread over formerly unwanted land, such as steep slopes and river banks.

The outskirts of the growing cities manifest activities other than squatter settlement. This is often where new economic activities are located, so a landscape of factories and warehouses is common. When government money is available, large high-rise apartment houses are built nearby for workers. There are also signs of middle-class suburbs growing up, which is a function both of jobs in the outlying area for white-collar workers and of "push" forces driving the affluent out of the city center. Traffic noise, air pollution, and congestion make the central city less desirable than before, so those who can afford new housing often relocate. This is obviously similar to the suburbanization of North American cities in the last decades.

Another parallel with the American experience is that the large central-city dwellings vacated by the middle class are often subdivided into smaller apartments for lower-income families. Chronic housing shortages are relieved with high-rise buildings. Where previously one middle-class family lived, the dwelling may now house six or seven families. Whether this structural change will eventually lead to the social disparity and ghetto pattern characteristic of North American cities remains to be seen (see Figure 10.21).

It must be emphasized once again that it is dangerous to assume that non-Western emerging cities will replicate the Western urban experience. Although we have noted some similarities with North American cities, the differences must also be kept in mind. As an example, many emerging cities will not undergo the same evolution of transportation systems found in Europe or America. They may evolve directly from foot and cart traffic systems to autos and trucks, skipping the electric streetcar and railroad period so important in molding the Western urban pattern.

Let us also appreciate how different national policies may affect emerging cities. China, for example, has been one of the few countries to contain urban growth. In 1963, China's leaders decided to stabilize the urban population. By requiring young people to locate in the countryside,

FIGURE 10.21
The landscape of Ibadan, Nigeria, contrasts high-rise office buildings, which are contemporary variants of colonial monuments, with middle-class housing in the foreground. Note also the high amount of pedestrian traffic along the street.

they created massive changes in the population distribution. It is estimated that by 1973, some 25 million people were permanently resettled in rural villages. This kind of planning can be effected only with a strong autocratic government; yet we must remember that many of the emerging countries are experimenting with socialistic or communistic institutions, and therefore they may have the power to force strong policies on their populations. Decisions regarding the nature and location of economic activities can also dramatically affect a country's urban pattern.

So, in conclusion, the future of the emerging city is unclear (see box, "Calcutta: Portrait of an Emerging City"). Certainly the urban problems faced in non-Western countries are some of the most important facing the

CALCUTTA: PORTRAIT OF AN EMERGING CITY

Although all cities are unique in their own ways, Calcutta illustrates many of the problems faced by hundreds of emerging cities around the globe. Thousands of migrants pour into Calcutta each day, leading to overburdened services, scarce housing, and high unemployment—in short, an overcrowded city.

Calcutta is one of India's largest urban centers, with almost 13 million people crowded into an area that sees population densities climbing to 177,000 people per square mile in the city center. This is three times the density of central Manhattan. United Nations estimates forecast that population will easily top 16 million by 2000.

Three-quarters of the city's population live in crowded tenements or *bustees.* These are mostly built of unbaked brick and lack adequate sanitary services. It is reported that generally 30 persons must share one water tap and that 20 share a single latrine. More than half of the city's families share one-room accommodations. But they are the lucky ones: Estimates on the homeless run well over half a million. These are the people who sleep on the city streets.

A recent study shows that 30 percent of the working force is unemployed. However, we can assume the figure to be much higher among the young, new migrants, and certain ethnic groups. As in many Third-World cities, scarce eco-

nomic resources aggravate tensions among ethnic groups, with the result that certain groups monopolize specific sectors of the economy, while others do without. For example, lower-class Muslims have been traditionally employed in soap and leather industries, work regarded by Hindus as polluting and therefore reserved for low-status people. Ethnic and kinship networks are tightly drawn so that group members share resources and exclude nonmembers. This is a typical pattern found in other emerging cities where the social fabric is made up of different ethnic and social groups.

What about Calcutta's future? It is difficult to be optimistic. City planners, working hand in hand with technical agencies of the United Nations, have constructed a two-tier plan. The first phase focuses on the immediate needs of the city, such as sewage, water, housing, and transportation. The second phase looks at the future of the city in the broad context of its hinterland and assumes responsibility for planning over a resource region encompassing some 500,000 square miles of the country. Ideally, such broad planning can control the flow of migrants by offering economic alternatives to city life. If Calcutta's growth can be slowed, then perhaps the city's services can be expanded to serve the existing population.

world. Some solutions may come from the Western experience; most will not. They will be local solutions, designed to meet specific needs; and therefore it is faulty to assume that non-Western cities will follow Western urban patterns. A totally new and unique urban landscape may emerge.

THE ECOLOGY OF URBAN LOCATION

The theme of cultural ecology is useful in understanding locational aspects of cities by examining how cultures have used and modified the physical environment during urban development. We should appreciate that interaction with the environment is a two-way street: Humans may respond to different physical characteristics; yet, equally, humans may modify those characteristics to suit their needs.

Site and Situation

There are two components of urban location, **site** and **situation.** Site refers to the local setting of a city, whereas the situation is the regional setting. Both are dynamic and change through time. This can result from changes in the physical environment, or, more commonly, from changes in cultural capabilities. To illustrate, think of San Francisco. The original site of the Mexican settlement was on a shallow cove on the eastern or inland shore of a peninsula. The importance of its situation, or regional location, was that it drew upon waterborne traffic coming across the bay from other, smaller settlements. Hence the town could act as a trans-shipment point. Hides and tallow were loaded onto deep-water clippers plying world trade routes.

But, through time, both the site and the situation of the city have changed. During the gold rush period, the small cove was filled to create flatland for warehouses and to facilitate extending wharves into deeper bay waters. The filled-in cove is now occupied by the heart of the central business district (see Figure 10.22). The geographic situation has also changed as patterns of trade and transportation technology have evolved. The original transbay situation was quickly replaced during the gold rush by a new role, supplying the mines and settlements of the gold country. Access to the two major rivers leading to the mines, plus continued ties to ocean trade routes, were the important components of the city's situation.

However, San Francisco's situation has changed dramatically in the last decade, for it is no longer the major port of the bay. The change in technology to containerized cargo was adopted more quickly by Oakland, the rival city on the opposite side of the bay, resulting in San Francisco's decline as a port city. One of the reasons that Oakland was able to adjust to containerized cargo was that it filled in huge tracts of shallow baylands, creating a massive area for the loading, unloading, and storage of cargo containers. This once again illustrates how urban sites and situations change.

Certain attributes of the physical environment have been important in the location of cities. Those cities with distinct functions, such as defense, have sought out specific physical characteristics in their original sitings. The locations of many contemporary cities can be partially explained by decisions made in the past that capitalized on advantages of certain sites. Trade and defense needs have been particularly important. The following classifications examine some of the different location possibilities.

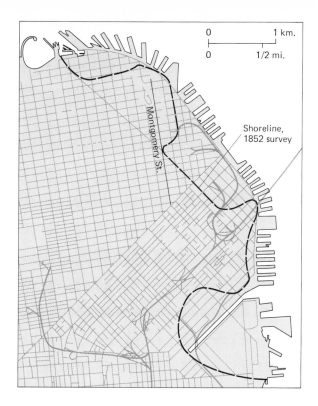

FIGURE 10.22
This map shows how San Francisco's site has been changed by human activity. During the late 1850s, shallow coves were filled, providing easier access to deeper bay waters and, as well, providing flat land near the waterfront for warehouses and industry.

Defensive Sites

There are many types of **defensive sites** (some are diagrammed in Figure 10.23). The river-meander site, with the city located inside a loop where the stream turns back on itself, leaves only a narrow neck of land unprotected by the waters. Cities as widely separated as Bern, Switzerland, and New Orleans are situated inside river meanders. Indeed, the nickname for New Orleans, Crescent City, refers to the curve of the Mississippi River.

Even more advantageous was the river-island site, which often combined a natural moat with an easier river crossing, because the stream was split into two parts. Paris began as a small settlement on the Ile de la Cité, or "island of the city," in the middle of the Seine River. Similarly, Montreal is situated on a large island surrounded by the St. Lawrence River and other water channels. Islands lying off the seashore or in lakes offered similar defensive advantages. Mexico City began as an Indian settlement on a lake island. Venice is the classic example of a city built on an offshore island in the sea. New York City began as a small Dutch town on Manhattan Island.

Peninsular sites were almost as advantageous as island sites, because they offered natural water defenses on all but one side (see Figure 10.24). Boston was founded on a peninsula for this reason, and a wooden palisade wall was built across the neck of the peninsula. Bombay is also built on a peninsula.

Danger of attack from the sea often prompted sheltered-harbor urban sites, where a narrow entrance to the harbor could easily be defended. Examples of sheltered-harbor cities include Rio de Janeiro, Tokyo, and San Francisco.

High points also were sought out. These are often referred to as acropolis sites, meaning "high city." Originally the city developed around

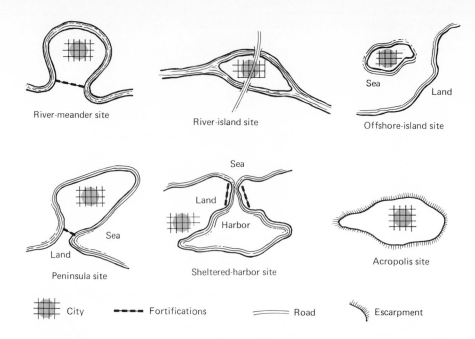

FIGURE 10.23
Defensive city sites make use of the natural protection offered by physical features such as water or hills.

FIGURE 10.24
A classic defensive site is Mont St. Michel, France, a small town clustered around a medieval abbey, which was originally separated from the mainland during high tides. A causeway now connects the island to shore, allowing armies of tourists to easily penetrate the town's defenses.

a fortification on the high ground and then spilled out over the surrounding lowland. Athens is the prototype of acropolis sites, but many other cities are similarly situated. Québec and Salzburg, Austria, occupy similar sites.

Trade-Route Sites

In many other instances, defense was not a primary consideration; instead, urban sites were frequently chosen because they lay at important points on trade routes. Here, too, the influence of the physical environment can be detected.

Especially common types of **trade-route sites** (see Figure 10.25) are bridge-point and river-ford sites, places where major land routes could easily cross over rivers. Typically, these were sites where streams were narrow and shallow with firm banks. Occasionally, such cities even bear in their names the evidence of their sites, as in Frankfurt ("ford of the Franks"), West Germany, and Oxford, England. The site for London was chosen because it is the lowest point on the Thames River where a bridge—the famous London Bridge—could easily be built to serve a trade route running inland from Dover on the sea.

Confluence sites are also common. They allow cities to be situated at the point where two navigable streams flow together. Pittsburgh, at the confluence of the Allegheny and Monongahela rivers, is a fine example (see Figure 10.26). So is St. Louis, near the confluence of the Mississippi and Missouri rivers. Head-of-navigation sites, where navigable water

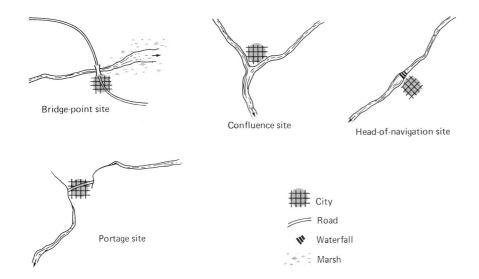

Bridge-point site

Confluence site

Head-of-navigation site

Portage site

City
Road
Waterfall
Marsh

FIGURE 10.25
Trade-route city sites are at strategic positions along transportation arteries. Is your city located on a trade-route site?

FIGURE 10.26
Pittsburgh's Golden Triangle, at the confluence of the Allegheny and Monongahela rivers, is a classic example of how an early fortified site has evolved into a commercial center.

WALTER CHRISTALLER
1893–1969

Although Christaller had a precocious beginning as a geographer, spending hours with an atlas as a youth, it was not until he was nearly 40 years of age that he began his study of geography at a university. Christaller became a "maverick" among the geographers in Germany. His ideas on models were too radical for most of his fellow geographers in Nazi Germany to accept. As a result, he was never offered a professorship.

Christaller's classic work, *The Central Places of Southern Germany,* was written in the early 1930s as his doctoral dissertation in geography. In it, he proposed the central-place theory described in this chapter. Acceptance of central-place theory came belatedly, among American and Swedish geographers. Only in his later years did Christaller receive the honors due him.

routes begin, are even more common, because goods must be transshipped at such points. Minneapolis-St. Paul, at the falls of the Mississippi River, occupies a head-of-navigation site. Basel, Switzerland, is on the Rhine River, and Louisville, Kentucky, is at the rapids of the Ohio River. Portage sites are very similar. Here, goods were portaged from one river to another. Moscow is on a portage site where the headwaters of streams flowing north and south are close. Similarly, Chicago is near a short portage between the Great Lakes and the Mississippi River drainage basin.

In these ways and others, an urban site can be influenced by the physical environment. There are, of course, many nonenvironmental factors that can influence the choice of site.

At this point, it is useful to distinguish between the specific urban site and the general location or **spatial distribution** of cities. Spacing or location implies a broader, overall view of the pattern of urban centers. Site is frequently influenced by the environment, but general location or spacing of cities is less likely to be. The theme of cultural integration will allow us to gain a better idea of why cities are spaced as they are.

■ CULTURAL INTEGRATION IN URBAN GEOGRAPHY

In recent decades, urban geographers have paid considerable attention to the distribution or spacing of towns and cities in order to determine some of the economic and political factors that influence the pattern of cities. In doing so, they have created a number of models that collectively make up "central-place" theory. These models represent examples of cultural integration.

Most urban centers are engaged mainly in the third, or **tertiary,** stage of production. Primary economic activities are extractive, such as agriculture, forestry, and mining. Construction and manufacturing are secondary activities, those that change the form of products. The tertiary activities of urban centers are to facilitate the distribution of manufactured goods to the people living in their vicinity and to provide political, medical, educational, transportational, communicational, and other services for consumers. Towns and cities that support such tertiary activities are called **central places.**

In the early 1930s, the German geographer Walter Christaller (see biographical sketch) first formulated **central-place theory,** a series of models designed to explain the spatial distribution of tertiary urban centers. Crucial to his theory is the fact that different goods and services vary both in **range,** the average maximum distance people will travel to purchase a good or service, and in **threshold,** the size of the population required to make provision of the service economically feasible. For example, it requires a larger number of people to support a hospital, university, or department store than to support a gasoline station, post office, or grocery store. Similarly, consumers are willing to travel a greater distance to consult a heart specialist, record a land title, or purchase an automobile than to buy a loaf of bread, mail a letter, or visit a movie theater. People will normally spend as little time and effort as possible in making use of services and purchasing goods in a central place, but they will be obliged to travel farther to use those services that require a large market.

Because the range of central goods and services varies, tertiary centers are arranged in an orderly hierarchy. Some central places are small and offer a limited variety of services and goods; others are large and offer an abundance. At the top of this hierarchy are regional metropolises, huge urban centers that offer all services associated with central places and that have very large tributary trade areas, or **hinterlands.** At the opposite extreme are small market villages and roadside hamlets, which may contain nothing more than a post office, service station, or café. Between these two extremes are central places of various degrees of importance. Each higher rank of central place provides all the goods and services available at lower-ranked centers, plus one or more additional goods and services. Central places of lower rank greatly outnumber the few at the higher levels of the hierarchy. One regional metropolis may contain thousands of smaller central places in its tributary market area (see Figure 10.27). The size of the market area is determined by the distance range of the goods and services it offers.

With this hierarchy as a background, Christaller then tried to measure the influence of three forces in determining the spacing and distribution of tertiary centers. He accomplished this by creating models. His first model measured the influence of market and range of goods on the spacing of cities. To simplify the model, he assumed that the terrain, soils, and other environmental factors were uniform; that transportation was universally available; and that all regions would be supplied with goods and services from the minimum number of central places. In such a model, the shape of the market area was circular, encompassing the range of goods and services, with the city at the center of the circle. However, when central places of the same rank in the hierarchy were nearby, the circle became a hexagon (see Figure 10.28a). If market and range of goods were the only causal forces, the distribution of tertiary towns and cities would produce a pattern of nested hexagons, each with a central place at its center.

Then Christaller created a second model. In this model, he tried to measure the influence of transportation on the spacing of central places. He no longer assumed that transportation was universally and equally available in the hinterland. Instead, Christaller assumed that as many demands for transport as possible would be met with the minimum expenditure for construction and maintenance of transportation facilities. As many high-ranking central places as possible would thus be on straight-line routes between important central places (see Figure 10.28b). The transportation factor causes a rather different pattern of central places from the pattern caused by the market factor. This is because direct routes between adjacent regional metropolises do not pass through central places of the next lowest rank. As a result, these second-rank central places are "pulled" from the points of the hexagonal market area to the midpoints in

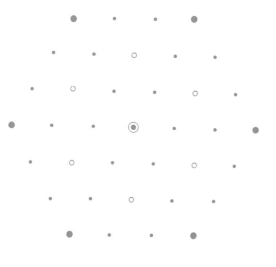

⊙ First order place
 (regional metropolis)

● Second order place

○ Third order place

• Fourth order place

FIGURE 10.27
Christaller's hierarchy of central places shows the orderly arrangement of towns of different sizes. This model is an idealized presentation of places performing central functions. For each large central place many smaller central places are located within the larger place's hinterland.

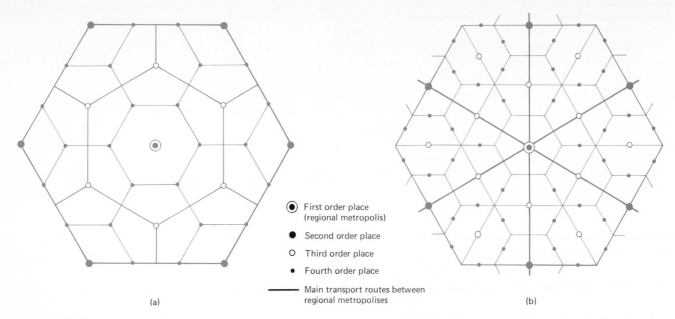

- ◉ First order place
  (regional metropolis)
- ● Second order place
- ○ Third order place
- • Fourth order place
- —— Main transport routes between
  regional metropolises

(a)　　　　　　　　　　　　　　　　　　　　(b)

FIGURE 10.28a
The influence of market area on Christaller's arrangement of central places is shown in this diagram. If marketing were the only factor controlling the distribution of central places, this diagram would represent the arrangement of towns and cities. Why, in this model, would hexagons be the shape to appear as opposed to a square, circle, or some other shape? (After Christaller, p. 66, by permission of the publisher.)

FIGURE 10.28b
This diagram shows the distribution of central places according to Christaller's model. If the availability of transportation is the determining factor in the location of central places, their distribution will be different than if marketing were the determining factor. Note that the second-order central places are pulled away from the apexes of the hexagon and become located on the main transport routes between regional metropolises. (After Christaller.)

order to be on the straight-line routes between adjacent regional metropolises.

Christaller felt that the market factor would be the greater force in rural countries, where goods were seldom shipped throughout a region, and that the transportation factor would be stronger in densely settled industrialized countries, where there were greater numbers of central places and more demand for long-distance transportation.

A third model devised by Christaller measured a type of political influence, the effect of political borders on the distribution of central places. Christaller recognized that political boundaries, especially within independent countries, would tend to follow the hexagonal market-area limits of each central place that was a political center. He also recognized that such borders tend to separate people and retard the movement of goods and services. Such borders necessarily cut through the market areas of many central places below the rank of regional metropolis. Central places in such border regions lose rank and size because their market areas are politically cut in two. Border towns are thus "stunted," and important central places are pushed away from the border, which distorts the hexagonal pattern.

Obviously, many other forces influence the spatial distribution of central places. Market area, transportation, and political borders are but three of them. For example, in all three of these models, it is assumed that the physical environment is uniform and, additionally, that people are evenly distributed. Of course neither of these is true, yet certain assumptions are necessary to construct a theoretical model that integrates different components of culture.

■ CONCLUSION

The first cities arose as new technologies, particularly the domestication of plants and animals, facilitated the concentration of people, wealth, and power in a few specific places. This transformation from village to city life was accompanied by new social organizations, a greater division of labor, and increased social stratification. These characteristics still distinguish rural and urban life-styles. Although the first cities developed in specific places, urban life has now been diffused worldwide and all suggestions are that our planet will become increasingly urban in the decades to come. Therefore an understanding of the city and its problems is crucial to understanding the human mosaic.

Many of the problems now plaguing the Western city are expressions of uncorrected ills from the past. Circulation and housing problems in Europe, for example, must often be understood in the context of the medieval urban landscape, for even though the landscape evolved 500 years ago, the narrow streets and cramped housing conditions of that period still pervade the typical European central city. Understanding the past is definitely necessary for correcting current problems.

This is also true of the North American city. Much of our urban environment evolved only during the last 200 years, when industrialism was the dominant force; yet this has in no way given us immunity from urban ills. Problems of land use, housing, transportation, and social services often trace their origins from the past century, and it is wise to attempt to understand the forces responsible for their use before we attempt solutions that may be unrelated to the true causes.

On the other hand, the problems of non-Western cities are mainly products of this century. Cities are bursting at the seams as thousands of new migrants crowd into urban places each day, seeking houses, jobs, and schooling. But jobs are scarce, so unemployment rates are often over 25 percent. Housing is also a problem. In some cities, over a third of the population lives in hastily constructed squatter settlements.

The future of the world's cities is unsure. Strong governmental planning measures might alleviate many of the present-day ills, but the long-range hope lies with decreased population growth and increased economic opportunities. Whether this is possible under contemporary conditions remains to be seen.

This chapter has examined the city at a broad-brush, worldwide level; the next chapter will look at cultural patterns within the city.

Suggested Readings

John Agnew, John Mercer, and David Sopher. *The City in Cultural Context.* Boston: Allen & Unwin, 1984.

Robert Aiken. "Squatters and Squatter Settlements in Kuala Lumpur," *Geographical Review,* 71 (1981), 460–471.

Abdullah Al-Mamum Khan. "Rural-Urban Migration and Urbanization in Bangladesh," *Geographical Review,* 72 (1982), 379–394.

Brian J. Berry. *The Human Consequences of Urbanization.* New York: St. Martin's Press, 1973.

Brian Berry. *Comparative Urbanization.* New York: St. Martin's Press, 1982.

Stanley Brunn and Jack Williams. *Cities of the World: World Regional Urban Development.* New York: Harper & Row, 1983.

R. J. Buswell and M. Barke. "200 Years of Change in a 900-year old City," *Geographical Magazine,* 2 (1980), 81–83ff.

Walter Christaller. *The Central Places of Southern Germany,* trans. C. W. Baskin. Englewood Cliffs, N.J.: Prentice-Hall, 1966.

Terry Christensen. *Neighborhood Survival: The Struggle for Covent Garden.* London: Prism, 1979.

Michael P. Conzen. "American Cities in Profound Transition," *Journal of Geography,* 82 (1983), 94–101.

Ben Crow and Allan Thomas. *Third World Atlas.* London: Open University Press, 1984.

Kingsley Davis. *Cities: Their Origin, Growth and Human Impact.* San Francisco: Freeman, 1973.

Thomas Detwyler and Melvin Marcus (eds.). *Urbanization and Environment: The Physical Geography of the City.* Belmont, Calif.: Duxbury Press, 1972.

Robert Dickinson. *The West European City.* London: Routledge & Kegan Paul, 1961.

A. A. Dike. "Environmental Problems in Third-World Cities: A Nigerian Example," *Current Anthropology,* 26 (1985), 501–505.

David Drakakis-Smith. *The Third World City.* London: Methuen, 1987.

James T. Fawcett, Siew-Ean Khoo, and Peter Smith. *Women in the Cities of Asia: Migration and Urban Adaptation.* Boulder, Colo.: Westview Press, 1984.

Arthur Field (ed.). *City and Country in the Third World.* Cambridge, Mass.: Schenkman, 1970.

Larry Ford. "Saving the Cities: Urban Preservation in America," *Focus,* 30 (1979).

Alan Gilbert and Joseph Gugler. *Cities, Poverty, and Development: Urbanization in the Third World.* Oxford: Oxford University Press, 1983.

Jean Gottmann. *Megalopolis.* Cambridge, Mass.: M.I.T. Press, 1961.

Jean Gottmann. "Third-World Cities in Perspective," *Area,* 15 (1983), 311–313.

Ernst Griffin and Larry Ford. "A Model of Latin American Urban Structure," *Geographical Review,* 70 (1980), 397–422.

Erwin A. Gutkind. *International History of City Development.* 4 vols. New York: Free Press, 1964–1969.

William Hance. *Population, Migration, and Urbanization in Africa.* New York: Columbia University Press, 1970.

Jorge Hardoy (ed.). *Urbanization in Latin America: Approaches and Issues.* Garden City, N.Y.: Doubleday (Anchor Books), 1975.

J. E. Hardoy and D. Satterthwaite. "Third-World Cities and the Environment of Poverty," *Geoforum,* 15 (1984), 307–333.

Spencer Havlik. "Third-World Cities at Risk: Building for Calamity," *Environment,* 28 (1986), 6ff.

J. V. Henderson. "Urbanization in a Developing Country: City Size and Population Composition," *Journal of Development Economics,* 22 (1986), 269–293.

Ruth Hottes. "Walter Christaller," *Annals of the Association of American Geographers,* 73 (1983), 51–54.

R. J. Johnston. *The American Urban System: A Geographical Perspective.* London: Longman, 1982.

J. A. Kahimbaara. "The Population Density Gradient and the Spatial Structure of a Third-World City: Nairobi, A Case Study," *Urban Studies,* 23 (1986), 307–322.

Nathan Keyfitz. "Do Cities Grow by Natural Increase or by Migration," *Geographical Analysis,* 2 (1980), 142–156.

Arnold S. Linsky. "Some Generalizations Concerning Primate Cities," *Annals of the Association of American Geographers,* 55 (1965), 506–513.

William J. Lloyd. "Understanding Late Nineteenth-Century Cities," *Geographical Review,* 71 (1981), 460–471.

Stella Lowder. *The Geography of Third-World Cities.* Totowa, N.J.: Rowman and Littlefield, 1986.

Laurence Ma and E. W. Hanten (eds.). *Urban Development in Modern China.* Boulder, Colo.: Westview Press, 1981.

L. D. McCann. *A Geography of Canada: Heartland and Hinterland.* Englewood Cliffs, N.J.: Prentice-Hall, 1982.

William Mangin. "Squatter Settlements," *Scientific American* (1967), 21–29.

Lewis Mumford. *The City in History.* New York: Harcourt Brace Jovanovich, 1961.

Michael Pacione (ed.). *Problems and Planning in Third World Cities.* London: Croom Helm, 1981.

John Pfeiffer. *The Emergence of Society.* New York: McGraw-Hill, 1977.

Henri Pirenne. *Medieval Cities.* Garden City, N.Y.: Doubleday (Anchor Books), 1956.

Charles Redman. *The Rise of Civilization.* San Francisco: Freeman, 1978.

D. A. Rondinelli. "Towns and Small Cities in Developing Countries," *Geographical Review,* 73 (1983), 379–395.

Lester Rowntree. "Creating a Sense of Place," *Journal of Urban History,* 8 (1981), 61–76.

Lester Rowntree and Margaret Conkey. "Symbolism and the Cultural Landscape," *Annals of the Association of American Geographers,* 70 (1980), 459–474.

Howard Saalman. *Medieval Cities.* New York: Braziller, 1968.

Christopher L. Salter. "The Paradox of the City," *Journal of Cultural Geography,* 1 (1981), 98–105.

D. Simon. "Third-World Colonial Cities in Context: Conceptual and Theoretical Approaches with Particular Interest to Africa," *Progress in Human Geography,* 8 (1984), 493–514.

Gideon Sjoberg. *The Preindustrial City.* New York: Free Press, 1960.

James E. Vance, Jr. *This Scene of Man: The Role and Structure of the City in the Geography of Western Civilization.* New York: Harper & Row, 1977.

Sam Bass Warner, Jr. *The Urban Wilderness: A History of the American City.* New York: Harper & Row, 1972.

11

The Urban Mosaic

URBAN CULTURE REGIONS

    Social Areas
    Neighborhoods

CULTURAL DIFFUSION IN THE CITY

    Centralization
    Decentralization
    The Costs of Decentralization

THE CULTURAL ECOLOGY OF THE CITY

    The Urban Ecosystem
    The Urban Geologic Environment
    Urban Weather and Climate
    Urban Hydrology
    Urban Vegetation

CULTURAL INTEGRATION AND MODELS OF THE CITY

    Concentric Zone Model
    Sector Model
    Multiple Nuclei Model
    Latin American Model

URBAN LANDSCAPES

    Themes in Townscape Study
    Components of the Landscape

CONCLUSION

Picking out patterns in your own city is, in some ways, a difficult matter. As you walk or drive through your city, its intricacy may dazzle, and its form may sometimes seem puzzlingly chaotic. It is often hard to imagine why city functions are where they are, why people cluster where they do. Why does one block have high-income housing and another, slum tenements? Why is an office building so near the airport? Why is the black ghetto next to the central business district? Why does the highway run through one neighborhood and around another? Why does the subway system connect the suburbs to the downtown area but provide no transportation to and from inner-city neighborhoods? And just when you think you are beginning to understand some patterns in your city, you note that those patterns are swiftly changing. The house you grew up in is now part of the business district. The row of houses across the street from your old grade school has been replaced by a bowling alley, laundromat, high-rise office building, or perhaps a giant parking lot. The central city that you roamed as a child looks dead. A suburban shopping center thrives on what was once farmland.

    Chapter 10 focused on cities as points in geographic space. The goal of this chapter is geographically quite different. We will try to orient ourselves within cities to gain some perspective on the patterns in them. In other terms, the two chapters differ in scale. The earlier chapter let us see cities from afar, as small dots diffusing across space and interacting with one another and with their environment. In this chapter, we will study the city as if we were walking its streets.

Our tour guides in this close-up view of the city will be five familiar themes of cultural geography. Through culture region, we will examine spatial differences within cities. Cultural diffusion will show how these internal and regional differences develop. Cultural ecology will permit us to see the role of the physical environment within the structure of the city. And through cultural integration, we will see what a finely woven fabric the city really is. Of course, the visual impact of these elements is revealed in the urban landscape, a "townscape" perceived in different ways by different people.

URBAN CULTURE REGIONS

Like society, the city is composed of many different groups; consequently, the theme of culture regions can be applied to those parts of the city where people live who share similar traits, such as values, income, language, religion, or race. Most city dwellers are intuitively aware of these urban culture regions. Visual clues — size and condition of housing, dress styles, or kinds of cars on a street — help categorize some areas as high-income, others as slums, some as Polish neighborhoods, others as Asian.

As we look at these urban regions, several questions concern the cultural geographer: How does one differentiate between ethnic and social areas, why do people of similar social traits cluster together, what subtle patterns might be found within these areas, and how does one delimit different kinds of urban districts?

Social Areas

To begin answering these questions, we should try to distinguish between **social culture regions** and **ethnic culture regions.** Although the distinction between the two may seem contrived, there is some usefulness in thinking about the differences that, often as not, are more a function of the researcher's emphases and interests than of the communities themselves. In studies that centralize the notion of social area, the emphasis is usually on socioeconomic traits, such as income, education, age, and family structure, while researchers use the notion of ethnic area to foreground traits of ethnicity, such as language, migration history, shared genetic traits, and so on. Obviously the two concepts overlap because there can be social regions within ethnic areas and vice versa. Let us also remember that some researchers choose to look at both social and ethnic regions as functions of the political and economic forces underlying and reinforcing residential segregation and discrimination. (More information on ethnic areas is found in Chapter 9.)

One way to define social areas is to isolate one social trait and plot its distribution within the city. The United States census is a common source of such information because the districts used to count population, called **census tracts,** are small enough to allow the subtle texture of social areas to show. For example, Figure 11.1 shows the rough distribution of income in Berkeley, California. Census tracts with similar average incomes have been lumped together, showing areas of high, middle, and low income. These areas, in a crude way, correspond to the social stratification of the

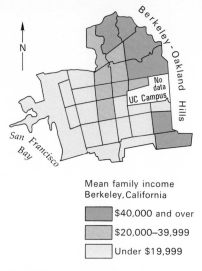

Mean family income
Berkeley, California

▓ $40,000 and over

▒ $20,000–39,999

□ Under $19,999

FIGURE 11.1
The map shows the high- and low-income areas of Berkeley based on the median family income for each census tract at the last census (1980). Although the figures are outdated, the point remains that income can be mapped as cultural regions. The areas of highest income are located in the Berkeley-Oakland hills, whereas the areas of lowest income are either directly adjacent to the UC campus on the south or in the flatlands on the west, where low-income housing is mixed with industrial and commercial uses. Students and ethnic minorities dominate the low-income areas and compete for the limited stock of low-rent housing in the city. The upper-income areas are predominantly white families living in better housing.

city. High-income areas are mostly in the hilly area to the east, where whites dominate. Lower-income areas are on the flatlands, closer to the bayfront industrial areas, and are made up of students and minorities. Similar mapping could be done with other social traits taken from the census, such as age, education, or percentage of families below poverty level. A visual field check is often a simple first step in mapping social areas (see Figures 11.2 and 11.3).

Another approach is to correlate various social indicators. For example, politicians have long known that districts with certain demographic characteristics (such as age, income, and occupation) tend to vote certain ways. There might be a correlation between, say, Democratic voting and Catholic working-class neighborhoods. What politicians know from experience, urban analysts try to formalize through statistical studies. They look at the degree of correlation among factors such as income, occupation, age, and ethnicity, and then their results can be translated into a pattern of multiple-factor urban social areas.

Neighborhoods

Social areas are not merely statistical definitions. They are also areas of shared values and attitudes, of interaction and communication. The concept of a **neighborhood** is often used to describe small social areas where people with shared values and concerns interact on a daily basis. For example, if we consider only census figures, we might find that parents between 30 and 45 years of age, with two or three children, and earning between $30,000 and $50,000 a year cover a fairly wide area in any given city. Yet, from our own observations, we know intuitively that this broad social area is probably composed of smaller units of social interaction where people link a sense of community to a specific locale.

A conventional sociological explanation for neighborhoods is that people of similar values cluster together to reduce social conflict; that is, where there is a social consensus regarding such mundane issues as home maintenance, child rearing, everyday behavior, and public order, there is little need to worry about these matters on a day-to-day basis. People who deviate from this consensus will face social coercion that could force them to seek residence elsewhere, thus preserving the values of the neighborhood. Because this definition of neighborhood emphasizes people of like mind and background choosing to live together, it celebrates the social homogeneity or sameness of small spatial communities.

But we increasingly find neighborhoods with far more heterogeneity than would be allowed by this traditional definition. Consequently, the current conceptualization of neighborhoods is more flexible and embraces traditional components of locality, such as geographic territoriality, political outlook and efficacy, or shared economic characteristics, but emphasizes the perceptual consensus that comes from both insiders and outsiders agreeing that a certain area or district constitutes a "neighborhood." For example, a neighborhood might contain a good deal of ethnic and social diversity, yet might also think of itself as a social community sharing similar political concerns, hold neighborhood meetings to address these problems, and achieve recognition with city hall as a legitimate group with political standing. Often this sense of neighborhood develops only when a community coalesces around a specific political issue, and this cohesion may actually erode or wane as the issue passes. Indeed, contemporary urban politics are characteristically caught up in this ever-changing network of neighborhood interest groups.

FIGURE 11.2
One of the most pressing problems facing the United States is reversing the continued decay of inner cities. This is the South Bronx.

FIGURE 11.3
Social areas within the city can be delimited by certain traits taken from the census, such as income, education, or family size. How would the social characteristics of this neighborhood in Palm Beach, Florida, differ from those in Figure 11.2?

The emphasis, then, is sensitive to residents constructing a sense of community and of place based on diverse criteria, independent of outsider definitions. The sociologist Herbert Gans learned that residents and city hall often have conflicting definitions of neighborhoods that aggravate political tensions. By all external sociological criteria, Boston's West End was a neighborhood; when Gans consulted the residents, however, he found they did not think of the West End as a single neighborhood, but instead broke it up into many subareas. Ironically, only with the threat of "redevelopment" did the residents come together and act as a single entity (see box, "Boston's West End and Urban Renewal").

In summary, the neighborhood concept is central to the cultural geography of cities because it recognizes the sentiment and attachment between people and places, and, furthermore, this becomes the basis for ongoing social and political action. More on this matter is found at the end of this chapter, where we discuss urban cultural landscapes. But we must also appreciate that many — if not most — contemporary urbanites do not share this sense of neighborhood; they live in perceptually undifferentiated residential areas.

■ CULTURAL DIFFUSION IN THE CITY

The patterns of activities we see in the city result from thousands of individual decisions made regarding location. Where should we locate our store, in the central city or in the suburbs? Where should we live, downtown or outside the city? The end result of such decisions might be expansion at the city's edge or the relocation of activities from one part of the city to another. The cultural geographer looks at such decisions in terms of expansion and relocation diffusion.

BOSTON'S WEST END AND URBAN RENEWAL

The West End, an aging Boston neighborhood dominated by Italians, was seen by outsiders as a slum. Planners and government officials viewed it as an eyesore contaminating elegant, upper-class Beacon Hill and the downtown shopping area. "Real estate men," according to sociologist Herbert Gans, "had long felt that the area was 'ripe' for higher — and more profitable — uses." In the late 1950s, the West End was slated for "urban redevelopment." This meant that the neighborhood's old, low-rent structures would be torn down and a new neighborhood of luxury apartment houses would be built — not, of course, for the West Enders, who would be "relocated" elsewhere.

Planners felt that, in addition to rebuilding the central city, they would be doing a favor to the West Enders by moving them out of a human cesspool. Unfortunately, the West Enders failed to agree. The vast majority of them had no desire to leave their "slum," which they saw as an attractive low-rent community. The day after the government gave the go-ahead signal for redevelopment, one young Italian told Gans: "I wish the world would end tonight . . . I wish they'd tear the whole damn town down, damn scab town . . . I'm going to be lost without the West End. Where the hell can I go?" A typical West Ender comment was: "It isn't right to scatter the community to all four winds. It pulls the heart out of a guy to lose all his friends."

To the West Enders, according to Gans, "The idea that the city could clear the West End, and then turn the land over to a private builder for luxury apartments seemed unbelievable." The average West Ender thought: "The whole thing is a steal, taking the area away from the people, and giving it to some guys who had paid off everyone else. . . . It is just someone making money at our expense."

In fact, the West Enders were not far wrong in defining the social injustice done to them. The financial effort expended on their needs (including relocation) amounted to about 1 percent of the clearance and rebuilding cost for the whole neighborhood. Yet, as Gans points out, "The real cost of relocation . . . was very much higher, and was paid in various ways by the people who had to move. In short, the redevelopment of the West End was economically feasible only because of the hidden subsidies which the residents provided — involuntarily, of course. . . ."

"I was told," Gans adds, "that before the West End was totally cleared — and even afterwards — West Enders would come back on weekends to walk through the old neighborhood and the rubble-strewn streets."

Adapted from Herbert J. Gans. *The Urban Villages.* Copyright © 1962 by The Free Press of Glencoe, Illinois, a Division of The Macmillan Company.

To understand the role of diffusion, let us divide the city into two major areas — the inner city and the outer city. Those diffusion forces that result in residences, stores, and factories locating in the inner or central city are **centralizing forces.** Those that result in activities locating outside the central city are called **decentralizing forces.** The pattern of homes, neighborhoods, offices, shops, and factories in the city results from the constant interplay of these two forces.

Centralization

We can best examine centralization by breaking it into two categories: economic and social advantages.

Economic Advantages. An important economic advantage to central-city location has always been accessibility. For example, imagine that a department store seeks a new location. Its success depends on whether customers can reach the store easily. If its potential market area is viewed as a full circle, then naturally the best location is in the center. There, customers from all parts of the city can gain access with equal ease. Before the automobile, a central-city location was particularly necessary because public transportation — such as the streetcar — was usually focused there. A central location is also important to those who must deliver their goods to customers because it provides equal transportation time and costs to all the customers. Bakeries and dairies usually were located as close as possible to the center of the city so that their daily deliveries would be most efficient.

Location near regional transportation facilities is another aspect of accessibility. Many a North American city grew up with the railroad at its center. Hence, any activity that needed access to the railroad had to locate in the central city. In St. Louis, Chicago, Minneapolis-St. Paul, Buffalo, and other urban areas, giant wholesale and retail manufacturing districts grew up around railroad districts. Thus they became "freight-yard and terminal cities" for the produce of the nation. Today, although many of these areas have been abandoned by their original occupants, a walk by the railroad tracks will give the most casual pedestrian a view of the modern "ruins" of the railroad city.

Another major economic advantage of the inner city is agglomeration, or clustering, which results in mutual benefits for businesses. For example, retail stores locate near one another to take advantage of the pedestrian traffic each generates. A large department store generates a good deal of foot traffic, so that any nearby store will also benefit. A number of cities around the world, including Atlanta, Pittsburgh, Montreal, and Munich, have actually closed specific downtown areas to motorized traffic, thereby creating pedestrian malls for downtown strollers and shoppers, hoping to create a pleasant environment that will attract more foot traffic.

Historically, offices have clustered together in the central city because of their need for communication. Remember, the telephone was invented only in 1875. Before that, messengers hand-carried the work of banks, insurance firms, lawyers, and many other services. Clustering was essential for rapid communication. Even today, there is a distinct tendency for office buildings to cluster, because face-to-face communication is still important for the business community. In addition, central offices take advantage of the complicated support system that grows up in a central city and aids everyday efficiency. Printers, bars, restaurants, travel agents, office suppliers, and others must be in easy reach.

Social Advantages.   Three social factors have traditionally reinforced central-city location: historical momentum, prestige, and the need to locate near work. The strength of historical momentum should not be underestimated. Many activities remain in the central city simply because they began there long ago. For example, the financial district in San Francisco is located mainly on Montgomery Street. This street originally lay along the waterfront, and San Francisco's first financial institutions were established there in the gold rush of 1849 because it was the center of commercial action. Goods were shipped from there to the Mother Lode region by river barge, and gold was brought down by packet. In later years, however, land filling extended the shoreline (see Figure 10.20). Today, the financial district is several blocks from the bay; consequently the district that began at wharfhead remained at its original location, even though other activity moved with the changing shoreline.

The prestige associated with the downtown area is also a strong centralizing force. For some activities, it is still necessary to have a central-city address. Think how important it is for some advertising firms to be on New York's Madison Avenue or for a stockbroker to be on Wall Street. This extends to many activities in cities of all sizes. The "downtown lawyer" and the "uptown banker" are examples. Residences have often been located in the central city because of the prestige associated with it. Most cities have remnants of high-income neighborhoods close to the downtown area. Although this trend has weakened in North America — downtown areas have become more congested and noisy, and transportation has encouraged suburban residences — it still is important elsewhere. London and Paris have very prestigious neighborhoods directly in the downtown area. The same is true for Latin American cities, where the power elite have traditionally lived in the city center.

Probably the strongest social force for centralization has been the desire to live near one's employment. Until the development of the electric trolley in the 1880s, there was little alternative for most urban dwellers but to walk to work. This meant that most people had to live near the central city, because most employment was there. Upper-income people had their carriages and cabs, but others had nothing. In his book, *Topophilia,* Yi-Fu Tuan notes that in early Victorian London, "Pedestrians rather than carriages dominated the street scene. Clerks, tradesmen, and workers thronged the sidewalks on their way to and from work in central London. Some 100,000 people a day, for example, walked over the toll-free London Bridge across the Thames, and about 75,000 over the toll-free Blackfriars Bridge."

The "horsecar," which came along in the 1850s, somewhat reduced central-city residential congestion. It was essentially a bus drawn along tracks by horses, and it traveled about 4 miles (6.5 kilometers) in three-quarters of an hour. However, only with the trolley — which covered 6 to 8 miles (9.5 to 13 kilometers), with stops, in one-half hour — did the middle class begin its exodus from the inner city. This electric-powered streetcar, first introduced in Richmond, Virginia, in the late 1880s, may have been an early factor in the declining prestige of the downtown area (see Figure 11.4). According to Sam Bass Warner, Jr., the electric streetcar's major failing "was its grinding gears and pounding steel wheels. . . . By raising the sound levels of urban streets to intolerable heights the streetcars drove the rich from their customary conspicuous locations on the city's main thoroughfares. Quiet isolation became a fundamental amenity in wealthy neighborhoods and the goal of middle-class homeowners."

The working poor had no possibility of escaping the noise. They accepted as well the elevated train whose tracks passed over (and through)

NORTH FROM 13TH & BROADWAY, OAKLAND.

FIGURE 11.4
The photograph of Oakland in 1916 shows the important role played by the electric streetcar in urban development. The straight avenues radiate out from the downtown and were planned to facilitate subdivision along streetcar lines. Residents could then use the streetcar for access to work and shopping opportunities in the central city while living in a less congested suburban environment.

their neighborhoods, creating a sunless world below. These poor, who still walked to work, were left in inner-city residences. Their residences were often the oldest in the city and consequently the most deteriorated and the cheapest to be found. Thus, as the middle class moved out to the "streetcar suburbs" on the edges of the city, the low-income workers increasingly dominated the inner city. Here began the clear-cut separation of rich and poor that we still see in urban areas today. In North American cities, this exodus of the middle class coincided with a period of great flow of European and Asian workers. Many inner-city areas became the ethnic neighborhoods that were discussed in Chapter 9.

Decentralization

Decentralizing forces encourage relocation diffusion, such as the movement of a shop or residence from the downtown to the suburbs. Decentralizing forces also promote expansion diffusion, such as the location of a new shop in the suburbs. The forces behind decentralization fall into the same two general categories (economic and social) that were used to explain centralization. Now, however, everything is reversed. People and businesses are moving from the city instead of into it (Figure 11.5).

Economic Advantages. Changes in accessibility have been a major reason for decentralization. The department store that originally located in the central city may now find that its customers have moved to the suburbs. They no longer shop downtown. As a result, the department store may move to a suburban shopping center. The same process also occurs among industries such as food-processing plants. They must move away to minimize transportation costs. The activities that were located downtown because of the railroad may now find trucking more effective. They relocate closer to a freeway system that skirts the downtown area. And many offices now locate near airports so that their executives and salespeople can fly in and out more easily.

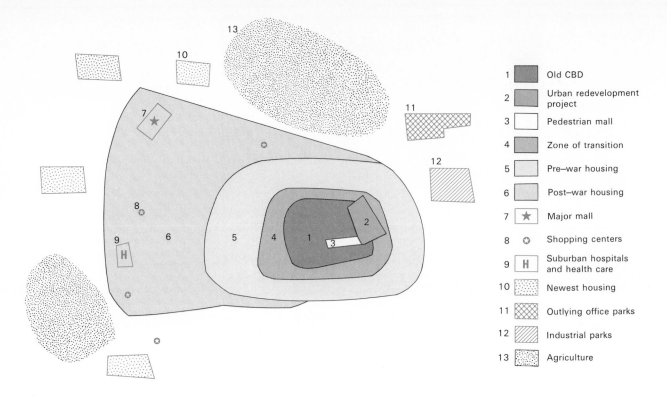

1		Old CBD
2		Urban redevelopment project
3		Pedestrian mall
4		Zone of transition
5		Pre–war housing
6		Post–war housing
7	★	Major mall
8	✿	Shopping centers
9	H	Suburban hospitals and health care
10		Newest housing
11		Outlying office parks
12		Industrial parks
13		Agriculture

FIGURE 11.5
This scheme for a hypothetical decentralized city depicts the various functional regions that might be found in a contemporary urban area. While the old CBD struggles (vacant stores and upper floors), newer activities locate either in the Urban Redevelopment Project (offices, convention center, hotel) or in outlying office parks, malls, or shopping centers; however, some new specialty shops might be found around the new downtown pedestrian mall. New industry locates in suburban industrial parks that, along with outlying office areas, form major destinations for daily lateral commuting.

Although agglomeration once served as a centralizing force, its former benefits have now become liabilities in many downtown areas. These disadvantages involve such things as increased rents as a result of the high demand for space; congestion in the support system, which means delays in getting supplies or standing in endless lines for lunches; and traffic congestion, which makes delivery to market time-consuming and costly. Some downtown areas are so congested that traffic moves more slowly today than it did at the turn of the century. Traffic studies of midtown New York City show that the average automobile moves at a snail's pace of 6 miles (9.5 kilometers) per hour. According to a 1907 study, horse-drawn vehicles moved through the same area at an average speed of 11.5 miles (18.5 kilometers) per hour, almost twice as fast.

Employees, experiencing high rents, traffic jams, and other inconveniences of central-city living, demand higher wages as compensation. This adds to the cost of doing business in the central city, and many firms choose to leave rather than bear such additional costs. As a result, many firms have left New York City. Most have chosen to locate in smaller suburbs removed from Manhattan. They claim that it costs less to locate there and that their employees are happier and more productive because they do not have to put up with the turmoil of city life.

There can also be benefits of clustering in new suburban locations, such as in industrial parks, where the costs of utilities and transportation links are shared by all the occupants. Similar benefits can come from residential agglomeration. Suburban real estate developments take advantage of clustering by sharing costs of schools, parks, road improvements, and utilities. New residents much prefer moving into a new development when they know that a full range of services is available nearby. Then they will not have to drive miles to find, say, the nearest hardware store. It is to the developer's advantage to encourage construction of nearby shopping centers.

Social Advantages.   A number of social factors reinforce decentralization, such as loss of downtown prestige, sentiment attached to the suburbs, and new employment patterns and transportation systems.

The downtown area might once have lured people and businesses into the central city because it was a prestigious location. But once it begins to decay, once shops close and office space goes begging, there may be a certain stigma attached to it. This may drive residents and commercial activities away. Investors will not sink money in a downtown area that they think has no chance of recovery, and shoppers will not venture downtown when streets are filled with vacant stores, transients, pawnshops, and secondhand stores. One of the persistent problems faced by cities is how to reverse this image of the downtown area so that people will once again consider it the focus of the city. Chambers of commerce spend millions of dollars each year putting out literature that tries to create a new image of the central city.

Sentiment and prestige attached to the suburbs are significant decentralizing forces. There has been a long-standing preference in the United States and Canada for the single-family dwelling and large lot. These have been most readily obtained where land values are lower, away from the city center. And because the suburbs were originally dominated by upper-income people, socially mobile families have considered a move in that direction a step upward.

The need to be near one's workplace has historically been a great centralizing force, but it can also be a very strong decentralizing force. At first the suburbs were "bedroom communities," from which people commuted to their jobs in the downtown area. This is no longer the case. In most metropolitan areas, most jobs are not in the central city but in outlying districts. Now people work in suburban industrial parks, manufacturing plants, office buildings, and shopping centers. Thus a typical journey to work involves **lateral commuting**—that is, travel from one suburb to another. As a result, most people who live away from the city center actually live closer to their workplaces. A testimony to this is a freeway system at rush hour; traffic is usually heavy in all directions, not just to and from the city center. A recent study by Muller shows that commuting from New England suburbs to central cities accounts for only 3 percent of daily traffic, whereas 61 percent involves lateral commuting.

The Costs of Decentralization

Unfortunately, decentralization has taken its toll. Many of the urban problems now burdening North American cities are direct products of the rapid decentralization that has taken place in the last 30 years (see box, "Trends and Themes for the Urban Geography of the 1990s"). These problems plague both inner cities and suburbs.

Vacant storefronts, empty offices, and deserted factories testify to the movement of commercial functions from central cities to suburbs. Retail sales in North American central cities have steadily declined, losing business to suburban shopping centers. Industries have relocated in spacious suburban industrial parks where taxes are lower, land costs cheaper, and transportation connections better. Even offices are finding advantages to suburban location. Like industry, offices capitalize on lower costs and easier access to new transportation networks.

What are cities doing to reverse this trend? Many cities have mounted special campaigns to combat central-city desertion. They offer tax incentives to those who stay or wish to locate in the downtown, and permits for

TRENDS AND THEMES FOR THE URBAN GEOGRAPHY OF THE 1990s

As this book goes to press late in the 1980s, there are several trends and themes pertinent to North American cities that, seeming significant for the 1990s, deserve monitoring. What follows is hardly a comprehensive list, but, instead, mentions several interesting topics that could significantly alter the structure of cities.

Continued Suburbanization and Counterurbanization

The 1960 census showed that the United States population was divided fairly equally among three categories: central cities, suburbs, and nonmetropolitan areas. But this had changed dramatically by the 1980 census, when fully 60 percent of the population lived in suburbs. What will the 1990 census show? All expectations are that a still larger percentage of the population will be in the suburbs, but of increasing interest is the phenomenon known as **counterurbanization.**

This term refers to the fact that some parts of North American nonmetropolitan areas, which are defined as small towns and rural areas removed from urban agglomerations, are growing faster than the traditional census-defined metropolitan centers. Taken to the extreme, the term suggests that more people are leaving cities than are moving in— hence the "counter-city" effect. Yet these people remain linked to cities in numerous ways. What is behind this? Several factors should be considered.

First, because of high housing prices in urban and suburban areas, many people are finding affordable housing in small towns and rural areas some distance from traditional metropolitan centers. However, this does not suggest a "return-to-the-farm" pattern. On the contrary, these counterurbanites are tied as ever to city jobs and services and have simply extended their commutes beyond what the census defines as the suburbs. Because most of these people commute by car, fluctuations in gasoline prices might profoundly affect this trend. Second, this pattern indicates further decentralization of jobs from the central city, either to the suburbs, or, in some cases, away from metropolitan areas into small towns. As jobs move farther from the city, workers move even farther out, creating the counterurban effect. And last, although affordable housing seems to be a major reason for counterurbanization, this trend is reinforced by an emotional blacklisting of the city as counterurbanites decide that urban life is too harried, complicated, and threatening, and vote with their cars.

The Future of Central Cities

If counterurbanization suggests population flight from central cities and suburbs, what will happen in the old urban cores? Several notions might help us think about central cities in the 1990s. The first concern is whether jobs continue moving to the suburbs and beyond. While new high-rise office buildings suggest an expanding job sector in some central cities, there is little question that, in general, white-collar jobs are decentralizing. Often a corporate headquarters will remain downtown while most day-to-day business activity takes place in outlying offices. Industrial blue-collar jobs left the central city early, so few central cities have much to lose in this category in the 1990s. Of concern,

though, are the "no-collar," or T-shirt, jobs that support low-income urbanites; janitors, bike messengers, entry-level office workers, and so on. Because these jobs are often filled by ethnic minorities who reside in the central cities, the movement of these jobs to the suburbs is a major problem: Rarely are these people able to shift residences to new suburban locations. Because many large urban areas experience ethnic in-migration, the proportion of central city populations that is low income and ethnic is growing, and finding employment becomes an increasing concern.

For years, urban analysts have predicted that large cities will become homes for only the rich and the poor, and that middle-income workers will abandon the city for the suburbs and small towns beyond. Many large North American cities have considerable affluent populations that reside (at least during the workweek) in condominiums, townhouses, and refurbished central-city housing; hints as to whether this population is growing will come from the 1990 census.

During the 1970s and 1980s, much was made of a "back to the city" movement, a perhaps exaggerated phenomenon fueled by highly visible neighborhood rehabilitation projects in some central cities—areas peopled by young, educated, middle-class singles and couples (remember the term *yuppie*?) who restored old housing and sometimes triggered gentrification (see box on "Reviving Old Neighborhoods," Chapter 10). While most cities have at least one trendy inner-city neighborhood that has been rehabilitated in the last decade, and some cities have many, this process varies highly from place to place and might be better examined in its local or regional context instead of being thought of as national or international movement. The still unanswered question is whether these young people stay in the city and become true city dwellers, marrying and raising children, or whether they flee for the suburbs and turn over their housing to other young, educated, middle-class replacements.

Finally, we should appreciate that there is a complicated dynamic of ethnic sorting taking place in North American central cities that will continue through the 1990s. For example, San Francisco's total population, which decreased in the immediate postwar decades as residents suburbanized, has been growing recently, primarily because of Asian immigration. Yet, as the Asian population increases, the city's black population decreases. This sorting and relocation process is found in other large cities as well, and has profound implications for the social, political, and economic structure of central cities.

"NIMBY": Not in My Backyard!

In the late 1980s, citizen revolt and rebellion against necessary yet problematic activities such as freeways, airports, firehouses, parking lots, schools, even parks were captured by the phrase "put it anywhere, but not in my backyard!" or NIMBY for short. This syndrome expresses an increasing public awareness that just about any urban activity carries with it some nuisance factor, such as crowds, traffic, or noise, that not only disturbs the quality of life, but—and this is not unimportant—might diminish housing and neighborhood real estate values. NIMBY protests are vexatious to city planners and governments. Yet these protests often provide the needed adhesive to bring neighborhoods together into viable social units with some degree of political clout.

new central buildings are often rushed through special channels that cut planning red tape. But most common is the downtown redevelopment project.

Urban renewal can have several goals, ranging from revival of retail trade, to construction of new central-city office space, to redevelopment of inner-city housing. The most common redevelopment strategy focuses on three interconnected components of city life: jobs, housing, and retail sales. The first task is to revive downtown employment patterns, often by constructing new office facilities competitive with outlying centers, or by concentrating on a specialized function. Many cities design redevelopment projects that cluster new financial institutions together. Banks, insurance firms, and stock brokerage houses can be found in the new high-rises.

Once people work in the city, they might be tempted to move back from the suburbs if appealing housing is available. So a second goal of redevelopment is construction of middle-income inner-city housing. Usually these projects will be located close to the new office complex. Finally, with people both working and living in the downtown once again, retail sales can be expected to pick up. This is the third phase of many renewal plans. Pedestrian malls, shops clustered around fountains and open spaces, restaurants, and numerous specialty shops can be found in the newly planned redevelopment shopping areas. These new retail centers are usually located near both offices and new housing so as to draw workers during lunch hours and the new residents on their way home from work. In fact, many redevelopment projects combine all three elements into one superblock: residences, shops, and workplaces connected by elevated pathways removed from street-level congestion.

Urban redevelopment can also be designed to renew the deteriorated housing stock of low-rent residences. However, because some see the continued presence of lower-income people in the central city as conflicting with revival of a viable retail sector, politicians are often reluctant to approve such plans. A constant criticism of renewal projects has been that they destroy low-rent housing and replace it with middle- or high-rent dwelling units. Poor people—who are usually the elderly and minorities—are displaced and forced to move into other low-rent areas of the city, aggravating the problem of urban poverty.

This is not to judge all urban renewal as bad. There are many humane renewal projects that have combined economic revitalization of the inner city with housing and jobs for society's less fortunate. It can be done. Yet all agree that it is politically and economically more difficult than the project that simply constructs housing for high- and middle-income city dwellers.

Decentralization has also cost society millions of dollars in problems brought to the suburbs. Where rapid suburbanization has been the case, sprawl has usually resulted. A common pattern is leapfrog or **checkerboard development,** where housing tracts jump over parcels of farmland resulting in a mixture of open lands with built-up areas. This pattern results because developers buy cheaper land farther away from built-up areas, thereby cutting their costs. Furthermore, home buyers often pay premium prices for homes in subdivisions surrounded by farmlands (see Figure 11.6).

This form of development is costly because it is more expensive to provide city services, such as police, fire protection, sewers, and electrical lines, to those areas laying beyond open, unbuilt-up parcels. Obviously, the most cost-efficient form of development is adding new housing directly adjacent to built-up areas. That way the costs of providing new

FIGURE 11.6
Residential decentralization, also known as suburbanization, gives us a familiar landscape of look-alike houses and yards, auto-efficient street and transportation patterns, and, in the background, remnants of agriculture, awaiting the day that they are converted into housing tracts.

services are minimal. Costs are considerably higher when parcels of open land must be bridged.

Furthermore, sprawl extracts high costs because of increased use of cars. Public transportation is extremely costly and inefficient when it must serve a low-density checkerboard development pattern; so costly that many cities and transit firms cannot extend lines into these areas. This means that the auto is the only form of transportation there. More energy is consumed for fuel, more air pollution is created by exhaust, and more time is spent in commuting and everyday activities in a sprawling urban area than in a centralized city. Thus, society pays again for the costs of decentralization.

We should not overlook the costs of losing valuable agricultural land to urban development. Farmers cultivating the remaining checkerboard parcels have a hard time making ends meet. They are usually taxed at extremely high rates because their land has high potential for development, and few can make a profit when taxes eat up all their resources. Often the only recourse is to sell out to subdividers. So the cycle of leapfrog development goes on.

But many cities are now taking strong measures to curb this kind of sprawling growth. Some cities, like San Jose, California, one of the fastest-growing cities of the 1960s, now try to focus new development on empty parcels of the checkerboard pattern. This is called **in-filling.** Instead of new growth extending the sprawling outer edge of the city, it will take place within the existing urban area, where services are already available and can be provided at lower costs.

Other cities are tying the number of building permits granted each year to the availability of urban services. If schools are already crowded, water supplies inadequate, and sewer plants overburdened, the number of new dwelling units approved for an area will reflect this lower carrying capacity (see box, "Controlling Suburban Growth").

So, in summary, the costs of decentralization are many. They range from decayed and moribund downtowns to sprawling suburbs lacking

---

CONTROLLING SUBURBAN GROWTH

Although the first suburban growth control measures were written more than a decade ago, the controversy continues today, with the issue enmeshed in drawn-out legal battles and bureaucratic red tape.

One of the earliest and precedent-setting growth control plans came from Petaluma, California, a small suburb of 50,000 people within the commuter zone north of San Francisco. Once a sleepy service center for chicken ranches, the town began sprawling with rapid growth in the late 1960s and, a few years later, the city council took strong measures to limit growth by adopting a plan whereby only 500 building permits would be issued yearly. This was roughly half the number granted in the previous years, so the intention was to slow growth by 50 percent. Five hundred permits would be awarded after careful review of all proposed building plans, with the coveted permits going to those structures that met rigorous criteria established by the City Council.

Adverse reaction and opposition to this plan was immediate. Not only did the building industry object because the plan would limit construction and jobs, but they were joined by civil rights groups who saw suburban growth control as a possible vehicle for racial discrimination. Because some types of suburban zoning, such as large-lot minimums and bans against apartment houses, tend to push up housing prices and discriminate against lower-income people, civil rights organizations saw the Petaluma plan as a threat to minority groups.

Consequently, this Petaluma plan was challenged in court as violating the constitutional "right to travel," a legal right traced to the Magna Carta, and the legal basis for housing without restrictive racial covenants. While a lobby of building industries, trade unions, and civil liberties groups supported a challenge to the Petaluma plan, the city, with financial backing and moral support from other cities interested in establishing a legal precedent for growth control, stood by its plan. Lower court decisions went both for and against the plan until a final decision was made by the Supreme Court in 1978 substantiating the legal basis for this approach to growth control.

However, even if the legal foundation for growth control was established, there are numerous other complexities to be faced by cities and neighborhoods battling unrestricted expansion. First, there is the question of whether growth control restrictions force up housing prices. A recent California study shows that housing prices in areas with growth control are 5 to 8 percent higher than in areas without controls, because of market demand for a scarce supply and because developers tack on additional costs to compensate for the paperwork and delays from a more complicated permit-approval process. A second issue is whether growth control restrictions discourage developers from building low- and moderate-priced homes. If only a limited number of permits are available for building (as in the Petaluma plan), then developers tend to maximize their investment by building higher-priced homes instead of a larger number of middle-income houses. Many cities have addressed this problem by granting incentives to developers who build for lower-income groups. Third, there are problems with how to limit the number of building permits. Some cities use lotteries, granting permits by chance, while others use a complicated point system that rewards plans with the desired attributes. Another common approach is limiting building to those areas of the city where services (such as water and sewers) are already available, thereby restricting leap-frog sprawl.

And, last, some cities link the number of building permits to the carrying capacity of public services, declaring building moratoria when schools, water systems, sewer plants, or roads become overloaded. Because cities prefer to plan their futures and control growth in an orderly manner, building moratoria are the least desirable vehicle for growth control from a city's viewpoint, yet they are often forced upon a municipality by citizen movements that place a moratorium on a local ballot by petition and then vote it into effect.

Working out an effective yet equitable way to limit and control suburban growth remains one of the challenges faced by cities and towns in the 1990s.

social-service infrastructures. While inner-city poverty and ghettoization can be partially blamed on decentralization, so can farmland loss, increased auto air pollution, and higher energy consumption. Though planning measures have alleviated some of these problems, many of these ills will multiply as our cities continue to decentralize.

THE CULTURAL ECOLOGY OF THE CITY

Cities are affected by their physical environments and equally, urbanization profoundly alters natural environmental processes. Consequently, the theme of cultural ecology is helpful in organizing information about these city-nature relationships. Perhaps one of the more valuable dimensions of this theme is that it allows us to conceptualize problematic components of the interaction between people and the environment, as we will see through our discussion of air pollution, flooding, and earthquake hazards. Although we talk in general terms about these topics in the next pages, we should not lose sight of how the differing cultural fabric within and between cities affects this city-nature relationship. Put differently, urban cultural ecology is a topic that differs vastly from place to place because of different physical environments and, equally important, because of varying cultural patterns.

The Urban Ecosystem

In the first chapter of this book, ecology is defined as the study of the relationship between an organism and its physical environment. To study this relationship, we examine both organism and environment as one unit through which the flow of energy or matter can be traced. This is called the **ecosystem.** We can apply this concept to the city in order to better understand the relationship between urban populations and the physical environment.

There are four important concepts related to the ecosystem approach: input, storage, output, and feedback. To illustrate, let us examine just one component of the urban ecosystem: water. Obviously, a city needs water to survive, so it imports a given amount each day, either from local sources, such as lakes and reservoirs, or from long distances via canals and aqueducts. This is the **input** of the system. What happens to it as it moves through the city?

Water is used in households, industry, stores, and offices. Using the terminology of the ecosystem, we say that it is transformed and leaves the system in other forms. These are the **outputs.** Some water is consumed by people; hence it temporarily becomes part of their body systems. Other water becomes part of different manufactured products, such as cheese or soft drinks, and, after transformation, may leave the city's system as goods exported to other markets. Still other water is used for industrial cooling and, as it evaporates, returns to the atmosphere system as vapor. And a small amount of water is not used, but rather is stored within the system for future use, just the way organisms store energy. But most of the water—about 95 percent—is simply used to convey wastes from one point to another; from home to sewer plant, from factory to river, from sidewalk to gutter. This output is a most troublesome aspect of the urban system.

Feedback is a crucial part of any system. It is the repercussions on a system when an element is returned in modified or changed form by other components of the system. An overly simplistic example would be if a city used water from a lake both for its water supply and also as a dumping area for sewage. As more effluent is discharged into the lake, water quality decreases, and the city must expend more energy (measured both in money and activity) to protect its freshwater supply.

A more complicated example—and in no way has this relationship been conclusively proven—is the way that city-produced air pollution may alter weather patterns so that an urban water supply system is strained, either by drought or by flooding. Further examples of the interconnectivity within the urban ecosystem will be apparent in the following discussion of the physical components of the urban environment.

The Urban Geologic Environment

In the previous chapter, under the discussion of site and situation, we saw that cities are both affected by—and affect—the physical environment. Let us explore further the relationships between urbanization and the geologic environment.

To begin with, topography can influence urban development in three ways: the direction of city growth, the routing of transportation, and the patterning of social areas. We must emphasize, however, that these potential effects are dependent on a number of cultural variables. The most important variables are a society's technological level, the amount of energy and capital available for modification of the geologic environment, and, lastly, the stage in a city's development. In other words, the geologic environment may have a great effect on those cities in early stages of growth, where there are spatial alternatives to expending energy and money on modifying terrain, or where the technology is lacking for bulldozing, landfill, or high-stress building construction. At later stages of growth, in a rich, highly industrialized culture, there will be far more examples of humans modifying the geologic environment (see Figure 11.7).

Let us look at the way terrain might influence early stages of city growth. Cities usually expand first on those areas where building costs are

FIGURE 11.7
When land values are high and pressure for housing intense, terrain rarely stands in the way of the developer, as illustrated by this cut-and-fill in California.

lowest. This means that flat, well-drained lands that are close to transportation and adjacent to existing urban activities will be built upon first. But as topography varies, building costs increase. Areas of hills, marshes, and floodplains may be built upon only at later stages of a city's growth when there are fewer alternatives.

The increased costs of site preparation, such as grading hills or draining swamps, can have two very different consequences. On the one hand, the increased cost of building may be passed on to the consumer—meaning that those who buy the houses pay more, and the area will be occupied by higher-income groups. On the other hand, aspects of construction may be cut in order to compensate for increased site preparation costs. Lots may be smaller, houses undersized, and shortcuts taken in construction methods so that the finished product is of lower quality. This means that lower-income groups will probably occupy the area.

Environmental feedback may also blemish an area. Former swamps or marshes may have flooding problems; hillsides may slide; or unstable foundations and flooded basements may lower market prices so that an area of former middle-priced homes declines in value, becoming accessible to lower-income residents. Unfortunately, they are the ones least able to bear the costs of pumping out basements or reinforcing foundations. It seems unjust that they must end up with and bear the costs of poor environmental planning.

Last, transportation systems can be affected by terrain. And since there is a close link between transportation and urban development, the resulting urban pattern may express these relationships. The first urban transportation system was the horse-drawn streetcar, which was obviously restricted to level parts of the city because horses could not pull car and passengers up or down hills. Slight gradients could be negotiated by smaller horse-drawn carriages; those who could afford such conveyances had access to hilltop building sites. But it was only with the cable car that hills became accessible to the middle class. Starting in San Francisco in 1873, cable cars came into widespread use in American cities. However, cable cars had problems in cold, wet climates because of freezing in the cable conduits, so a better solution to public transportation needs was sought.

Electric trolley systems profoundly altered the pattern of urban development beginning in the 1890s. But, like the horse-drawn carriage, they had limited hill-climbing abilities. Only slight gradients could be negotiated, so trolley lines ascended slopes only when it was possible to follow hillside contours. Often a network of steep stairways and paths connected neighborhoods with streetcar lines. In the end, it was only the automobile that led to widespread building on steep urban slopes. And even this form of development has been influenced by factors such as frequency of heavy snowfalls and ice storms.

The possibility of serious geologic feedback can influence extant urban patterns. In some parts of the world, the potential of damage from earthquakes is severe. The threat of destruction from earthquakes has always been great in California, yet if one examines the pattern of development, it is appalling to see how much construction has taken place in vulnerable areas. Filled lands, such as on bay margins, are areas where ground shaking will be worst, yet millions of people reside in these areas in California. Other construction has taken place directly on major faults where continual movement—known as creep—slowly rips buildings apart. Widespread development is found in floodplains immediately downstream from huge dams that could collapse from a major quake.

Only since the 1970s has California taken steps to prevent construction on the hundreds of active faults crisscrossing urban areas. When the inevitable major earthquake comes, the toll will be high.

Although California is notorious for its earthquake hazard, the possibility of major damage from a quake is not limited just to that area. Some of the strongest recorded earthquakes have been in the central and eastern portions of the United States. But few measures are being taken in those areas to protect urban dwellers from potential disaster, either by requiring adjustments to existing buildings or planning growth for areas less vulnerable to earthquake damage.

Urban Weather and Climate

Cities alter just about all aspects of local weather and climate. Temperatures are higher in cities, rainfall increases, the incidence of fog and cloudiness is greater, and atmospheric pollution is much higher near cities.

The causes behind these alterations are no mystery. Because cities pave over large areas of streets, buildings, parking lots, and rooftops, about 50 percent of the urban area is a hard surface. Rainfall is quickly carried into gutters and sewers, so that little standing water is available for evaporation. Because heat is removed from the air during the normal evaporation process, where moisture is reduced, evaporation is lessened, and air temperatures are higher.

Furthermore, cities generate enormous amounts of heat. This comes not just from heating system of buildings, but also from automobiles, industry, and even from human bodies. One study shows that on a winter day in Manhattan, the amount of heat produced in the city is 2½ times that reaching the ground from the sun. (During the summer, solar heating is greater than human-produced heat.) The end result of this heat generation is to produce a large mass of warmer air sitting over the city. This is called the urban **heat island** (see Figure 11.8).

As a result of the heat island, yearly temperatures will average 3.5 degrees Fahrenheit warmer than in the countryside; during the winter, when city-produced heat is higher, the temperature difference can easily be 7 to 10 degrees.

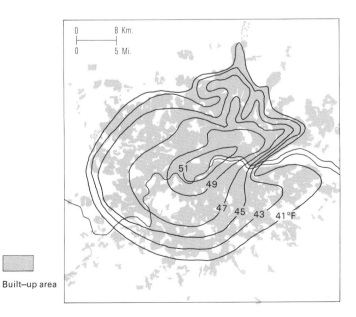

FIGURE 11.8
The London heat island forms a dome over the city. Notice the marked contrast in temperature between the built-up central part of the city and the surrounding "Green Belt." (After Chandler.)

There will also be significant temperature differences within the city. In winter, heavily traveled streets will be 2 or 3 degrees Fahrenheit warmer than untraveled side streets; places where autos stand for a while, like stoplights, can be another 3 degrees Fahrenheit warmer. Furthermore, low spots in the city, where cold air collects, will be much colder than higher places. And wooded areas are warmer than bare blocks.

During the summer, the city center is warmer than the suburbs. Often there can be a 10 degree Fahrenheit difference between downtown and outlying residential areas, which is a result of suburban lawns and parks stabilizing temperatures by using up heat through evaporation and releasing heat at night faster than paved areas. Concrete areas tend to store heat longer at night, which leads to a buildup of temperatures over a series of warm days.

Precipitation (rain and snowfall) is also affected by urbanization. Because of higher temperatures within the urban area, snowfall will be about 5 percent less than in the surrounding countryside. However, rainfall can be 5 to 10 percent higher. This is a function of two factors: first, the large number of dust particles in urban air, and, second, the higher city temperatures. Dust particles are a necessary precondition for condensation, for they offer a focus around which moisture can adhere. So where there is a greater number of dust particles, condensation will take place more easily. That is why fog and clouds are usually more frequent around cities (see Figure 11.9).

Once condensation takes place, rainfall is not far behind. Rainfall increases on the order of 10 percent have been documented immediately downwind from cities. For example, thunderstorms in the London area produce 30 percent more rainfall than in the countryside. Some urban climatologists argue that they can see a weekday rainfall increase pattern: Rainfall is less on weekends because dust particle generation—from autos and industry—is reduced.

City-generated air pollution is one of the most serious problems of our times. No longer is air pollution simply a nuisance; it can cause serious illness, at times death. Pollution damages agriculture near cities; and it extracts a high cost from every urban dweller. Unless pollution can be halted, it may actually be the limiting factor on growth. Some suggest that fresh air—not water—will determine the ultimate carrying capacity of the Los Angeles basin. Federal and local air quality agencies are experimenting with regulations limiting further growth and development in those areas suffering from persistent air pollution.

Much has been written about air pollution, and we refer readers to references listed at the end of this chapter for additional material.

Urban Hydrology

The city is not only a great consumer of water, but it also alters runoff patterns in a way that increases the frequency and magnitude of flooding. We will first discuss urban water demands, then the problems of urban flooding.

Within the city, residential areas are usually the greatest consumers of water. This could vary depending on the kind of industry found in a city, but as a general statement, each person uses about 60 gallons per day in a residence.

Of course, residential demand varies. It is higher in drier climates than where rainfall is adequate for garden water; it is greater where lots are larger; and it is also higher in middle- and high-income neighborhoods

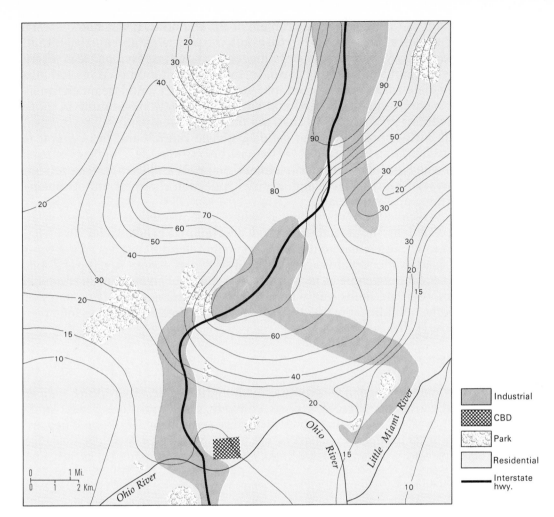

FIGURE 11.9
The dust dome over Cincinnati, Ohio. Values show the concentration of particulate matter in the air at 3000 feet elevation. The higher the value, the greater the amount of particulate matter. (After Bach and Hagedorn.)

than in lower-income areas. Higher-income groups usually have a larger number of water-using appliances, such as washing machines, dishwashers, and swimming pools.

However, price influences water demand. People use less water when price increases. Periods of drought in the west demonstrated that residents can both use considerably less water and find alternatives to freshwater consumption. Many of the rationing plans adopted during the California drought of the late 1980s restricted per capita daily use to around 40 gallons. Toilets (which use about seven gallons per flush) were flushed less, showers were shortened, and household "gray water" was used for gardens.

This is not to suggest that only western cities are vulnerable to drought. The eastern United States experienced severe water shortages in the mid-1960s, and England suffered from a two-year drought in the mid-1970s. In both cases, city dwellers were forced to ration water. As meteorologists forecast increased climatic variability, meaning that more frequent droughts are a distinct possibility, cities must prepare for more efficient water usage.

Let us turn now to the problem of urban floods. It was noted earlier that urbanization seems to increase both the frequency and the magnitude of flooding. Why might this be? Cities create large impervious areas where water cannot soak into the earth. Instead, precipitation is converted into immediate runoff. It is forced into gutters, sewers, and stream channels that have been straightened and bared of vegetation, resulting in more frequent high-water levels than are found in a comparable area of rural land. Furthermore, the time period between rainfall and peak runoff is reduced in cities; there is less lag than in the countryside, where water runs across soil and vegetation into stream channels and then into rivers. So, because of hard surfaces and artificial collection channels. runoff is concentrated and immediate.

Several studies show that flooding becomes five or six times more frequent in an urbanized watershed, and because pressures on land from city growth often lead to the development of floodplains, a scenario is set for disaster. Floodplains are, by definition, areas subject to natural flooding, so it should come as no surprise that rivers reclaim their full channels every now and then. And when urbanization increases the frequency of flooding, building on floodplains becomes increasingly hazardous (see Figure 11.10).

Urban Vegetation

Until a decade ago, it was commonly thought that the city was made up of mostly artificial surfaces: asphalt, concrete, glass, and steel. Recent studies, however, show that about two-thirds of North American cities are comprised of trees and herbaceous plants (mostly cultivated grasses for lawns and weeds in vacant lots). Only a third is made up of artificial

FIGURE 11.10
Often urbanization disturbs the natural hydrology, so that both frequency and magnitude of flooding are increased. This flood resulted from a locally severe thunderstorm in Virginia.

FIGURE 11.11
Vegetation is linked closely to the different components of the urban ecosystem. One of its primary functions in the city, as shown by this photo, is to reduce air temperatures by absorbing ambient heat and solar radiation and transpiring water from the millions of square feet of leaf surfaces. This can result in distinct temperature differences between vegetated and nonplanted areas.

surfaces. This urban vegetation is usually a mix of natural and introduced species and is a critical component of the urban ecosystem because it affects the city's geology, hydrology, and meteorology (see Figure 11.11).

More specifically, urban vegetation affects the quantity and quality of surface and ground water; reduces wind velocity and turbulence and temperature extremes; affects the pattern of snow accumulation and melting; absorbs thousands of tons of airborne particulates and atmospheric gases; and offers habitat for mammals, birds, reptiles, and insects, all of which play some useful role in the urban ecosystem. Furthermore, trees, shrubs, and grasses in the city influence the propagation of sound waves by masking out much of the city's noise, affect the distribution of natural and artificial light within urban areas, and, finally, are an extremely important component in the development of soil profiles, which, in turn, control hillside stability.

As an example of how urban vegetation affects the ecosystem, we learned in the previous section that runoff from rain collects very quickly in gutters and sewers because of the large amount of impervious surface throughout the city. United States Forest Service scientists used Dayton, Ohio, as a field laboratory to determine the quantitative effects of vegetation on hydrology and climate. They found that vegetation was responsible for intercepting and holding about 25 percent of the rainfall from a storm, rainfall that would — if it were not for vegetation — create frequent and costly flooding in the city.

These Forest Service researchers also found that selective revegetation of the Dayton business district could reduce the heat island effect by 25 to 50 percent. This would mean a more comfortable downtown, especially for the elderly who are more sensitive to temperature extremes, and reduce energy costs for air conditioning in the central business district. Vegetation reduces air temperatures by, first, providing a mass that absorbs heat and solar radiation, and, second, using energy in evaporating water off millions of square feet of leaf surfaces.

Vegetation and the geologic components of the urban ecosystem are also closely associated. The amount of slope and physical-chemical properties of the bedrock determine what kinds of vegetation will be able to exist on a site. In turn, the vegetation impacts on the soil and geology of a location. For example, about 25 percent of Cincinnati is hilly. As housing developers and highway builders cut the oak-hickory forests on these urban hillsides, the soils and loose bedrock begin to slip. Over a recent six-year period, this gradual landsliding has become so serious that it has cost the city residents $5 million each year for repairs and relocations. Engineering solutions are unable to solve the problem, so the city is now managing its urban forest for hillside stability. These forests also reduce downslope winds, cool summer air, and filter air pollution from stagnant air trapped in the river valley.

Although urban vegetation generally contributes in a positive way to the urban ecosystem, there are always costs involved that cities must bear; these costs can be expressed in dollars and cents, human morbidity (sickness and injury), and a lowered quality of life. To start with, think of the obvious monetary costs of caring for urban vegetation: selecting, planting, watering, pruning, spraying, sweeping leaves from city streets. Hundreds of thousands of dollars are spent on this in every city each year, dollars that could be allocated for other public services. In the humid eastern half of the United States, for example, mowing lawns amounts to about $2 per capita, which means that in a medium-sized city of 500,000, a million dollars in gasoline is consumed simply to keep grass from getting beyond what cultural values dictate.

High pollen counts from certain kinds of vegetation aggravate respiratory diseases for some people, or, minimally, hay fever and nuisance allergies take a toll on segments of the city's population. There are also costs from trees falling on houses and cars during a storm.

In the city, vegetation, like all components of the physical environment, generates both costs and benefits. People must, then, decide how best to manage these components to maximize the positive dimensions of the urban ecosystem.

To conclude this section on the cultural ecology of the city, let us remember that our urban settlements are still closely tied to the physical environment. Our cities change these natural processes in profound ways, and we must understand these disturbances in order to make better decisions about adjustments and control. Yet the physical environment must not be thought of simply as an antagonist to be conquered. This last section on urban vegetation demonstrates that there are many benefits to be gained from proper management of the ecosystem. Management, however, is rooted in the cultural context, in the values, ethics, goals, and priorities of a people, which is why the issue is ultimately tied to cultural geography.

CULTURAL INTEGRATION AND MODELS OF THE CITY

In our look at centralizing and decentralizing forces, we saw that many factors influence the location of an activity within a city. A logical follow-up question is this: Does a predictable land-use pattern result from the interplay of these factors? One method of seeking answers is to create models that describe and simplify the relationships among the different social, economic, and geographic factors. Various academic disciplines have long sought to isolate the most important processes at work in a city. The goal is to derive a model that describes the pattern of a city and explains how it evolved. Following a discussion of urban processes, the four most widely used models are described below. The first three were formulated from North American cities, and the fourth from non-Western urban places. It is used to remind us of the important international dimension to urban cultural geography.

There are a number of processes at work in a city, leading to different social and economic patterns. Six are briefly discussed here. The first is *concentration,* which refers to the differential distribution of population and economic activities in a city and the manner in which they have focused on the center of the city. *Decentralization,* defined earlier, refers to the location of activity away from the central city. *Segregation* is the sorting out of population groups due to conscious preferences for associating with one group or another through bias and prejudice. A somewhat similar process operates among economic activities; we call this *specialization.* The process through which a new activity or social group enters an area has traditionally been called *invasion.* And if that new use or social group gradually replaces the former occupants, this illustrates the process of *succession.* These last two terms have been adopted from plant ecology and were originally used to describe changes in vegetation. Because the term *invasion* connotes a hostile, warlike environment, it is used cautiously by social scientists when referring to cultural and ethnic groups.

With these six processes in mind, let us examine how they might influence urban patterns. We shall do so by looking at four widely used models of city structure. Let us remember, though, that these models were constructed to examine single cities and do not apply to or explain the urban process of conurbation or metropolitan coalescence so common in the world today.

Concentric Zone Model

The **concentric zone model** was developed in 1925 by Ernest W. Burgess, a sociologist at the University of Chicago. Although his model closely resembles Chicago (if the east side were not cut off by Lake Michigan), his intent was simply to construct a theoretical model of urban growth.

Figure 11.12 shows the concentric zone model with its five zones. At first glance, you can see the effects of residential decentralization. There is a distinct pattern of income levels from the **CBD** (central business district) out to the commuters' zone. This shows that even at the beginning of the auto age, American cities expressed a clear separation of social groups. The extension of trolley lines into the surrounding countryside had a lot to do with this pattern.

Zone 2, a transitional area between the CBD and residential Zone 3, was characterized by a mixed pattern of commercial and residential land

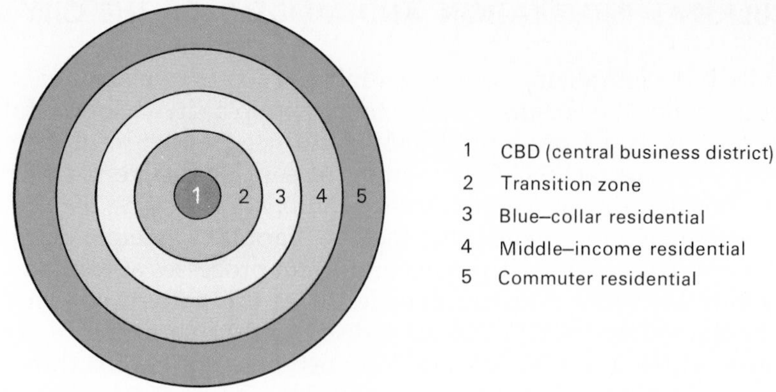

1   CBD (central business district)
2   Transition zone
3   Blue—collar residential
4   Middle—income residential
5   Commuter residential

FIGURE 11.12
The concentric zone model is shown in this diagram. Each zone represents a different type of land use in the city. Can you identify examples of each zone in your community?

use. Rooming houses, small apartments, and tenements attracted the lowest-income segment of the urban population. Often this zone included slums and skid rows. Here, also, many ethnic ghettos began. Landowners, while waiting for the CBD to reach their land, erected shoddy tenements to house a massive influx of foreign workers. An aura of uncertainty was characteristic of life in Zone 2, because commercial activities rapidly displaced residents as the CBD expanded. Today, this area is often characterized by physical deterioration (see Figure 11.13).

Zone 3, the "workingmen's quarters," was a solid blue-collar arc, located close to the factories of Zones 1 and 2. Yet Zone 3 was more stable than the zone of transition around the CBD. It was often characterized by ethnic neighborhoods: blocks of immigrants who had broken free from the ghettos in Zone 2 and moved outward into flats or single-family dwellings. Burgess suggested that this working-class area, like the CBD, was spreading outward, because of pressure from the zone of transition and because blue-collar workers demanded better housing.

FIGURE 11.13
The transitional zone in the city contains vacant and deteriorated buildings. Broken windows and boarded storefronts are part of the landscape.

Zone 4 was a middle-class area of "better housing." From here, established city dwellers, many of whom moved out of the central city with the first streetcar network, commuted to work in the CBD.

Zone 5, the commuters' zone, consisted of higher-income families clustered together in older suburbs, either on the farthest extension of the trolley or on commuter railroad lines. This zone of spacious lots and large houses was the growing edge of the city. From here, the rich pressed outward to avoid the increasing congestion and social heterogeneity brought to their area by an expansion of Zone 4.

Burgess's concentric zone theory represented the American city in a new stage of development. Before the 1870s, an American metropolis, such as New York, was a city of mixed neighborhoods where merchants' stores and sweatshop factories were intermingled with mansions and hovels. Rich and poor, immigrant and native-born rubbed shoulders in the same neighborhoods. However, in Chicago, Burgess's hometown, something else occurred. In 1871, the great Chicago Fire burned out the core of the city, leveling almost one-third of its buildings. As the city was rebuilt, it was influenced by late nineteenth-century market forces: real estate speculation in the suburbs, inner-city industrial development, new streetcar systems, the need for low-cost working-class housing. The result was a more explicit social patterning than existed in other large cities; Chicago became essentially a segregated city with a concentric pattern working its way out from the downtown in what one scholar called "rings of rising affluence." It was this rebuilt city that Burgess used as the basis for his concentric zone model.

However, as you can see from Figure 11.14, the actual residential map of Chicago does not exactly match the simplicity of Burgess's concentric zones. For instance, it is evident that the wealthy continue to monopolize certain high-value sites within the other rings, especially Chicago's "Gold Coast" along Lake Michigan. According to the concentric zone theory, this area should have been part of the zone of transition. Burgess accounted for certain of these exceptions by noting how the rich tended to monopolize hills, lakes, and shorelines, whether they were close to or far from the CBD. Critics of Burgess's model also were quick to point out that even though portions of each zone did exist in most cities, rarely were they linked in such a way as to totally surround the city. Burgess countered that there were distinct barriers, such as old industrial centers, that prevented the completion of the arc. Still other critics felt that Burgess, as a sociologist, overemphasized residential patterns and did not give proper credit to other land uses—such as industry, manufacturing, and warehouses—in describing the urban mosaic.

Despite these criticisms, concentric zone theory was fairly accurate in describing the cities of 1925. In fact, many of the zones can still be seen in contemporary cities, particularly the zone of transition around the central business district. It is still a jumbled mixture of land uses, neither totally residential nor totally commercial. Usually it is still the area of skid rows and slums. It is easily recognized by its pawnshops, rescue missions, large parking lots, rooming houses, transient hotels, old factories, and—since the 1950s—massive urban renewal projects, which seek to "upgrade" the land by replacing older residential buildings with convention centers, offices, and parking garages. Because these projects usually displace the transient population, they in effect expand the zone of transition. Skid rows are like bumps under the carpet: They can be moved by sweeping the surface, but they never completely disappear.

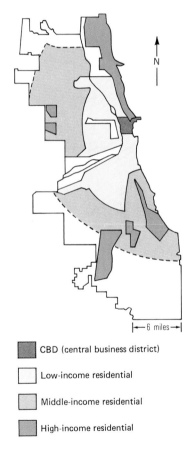

|◄— 6 miles —►|

█ CBD (central business district)

☐ Low-income residential

▨ Middle-income residential

█ High-income residential

FIGURE 11.14
Residential areas of Chicago in 1920 were used as the basis for many studies and models of the city. Compare this pattern with the concentric zone and sector models.

Sector Model

Homer Hoyt, an economist who studied housing data for 142 American cities, presented his **sector model** of urban land use in 1939. He maintained that high-rent residential districts ("rent" meaning capital outlay for the occupancy of space, including purchase, lease, or "rent" in the popular sense) were instrumental in shaping the land-use structure of the city. Because these areas were reinforced by transportation routes, the pattern of their development was one of sectors or wedges (see Figure 11.15) rather than concentric zones.

Hoyt suggested that the high-rent sector would expand according to several factors. First, a high-rent sector moves from its point of origin near the CBD, along established routes of travel, toward another nucleus of high-rent buildings; that is, a high-rent area directly next to the CBD will naturally head in the direction of a high-rent suburb, eventually linking the two in a wedge-shaped sector. Second, a high-rent sector will progress toward high ground or along waterfronts, when these areas are not used for industry. The rich have always preferred such environments for their residences. Third, a high-rent sector will move along the route of fastest transportation. Fourth, a high-rent sector will move toward open space. A high-income community rarely moves into an occupied lower-income neighborhood. Instead, the wealthy prefer to build new structures on vacant land where they can control the social environment.

As high-rent sectors develop, the areas between them are filled in. Middle-rent areas move directly next to them, drawing on their prestige. Low-rent areas fill in the remaining areas. Thus, moving away from major routes of travel, rents go from high to low.

There are distinct patterns in today's cities that echo Hoyt's model. He had the advantage over Burgess in that he wrote later in the automobile age and could see the tremendous impact that major thoroughfares were having on cities. However, when we look at today's major transportation arteries—which are generally freeways—we see that the areas surrounding them are often low-rent districts. According to Hoyt's theory, they should be high-rent districts. Freeways are rather recent additions to the city, coming only after World War II. In a sense, they were imposed on an existing urban pattern. To minimize the costs of construction, they were built as often as possible through low-rent areas, where the costs of land purchase for the rights of way were less. This is why so many freeways rip

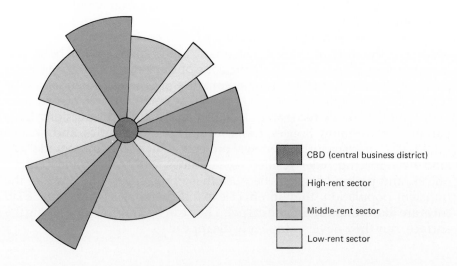

FIGURE 11.15
Another model of urban land use is the sector model. In this model zones are pie-shaped wedges radiating along main transportation routes.

CBD (central business district)

High-rent sector

Middle-rent sector

Low-rent sector

through ethnic ghettos and low-income areas. Economically speaking, this is the least expensive route. This problem will persist until low-income neighborhoods organize effective political resistance against such disturbances.

Multiple Nuclei Model

Both Burgess and Hoyt assumed that a strong central city affected patterns throughout the urban area. However, as the city increasingly decentralized, districts developed that were not directly linked to the CBD. In 1945, two geographers, Chauncey Harris and Edward Ullman, suggested a new model, the **multiple nuclei model.** They maintained that a city developed with equal intensity around various points, or "multiple nuclei" (see Figure 11.16). In their eyes, the CBD was not the sole generator of change. Equal weight must be given to an old community on the city outskirts around which new suburban developments clustered; to an industrial district that grew from an original waterfront location; or to a low-income area that began because of some social stigma attached to the site. In other words, the city grew from a number of unrelated points, not from a single center.

Harris and Ullman rooted their model in four geographic principles. First of all, certain activities require highly specialized facilities, such as accessible transportation for a factory or large areas of open land for a housing tract. The second principle is that certain activities cluster together because they profit from mutual association. Examples would be banks, used-car lots, and jewelry stores. Third, certain activities repel each other and will not be found in the same area. Examples would be high-rent residences and industrial areas, or slums and expensive retail stores. Fourth, certain activities could not make a profit if they paid the high rent of the most desirable locations. Therefore, they seek lower-rent areas. For example, new-car dealers may like to locate where pedestrian traffic is greatest in order to lure the most people into their showrooms. However, they need great amounts of space for showrooms, storage, service facilities, and used-car lots. Therefore, they cannot afford the high rents that the most accessible locations demand. They compromise by finding an area of lower rent that is still relatively accessible.

The multiple nuclei model, more than the other models, seems to take into account the varied factors of decentralization in the structure of the North American city. Many criticize the concentric zone and sector theories as being rather deterministic, for they emphasize one single factor (residential differentiation in the concentric zone theory or rent in the

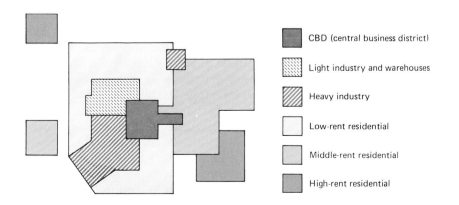

CBD (central business district)

Light industry and warehouses

Heavy industry

Low-rent residential

Middle-rent residential

High-rent residential

FIGURE 11.16
The multiple nuclei model is shown in this diagram. This model was devised to show that the CBD is not the sole force in creating land-use patterns within the city. Rather, land-use districts may evolve for specific reasons at specific points elsewhere in the city, hence the name *multiple nuclei.*

sector theory) to explain the city. But the multiple nuclei theory encompasses a larger spectrum of economic and social possibilities. Harris and Ullman could probably appreciate the variety of forces working on the city because they did not confine themselves to seeking simply a social or an economic explanation. As geographers, they tried to integrate the disparate elements of culture into a workable model. Most urban scholars agree that they succeeded.

Latin American Model

While these first three models were developed out of the North American urban experience, we should not overlook the international component of urban cultural geography, and, to remind us of that, we now turn our attention to models of non-Western cities. This is a more complex subject because of the profound influence local cultures have on urban development and form, so it is difficult to generalize non-Western cities into one or two comprehensive models comparable to those formulated from the relatively homogenous conditions of the United States and Canada. But to illustrate cultural integration in non-Western cities, we draw upon a model specific to one region—Latin America—while reminding readers that there are several other models applicable to other parts of the non-Western world; readings are found at chapter's end that elaborate on these points.

The Latin American city model is found as Figure 1.14, in the first chapter. Refer to that figure as you read this section. This model is a generalized scheme that both is sensitive to local cultures in South America, and also articulates the pervasive influence of international forces, both Western and non-Western, as they influence urban structure. This dimension comes through in the description and explanation of each element of the model.

In contrast to contemporary North American cities, the CBDs of Latin American cities are vibrant, dynamic, and increasingly specialized. The dominance of the CBD is explained in part by a reliance on public transit that serves the central city and, equally, on the existence of a large and relatively affluent population close to the CBD. Outside of the CBD, the dominant component is a commercial spine surrounded by an elite residential sector; because these two zones are interrelated, they are referred to as the spine/sector. This is essentially an extension of the CBD down a major boulevard, along which are the city's important amenities, such as parks, theaters, restaurants, and even golf courses. Strict zoning and land controls assure continuation of these activities and protect the elite from incursions by low-income squatters.

Somewhat less prestigious is the inner-city zone of maturity, a collection of traditional colonial homes and upgraded self-built homes occupied by people unable to participate in the spine/sector. This is an area of upward mobility. The zone of accretion is a diverse collection of housing types, sizes, and quality, which can be thought of as a transition between the zone of maturity and the zone of peripheral squatter settlements. It is an area of ongoing construction and change, emblematic of the explosive population growth that characterizes the Latin American city. While some neighborhoods within this zone have city-provided utilities, other blocks must rely on water and butane delivery trucks for essential services.

The most recent migrants to the Latin American city are found in the zone of peripheral squatter settlements; this fringe of poor people and inadequate housing contrasts dramatically with the affluent and comfortable suburbs that ring North American cities. Squatter houses are often built from scavenged materials, and the appearance of these areas is that of a refugee camp, surrounded by a denuded landscape bare of vegetation that was cut for fuel and building materials. Streets are unpaved and open trenches carry wastes; residents carry water from long distances, and electricity is often "pirated" by attaching illegal wires to the closest utility pole. If residents have work, their commute is a long one that consumes much of the day. Although this zone's quality of life seems marginal, many squatter settlements are transformed through time by their residents into permanent neighborhoods with minimal amenities.

In concluding this section, we again remind you of both the assets and liabilities of these models of urban structure. There is a delicate and sometimes dangerous balance between compressing vast and varied information into generalizations, for much information must, by definition, be suppressed. For cultural geographers who celebrate the cultural distinctiveness of places and people, this is often an uncomfortable compromise—and yet, we must start somewhere. These four urban models offer a beginning, not an end.

■ URBAN LANDSCAPES

Cities, like all places inhabited by humans, demonstrate an intriguing array of cultural landscapes that gives varied insights to the complicated interactions between people and their surroundings. By reading these townscapes, we gain access to the past, open doors on the future, and better understand the different social forces shaping our settlements (see Figure 11.17). Grady Clay, in his enchanting book on reading American cityscapes, says:

> No true secrets are lurking in the landscape, but only undisclosed evidence, waiting for us. No true chaos is in the urban scene, but only patterns and clues waiting to be organized.

We agree, and in this section we offer some thoughts on how to view North American urban landscapes. We begin by discussing some themes,

FIGURE 11.17
There are various ways of looking at cityscapes: as indicators of change, as palimpsests, as expressions of visual biases, and as manifestations of symbolic traditions. This photo of Boston's central city offers evidence for all approaches. Which clues would you select to illustrate each cityscape theme?

geographical reference points, one might say, for investigating cityscapes. This is followed by a brief discussion of the different components of urban landscapes. Much of what we say will strike a familiar chord because our urban scene is the basis of so much of our life; you will find that you have great depths of intuitive knowledge about cityscapes.

Themes in Townscape Study

Cultural geographers look to cityscapes for many different kinds of information, and here we discuss five interconnected themes that are commonly used as organizational themes for landscape research.

Landscape Dynamics. Because North Americans are a restless people with little remorse about incessantly reshaping environments, our settlements are cauldrons of change. Think of some familiar indicators in the cityscape: downtown uses creeping into residential areas; deteriorated farmland on the city's outskirts; older buildings demolished for the new. These are all signs of specific processes effecting urban change; the landscape faithfully reflects this dynamic.

When these visual clues are systematically mapped and analyzed, they offer unquestionable evidence for the currents of change expressed in our cities. Of equal interest is to note where change is not occurring, those parts of the city where, for different reasons, the city remains relatively static. An unchanging landscape, then, also conveys an important message. Perhaps that part of the city is stagnant because it is removed from those forces effecting change in other parts. Or perhaps there is a conscious attempt by local residents to inhibit change, to preserve open space by resisting suburban development, for example, or by preserving a historic landmark.

In summary, look to the landscape to understand how our cities are changing. Not only is it where change first appears, but documenting landscape changes through time gives valuable insight into the paths and trajectories of settlement development.

The City as Palimpsest. Because cityscapes change through time, they offer a rich field for uncovering remnants of the past. A **palimpsest** is an old parchment used over and over for written messages. Before a new missive could be written, the old was erased; yet rarely were all the previous characters and words completely obliterated, so remnants of earlier messages showed through. This mosaic of old and new is called a palimpsest, a word geographers use fondly to describe the visual mixture of old and new in cultural landscapes.

The city is full of palimpsestic offerings, replete with historic artifacts scattered amidst the contemporary fabric. How often have you noticed an old Victorian farmhouse surrounded by new tract homes, or a historic street pattern obscured by a recent urban redevelopment project, or a brick factory shadowed by new high-rise office buildings? All of these give clues to past settlement patterns, and, again, all are mute testimony to the processes of change in the city.

But our interest in this historical mosaic is more than romantic nostalgia, for a systematic collection of these urban remnants provides us with glimpses of the past that might otherwise be hidden. All societies pick and choose what they wish to preserve for future generations and, in this process, a filtering takes place that often excludes and distorts information. But the landscape does not lie.

The urban palimpsest, then, is a way of finding the past in the contemporary landscape, of evaluating these remnants so as to glean a better understanding of historic settlement.

Landscape Tastes: The Look of the City.   Contrary to what many think, our North American cities should not be stereotyped as aesthetic junkyards, places where visual chaos reigns because of individualistic collections of cost-effective architectural solutions. Instead, there is much to be learned from a closer examination of urban scenic qualities.

First, look for places where there is some sort of control on visual change. People generally have "landscape tastes," visual biases that guide the scenic qualities of our environment. Some communities are more explicit than others in putting these tastes into legal form. San Franciscans, for example, have argued for more than a decade over the question of high-rise restrictions, in part because one segment of the community is interested in protecting traditional views of hills and bay. And many towns have sign ordinances that limit size and content of outdoor advertising. This too is a good focus for a study of landscape tastes.

Other communities go even further and attempt to legislate how all buildings should look. Some towns, for example, have strict controls on new construction, and it must fit in with building guidelines that articulate the community's conceptions of an idealized landscape. But geographers are not content simply to document that such restrictions exist; we also attempt to understand how they came about. Is there a consensus about landscape appearance? If so, how are these tastes effected, and what is the impact of these restrictions on the community? Restrictions usually mean sacrifices on someone's part, and forfeit is not often equally shared in any society; some people always pay more than others.

Another approach to visual analysis is to isolate those landscape traits that convey some sort of regional distinctiveness to a place. Why, for example, does Pittsburgh look different from Vancouver, or Eugene not like Salt Lake City? Obviously, many factors are responsible, factors such as different natural settings, distinctive human modification of the environment, different building materials and architectural style; all of these are important. We can call this regional distinctiveness a **sense of place,** the personality, one might say, that sets one city off from another, that makes it unique.

Major threats to a city's sense of place come from **visual convergence,** the tendency for our cities to take on similar appearances at the expense of regional traits. Much of this comes from widely shared solutions to building problems: similar construction technology, similar approaches to satisfying space and business needs, similar architecture. Warehouses, shopping malls, and high-rises are usually built the same way and for the same reasons in Atlanta as in Des Moines; consequently they tend to look alike. And the same is true for smaller-scale buildings, components of what we might call the "franchised landscape"—strip developments of similar-appearing motels, fast-food stores, service stations, clothing chains. Most of these structures are built on a national model; hence they are often insensitive to local visual traits. Although few would argue the convenience and economic efficiency of these developments, they do raise serious questions about continued regional distinctiveness.

Resistance to visual convergence is increasingly widespread, and offers a fascinating laboratory on how communities control their sense of place. As an illustration, a small coastal Maine town resisted plans by a well-known hamburger chain to construct one of its easily identifiable fast-food spots on a crucial corner of town. The community argued that the franchised architecture violates the New England townscape, that it is contrary to the town's sense of place. But the hamburger chain offered to compromise, to integrate its outlet into a large Victorian house instead of demolishing the historic structure. That confused the town. Were they genuinely concerned about appearance, in preserving the aesthetics of the community, or were they objecting mainly to the idea of a fast-food outlet in their town? The hamburger chain won. Because people always feel strongly about how their towns look, yet often feel equally strongly about economic development, there is a complicated social dynamic involved in protecting a settlement's sense of place from visual convergence.

Symbolic Townscapes.   Landscapes contain much more than literal messages about economic function. They are also loaded with figurative or metaphorical meaning, highly subjectivized emotion, memories, and content essential to the social fabric. To some, skyscrapers are more than high-rise office buildings: They are symbols of progress, economic vitality, downtown renewal, or corporate identities. Similarly, historic landscapes, those parts of the city where the past has been preserved, help people define themselves in time, establish social continuity with the past, and codify a forgotten, yet sometimes idealized, past.

D. W. Meinig, a geographer who has given much thought to these landscapes, maintains that there are three highly symbolized townscapes in the United States. They are the New England village, with its white church, commons, and tree-lined neighborhoods (Figure 11.18); Main Street of Middle America, the string street of a small Midwestern town, with storefronts, bandstand, and park; and what Meinig calls California Suburbia, suburbs of quarter-acre lots, effusive garden landscaping, swimming pools, and ranch-style homes.

> Each is based upon an actual landscape of a particular region. Each is an image derived from our national experience . . . simplified . . . and widely advertised so as to become a commonly understood symbol. Each has . . . influenced the shaping of the American scene over broader areas.

In a more political and problematic sense, we should be aware that the cultural landscape is an important vehicle for constructing and maintaining social and ethnic distinctions, and that this is often done in subtle and implicit ways that are intertwined with landscape symbols. To illustrate, geographers Jim and Nancy Duncan found that because conspicuous consumption is a major means for conveying social identity in our culture, elite landscapes are created and preserved through large-lot zoning, imitation country estates, and a constellation of detailed ornamental iconography; thus the residential landscapes in upper-income areas are controlled and managed so as to reinforce class and status categories. Their study of elite suburbs near Vancouver and New York sensitize us to how the cultural landscape can be thought of as a repository of symbols used by our society to differentiate itself and protect vested interests.

Cultural geographers are interested in how townscapes and landmarks take on symbolic significance, whether these idealizations are based on some sort of reality or, instead, are fabricated from diverse predilections. In addition, we are interested in how to assess the impact of these symbolic landscapes. After all, the hidden and shared messages inherent in loaded landscapes usually determine how we treat our environment; how it is managed, changed, or protected.

FIGURE 11.18
This view of a New England village (Springfield, Vermont, in this case) strikes a familiar chord for most of us because the landscape has become a symbol with diverse meanings. Think of the ways this symbol is used in art, literature, film, and television, and of the messages and emotion conveyed by this landscape.

Perception of the City.   During the last 20 years, social scientists have been concerned with measuring people's perceptions of the urban landscape. They assume that if we really know what people see and react to in the city, we can ask architects and urban planners to design and create a more humane urban environment, one that we would respond to in a positive manner.

Kevin Lynch, an urban designer, pioneered a method for recording people's images of the city. He assumed that all people have a mental map. After all, they must find their way about their cities in the course of daily life. Lynch then figured out ways that people could convey their mental maps to others. With this information, he could discover which parts of the urban landscape are being used as visual clues by which people. What do people react favorably or negatively to? What do they block out?

On the basis of interviews conducted in Boston, Jersey City, and Los Angeles, Lynch suggested five important elements in mental maps of cities:

1. *Pathways* are the routes of frequent travel, such as streets, freeways, and transit corridors. We experience the city from the pathways. Therefore, they become the threads that hold our maps together.
2. *Edges* are boundaries between areas, or the outer limits of our image. Mountains, rivers, shorelines, and even major streets and freeways are commonly used as edges. They tend to define the extremes of our urban vision; then we fill in the details.
3. *Nodes* are strategic junction points, such as breaks in transportation, traffic circles, or any place where important pathways come together.
4. *Districts* are small areas with a common identity, such as ethnic areas and functional zones (for instance, the CBD or a row of car dealers).
5. *Landmarks* are reference points that stand out because of shape, height, color, or historic importance. The city hall in Los Angeles, the Washington Monument in Washington, D.C., or the golden arches of a McDonald's are all landmarks.

Using these concepts, Lynch saw that some parts of the cities were more **legible** than others. Overall, Lynch discovered, legibility comes when the urban landscape offers clear pathways, nodes, districts, edges, and landmarks. The less legible parts of the city do not offer such a precise landscape. Thus it is more difficult for a person to form a mental map of that area. And further, some cities—such as Boston—are more legible than other cities. For example, Lynch found that Jersey City is a city of low legibility. Wedged between New York City and Newark, Jersey City is fragmented by railroads and highways. Residents' mental maps of Jersey City have large blank areas in them. When questioned, they can think of few local landmarks. Instead, they tend to point to the New York City skyline just across the river.

In the 1970s, the planning department of the City of Los Angeles undertook a comprehensive study to see what images different residents held of Los Angeles. Figure 11.19b shows the composite mental map of hundreds of residents. Note the important role of the mountains as visual edges (see Figure 11.19a). When visible, they set limits to the image of the

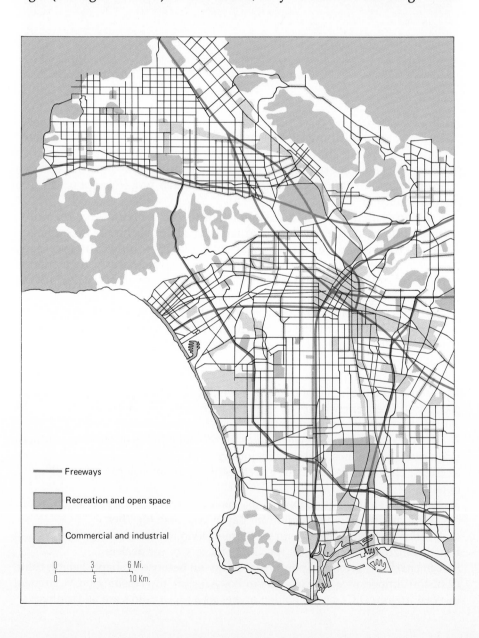

Freeways

Recreation and open space

Commercial and industrial

0   3   6 Mi.

0   5   10 Km.

FIGURE 11.19
Compare the map of physical form and land used in Los Angeles to the images of the city. The image is a map compiled from many mental maps described by residents. How do you think this exercise would turn out in your city?

Los Angeles basin. However, the mountains often are hidden by smog, which deprives Angelenos of an important point of reference.

In Los Angeles, freeways obviously serve as the major pathways. Note that in areas without freeways, there are large voids in the mental maps. This demonstrates the important role that pathways play in our image of a place. Some people seem to know how to get to a certain point only by the freeway, even though it may be faster and shorter to cut across town. However, rarely is a person's mental map changed with updated information.

Figure 11.20 illustrates how different social groups have vastly different images of the same city. Residents of the upper-income communities of Westwood and Northridge are highly mobile, traveling throughout Los Angeles for work, recreation, and services. As a result, their mental maps are rather comprehensive. In contrast, Avalon and Boyle Heights are

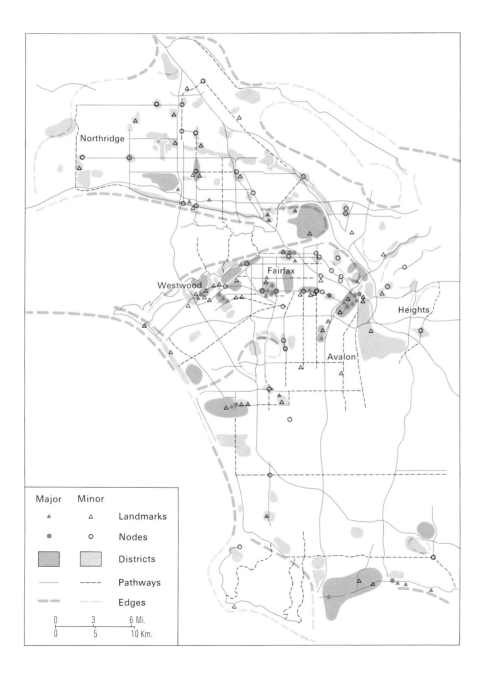

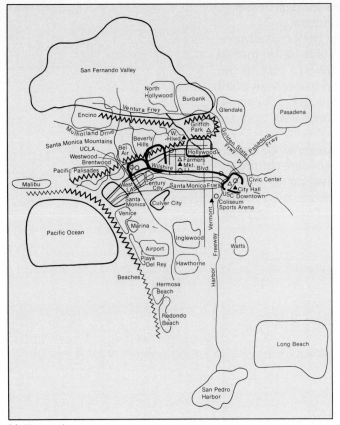

(a) Westwood

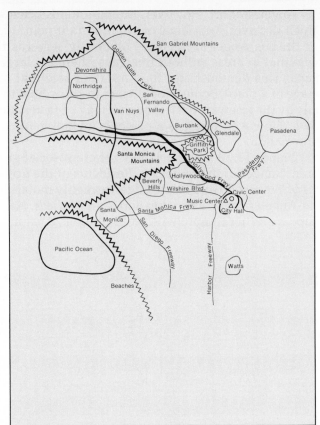

(b) Northridge

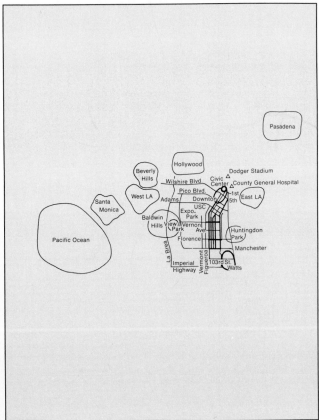

(c) Avalon

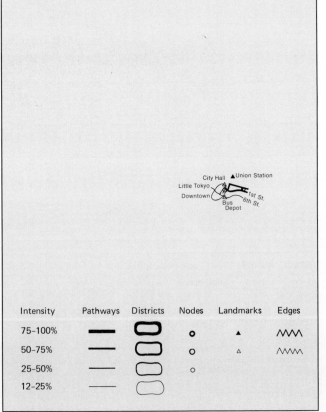

(d) Boyle Heights

Intensity	Pathways	Districts	Nodes	Landmarks	Edges
75–100%			o	▲	∧∧∧∧
50–75%			o	△	∧∧∧∧
25–50%			o		
12–25%					

low-income communities where social discrimination and economic hardship inhibit physical mobility. Boyle Heights is largely Mexican-American, so a language barrier further aggravates the situation. As you can see, the mental maps held by residents of these two communities are far less comprehensive than the images held by Westwood and Northridge residents. It is important to recognize that a limited mental map reinforces social isolation, which in turn furthers the plight of these communities. People rarely venture into unfamiliar areas; thus they miss potential job opportunities or other activities that might better their situations. Therefore, the mental map is both a product of isolation and a cause of it. People rarely have images of places where they haven't been, and they don't go into areas where they lack psychological reference points in the form of an urban image. We should remember that there are distinct ethnic, gender, and age variables to mental maps of cities, and these differences often influence everyday behavior.

Components of the Landscape

Now that you have seen some of the ways information can be organized about the cityscape, let us briefly discuss different components of this visual mosaic. Because much of this material about landscape has been touched upon in other parts of the book, we treat it here in succinct form, striving mainly to tie some new thoughts about your surroundings to familiar experiences. We have categorized this information under broad headings that may be helpful in organizing components of the cityscape.

Natural Elements.   Look again at how different physical elements, such as topography, vegetation, hydrology, even weather and climate, are integrated into the cityscape. While many cities have remolded their topographic surroundings by cutting into hills and filling depressions, most likely terrain still plays some role in contributing to the urban sense of place. Even Manhattan, which is often thought of as a flat island, takes some character from the subtleties of its topography. And how would Chicago look if it were built on hills instead of on a flat lake plain? Vegetation also plays an important role in giving some visual uniqueness to a town and, as well, it can help us decipher information about social patterns and settlement history. Contrast the stately elms of older neighborhoods with the often barren curbsides of newer suburbs. Think about how gardens express people's preferences, how they give us some clue to their own personal landscape tastes, or what garden landscaping tells us about ethnic heritage and income level.

   Weather and climate also are part of the landscape. Think of London and its fog, desert temperatures in Phoenix, rain in Seattle, and how the appearance of a city changes remarkably from summer to winter.

Street Patterns.   The gridiron pattern was discussed in Chapter 10. Although this is by far the most common street pattern in North America,

FIGURE 11.20
Compare these four mental maps of Los Angeles. Those for Westwood and Northridge illustrate the comprehensive mental images carried by upper middle-income people who have high mobility and move freely around the urban region. In contrast, the mental maps for two low-income groups, Avalon and Boyle Heights, show less knowledge of the city, which is a function of limited mobility. What causes a group to have reduced mobility? Both are minority areas. (From *The Visual Environment of Los Angeles,* Los Angeles Department of City Planning, 1971.)

look for departures from this form, places where the street pattern might predate the range and township survey, or where streets have been added on to the grid to break the monotony. Postwar suburbs rarely have streets laid out on the rectangular grid. Instead, most curve about the subdivision. Places where different street patterns converge usually convey important information about a settlement's past.

And take another look at street names. Toponyms (which are names on the land) have been discussed throughout this book, and cities are wonderful places to read this encyclopedia. Often they tell us much about unfulfilled aspirations (such as a Main Street that isn't); about a developer's family, where streets are named for children; or about longings for an idealized environment: Pastoral Place, Halcyon Drive, Sunset Drive. All sorts of fascinating stories are contained in place-names, and the city is no exception.

Open Spaces.   Open spaces come in all sorts of shapes and sizes, each with its own history. Look not just at the most apparent open spaces, although large parks and gardens do tell us much about the planning history of a city, but also at smaller places, at vacant lots, neighborhood parks, areas of apparent neglect where buildings have been demolished. These "leftover" spaces can give us information about recent changes in the city, city values and finances, and the pressures (or lack of them) on the town's land inventory. Rarely are there vacant lots in towns with a high building demand, while cities with a high number of vacant parcels often are stagnating or depressed areas.

Building Architecture and Material.   Probably nothing in the cityscape is quite so informative as a building's shape, architecture, and the materials used in construction. A little knowledge about different building styles can tie buildings to specific periods in the past. Construction techniques have differed through time; this too is an important aspect of the landscape. Brick cities look and feel very different from those where wood frame houses prevail. Steel framing for high-rises came about only in the late nineteenth century, so multistory buildings built before that time were usually restricted to five floors or less, which was the height limitation of nonframe construction.

Architectural styles tell us not only about a building's period, but also about its role in the city, about its original function. Note the differences between buildings designed by professionals and those that are owner-built: "vernacular" architecture, or what some call "folk" building.

Look also at those structures where there has been an apparent change of use, for the gas stations that harbor health food stores, or the boutiques in renovated brick factories, then tie these clues to different kinds of social and land use change.

Odds and Ends.   Last, think about some of the unique components of landscape, of the smells and odors, sounds and noises, of how they differ from city to city, and between neighborhoods. Lawn mowers buzzing on a Saturday afternoon and the smell of steaks broiling in the evening tell us it's suburbia; other parts of the city sound and smell different.

Look at signs and billboards to tell you about activities in various parts of the city. Take another look at the faded ones, the out-of-date posters, even the grafitti on the walls.

See how people bound their space, how they use fences between properties—or do without. Note how city institutions, factories, and industrial parks keep people out, or allow them in.

And look closely at the people in the landscape, at their dress, behavior, activities, style. One of the most important intuitive clues we have learned through time is to evaluate strangers. Take another look; stand back from your preconceptions and try to decipher more about the people you see on the street, for they are often the architects of a unique landscape.

■ CONCLUSION

People and activities spread themselves across the city in an intricate urban mosaic, and we have examined various components of this urban structure. Culture regions are found at a smaller scale than previously explored; in the city, neighborhoods and census units can be thought of as social areas and cultural regions.

We also see two major forces at work in the city that can be conceptualized as diffusion processes. One works to centralize activities within the city, the other to decentralize different activities into the suburbs. The latter is the dominant force currently at work in North American cities. But the costs of decentralization run high, not just to the suburbs, where unplanned growth takes its toll, but also to the inner cities, which are left with decayed and stagnant cores.

The cultural ecology of the city is a complicated issue because urbanization has modified natural ecosystems in a profound manner. Feedback from these systems, in the form of floods, landslides, and earthquakes, is a significant concern to urban dwellers everywhere. Urban vegetation can mitigate many of these problems if properly managed, yet that becomes an issue of public values, of weighing benefits against costs.

Cities, as a dense expression of human artifacts, offer a fascinating array of cultural landscapes that tell us much about ourselves and our interaction with the environment. These cityscapes convey different kinds of information, telling us about contemporary change, the past, our scenic values, our symbolic storehouse, all of which are subject to the vagaries of individual perception.

Because our cities are cultural creations, hewn from nature and reflecting the spectrum of social goals, technologies, values, and institutions, they are fitting topics of study for cultural geography and offer endless insight into our human mosaic.

Suggested Readings

John S. Adams (ed.). *Contemporary Metropolitan American.* Cambridge, Mass.: Ballinger, 1976.

John S. Adams. "The Geography of Riots and Civil Disorders in the 1960's," *Economic Geography,* 67 (January 1972), 24–42.

John Agnew, John Mercer, and David Sopher (eds.). *The City in Cultural Context.* Boston: Allen & Unwin, 1984.

Kay Anderson. "The Idea of Chinatown: The Power of Place and Institutional Practice in the Making of a Racial Category," *Annals of the Association of American Geographers,* 77 (1987), 580–598.

Wilfrid Bach and Thomas Hagedorn. "Atmospheric Pollution: Its Spatial Distribution over an Urban Area," *Proceedings of the Association of American Geographers,* 3 (1971), 22.

Brian J. Berry. *The Human Consequences of Urbanization.* New York: St. Martin's Press, 1973.

Brian Berry. *Comparative Urbanization.* New York: St. Martin's Press, 1982.

Stanley Brunn and Jack Williams (eds.). *Cities of the World: World Regional Urban Development.* New York: Harper & Row, 1983.

Manuel Castells. *The City and Grassroots: A Cross-Cultural Theory of Urban Social Movements.* Berkeley: University of California Press, 1983.

T. J. Chandler. "The Changing Form of London's Heat Island," *Geography,* 46 (1961).

City of Los Angeles. *The Visual Environment of Los Angeles.* Los Angeles: Department of City Planning, 1971.

Grady Clay. *Close-Up. How to Read the American City.* New York: Praeger, 1973.

Michael P. Conzen. "American Cities in Profound Transition: The New City Geography of the 1980s," *Journal of Geography,* 82 (1983), 94–101.

Roman Cybriwsky. "Social Aspects of Neighborhood Change," *Annals of the Association of American Geographers,* 9 (1983), 99–109.

Thomas Detwyler and Melvin Marcus (eds.). *Urbanization and Environment: The Physical Geography of the City.* Belmont, Calif.: Duxbury Press, 1972.

David Drakakis-Smith. *The Third World City.* London: Methuen, 1987.

James Duncan. "Review of Urban Imagery: Urban Semiotics," *Urban Geography,* 8 (1987), 473–483.

James Duncan and Nancy Duncan. "A Cultural Analysis of Urban Residential Landscapes in North America: The Case of Anglophile Elite," in John Agnew, John Mercer, and David Sopher (eds.), *The City in Cultural Context.* Boston: Allen & Unwin, 1984, pp. 255–276.

L. J. Evenden (ed.). "Vancouver: Western Metropolis," *Western Geographical Series,* 16 (1978).

Richard Fusch and Larry Ford. "Architecture and the Geography of the American City," *Geographical Review,* 73 (1983), 460–471.

Brian Godfrey. *Neighborhoods in Transition: The Making of San Francisco's Ethnic and Nonconformist Communities.* Berkeley: University of California Press, 1988.

Ernst Griffin and Larry Ford. "Cities of Latin America," in Stanley Brunn and Jack Williams (eds.), *Cities of the World: World Regional Urban Development.* New York: Harper & Row, 1983, pp. 199–240.

John Fraser Hart. "The Bypass Strip as an Ideal Landscape," *Geographical Review,* 72 (1982), 218–222.

Gerald Hodge and M. A. Qadeer. "The Persistence of Canadian Towns and Villages: Small Is Viable," *Urban Geography,* 1 (1980), 335–349.

George Hopkins (ed.). *Proceedings of the National Urban Forestry Conference.* Syracuse: State University of New York, 1980.

Homer Hoyt (ed.). *Structure and Growth of Residential Neighborhoods in American Cities.* Washington, D.C.: Federal Housing Administration, 1939.

J. B. Jackson. *The Necessity for Ruins and Other Topics.* Amherst: University of Massachusetts Press, 1980.

J. B. Jackson. *Discovering the Vernacular Landscape.* New Haven, Conn.: Yale University Press, 1985.

James H. Johnson (ed.). *Suburban Growth: Geographical Processes at the Edge of the City.* New York: Wiley, 1974.

R. J. Johnson. *The American Urban System: A Geographical Perspective.* London: Longman, 1982.

R. J. Johnson and D. T. Herbert. *Social Areas in Cities.* 2 vols. New York: Wiley, 1976.

Paul Knox. "Symbolism, Styles, and Settings," *Architecture and Behavior,* 2 (1984), 107–122.

David Lanegran. "Enhancing and Using a Sense of Place Within Urban Areas: A Role for Applied Cultural Geography," *The Professional Geographer,* 38 (1986), 224–228.

Peirce Lewis. "Learning from Looking: Geographic and Other Writing About the American Cultural Landscape," *American Quarterly,* 35 (1983), 242–261.

David Ley. *A Social Geography of the City.* New York: Harper & Row, 1983.

David Ley. "Styles of the Times: Liberal and Neo-Conservative Landscapes in Inner Vancouver, 1968–1986," *Journal of Historical Geography,* 13 (1987), 40–56.

William J. Lloyd. "Understanding Late Nineteenth-Century Cities," *Geographical Review,* 71 (1981), 460–471.

Kevin Lynch. *The Image of the City.* Cambridge, Mass.: M.I.T. Press, 1960.

L. D. McCann (ed.). *A Geography of Canada: Heartland and Hinterland,* 2nd ed. Englewood Cliffs, N.J.: Prentice-Hall, 1987.

K. MacDonald. "The Commercial Strip: From Main Street to Television Road," *Landscape,* 28 (1985), 12–19.

D. W. Meinig (ed.). *The Interpretation of Ordinary Landscapes. Geographical Essays.* New York: Oxford University Press, 1979.

Peter A. Morrison. "Urban Growth and Decline: San Jose and St. Louis in the 1960's," *Science,* 185 (August 1974), 757–762.

Lewis Mumford. *The City in History.* New York: Harcourt Brace Jovanovich, 1960.

Howard Nelson. "The Form and Structure of Cities: Urban Growth Patterns," *Journal of Geography,* 68 (1969), 198–207.

Risa Palm. "Reconsidering Contemporary Neighborhoods," *Landscape,* 26 (1982), 17–20.

Edward Relph. *The Modern Urban Landscape, 1880 to the Present.* Baltimore: Johns Hopkins University Press, 1987.

Lester Rowntree. "Creating a Sense of Place," *Journal of Urban History,* 8 (1981), 61–76.

Lester Rowntree and Margaret W. Conkey. "Symbolism and the Cultural Landscape," *Annals of the Association of American Geographers,* 70 (1980), 459–474.

Christopher L. Salter. "What Geographers See," *Journal of Geography,* 82 (1983), 50–53.

Forest Stearns and Thomas Montag. *The Urban Ecosystem: A Holistic Approach.* Stroudsburg, Pa.: Dowden, Hutchinson and Ross, 1974.

Fritz Steele. *The Sense of Place.* Boston: CBI Publishing, 1981.

George Sternlieb and James W. Hughes. "The Changing Demography of the Central City," *Scientific American,* 243 (1980), 48–53.

Gerald Suttles. *The Social Construction of Communities.* Chicago: University of Chicago Press, 1972.

Yi-Fu Tuan. *Topophilia: A Study of Environmental Perception, Attitudes and Values.* Englewood Cliffs, N.J.: Prentice-Hall, 1974.

U.S. Forest Service. *Proceedings of the Conference on Metropolitan Physical Environment.* Broomall, Pa.: Northeastern Forest Experiment Station, 1977.

James E. Vance, Jr. *This Scene of Man: The Role and Structure of the City in the Geography of Western Civilization.* New York: Harper & Row, 1977.

David Ward. "The Ethnic Ghetto in the United States: Past and Present," *Transactions, Institute of British Geographers,* 7 (1982), 258–275.

David Ward. *Cities and Immigrants.* New York: Oxford University Press, 1971.

Sam Bass Warner, Jr. *The Urban Wilderness: A History of the American City.* New York: Harper & Row, 1972.

Wilbur Zelinsky. "Where Every Town Is Above Average: Welcoming Signs Along America's Highways," *Landscape,* 30 (1988), 1–10.

Chapter 12

Industrial Geography

INDUSTRIAL REGIONS

Primary Industry
Secondary Industry
Tertiary Industry
Quaternary Industry
Quinary Industry

DIFFUSION OF THE INDUSTRIAL REVOLUTION

Origins of the Industrial Revolution
Diffusion from Britain

INDUSTRIAL ECOLOGY

Acid Rain
The Greenhouse Effect

Environmental Factors in Industrial Location

INDUSTRIAL CULTURAL INTEGRATION

Labor Supply
Markets
The Political Element in Industrial Location
Industrialization as an Agent of Cultural Change

INDUSTRIAL LANDSCAPES

CONCLUSION

Two great economic "revolutions" occurred in human development. The first of these was the domestication of plants and animals, which occurred in our dim prehistory. This agricultural revolution, discussed in Chapter 3, ultimately resulted in a huge increase in human population, a greatly accelerated modification of the physical environment, and major cultural readjustments. The second of these upheavals, the **industrial revolution,** is still taking place, and it involves a series of inventions leading to the use of machines and **inanimate power** in the manufacturing process. We live today at a pivotal point in the destiny of our species, for we are witnesses to this second revolution.

The industrial revolution, which began in the eighteenth century, released for the second time undreamed-of human productive powers. Suddenly, whole societies were able to engage in the seemingly limitless multiplication of goods and services. Rapid bursts of human inventiveness followed, as did gigantic population increases, and a massive, often unsettling remodeling of the environment. Today, the industrial revolution,

418

with its churning of whole populations and its restructuring of ancient cultural traditions into popular forms (see Chapter 8), is still running its course. There are few lands still largely untouched by its machines, factories, transportation devices, and communication techniques. Western nations, where this revolution has been under way the longest, are still feeling its sometimes painful, sometimes invigorating effects.

On an individual level, there is scarcely a facet of American life that has not been affected in a major way by the industrial revolution. A Friday night out might involve a drive in a car to a single outlet in a nationwide chain of restaurants, where you can order fried chicken raised several states away on special enriched grain, brought by refrigerated truck to a deep freeze, and cooked in an electric oven. Later, at a movie, you might buy a candy bar manufactured halfway across the country and have a soft drink delivered to you by a machine that has its own ice. Then you would enjoy a series of machine-produced pictures flashed in front of your eyes so fast that they seem to be moving. You could just as easily pick almost any other moment in your life, from sleep, with its permanent-press contoured sheets and its mass-manufactured alarm clocks, to your pet cat, with its chemical flea collar, canned food, and distemper shots. What you discover is that just about every object and every event in your life is affected, if not actually created, by the industrial revolution.

This chapter concentrates on industry and the industrial revolution as the cultural geographer sees it. In Western culture, the majority of the population owe their livelihoods either directly or indirectly to industry and its related products and services. Add to this the uneven spatial distribution of industry and its ecological ramifications, and you can understand the geographer's interest in this subject.

Five types of industrial activity can be distinguished. **Primary industries** are those involved in extracting natural resources from the earth. Fishing, hunting, lumbering, and mining are examples of primary industries (Figure 12.1). Agriculture, also a primary industry, was treated in Chapter 3. **Secondary industry** is the processing stage, commonly called manufacturing. It lies at the very heart of industrial activity. Secondary industries process the raw materials extracted by primary industries, transforming them into more usable form. Ore is converted into steel; logs are milled into lumber; fish are processed and canned. As a rule, several steps are involved in manufacturing. In this secondary stage, many factories turn out products that serve as raw materials for other secondary industries. Thus, steel mills provide steel for automobile factories, and lumber mills provide building materials for the construction industry. Construction is also a secondary industry.

The other three types of industrial activity all involve *services* of some sort, rather than the extraction or production of commodities. So wide is the range of services that industrial geographers find it useful to distinguish three sectors. **Tertiary** activities include transportation and communication facilities, which permit the distribution of goods and services. Highways, railroads, airlines, pipelines, telephones, radios, and television are all vital to the distribution of goods and services. Utilities also fall in the tertiary industrial sector. **Quaternary industry** includes most other producer services, such as trade, banking, insurance, law, wholesaling, and real estate, while **quinary industry** provides consumer services such as health, education, government, research, tourism, and recreational facilities. A rising focus of the quinary sector is the generation of knowledge and information, which is both a producer and consumer service.

FIGURE 12.1
An example of a secondary industry, this lumber mill is in Gabon, a nation of equatorial Africa. The oil industry has become one of the most controversial primary activities in recent decades. Periodic shortages and repeated price increases have made every citizen of the industrialized world aware of our dependence on this primary industry. The oil wells shown here are in Lake Maracaibo, Venezuela.

In the United States, the work force is divided among the five industrial sectors as follows; primary 4 percent, secondary 29 percent, tertiary 7 percent, quaternary 25 percent, and quinary 35 percent. Increasingly, American industry shifts toward the service sectors.

The five types of industry should not be thought of as totally separate operations that can be dealt with separately from one another. The worker in Detroit who gets laid off because her plant is moved to Singapore, the Argentinian who drinks a cola bottled in Argentina while watching "Miami Vice" on his Japanese-made TV, and the lumberman who buys a Taiwanese table made with wood he cut in Oregon are all involved in an interconnected economic system of global proportions. Single corporate entities called *conglomerates* may own scores of industries of all five types in a variety of fields. As a result, corporate planning, whether in the United States, Japan, Germany, or elsewhere, goes on at all levels at once. Scholars, for instance, have pointed out that labor costs and other factors have increasingly led United States corporations to send secondary industries overseas and export their products back to the United States, now a base for the service sectors.

Because industrialization is closely interwoven with the physical environment and with other facets of culture, because industry is unevenly distributed, because the industrial revolution is a series of ideas spreading by means of cultural diffusion, and because entire landscapes have been remolded and often deformed by industrialization, we can profitably apply the five themes of cultural geography to the study of industry. Thus, we will discuss industrial regions, the diffusion of industrial innovations, industrial ecology, the place of industry in cultural integration, and the industrial landscape.

▨ INDUSTRIAL REGIONS

Each type of industrial activity—primary, secondary, tertiary, quaternary, and quinary—displays unique spatial patterns. Geographers, applying the theme of culture region, refer to these as industrial regions, and Figure 12.2 reveals some of these patterns.

Primary Industry

Primary industries extract both renewable and nonrenewable resources. **Renewable resources** are those that can be used without being permanently depleted, such as forests, water, fishing grounds, and agricultural land. **Nonrenewable resources** are those that are depleted when they are used, such as minerals.

Many primary industries, especially those engaged in miming, are spread widely across the Earth. In fact, many regions that lack significant manufacturing activity have major primary industries. Figure 12.2 shows the main areas of primary and secondary industry. As a rule, however, primary industries are more likely to develop in conjunction with manufacturing districts. Zones of primary industry distant from manufacturing centers are likely to spring up only if the resource is very valuable and rare, and thus worth enough to withstand the cost of transporting it long distances. Almost every major area of secondary industry is surrounded by a "halo" of primary activity.

Secondary Industry

Most of the world's industrial activity is found in the developed market countries of the midlatitude Northern Hemisphere, especially in parts of Anglo-America, Europe, the Soviet Union, and Japan. This is particularly true of manufacturing. In the United States, many secondary industries are clustered in the northeastern part of the country, a region often referred to as the American Manufacturing Belt (see Figure 12.3). On the opposite Atlantic shore, manufacturing is concentrated in the central core of Europe, surrounded by a less industrialized periphery (see Figure 12.4). Most Soviet manufacturing is in the western third of the Soviet Union, while Japan's industrial complex is concentrated around the shore of the Inland Sea and throughout the southern part of the country (see Figures 12.5 and 12.6).

Many different types of manufacturing are found within the world's major regions. These often display considerable spatial segregation, so that a single industrial district might be composed of several zones, each dominated by a particular kind of industry. Figure 12.7 shows this segregation in the Ruhr district of West Germany. Iron and steel manufacture might be concentrated in one of these zones, chemical factories in another, textiles in a third, and automobile manufacture in a fourth. This pronounced regional specialization arose with the industrial revolution in the 1700s, causing manufacturing to take on a heightened geographical character.

Core and Periphery. Reflecting the enhanced regionalism that accompanied the industrial revolution was the development of economic **core and periphery.** The evolving industrial core consisted of the developed countries, with their collective manufacturing regions, while the periphery was

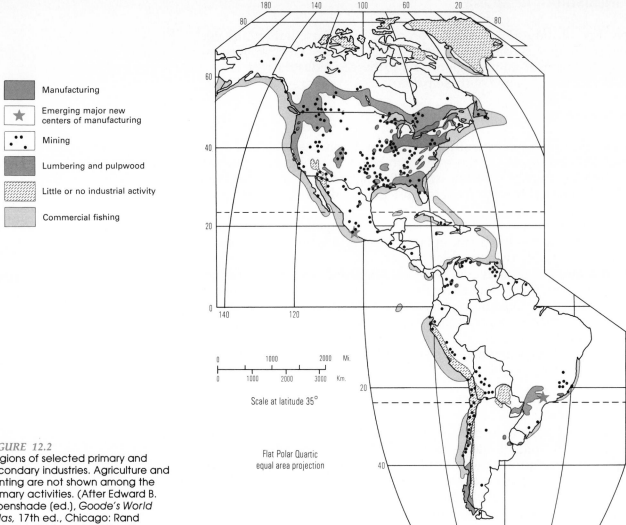

Manufacturing

Emerging major new centers of manufacturing

Mining

Lumbering and pulpwood

Little or no industrial activity

Commercial fishing

0   1000   2000   Mi.
0   1000   2000   3000   Km.

Scale at latitude 35°

Flat Polar Quartic
equal area projection

FIGURE 12.2
Regions of selected primary and secondary industries. Agriculture and hunting are not shown among the primary activities. (After Edward B. Espenshade (ed.), *Goode's World Atlas,* 17th ed., Chicago: Rand McNally, 1982, pp. 28–29, with modifications and simplification.)

formed of nonindustrial and weakly industrialized lands, including many colonies. Surplus value and resources were extracted from the increasingly impoverished peripheries and drawn to the core. The resultant geographical pattern—one of the fundamental realities of our age—is often referred to as **uneven development,** or regional disparity. Opinion differs concerning whether this industrial manifestation of the core/periphery concept is a correctable or inherent geographical feature of the world economy, capitalist and socialist alike. Uneven development has proven to be increasingly and unyieldingly present (see Figure 2.14).

Although the manufacturing dominance of the developed countries of the core persists, a major global geographical shift is currently under way in secondary industry. In virtually every core country, the secondary sector is in marked decline, factories are closing, blue-collar unemployment rates are the highest since the Great Depression of the 1930s, and a "deskilling" of the work force proceeds. In the United States, for example, where manufacturing employment began a relative decline about 1950, nine out of every ten new jobs in recent years have been unskilled, low-

paying service positions. The old, established manufacturing countries have adopted widely different strategies to cope with the decline, adding still more geographical contrasts to the industrial scene. West Germany, for example, has maintained an unusually high proportion of its work force in manufacturing by reinvesting for high productivity, offering high wages, specializing in expensive export-oriented products, and protecting the high level of labor skill through a well-developed apprenticeship system.

Manufacturing industries lost by the core countries are being relocated to newly industrializing lands of the periphery. South Korea, Taiwan, Singapore, Brazil, Mexico, and India, in particular, have experienced a major recent expansion of manufacturing, a movement that is continuing and beginning to involve many other peripheral countries.

Global Corporations. The ongoing locational shift in manufacturing regions is largely the work of **global corporations,** also called **multinationals** or **transnationals.** We can no longer think of decisions on market

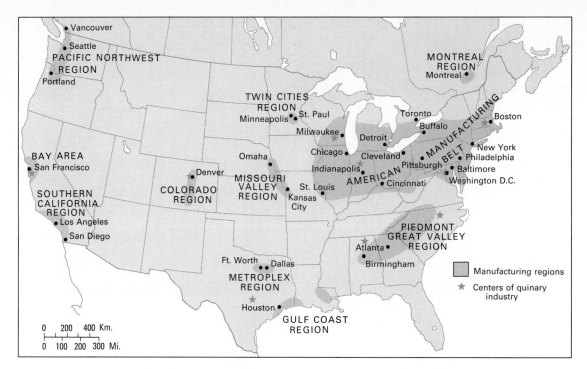

FIGURE 12.3

Major manufacturing regions and centers of quinary industry in Anglo-America. The largest and most important region is still the American Manufacturing Belt, the traditional industrial core of the United States. Dispersal of manufacturing to other regions has occurred mainly since World War II. What factors might explain the location of these regions?

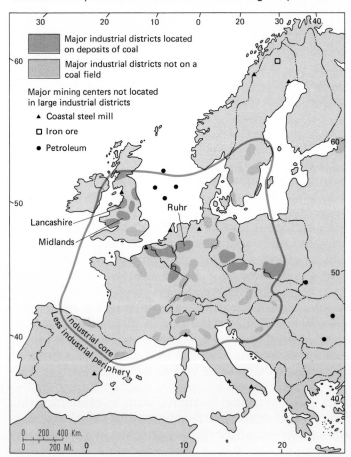

FIGURE 12.4

Industrial areas of Europe are plotted on this map. An industrialized core is surrounded by a less industrialized area. Does North America reveal a similar core/periphery pattern (see Figure 12.3)?

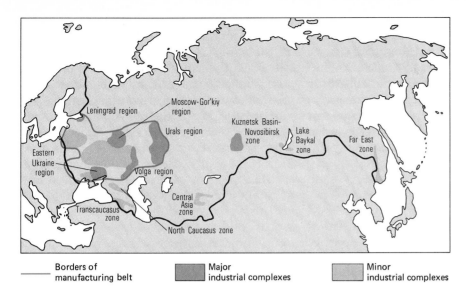

Borders of
manufacturing belt

Major
industrial complexes

Minor
industrial complexes

FIGURE 12.5
The Soviet manufacturing belt
developed close to Europe. In spite
of Soviet attempts to disperse their
industry, it remains concentrated in
the western third of the country.
What political and economic
problems does this cause for the
nation? (In part, after R. E. Lonsdale
and J. H. Thompson, "A Map of the
U.S.S.R.'s Manufacturing," Economic
Geography, 36 (1960), 36–52.)

location, labor supply, or other aspects of industrial planning within the framework of a single plant controlled by a single owner. Instead, we are dealing with a highly complex international corporate structure that plans on a gargantuan scale. Working through great corporations that straddle the Earth, people are able for the first time to utilize world resources with an efficiency dictated by the objective logic of profit.

Today, the size of corporate conglomeration is breathtaking. The total sales of global corporations are greater than the gross national product of every country except the United States and the Soviet Union. These corporate giants based mainly in the United States, Europe, and Japan have such sweeping control over international communications networks, the latest advances in modern technology, and large amounts of investment capital that they have effectively penetrated and often control the economic structures of underdeveloped states. Already 20 years ago, foreign interests controlled 67 percent of the metal-products industry in Mexico, 84 percent of the tobacco industry, and 100 percent of the rubber, electrical machinery, and automobile industries. In Argentina, global corporations

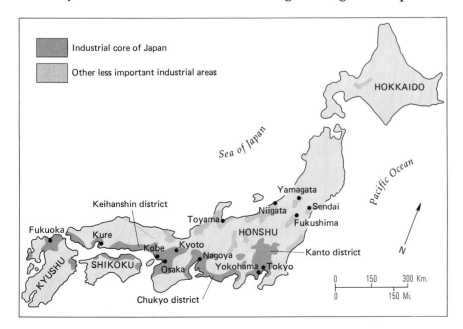

FIGURE 12.6
Japanese industrial areas
manufacture products for the entire
world. (In part, after John H.
Thompson and Michihiro Miyazaki,
"A Map of Japan's Manufacturing,"
Geographical Review, 49 (1959),
1–17.)

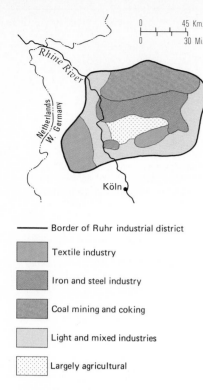

——— Border of Ruhr industrial district

Textile industry

Iron and steel industry

Coal mining and coking

Light and mixed industries

Largely agricultural

FIGURE 12.7
The Ruhr industrial district in West Germany is the single most important industrial area in all of Europe. Note the spatial segregation of different types of industry and the relatively small size of this particular district.

control more than 50 percent of each company in the top 50. Since the decision-making mechanisms of these locally based companies are geared toward the profit structure of the parent corporation and not toward the local economies in which they exist, their decisions, some scholars have argued, may well result in the further impoverishment of already poor peripheral countries, even as they develop their manufacturing sectors. Certainly, the global corporations have done little to reverse the widening gap between core and periphery.

The decline of primary and secondary industries in the older developed core, or **deindustrialization,** has ushered in an era widely referred to as the **postindustrial** phase. The three service sectors—tertiary, quaternary, and quinary—achieve dominance in the postindustrial phase. Both the United States and Canada can now be regarded as having entered the postindustrial era. The aging coal miner of Pennsylvania and veteran auto assembler in Ontario, born into an era of robust primary and secondary industry, now struggle for financial survival in countries that become increasingly deindustrialized.

Tertiary Industry

The tertiary industrial sector, part of the postindustrial phase, includes transportation, communication, and utility services. These developed originally in the period when manufacturing was dominant, and the geographical distribution of transportation facilities still closely parallels the spatial pattern of primary and secondary industry. Modern industries require well-developed transport systems, and every industrial district is served by a network of such facilities. Figure 12.8 maps the number of persons per motor vehicle by country. Major regional differences exist in the relative importance of the various modes of transport. In the Soviet Union, for example, highways are of little significance; railroads, and to a lesser extent waterways, carry most of the transport load. In the United States, on the other hand, highways are very important, while the railroad system is in decline. Many western European nations rely heavily on inland waterways. However, regional contrasts can be seen even within an area as small as Europe: The Netherlands moves the far greater part of all goods by river and canal; France has traditionally emphasized railroads at the expense of highway construction; and Italy uses highways far more than either railways or waterways. Beyond the industrialized regions, transport systems are much less developed. In most of Africa, interior Asia, and other weakly industrialized regions, motorable highways and railroads are rare.

The tertiary sector is changing rapidly with technological advances. In the postindustrial era, such services as electronic transfer of funds and telecommunications between computers that are cities or continents apart now rival the traditional importance of coal-carrying railroads or freight-moving trucks.

Quaternary Industry

Most industrial geographers understand the quaternary industrial sector to include those services required by producers, such as trade, insurance, legal services, banking, advertising, wholesaling, retailing, and real estate transactions. Such activities represent one of the major growth sectors in postindustrial economies, and a geographical segregation seems to

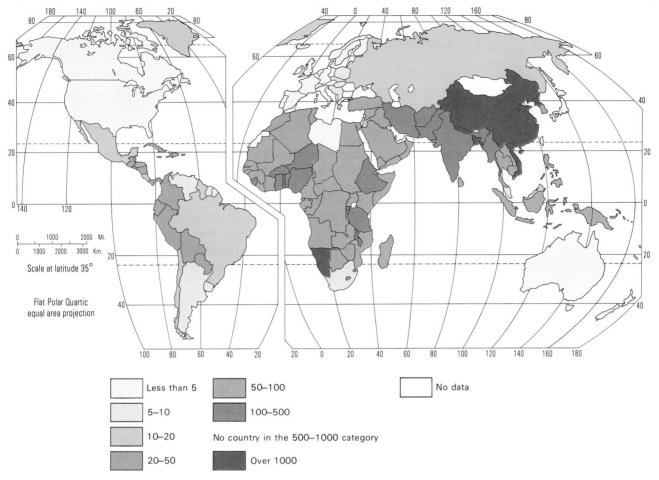

Less than 5	50–100	No data
5–10	100–500	
10–20	No country in the 500–1000 category	
20–50	Over 1000	

FIGURE 12.8
The number of persons per motor vehicle (cars and trucks) is mapped here. The most highly industrialized nations have the largest numbers of cars and trucks per unit of population. (United Nations, *Statistical Yearbook,* 1983–84, pp. 1011–1017.)

be developing, in which manufacturing is increasingly shunted to the peripheries while corporate headquarters, markets, and the producer-related service activities remain in the core. An inherent problem in this spatial arrangement is **multiplier leakage.** Capital is invested by global corporations in secondary industry in the peripheries, but most of the profits flow back to the core, since the headquarters and service sectors remain there. Between 1960 and 1970, for instance, American-based corporations took, on the average, 79 percent of their net profits out of Latin America. As a result, the industrialization of less-developed countries is actually increasing the power of the world's established industrial nations. In fact, while industrial technology has spread everywhere, today we face a world in which the basic industrial power of the planet is more centralized than ever. The responsible global or multinational corporations are headquartered mainly in quaternary areas where the industrial revolution took root earliest—the midlatitude countries of the Northern Hemisphere. Similarly, loans for industrial development are made by banking institutions in Europe and the United States, with the result that crippling interest payments drain away from the poor to the rich countries.

Within the quaternary sector, regional contrasts other than core/periphery also generally develop. Some cities become centers of banking and finance; others focus on trade or insurance. No matter what sector of industry we consider, the geographical dimension is at once evident.

Quinary Industry

Quinary industrial activity centers on various consumer or household-related services, such as education, administration or government, recreation/tourism, and health/medicine. Its focus, however, is upon collection, generation, storage, retrieval, and processing of knowledge and information, including research, publishing, consulting, and forecasting. Postindustrial society is organized around knowledge and innovation, which are used to acquire profit and exert social control. New knowledge leads to new ways of doing things and to new products and services. Change thereby spreads from the quinary sector to the other four types of industrial activity.

Quinary industry depends on a highly skilled, intelligent, creative, and imaginative labor force, and as such is elitist. While focused geographically in the old industrial core, the distribution of quinary activity, if viewed on a more local scale, can be seen to coalesce around major universities and research centers. The presence of Stanford and the University of California at Berkeley, for example, helped make the San Francisco Bay area a major center of quinary industry, and similar foci have developed near Harvard and M.I.T. in New England and the triuniversity Raleigh-Durham-Chapel Hill "Research Triangle" of North Carolina (Figure 12.3).

At the heart of the quinary sector is the modern electronic computer. A fierce competition to upgrade the technology of this remarkable invention accounts for a considerable portion of quinary activity. The massively funded Sematech Corporation, drawing on both private and public financing, has been created to help preserve the American advantage in computer technology, and the choice of Austin, Texas, as a site for its main center, following competitive bids from many areas, boosted that city firmly into the quinary industrial age. The equally fierce national competition to obtain the new "superconducting supercollider" facility for experimental physics represents yet another reminder of the growing importance of quinary activity.

Activities such as tourism are also classified in the quinary sector by many industrial geographers. Tourism is a nearly universal behavior in postindustrial societies and is much less common in areas dominated by primary and secondary industries. In common with all industrial activity, tourism also displays major regional differences. Environmental and cultural amenities often serve as magnets for tourist movement.

The theme of culture region allows, at best, a rather static description of industrial regionalization, of uneven development and the core/periphery pattern. By turning now to our second theme, diffusion, we can better see how these distributions came to be.

■ DIFFUSION OF THE INDUSTRIAL REVOLUTION

The world map of industrial regions is a good measure of how far the industrial revolution has spread, how far the cultural diffusion of this revolution's constantly evolving technology and ideas has proceeded. Until the industrial revolution, the large majority of people were concerned with the most basic of primary economic activities—acquiring from the land the necessities of survival. Society and culture were overwhelmingly rural and agricultural. To be sure, industry existed in this setting, since humans are by nature makers of things. For as long as our biological species has existed, we have fashioned tools, weapons, utensils, clothing, and other objects, but traditionally these items were made by hand, laboriously and slowly. Before about 1700, virtually all such manufacture was carried on in two rather distinct systems: **cottage (household) industry** and **guild industry.**

Cottage industry, by far the most common, was practiced in farm homes and rural villages, usually as a sideline to agriculture. Objects for family use were made in each household, and most villages had a cobbler, miller, weaver, and smith who worked part time at these trades in their homes. Skills were passed from parents to children with little formality.

By contrast, the guild system consisted of professional organizations of highly skilled, specialized artisans engaged full time in their trades and living in towns and cities. Membership in a guild was attained through a long apprenticeship, during which the master craftsman taught the apprentice the secrets of the profession. The guild was a fraternal organization of artisans skilled in a particular craft, so that there were guilds for weavers, glassblowers, silversmiths, steel makers, and potters. While the cottage and guild systems were different in many respects, they did share one trait: Both depended on hand labor and human power.

Origins of the Industrial Revolution

The industrial revolution arose mainly among English cottage craftspeople, and fundamentally restructured secondary industry. First, human hands were replaced by machines in the fashioning of finished products, rendering the word *manufacturing* ("made by hand") technically obsolete. No longer would the weaver sit at a hand loom and painstakingly produce each piece of cloth. Instead, large mechanical looms were invented to do the job faster and more economically (though not necessarily better). Second, human power was replaced by various forms of inanimate power. The machines were driven by water power, the burning of fossil fuels, and later by hydroelectricity and the energy of the atom. Men and women, once the proud producers of fine handmade goods, became tenders of machines.

We know a lot more about the origins and diffusion of the industrial revolution than we do about the beginnings of agriculture. The industrial revolution is a matter of recorded history and has been studied in great detail. We can pinpoint its origin. The industrial revolution began in England in the early 1700s, though it is possible to trace its antecedents back even earlier. Within a century and a half of its beginnings, this economic revolution had greatly altered all three levels of industrial activity.

Textiles. The initial breakthrough came in the secondary or manufacturing sector. More exactly, it occurred in the British cotton textile cottage industry, centered at that time in the district of Lancashire in western England. At first the changes were modest and on a small scale. Mechanical looms were invented, and flowing water, long used as a source of power by local grain millers, was harnessed to drive the looms. During this stage, manufacturing industries remained largely rural, scattered about at the sites where rushing streams could be found, especially waterfalls and rapids. Later in the eighteenth century, the invention of the steam engine provided a better source of power, and a shift away from water-powered machines was made.

In the beginning, the industrial revolution was really a cotton revolution. In England, until about 1830, "factories" or "industry" meant the production of cotton cloth (Figure 12.9). No other industry even remotely

FIGURE 12.9
The first major industry of the industrial revolution was the production of cotton cloth. This etching, dated 1835, shows cotton being spun into thread. The textile industry was characteristic of manufacturing in the United Kingdom.

approached the million and a half people directly or indirectly involved in Britain's textile production. In the United States, too, the first factories were textile plants.

Metallurgy. Traditionally, metal industries had been small-scale, rural enterprises. They were carried on in small forges situated near ore deposits and relied on forests to provide charcoal for the smelting process. The chemical changes that occurred in the making of steel were not understood even by the craftspeople who used them, and much ritual, superstition, and ceremony were associated with steel making. Techniques had changed little since the beginning of the Iron Age, 2000 years before.

The industrial revolution radically altered all this. In the eighteenth century, a series of inventions by master ironmakers living in the valley of the Severn River in Shropshire, at the Coalbrookdale south of Lancashire in the English Midlands, allowed the old traditions, techniques, and rituals of steel making to be swept away and replaced with a scientific, large-scale industry. Coke, which is nearly pure carbon and is derived from high-grade coal, replaced charcoal in the smelting process. Large blast furnaces were invented to replace the forge, and efficient rolling mills took the place of hammer and anvil. Mass production of steel was the result, and the new industrial order was built of steel. Other manufacturing industries made similar transitions, and entirely new types of manufacturing arose, such as machine making.

Mining. Primary industries were also revolutionized. The first to feel the effects of the new technology was coal mining. The adoption of the steam engine necessitated huge amounts of coal to fire the boilers, and the conversion to coke in the smelting process further increased the demand for coal. Fortunately, Britain had large coal deposits. New mining techniques and tools were invented, so that coal mining became a large-scale, mechanized industry. Because coal was heavy and bulky, it was difficult to transport. As a result, manufacturing industries began flocking to the coalfields in order to be near the supply. Similar modernization occurred in the mining of iron ore, copper, and other metals needed by rapidly growing industries.

FIGURE 12.10
The invention of the railroad played a vital role in the development of the industrial revolution. This old print depicts the Phoenix locomotive and carriage.

Railroads. The industrial revolution also affected the tertiary sector, most notably in the form of rapid bulk transportation. The traditional wooden sailing ships gave way to steel vessels driven by steam engines, canals were built, and the British-invented railroad came on the scene (Figure 12.10). The principal stimulus that led to these transportation breakthroughs was the need to move raw materials and finished products from one place to another, both cheaply and quickly. The impact of the industrial revolution would have been minimized had not the distribution of goods and services also been improved (see box, "Distance in the Preindustrial Age"). It is no accident that the British, creators of the industrial revolution, also invented the railroad and initiated the first large-scale canal construction. Nor is it accidental that the British also revolutionized the shipbuilding industry and dominated it from their Scottish shipyards even into the twentieth century.

It should be realized, however, that the development of these three sectors of industry was closely intertwined. The English railroad was the creation of the coal mines. The first modern railway ran from the inland coalfield of Durham to the English coast. The earliest locomotive drivers were all hired out of coal areas. In turn, the iron and steel industries, the

DISTANCE IN THE PREINDUSTRIAL AGE

Our lives are a constant adventure in shrinking space. With a car, we're just minutes from a friend miles away. The airplane has put us within jet-lag distance of Paris, Moscow, or Calcutta. Rockets are bringing the solar system into our distance calculations. In such an age, it is hard to imagine what an obstacle distance often proved to be before the industrial revolution.

A record of 10,000 letters sent to Venice, Italy, in the early sixteenth century shows clearly what a factor distance was in the preindustrial world. Letters from nearby Genoa took an average of 6 days to arrive; London, 27; Constantinople, 37; Lisbon, 46; Damascus, 80. But these average figures hardly tell the whole tale. Changing human and climatic conditions lent a striking elasticity to mail delivery. Deliveries from Paris ranged from a maximum of 34 days to a minimum of 7 days; Barcelona, 77 to 8; and Florence, 13 to 1, to pick three places at random. Zara, which was separated from Venice by only a short stretch of the Adriatic Sea, held the record. Its letters, depending upon sailing conditions, took from a maximum of 25 to a minimum of 1 day to arrive. Compared to other goods, however, letters moved briskly across the map. Sixteenth-century Italian businessmen normally assumed that it took even their privileged goods three months to reach London.

In fact, before the eighteenth century, distance had been a relatively constant factor for centuries. In terms of travel, the Mediterranean was about the same "size" in the sixteenth century as it had been in Roman times over 1000 years earlier. Traveling times did not change much until the nineteenth century.

From Fernand Braudel, *The Mediterranean and the Mediterranean World in the Age of Phillip II* (New York: Harper & Row, 1972), vol. 1, p. 356.

basic core of the industrial system, were mainly the creation of the railroad. It was the burst of railroad building that provided Britain's tiny iron industry with a demand large enough to justify investment in its expansion. For a single mile (1.6 kilometers) of rail, 300 tons (272 metric tons) of steel were needed for track alone. As a result, the first two decades of railroad building, 1830–1850, saw iron and steel production increase from 680,000 to 2,250,000 tons (617,000 to 2,041,000 metric tons). In the same period, the output of coal, which first fostered the development of the railroad, soared from 15 million to 49 million tons (13.6 to 44.4 metric tons), in part to stoke the growing steel industry.

Diffusion from Britain

For a century, Britain maintained a virtual monopoly on its industrial innovations. Indeed, the British government actively tried to prevent the diffusion of the various inventions and innovations that made up the industrial revolution, because they gave Britain an enormous economic advantage and contributed greatly to the growth and strength of the British Empire. Nevertheless, this technology finally diffused beyond the bounds of the British Isles (see Figure 12.11). Continental Europe was the first to receive its impact. In the last half of the nineteenth century, the industrial revolution took firm root in Germany, Belgium, and other nations of northwestern and central Europe. The diffusion of railroads in Europe provides a good index to the spread of the industrial revolution there (Figure 12.12). The United States began rapid adoption of this new technology about 1850, followed a half-century later by Japan, the first major non-Western nation to undergo full industrialization. In the first third of the present century, the diffusion of industry and modern transport spilled over into the Soviet Union, and more recently, as we have

FIGURE 12.11
The diffusion of the industrial revolution has changed cultures in much of the world.

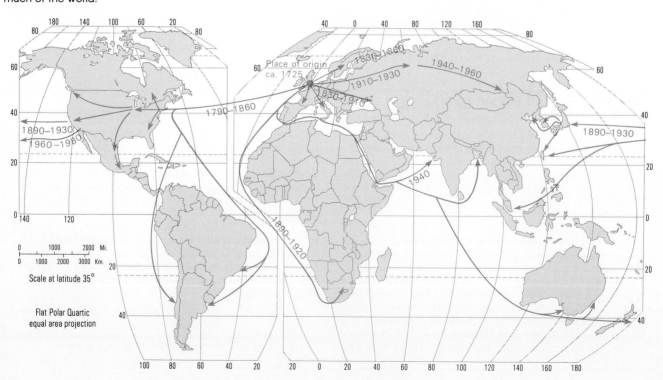

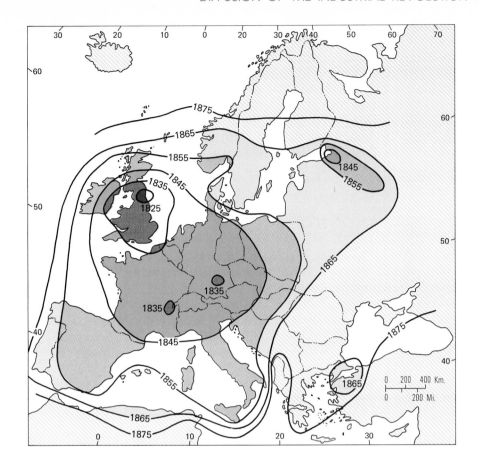

FIGURE 12.12
The diffusion of the railroad in Europe. The industrial revolution and the railroad spread together across much of the continent.

seen, countries such as Taiwan, South Korea, Hong Kong, and Singapore have joined the manufacturing age.

In the United States, the spread of the railroad affected the distribution of industries both within cities and within regions. Steel mills, refineries, meat-packing plants, and other industrial complexes sprang up at major rail terminals. Wherever it went, the railroad concentrated industry; yet, at the same time, its presence allowed for a greater regional diversification of industrial tasks. Small cities began to specialize in the production of specific industrial goods based on local skills and resources, as parts of large, railroad-linked industrial clusters. By 1916, the American rail network had reached its height with 254,000 miles (409,000 kilometers) of track, carrying 77 percent of all intercity freight tonnage, and 98 percent of intercity passengers.

Few cultures exposed to industrial innovations have proved resistant to them. However, the spread of the industrial revolution could be halted or even reversed by determined political administrators. A striking example was Britain's deliberate deindustrialization of its Indian colony to create a market for its cotton products. India's textile industry had traditionally exported cotton goods to all parts of the world. As late as 1815, India exported to England cotton goods worth 50 times the British cotton goods it imported. However, imperial Britain, which had used high tariffs to protect its own cotton production, opened India to "free trade." Using its imperial power, it caused India's old industrial centers to die. Dacca, now in Bangladesh, became partly overgrown with jungle, and skilled Indian workers were forced into the countryside to take up agricultural pursuits. In the end, India, once a great cotton textile producer, exported only raw cotton to Britain, where it was turned into textile goods and sent back to India to be bought.

Britain's political and military pressure helped it to conquer a world market for its exploding industrial plant. In a sense, then, it spread the industrial revolution across the planet. However, in practical terms, it turned its colonies into giant plantations or mines for the production of raw materials to be processed in Britain. India's actual industrialization was set back at least half a century. Perhaps only the independence of the United States, through its revolutionary war against Britain, saved it from a similar fate.

▮ INDUSTRIAL ECOLOGY

The diffusion of the industrial revolution has occurred only at enormous environmental expense. By its very nature, the technology of modern industry consumes nonrenewable resources and damages the natural environment. Massive pollution of the air and water seems to be an unavoidable by-product of mechanized secondary industrial processes, at least in our present state of knowledge. While pollution and environmental alteration could be significantly reduced, can they ever be totally eliminated if mechanized culture is to maintain its industrial base? Perhaps in the final analysis we will find that industrialization, which has become so integral a part of our culture in the past two centuries, is simply ecologically untenable and cannot be maintained. In short, our modern industrial way of life may prove a maladaptive strategy in terms of cultural ecology.

Our experience with industrialization has been too short and shallow to permit an adequate perspective on the problem. In the United States, we have lived with the industrial revolution for a little over one century. What would the ecological impact of this system be after two centuries, ten centuries, twenty centuries? We can only guess, but many experts are not optimistic. What we do know is that the technology of the industrial revolution has demanded that we modify our habitat on a previously undreamed-of scale, and at the same time it has provided us with the tools and techniques to carry out that massive modification.

Acid Rain

In almost every decade, it seems, we learn of some new, previously unsuspected impact of our industrial economy on the environment. Most often, these rapidly developing crises involve the generation of energy so essential in the industrial world.

Acid rain, known to researchers since the 1950s, attained public awareness about 1980. The burning of fossil fuels by power plants, factories, and automobiles releases into the air acidic sulfur oxides and nitrogen oxides, which are in turn flushed from the atmosphere by precipitation. The resultant rainfall has a much higher than normal acidity. For example, a shower that fell on the town of Kane, in northern Pennsylvania, on September 19, 1978, had a pH reading equivalent to vinegar. Overall, 84 percent of energy in the world is generated by burning fossil fuels, making acid rain a prevalent phenomenon.

Acid rain is capable of poisoning fish, damaging plants, and diminishing soil fertility. Such problems have been intensively studied in West Germany, one of the most completely industrialized nations in the world. German scholars have been impressed by the dramatic suddenness with which the catastrophic effects of acid rain have arrived. In 1982, only 8 percent of West German forests showed damage, but by 1984 the proportion had risen to half. Only a crash program of pollution control and energy conservation can now save the woodlands of Germany. In the words of geographer Wilfrid Bach, "The ongoing forest dieback demands that without any further delay, emission of these pollutants must be controlled at the source much more effectively," if the German forests are not to perish.

In North America the effects of acid rain are accumulating, but not with the catastrophic speed seen in central Europe (Figure 12.13). Over 90 lakes in the seemingly pristine Adirondack Mountains of New York were "dead," devoid of fish life, by 1980, and 50,000 lakes in eastern Canada face a similar fate. Recent studies suggest that acid rain is now causing mass killings of marine life along the northeastern coast of the United States. Oxides of nitrogen seem to be the principal culprit in the coastal waters, and the impact has been noted in Chesapeake, Delaware, and Narragansett bays, as well as Long Island Sound. The government of

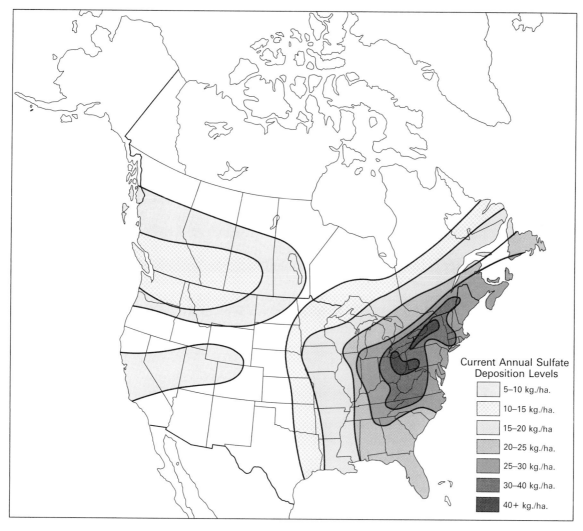

Current Annual Sulfate
Deposition Levels

5–10 kg./ha.

10–15 kg./ha.

15–20 kg./ha

20–25 kg./ha.

25–30 kg./ha.

30–40 kg./ha.

40+ kg./ha.

FIGURE 12.13

Distribution of acid rain in North America, as measured by the annual sulfate deposition, derived from airborne sulfur oxides (SO₂). Deposition levels of 20 kg/ha. (or 18 lb per acre) are generally regarded as threatening to some aquatic and terrestrial ecosystems. Nitrate components of acid rain are not shown. (Source: Canadian Embassy, Washington, D.C., 1984.)

ALFRED WEBER
1868–1958

Weber, the most influential pioneer theorist of industrial location, in 1909 published his seminal work, later translated as *Theory of the Location of Industry*. Most subsequent research in industrial location theory represents attempts by others to refine or refute his model. Many aspects of Weber's theory remain viable today and are presented in this chapter.

Weber's wide-ranging intellect defies academic disciplinary boundaries. He dealt at one time or another with sociology, culture history, economic geography, philosophy, political science, art, poetry, law, and economics; his writings are far too diverse to classify. Born in Erfurt, Germany, Weber earned a doctorate at Berlin in 1897. A decade later he assumed the chair of social science and political economy at Heidelberg University in southwestern Germany, a position he occupied for the remainder of his long career. The Alfred Weber Institute for Social and Political Sciences at Heidelberg commemorates his achievements. He represents yet another of the German founding fathers of modern geography.

Canada has for some years urged United States officials to take stringent action to help alleviate acid-rain damage, since much of the problem on the Canadian side of the border derives from American pollution, but so far their pleas have been to little avail.

Now even China's forests are beginning to succumb to acid rain. The problem, clearly, has assumed global proportions.

The Greenhouse Effect

Also produced by the burning of fossil fuels, the **greenhouse effect** offers the possibility of catastrophic change of the Earth's climate. Every year, 22,000,000,000 tons (20 billion metric tons) of carbon dioxide are produced worldwide by fossil fuel burning, a level 50 times that prevalent in 1860. In addition, the ongoing destruction of the world's rain forests adds huge additional amounts of CO_2 to the atmosphere. While CO_2 is a natural component of the Earth's atmosphere, the freeing of this huge additional amount is altering the chemical composition of the air. Carbon dioxide, only one of the absorbing gases involved in the greenhouse effect, permits solar shortwave heat radiation to reach the Earth's surface, but acts to block or trap longwave outgoing radiation, causing a thermal imbalance and global heating.

The result could be, at worst, a runaway buildup of solar heat that would evaporate all water and make any form of life impossible, causing planted Earth to resemble more closely hostile Venus. Less catastrophically, the greenhouse effect could warm the global climate only enough to melt or partially melt the polar icecaps, causing the sea level to rise as much as hundreds of feet and inundate the world's coastlines. The long-term effects of even this lesser change could have disastrous results for humankind. The worst-case scenario for the year 2030 seems to include a climatic warming to the level known 4 million years ago, in the mid-Pliocene age.

The onset of the greenhouse effect could be sudden, as some critical, unknown threshold is reached in atmospheric carbon dioxide. This doomsday is possibly being delayed by another industrial-related environmental alteration—the addition of huge amounts of **particulate matter** to the atmosphere. Such pollution acts to block out solar radiation and cool the climate. The two atmospheric processes, greenhouse effect and particulate pollution, may have acted to neutralize each other, at least so far. If this is the case, the balance achieved is a precarious one. Citizens of the industrial age need to be aware of the possible impacts of our newfound adaptive strategy.

Environmental Factors in Industrial Location

If the industrial revolution has brought accelerated physical environmental change, it has also been governed in part by the same environment. The spatial distribution of industry in particular has been influenced by environmental considerations.

Industrial location theory, pioneered by Alfred Weber (see biographical box), seeks the optimal siting for each firm. The underlying assumption is that the usual goal in locating an industry is cost minimization. Various environmental factors must be figured into cost, including raw materials, energy sources, and restrictions related to climate and terrain.

Raw Materials.   In the early stages of the industrial revolution, industries grew where the raw materials were. The reason was simple. The development of efficient means of mass transportation only came about a century after the beginning of the revolution. Before about 1830 or 1840, it was impossible to move bulky, heavy raw materials very far. In the last century and a half, the attraction of industry to raw materials has steadily decreased because of improved transportation facilities, yet it has not been eliminated altogether.

As a rule, we can say that manufacturers, in attempting to minimize the costs of production, will locate near their raw materials if there is a great loss of weight or bulk in the manufacturing process, or if the finished product is less perishable than the raw materials from which it is made (Figure 12.14). The refining of minerals, the manufacture of iron, steel, and paper, and the canning of fish are examples of industries attracted for these reasons to the source of raw materials.

In industrial location, we should also recognize the phenomenon called **industrial inertia.** This refers to the tendency of industries to remain in their initial locations, even after the forces that attracted them there cease to act. Some industries that were drawn to the sources of raw materials in the 1700s or early 1800s, before the advent of modern modes of transportation, remain in the same location. This inertia occurs because capital investment in the form of land and structures would have to be sacrificed if the industry were relocated. In addition, the present labor force would be difficult to relocate with the industry. It is not uncommon to find industries that remained in the same place even after the non-renewable raw materials that originally attracted them were completely exhausted. Even so, the continued improvement of transport facilities has caused the locational pull of raw materials to become rather inconsequential in most industries. In 1909, Alfred Weber concluded that transport costs for raw materials were of fundamental importance in factory location, but that no longer is true.

FIGURE 12.14
The location of industry is influenced by the location of raw materials and energy supply, among other factors. This steel plant benefits by locating close to sources of coal in Pennsylvania. Enormous quantities wait nearby for use in the manufacturing process.

Energy Supply. The quantity of energy consumed by industries, measured either as a total amount or per unit of goods produced, has increased greatly since the beginning of the industrial revolution. In a proper sense, energy was not "consumed" at all when water power was used, because water is a renewable power source. Rather, the rapid increase of power use began with the shift from water power to the steam engine and accelerated with the subsequent adoption of other power sources, in particular, electricity.

During the early part of the industrial revolution, long-distance shipment of fossil fuels, from which inanimate power was derived, was too costly to be economically feasible. As a result, industrial plants requiring large amounts of energy were forced to locate where water power or coal was available. Later inventions, such as the railroad, pipeline, motorized barges, and seagoing tankers, have largely removed this restriction on location. The harnessing of electricity and development of high-tension power lines further reduced the locational pull of power supplies.

A few types of manufacturing are still strongly attracted to the sites of energy production. One of these is the aluminum industry, which consumes huge amounts of electricity in the process of converting the raw material bauxite into aluminum. Hydroelectric sites are preferred, since the electricity generated by falling water is renewable and hence cheaper than electricity produced by burning coal or petroleum products. Since electricity cannot be transmitted great distances without considerable loss of power from the transmission lines, location near the hydroelectric facility is best, though recent developments in superconductivity may alter this situation. Hydroelectric sites have attracted aluminum industries to relatively remote places such as Soviet Siberia and the Pacific coastal mountains of Canada. So great are the needs for electric power in this industry that such remote places, hundreds or even thousands of miles removed from the sources of bauxite and the markets for aluminum, are economically practical.

The world entered a new phase of energy consumption when many of the leading oil-producing nations banded together to form OPEC, the Organization of Petroleum Exporting Countries. Because of OPEC actions, the price of petroleum soared, reaching more nearly its valid market value. The problem in this case, however, is not one of industrial location as related to energy source and not one of energy transport, but rather the cost of energy at the wellhead. It seems unlikely, therefore, that rapidly increasing energy costs will cause any significant relocation of manufacturing industries, because transportation expenses constitute a smaller than ever proportion of total energy costs. Nuclear energy, though plagued by serious ecological problems, offers even more freedom from the locational constraints of energy supply, and current research in superconductivity of electricity could well lead to a further dramatic weakening of such constraints.

Restrictions of Terrain and Climate. Few industries are excluded from an area because of the nature of the terrain, the surface of the land. Only in cases where very large amounts of land are required, or where special characteristics such as the ability to support heavy loads are required, does terrain become a major factor in industrial location. Since suitable terrain can generally be found within a region, terrain becomes an important factor only when specific terrain characteristics must be paired with other site characteristics. One example would be an industry that requires both level land and a port, which is true of some steel mills relying on imported ore.

The role of climate in industrial location is now hardly more significant than that of terrain. Our increasing ability to control indoor atmospheric conditions has greatly reduced the impact of climate and weather in choosing location. We can now heat, cool, humidify, or dehumidify any structure. However, modifications of natural atmospheric conditions can be achieved only through the application of energy and the use of machinery, each of which adds to the cost of operations. For this reason, the location of a factory in an area where substantial air conditioning is required will be practical only if there are compensating advantages. For example, the cost of humidifying cotton textile mills in dry climates, necessary to prevent fibers from breaking in the cloth-making process, can be justified only if the needed cotton is grown nearby.

▓ INDUSTRIAL CULTURAL INTEGRATION

The causal factors influencing industrial location extend beyond the physical environmental elements to include various cultural and economic features. Industrial location theory explains the spatial distribution of industry by referring mainly to other aspects of society. From the time of Alfred Weber, location theorists have placed enormous importance on labor as a locational factor.

Labor Supply

Labor-intensive industries are those for which labor costs form a large part of total production costs (Figure 12.15). Examples are industries depending on highly skilled workers producing small objects of high value, such as transistors, cameras, and watches. Manufacturers consider several characteristics of labor in deciding where to locate factories: availability of workers, average wages, necessary skills, and worker productivity. Traditionally, workers with certain skills tended to live and work in a small number of places, partly as a result of the need for person-to-person training in handing down such skills. Consequently, manufacturers often sought locations where these skilled workers lived.

In recent decades, the increasing mobility of labor throughout the Western world has lessened the locational influence of labor. Migration of labor has accelerated since World War II, especially in Europe and the United States. Large numbers of workers in Europe have migrated from south to north, leaving homes in Spain, southern Italy, Greece, Turkey, and Yugoslavia to find employment in the main European manufacturing belt.

Factory "migration" itself is an increasingly powerful force on the labor market. For those industries dependent on largely unskilled labor, or labor that can be trained quickly and cheaply, relocation to economically depressed rural areas can result in higher profits. The main attraction of such areas is the large supply of cheap labor, a contrast to the high wages typical in established industrial districts. Much industry has been attracted to the American South for this reason.

Nonetheless, this pattern is now being repeated on an international scale, and a new global division of labor seems to be in the works. Behind these changes in the international labor market lies the strategic thinking by directors of the global corporations. According to a Department of Commerce study, as early as the mid-1970s, 298 American-based global corporations employed as many as 25 percent of their workers outside the United States. A typical example was General Electric, which shipped

FIGURE 12.15
Some industries depend on a supply of skilled workers. One example is this transistor factory near Tokyo. The women in the assembly line are working on printed circuits.

component parts to Singapore. There, by workers who were paid 30 cents an hour, they were assembled into products to be exported back to the United States. Other major corporations, like Fairchild Camera, Bulova, RCA, and Zenith, early on moved their plants to Hong Kong, Taiwan, and other Asian cheap-labor areas, where the labor pool included children as well as adults who worked up to seven days a week.

Such factories, despite relocation costs, quickly drive up corporate profit margins. In addition, the ability of these corporations to plan on such an international scale and to shift the production of a given product thousands of miles away is having a strong effect on the organized labor movements inside the United States.

Markets

A market is the area in which a product may be sold in a volume and at a price profitable to the manufacturer. The size and distribution of markets are generally the most important factors in determining the spatial distribution of industries. Many experts who have studied industrial location consider the market attraction so great that they regard locating an industry near its market as the norm.

Certain industries, in an economic sense, *must* locate at the market. That is, some manufacturers must situate their factories among their customers if they are to minimize costs and maximize profits. Such industries include those manufacturing a **weight-gaining** finished product, such as bottled beverages, or a **bulk-gaining** finished product, such as metal containers or bottles. In other words, if weight or bulk is added to the raw materials in the manufacturing process, location near the market is economically desirable due to the transport cost factor. Similarly, if the finished product is more perishable than the raw materials, which is the case with bakery goods and local newspapers, a location near market is also required. In addition, if the product is more fragile than the raw materials that go into its manufacture, as in the making of glass, the industry will be attracted to its market. In each of these cases—gain in weight, bulk, perishability, or fragility—transportation costs on the finished product are much higher than on the raw materials.

Obviously, the degree of importance of market as an attractive force increases with the degree of clustering of population. If population is relatively evenly distributed across a country, no single location can be said to be nearest to the market, but the clustering in cities so typical of modern industrial societies pulls manufacturers to the urban centers. Similarly, the type of market being served can affect the location of industries. Some manufacturers supply highly clustered urban markets, while others, such as the makers of farm machinery, cater to a more dispersed body of consumers. Industries selling goods to dispersed markets have greater freedom in their choice of locations.

As a rule, though, we can say that in Western industrial cultures, the greatest market potential exists where the largest numbers of people are found. This is the result of what is sometimes called **agglomeration.** Once an industry locates in a particular place, it provides additional jobs, attracting laborers into the area. This additional population in turn enlarges the local market, thereby attracting other industries. In the same way, the industries arriving later attract still more people and still more industries. This is how industrial districts develop, through a snowballing increase in people, infrastructure, and industries. It is a process that is very difficult to control in free-enterprise systems, and if it is allowed to run its course, agglomeration will produce serious overcrowding and excessively clustered population. This intense concentration of industries and population is characteristic of most industrialized nations. Consequently, most such countries suffer from associated problems such as congestion, inadequate housing and recreational facilities, and extreme local pollution of the environment.

The Political Element in Industrial Location

Political influence on the spatial distribution of industrialization is common. Governments often intervene directly in decisions concerning industrial location. Such intervention typically results from a desire to establish strategic, militarily important industries that would otherwise not develop; to decrease vulnerability to attack by artificially scattering industry to many parts of the country; to create national self-sufficiency by diversifying industries; to bring industrial development and a higher standard of living to poverty-stricken provinces; to place vital strategic industries in remote locations, far removed from possible war zones; or to halt the multiplier effect in existing industrial areas. Such governmental influence is most pronounced in highly planned economic systems, particularly in Communist or socialist countries such as the Soviet Union and China, but it can be seen to some extent in almost every industrial nation (Figure 12.16).

The existence of armaments factories in the Republic of South Africa, a country that fears a United Nations arms embargo, is a good example of the artificial development of government-encouraged strategic industries.

FIGURE 12.16
In the Soviet Union the government
has supervised the location of
industry. These women work in a
machinery plant near Moscow.

The scattering of industry in the Soviet Union, motivated partly by a desire to lessen the catastrophic effect of a military attack, is another. The development of a major industrial complex in the Soviet Ural Mountains, deep in the interior of the country, was partially in response to the German military advance in 1941. For similar strategic reasons, the United States government during World War II encouraged the development of an iron and steel industry in Utah, an economically inefficient location that would not have attracted such industry without government intervention. The American aircraft industry was similarly dispersed as a result of government policy. The peacetime Italian government has deliberately caused industries to be established in the impoverished southern part of the country in an effort to improve the standard of living there. Similarly, the American government has encouraged new industrial development in economically depressed Appalachia. The United Kingdom, with some limited success, has attempted to retard further industrial development in existing population centers, causing many new factories to be situated in rural or small-town areas.

Local and state governments are often directly involved in efforts to influence industrial locations. Action by such governments sometimes takes the form of tax concessions, such as those granted by a number of states, counties, and cities in the United States. These concessions commonly last for a specified period of time, frequently ten years or less, and are designed to persuade industries to locate in areas under their jurisdiction. Conversely, governments can act to prevent the establishment of industries viewed as undesirable. A brewery, for example, could be kept out of an area where influential local church leaders had prohibitionist views and brought their influence to bear on government officials. Oil refineries and "superport" facilities for large tankers are presently being blocked from New England by state action, and some American municipalities have refused to allow development of particularly pollution-prone industries such as copper smelters and paper mills.

Another type of government influence comes in the form of tariffs, import-export quotas, political obstacles to the free movement of labor and capital, and various types of hindrance to transportation across borders (see box, "Tariffs and Toyotas"). Tariffs, in effect, reduce the size of a market area proportional to the amount of tariff imposed (see Figure 12.17). A similar effect is produced when the number of border crossing points is restricted. In some parts of the world, especially Europe, the impact of tariffs and borders on industrial location has been greatly reduced by the establishment of free-trade blocs, groups of nations that have banded together economically and abolished most tariffs. Of these associations, the European Common Market is perhaps the most famous. Composed of ten nations of non-Communist Europe, the Common Market has succeeded in abolishing most tariffs within its area.

Global corporations, which scatter their holdings across international borders, would seem to diminish the political factor in industrial location. In reality, however, even the multinational enterprises must pay heed to boundaries. Different countries act variously to encourage or discourage foreign investment, creating major discontinuities in opportunities for the global corporations. Even in an era when industrial decisions have worldwide impact, the political locational factor remains viable.

Industrialization as an Agent of Cultural Change

In these various ways, different aspects of culture are integrated with industrial location, but equally pronounced are the effects of industry on culture. Indeed, industrialization is the most potent and effective agent of cultural change ever to operate. Entire cultures have been reshaped as a consequence of the industrial revolution. Traditions thousands of years old have been discarded almost overnight. Much of the replacement of folk culture by popular culture can be attributed at least indirectly to the industrial revolution (Figure 12.18). With spreading industrialization went the most concentrated burst of invention in history. From the steamship and the simple tack to the revolver and the ballistic missile, from the typewriter and the rotary printing press to the computer and the atom bomb, the list of innovations is almost endless.

Some of the more important and far-reaching changes brought by industrialization include increased interregional trade and intercultural contact, basic alterations in employment patterns, a shift from rural to urban residence for vast numbers of people, the release of women from the home, the ultimate disappearance of child labor, an initial increase in the rate of population growth followed by a drop to unprecedented low birth rates, greatly increased individual mobility and mass migrations of people, a decline in the role of organized religion, the decline of the

TARIFFS AND TOYOTAS

In the summer of 1980, the impact of tariffs on industrial location found expression in a dispute between the United States and Japan. According to U.S. tariff law, motor vehicles imported fully assembled are subject to a 25 percent tariff, while importers pay only a 4 percent tariff on vehicle parts. The Japanese Toyota firm had for years imported vehicles that were almost fully assembled, lacking only superficial work to be ready for sale. Toyota paid the 4 percent "parts" tariff on these vehicles. The "final touch" assembly took place at a Long Beach, California, plant which, owing to the large volume of imports, employed a sizable labor force. When the United States acted to reclassify the vehicles as "fully assembled," thereby raising the tariff to 25 percent, Toyota countered by threatening to close the Long Beach plant on the grounds that it would no longer be economically profitable.

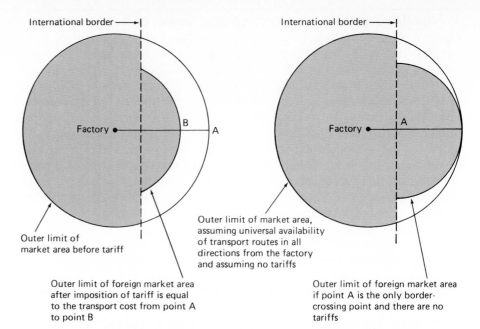

International border →

International border →

Factory ●————————|———B——A

Factory ●————————|———A

FIGURE 12.17
The impact of political borders on market area is illustrated in this diagram. The presence of a political border reduces the market area of a factory if a tariff is imposed or if the number of border-crossing points is restricted. As a result, factories tend not to be located in border zones. (After Herbert Giersch, "Economic Union Between Nations and the Location of Industries," *Review of Economic Studies,* 17 (1949–50), 87–97.)

Outer limit of
market area before tariff

Outer limit of foreign market area
after imposition of tariff is equal
to the transport cost from point A
to point B

Outer limit of market area,
assuming universal availability
of transport routes in all
directions from the factory
and assuming no tariffs

Outer limit of foreign market area
if point A is the only border-
crossing point and there are no
tariffs

multigeneration family, greatly increased educational opportunities for the nonwealthy, and an increase of government influence and functions.

Perhaps the most basic change, however, is the way people make their livings. Industrial development in a region typically produces a restructuring of employment. A marked increase occurs in the proportion of the labor force employed in secondary and tertiary activities, as well as in such primary activities as lumbering and mining. There is a resultant decline in agricultural employment. Worker productivity increases greatly, both in industry and agriculture, mainly due to the adoption of machinery in the production process. This increased productivity allows the number of children and elderly persons in the labor force to decline substantially, but the number of women working outside the home increases.

FIGURE 12.18
Industrialization brings culture change. Today we see men in Senegal, Africa, pouring molten metal in a factory, but their clothes remind us that only a few years ago their lives and occupations were very different.

The large-scale expansion of interregional trade is largely due to industrialization, for no industrial region is self-sufficient. Each must rely on other regions for raw materials, foodstuffs, laborers, and markets. Such trade contacts, often between peoples with very different cultural heritages and social patterns, naturally accelerate the processes of cultural diffusion. While intercultural contacts can serve to reduce prejudice and suspicion, too great a dependence upon an unfamiliar people for basic necessities can result in feelings of hostility if one or both trading partners feel they are being cheated. The rise of anti-Arab sentiment in the United States after 1973 was in part the result of greatly increased oil prices.

Before the industrial revolution, education was a luxury available only to the wealthy. In an industrial society, however, worker productivity is closely related to the educational level of the labor force. This recognition has led all industrial countries to devote large portions of their financial resources to the support of education. This has been facilitated by release of children from the labor force.

As a rule, people strongly resist substantial changes in their basic cultural patterns unless some immediate and great personal benefit is perceived. It is some measure of the appeal and promise of the industrial revolution that so many people in such a great variety of cultures have been willing to discard tradition in order to adopt this new way of life.

■ INDUSTRIAL LANDSCAPES

The industrial landscape is part of our daily life, for industry is a prominent and often disturbing visible feature of our surroundings. It is a landscape not normally designed for beauty, charm, or aesthetic appeal, but rather for utility. Often it is, by almost anyone's standards, ugly. As a rule, industrial landscapes are poor places for humans to have to spend their lives.

Each level of industrial activity produces its own distinctive landscape. Primary industries have perhaps the most drastic impact on the land. The resultant landscapes contain slag heaps, strip-cut commercial forests, massive, strip-mining scars, gaping open-pit mines, and "forests" of oil derricks. But primary industrial landscapes can also be pleasing, as in the comfortable fishing villages of New England and Portugal (Figure 12.19).

The manufacturing landscapes of secondary industry are most notable in the form of factory buildings. Some of these are imaginatively designed and well landscaped, others are less appealing and surrounded by gray seas of parking lots. They range from the futuristic, harsh, solid geometry of chemical refineries and formless, stark "brick-pile" factories to award-winning structures designed by famous architects (Figure 12.20).

Manufacturing landscapes first appeared in Britain, since that island was the first area touched by the industrial revolution. It is interesting to observe how British poets and artists of the eighteenth and nineteenth centuries reacted to the emerging manufacturing landscape. Poets and artists are widely acknowledged to be aesthetically sensitive and more perceptive than the average person, so their reactions should interest us. Geographers Gary Peters and Burton Anderson studied the works of such writers and painters. They found that after an early period of optimism about industrialization, some poets and artists quickly sensed that something was amiss in the landscape. Their warnings, in the form of paintings and poems, began appearing in the 1775–1800 period. Typical is the

FIGURE 12.19
Sacramento Hill, once a prominent landmark in the Warren-Bisbee copper mining district of Arizona, gave way as the landscape was industrialized. These three views show the original hill, the remnant in the early 1920s, and what was left in 1982. The artificial abyss called Lavender Pit yawns at the center of the latter view. (From Francaviglia, ''Copper Mining and Landscape Evolution,'' pp. 282, 283, 288, with the permission of Richard V. Francaviglia and the Arizona Historical Society, Tucson.)

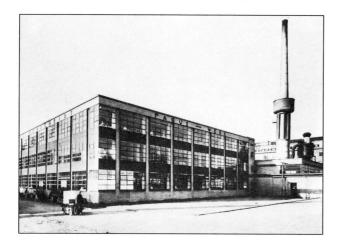

FIGURE 12.20
The famous architects Walter Gropius and Adolf Meyer designed this German factory about 1910, in the town of Alfeld. (Photo courtesy of the Museum of Modern Art, New York City.)

description of an iron foundry written by the poet Robert Burns in his native Scottish dialect:

We cam na here to view your warks,
In hopes to be mair wise,
But only, lest we gang to Hell,
It may be nae surprise.

Some artists of the period left us paintings that convey a sinister, forbidding, unpleasant landscape. By the time ordinary people began to see with the eyes of poets and artists, the manufacturing landscape was seemingly out of control, and much of the British industrial region was already known, appropriately, as the "Black Country" (see box, " 'How Green Was My Valley' ").

"HOW GREEN WAS MY VALLEY"

Richard Llewellyn, a Welshman, wrote a beautiful novel about growing up in the coal mining district of Wales in the late nineteenth century. He saw the industrial landscape expand across his native valley, and he lamented it:

Bright shone the sun, but brighter shone the Valley's green, for each blade of grass gave back the light and made the meadows full of gold and greens, and yellows and pinks and blues were poking from the hedges where the flowers were hard at work for the bees. May and almond were coming, and further down, early apple was doing splendid in four tidy rows behind Meirddyn Jones' farm. His herd of black cows were all down in the river up to their bellies in the cool quiet water, with their tails making white splashes as they dropped after slapping flies, and up nearer to us, sheep were busy with their noses at the sweet green. When the wind took breath you could hear the crunching of their jaws.

Beautiful was the Valley this afternoon, until you turned your head to the right. Then you saw the two slag heaps. . . .

Below us, the river ran sweet as ever, happy in the sun, but as soon as it met the darkness between the sloping walls of slag it seemed to take fright and go spiritless, smooth, black, without movement. And on the other side it came forth grey, and began to hurry again, as though anxious to get away. But its banks were stained, and the reeds and grasses that dressed it were hanging, and black, and sickly, ashamed of their dirtiness, ready to die of shame, they seemed, and of sorrow for their dear friend, the river. . . .

Big it had grown, and long, and black, without life or sign, lying along the bottom of the Valley on both sides of the river. The green grass, and the reeds and the flowers, all had gone, crushed beneath it. And every minute the burden grew, as cage after cage screeched along the cables from the pit, bumped to a stop at the tipping pier, and emptied dusty loads on to the ridged, black, dirty back.

On our side of the Valley the heap reached to the front garden walls to the bottom row of houses, and children from them were playing up and down the black slopes, screaming and shouting, laughing in fun. On the other side of the river the chimney-pots of the first row of houses could only just be seen above the sharp curving back of the far heap, and all the time I was watching, the cable screeched and the cages tipped. . . .

Geographer C. S. Davies, a son of the Welsh coalfields, offers a different, even nostalgic view of the industrial landscape. Noting the decline of the coal mining industry in South Wales and the accompanying deindustrialization since 1930, he laments the deliberate, government-supported obliteration of the defunct mining landscape, a removal prompted, he believes, by the British preference for agrarian scenes. Wales, "its spirit and wealth now broken," is losing its coal mining landscape. "So rapid," he writes, "is the ongoing erasure of the mining scene — the dark, inner landscape of the pit and the more familiar surface features of pithead gear, slag heaps and grey streaked villages — that soon there will be no palpable evidence of how thousands of ordinary people . . . worked and lived." In this manner, Britain seeks "to sanitize landscapes pillaged while forging an industrial empire."

Service industries, too, produce a cultural landscape. Its visual content includes elements as diverse as high-rise bank buildings, hamburger stands, and the concrete and steel webs of highways and railroads. Some highway interchanges can only be described as a modern art form, but perhaps the aesthetic high point of the tertiary landscape is found in bridges, often graceful and beautiful structures (Figure 12.21). Few sights of the industrial age can match a well-designed rail or highway bridge.

Industrialization has even changed the way we view the landscape. As the geographer Yi-Fu Tuan has commented, "It was only in the early decades of the twentieth century that vehicles began to displace walking as the prevalent form of locomotion, and street scenes were perceived increasingly from the interior of automobiles moving staccato-fashion through regularly spaced traffic lights." Los Angeles, the ultimate automobile city, is perhaps the best example of the new viewpoints provided by the industrial age. Its freeway system allows individual motorists to observe their surroundings at nonstop speeds up to 55 miles per hour. It also allows the driver to look *down* on the world. The pedestrian, on the other hand, is slighted. The view from the street is not encouraged. In some areas of Los Angeles, streets actually have no sidewalks at all, so that the nonautomobile viewpoint is functionally impossible. In other areas, the layout of the main avenues has been planned with the car in mind,

FIGURE 12.21
This Belgian landscape includes many elements of tertiary industrial activity, including roads, a bridge, and river transport.

The themes and concepts of cultural geography should be taken beyond the classroom to both understand and improve our increasingly complex and troubled world. This essay and the accompanying color photographs will remind you of this personal challenge and responsibility. The photographs are ordered in the same sequence as the book's chapters and serve as cues to link the topics of each chapter to the world beyond your college campus.

Because culture and humanity are inseparably linked, the tools of cultural analysis are fundamental to understanding the human condition. For example, as we look at an Algerian marketplace, the five themes of cultural geography remind us of how that part of the world forms a distinct cultural region and how the traits that make it unique have diffused through time and space. We can recognize that fundamental to any people's survival and subsistence is a tenuous ecological relationship with the environment, producing an artifact—the cultural landscape. Some adaptive strategies are more successful than others, and one of the challenges faced by peoples in the developing world is how to adapt to and maximize the benefits of a global economy. The soft-drink billboard dominating a harbor scene in Aberdeen,

The human mosaic: A marketplace in Algeria

Converging cultures, local and global: Hong Kong

An increasingly crowded world: New York City

A hungry world: Ethiopian relief camp

Hong Kong, reminds us of both the costs and benefits of converging economies and cultures.

Population growth underlies many of the world's problems, from personal crowding and congestion (as in this New York City street scene) to life-or-death competition for scarce resources such as land, food, and clean water (Chapter 2). Populations increase because of diverse cultural factors that demand understanding: High birth rates have often been driven by poverty, sickness, and desperation as parents seek survival strategies through large families. But in the aggregate, individual family solutions become world problems. Therefore, international family planning policies must involve a sensitive understanding of cultural contexts. Furthermore, we should not forget that recent population growth has come mainly from reduced death rates, primarily through diffusion of Western medicine and hygiene. We must think through the wisdom of using this two-edged sword.

Food equals survival, and as the photo of an Ethiopian refugee camp reminds us, it is a scarce resource in many parts of the world; each year at least 20 million people (mainly children) die from the effects of malnutrition. Yet this happens in a world of plenty, where, theoretically at least, there is more than adequate food for each world citizen—some say enough to provide each person with over 5 pounds a day (Chapter 3). So what's the problem, then? Cultures, politics, economies. Society, not nature, is to blame, so finding solutions will involve comprehensive understanding of world cultural geographies.

Political unrest, driven by demands for cultural independence, is rampant in this world, and it often starts among the young, as expressed by the photograph of stone- and bottle-throwing Palestinian youths in the occupied West Bank (Chapter 4). World systems and world powers are consistently challenged as smaller-scale cultural groups find their voices.

Cultural imperialism comes in many forms; the photograph of billboards on a Tokyo street indicates the hegemony of world trade and advertising systems that have created an international language of signs and symbols to promote goods and services of questionable social value (Chapter 5). Interacting with these systems is the culture of global tourism, which brings mixed blessings to peoples and countries throughout the world. The Great Wall of China, originally built to keep out foreign invaders, now attracts them. Yet some countries are reluctant to open their doors to international visitors, for with foreign tongues come foreign ideas and influences.

Religion has been and continues to be a powerful vehicle for the spread of culture (Chapter 6). Furthermore, because religion

Cultures in conflict: The West Bank occupied lands, Israel

A sign of our time: Tourism, China

International languages, signs, and symbols: Tokyo

Life and death: Muslim funeral, Soviet Union

Religious and cultural minorities: Sikhs, Punjab region

integrates so many facets of culture, it often links
spiritual and secular concerns. In many parts of
the world, such as with the Muslim minorities in
the USSR, religion becomes the basis for political
actions toward cultural autonomy. Islam is the
world's fastest-growing religion and will
probably encompass a quarter of the world's
population by the year 2000; as global citizens,
regardless of creed, we should understand the
cultural and political importance of this major
world institution. Crucial to comprehension of
world religions is a sensitivity to sacred
landscapes and places, such as this Sikh shrine in
the Punjab; these holy places act both to focus
and to unify a group at odds with the dominant
Islamic and Hindu societies.

Chapters 7 and 8, on folk and popular geography, contrast the extreme ends of a cultural spectrum while also speaking to the increasingly interactive tension between the two. Looking at the village of Secret Corners, Zaire, we have little trouble comparing the life-styles of that place with those of the people eating and socializing at McDonald's in Tokyo, and, further, we may wonder about the assets and liabilities of each contrasting culture. While the neon landscape of McDonald's exemplifies well-known and often intrusive world cultural systems, so the folk village of Secret Corners triggers images of a simpler, less frantic, regional life. But we should not argue about the benefits of one over the other; instead, as cultural geographers, we should understand the impact of one on the other and the interaction between the two.

Today, around the world and in our own country, we see a renewed celebration of ethnicity. Some of this ethnic pride takes political form in independence movements and resistance to imperialism. As we watch the resurgence of ethnic politics in today's world, we should not overlook the fundamental reasons behind much of this ethnic unrest, remembering that it is often fueled by discrimination and racism, segregation and exclusion (Chapter 9).

Folk cultures in a modernizing world: Zaire

The dominance of popular culture: Tokyo

Ethnicity and racism: Miami

Urban inequities: Hong Kong

We are—or will soon be—a predominantly urban world, with most of the Earth's inhabitants dwelling in cities (Chapters 10 and 11). This phenomenon reflects the largest movement of humans in history—this century's migration from country to city. Yet migration to cities does not always provide solutions; often, it simply reinforces existing inequities, as attested to in the photograph of a squatter settlement in otherwise affluent Hong Kong. The most rapid urban growth is in the developing world, not only because cities offer some glimmer of economic hope, but also because the "push" forces from the countryside are so strong. There, population has outstripped resources, and rural peoples are caught in a downward spiral. As a last resort, people move to the squatter settlements found everywhere in the developing world.

In the developed world, by contrast, urban growth has slowed, as urbanites move from city to suburbs or beyond. Paris, for example, has channeled its growth into nodes ringing the Paris Basin. In the United States, suburban growth has

Landscapes of our urban world: Paris

Coalescing cities: Megalopolis, USA

Contrasting landscapes: Denver

led to coalescing cities, creating the conurbation known as megalopolis. Boston is in the north of the Landsat photograph; Providence, Rhode Island, in the center. The cultural landscape theme proves valuable for examining city life because of the overt distinctions between social areas, as seen in this photograph of Denver, Colorado.

Western industrialization, as shown here in Detroit, the auto capital of the world, is a much-desired model for economic development in the world today, despite the associated social and environmental costs. Cultural geography reminds us that benefits and costs are unequally distributed in the world today (Chapter 12). We in the Western world, a numerical minority, have exploited a majority of the world's ecosystems for our benefit, and, in doing so, have irrevocably harmed the world's atmosphere, forests, and waters. Because of the damage we have done, the attempts of developing countries to industrialize are hindered.

The costs and benefits of industrialization: Detroit

Developed and developing worlds: Zaire

The last chapter of this textbook (Chapter 13) uses case studies to show you how cultural geography is valuable in addressing world problems. As you read these, think back to the themes and concepts you studied in the first twelve chapters of the book, thinking of the examples used and the links made to the world at large. Look again at the photographs accompanying this essay. Enjoy the cultural diversity displayed, celebrate the variability of people and places found on this Earth, and yet remember that you, as a member of a privileged world elite—college students—are in a unique position to help rectify these problems; some would say that you have a moral and ethical responsibility to do so. We'll leave that for you to decide, but end by simply reminding you that the first step toward solving any problem is a better understanding of its causes and context. Now that you've studied cultural geography, you have additional tools to work with. Use them well.

Subsistence and survival: Kashmir, India

and the pedestrian is likely to feel ill at ease amid the nonhuman surroundings — noise, traffic jams, drive-in banks, and parking lots. Often the shopping street is no longer scaled to the pedestrian — Los Angeles's Ventura Boulevard extends for 15 miles.

There are areas where such industrial landscapes are overwhelmingly dominant, but the imprint remains rather local, reflecting the highly centralized nature of industrial activity. It is possible, even in industrial districts such as the Ruhr region of West Germany, to find rural scenes and functioning farms.

■ CONCLUSION

One of the most significant events of our age is the spread of industrialization. This has brought a host of far-reaching cultural changes. Already the industrial revolution has modified the cultures and landscapes of some lands so greatly that people who lived there a century ago would be completely bewildered by the modern setting.

We discussed the five types of industry — primary, secondary, tertiary, quaternary, and quinary. Through the theme of culture region we noted the spatial patterns of these five types. We traced the spread of the innovations that made up the industrial revolution, following the routes of diffusion from Britain to the rest of the world.

The impact of industrial activity on the environment becomes apparent through the study of cultural ecology. In some places, the ravages of industry have reached an alarming state, but the relationship between industry and the land is not one-sided. The environment influences industrial location.

Through the approach of cultural integration, we found that industry is related in countless ways to other elements of culture. In particular, industrial location is often governed by economic and political factors.

The characteristics of industrial landscapes are familiar to us. The theme of cultural landscape allowed us some deeper insight into these visible manifestations of the industrial revolution.

Suggested Readings

Gunnar Alexandersson. *Geography of Manufacturing.* Englewood Cliffs, N.J.: Prentice-Hall, 1967.

John Allen. "Service Industries: Uneven Development and Uneven Knowledge," *Area,* 20 (1988), 15–22.

Wilfrid Bach. "The Acid Rain/Carbon Dioxide Threat — Control Strategies," *GeoJournal,* 10 (1985), 339–352.

Brian J. L. Berry. *Geography of Market Centers and Retail Distribution.* Englewood Cliffs, N.J.: Prentice-Hall, 1967.

Keith Chapman and David Walker. *Industrial Location: Principles and Policies.* New York: Basil Blackwell, 1987.

David Clark. *Post-Industrial America: A Geographical Perspective.* New York: Methuen, 1985.

Peter W. Daniels. "The Geography of Services," *Progress in Human Geography,* 10 (1986), 436–444; 11 (1987), 433–447.

Peter W. Daniels. *Service Industries: A Geographical Appraisal.* New York: Methuen, 1986.

Christopher Shane Davies. "Dark Inner Landscapes: The South Wales Coalfield," *Landscape Journal,* 3 (1984), 36–44.

Peter Dicken. *Global Shift: Industrial Change in a Turbulent World.* London: Harper & Row, 1986.

R. C. Estall and R. Ogilvie Buchanan. *Industrial Activity and Economic Geography: A Study of the Forces Behind the Geographical Location of Productive Activity in Manufacturing Industry,* 2nd ed. London: Hutchinson, 1966.

Dean K. Forbes. *The Geography of Underdevelopment.* Baltimore: Johns Hopkins University Press, 1984.

Dean K. Forbes and Peter J. Rimmer (eds.). *Uneven Development and the Geographical Transfer of Value.* Human Geography Monograph 16, Research School of Pacific Studies. Canberra: Australian National University, 1984.

Richard V. Francaviglia. "Cooper Mining and Landscape Evolution," *Journal of Arizona History,* 23 (1982), 267–298.

Andreas Grotewold. "The Growth of Industrial Core Areas and Patterns of World Trade," *Annals of the Association of American Geographers,* 61 (1971), 361–370.

Nathaniel B. Guyol. *Energy in the Perspective Geography.* Englewood Cliffs, N.J.: Prentice-Hall, 1971.

Peter Hall and Ann Markusen (eds.). *Silicon Landscapes.* Boston: Allen & Unwin, 1985.

Susan Hanson (ed.). *The Geography of Urban Transportation.* New York: Guilford, 1986.

A. G. Hoare. *The Location of Industry in Britain.* Cambridge: Cambridge University Press, 1983.

Peter J. Hugill. "Good Roads and the Automobile in the United States, 1880–1929," *Geographical Review,* 72 (1982), 327–349.

John A. Jakle. *The Tourist: Travel in Twentieth-Century North America.* Lincoln: University of Nebraska Press, 1987.

H. R. Jarrett. *A Geography of Manufacturing,* 2nd ed. Plymouth, England: Macdonald and Evans, 1977.

Gerald J. Karaska and David F. Bramhall. *Locational Analysis for Manufacturing: A Selection of Readings.* Cambridge, Mass.: M.I.T. Press, 1969.

Russell King. *The Industrial Geography of Italy.* New York: St. Martin's Press, 1985.

Thomas J. Kirn. "Growth and Change in the Service Sector of the U. S.: A Spatial Perspective," *Annals of the Association of American Geographers,* 77 (1987), 353–372.

John Langton. *Geographical Change and Industrial Revolution: Coalmining in Southwest Lancashire, 1590–1799.* Cambridge Geographical Studies, No. 11. New York: Cambridge University Press, 1980.

John Langton. "The Industrial Revolution and the Regional Geography of England," *Transactions of the Institute of British Geographers,* 9 (1984), 145–167.

Frank Leeming. "Chinese industry—Management Systems and Regional Structures," *Transactions of the Institute of British Geographers,* 10 (1985), 413–426.

Ann Markusen, Peter Hall, and Amy Glasmeier. *High Tech America.* Winchester, Mass.: Allen & Unwin, 1986.

Ron Martin and Bob Rowthorn (eds.). *The Geography of De-Industrialization.* Dobbs Ferry, N.Y.: Sheridan House, 1986.

Doreen Massey. *Spatial Divisions of Labor: Social Structures and the Geography of Production.* New York: Methuen, 1985.

Doreen Massey and Richard Meegan (eds.). *Politics and Method: Contrasting Studies in Industrial Geography.* London: Methuen, 1986.

David R. Meyer. "Emergence of the American Manufacturing Belt: An Interpretation," *Journal of Historical Geography,* 9 (1983), 145–174.

Michael Pacione (ed.). *Progress in Industrial Geography.* London: Croom Helm, 1985.

Douglas Pearce. *Tourism Today: A Geographical Analysis.* New York: Longman, 1987.

Richard Peet. *International Capitalism and Industrial Restructuring.* Winchester, Mass.: Allen & Unwin, 1987.

Gary L. Peters and Burton L. Anderson. "Industrial Landscapes: Past Views and Stages of Recognition," *Professional Geographer,* 28 (1976), 341–348.

Richard Pillsbury. "From Hamburger Alley to Hedgerose Heights: Toward a Model of Restaurant Location Dynamics," *Professional Geographer,* 39 (1987), 326–344.

Norman J. G. Pounds. *The Ruhr: A Study in Historical and Economic Geography.* London: Faber, 1952.

David Rich. *The Industrial Geography of Australia.* London: Croom Helm, 1987.

Peter J. Rimmer. "Transport Geography," *Progress in Human Geography,* 9 (1985), 271–277; 10 (1986), 397–406, 12 (1988), 270–281.

Stephen W. Sawyer. *Renewable Energy: Progress, Prospects.* Washington, D.C.: Association of American Geographers, Resource Publication, 1986.

Allen J. Scott and Michael Storper (eds.). *Production, Work, Territory: The Geographical Anatomy of Industrial Capitalism.* Winchester, Mass.: Allen & Unwin, 1986.

Kenneth R. Sealy. *The Geography of Air Transport.* London: Hutchinson, 1957.

David M. Smith. *Industrial Location: An Economic Geographical Analysis,* 2nd ed. New York: Wiley, 1981.

Wilfred Smith. *Geography and the Location of Industry.* Liverpool: University Press, 1952.

Edward J. Taaffe and Howard L. Gauthier, Jr. *Geography of Transportation.* Englewood Cliffs, N.J.: Prentice-Hall, 1973.

Michael Taylor. "Industrial Geography," *Progress in Human Geography,* 10 (1986), 407–415.

Michael Taylor and Nigel Thrift (eds.). *The Geography of Multinationals.* New York: St. Martin's Press, 1982.

Richard S. Thoman and Edgar C. Conkling. *Geography of International Trade.* Englewood Cliffs, N.J.: Prentice-Hall, 1967.

Barrie Trinder. *The Making of the Industrial Landscape.* London: J. M. Dent & Sons, 1982.

James E. Vance, Jr. *Capturing the Horizon: The Historical Geography of Transportation.* New York: Harper & Row, 1986.

Hugh D. Watts. *Industrial Geography.* London: Longman Scientific & Industrial Publication, 1987.

Michael J. Webber. *Industrial Location.* Newbury Park, Calif.: Sage Publications. Volume 3 in the Scientific Geography Series, 1984.

Alfred Weber. *Theory of the Location of Industries.* Translated and edited by Carl J. Friedrich. Chicago: University of Chicago Press, 1929.

Christian Werner. *Spatial Transportation Modeling.* Newbury Park, Calif.: Sage Publications. Volume 5 in the Scientific Geography Series, 1985.

Hubert G. H. Wilhelm. "The Borrow Pit Landscape," *Journal of Cultural Geography,* 8 (Fall–Winter 1987), 25–34.

Chapter 13

Applying Cultural Geography: A Case Study Approach

COMMON THEMES IN THE CASE STUDIES

PROBLEMS OF REGIONAL LANDSCAPE CHANGE: BOLINAS LAGOON, CALIFORNIA

SETTLEMENT CHANGE AND HEALTH IN WEST MALAYSIA

CULTURAL DIFFUSION IN INDIA: PROBLEMS WITH THE GREEN REVOLUTION

THE CULTURAL ECOLOGY OF DESERTIFICATION: DROUGHT IN THE GREAT PLAINS

THE AMISH CULTURE REGION: A STUDY IN ENERGY EFFICIENCY

THE CULTURAL GEOGRAPHY OF DROUGHT, FAMINE, AND CONFLICT: THE CASE OF ETHIOPIA

CONCLUSION

We have used diverse material in this text to explain and illustrate the different themes and topics of cultural geography. Examples have come from various cultures and assorted time periods; some are local, others global, some current, others historical. This far-reaching eclecticism is an exciting part of the field and is one of the respected traditions of cultural geography. Yet, within this disparate material, you have probably noticed different degrees of pragmatism. While some studies link cause and effect into equations that have obvious applications to world problems, other examples are more arcane, mainly suited to illustrating abstract principles. Their value to the problem-ridden world outside the classroom might seem questionable.

In this concluding chapter we show more explicitly how cultural geography can be applied to the different social and environmental problems nagging our world, and demonstrate that this field has a viable life outside the confines of the university. We do this for several reasons. First, there is a long tradition of applied cultural geography traced back to Carl Sauer, a founding father of American geography, who was deeply involved with Depression-era land-use planning and environmental assessment. Appreciation and understanding of the varied expressions of this tradition are important for a full comprehension of the topic.

Second, we think that students should leave all introductory classes with some idea of how the course material might be applied to our world. Although most knowledge serves a useful end in itself, knowledge that can be applied to solving the world's problems embodies the highest goals of education.

Third, many of our students show an interest in pursuing geography as a course of study; yet, before committing themselves to a major, they wish to know more about the field, about the range of employment possibilities, and about the kinds of work one can expect and strive for. Although these case studies were all done by professional geographers with extensive graduate training, they illustrate, nonetheless, the spectrum of geographic research and the range of possibilities within the field. In many cases similar work is done by geographers with BA or BS degrees. We return to the question of geographic education later in the chapter.

Last, these case studies are a way of reiterating and expanding upon the themes, concepts, and skills important to geographic research. A short summary to that end follows each case study. The color photo essay preceding this chapter also reinforces the linkages between global problems and the themes and concepts you have studied in cultural geography.

■ COMMON THEMES IN THE CASE STUDIES

As you read these case studies, pay particular attention to the following:

1. All the case studies are tied rather directly to some form of interaction between humans and the physical environment. This ranges from human disturbance and protection of a valued ecosystem to problems in agricultural adaptation. This relationship between nature and culture is a fundamental theme in geography.
2. Note also that culture—in its varied expressions—is central to these studies; the problem cannot be understood or solved without explicit concern with the cultural context.
3. Unlike some research that is rather open-ended, these case studies are focused on a specific social or environmental problem and, because of this, generate conclusions that can be translated into guidelines and suggestions for solving that problem. How easily and readily this can be done depends, of course, on the nature of the problem and the research questions. In the first case study, on Bolinas Lagoon, providing solutions was the major impetus for the work; in another, the case study on Amish energy, conclusions are important at a more general level and cannot be easily translated into specific policy or regulations.
4. We have used the five themes of cultural region, diffusion, ecology, integration, and landscape as the framework for this book, and, indeed, these themes are major reference points for the field of cultural geography. As you look through these case studies, note how the themes have been operationalized into research strategies. Sometimes—such as with the diffusion study of grain in India—one theme clearly dominates. In most cases, however, researchers have integrated different themes into their research design. In the study of Malaysian settlement, for example, landscape change is important, yet so are the ecological aspects of health, a topic that would fit under our cultural ecology theme. This demonstrates again that as useful as this thematic framework is for study and research organization, it is a flexible framework that is to be adjusted to fit specific problems.

These points will become clearer as we look at the first case study, a problem of understanding and controlling landscape change in coastal California in order to preserve a threatened saltwater lagoon.

■ PROBLEMS OF REGIONAL LANDSCAPE CHANGE: BOLINAS LAGOON, CALIFORNIA

An excellent example of how the cultural landscape concept can be used in regional land-use planning takes us to the coast of California just north of San Francisco, where a team of professionals worked for years to understand how an area of roughly 20 square miles was evolving and, equally important, how these processes might be managed so as to preserve its ecological integrity. The complicating factor was that guidelines had to be worked out to allow continued human use of the surrounding area; this watershed could not become a scientific preserve, locked up and removed from the public.

Bolinas Lagoon and its watershed lie on the western boundary of Marin County, at precisely the point where the solid floor of the Pacific Ocean meets the continental geology of North America (see Figure 13.1). This is the infamous San Andreas Fault, the seismic zone responsible for the great San Francisco earthquake of 1906, a rift zone running north and south the length of California. To watch the tide come in, filling the lagoon slowly on a misty morning while pelicans, herons, and egrets feed on mudflats and marshes, is to disguise the dramatic geologic history of the area. Equally, to gaze upon this bucolic scene is to deny its ecological future. Earthquakes created the lagoon; erosion and sedimentation will extinguish it.

Bolinas Lagoon has been filling with sediments brought in by ocean tides, onshore winds, and the streams draining its watershed. In the late 1960s, people became alarmed that this precious resource was nearing extinction. Concerned citizens thought that human use of the area — sea cliff housing, logging, and dairy farming — were increasing sediment deposition in the lagoon. The result, they said, would be a premature death for one of the most important fish and bird breeding areas on the Pacific coast. What could be done to control these impacts?

FIGURE 13.1
Bolinas Lagoon, California, offered a challenging focus for a study in applied cultural geography, a study necessitating an integrative comprehension of the change in local landscape, the cultural ecology, and the regional dynamics. This view is looking north along the San Andreas fault and shows most of the lagoon's watershed.

Governmental agencies, along with several private conservation foundations, joined together to fund a study of the lagoon to understand better this complicated ecosystem, with the goal of providing Marin County with a sound land-use plan that might balance surrounding land uses with an assured life for the lagoon. The scientific team was led by geographer Rowan Rowntree, who was charged with answering the following questions:

> How fast is Bolinas Lagoon filling and how many years until this resource is lost?
>
> Is the sedimentation primarily of natural or human causes? Put another way, which is to blame for the lagoon's demise, nature or culture?
>
> As the watershed evolves in the future, how will the ecosystem change?
>
> Finally, how can the lagoon and the watershed be managed to retard sedimentation without unreasonably restricting existing land use?

To answer these questions and to generate a sound land-use plan for the area, the team had to fully evaluate the historical roles of both nature and culture as they had worked together to form the present ecosystem. The cultural landscape of the lagoon and its watershed presents a serene mosaic of fields and forests, dairy farms, two small villages, and the sinuous channels and marshes of the estuary. How had these components interacted through time to have an impact on the lagoon?

To conceptualize the research, the team divided all sedimentation processes into two categories: those occurring inside the ecosystem (such as logging and field erosion from farms), and those occurring outside the lagoon (such as Pacific storms that bring sediments to the estuary's mouth). A second conceptual distinction was made between events and processes thought to be natural and those considered to be of human doing. Discriminating between natural and cultural phenomena is a common task faced by many research geographers, primarily because it is thought that once this distinction is made, then human activities can be regulated to reduce their impact.

A first step was to determine what the natural sedimentation rate for the lagoon landscape might have been through its geologic history. This was done by sending low-frequency acoustic pulses from the water surface down hundreds of feet to bedrock, measuring the echo, then calculating the depth of sedimentation since the Ice Age. Dividing this by the number of years since the sea level stabilized and lagoon formation began yielded figures for the natural rate of deposition. This established a baseline to compare with historical sedimentation rates tied to human disturbance in the watershed and on the nearby coastal cliffs.

Following this, a sequential analysis of the historical maps, taken from university archives, showed how the marshes and mudflats had expanded since the first official coastal survey was taken in 1850. This gave the researchers some feel for recent morphological change to the lagoon; this, in turn, gave clues to how the marsh had changed with the onset of widespread human settlement.

At hydrological gauging stations in the watershed, runoff and sediment loads were measured to learn how land use and soil erosion contributed to lagoon deposition. Because redwood logging was thought to be a major culprit in accelerating erosion, special analyses were made in that portion of the landscape. With these watershed figures, calculations were made to determine whether regulated forms of logging could be allowed to continue without speeding the evolution—and extinction—of the estuary.

Measurements were also taken along the edges of expanding marshes to determine which species of marsh plants were colonizing the newly deposited mud and at what rates. This was important because sediment is trapped and deposited at a much faster rate once the bare mudflats are occupied by plants. Once the marsh food chain was understood, experiments were made to predict how the species mix might change as the lagoon evolved in the future. This was critical because the large bird species at the top of the chain, such as great blue herons and American egrets, birds with large nesting populations in the watershed, were a major aesthetic attraction of the marsh, and would be affected dramatically by food-chain atrophy.

Finally, prospective land-use patterns that might occur from population pressure on this area, which is within San Francisco's commute zone, were mapped and calculations made as to how these changes would affect sedimentation rates in the lagoon's watershed. Urbanization, as we know, can change watershed sedimentation and flow in profound ways.

Once the results of these research components were compiled, Rowntree and his staff drew on the integrative tradition of cultural geography to tie together the pieces into an ecologically based land-use plan for the Bolinas Lagoon watershed and its estuary. An important preliminary stage to formulating regulatory guidelines involved clarifying values about nature's workings. A social and political consensus was necessary on how the lagoon's life was perceived and, more important, how much human interference into ecological processes was acceptable. Should all sedimentation be stopped and the lagoon dredged, returning it to an earlier, predisturbed state? Or should its current state be recognized and a land-use plan worked out allowing an "acceptable" rate of deposition?

After long debate, agreement was reached conceptualizing the landscape as an ongoing natural process. Some sedimentation was allowable, mainly because it provided essential nutrients to the lagoon's bird life, but those human activities that produced "unnatural" erosion and deposition—mainly logging and high-density residential uses—were banned from the watershed. And even though the lagoon and its spectacular bird life were a major resource to the county, the planning and political bodies decided it should not be regulated into a static state. Nature would take its course and the estuary would eventually fill. Dredging was ruled out as unacceptable meddling in this natural process.

Although the Bolinas project brought together experts from various scientific fields, many facets of the problem were central to cultural geography. Conceptualizing and translating natural processes into political terms involved explicit consideration of cultural values and ethics; placing human disturbance of ecological processes into the cultural context was a prime necessity.

Historical reconstruction of landscape change has been mentioned throughout this book, and the reader can readily see how important this theme was to the Bolinas project. Although the project leader found a strong background in physical geography essential to working with consultants from the natural sciences, equally important was his ability to place these findings into a cultural framework. Another important facet of geographic thinking that served the project well was the ability to conceptualize problems in different scales, to ponder and organize information on the total watershed one day, then concentrate on microprocesses of marsh grass invasion the next.

Last, the geographic tradition of field involvement was of obvious importance to successful completion of the work. Most geographers find no substitute for time in the field to map, measure, and experience the diverse forces shaping the cultural landscape.

Whereas the Bolinas study focused on human interference in physical systems as they impinged on a natural resource, the next case study looks at the implications of landscape change as they affect the human resource, specifically, health and mortality.

SETTLEMENT CHANGE AND HEALTH IN WEST MALAYSIA

Geographer Melinda Meade examined the relationship between human health and land development in Malaysia to determine whether modification of the natural landscape resulting from agricultural expansion might aggravate or alleviate health problems.

This question was raised by evidence in other parts of the world that agricultural expansion often changes natural systems in such a way as to offer disease-bearing organisms an expanded habitat, resulting in increased sickness for the human population. Probably the best example involves the snail-dependent *schistosomiasis,* which is now one of humankind's greatest plagues because the snail's habitat is enlarged through irrigation schemes. Professor Meade points out that land development planners rarely consider the potential health problems that might result from disruption of the natural environment. Instead, they automatically assume that health will improve if the people's standard of living is improved. But this is not always the case.

To test her ideas, Meade analyzed a major land development scheme in Malaysia to see if human health had actually improved as a result of rain-forest clearance, expansion of rubber plantations, and resettlement of the native population into a new plantation village. This plan, called Project Gedangsa after the name of the plantation on which it was carried out, was executed in 1962 and is typical of development now taking place in Malaysia. Some 200,000 people have been recently relocated onto plantation villages; over one million acres of rain forest have been replaced with rubber or palm oil crops (Figure 13.2).

The first part of Meade's study documents the modification of the natural environment by the land development plan. Her approach is an excellent example of how the cultural ecology theme can be used to guide research. As she examines changes in the natural landscape, Meade is particularly interested in whether rain-forest clearance has enlarged the habitat of the malaria-bearing mosquito. She notes that in its natural condition the Malaysian rain forest supports hundreds of different mosquito species because the environmental niches are so varied and numerous that no single species can attain great numbers. But when the rain forest is cleared and burned, one niche is expanded as others are wiped out. If a malarial mosquito occupies that expanded niche, its population will explode and a higher incidence of malaria in the nearby human population will result. In the past, the history of plantation expansion in Malaysia has been the history of malaria epidemics. Today there is almost total dependence on insecticides to control mosquitos in the new plantations, but the last few years have seen mosquito species emerge that are resistant to several types of pesticides.

Meade finds that because the Gedangsa plantation is more than 15 years old, trees are now mature enough to shade many of the streams and

FIGURE 13.2
Some argue that rain-forest lands offer great potential for the expansion of agriculture and human settlement. Others maintain that tampering with this fragile ecosystem will have far-reaching negative consequences.

ponds where malaria mosquitos might breed. The mosquito prefers waters exposed to sunlight, so it is mainly in the early years of land development, before trees grow up, that the mosquito's habitat is expanded. At this later stage the main danger has passed.

In a second phase of Meade's study, she examines the plantation settlement pattern to see if it promotes or inhibits sickness and disease. This question touches upon another of the themes introduced in this book, cultural landscape. House types, road patterns, and settlement location are all components of the cultural landscape. As Meade analyzes the plantation's settlement landscape, she finds problems. Settlers are provided with simple three-room, iron-roof houses, oriented to the road network rather than to prevailing winds. Houses are poorly ventilated and debilitatingly hot, which could have an adverse effect on health. But there are some improvements over native villages: Most important, latrines and piped water are provided. The latrines deprive infectious worms of a habitat in soiled earth; piped water means that women no longer are exposed to mosquitos as they spend long hours doing laundry in streams. Both of these features have reduced the usual health problems.

So when all factors are considered, Meade finds that the health advantages of this particular land development scheme outweigh the disadvantages. As a result, the plantation's population is expanding due to a lowered mortality rate. Malaria is momentarily under control due to spraying and other precautionary measures. The incidence of worm-carried infections in small children (who normally crawl about in contaminated soil) is down, mainly because of the latrine system.

The broader demographic implications coming from Malaysian land development schemes are varied and could affect the country's population in several ways. First, new plantation schemes might trigger malaria epidemics as rain-forest clearing takes place unless precautionary measures are taken; there is also some danger that population mobility—

travel and migration — might introduce new strains of malaria and other diseases into previously resistant populations. But the most important effect is that improved health facilities generally reduce mortality rates; therefore the country's population will express this growth.

Because similar development programs are found in many other emerging countries, Meade's study serves as an excellent model for evaluating the health problems and advantages accompanying development and for calculating potential population growth resulting from improved health conditions.

In this study, as in the previous one, the major research questions are answered by looking at changes in the cultural landscape. And once again, this study expresses the common geographic focus on interaction between humans and their physical environment: in this case, how anthropogenic forces have altered the mosquito's habitat and, second, whether the disturbance has significant effects on human health. A third theme is evaluating the costs and benefits of a new settlement landscape.

Meade draws upon an impressive array of skills in her work, bringing together diverse material from aquatic biology, forest ecology, epidemiology, and settlement planning. These talents were focused on specific questions and, once answered, her conclusions could be readily translated into guidelines that would improve the resettlement process and contribute to a more healthful condition for humanity.

Human health is closely linked to diet and food availability. The next case study looks at some social problems in agricultural productivity in India.

■ CULTURAL DIFFUSION IN INDIA: PROBLEMS WITH THE GREEN REVOLUTION

Major breakthroughs in world food production came in the 1960s through the "Green Revolution" when new hybrid seeds and intensive cultivation methods doubled wheat and rice yields in many areas of the world. But this revolution brought mixed blessings to some regions because these new hybrid seeds usually demanded more irrigation water and artificial fertilizers that added to farmers' costs.

In this study, the Canadian geographer A. K. Chakravarti uses the theme of cultural diffusion to assess the impact of new agricultural technologies on India's social structure. Specifically, he traces the spread of high-yield seeds across India, then evaluates the results on a region-by-region basis.

Some background material is necessary to fully appreciate the impact of high-yield seeds on India's agriculture. First, most of the country's farming is subsistence cultivation of food grains for family use; there is little commercial, export-oriented agriculture. Second, there are many regions that must draw on grains from other parts of India, and one goal of agricultural planning is to make all regions self-sufficient. Lastly, since there is no land available for farm expansion, increased food production must come only from improved yields.

Chakravarti points out that earlier attempts to raise production through fertilization and irrigation of native grain seeds were not encouraging. Local plant strains evolved over centuries and are suited to the specific conditions of low soil fertility and periodic drought. They did not respond well to fertilizers and supplemental watering, so new hybrid seeds were developed that would benefit from improved conditions. The new seeds first appeared in 1966 and at first glance led to major progress. Total food-grain production in 1970 was twice that of 1950.

But the benefits have not been shared equally. As Chakravarti examined the diffusion of the new grain seeds, it became apparent to him that major improvements in production came in those areas best able to bear the higher costs of cultivating the new seeds. Poorer people, who could not afford expensive changes in production techniques, saw their relative position in the country's agricultural spectrum actually worsen. What are the reasons behind this differential response? The problem is capital.

The new hybrid seeds are highly responsive to fertilization, but many farmers cannot afford chemical fertilizers and the banks are unwilling to lend money to marginal farmers. Even the agriculturists themselves are reluctant to borrow, knowing that they will lose their land if payments are not met. Most farmers would rather struggle on, secure with their traditional seeds and poor crops, than face the risk of becoming landless. Consequently, yields remain low even with the new seeds, since many farmers cannot afford commercial fertilizers.

A similar problem keeps many poorer farmers from using pesticides and developing irrigation systems that are necessary to bring the best yields from the new seeds. Chakravarti notes that high-yield seeds are more susceptible to disease and pests than traditional seed varieties, since the former have adapted over thousands of years to local conditions. Because the new seeds are more vulnerable, they need more protection in the form of expensive chemical pesticides. Once again, the author finds that in the richer agricultural regions pesticides are implemented, while in the poor areas the crops do without. Damage from insects and disease takes a very high toll.

Irrigation is also necessary to gain full benefits from the new seeds, while native grains are adapted to the normal Indian pattern of drought and monsoon. But irrigation, like fertilizer and pesticides, costs money; so once again the rich farmers who can afford these changes reap the benefits and the poor do without.

In summation, Chakravarti finds that the new hybrid wheat seeds are about 155 percent more expensive to farm than native seed varieties. However, this higher cost is compensated for by yields that are twice as high and a net income that is 190 percent greater than that of native seeds. So, looking at the higher costs, and higher returns, it is easy to see how a vicious cycle is perpetuated. The richer farmers can afford the additional expense of the new seeds, while those in poor regions cannot. The prosperous areas gain the benefits, the poor ones do not. Furthermore, poor farmers suffer additionally because the demand for new hybrid wheat is higher than for the traditional wheat, causing prices for native grain to drop.

This disparity between rich and poor is not quite so apparent in the rice-growing regions. The author points out that new hybrid rice strains have not been as successful as wheat because of several problems. First, the new rice crops are extremely susceptible to disease, and because the cash return is not high, even well-to-do farmers cannot afford pesticides to protect their crops. Also, returns are low because market demand is low. Buyers prefer the taste of traditional rice for food purposes, and the native rice has longer stems than can be used for cattle feed. Consequently, prices paid for the new hybrid rice are lower than for traditional crops and few farmers are interested in converting to the new rice seeds.

In conclusion, Chakravarti's study shows that the Green Revolution has actually aggravated long-standing economic and social disparities in

India; the rich have become richer, while the plight of the poor has worsened (Figure 13.3). Although the author does not mention it in his study, recent evidence suggests that tenant farmers are being evicted from rented lands, now that landlords see the possibility of increased profits by growing new high-yield wheat strains. In the past, the poor at least had the security of their own land, even though it may have been rented, and the knowledge that some sort of crop could be harvested. But now, a whole new class of displaced poor plagues India, placing additional burdens on the country's food supplies and adding social complications to the Green Revolution.

This case study shows how the theme of cultural diffusion can be applied to a pressing resource problem. Chakravarti concentrates on one innovation, hybrid seeds, and explicates conditions of acceptance and rejection of this trait through close examination of the cultural context of agricultural adoption. He finds unresolved barriers to this Green Revolution hybrid among certain social classes, rapid adoption by other groups, and a widening of class boundaries as a result of this differential diffusion.

Whereas the previous two studies emphasized geographic skills focused on ecosystemic change resulting from human disturbance, Chakravarti's study draws on a different facet of geographic training. This study involved widespread quantitative analysis, initially in tracing the spread of hybrid seeds, then in examining the economic conditions of acceptance and rejection. Furthermore, economic analysis was important in assessing the cost-benefit ratios of this new technology.

FIGURE 13.3
One strategy for solving the global food crisis is to make farming more efficient. Yet that approach often aggravates social problems. This is a scene from southern India.

In spite of this quantitative aspect, this study remains firmly rooted in cultural geography because of the compelling need to understand those cultural assemblages forming the backdrop for diffusion. A profound comprehension of Indian farming structure was imperative to move this study beyond the impersonal equations of mechanical economic analyses.

Although conclusions from this study are clear, implementing solutions is a vexing problem. Improving food production is a primary economic and political goal for India, yet achieving these aims is complicated by such problems as highlighted in this study. Politicians are not sure whether the costs of increased social disparity are high enough to warrant intervention in the diffusion of hybrid seed agriculture, for, as Chakravarti pointed out, even though the rich get richer and the poor get poorer, overall food production has increased. This might be enough to offset the attendant social problems.

Expanding the world's food supply has forced farming into marginal lands where, by definition, there is a greater risk of environmental and social hazards. One common agricultural strategy has been to push farming into semiarid lands, places where drought is common and soils fragile. Farming these lands can lead to desertification, which is the expansion of desertlike conditions due to human misuse of the land. This next case study looks at this problem in North America.

◼ THE CULTURAL ECOLOGY OF DESERTIFICATION: DROUGHT IN THE GREAT PLAINS

Martyn Bowden, a geographer at Clark University, looks at the cultural ecology of North America's Great Plains agricultural region to determine whether the area is vulnerable to desertification (Figure 13.4). Using the cultural-historical method common to cultural geography, Bowden examines three issues central to continued agricultural viability:

1. Will the Great Plains climate change?
2. Will the region's soil and water resources be depleted by current livelihood systems?
3. Will people continue to farm the Great Plains?

The topic of climatic change is clouded by controversy and contradiction. Some scientists see us entering a new Ice Age resulting from human-caused industrial pollution modifying our atmosphere so that gradual cooling is taking place. Even if this is true, Bowden concludes that global cooling will not affect Great Plains productivity — except possibly in the Canadian wheat belt, where the growing season could be critically shortened.

Other climatologists argue that pollution is actually causing a warming of the world's climate, the greenhouse effect, which might increase the possibility of drought in semiarid regions like the Great Plains. Still others argue that droughts occur on fairly regular cycles and that these are totally removed from whether the Earth is warming or cooling. Bowden reviews each of the theories concerning drought periodicity and concludes that the Great Plains will not experience another prolonged period of extreme warmth and dryness until the early twenty-second century, although it is likely that there will be some short-term droughts before that.

Bowden next examines human demands on soil and water resources, asking whether these essential components of agriculture will remain

FIGURE 13.4
The Great Plains of North America provide foodstuff for many countries, but are they being managed correctly in terms of climatic fluctuations, domestic needs, and world food problems?

intact to meet the needs of future Great Plains farming. The author treats the soil resource question by critically evaluating claims made during the 1930s Dust Bowl period that the region suffered irreparable damage from misuse, drought, and wind. At that time, experts estimated that 75 percent of the soil surface in western Kansas was lost and ruined for crop production. Yet, Bowden finds that in 1945 this same area produced some of the highest yields in the state. Obviously, the extent of soil damage was overestimated. Indeed, some areas abandoned in the 1930s are still out of production, but the author calculates that this acreage totals only one-fifth of one percent of the entire arable land in the Great Plains.

Bowden concludes that further abandonment is unlikely for several reasons. First of all, there is slight prospect that conditions of the 1930s will be repeated, since farmers are now much more familiar with sound soil conservation practices such as summer fallowing and contour plowing. Furthermore, farms are now larger, so there is less pressure for unrealistically high yields from small parcels.

Even if soil conditions are not a problem, water for irrigated agriculture might be. Bowden examines the contemporary pattern of water usage in the Great Plains, finding that consumption is higher than natural replenishment, and that irrigated farming will suffer serious shortages in the future, particularly in the Texas and Oklahoma panhandles, where subsurface waters are being "mined" at a rapid rate. At present rates of use, shortages will force drastic reductions of irrigated acreage in those areas by the year 2015. Even in areas dependent on surface runoff, such as the Platte regions of Colorado and Nebraska, shortages have already been experienced.

One major reason for scarce water supplies is that Great Plains urban areas have grown rapidly and now use water that was formerly available for irrigated agriculture. The trade-off between urban and rural use is taking its toll.

The last topic examined by Bowden is the possibility of farm abandonment during periods of resource stress. Have people left the Great Plains in the past during hard times, and might they desert their farms in the future? The author begins by taking a historical look at periods of stress in the region. Droughts in the 1870s and 1890s caused widespread food shortages among new settlers. In fact, evidence suggests that people got by only because military garrisons shared food supplies. Still, there were numerous drought-caused deaths from starvation, and hundreds of new farms were abandoned. Bowden suggests that Americans were then still novices in coping with dry lands and periodic drought. Farmers lacked experience in how to adapt to stressful times.

Again in 1916, the region was hit by drought, particularly the Dakotas and Montana, where farmers had just settled the land. Droughts take a particularly high toll when farms have just been settled, since farmers will not have any savings or capital to fall back on when crops fail. Bowden notes that in this 1916 drought, government aid was slow in coming because Washington blamed the problem on careless farming. As a result, thousands of farmers pulled up stakes and headed north to Canada, where the government played a more active supporting role in helping new settlers.

The next period of stress was during the 1930s. Our stereotype is of thousands of farmers abandoning the Dust Bowl and heading west to seek their fortunes in California. Steinbeck's Joad family in *The Grapes of Wrath* did much to further the myth of the Dust Bowl farmer (Figure 13.5). But as Bowden points out, these people were not all from the Great Plains; most of them were southern tenant farmers who had been displaced by banks foreclosing on loans in order to consolidate small parcels into larger holdings. Consolidation of parcels also took place in the Great Plains, and many farmers were indeed dislocated because of this process. But the end result was larger holdings better suited to periodic drought. Larger farms have more cushion to fall back on during hard times.

FIGURE 13.5
Numerous factors converged to create the Dust Bowl in the 1930s. Here, dust clouds roll over Lamar, Colorado.

Bowden argues that the time was ripe for farm consolidation, both because large farms are better suited to the environmental conditions and because mechanization was beginning to play a major role in Great Plains agriculture. Large parcels are better suited for machines. So the dislocations that resulted were not totally a product of drought; social and technological change was equally responsible. Bowden is not attempting to minimize the Dust Bowl tragedy. He is interested only in setting the record straight by explaining various causes behind the disruptions of the 1930s. However painful this period of adjustment might have been, Bowden sees it as having had positive consequences. Today, because parcels are larger, because banks understand the needs of Great Plains farmers, and because the government is more supportive of agriculture in the region, future droughts will not be as disruptive as in the past. A wealth of experience has built up in the Great Plains concerning the optimum use of the resource base, so the future, in Bowden's opinion, appears fairly secure. The Great Plains will continue to serve the needs of the country and, to a smaller degree, the food needs of the world. Problems experienced in the past will not be repeated.

Bowden's research is an outstanding example of how the cultural-historical method can be used to analyze the past adjustments and modifications of the environment in order better to predict the future. A systematic examination of human adaptation to resource stress tells us much about how problems were met in the past. This gives us strong footing for making statements about how problems will be met in the future and illustrates the valuable contributions that historical-cultural ecology can make to understanding current resource problems.

More specifically, this study elaborated on the topic of social vulnerability as it pertains to a serious natural hazard: drought. By dissecting historical impacts and adaptation to drought in the Great Plains, Bowden elucidated those social conditions that, first, aggravate vulnerability to moisture shortages, and, second, engender resiliency, which is the ability to recover from a stressing episode. As a result, an evaluative statement can be made about which strategies constitute the most effective measures. These findings can then be applied to formulating effective governmental policies on drought aid.

Agricultural adjustment is a common theme in geographic research because of the explicit concern with the interface between nature and culture. Research on the diffusion of hybrid seeds in India illustrated one approach, the study of drought adaptation in the Great Plains another. The next case study uses still another conceptual theme, that of cultural region, to compare the energy-conservative agriculture of the Amish peoples with their mechanized neighbors; the research goal is to determine which form of agriculture is more efficient in terms of energy use. This study was done by Warren Johnson, Victor Stolzfus, and Peter Craumer.

■ THE AMISH CULTURE REGION: A STUDY IN ENERGY EFFICIENCY

Although most people look upon the Amish as remnants of traditional America, the authors suggest that because of their energy conservation, the Amish might offer insights into how the world could get along with less energy. The Amish use less energy than typical American communities and farms because the sect generally avoids modern mechanized technology (see Figure 13.6). Many of them do not use public electricity or

FIGURE 13.6
Because the Amish do not use mechanized agriculture, they use considerably less energy than their "modern" neighbors.

natural gas, for their literal interpretation of the biblical passage "Be ye not unequally yoked together with unbelievers" prevents them from drawing on secular society's utilities. Instead, the most conservative Amish generate their own power with a central engine, then transmit it to outlying buildings with a complicated system of belts and pulleys. This system has obvious limitations for running machinery, so little mechanization is apparent in Amish homes or farms. Other Amish, however, are more open to machinery and do use small engines for power milkers, mechanical hay balers, and feed grinders. Nevertheless, even among the less conservative Amish, their level of mechanization is still far lower than their non-Amish neighbors (see Figure 13.7).

The authors designed their study with two goals in mind: First, they wished to calculate just how much less energy Amish use than non-Amish farmers; second, they then determined whether Amish farmers pay a penalty for low energy use through reduced yields. The first step was to calculate the energy ratio or caloric gain for both Amish and non-Amish farms. Caloric gain is a rather complicated term—and we refer you to the study for details on how it is actually calculated—but, stated most simply, it measures the amount of food energy produced per unit of energy spent to produce food. An energy ratio greater than 1.0 indicates that the farming process produces more food energy than total energy used; less than 1.0 indicates that the farm consumes more energy than it produces in food form.

Three different groups of Amish were studied: in central Pennsylvania, eastern Illinois, and southwestern Wisconsin. This was done to obtain results from different environments, ranging from ridge and valley dairy country to Midwestern corn belt. A small number of non-Amish farmers

FIGURE 13.7
Corn-belt farms, such as this one in Iowa, are highly mechanized and, as a result, use great amounts of energy. As energy costs increase, so must food prices.

were studied in each of the three areas for the sake of comparison. The resulting energy ratios and yields are presented in Table 13.1

In central Pennsylvania, the Amish sample consisted of two groups: an extremely conservative group (the Nebraska Amish) and less conservative Amish (Old Order Amish). Both groups of Amish, along with the non-Amish, are primarily dairy farmers.

The results show that the less conservative Old Order Amish produce milk rather efficiently. Their yield is actually higher than that of the non-Amish, who use 83 percent more energy to produce a gallon of milk.

TABLE 13.1

	Energy Ratio	Yield[a]
Pennsylvania		
Old Order Amish	1.0	3,151
Nebraska Amish	1.5	1,710
non-Amish	0.5	3,071
Illinois		
Amish	0.9	3,165
non-Amish	2.0	11,444
Wisconsin		
Amish	1.6	1,305
non-Amish	0.2	1,668

[a] The yield figure is in the number of 1,000 kilocalories, abbreviated Mcal, per hectare. A hectare is an area measurement in the metric system. One acre equals 0.405 hectare.

Source: Johnson, Stolzfus, and Craumer, p. 376. Copyright 1977 by the American Association for the Advancement of Science.

In this case, Old Order Amish pay no penalty in the form of reduced yields. But the more conservative Nebraska Amish, who use less machinery, do pay a penalty: Yields are much lower, mainly because they use less fertilizer and can only milk up to 20 cows without milking machines. Without refrigeration, their milk must be sold as Grade B, cooled only by spring water. Their farms are smaller than those among the Old Order Amish, and they have fewer cows, in large part because they do not use milking machines. All milking is done by hand.

The eastern Illinois study was done in an area of corn growing and hog raising. Because the Amish are not highly mechanized, their farms are considerably smaller than those of the non-Amish (495-acre average for non-Amish, 96 acres for the Amish). The Amish energy ratio of 0.9 suggests that their farms actually consume more energy than is produced in food form; whereas the non-Amish, with an energy ratio of 2.0, are relatively efficient. However, it is important to realize the two types of farming are not directly comparable, since the Amish concentrate on pigs, the non-Amish on corn. Looking at this sample area, the authors suggest that scarce energy would drastically limit yields from intensive farming, while Pennsylvania-type farming would better adjust to lower energy consumption without paying high penalties. Illinois farming is ideally suited to mechanization, with its large parcels, needs for heavy applications of fertilizers and pesticides, and efficient food-processing machinery. Dairy farming, on the other hand, might be able to adjust more readily by using more manual labor.

The southwestern Wisconsin study was done in dairy country similar to Pennsylvania and demonstrates once again that Amish dairy farming is highly efficient. Although Amish yields are slightly lower than those of their non-Amish neighbors, the energy ratio of 1.6 shows that they are net producers of food energy, whereas the non-Amish are energy consumers. Note also that the Wisconsin yields — for both Amish and non-Amish — are considerably lower than those in Pennsylvania. This can be attributed to poorer soils and modest herd size. Also, the Wisconsin Amish are almost as conservative as the Nebraska Amish in Pennsylvania, so little machinery is used on their farms.

The authors are cautious in drawing conclusions from their study. Based on the data collected, they are not optimistic about all types of agriculture adjusting to conditions of scarce energy. Certain kinds of farm production will suffer more than others. The penalty paid by intensive crop cultivation might be extremely high in the form of reduced yields, whereas other kinds of agriculture, where human labor can more easily replace mechanization, might be able to adapt without paying penalties. And if workers are displaced from industry as energy becomes scarce and factories close down, perhaps farm employment can profit by absorbing former industrial workers.

In this study of the Amish, their agricultural activities are treated as a formal cultural region, an area bounded by distinct social borders, within which their energy efficiency is analyzed. This aspect of their culture is measured in objective terms (units of energy) so that unbiased comparisons can be made with neighboring agricultural strategies.

Energy analysis is a common research theme in cultural geography because any sort of work, performed by either animate or inanimate sources, can be transformed into comparable units of measurement. Equally, manufactured substances, such as fodder, fertilizer, and fuel, can be similarly translated into units of energy, allowing comparisons to be made between energetic systems. This is much like energy flow is measured through a natural ecological system, such as a marsh food chain.

This study, like the one on hybrid seed diffusion, involved an impressive combination of cultural and quantitative analysis. First, a comprehensive understanding of both Amish and non-Amish agricultural systems was necessary. This alone is a formidable task. Once the salient characteristics of each system were understood, the components were then translated into energy units, which, as the reader can readily imagine, involved considerable amounts of statistical transformation. Once this was accomplished, the quantitative comparison could proceed, and the data could be analyzed.

■ THE CULTURAL GEOGRAPHY OF DROUGHT, FAMINE, AND CONFLICT: THE CASE OF ETHIOPIA

Widespread food shortages, or famines, periodically cripple many developing countries by causing thousands of deaths from starvation and malnutrition. While these famines are often triggered by some sort of natural disaster, such as drought or floods, emergency relief is commonly complicated, slowed, and even denied by internal and international politics. Ethiopia, a country of about 48 million people in northeast Africa, has suffered numerous famines in the last decades that have been given much attention by the world press, yet the linkages among drought, politics, and famine have been incompletely analyzed. This case study, which draws upon the work of the geographers Girma Kebbede and Mary Jacob, points out that these famines are a combination of (1) drought conditions resulting from normal climatic fluctuations accentuated by years of environmentally destructive land uses, (2) internal political problems that inhibit timely relief measures, and (3) external politics that have also forestalled emergency relief. Although the specifics of this case study are drawn from Ethiopia, the general findings can be applied to many developing countries.

Before we look at the problems of Ethiopia, we should say a few words linking this study to cultural geography. At one level, the work of Kebbede and Jacob best fits into the theme of cultural ecology because it focuses on the interaction between humans and the physical environment. And yet, other themes also come into play: Their analysis of environmental degradation comes from reading the cultural landscape; the movement (or lack) of people and supplies can be conceptualized as cultural diffusion; and understanding the extremely complex internal politics of Ethiopia draws upon notions of cultural areas and regions. Consequently, as with other case studies in this chapter, Kebbede and Jacob's research effectiveness comes from building their analytic framework from a range of geographic themes and concepts.

Let us begin with a quick look at the physical and cultural geography of Ethiopia (see Figure 13.8). Generally speaking, the country can be divided into two major topographic categories: the highland core and the lowland periphery. Peaks in the highlands reach 15,000 feet (4,500 meters), and some lowland areas are actually below sea level. As might be expected, the highlands are relatively wet while the lowlands are extremely dry.

The cultural geography is far more complicated because Ethiopia has long been a meeting ground between peoples from Asia and Africa; what follows is oversimplified, yet it is also necessary to a basic understanding of that country's problems. Emblematic of the country's complex ethnic and cultural mosaic is that there are over 100 distinct languages, the most important of which are within the Semitic group. In religious makeup,

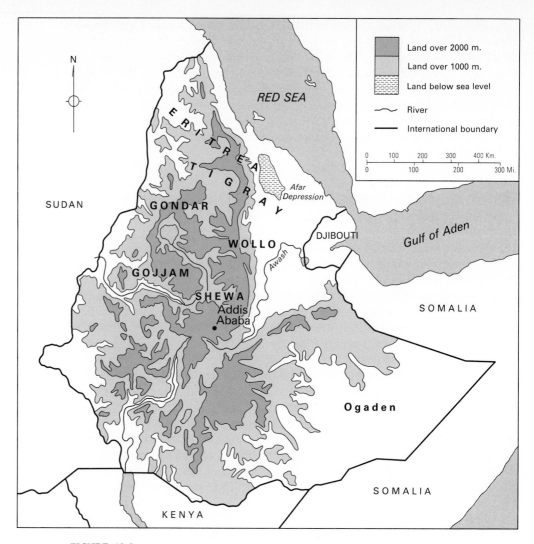

FIGURE 13.8
This map of Ethiopia shows, first, the distinction between the upland core and the lowland periphery, and, second, the location of the various regions within the country. The major separatist movements are in Eritrea and Tigray in the north. (Adapted from Kebbede and Jacob, *Geography*, 1988.)

Christians constitute about half of the population, Muslims around 40 percent, and the remainder are mostly animists. Strong regional traditions, often but not always drawn along cultural lines, characterize and constrain national politics; as this book goes to press, the central government is fighting no fewer than six separate internal wars, a fact that is all-important to understanding how famine aid is dispensed. The strongest separatist movements are in the northern provinces of Eritrea and Tigray. Ethiopia was long ruled by a monarchy, but this was abolished in 1975 following a socialist revolution the year before, and a formal Communist regime was proclaimed in 1984.

The northern region of Ethiopia, which includes Eritrea, Tigray, and Wollo, is the area hardest hit by drought and famine; in Tigray alone, five major famines have hit the province in the last 30 years. Kebbede and Jacob find that, although drought has become almost a "normal" phenomenon in recent decades, centuries of relentless exploitation of the land have resulted in severe environmental degradation that aggravates climatic fluctuations. Specifically, the topsoil is so devoid of organic matter that its ability to hold water and moisture is much reduced; hence, over the years the same amount of rainfall has become less and less effective for growing crops. In addition, heavy rainfall results in severe flooding that erodes away thousands of tons of topsoil. What we see, then, is that two thousand years of sedentary agriculture have taken their toll through soil exhaustion resulting in a loss of environmental resiliency; instead of the land buffering against wet and dry climatic extremes, it accentuates both drought and flooding, so that the local population is caught in a downward spiral of lowered fertility and more frequent droughts and floods, resulting in famine. Unfortunately, this problem is not unique to Ethiopia and is fairly widespread in the developing world.

Also common are the problems resulting from governmental efforts to improve finances by expanding cash crops for export. In Ethiopia, Kebbede and Jacob found that the Afar people of the northeast lowlands have been particularly hard-hit by recent droughts, less because of the harsh environment than because these traditionally pastoral people were displaced to marginal environments when the central government confiscated their grazing lands to grow irrigated cotton and sugar for export. A traditional adaptation to environmental uncertainty was subverted by the government's fixation on cash flow.

As noted earlier, internal political tensions and civil war complicate and distort famine relief. Because the central government is determined to suppress regional liberation fronts, Ethiopia has one of the largest armies in Africa. This comes at considerable cost: About half of the nation's annual budget is spent on defense and internal security—monies, one could argue, that otherwise might be spent on development and aid. Furthermore, many observers believe that the government has not done enough to prevent, or at least ease, the worsening conditions in the northern provinces, and instead dispenses aid and relief congruent with its political goals. Famine was also used as a political tool by the prerevolutionary government, which committed crimes against its own people by deliberately covering up the existence of the 1972–1974 famine, attempting, critics would say, to starve the separatist movements of the north into submission. Many would argue the current government is using the same strategy, since it distributes famine relief mainly to those supporting the central government.

International politics also affect famine aid. The pre-1974 monarchy was friendly to the West and the United States, but since Ethiopia's political allegiance shifted to the Soviet Union with its revolution, some Western relief agencies have been less helpful and have deliberately delayed aid to punish an outspoken Marxist government. Not that the Soviets are blameless: According to Kebbede and Jacob, the Soviet Union has sold Ethiopia over $5 billion worth of military hardware since 1977, but gave less than $100 million in economic aid.

What is to be learned from this case study from Ethiopia? In terms of understanding world problems, probably the most important lesson is that famine is rarely caused by natural disasters, but instead is more commonly a product of the interaction between nature and culture. Although fluctuations in climate produce wet and dry years, Kebbede and Jacob remind us that the impact of these events is often multiplied by human activities and political complexities. Tragically, the conditions that produce famine will increase as world population grows during the 1990s. We might also remember that cultural geography gives us an effective and sensitive framework for understanding such global problems. Because this brief case study has necessarily simplified the work of geographers Girma Kebbede and Mary Jacob, we refer readers to their original works, listed at chapter's end.

■ CONCLUSION

Unfortunately, students often get caught up in the detailed minutiae of introductory courses and lose a broader perspective on the world. Sometimes they leave the classroom with a narrow view of facts, figures, and memorized trivia that obscure what they have actually learned in the class; a myopia hinders them in applying new terms, themes, concepts, and material to experiences beyond the final exam.

We have used the six case studies as a device to counteract that syndrome by showing you how cultural geography can be applied to a wide range of social and environmental problems. These studies illustrate the different scales of problem solving and indicate how research findings are translated into policy guidelines to solve certain kinds of problems; furthermore, these case studies reiterate and expand on the themes and concepts used throughout this book. Last, we have used this opportunity to add a few words about the skills and methods used in the field to illustrate how professional geographers approach different research problems.

Some of you may go on to become professional geographers; most will not. Yet all of you who have read this book have new intellectual skills useful for organizing information about yourselves, your society, your surroundings, and the world beyond. And just in case you have lost perspective on how much you have learned, let us take this last opportunity to remind you of your new talents.

First of all, you have a new understanding of the power of culture and of its varied expressions. You see the importance of belief systems in shaping resource exploitation, of social constraints on livelihood systems, and of the way culture transforms our experiences with the physical environment. Primarily, you are able to view culture in a spatial context, to translate diverse information into a new dimension. You can conceptualize the movement of cultural phenomena through space using diffusion models, differentiate areas of similarity into cultural regions, and decipher visual expressions of human habitation through the cultural landscape. You can understand and assess the different forms of human interaction with the physical environment given the precepts of cultural ecology, and you can model how phenomena might behave in theory through cultural integration.

Furthermore, you can think in different scales, from neighborhood to global. This ability will serve you well, for one of the intellectual shortcomings of specialization seems to be spatial inflexibility, a rigidity that inhibits examining problems at different scales. Complementing these new skills are heightened abilities in spatial interpretation, in reading maps, and in cartographic data interpretation.

And, because time and space are inseparable, you have an enhanced temporal perspective that should facilitate moving beyond "presentism," that shortsighted, confining state that limits the temporal dimension to contemporary events. You have seen the importance of historical explanation for environmental change and for various cultural patterns, you have seen how this allows both a more refined view of the present and, equally important, a degree of predictability concerning the future. To understand the present, one must know the past; to know both allows comprehension of the future.

You recognize the value of time in understanding landscape changes and the importance of gauging human interference in natural systems by examining physical processes through time. You see that cultural movement and transmission must have a time dimension. Remember the value of a historical approach, whatever the topic.

Although the emphasis in this book has been on culture, you also have an improved understanding of the physical world, our natural environment, specifically of the ways in which humans have modified this milieu. Geography sits squarely between the natural and social sciences, and any introduction to this discipline is not complete without a course from both sides. If you have not studied physical geography, you should do so before you can call your introduction complete; the dynamic between nature and culture yields gratifying insight to the human condition.

Most students seek a delicate balance in their college educations between general courses that will expand their horizons and the specialized skill classes that will prepare them for employment in this increasingly technical world. Both are important; both are necessary. This was illustrated over and over again in the case studies where immense breadth was necessary to understand a problem's complexity or to synthesize information from disparate sources, and yet specific skills, such as ecosystem analysis or quantitative methods, were necessary to effect the research.

Cultural geography is a framework for the rest of your education, for it combines far-ranging breadth with technical skills; it offers pathways that lead in both directions, each feeding back to engender a better understanding of the world, of the global village that makes up the human mosaic.

Suggested Readings

Martyn Bowden. "Desertification of the Great Plains: Will it Happen?" *Economic Geography,* 53 (1977), 397–406.

Martyn Bowden et al. "The Effect of Climate Fluctuations on Human Populations: Two Hypotheses," in T. M. L. Wigley, M. J. Ingram, and G. Farmer (eds.), *Climate and History: Studies in Past Climates and Their Impact on Man.* Cambridge: Cambridge University Press, 1981, pp. 479–513.

Reid Bryson and Thomas Murray. *Climates of Hunger: Mankind and the World's Changing Weather.* Madison: University of Wisconsin Press, 1977.

A. K. Chakravarti. "Green Revolution in India," *Annals of the Association of American Geographers,* 63 (1973), 319–330.

John Clarke. *Resettlement and Rehabilitation: Ethiopia's Campaign Against Famine.* London: Speediprinters, 1987.

Jason Clay and Bonnie K. Holcomb. *Politics and the Ethiopian Famine, 1984–1985.* Cambridge, Mass.: Cultural Survival, Inc., 1987.

County of Marin. *Bolinas Lagoon Resource Management Plan.* San Rafael, Calif.: Marin County Department of Parks and Recreation, 1981.

John W. Frazier (ed.). *Applied Geography: Selected Perspectives.* Englewood Cliffs, N.J.: Prentice-Hall, 1982.

G. Hancock. *Ethiopia: The Challenge of Hunger.* London: Gollancz, 1985.

K. Jansson, M. Harris, and A. Penrose. *The Ethiopian Famine.* London: Zed Books, 1987.

Warren Johnson, Victor Stolzfus, and Peter Craumer. "Energy Conservation in Amish Agriculture," *Science,* 198 (October 28, 1977), 373–378.

Robert Kates. "The Human Environment: The Road Not Taken, the Road Still Beckoning," *Annals of the Association of American Geographers,* 77 (1987), 525–534.

Girma Kebbede. "Cycles of Famine in a Country of Plenty: The Case of Ethiopia," *GeoJournal* 17:1 (1988), 125–132.

Girma Kebbede and Mary J. Jacob. "Drought, Famine and the Political Economy of Environmental Degradation in Ethiopia," *Geography,* 73:1 (1988), 65–70.

John Leighly. "Ecology as Metaphor: Carl Sauer and Human Ecology," *Professional Geographer*, 39 (1987), 405–412.

H. Lemma. "The Politics of Famine in Ethiopia," *Review of African Political Economy*, 33 (1985), 44–58.

Melinda Meade. "Land Development and Human Health in West Malaysia," *Annals of the Association of American Geographers*, 66 (1976), 428–439.

G. Tyler Miller, Jr. *Living in the Environment*, 5th ed. Belmont, Calif.: Wadsworth, 1988.

Rowan Rowntree. "Evolutionary and Cyclical Change as Fundamental Attributes of the Estuary," in R. C. Smardon (ed.), *The Future of Wetlands: Assessing Visual-Cultural Values*. Totowa, N.J.: Allanheld, Osnun, 1983, pp. 120–145.

Rowan Rowntree. *Biological Considerations in Bolinas Lagoon Planning*. Washington, D.C.: The Conservation Foundation, 1976.

Christopher L. Salter. "What Can I Do with Geography?" *Professional Geographer*, 35 (1983), 266–273.

Glossary

absorbing barrier A barrier that completely halts diffusion of innovations and blocks the spread of cultural elements. (Chapter 1)

acculturation The process by which an ethnic group changes in order to function in the host society. (Chapter 9)

acid rain A result of the burning of fossil fuels, acid rain results when sulfur and nitrogen oxides are flushed from the atmosphere by precipitation, with lethal effects for many plants and animals. (Chapter 12)

agglomeration A snowballing geographical process by which secondary through quinary industrial activities become clustered in cities and compact industrial regions in order to share infrastructure and markets. (Chapters 10, 12)

agribusiness Highly mechanized, large-scale farming usually under corporate ownership. (Chapter 3)

agricultural landscape The cultural landscape of agricultural areas. (Chapter 3)

agricultural region A culture region based on characteristics of agriculture, within which a given type of agriculture occurs. (Chapter 3)

agriculture The cultivation of domesticated crops and the raising of domesticated animals. (Chapter 3)

agro-town A very large, clustered, rural settlement, consisting of many thousands of people who are employed in agriculture. (Chapter 2)

animism The belief that inanimate objects, such as trees, rocks, and rivers, possess souls. (Chapter 6)

antecedent boundary A political border drawn prior to the settlement of an area. (Chapter 4)

assimilation The loss of all ethnic traits and complete blending into the host society. (Chapter 9)

birth rate The number of births in one year per thousand persons in the population. (Chapter 2)

buffer state An independent but small and weak state lying between two powerful, potentially belligerent states. (Chapter 4)

bulk-gaining product A product in which volume is added to the raw materials in the manufacturing process. (Chapter 12)

cadastral pattern The shapes formed by property borders; the pattern of land ownership. (Chapter 3)

CBD The central business district of a city. (Chapter 11)

census tracts Small districts used by the United States Census Bureau to survey the population. (Chapter 11)

centralizing forces Diffusion forces that encourage people or businesses to locate in the central city. (Chapter 11)

central place A town or city engaged primarily in the tertiary stage of production; a regional center. (Chapter 10)

central-place theory A set of models designed to explain the spatial distribution of tertiary urban centers. (Chapter 10)

centrifugal force Any factor that disrupts the internal order of a state. (Chapter 4)

centripetal force Any factor that supports the internal unity of a state. (Chapter 4)

chain migration The tendency of people to migrate along channels, over a period of time, from specific source areas to specific destinations. (Chapter 9)

checkerboard development A mixture of farmlands and housing tracts. (Chapter 11)

coercion and warfare model An explanatory model for the rise of cities that argues competition for scarce resources engenders a pattern of fortified settlements. (Chapter 10)

colonial city A city founded by colonialism, or an indigenous city whose structure was deeply influenced by Western colonialism. (Chapter 10)

concentric zone model A social model that depicts a city as five areas bounded by concentric rings. (Chapter 11)

contact conversion The spread of religious beliefs by personal contact. (Chapter 6)

contagious diffusion A type of expansion diffusion; the spread of cultural innovation by person-to-person contact, moving wavelike through an area and population without regard to social status. (Chapter 1)

convergence hypothesis A hypothesis holding that cultural differences between places are being reduced by improved transportation and communications systems, leading to a homogenization of popular culture. (Chapter 8)

core area The territorial nucleus from which a state grows in area and through time, often containing the national capital and the main center of commerce, culture, and industry. (Chapter 4)

core/periphery A concept based on the tendency of both formal and functional culture regions to consist of a core or node, in which defining traits are purest or functions are headquartered, and a periphery that is tributary and displays fewer of the defining traits. (Chapters 1, 3, 4, 5, 12)

cottage (household) industry A traditional type of manufacturing in the preindustrial revolution era, practiced on a small scale in individual rural households as a part-time occupation and designed to produce handmade goods for local consumption. (Chapter 12)

counterurbanization A term describing the apparent population movement away from urban and suburban areas; rapid population growth in formerly rural counties is the major indicator of counterurbanization. (Chapter 11)

cultural adaptation The concept, central to cultural ecology, that culture is the uniquely human method of meeting physical environmental challenges— that culture is an adaptive system. (Chapter 1)

cultural determinism The viewpoint that the immediate causes of all cultural phenomena are other phenomena. (Chapter 1)

cultural diffusion The spread of elements of culture from the point of origin over an area. (Chapter 1)

cultural ecology Broadly defined, the study of the relationships between the physical environment and culture; narrowly (and more commonly) defined, the study of culture as an adaptive system serving to facilitate human adaptation to nature and environmental change. (Chapter 1)

cultural geography The description and explanation of spatial patterns and ecological relationships in human culture. (Chapter 1)

cultural integration The relationship of different elements within a culture. (Chapter 1)

cultural landscape The artificial landscape; the visible human imprint on the land. (Chapter 1)

cultural rebound The belated appearance, after the early difficult years of pioneering are past, of Old World cultural traits among ethnic groups that have migrated. (Chapter 9)

culture A total way of life held in common by a group of people, including such learned features as speech, ideology, behavior, livelihood, technology, and government. (Chapter 1)

culture area A composite formal culture region based on whole cultures, on the totality of cultural traits. (Chapter 1)

culture region An area occupied by people who have something in common culturally; or a spatial unit that functions politically, socially, or economically as a distinct entity. (Chapter 1)

death rate The number of deaths in one year per thousand persons in the population. (Chapter 2)

decentralization The movement of households, business, and industry away from the central city. (Chapter 10)

decentralizing forces Diffusion forces that encourage people or businesses to locate outside the central city. (Chapter 11)

defensive site An easily defended place to locate a city. (Chapter 10)

deindustrialization Decline of primary and secondary industry, accompanied by a rise of the service sectors of the industrial economy. (Chapter 12)

demographic region A culture region based on characteristics of demography. (Chapter 2)

demographic transformation A change in population growth that occurs when a nation moves from a rural, agricultural society with high birth and death rates to an urban, industrial society in which death rates decline first and birth rates decline later. (Chapter 2)

demography The statistical study of population size, composition, distribution, and change. (Chapter 2)

denomination A subdivision of a major religion, such as Lutheran or Baptist. (Chapter 6)

dialect A regional variety of a language. (Chapter 5)

diversifying selection Adaptive strategies that are versatile and diverse, including multiple strategies, a tolerance of deviant behavior, and an openness to new ideas or strategies; typical of marginal, stressful physical environments. (Chapter 1)

domesticated animal An animal kept for some utilitarian purpose whose breeding is controlled by humans and whose survival is dependent on humans; differing genetically and behaviorally from wild animals. (Chapter 3)

domesticated plant A plant willfully planted and tended by humans that is genetically distinct from its wild ancestors as a result of selective breeding. (Chapter 3)

dominant personality A forceful, ambitious, influential person, a natural leader, who emigrates and is able to convince others to follow. (Chapter 9)

double-cropping Harvesting twice a year from the same parcel of land. (Chapter 3)

dust dome A pollution layer over a city that is thickest at the center of the city. (Chapter 11)

ecology The study of the relationship between an organism and its physical environment. (Chapter 1)

economic determinism The belief that human behavior, including spatial or geographical attributes, is largely or wholly dictated by economic factors and motivation. (Chapter 1)

ecosystem The functioning ecological system in which biological and cultural *Homo sapiens* live and interact with the physical environment. (Chapter 1); a unit through which the flow of matter or energy is traced. (Chapter 11)

emerging city A city of a current developing or emerging country. (Chapter 10)

emigrant letters Including "American letters," those letters written back to friends and relatives in their former homes by early immigrants, describing their new homeland in glowing terms, serving to induce others to follow them. (Chapter 9)

enclave A piece of territory surrounded by, but not part of, a state. (Chapter 4)

environmental determinism The school of thought based on the belief that cultures are, directly or indirectly, shaped by the physical environment, that cultures are molded by physical surroundings. (Chapter 1)

environmental perception The school of thought based on the belief that cultural attitudes shape perception of the environment, causing people of different cultures to perceive their surroundings differently and to make different decisions as a result. (Chapter 1)

environmental stress model An explanatory scheme for urban origins emphasizing a changing physical environment. Social advantage goes to that group best adapting to the new conditions. (Chapter 10)

ethnic culture region An area shared by people of similar ethnic background, who share race or language. (Chapter 11)

ethnic geography The study of the spatial and ecological aspects of ethnicity. (Chapter 9)

ethnic island A small ethnic area in the rural countryside; sometimes called a "folk island." (Chapter 9)

ethnic neighborhood An area within a city containing members of the same ethnic background; a voluntary segregation of urban people along ethnic lines. (Chapter 9)

ethnic province A large district dominated by a single ethnic group, usually including both rural areas and cities. (Chapter 9)

ethnic religion A religion identified with a particular ethnic or tribal group; does not seek converts. (Chapter 6)

ethnographic boundary A political boundary that follows some cultural border, such as a linguistic or religious border. (Chapter 4)

exclave A piece of a state separated from the main body of it by the intervening territory of another state. (Chapter 4)

expansion diffusion The spread of innovations within an area in a snowballing process, so that the total number of knowers becomes greater and the area of occurrence grows. (Chapter 1)

farmstead The center of farm operations, containing the house, barn, sheds, and livestock pens. (Chapter 2)

farm village A clustered rural settlement of moderate size, inhabited by people who are engaged in farming. (Chapter 2)

faubourg The suburbs of a medieval city. The term means "beyond the fortress," which translates to outside the city walls. (Chapter 10)

federal state An independent state in which considerable autonomy and power are given to individual provinces and the central government is relatively weak. (Chapter 4)

feedback Repercussions on a system when an element is returned in modified form. (Chapter 11)

feedlot A factorylike farm, devoted to either livestock fattening or dairying; all feed is imported and no crops are grown on the farm. (Chapter 3)

floating activities Those activities not tied to a specific location. (Chapter 10)

folk Traditional, rural, nonpopular. (Chapter 7)

folk architecture Structures built by members of a folk society or culture in a traditional manner and style, without the assistance of professional architects or blueprints, using locally available raw materials. (Chapter 7)

folk culture A small, cohesive, stable, isolated, nearly self-sufficient group that is homogeneous in custom and race; characterized by a strong family or clan structure; order maintained through sanctions based in the religion or family; little division of labor other than between the sexes; frequent and strong interpersonal relationships, and a material culture consisting mainly of handmade goods. (Chapter 7)

folk fortress A stronghold area with natural defensive qualities, useful in the defense of the state against invaders. (Chapter 4)

folk geography The study of the spatial patterns of elements of folklife; a branch of cultural geography. (Chapter 7)

folklife The totality of the material and nonmaterial folk culture. (Chapter 7)

folklore Nonmaterial folk culture; the teaching and wisdom of a folk group; the traditional tales, sayings, beliefs, and superstitions that are transmitted orally. (Chapter 7)

formal culture region A region inhabited by people who have one or more cultural traits in common. (Chapter 1)

forward-thrust capital A capital city situated near the frontier of the most rapid territorial expansion or new settlement in a state. (Chapter 4)

functional culture region An area that functions as a unit politically, socially, or economically. (Chapter 1)

functional zonation The division of the city into different areas for different functions, such as industry and housing. (Chapter 10)

generic toponym The descriptive part of many place-names, often repeated throughout a culture area. (Chapter 5)

gentrification Replacement of lower-income groups by higher-income people as buildings are restored. (Chapter 10)

geography The study of spatial patterns, of differences and similarities from one place to another in environment and culture. (Chapter 1)

geomancy A traditional East Asian form of environmental perception, also called *feng shui*, by which particular configurations of terrain, compass directions, soil textures, and watercourse patterns become more auspicious than others, influencing the siting of houses, villages, cities, temples, and graves. (Chapters 1, 6)

geometric boundary A political border drawn in a regular, geometric manner, often a straight line, without regard for environmental or cultural patterns. (Chapter 4)

geophagy The deliberate eating of earth. (Chapter 7)

geopolitics The portion of political geography dealing with international strategic matters such as conquest and power balances as they relate to the spatial patterns of physical and cultural geography. (Chapter 4)

ghetto A segregated ethnic area within a city, caused by residential discrimination against the will of the people involved. (Chapter 9)

global corporations Also called multinationals or transnationals, these corporations are industries that operate in more than one country, dispersing their factories, headquarters, marketing, and service functions across international boundaries. (Chapter 12)

greenhouse effect The results from the increased addition of carbon dioxide and certain trace gases to the atmosphere through industrial activity and deforestation causing more of the sun's heat to be retained, thus warming the climate of the Earth. (Chapter 12)

green revolution The recent introduction of high-yield hybrid crops and chemical fertilizers and pesticides into traditional Asian agricultural systems, most notably paddy rice farming, with attendant increases in production and ecological damage. (Chapter 3)

guild industry A traditional type of manufacturing in the preindustrial revolution era, involving handmade goods of high quality manufactured by highly skilled artisans who resided in towns and cities. (Chapter 12)

head-link capital A capital city situated near the border along the main route of foreign trade and cultural contact. (Chapter 4)

heartland The interior of a state or landmass, removed from maritime connections; in particular, the interior of the Eurasian continent. (Chapter 4)

heartland theory A 1904 proposal by Mackinder that the key to world conquest lay in control of the interior of Eurasia. (Chapter 4)

heat island An area of warmer temperatures at the center of a city, caused by the urban concentration of heat-retaining concrete, brick, and asphalt. (Chapter 10)

hierarchical diffusion A type of expansion diffusion; innovations spread from one important person to another or from one urban center to another, temporarily bypassing persons of lesser importance and rural areas. (Chapter 1)

hinterland The area surrounding a city and influenced by it. (Chapter 10)

host culture The dominant, majority cultural group within a country or society, which usually occupies a dominant social-economic position. (Chapter 9)

humanistic geographers Those geographers who stress that an understanding of culture and of the subjectivity and individuality of humans is essential to an analysis of spatial variations and the understanding of places; they reject the notion that human geography is a science. (Chapter 1)

hybrid A special plant or animal that results from breeding two different varieties. (Chapter 3)

hydraulic civilization A civilization based on large-scale irrigation. (Chapter 10)

idiographic research Research that involves the study of phenomena that are never alike and that therefore do not lend themselves to the development of explanatory laws. (Chapter 1)

immigrant's ladder The movement of people from a core ethnic neighborhood to progressively higher-status neighborhoods. (Chapter 9)

inanimate power Power derived from sources other than humans and work animals; in particular, the use of water or wind power, steam, and electricity. Today it is generated through the burning of fossil fuels such as coal or oil or by means of nuclear fission. (Chapter 12)

independent inventions Cultural innovations that are developed in two or more locations by persons or groups working independently. (Chapter 1)

indigenous city A city formed by local forces. (Chapter 10)

industrial inertia The tendency of industries to remain in their original locations, even after the forces that originally attracted them there have disappeared. (Chapter 12)

industrial revolution A series of inventions and innovations, arising in England in the 1700s, which led to the use of machines and inanimate power in the manufacturing process. (Chapter 12)

infanticide The killing of newborn children, often for purposes of population control. (Chapter 2)

in-filling New building on empty parcels of land within a checkerboard pattern of development. (Chapter 11)

innovation model A model arguing that the first cities were closely tied to a breakthrough innovation in technology, food production, or social organization. (Chapter 10)

input A resource, such as water, flowing into an ecosystem. (Chapter 11)

insurgent state A state within a state, the result of a guerrilla insurgency directed toward secession or overthrow of the existing government. (Chapter 4)

intensive agriculture The expenditure of much labor and capital on a piece of land to increase its productivity. In contrast, extensive agriculture involves less labor and capital. (Chapter 3)

intertillage The raising of different crops mixed together in the same field, particularly common in shifting cultivation. (Chapter 3)

isogloss The border of usage of an individual word or pronunciation. (Chapter 5)

labor-intensive industry An industry for which labor costs represent a large proportion of total production costs. (Chapter 12)

laissez-faire utilitarianism The belief that economic competition without government interference produces the most public good. (Chapter 10)

language family A group of related languages derived from a common ancestor. (Chapter 5)

lateral commuting Traveling from one suburb to another in going from home to work. (Chapter 11)

legible city A city that is easy to decipher, with clear pathways, edges, nodes, districts, and landmarks. (Chapter 11)

lingua franca An existing, well-established language used widely where it is not a mother tongue, for the purposes of government, trade, business, and other contacts among persons. (Chapter 5)

linguistic refuge area An area, isolated or protected by environmental conditions, in which a language or dialect has survived. (Chapter 5)

logical positivism The worldly, secular, antitheological view that knowledge derives only from an empirical analysis, employing the scientific method and normally involving quantification, of the properties and relationships of sensed phenomena; strict adherence to the testimony of observation is maintained. (Chapter 1)

manifest destiny The belief that a nation should follow its natural course by expanding to some clear environmental limits. (Chapter 4)

march or marchland A strip of territory, traditionally one day's march for infantry, that served as a boundary zone for independent states in premodern times. (Chapter 4)

market garden A farm devoted to specialized fruit, vegetable, or vine crops for sale rather than consumption. (Chapter 3)

material culture All physical, material objects made and used by members of a cultural group, such as clothing, buildings, tools and utensils, instruments, furniture, and artwork; the visible aspect of culture. (Chapter 7)

megalopolis A large urban region formed as several urban areas spread and merge, such as Boswash, the region including Boston, New York, and Washington, D.C. (Chapter 10)

melting pot In multiethnic societies, the assumption that all diverse cultures present will assimilate to produce a national culture, and that each culture will lose its distinctiveness. (Chapters 1, 9)

mental map A map, often including positive or negative images of different areas, as perceived in the mind of the individual person. (Chapter 2)

migration region A geographical area, usually contiguous, within which the segment of the population that migrates tends to stay, rather than leaving the region. (Chapter 2)

model An abstraction, an imaginary situation, proposed by geographers to simulate laboratory conditions so that they may isolate certain causal forces for detailed study. (Chapter 1)

monotheism The worship of only one god. (Chapter 6)

multiple nuclei model A model that depicts a city growing from several separate focal points. (Chapter 11)

multiplier leakage The process by which industrial profits "drain" back to major industrial districts from factories established in outlying provinces or countries. (Chapter 12)

nation-state An independent state inhabited by a relatively homogeneous cultural group. (Chapter 4)

natural boundary A political border that follows some feature of the natural environment, such as a river or mountain ridge. (Chapter 4)

neighborhood A small social area within a city where residents share values and concerns and interact with one another on a daily basis. (Chapter 11)

neighborhood effect The rapid acceptance of an innovation in a small area or cluster around an initial adopter. (Chapter 1)

node In a functional culture region, a central point where functions are coordinated and directed. (Chapter 1)

nomothetic science A law-giving science. (Chapter 1)

nonmaterial culture Includes the oral aspect of a culture, such as songs, dialect, tales, beliefs, and customs. (Chapter 7)

nonrenewable resources Resources that must be depleted in order to be used, such as minerals. (Chapter 12)

outputs Elements produced by and flowing out of an ecosystem; for example, water may leave a system in many forms—as sewage, as a component of food or drinks for export, as vapor produced by industry. (Chapter 11)

paddy A small flooded field enclosed by mud dikes, used for rice cultivation in the Orient. (Chapter 3)

palimpsest A term used to describe cultural landscapes with various layers and elements of historical "messages." Geographers use this term to reinforce the notion of the landscape as a text that can be read; a landscape palimpsest has elements of both modern and past periods. (Chapter 11)

particulate matter Bits of matter spewed into the air by incinerators, car exhausts, tire wear, industrial combustion, and so forth. (Chapters 11, 12)

permeable barrier A barrier that permits some aspects of an innovation to diffuse through but weakens and retards continued spread; an innovation can be modified in passing through a permeable barrier. (Chapter 1)

personal space The amount of space that individuals feel "belongs" to them as they move about their everyday business. (Chapter 2)

phenomenology The view that the primary objective of research is the direct investigation and description of phenomena, both sense-experienced and nonsenuous, free of theories about their causal explanation and as free as possible from unexamined preconceptions and presuppositions. (Chapter 1)

physical environment All aspects of the natural physical surroundings, such as climate, terrain, soils, vegetation, and wildlife. (Chapter 1)

pidgin A composite language consisting of a small vocabulary borrowed from the linguistic groups involved in international commerce. (Chapter 5)

pilgrimage A journey to a place of religious importance. (Chapter 6)

place A term used to connote the subjective, idiographic, humanistic, culturally oriented type of geography that seeks to understand the unique character of individual regions and places, rejecting the principles of science as flawed and unknowingly biased. (Chapters 1, 11)

plantation A large landholding devoted to specialized production of a tropical cash crop. (Chapter 3)

polyglot Characterized by many different languages. (Chapter 5)

polytheism The worship of many gods. (Chapter 6)

popular culture A dynamic culture based in large, heterogeneous societies permitting considerable individualism, innovation, and change; having a money-based economy, division of labor into professions, secular institutions of control, and weak interpersonal ties; producing and consuming machine-made goods. (Chapter 8)

population density The number of people in an area of land, usually expressed as people per square mile or people per square kilometer. (Chapter 2)

population explosion The rapid, accelerating increase in world population since about 1650 and especially since 1900. (Chapter 2)

population geography The study of spatial differences in the distribution, density, and demographic types of people. (Chapter 2)

population pyramid A bar graph used to show the age and sex composition of a population. (Chapter 2)

port of entry The area at the core of an ethnic neighborhood in a city where recent migrants to the city are likely to seek housing. (Chapter 9)

possibilism The school of thought based on the belief that humans, rather than the physical environment, are the primary active force; that any environment offers a number of different possible ways for a culture to develop; and that the choices among these possibilities are guided by cultural heritage. (Chapter 1)

postindustrial phase The way of life produced by dominance of the tertiary, quaternary, and quinary sectors of economic activity. (Chapter 12)

preadaptation A complex of adaptive traits and skills possessed in advance of migration by a group, giving them survival ability and competitive advantage in occupying the new environment. (Chapters 2, 9)

preindustrial model A city scheme that places the highest status groups in the city center; group status lessens toward the periphery. (Chapter 10)

primary industries Industries engaged in the extraction of natural resources, such as agriculture, lumbering, and mining. (Chapter 12)

primate city A city of large size and dominant power within a country. (Chapters 4, 10)

push-and-pull factors Unfavorable, repelling conditions and favorable, attractive conditions that interact to affect migration and other elements of diffusion. (Chapter 2)

quasi-religion A system of belief similar to a religion but lacking worship services. (Chapter 6)

quaternary industry A service sector of industry; includes business services such as trade, insurance, banking, advertising, and wholesaling. (Chapter 12)

quinary industry A service sector of industry; includes services such as health, education, research, government, retailing, tourism, and recreational facilities. (Chapter 12)

raison d'être In French, literally "reason for being"; the main unifying force within a state, the principal basis of nationalism. (Chapter 4)

ranching Commercial raising of herd livestock, on a large landholding. (Chapter 3)

range In central-place theory, the average maximum distance people will travel to purchase a good or service. (Chapter 10)

region A grouping of like places or the functional union of places to form a spatial unit; see also *culture region.* (Chapter 1)

relic boundary A former political border, no longer functioning as a boundary. (Chapter 4)

religion A social system involving a set of beliefs and practices through which people seek harmony with the universe and attempt to influence the forces of nature, life, and death. (Chapter 6)

relocation diffusion The spread of an innovation or other element of culture that occurs with the bodily relocation (migration) of an individual or group that has the idea. (Chapter 1)

renewable resources Resources that are not depleted if wisely used, such as forests, water, fishing grounds, and agricultural land. (Chapter 12)

rimland The maritime fringe of a country or continent; in particular, the western, southern, and eastern edges of the Eurasian continent. (Chapter 4)

rimland theory A 1944 proposal by Spykman that the key to world conquest lay in domination of the Eurasian rimland. (Chapter 4)

sacred space An area recognized by a religious group as worthy of devotion, loyalty, esteem, or fear, to the extent that it becomes sought out, avoided, inaccessible to the nonbeliever, and/or removed from economic use. (Chapter 6)

satellite state A small, weak state dominated by one powerful neighbor to the extent that some or much of its independence is lost. (Chapter 4)

secondary industries Industries engaged in processing raw materials into finished products; manufacturing. (Chapter 12)

sector model An economic model that depicts a city as a series of pie-shaped wedges. (Chapter 11)

sedentary cultivation Farming in fixed and permanent fields. (Chapter 3)

sequent occupance An historical sequence of land use, implying distinct occupance phases. (Chapter 1)

sex ratio The numerical ratio of males to females in a population. (Chapter 2)

shatter belt A zone of great cultural complexity containing many small cultural groups. (Chapter 5)

shifting cultivation A type of agriculture characterized by land rotation, in which temporary clearings are used for several years and then abandoned to be replaced by new clearings; also known as slash-and-burn agriculture. (Chapter 3)

site The local setting of a city. (Chapter 10)

situation The regional setting of a city. (Chapter 10)

social culture region An area in a city where many of the residents share social traits such as income, education, and stage of life. (Chapter 11)

social geography The study of the spatial attributes of social phenomena such as crime, aging, health, marriage, divorce, and quality of life. (Chapter 2)

space A term used to connote the objective, quantitative, nomothetic, theoretical, model-based, economic-oriented type of geography that seeks to understand spatial systems and networks through application of the principles of social science. (Chapter 1)

spatial distribution The general pattern of location, as opposed to specific sites. (Chapter 10)

stabilizing selection Adaptive strategies that are specialized and lack diversity, characterized by conservatism and intolerance of deviant behavior; typical of fruitful physical environments not subject to significant fluctuation. (Chapter 1)

state church A church designated by the government as the official, legal faith in a political state, usually receiving financial support from the government. (Chapter 6)

stimulus diffusion When a specific trait fails to diffuse but the underlying idea or concept is accepted. (Chapter 1)

subsequent boundary   A political border drawn after the settlement of an area. (Chapter 4)

subsistence agriculture   Farming to supply the minimum food and materials necessary to survive. (Chapter 3)

suitcase farm   In American commercial grain agriculture, a farm on which no one lives, that is planted and harvested by hired migratory crews. (Chapter 3)

survey pattern   A pattern of original land survey in an area. (Chapter 3)

teleology   A philosophy proposing that the Earth was created specifically as the abode for humans, that the Earth belongs to humans by divine intention. (Chapter 6)

territorial imperative   The instinctual need to posses and defend territory; observed in many animal species and perhaps also inherent in humans. (Chapter 4)

tertiary industry   A service sector of industry; includes transportation, communications, and utilities. (Chapter 12)

theocracy   A government guided by a religion. (Chapter 6)

threshold   The population required to make provision of services economically feasible. (Chapter 10)

time-distance decay   The decrease in acceptance of a cultural innovation with increasing time and distance from its origin. (Chapter 1)

topical geography   The division of geographical subject matter into topics, such as agricultural geography, rather than into regions. (Chapter 1)

toponym   A place-name. (Chapter 5)

trade-route site   A place for a city that is at a significant point on transportation routes. (Chapter 10)

uneven development   The tendency for industry to develop in a core/periphery pattern, enriching industrialized countries of the core and impoverishing the less industrialized periphery. (Chapter 12)

unitary state   An independent state in which power is highly concentrated in the central government. (Chapter 4)

universalizing religion   A religion that actively seeks converts and has the goal of converting all humankind. (Chapter 6)

urban hearth areas   The five regions—Mesopotamia, the Nile Valley, Pakistan's Indus Valley, China's Yellow River area, and Mesoamerica—where the world's first cities evolved. (Chapter 10)

urbanized area   The complete metropolitan region, including both central city and suburbs. (Chapter 10)

urbanized population   The proportion of a country's population living in cities. (Chapter 10)

urban morphology   The form and structure of cities, including street patterns and the size and shape of buildings. (Chapter 10)

vernacular culture region   A region perceived to exist by its inhabitants; based in the collective spatial perception of the population at large; bearing a generally accepted name or nickname. (Chapters 1, 8)

visual convergence   The tendency for places to look alike; to converge in appearance because of similar building and design technologies. (Chapter 11)

weight-gaining product   A product in which weight is added to the raw materials in the manufacturing process. (Chapter 12)

zero population growth   A stabilized population created when the average of only two children per couple survives to adulthood, so that, eventually, the number of deaths equals the number of births. (Chapter 2)

Index

Abler, Ronald F., 279, 280
Aborigines, 94, 160–161, 164, 310
Acadiana, 52, 229, 230, 232
Acculturation, 294, 308
Acid rain, 434–436
Acropolis, 343
Adaptation, cultural, 19, 21, 59,
    62–63, 82, 101, 174, 203, 240,
    310, 434. *See also* Preadaptation
Addis Ababa, 108, 331, 470
Adirondack Mountains, 435
Afar, 471
Afghanistan, 143, 144, 194, 251,
    358
Africa
    agriculture in, 5, 72, 81, 85, 87,
        88, 89, 102, 106, 469–471
    architecture in, 251
    birth rate in, 40
    cities in, 362
    colonialism in, 137, 174, 360
    culture regions in, 7, 470
    diffusion from, 221
    disease in, 60, 61
    economy of, 420, 441, 471
    ethnic groups in, 21, 88, 106
    geophagy in, 241
    languages in, 162–164, 174,
        179, 469
    material culture in, 238
    origin of humankind in, 53–54
    pilgrims from, 214–215
    political geography of, 137–138
    population of, 38, 59, 60, 61, 71
    religions in, 194, 195, 197, 201,
        470

as source of slaves, 67, 175
transport in, 426
urbanization in, 331
African-Americans. *See* Blacks
Age distribution, population, 49–51
Agglomeration, 353, 381, 441
Agora, 343
Agribusiness, 92–93
Agriculture, 459–471
    chapter on, 80–120
    and climate, 101
    defined, 80, 419
    and drought, 462–465
    ecology of, 101–104, 244
    ethnic groups in, 105, 106, 317–
        319, 469–471
    fairs of, 236–237
    intensive, 83, 107
    Mediterranean, 82–83, 85, 87
    origin and diffusion of, 95–99
    plantation, 82–83, 89–90
    and politics, 147, 148
    as related to cities, 333–336,
        387–388
    as related to religion, 209–212
    subsistence, 81–89
    and terrain, 101, 102
    types of, 81–94
Agro-town, 69
Ahimsa, 195, 207
AIDS (acquired immune deficiency
    syndrome), 52
Alabama, 13, 208, 219, 242, 265,
    267, 269, 318
Alaska, 50, 127
    highway, 179

Alberta, 299
Alcoholic beverages, 12, 24,
    209–210, 212–213, 245–247,
    263–264
Algeria, 60, 134, 163
Allen, James P., 296, 308
Alpacas, 85, 99
Alps, 60, 141, 172, 174, 215
Altaic languages, 160–161, 163,
    170
Aluminum, 438
Alwin, John A., 237, 239
Amazon basin, 59, 84, 197
American Manufacturing Belt, 421,
    424
Amerindians, 5
    agriculture of, 82, 84, 95, 97, 99,
        336
    Aztec, 54–55
    blowgun among, 238, 239
    cities of, 336
    environmental perception of, 208
    forest removal by, 185
    Fox, 319
    Haida, 204
    houses of, 252
    Inca, 252. *See also* Quechua
    languages of, 159, 160, 164, 172,
        175, 176, 179
    in Louisiana, 232
    Maya, 74–76
    Navaho, 65–66, 208
    numbers of, 304
    Odawa, 176
    Pueblo, 204, 322–323
    religion of, 203, 204, 208

Amerindians (*Continued*)
 reservations of, 10, 311, 319
 Tapirapé, 64
 Tenetehara, 64
 toponyms of, 183, 184
 in urban areas, 300
 Yanoama, 208
 Zuñi, 208
Amharic, 163, 178
Amish, 100–101, 228, 294, 299, 465–468
Anderson, Burton, 445
Andes, 59, 172, 251, 252
Anglo-America, 421, 424. *See also* Canada; United States
Animism, 191, 197, 201, 203, 204, 205, 221, 245
Ankara, 128
Antarctica, 36, 54
Appalachians, 231, 242, 243, 244, 245–248, 269, 309, 312, 442
Apples, 90
Aqueducts, 81
Arabia, 40, 54, 87, 162, 163, 172, 179, 195, 199, 205, 214. *See also* Oman; Saudi Arabia; Yemen
Arabic, 162, 163, 175, 178, 179, 185, 195
Arab League, 133, 134
Arabs, 2, 124, 137, 163, 175, 178, 179, 183, 185, 205, 445
Architecture, 28–30
 ethnic, 319–321, 322–323
 folk, 74, 152, 231, 240, 249–257
 industrial, 445, 447
 of popular culture, 274, 288–289
 religious, 4, 217–218
 urban, 342, 414
Ardrey, Robert, 125
Argentina, 41, 91, 94, 111, 332, 420, 425
Arizona, 51, 61, 274, 277, 280, 283, 446
Arkansas, 91, 235, 248
Arreola, Daniel D., 323
Asia. *See also entries for various countries*
 agriculture in, 81, 82, 84, 85, 97, 100
 animal domestication in, 99
 colonialism in, 137, 174
 crop domestication in, 97
 drug trade from, 274
 emigration from, 300, 301
 languages in, 161, 162–164
 religions in, 194–197
 as religious hearth area, 198–201
 urbanization in, 331, 336, 341, 359, 365

Assimilation, 295
Athens, 23, 343
Atlanta, 381
Australia
 agriculture in, 91, 92, 94, 98
 architecture in, 252
 birth rate in, 41
 diet in, 106
 ethnic groups in, 94, 164, 295
 immigration to, 55, 174
 political geography of, 129, 136, 141
 popular culture in, 263
 population of, 38, 40, 60, 146
 survey pattern in, 110
Austria, 60, 141, 162, 368. *See also* Salzburg; Vienna
Austro-Asiatic languages, 160–161, 164
Austro-Hungarian Empire, 145
Aztecs. *See* Amerindians, Aztec

Bach, Wilfrid, 435
Bahrain, 194
Bali, 196
Bananas, 74, 82, 89, 96
Bangladesh, 39, 73, 127, 162, 433
Bantu languages, 138, 163, 167, 172, 179
Baptists, 192, 193, 194, 212, 213, 245
Barcelona, 136
Barley, 85, 87, 97, 333
Barns, 230, 231, 254, 322
Barriadas, 363
Barriers, 134, 174, 201–203, 236, 239, 242, 274, 275, 461
 absorbing, 15, 138, 202, 203, 272, 307
 permeable, 15, 138, 202, 242, 307
Basques, 130, 145, 316
Baumann, Duane, 208
Bavaria, 141, 219
Bedouin, 179
Beer, 12, 263–264, 442
Belfast, 145
Belgium, 135, 215, 432, 448
Bennett, Charles, 174
Berbers, 163
Berkeley, 378, 428
Berlin, 126, 149, 151, 183
Bible Belt, 193, 194
Bilash, O. S. E., 28
Birth control, 42–49, 56–57
Birth rate, 40–46
Bjorklund, Elaine M., 315, 316
Black Forest, 63
Blacks
 dialects of, 165–166, 172, 175

 diet of, 241–242
 music of, 235
 in South Africa, 302
 in the United States, 9, 165–166, 175, 231, 235, 241–242, 294, 297, 300, 301, 302, 304, 305, 314, 315, 386
Blaut, James M., 16
Blowguns, 237–239
Boers, 136
Bolinas Lagoon, 454–457
Bolivia, 137, 275
Bombay, 329, 332, 367
Borders
 cultural, 8–11, 86
 linguistic, 158–160
 political, 128, 141–142
Borneo, 238
Boston, 2, 222, 275, 293, 301, 304, 316, 356, 380, 409
Bowden, Leonard, 100
Bowden, Martyn, 462–465
Brasilia, 129, 358
Brazil
 agriculture in, 5, 84, 90, 91
 cities in, 332
 ethnic groups in, 64, 84, 179, 208, 295
 industry in, 423
 land survey in, 111
 language in, 175, 179
 political geography of, 126, 129
 population of, 39, 146
Bretons, 130
Bridges, 20, 215, 257, 448
Brierley, J. S., 318, 319
British Columbia, 204
British Commonwealth, 133
British Empire, 140
Brooklyn, N.Y., 28
Brownell, Joseph, 269, 270
Brunn, Stanley D., 123, 124
Buchanan, Keith, 178
Buddhism
 in China, 202, 203
 diffusion of, 199, 201
 distribution of, 191, 196–197
 and environmental change, 207
 and geomancy, 203–204
 imprint on landscape, 196, 219
 in Japan, 196
 Lamaist, 191, 196, 205
 Zen, 196–197
Buffalo, N.Y., 381
Buffer state, 128, 148
Bunge, William W., 40
Burgess, Ernest W., 399–401
Burma (Myanmar), 100, 132
Burmese, 164
Butt, Paul L., 264

Cacao, 89
Cadastral pattern, 110–116
Cahokia, 336
Cairo, 332
Cajuns (Acadiens), 52, 172, 232.
  See also Acadiana; French, in
  Louisiana
Calcutta, 209, 332, 365
California
  agriculture in, 90, 91, 98
  alteration of environment in,
    103–104, 454–457
  cities in, 332, 366, 389, 392
  developers in, 389
  diffusion from, 271
  ethnic groups in, 386
  and migration, 53, 55, 248
  natural hazards in, 276
  politics in, 123, 124
  sports in, 267
Camels, 87, 88, 179, 212
Canada
  agriculture in, 91, 94, 147, 148
  architecture in, 251, 254, 255, 257
  birth rate in, 41
  borders of, 147, 148
  culture regions in, 9, 10
  divorce in, 38
  ethnic groups in, 57, 58, 179–
    180, 295–301, 304–306, 308,
    310, 312, 322
  folk culture in, 232, 233, 236, 237
  French in, 57, 58, 129, 149,
    179–180, 222–223, 232, 233,
    236, 251, 255, 257, 258, 297,
    300, 301, 304–305
  industry in, 424, 438
  land survey pattern in, 111, 113,
    149, 180
  languages in, 179–180
  newspapers in, 276
  political geography of, 128, 129,
    144, 180
  pollution in, 435, 436
  population of, 49, 57, 58, 146
  religious groups in, 192–193,
    222–223
  sex ratios in, 50
  sports in, 274
  toponyms in, 222–223, 272
Cape Town, 136
Capital city, 128–129, 135
Caracas, 363
Cargo cults, 209
Carney, George O., 248, 268
Caste system, 24, 195
Catalonia, 136, 145
Cattle
  in Africa, 60, 61, 72, 87, 88
  in Asia, 84

dairy, 92–93
  domestication of, 99
  fattening of, 90–91
  herding of, 85, 87, 88, 212
  ranching, 94
  sacred status of, 205
Caucasian race, 41, 54
Caucasus Mountains, 172, 173
CBD (central business district), 25,
  399, 402, 403
Celtic, 161, 171, 178, 245, 247, 311
Cemeteries, 219–221
Census tracts, 377–378
Central business district. *See* CBD
Central place theory, 370–372
Centrifugal forces, 130
Centripetal forces, 130
Centuriation, 111
Chain migration. *See* Migration,
  chain
Chakravarti, A. K., 68, 459–462
Checkerboard development, 387
Chesapeake Bay, 435
Cheyenne, 274
Chicago, 300, 304, 370, 381, 401
Chicano. *See* Mexican-Americans
Chile, 126, 128, 146
China. *See also* Taiwan
  agriculture in, 5, 83, 86, 97
  alteration of environment in, 102
  architecture in, 249, 251
  birth control in, 48–49
  cities in, 20, 332, 348
  Great Wall of, 150, 152
  languages in, 163–164
  political geography of, 129, 135,
    146
  pollution in, 436
  population of, 38, 39
  religion in, 196–197, 201,
    202–203, 205, 206, 207, 220,
    222
  as urban hearth, 337, 341
Chinese people, 65, 163, 176, 220,
  222, 300, 302, 304, 315, 317,
  354
Chongqing, 20
Christaller, Walter, 370
Christianity
  in China, 202–203
  Coptic, 191
  in Cyprus, 145
  diffusion of, 199–201
  distribution of, 191–194, 209
  Eastern, 191
  and economy, 209–210, 215
  environmental ethic of, 206–
    207, 208
  Maronite, 191
  Mormon. *See* Mormons

Nestorian, 191
  Orthodox, 191, 216–217, 222
  Protestant, 191, 192, 193, 194,
    207, 208, 219, 222
  Roman Catholic, 57, 145, 178,
    191, 192, 193, 194, 210, 212,
    213, 214, 215, 219, 222–223
  Uniate, 299
  Western, 191–193
Cincinnati, 398
Cities. *See also* Geography, urban
  agglomeration within, 353, 381
  capital, 128–129
  centralization of, 381–385
  as central places, 370–372
  checkerboard development in,
    387
  colonial, 358, 360–362
  cultural landscape of, 341–343,
    405–415
  culture regions within, 377–380
  in Dark Ages, 346
  decentralization of, 383–390
  as defensive sites, 357–368
  development of, 341–366
  diffusion of, 333–341
  diffusion within, 380–390
  ecology of, 366–370, 390–398
  ethnic groups in, 299–304,
    314–316, 323–324, 386
  Greek, 343–344
  growth control in, 389
  hydrology of, 394–396
  industrial, 352–355
  largest, 331–332
  Latin American, 24–25, 332,
    404–405
  medieval, 346–349
  Mesoamerican, 339
  Mesopotamian, 333, 336–340
  migration and, 363–364
  models relating to, 24–25,
    358–366, 370–372, 399–405
  morphology of, 20, 342, 349, 351
  neighborhoods in, 299–304,
    378–380
  nonwestern, evolution of,
    357–366
  origin of, 333–336
  perception of, 409–413
  planning of, 339, 344, 350, 386,
    389
  pollution in, 393–394
  preindustrial, 359
  primate, 128, 332
  Renaissance and baroque,
    349–352
  renewal of, 380, 386–387
  Roman, 344–346
  siting of, 345, 366–370

Cities (*Continued*)
  social areas in, 377–378
  suburbanization of, 383–390
  trade route sites of, 368–370
  transport within, 382, 385, 402
  vegetation in, 396–398
  weather and climate in, 393–394
Citrus, 74, 90, 98, 101
Clay, Grady, 405
Cleveland, 300, 302
Climate, 59, 101–102, 171, 172,
    174, 335, 393–394, 438–439,
    462–465, 469
Coal, 60–61, 424, 426, 430, 431,
    437, 438
Cocaine, 274–275
Coconuts, 89
Coercion and warfare model, 335
Coffee, 89, 106, 107
Colombia, 275
Colonialism, 137, 174–175,
    360–362
Colorado, 52, 99–100
Columbus, Ohio, 356
Common Market, 6, 133, 443
Communism, 72, 101, 114, 116,
    124, 132, 137, 142–144, 148,
    152, 153, 197–198
Commuting, 385
Compton, P. A., 57
Confucianism, 191, 196, 220
Connecticut, 52
Contagious diffusion. *See*
    Diffusion, contagious
Convergence hypothesis, 265, 279,
    280
Coptic Christianity, 191
Core area, political, 131, 134–136,
    140, 141
Core/periphery, 11, 12, 107–109,
    129, 134–135, 421–423, 427
Corn (Indian corn, maize), 74, 82,
    90, 91, 97, 99, 100, 336
Corn Belt, 90, 466
Cornish, Vaughan, 140
Corsica, 130
Costa Rica, 95
Cotton, 85, 89, 429, 430, 433, 439
Council for Mutual Economic
    Assistance (COMECON), 133
Counterurbanization, 386
Cuba, 141, 300
Cultural adaptation. *See*
    Adaptation, cultural
Cultural diffusion. *See* Diffusion,
    cultural
Cultural ecology. *See* Ecology,
    cultural
Cultural integration. *See*
    Integration, cultural

Cultural landscape. *See* Landscape,
    cultural
Cultural rebound, 309–310
Culture, 472
  in applied geography, 453
  area, 9
  definition of, 4
  folk. *See* Folk culture
  popular. *See* Popular culture
Culture region, 6–13
  agricultural, 81–94
  in ethnic geography, 295–306,
    311, 316
  in folk geography, 229–234,
    465–469
  formal, 6–11, 12, 81–94,
    122–124, 190
  functional, 11–12, 125–134, 190
  in industry, 421–428
  in linguistic geography, 158–166
  migration, 52–53
  in political geography, 122–134
  in popular culture, 263–270
  in population geography, 38–53
  in religious geography, 190–198
  in urban geography, 330–333,
    377–380
  vernacular, 13, 268–270
Cushites, 163
Cybriwsky, Roman, 151
Cyprus, 145, 216–217
Czechoslovakia, 67, 116
Czechs, 294, 296, 298, 300, 305,
    312–313, 316

Dacca, 433
Dairying, 92–93, 94, 105, 108, 109
Dallas, 280
Danube, 183
Davies, C. S., 448
Dayton, Ohio, 397–398
Death rate, 37, 42
Deccan Plateau, 174
Deforestation. *See* Forest removal
Deindustrialization, 426
Delaware, 52, 230
Demographic regions, 38–53
Demographic transformation, 45
Demography, 36
Denmark, 73, 144, 149
Desertification, 103, 462–465
Determinism
  cultural, 26–27
  economic, 25
  environmental, 18, 19, 140, 205,
    240
Detroit, 272, 420
Dialects, 158, 159, 164–166, 176,
    182, 280

Diet, 106, 107, 209–212, 229, 230,
    241–242, 245–247, 263–265
Diffusion, cultural
  in agriculture, 95–101, 459–462
  of cities, 333–341
  contagious, 14, 15, 57–58, 101,
    137, 139, 168, 199, 201, 271
  defined, 14–17
  in ethnic geography, 306–312
  expansion, 14, 15, 99, 134–137,
    167, 168, 199, 201, 234, 236,
    271, 380
  in folk geography, 234–239
  hierarchical, 14, 15, 52, 58, 167,
    199, 201, 270
  in industrial geography, 428–434
  in linguistic geography, 166–170
  in political geography, 134–139
  in popular culture, 270–276
  in population geography, 53–58
  in religious geography, 198–203
  relocation, 14, 15, 53, 58, 98,
    134–137, 166, 167, 168–169,
    199, 234, 235, 238, 272, 306,
    380
  stimulus, 15, 97
  in urban geography, 380–390
Diseases, 37, 50, 52, 57–58,
    60–61, 276–277
Distance decay, 15, 201–202, 270
Diversifying selection, 21, 101,
    102, 106
Divorce, 37, 38
Dixie, 13, 269
Domestication, 95, 99, 205,
    333–334
Dominican Republic, 67
Double-cropping, 84
Doughty, Robin W., 207
Dravidian languages, 160–161,
    164, 174, 195
Drought, 462–465, 469
Drucker, Johanna, 180
Drugs, 132, 274–275
Duncan, James, 408
Duncan, Nancy, 408
Dust Bowl, 103, 464
Dust dome, 394–395
Dutch, 28, 68, 296, 298, 304, 305,
    315–316

Earthquakes, 276, 392, 454
Easter Island, 164, 168, 169
East Indies, 239. *See also* Indonesia
Ecology, cultural
  in agricultural geography,
    101–104
  in applied geography, 453
  defined, 17–23
  of ethnic groups, 310–312

of folk culture, 240–245, 249
in industrial geography, 434–439
in linguistic geography, 170–174
in political geography, 139–144
of popular culture, 276–279
in population geography, 59–64
in religious geography, 203–208
in urban geography, 366–370, 390–398
Economy, 80–120, 418–451
and demography, 67–68
and language, 179
and political geography, 147–148
and religion, 209–215
Ecosystem, 17, 390, 455
Ecuador, 42, 159
Edmonton, 299
Egypt, 135, 140, 146, 191, 220, 334
Electricity, 438
El Paso, 283
Emerging city model, 362–366
Enclave, 126
Energy, 438, 465–469
England, 51, 140, 150, 151, 185, 352, 353, 355, 395, 429–431. See also United Kingdom
English language, 158, 162, 164–166, 170, 171, 172, 175, 178, 179, 180, 182
English people, 230, 233, 247, 304, 305, 311
Environment
influence on humankind, 18–19, 21, 59–60, 101–102, 139–144, 170–174, 203–206, 240–243, 310–312, 366, 390, 436–439
as modified by people, 22–23, 102–104, 139, 206–207, 278–279, 390–398, 434–436, 445–448, 455, 462, 469, 472
Environmental determinism. See Determinism, environmental
Environmental perception. See Perception, environmental
Environmental stress model, 335
Eritrea, 470
Eskimos, 7, 9, 15, 59, 94, 160, 164, 172, 304
Estonia, 146
Ethiopia, 72, 106, 108, 137, 163, 178, 191, 331, 469–471
Ethnic groups
in cities, 299–304, 354, 356, 378, 386
definition of, 294
geography, 293–327
ghetto, 301–302
island, 297–299, 311, 315, 316

neighborhood, 299–304, 378, 380
in politics, 130, 144–146
province, 296–297
religions, 190, 195, 200, 212
Euphrates River, 97, 211, 336. See also Fertile Crescent; Mesopotamia
Eurasia, 38, 87, 142–144, 199
Europe
agriculture in, 85, 90, 92
cities in, 332, 343–355
culture regions in, 8, 11
forest clearance in, 63, 102–103, 185
industry in, 421, 424–426, 429–434
language in, 160–161, 162, 176
migration in, 439
political geography of, 142–144, 177, 217
population of, 40
religion in, 192, 195, 197, 198, 200, 209, 210, 215, 217
transportation in, 201, 215, 431–433
Evans, E. Estyn, 253
Ewald, Ursula, 108–109
Exclave, 126–127
Expansion diffusion. See Diffusion, expansion

Farm abandonment, 464–465
Farmsteads, 251–258
Feedlots, 90, 93
Fences, 114–116, 232
Feng-shui. See Geomancy
Fertile Crescent, 97, 99, 162, 174, 199. See also Mesopotamia
Field patterns, 110–116, 149, 153
Filipino-Americans, 300
Finland, 168
Finnish, 163, 168
Finnish-Americans, 305, 311, 319–321
Fishing, 212, 421–423, 445
Flax, 85
Floating activities, 359
Florida, 51, 53, 61, 192, 283, 316
Folk culture, 227–260
cultural integration in, 245–248
definition of, 227–228
diffusion in, 234–239
ecology of, 240–245, 465–469
landscape of, 249–258
medicines of, 242–243
regions of, 229–234
Folk fortress, 140
Folklife, 229
Folklore, 229, 233–234, 235, 236

Foods, 5, 9, 64–65, 83–94, 106, 210–212, 230, 232, 241–242, 263–265, 293, 294. See also Alcoholic beverages
Ford, Larry, 25, 356
Forest removal, 63, 102–103, 109, 185, 241, 457
Forum, 345
Francaviglia, Richard V., 276, 446
France
agriculture in, 72, 105
cities in, 128, 135, 214, 332, 344, 351
cultural landscape of, 72, 111, 284
migration to, 50
political geography of, 121, 126, 130, 141, 147, 150
population of, 57, 58, 295
religion in, 214, 215
transport in, 426
Frankfurt, 369
French
in Canada. See Canada, French in
Community, 133
language, 162, 167–168, 172, 174, 179–180
in Louisiana, 10, 111, 114, 172, 221, 232, 296, 297, 298. See also Acadiana
in Maine, 308
in the United States, 10, 298, 304, 305, 308
Friends and neighbors effect, 139

Gabon, 420
Gade, Daniel W., 26, 284
Gambia, The, 127, 128
Ganges River, 204, 214, 220
Plain, 40, 70, 174, 199, 201
Gans, Herbert, 380
Gardening, market, 82–83, 87, 90, 108, 109
Gentrification, 356
Geography
agricultural, 5–6, 80–120
applied, 452
cultural, defined, 4–5
definition of, 1–4
economic, 80–120, 418–451
and education, 472–473
ethnic, 293–327
folk, 227–260
history of, 1–5
humanistic, 26
industrial, 418–451
linguistic, 157–188
political, 121–156
of popular culture, 261–292
population, 36–79
regional, 3, 6–13

Geography (*Continued*)
  of religion, 189–226
  social, 37
  topical, 3
  transportation, 426, 431–433,
    437, 441, 444, 448–449
  urban, 328–417
Geomancy, 22, 203–204, 220, 222
Geophagy, 241–242
Geopolitics, 122, 142
Georgia, 172, 218, 244, 249, 265
Georgian Republic, 173
Gerlach, Russel L., 312, 318, 321
German Democratic Republic. *See*
  Germany, East
Germanic languages, 7, 8, 60,
  160–161, 174, 185
Germans, 67
  as geographers, 2–5, 28
  in Canada, 296, 304, 305
  language of, 174, 179
  migrations of, 175
  Russian-, 311–312, 321
  in the United States, 176, 228,
    230, 231, 264, 294, 296, 298,
    299, 304–305, 306, 307, 310,
    312, 317–318, 321, 323, 356
Germany
  agriculture in, 6, 98, 153,
    209–210
  architecture in, 252
  cities in, 349, 351, 356
  cultural borders in, 11
  East, 58, 71, 153, 183, 184
  forest clearance in, 63, 103, 109,
    185
  industry in 421, 423, 426, 432
  inheritance systems in, 65, 67
  political geography of, 126, 135,
    144, 149, 153
  pollution in, 434–435
  population of, 44, 49, 58, 63, 67
  religion in, 219
  settlement forms in, 71, 149, 153
  toponyms in, 183–185
  transport in, 151
  West, 40, 49, 50, 126, 135, 149,
    153, 423, 434–435
Ghettoes, 301–302, 304, 403
Global corporations, 423–424,
  425–426, 439–440
Goats, 85, 87, 99, 102, 212
Gottmann, Jean, 122, 356
Gould, Peter, 2, 134
Graffiti, 151
Grains, 83–87, 91–92, 97, 102.
  See also Barley; Corn; Millet;
  Rice; Wheat
Grapes. *See* Viticulture
Great Britain, 51, 55. *See also*
  England; United Kingdom

Great Plains, 5, 22, 91, 99, 103,
  104, 205, 251, 312, 462–465
Greece, 4, 5, 23, 87, 102, 133, 134,
  144, 151, 343–344, 439
Greeks, 2, 9, 161, 176, 191, 304,
  343–344
Greenhouse effect, 436
Green revolution, 84, 100, 102,
  459–462
Griffin, Ernst, 25, 109
Gritzner, Charles F., 239, 240
Growth control, 389
Guerrilla warfare, 132
Guinea-Bissau, 53
Guyana, 145

Hägerstrand, Torsten, 14–17, 24
Hahn, Eduard, 95
Haiti, 67, 256
Hamitic, 160–161, 162–163, 172
Hamito-Semitic languages, 160–
  161, 162–163, 170, 469
Hamlet, 69, 73, 310
Hance, William, 362
Hangchow, 348
Harries, Keith D., 314–315
Harris, Chauncey, 403
Hawaii, 141, 164, 168, 169
Haymaking, 92, 237–239
Hazards, natural, 203, 276
Hearth areas
  agricultural, 96–99
  industrial, 429–432
  linguistic, 167, 168
  political, 134–136
  religious, 198–201
  urban, 336–341
Heartland theory, 142–144
Heat island, 393
Hebrew, 162, 163, 178, 205. *See
  also* Judaism
Hecht, Melvin E., 283
Hecock, Richard D., 285
Hemp, 85, 89
Heyerdahl, Thor, 340
Hierarchical diffusion. *See*
  Diffusion, hierarchical
Himalayas, 174
Hindi, 162
Hinduism, 24, 68, 191, 195–196,
  199, 201, 204, 205, 207, 209,
  212, 213, 214, 215, 216, 218,
  219, 220
Hinterland, 371
Homosexuality, 280, 281
Hong Kong, 358, 433, 440
Horvath, Ronald J., 108
Host culture, 294
House types, 249–258. *See also*
  Architecture
Houston, 281, 282

Hoyt, Homer, 402
Hsu, Shin-Yi, 206
Humboldt, Alexander von, 3, 4
Hungarian, 163, 174
Hunting and gathering, 94, 240
Hurricanes, 249, 276
Hybrids, 84, 99–100, 101, 459
Hydraulic civilization model, 334

Iceland, 4, 141, 142
Icelanders, 311
Ideology, 136–138, 146–147,
  152–153, 324
Idiographic science, 26
Illinois, 100, 192, 208, 267, 272,
  298, 466
Immigrant's ladder, 304
Inca. *See* Amerindians, Inca
Independent invention, 14, 97,
  237–239
India
  agriculture in, 83, 100, 459–462
  alteration of environment in, 102
  birth control in, 47, 48, 56
  cities in, 204, 209, 214, 220, 332,
    365
  diet in, 68
  emigration from, 300
  field pattern in, 110
  industry in, 423, 433
  irrigation in, 459
  languages in, 161, 164, 174
  migration in, 66
  political geography of, 142, 144,
    146, 216
  popular culture in, 274
  population of, 38, 39, 45, 49
  religions in, 24, 194, 195, 196,
    201, 204, 207, 214, 215, 216,
    220
  villages in, 70
Indian Ocean, 142
Indiana, 267, 272, 299
Indians, American. *See* Amerindians
Indic languages, 160–161
Indigenous city model, 358–359
Indochina, 97. *See also* Vietnam
Indo-European languages, 160–
  162, 166–167, 170, 173, 174,
  195, 209
Indonesia, 39, 68, 81, 128, 164,
  195, 196, 201, 214, 215, 332.
  See also Borneo; East Indies;
  Java
Indus River Valley, 174, 201, 336,
  340
Industrial revolution, 418–419,
  428–434
Industry
  chapter on, 418–451
  and cities, 352–355, 383, 393

cottage, 429
diffusion of, 428–434
guild, 429
locational factors of, 436–444
primary, 419–423, 430
quaternary, 419–420, 426–427
quinary, 419–420, 424, 428
secondary, 419–426, 429–430
tertiary, 419–420, 426, 430
Infanticide, 46
Innovation model, 334
Insurgent state, 131–133
Integration, cultural, 23–27
    in agricultural geography, 104–109
    in ethnic geography, 312–319
    in folk geography, 245–248
    in industrial geography, 439–445
    in linguistic geography, 174–180
    in political geography, 144–148
    in popular culture, 279–282
    in population geography, 64–68
    in religious geography, 208–217
    in urban geography, 370–373, 399–405
Intertillage, 82
Iowa, 100, 221, 271, 319
Iran, 99, 161, 172, 194
Iranic languages, 160–161
Iraq, 97, 99, 162, 194, 333, 336
Ireland, 55, 56, 65, 253
    Northern, 131, 144, 216, 217, 245
    Republic of, 216
Irish
    in Canada, 304, 310
    Scotch-, 233, 245, 247, 318
    in the United States, 295, 296, 298, 299, 304, 305, 310, 315
Iron Curtain, 153
Irrigation, 83, 85, 99, 100, 104, 135, 334, 459, 462
Ise, 214
Islam
    and Arabic, 179
    and cities, 300
    and diet, 210–212
    diffusion of, 198–201
    distribution of, 191, 194–195
    ecology of, 204, 205
    holy places of, 190, 204, 205, 214–215
    imprint on landscape, 217–218, 220, 221
    and nationalism, 145, 216
    pilgrimages, 214–215
    Shiah, 191, 194–195
    Sunni, 191, 195
    in the U.S.S.R., 124
Isogloss, 158–159, 166
Israel, 144, 163, 181, 195, 198, 216
Istanbul, 128, 191

Italians
    in Canada, 301, 304, 309, 310
    language of, 174, 176, 293
    in the United States, 264, 293, 299, 300, 301, 302, 304, 305, 315, 316, 317, 380
Italy, 57, 58, 60, 142, 146, 147, 431, 439

Jacob, Mary, 469
Jakle, John A., 286, 287
Japan
    agriculture in, 83, 84, 85
    birth rate in, 40
    cities in, 332
    cultural landscape of, 110, 111, 181
    industry in, 421, 425, 432, 440, 443
    political geography of, 144
    population of, 39
    religions in, 196, 201, 204, 214
Japanese, 163, 181
Jarmo, 333
Java, 68, 106
Jefferson, Mark, 19
Jersey City, 409, 410
Jerusalem, 190, 199
Jett, Stephen C., 238–239
Jews. See Judaism
Johannesburg, 302
Johannessen, Carl L., 95
Jones, Richard C., 306, 309
Jordan River, 199, 204
Judaism, 67, 131, 163, 178, 190, 191, 195, 198–200, 205, 211, 216, 299–302, 304, 315, 316
Judeo-Christian tradition, 23, 206–208
Jute, 84, 89

Kain, John F., 302
Kalahari Desert, 164
Kansas, 272, 298
Kant, Immanuel, 3, 30
Kaups, Matti, 319–321
Kay, Jeanne, 278
Kebbede, Girma, 469
Kentucky, 23, 244, 247, 248, 267, 285–286
Kenya, 61, 88, 106
Khoisan languages, 160–161, 164, 172
Kluckhohn, Florence, 208
Knapp, Gregory, 159
Kniffen, Fred B., 236, 238, 262
Knight, David B., 130
Kollmorgen, Walter M., 295, 318
Korea, 140, 175, 201, 300, 423, 433
Korean language, 163
Kurath, Hans, 164, 165

Kurdistan, 191
Kuwait, 194

Labor, 439–440
Lai, Chuen-yan David, 220, 222
Laissez-faire utilitarianism, 353
Landscape, cultural, 27–30
    agricultural, 68–76, 110–116
    amenity, 285
    change of, 452–457
    elitist, 284–285
    of ethnic groups, 319–324
    of folk culture, 249–258
    industrial, 445–449
    of language, 180–185
    political, 149–153
    of popular culture, 282–290
    religious, 217–223
    of rural settlements, 68–76, 110–116, 249–258
    urban, 341–366, 405–415
Language, 157–188
    and demography, 57
    and economy, 179
    and environment, 170–174, 240
    families of, 160–164, 166–170
    origins of, 170
    pidgin, 165, 179
    and politics, 144–146, 174–176, 180
    and religion, 178–179
Lapps, 59, 310
Latin, 167, 178, 183, 201
Latin America, 56, 85, 137, 332, 360, 404, 427
Latvia, 146, 170, 176
Laws of the Indies, 360
Lebanon, 121, 144, 145, 191, 194, 217
Legal systems, 64, 65, 67–68, 122, 124, 149
Leipzig, 183
Lemon, James T., 318
Leningrad, 129
Lesotho, 126
Lewis, Thomas R., 255
Ley, David, 151
Liberia, 137
Lima, 363
Lingua franca, 179
Liquor. See Alcoholic beverages
Lithuania, 146
Liverpool, 354
Llamas, 85, 99
Lodrick, Deryck O., 207
Log construction, 30–32, 230, 231, 232, 240, 249, 251, 255, 256, 257, 310, 319, 320
London, 275, 332, 353, 369, 393
Long-lots, 111–114, 149

Los Angeles, 275, 301, 303, 314–315, 332, 394, 410–413, 448, 449
Louisiana, 52, 91, 111, 114, 172, 192, 193, 221, 232, 236, 256, 265, 296, 297. *See also* French, in Louisiana
Louisville, 370
Lourdes, 214
Lowenthal, David, 288–290
Lower South. *See* South, subcultures in
Lutheranism, 192, 193, 194, 212, 213
Lynch, Kevin, 409

Macao, 36
Mackinder, Halford J., 142–144
Madagascar, 164, 168, 174, 238. *See also* Malagasy Republic
Madrid, 136
Maine, 272, 308, 407
Maize. *See* Corn
Malagasy Republic, 141
Malawi, 50
Malaya, 168
Malayo-Polynesian languages, 160–161, 164, 168–169, 174, 186, 238, 239, 249. *See also* Maori
Malaysia, 214, 215, 457–459
Malthus, Thomas R., 43–45
Manchester, 354–355
Manifest destiny, 142
Manila, 363
Manioc, 82, 971
Manitoba, 301, 318, 322
Manufacturing, 419, 421–426, 429–430
Maori, 184, 206, 310
March (Marchland), 128
Market gardening. *See* Gardening, market
Markets, 107–108, 370–372, 440–441
Maronites, 191
Marsh, George Perkins, 22
Marxism. *See* Communism
Maryland, 52, 230
Masai, 88
Massachusetts, 135, 236, 237
Mather, Cotton, 319–321
Mattson, Richard L., 286, 287
Matwijiw, Peter, 301
Mayas. *See* Amerindians, Maya
Meade, Melinda, 457–459
Mecca, 199, 204, 205, 214, 215
Media, mass, 270, 274, 275–276, 279–280
Medina, 199, 214

Medicine, folk, 242–243
Mediterranean
  agriculture, 82–83, 85, 87, 251
  alteration of environment in, 102
  political geography of, 142
Megalopolis, 356–357
Meinig, Donald W., 408
Meitzen, August, 28, 110
Melanesia, 209
Memphis, 276
Mennonites, 221, 228, 318, 322. *See also* Amish
Mental maps, 2, 61, 62, 134, 409–413
Mesoamerica, 339
Mesopotamia, 2, 336–340. *See also* Euphrates River; Fertile Crescent; Tigris River
Metes and bounds, 112–113, 115
Methodism, 192, 193, 194, 212, 213, 245
Mexican-Americans, 123, 176, 208, 213, 234, 297, 300, 301, 303, 304, 305, 306–307, 309, 314–315, 316, 317, 323, 324
Mexico
  agriculture in, 81, 109
  Amerindians in, 54–55, 74–76
  emigration from, 306–307, 309
  folk architecture in, 251
  folk medicine in, 242
  industry in, 423, 425
  languages in, 172
  migration in, 54–55
  pilgrimages in, 213
  political geography of, 128, 153
  population of, 49
  religion in, 203, 213
  sports in, 274
  urbanization in, 332
Mexico City, 128, 332, 367
Michigan, 272, 315, 316, 319–321
Middle East, 85
Midwest, 102, 182, 192, 193, 208, 230, 231–232, 236, 269, 270, 296
Migration, 52–56, 61–62, 65, 66, 167–170, 173–174, 243–244, 304, 306–309, 311–312
  chain, 306, 307
  region, 52–53
  urban, 363–364
Milbauer, John A., 268
Miller, E. Joan Wilson, 235
Millet, 85
Mining, 419, 421, 422–423, 424, 430, 446, 447
Minneapolis, 370, 381
Minnesota, 193, 285, 298, 319–321
Mississippi, 50, 242, 265, 282

Mississippi River, 274, 276, 336
Missouri, 235, 248, 267, 296, 298, 312, 318, 321
Missouri River, 274
Models
  agricultural land-use, 24, 106–109
  central place, 370–372
  coercion and warfare, 335
  concentric zone, 24, 106–109, 399–401
  defined, 24–25
  of diffusion, 14, 17
  emerging city, 362–366
  environmental stress, 335
  hydraulic civilization, 334
  indigenous city, 358–359
  innovation, 334
  linguistic, 170, 177
  multiple nuclei, 403–404
  preindustrial urban, 359
  sector, 401–403
  urban, 24–25, 358–365, 399–405
Mongolia, 128, 196, 201, 205
Mongols, 88, 173, 205
Monotheism, 9, 190, 194, 195, 198, 200, 205–206
Montana, 237, 238
Montréal, 53, 367, 381
Moors. *See* Arabs
Mormons, 10, 192, 193, 202, 216, 288
  dietary restrictions of, 24, 202, 212
  environmental perception of, 208
  farm villages of, 70, 221
  material culture of, 239, 288
Morocco, 7, 60, 134, 163, 210
Morphology, urban, 342, 349, 358, 404
Morrill, Richard, 122
Moscow, 129, 135, 136, 218, 370, 442
Multiplier effect, 370
Multiplier leakage, 427
Mumford, Lewis, 353
Munich, 349, 381
Music
  folk, 231, 233–235, 247–248
  popular, 274, 275, 276
Muslims. *See* Islam
Myanmar. *See* Burma

Nationalism, 125–126, 130, 144–146, 147, 175–176
Nation-state, 144
NATO. *See* North Atlantic Treaty Organization

Navaho. *See* Amerindians, Navaho
Nazism, 195, 198, 295
Nebraska, 91, 272, 273, 294
Neighborhood effect, 16
Neighborhoods, 299–304, 378–380
Nepal, 128
Nestorians, 191
Netherlands, 40, 140, 197, 426
Nevada, 267
New Brunswick, 182
New Delhi, 332, 360–361
New England
　agriculture in, 100
　architecture of, 254–256, 258, 408
　folk culture in, 230, 234, 236
　industry in, 428, 442, 445
　religious groups in, 221, 222
　subculture, 9–10, 182–183
　suburbs in, 385
　villages in, 221, 222
Newfoundland, 52, 309, 310
New Guinea, 197. *See also* Papuan
New Hebrides, 209
New Jersey, 230
New Mexico, 111, 170, 204, 240, 323
New Orleans, 266, 367
New York (state), 182, 231, 232, 271, 272, 435
New York City
　architecture in, 28–30
　death rate in, 354
　ethnic groups in, 195, 300, 354
　morphology of, 149, 150, 401, 410
　music in, 275
　pollution in, 63
　population of, 45
　quality of life in, 384
　site of, 367
　size of, 332
　sports in, 274
　zoning in, 354, 382
New Zealand
　agriculture in, 92, 93, 94, 98
　architecture in, 252
　ethnic minority in, 184, 206
　immigration to, 55, 98, 168, 169, 174
　languages in, 164, 168, 169
　migration in, 61
　political geography of, 136
　survey pattern in, 110
Niger-Congo languages, 160–161, 163
Nigeria, 38, 39
Nile River Valley, 40, 60, 135, 140, 146, 211, 336

Nilo-Saharan languages, 160–161, 164
Node, of culture areas, 11–12, 134–136
Nolan, Mary Lee, 213
Nomadic herding, 82–83, 87–89
Nomads, 87–89, 205–206, 211–212, 251
Nomothetic science, 25–26
North America, 435. *See also* Canada; Mexico; United States
North Atlantic Treaty Organization (NATO), 133, 134
North Carolina, 248, 428
North Dakota, 71, 193
Northern Ireland. *See* Ireland, Northern
Norway, 128, 176, 216
Norwegians, 298, 312
Norwine, Jim, 19
Nova Scotia, 172, 232

Ohio, 115, 256, 267, 269, 272, 282, 356
Oil, 420, 438
Oklahoma, 248, 267, 268, 274, 282, 288, 289
Oklahoma City, 288, 289
Olives, 85, 87
Omaha, 273
Oman, 172
Ontario, 149, 176, 182, 232, 255, 257, 269, 272, 310, 426
Oregon, 62, 254
Organization of Petroleum Exporting Countries (OPEC), 438
Overpopulation, 40–49
Ozarks, 231, 235, 312, 313, 318, 321, 323

Pacific Ocean, 168, 169, 212, 238, 239
Paddy, 83–84, 86, 101, 110
Pakistan, 39, 104, 127, 194, 216, 271
Palestine, 67, 144
Paleosiberian languages, 160–161, 164
Palimpsest, 406–407
Papuan, 160–161, 164
Paris, 128, 135, 141, 214, 346, 350, 351, 367
Parsees, 219–220
Parties, political, 123–124
Pennsylvania, 61–62, 100, 202, 230, 231, 232, 267, 269, 282, 296, 317, 318, 426, 434, 465–469
Peppers, 74

Perception, environmental, 21–22, 208, 243–244, 311–312
　and agriculture, 22, 104
　in cities, 409–413
　and migration, 22, 55, 61–62
　and population distribution, 60–62
Personal space, 66
Peru, 97, 141, 275
Peters, Gary, 445
Petroleum. *See* Oil
Phenomenology, 26
Philadelphia, 151
Philippines, 27, 141, 162, 175, 194, 201, 217, 300
Phoenicians, 2, 162
Pidgin, 165, 179
Pierce, Robert M., 123, 124
Pilgrimage, 212–215
Pitcairn Island, 212
Pittsburgh, 369
Place, sense of, 26, 409
Placelessness, 262, 263
Place names. *See* Toponyms
Planning, city, 149, 150, 339, 343, 344, 349, 350, 380, 386, 389
Plantations, 82–83, 89–90, 101, 165
Poland, 60, 67, 126, 131, 140, 195, 274
Poles, 296, 298, 299, 300, 301, 302, 304–305, 309, 323
Political geography, 121–156, 175–176, 215–217, 441–443
Pollution, environmental, 63, 278–279, 393, 398, 434–436, 447
Polynesia, 168–169, 174, 184. *See also* Malayo-Polynesian languages
Polytheism, 195, 206
Popular culture, 228–229, 261–292
Population
　chapter on, 36–79
　density, 36, 38–40, 59–64, 106
　distribution of, 36–40, 59–64, 146
　ecology, 59–64
　explosion, 42–49, 56–57
　geography of, 36–79
　pyramid, 49–50
　urban, 332, 386
　world, 36, 38–40
Pork. *See* Swine
Portugal, 50, 141, 146, 147, 167, 174, 175, 445
Portuguese, 174, 175
Positivism, logical, 26
Possibilism, 18–19, 21, 59, 205, 241
Postindustrial society, 426

Potato, 65, 85, 90, 96, 97, 98
Preadaptation, 59, 311
Preindustrial urban model, 359
Price, Edward T., 242
Primate city, 128, 332
Protestantism. *See* Christianity, Protestant
Pueblo Indians. *See* Amerindians, Pueblo
Puerto Ricans, 300, 304
Punjab, 199, 201
Push-and-pull factors, 54, 244
Pygmies, 21
Pyle, Gerald F., 57–58
Pyrenees, 141

Quaternary industry. *See* Industry, quaternary
Québec, 57, 58, 111, 129, 149, 179–180, 222–223, 251, 257, 258, 308
Quechua, 19, 172
Quinary industry. *See* Industry, quinary

Railroads, 179, 419, 426, 431–433
Raitz, Karl, 285–286
Ranching, livestock, 82–83, 93–94, 108, 109
Range of goods, 370
Raw materials, 436–437
Rechlin, Alice, 298, 299
Region, 3. *See also* Culture, area; Culture region
Reindeer, 15, 87
Religion, 189–226
   cultural landscape of, 4, 217–223
   and demography, 57, 65
   defined, 189
   and economy, 104, 209–215
   ethnic, 190, 195, 200, 212
   and ethnicity, 294, 299, 322
   and language, 178–179
   and political geography, 144–145, 215–217
   quasi, 197–198
   and rise of cities, 333–334
   universalizing, 190, 191, 194, 195, 196, 200, 201, 212
Relocation diffusion. *See* Diffusion, relocation
Relph, Edward, 262
Rhine River, 67, 183, 209–210
Rice, 27, 65, 68, 82, 83–85, 91, 97, 101, 102
Rimland theory, 143–144
Rio de Janeiro, 129, 149, 151, 332, 367
Rio Grande, 242
Ritter, Carl, 3, 5

Rocky Mountains, 269, 274
Rodeos, 272–274
Roman Catholic Church. *See* Christianity, Roman Catholic
Romance languages, 57, 160–161, 167
Romania, 60, 171
Romans, 2, 11, 65, 67, 111, 150, 167, 183, 195, 201, 341, 344–346
Rome, 199, 214, 216, 345
Rooney, John F., 264, 265, 266, 282
Rowntree, Rowan, 455
Ruhr, 151, 356, 421, 424, 426, 449
Russia. *See* Union of Soviet Socialist Republics
Russian language, 162, 176, 179

Saarinen, Thomas, 104
Sack, Robert, 125, 285
Sacred space, 190
Sahara Desert, 59, 60, 63, 87, 89, 103, 163
Sahel, 103
St. Lawrence Valley, 322
St. Louis, 381
Salt Lake City, 216, 288
Salzburg, 347, 349, 368
San Diego, 324, 356
San Francisco, 20, 149, 163, 280, 288, 300, 301, 302, 366, 386, 428
San Jose, 389
São Paulo, 332
Satellite state, 128, 148
Saudi Arabia, 205, 214
Sauer, Carl O., 95–97, 238–239, 452
Saunas, 319–321
Scandinavians, 296, 298
Schlichtmann, Hansgeorg, 313
Selection, 21, 101, 102, 106
Scotch-Irish. *See* Irish, Scotch-
Scotland, 172, 431
Scots, 295, 304
Semitic languages, 160–161, 162–163, 174, 198, 200
Semple, Ellen Churchill, 19, 205, 207
Senegal, 127, 194, 444
Seoul, 332
Sequent occupance, 31
Services, industrial, 419, 420, 426–428
Settlement, rural, types of, 68–76, 110–116, 149, 151
Seventh-Day Adventism, 212
Sex ratio, 50–51
Shanghai, 332

Sheep, 85, 87, 94, 99, 102, 147, 148, 212
Shifting cultivation, 81–83, 101, 250
Shintoism, 191, 196, 204, 213
Shortridge, James R., 193–194, 270
Siberia, 15, 88, 94, 438
Sikhs, 146
Sims, John, 208
Singapore, 163, 420, 423, 433, 440
Sino-Tibetan languages, 160–161, 163–164
Sisal, 89
Sitwell, O. F. G., 28, 29
Sjoberg, Gideon, 359
Slavs, 160–161, 175, 183, 191, 298
Smole, William J., 208
Sorghum, 85
South, the
   agriculture in, 99, 100
   architecture in, 254–258
   dialects in, 164–166, 182
   ethnic groups in, 296, 297
   folk culture in, 230–233, 235–236, 241–248
   personal names in, 280
   politics in, 122, 123, 138
   religion in, 192, 193, 208, 219, 221, 222
   sports in, 265, 267
   subcultures in, 9, 10, 122, 123, 138, 164–166, 229–233, 245–248, 254–256
   toponyms in, 171, 182, 222
   as vernacular region, 13, 269
South Africa, Republic of, 90, 94, 98, 110, 126, 136–138, 302, 441
South America, 38, 59, 85, 108, 172, 175, 238, 251, 274, 275
South Carolina, 123, 172
South Dakota, 193
Soviet Union. *See* Union of Soviet Socialist Republics
Soybeans, 85, 90
Spain, 50, 124, 136, 141, 146, 167, 174, 175, 183, 185, 210, 295, 439
Spaniards, 74
Spanish, 158, 161, 162, 171, 174, 175, 297, 305
Sports, 232, 247, 263, 264–268, 272–274, 277, 282
Spykman, Nicholas, 143–144
Squatter settlements, 363
Sri Lanka (Ceylon), 89, 141, 162, 164, 196
Stabilizing selection, 21, 101, 106
Standard of living, 51–53
Steel, 419, 421, 424, 426, 430, 432, 437

Structuralism, 26
Stump, Roger W., 193
Suburbanization, 383–390
Sudan, 61, 106, 221
Sugar cane, 84, 89, 101
Suitcase farming, 91–92
Survey, land, 110–116
Swahili, 163, 179
Swaziland, 148, 156
Sweden, 53, 59, 73, 295
Swedes, 295
Swedish language, 168
Swine, 74, 84, 85, 90, 99, 147, 148, 210–212
Swiss, 296, 298
Switzerland, 19, 30, 60, 123, 129, 152, 234, 252
Syria, 99, 162

Tai language, 160–161, 164
Taiwan, 57, 86, 164, 249, 423, 433, 440
Taoism, 191, 196
Tariffs, 433, 443, 444
Tartars, 87, 88
Tauregs, 163
Tea, 84, 89, 106, 107
Teleology, 206–207
Tennessee, 242, 246, 247, 248
Teotihuacán, 339
Tepe Yahya, 340
Terracing, 27, 83
Terrain
    and cities, 20, 391–393
    influence of culture, 59–60, 101–102, 171–174, 243–244
    influence on industry, 438
    modified by industry, 446–447
    role in political geography, 139–142
Territorial imperative, 125
Tertiary industry, 370, 419, 426, 431–432
Texas
    agriculture in, 91, 104
    alcoholic beverages in, 212–213, 263
    architecture in, 257, 258, 323
    cadastral pattern in, 111
    economy of, 62
    ethnic groups in, 296, 298, 307, 309, 312–313, 317–318, 323
    folk medicine in, 242–243
    language in, 158
    migration to, 244, 248
    political geography of, 124, 136
    religion in, 212, 213
    sports in, 265, 267, 282
    toponyms in, 172, 185
Textiles, 421, 426, 429–430, 439

Thailand, 42, 97, 102
Theocracy, 147, 216
Thünen, Johann Heinrich von, 24, 106–109
Tibet, 146, 196, 201, 205
Tibetans, 164, 205
Tigray, 490
Tigris River, 97, 211. See also Fertile Crescent; Mesopotamia
Time-distance decay, 15, 100, 201–202, 270
Tobacco, 85, 89, 202
Todd, D., 318, 319
Tokyo, 45, 332, 367, 440
Toponyms, 180, 182–185, 222–223, 256, 271–272, 414
Tourism, 428
Transportation. See also Railroads
    as agent of diffusion, 271, 277, 308
    and cities, 349, 364, 370–372, 382, 385, 392, 400, 402
    influence on agriculture, 107–109
    influence on language, 179
    and political geography, 151
    and religion, 201, 214–215
    river and canal, 426
    road, 426, 427
    as tertiary activity, 419, 426, 448
Trans-Siberian railroad, 179
Truck farming. See Gardening, market
Tuan, Yi-fu, 207, 290, 382, 448
Tucson, 283, 301
Tundra, 87, 163
Turkey, 42, 99, 128, 134, 142, 145, 172, 194, 439
Turkeys, 76, 99
Turks, 9, 145, 173, 201

Uganda, 61, 71
Ukraine, 176
Ukrainians, 176, 296, 298, 299, 300, 301, 304–305
Ullman, Edward, 403–404
Union of Soviet Socialist Republics (U.S.S.R.). See also Estonia; Latvia; Lithuania; Siberia; Ukraine
    agriculture in, 87, 88, 91
    emigration from, 176, 195, 312, 322
    ethnic groups in, 124, 146, 172, 173, 176
    industry in, 421, 425, 426, 432, 438, 441, 442
    languages in, 170, 176
    political geography of, 123, 124, 128, 129, 135, 136, 140, 142–144, 146, 152

population of, 38, 39
religion in, 191, 197
transport in, 179, 426
United Kingdom. See also England; Ireland, Northern; Scotland; Wales
    cities in, 353–354
    language groups in, 178
    political geography of, 131, 133, 136, 137, 140, 142, 145, 150
    population of, 51, 55, 295
    religion in, 145, 217
    sports in, 266
United Nations, 134, 441
United States
    agriculture in, 22, 89–94, 99–102, 104, 147–148, 462–469
    architecture in, 251–257, 319–323
    birth rate in, 41
    blacks in. See Blacks, in the United States
    cultural landscape of, 111–115, 251–257, 319–324
    culture regions in, 9–10, 13, 122–123, 138, 165, 182–183, 229–233, 253–257, 297, 305
    destruction of environment in, 103–104
    dialects in, 164–166
    dietary preferences in, 106, 263–265
    divorce in, 38
    drugs in, 274, 275
    ethnic groups in, 165–166, 172, 176, 195, 293–324
    folk culture in, 229–249, 253–257
    forest clearance in, 102, 185
    immigration to, 62, 295–300, 303–304, 306–307
    industry in, 421, 422, 424, 425, 428, 432
    land survey in, 111–115
    migration within, 51–53, 55, 61, 243–244, 439
    newspapers in, 276
    political geography of, 122–123, 124, 128, 129, 130, 135, 136, 138, 139, 142, 144, 147, 148, 149, 150, 151, 152, 217
    pollution in, 434–435
    popular culture of, 262–290
    population of, 38, 39
    religion in, 192–194, 195, 196, 202, 204, 205, 208, 212, 213, 216, 217, 218, 219, 221–222
    sports in, 263–268, 272–274, 277, 282

United States (*Continued*)
  toponyms in, 172, 182–184,
    185, 222, 256, 271–272
  transport in, 426
  urbanization in, 330, 332, 352,
    386
Upland South. *See* South,
  subcultures in
Ur, 339
Uralic languages, 160–161, 163,
  170, 174
Ural Mountains, 442
Urban geography, 328–417
Urbanization, 330–333, 352–353,
  362
Urban renewal, 387
Uruguay, 108–109
Utah, 70, 192, 193, 202, 216, 239,
  263, 282, 288, 442

Vance, James, 360
Varanasi (Benares), 204, 214, 220
Vatican City, 178, 216
Vegetation, 102–103, 207, 396–
  398, 457
Venezuela, 208, 363, 420
Venice, 367, 431
Vermeer, Donald E., 242
Vidal de la Blache, Paul, 28, 30
Vienna, 346, 349

Vietnam, 73, 143, 151, 196, 295, 300
Villages, farm, 69–72, 74–76,
  221–222, 322, 333
Virginia, 52, 135, 172, 248, 357, 382
Viticulture, 85, 87, 90, 209–210
Vogeler, Ingolf, 93
Voting patterns, 122–124, 138, 147

Wales, 178, 235, 447
Ward, Gerard, 168–169
Warsaw, 131
Washington, D.C., 349, 352, 356,
  409
Washington (state), 122, 243, 244,
  254
Webb, John, 168–169
Weber, Alfred, 436, 439
Welsh, 178, 179, 235, 295
West Indies, 128
West Virginia, 282
Wheat, 5–6, 85, 87, 91–92, 97,
  101, 460
White, Rodney, 2, 134
Wilhelm, Eugene, 229
Windmills, 232, 257
Wine, 90, 209–210
Winnipeg, 300, 301
Wisconsin, 182, 193, 298, 311
Withers, Charles, 170, 177

Women
  as farmers, 98
  as gatherers, 94
  as geographers, 19, 108, 180,
    205, 207, 213, 235, 278,
    298–299, 315, 316, 408, 457,
    469
  life expectancy of, 49–50
  migration of, 66
  rights of, 138
  in sports, 267, 274
Wyoming, 274

Yams, 82
Yellow River (Huang Ho), 336
Yellowstone Park, 289
Yemen, 194
Yoon, Hong-key, 184
Yucatan, 74–75
Yugoslavia, 439

Zaire, 126, 135
Zambia, 364
Zelinsky, Wilbur, 269, 270, 271,
  272, 279–281, 317
Zero population growth, 44–45
Ziggurat, 337
Zonation, functional, 342
Zoning, 354
Zoroastrians, 219–220

Major Linguistic Culture Areas of the World

Indo-European

- Slavic
- Germanic
- Romance
- Iranic
- Indic
- Other Indo-European

Hamito-Semitic (Afro-Asiatic)

- Semitic
- Hamitic

- Altaic
- Niger-Congo
- Malayo-Polynesian
- Uralic
- Sino-Tibetan
- Austro-Asiatic
- Other groups

E = Eskimoan	D = Dravidian
A = Amerindian	T = Tai
N-S = Nilo-Saharan	P = Papuan
K = Khoisan	Ab = Aborigine
Ps = Paleosiberian	

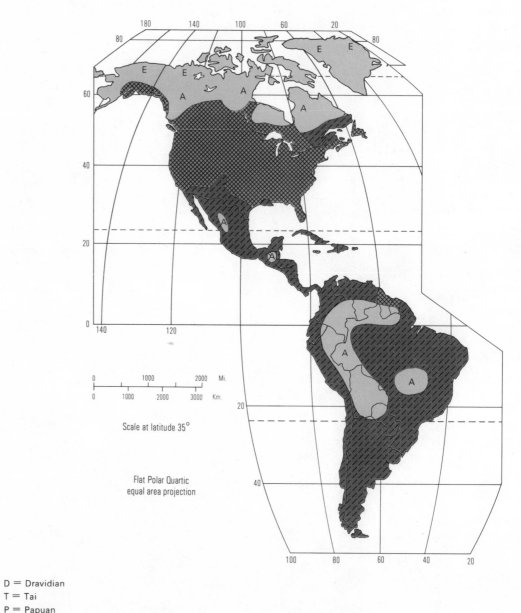

Scale at latitude 35°

Flat Polar Quartic
equal area projection